Teach Yourself VISUALLY™ Word 2002

Save Time!

Download the examples used in this book from our Web site to easily follow along with the steps!

www.maran.com/resources/teachyourself/word2002

Visual

From maranGraphics®

&

Hungry Minds™

Best-Selling Books • Digital Downloads • e-books • Answer Networks • e-Newsletters • Branded Web Sites • e-learning

New York, NY • Cleveland, OH • Indianapolis, IN

Teach Yourself VISUALLY™ Word 2002

Published by
Hungry Minds, Inc.
909 Third Avenue
New York, NY 10022
www.hungryminds.com

Library of Congress Control Number: 2001096759
ISBN: 0-7645-3587-0
Printed in the United States of America
10 9 8 7 6 5 4 3 2 1

1K/QW/QR/QS/MG

Distributed in the United States by Hungry Minds, Inc.
Distributed by CDG Books Canada Inc. for Canada; by Transworld Publishers Limited in the United Kingdom; by IDG Norge Books for Norway; by IDG Sweden Books for Sweden; by IDG Books Australia Publishing Corporation Pty. Ltd. for Australia and New Zealand; by TransQuest Publishers Pte Ltd. for Singapore, Malaysia, Thailand, Indonesia, and Hong Kong; by Gotop Information Inc. for Taiwan; by ICG Muse, Inc. for Japan; by Intersoft for South Africa; by Eyrolles for France; by International Thomson Publishing for Germany, Austria and Switzerland; by Distribuidora Cuspide for Argentina; by LR International for Brazil; by Galileo Libros for Chile; by Ediciones ZETA S.C.R. Ltda. for Peru; by WS Computer Publishing Corporation, Inc. for the Philippines; by Contemporanea de Ediciones for Venezuela; by Express Computer Distributors for the Caribbean and West Indies; by Micronesia Media Distributor, Inc. for Micronesia; by Chips Computadoras S.A. de C.V. for Mexico; by Editorial Norma de Panama S.A. for Panama; by American Bookshops for Finland.
For U.S. corporate orders, please call maranGraphics at 800-469-6616 or fax 905-890-9434.
For general information on Hungry Minds' products and services, please contact our Customer Care Department within the U.S. at 800-762-2974, outside the U.S. at 317-572-3993 or fax 317-572-4002.
For sales inquiries and reseller information, including discounts, premium and bulk quantity sales, and foreign-language translations, please contact our Customer Care Department at 800-434-3422, fax 317-572-4002, or write to Hungry Minds, Inc., Attn: Customer Care Department, 10475 Crosspoint Boulevard, Indianapolis, IN 46256.
For information on licensing foreign or domestic rights, please contact our Sub-Rights Customer Care Department at 212-844-5000.
For information on using Hungry Minds' products and services in the classroom or for ordering examination copies, please contact our Educational Sales Department at 800-434-2086 or fax 317-572-4005.
For press review copies, author interviews, or other publicity information, please contact our Public Relations department at 317-572-3168 or fax 317-572-4168.
For authorization to photocopy items for corporate, personal, or educational use, please contact maranGraphics at the address above.

Trademark Acknowledgments

Permissions

U.S. Corporate Sales
Contact maranGraphics at (800) 469-6616 or fax (905) 890-9434.

U.S. Trade Sales
Contact Hungry Minds at (800) 434-3422 or fax (317) 572-4002.

Some comments from our readers...

"I have to praise you and your company on the fine products you turn out. I have twelve of the *Teach Yourself VISUALLY* and *Simplified* books in my house. They were instrumental in helping me pass a difficult computer course. Thank you for creating books that are easy to follow."

–Gordon Justin (Brielle, NJ)

"I commend your efforts and your success. I teach in an outreach program for the Dr. Eugene Clark Library in Lockhart, TX. Your *Teach Yourself VISUALLY* books are incredible and I use them in my computer classes. All my students love them!"

–Michele Schalin (Lockhart, TX)

"Thank you so much for helping people like me learn about computers. The Maran family is just what the doctor ordered. Thank you, thank you, thank you."

–Carol Moten (New Kensington, PA)

"I would like to take this time to compliment maranGraphics on creating such great books. Thank you for making it clear. Keep up the good work."

–Kirk Santoro (Burbank, CA)

"I write to extend my thanks and appreciation for your books. They are clear, easy to follow, and straight to the point. Keep up the good work!"

–Seward Kollie (Dakar, Senegal)

"What fantastic teaching books you have produced! Congratulations to you and your staff. You deserve the Nobel prize in Education in the Software category. Thanks for helping me to understand computers."

–Bruno Tonon (Melbourne, Australia)

"Over time, I have bought a number of your 'Read Less-Learn More' books. For me, they are THE way to learn anything easily."

–José A. Mazón (Cuba, NY)

"I was introduced to maranGraphics about four years ago and YOU ARE THE GREATEST THING THAT EVER HAPPENED TO INTRODUCTORY COMPUTER BOOKS!"

–Glenn Nettleton (Huntsville, AL)

"Compliments To The Chef!! Your books are extraordinary! Or, simply put, Extra-Ordinary, meaning way above the rest! THANK YOU THANK YOU THANK YOU! for creating these."

–Christine J. Manfrin (Castle Rock, CO)

"I'm a grandma who was pushed by an 11-year-old grandson to join the computer age. I found myself hopelessly confused and frustrated until I discovered the Visual series. I'm no expert by any means now, but I'm a lot further along than I would have been otherwise. Thank you!"

–Carol Louthain (Logansport, IN)

"Thank you, thank you, thank you...for making it so easy for me to break into this high-tech world. I now own four of your books. I recommend them to anyone who is a beginner like myself. Now... if you could just do one for programming VCR's, it would make my day!"

–Gay O'Donnell (Calgary, Alberta, Canada)

"You're marvelous! I am greatly in your debt."

–Patrick Baird (Lacey, WA)

maranGraphics is a family-run business
located near Toronto, Canada.

At **maranGraphics**, we believe in producing great computer books—one book at a time.

Each maranGraphics book uses the award-winning communication process that we have been developing over the last 25 years. Using this process, we organize screen shots, text and illustrations in a way that makes it easy for you to learn new concepts and tasks.

We spend hours deciding the best way to perform each task, so you don't have to! Our clear, easy-to-follow screen shots and instructions walk you through each task from beginning to end.

Our detailed illustrations go hand-in-hand with the text to help reinforce the information. Each illustration is a labor of love—some take up to a week to draw!

We want to thank you for purchasing what we feel are the best computer books money can buy. We hope you enjoy using this book as much as we enjoyed creating it!

Sincerely,

The Maran Family

Please visit us on the Web at:

www.maran.com

CREDITS

Author:
Ruth Maran

Copy Development Director:
Wanda Lawrie

Copy Editing and Screen Captures:
Roxanne Van Damme
Megan Kirby

Technical Consultant:
Paul Whitehead

Project Manager:
Judy Maran

Editor:
Norm Schumacher

Layout Artist:
Treena Lees

Illustrators:
Russ Marini
Steven Schaerer

Screen Artist and Illustrator:
Darryl Grossi

Indexer:
Roxanne Van Damme

Permissions Coordinator:
Jennifer Amaral

Senior Vice President and Publisher, Hungry Minds Technology Publishing Group:
Richard Swadley

Publishing Director, Hungry Minds Technology Publishing Group:
Barry Pruett

Editorial Support, Hungry Minds Technology Publishing Group:
Jennifer Dorsey
Sandy Rodrigues
Lindsay Sandman

Post Production:
Robert Maran

ACKNOWLEDGMENTS

maranGraphics™

Thanks to the dedicated staff of maranGraphics, including Jennifer Amaral, Roderick Anatalio, Darryl Grossi, Kelleigh Johnson, Megan Kirby, Wanda Lawrie, Treena Lees, Cathy Lo, Jill Maran, Judy Maran, Robert Maran, Ruth Maran, Russ Marini, Steven Schaerer, Norm Schumacher, Raquel Scott, Roxanne Van Damme and Paul Whitehead.

Finally, to Richard Maran who originated the easy-to-use graphic format of this guide. Thank you for your inspiration and guidance.

TABLE OF CONTENTS

Chapter 1 — GETTING STARTED

Introduction to Word 4
Start Word 6
The Word Window 7
Enter Text 8
Select Text 10
Move Through a Document 12
Select a Command 14
Using the Task Pane 16
Getting Help 18

Chapter 2 — SAVE AND OPEN DOCUMENTS

Save a Document 22
Save a Document in a Different Format 24
Close a Document 26
Exit Word 27
Open a Document 28
Open a Document in a Different Format 30
Search for a Document 32
Protect a Document 34

Chapter 3 — CHANGE DISPLAY OF DOCUMENTS

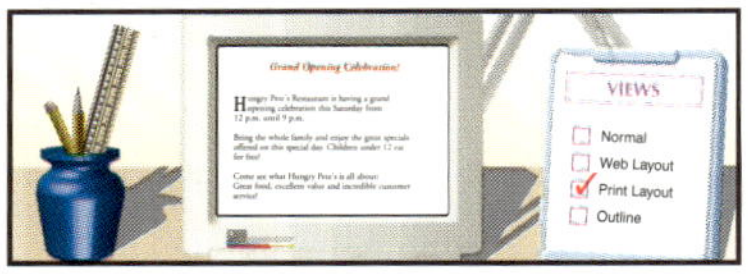

Change the View of a Document 40
Display or Hide the Ruler 42
Display or Hide a Toolbar 43
Move a Toolbar 44

Size a Toolbar 45
Zoom In or Out 46
Split a Document 47
Display or Hide White Space 48
Display or Hide Formatting Marks 49
Using the Document Map 50

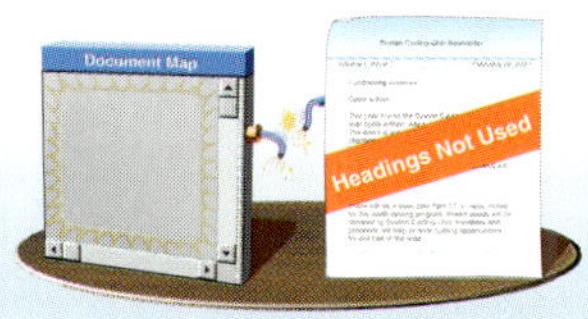

Chapter 4

EDIT TEXT

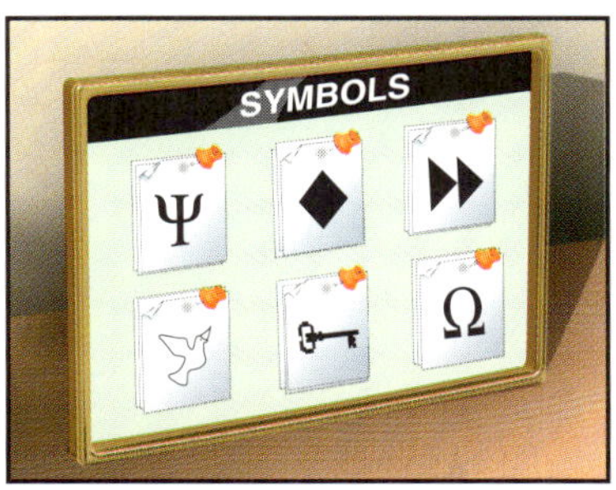

Insert and Delete Text 54
Move or Copy Text 56
Insert the Date and Time 58
Undo Changes 59
Count Words in a Document 60
Find Text 62
Replace Text 64
Check Spelling and Grammar 66
Turn Off Spelling and Grammar Check 68
Using the Thesaurus 70
Using AutoCorrect 72
Using AutoText 74
Insert Symbols 76
Add a Comment 78
Track Changes 80
Review Tracked Changes 82
Translate Text 84

TABLE OF CONTENTS

Chapter 5 — FORMAT TEXT

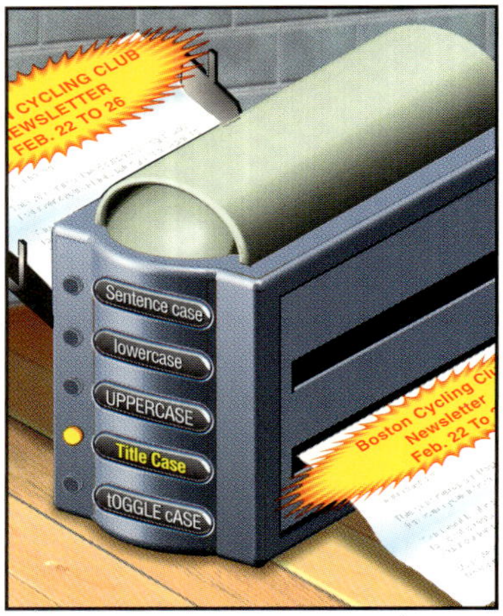

Change Font of Text 88
Change Size of Text 89
Bold, Italicize or Underline Text 90
Change Case of Text 91
Change Color of Text 92
Highlight Text 93
Change Alignment of Text 94
Change Appearance of Text 96
Change Font for All New Documents 98
Animate Text 100
Copy Formatting 102
Change Line Spacing 104
Remove Formatting From Text 105

Chapter 6 — WORK WITH FORMATTING AND STYLES

Check Formatting 108
Apply Formatting 110
Create a Style 114
Change a Style 116
Review Formatting 118

Chapter 7 — FORMAT PARAGRAPHS

Create a Bulleted or Numbered List 124
Indent Paragraphs 128
Change Tab Settings 130
Create a Drop Cap 134
Add a Border 136
Add Shading 138

Chapter 8 FORMAT PAGES

Insert a Page Break....142
Insert a Section Break....144
Add Page Numbers....146
Add a Header or Footer....148
Add Footnotes or Endnotes....152
Change Margins....156
Center Text on a Page....158
Change Page Orientation....159
Control Page Breaks....160
Add a Watermark....162
Add a Page Border....164
Create Newspaper Columns....166

Chapter 9 PRINT DOCUMENTS

Preview a Document Before Printing....170
Print a Document....172
Print an Envelope....174
Print Labels....176
Change Paper Size and Source....180

Chapter 10 WORK WITH MULTIPLE DOCUMENTS

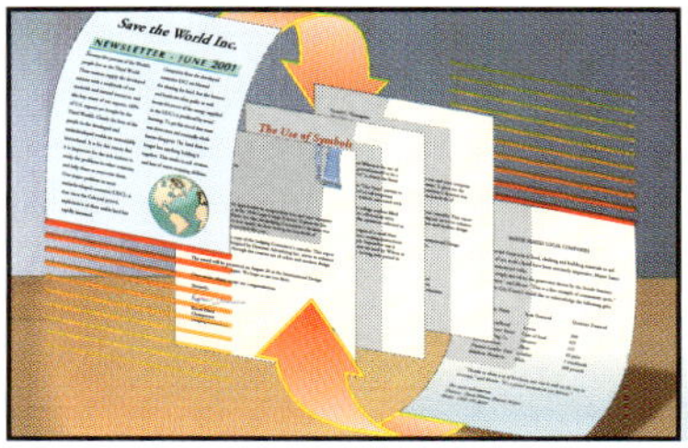

Create a New Document....184
Switch Between Documents....185
Arrange Open Documents....186
Move or Copy Text Between Documents....188

Chapter 11 WORK WITH TABLES

Create a Table 192
Add a Row or Column 194
Delete a Row or Column 196
Change Row Height or Column Width 198
Move a Table 200
Resize a Table 201
Combine Cells 202
Split Cells 203
Align Text in Cells 204
Add Shading to Cells 205
Change Table Borders 206
Format a Table 208

Chapter 12 WORK WITH GRAPHICS

Add an AutoShape 212
Add WordArt 214
Add a Text Box 216
Add a Picture 218
Add a Clip Art Image 220
Move a Graphic 224
Resize a Graphic 225
Change Color of a Graphic 226
Rotate a Graphic 227
Create a Drawing Canvas 228
Wrap Text Around a Graphic 230
Add a Diagram 232

Chapter 13 TIME-SAVING FEATURES

Using Smart Tags 240
Using Templates and Wizards 242
Create a Template..244
Customize a Toolbar 246
Create a New Toolbar 250
Record a Macro 252
Run a Macro 256

Chapter 14 USING MAIL MERGE

Create Letters Using Mail Merge 260
Create Labels Using Mail Merge 270

Chapter 15 USING SPEECH RECOGNITION

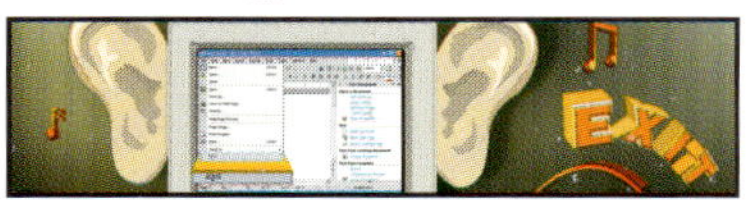

Set Up Speech Recognition 280
Using Dictation Mode 286
Using Voice Command Mode..........................288

Chapter 16 WORD AND THE INTERNET

E-mail a Document 292
Create a Hyperlink 294
Save a Document as a Web Page 296

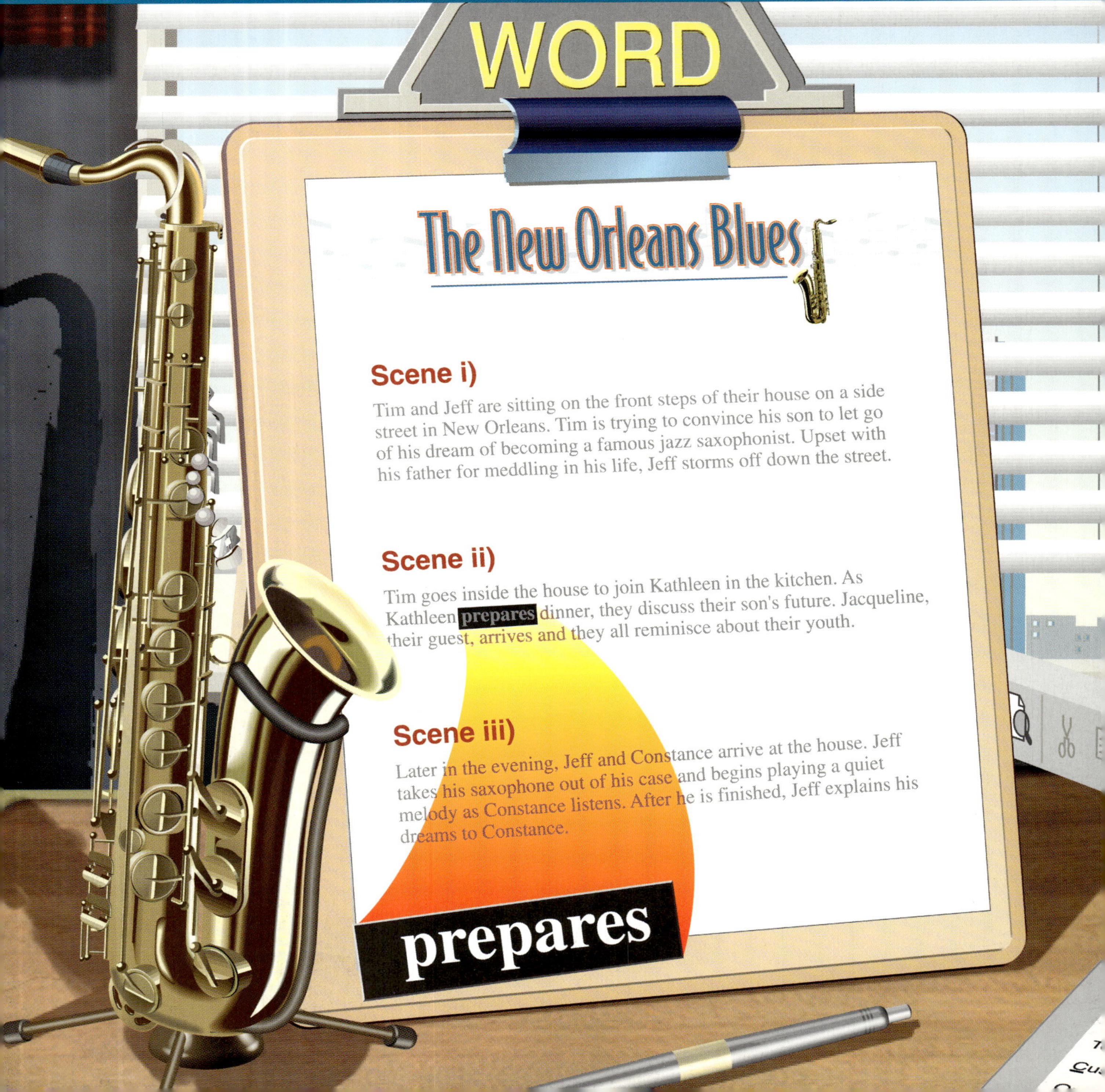
WORD
The New Orleans Blues
Scene i)
Tim and Jeff are sitting on the front steps of their house on a side street in New Orleans. Tim is trying to convince his son to let go of his dream of becoming a famous jazz saxophonist. Upset with his father for meddling in his life, Jeff storms off down the street.
Scene ii)
Tim goes inside the house to join Kathleen in the kitchen. As Kathleen prepares dinner, they discuss their son's future. Jacqueline, their guest, arrives and they all reminisce about their youth.
Scene iii)
Later in the evening, Jeff and Constance arrive at the house. Jeff takes his saxophone out of his case and begins playing a quiet melody as Constance listens. After he is finished, Jeff explains his dreams to Constance.
prepares

CHAPTER 1

Getting Started

Are you ready to begin using Microsoft Word 2002? This chapter will help you get started.

Introduction to Word 4

Start Word 6

The Word Window 7

Enter Text 8

Select Text 10

Move Through a Document 12

Select a Command 14

Using the Task Pane 16

Getting Help 18

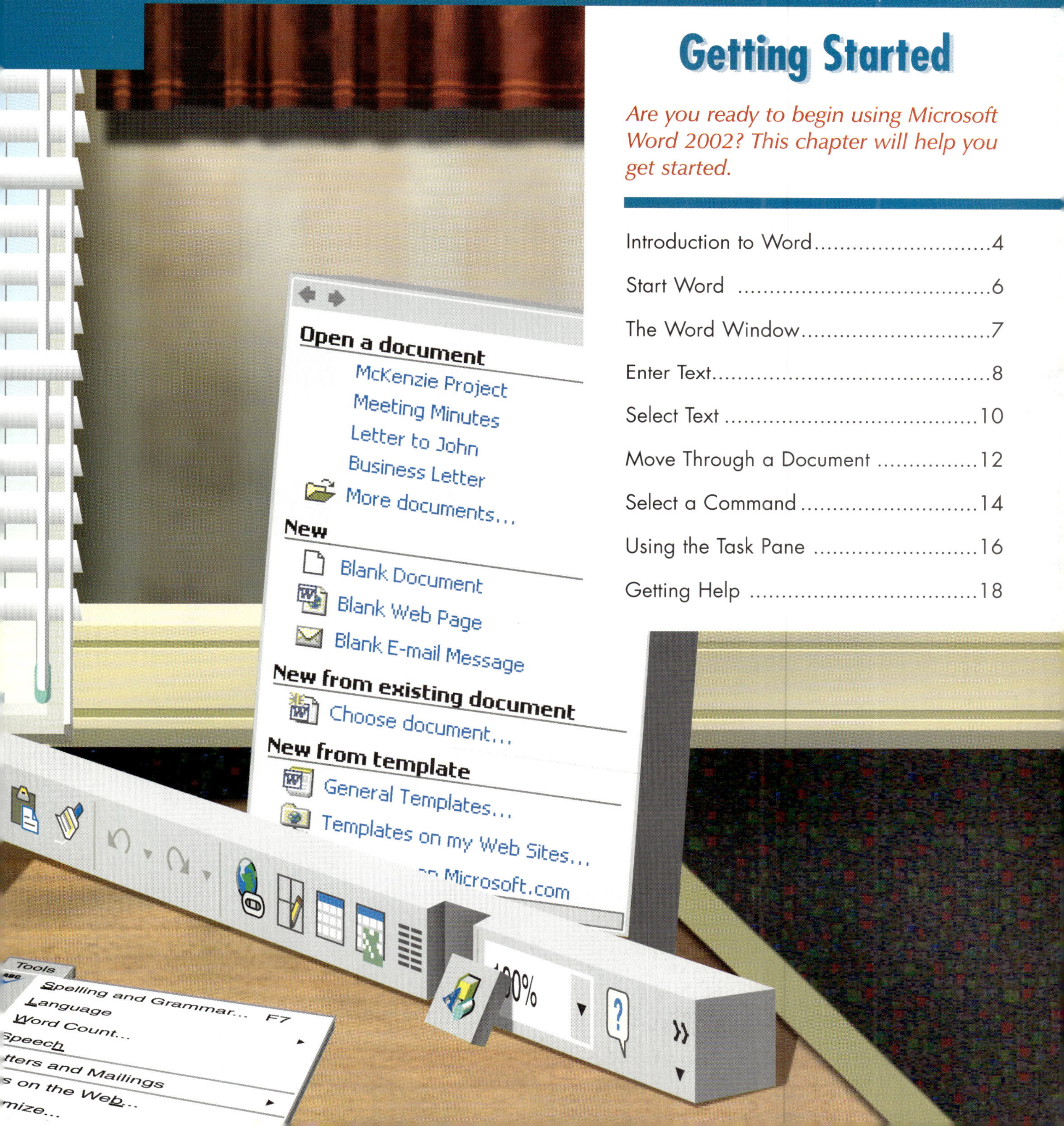

INTRODUCTION TO WORD

Word is a word processing program you can use to efficiently produce professional-looking documents, such as letters, reports, essays and newsletters.

Edit Documents

Word offers many time-saving features to help you edit text in a document. You can add, delete and rearrange text. You can also quickly count the number of words in a document, check your document for spelling and grammar errors and use Word's thesaurus to find more suitable words.

Format Documents

You can format a document to enhance the appearance of the document. You can use various fonts, styles and colors to emphasize important text. You can also adjust the spacing between lines of text, change the margins, center text on a page and create newspaper columns.

Print Documents

You can produce a paper copy of a document you create. Before printing, you can preview how the document will appear on a printed page. Word also allows you to print envelopes and labels.

Work With Tables and Graphics

Word can help you create tables to neatly display columns of information in a document. Word's ready-to-use designs allow you to instantly give a table a professional appearance. You can also add graphics, such as AutoShapes, clip art images and diagrams, to a document to illustrate ideas.

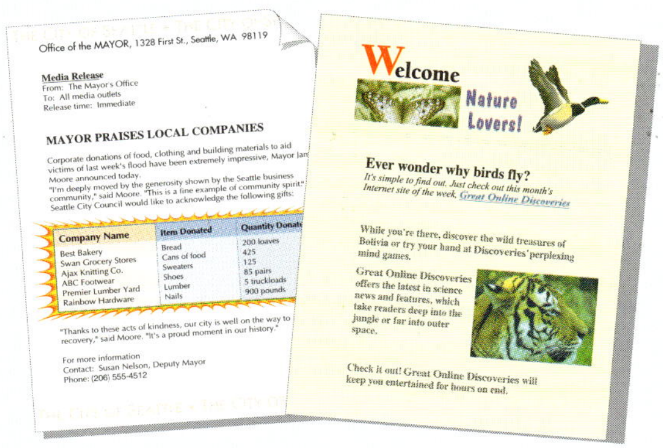

Use Mail Merge

Word's Mail Merge Wizard can help you quickly produce personalized letters and labels for each person on a mailing list. This is useful if you often send the same document, such as an announcement or advertisement, to many people.

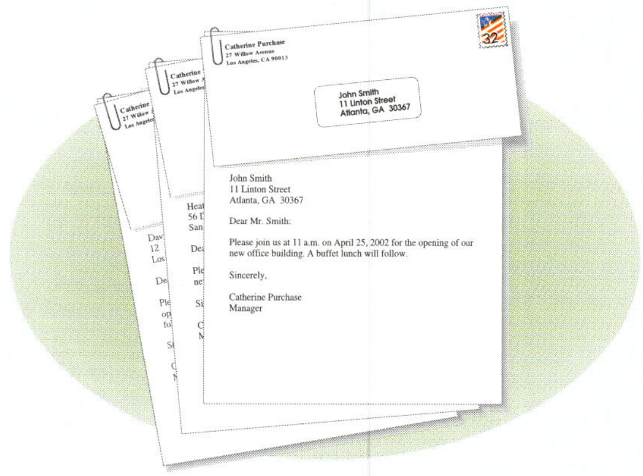

Use Speech Recognition

The speech recognition feature allows you to use your voice to enter text into a document. You can also use speech recognition to select commands from menus, toolbars and dialog boxes using your voice.

Word and the Internet

Word offers features that allow you to take advantage of the Internet. You can create a hyperlink in a document to connect the document to a Web page. You can also save a document as a Web page. This allows you to place the document on the Internet for other people to view.

START WORD

You can start Word to create and work with documents.

When you start Word, a blank document appears on your screen. You can type text into this document.

START WORD

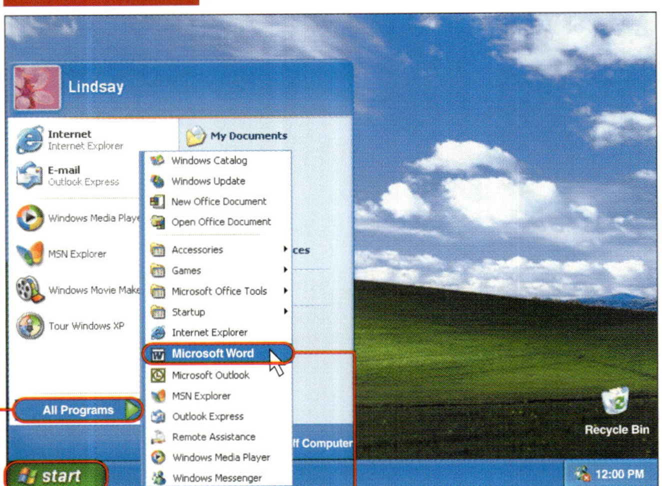

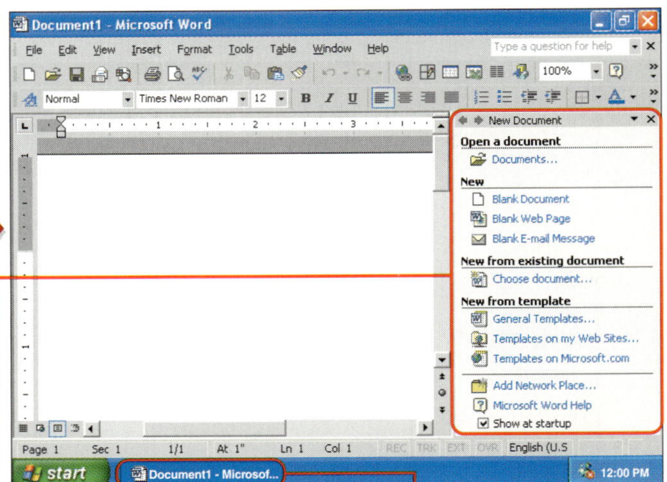

1 Click **start**.

2 Click **All Programs** to view a list of the programs on your computer.

Note: If you are using an earlier version of Windows, click ***Programs*** *in step* ***2****.*

3 Click **Microsoft Word**.

■ The Microsoft Word window appears, displaying a blank document.

■ This area displays a task pane, which allows you to quickly perform common tasks. For information on using the task pane, see page 16.

■ A button for the Microsoft Word window appears on the taskbar.

THE WORD WINDOW

The Word window displays many items you can use to create and work with your documents.

Title Bar

Shows the name of the displayed document.

Menu Bar

Provides access to lists of commands available in Word and displays an area where you can type a question to get help information.

Standard Toolbar

Contains buttons you can use to select common commands, such as Save and Print.

Formatting Toolbar

Contains buttons you can use to select common formatting commands, such as Bold and Italic.

Ruler

Allows you to change tab and indent settings for your documents.

Task Pane

Contains options you can select to perform common tasks, such as opening or creating a document.

Insertion Point

The flashing line on the screen that indicates where the text you type will appear.

Document Views

Provides access to four different views of your documents.

Scroll Bars

Allow you to browse through a document.

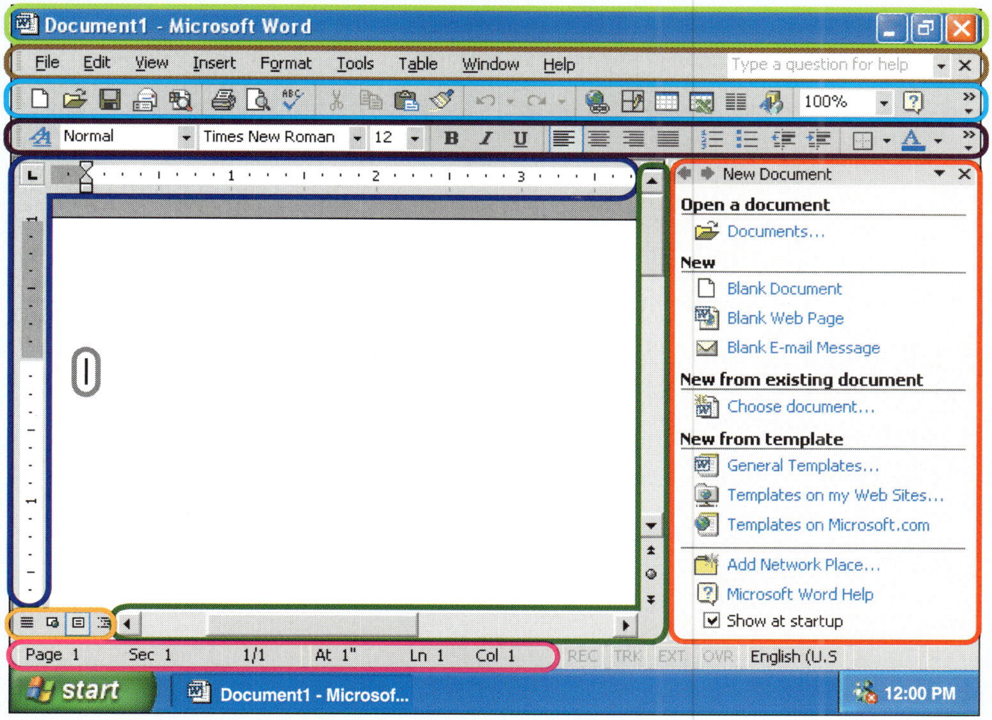

Status Bar

Provides information about the area of the document displayed on the screen and the position of the insertion point.

Page 1

The page displayed on the screen.

Sec 1

The section of the document displayed on the screen.

1/1

The page displayed on the screen and the total number of pages in the document.

At 1"

The distance from the top of the page to the insertion point.

Ln 1

The number of lines from the top margin to the insertion point.

Col 1

The number of characters from the left margin to the insertion point, including spaces.

ENTER TEXT

Word allows you to type text into your document quickly and easily.

ENTER TEXT

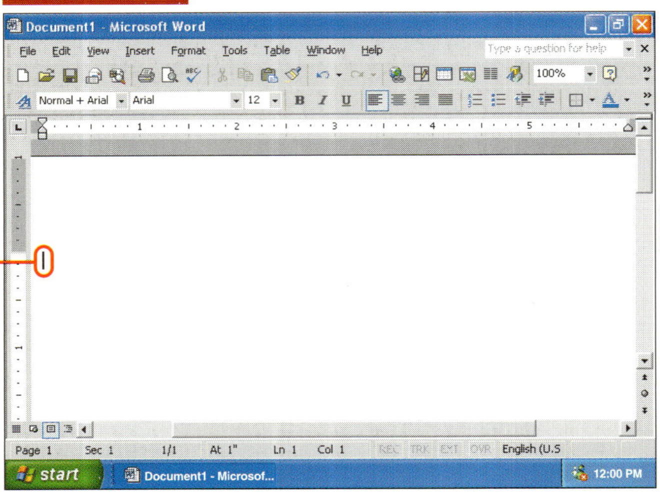

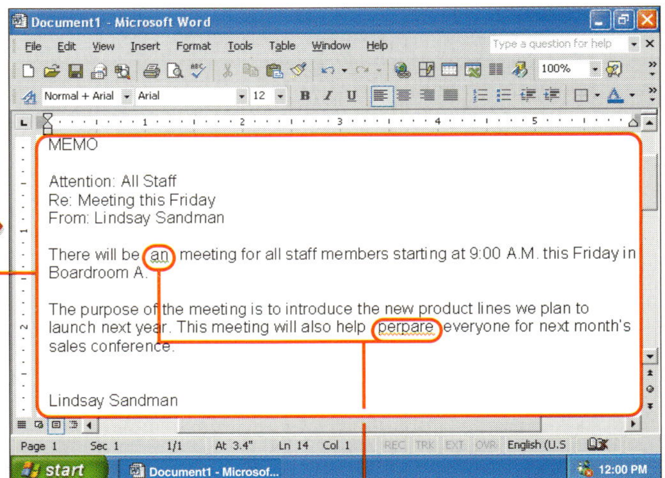

■ The text you type will appear where the insertion point flashes on your screen.

1 Type the text for your document.

Note: In this book, the font of text was changed to Arial to make the examples easier to read. To change the font of text, see page 88.

■ When you reach the end of a line, Word automatically wraps the text to the next line. You only need to press the **Enter** key when you want to start a new paragraph.

■ Word automatically underlines misspelled words in red and grammar errors in green. The underlines will not appear when you print your document. To correct misspelled words and grammar errors, see page 66.

How can I quickly enter text in a new location in my document?

Word's Click and Type feature allows you to quickly position the insertion point in a new location so you can enter text. Double-click a blank area where you want to position the insertion point and then type the text you want to enter. The Click and Type feature is only available in the Print Layout and Web Layout views. To change the view of a document, see page 40.

Where can I find a sample document like the one used in this chapter?

The sample documents used in each chapter of this book are available on the Web at www.maran.com/resources/teachyourself/word2002. You can download the sample documents so you can perform the tasks in this book without having to type the documents yourself.

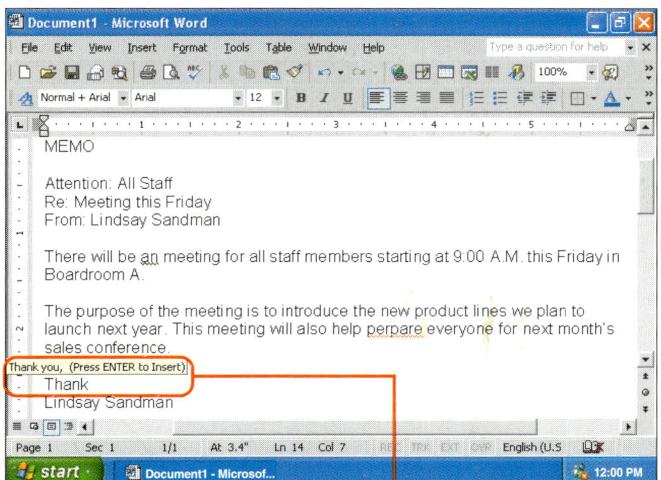

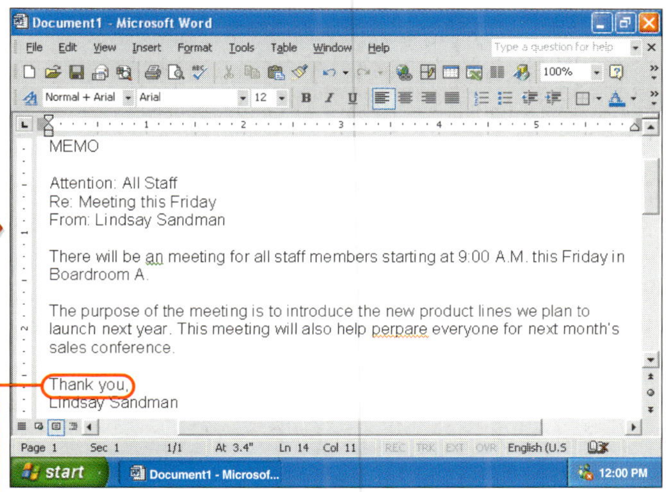

ENTER TEXT AUTOMATICALLY

■ Word's AutoText feature helps you quickly enter common words and phrases.

■ When you type the first few characters of a common word or phrase, a yellow box appears, displaying the text.

1 To insert the text, press the Enter key.

■ To ignore the text, continue typing.

Note: For more information on the AutoText feature, see page 74.

Before performing many tasks in Word, you must select the text you want to work with. Selected text appears highlighted on your screen.

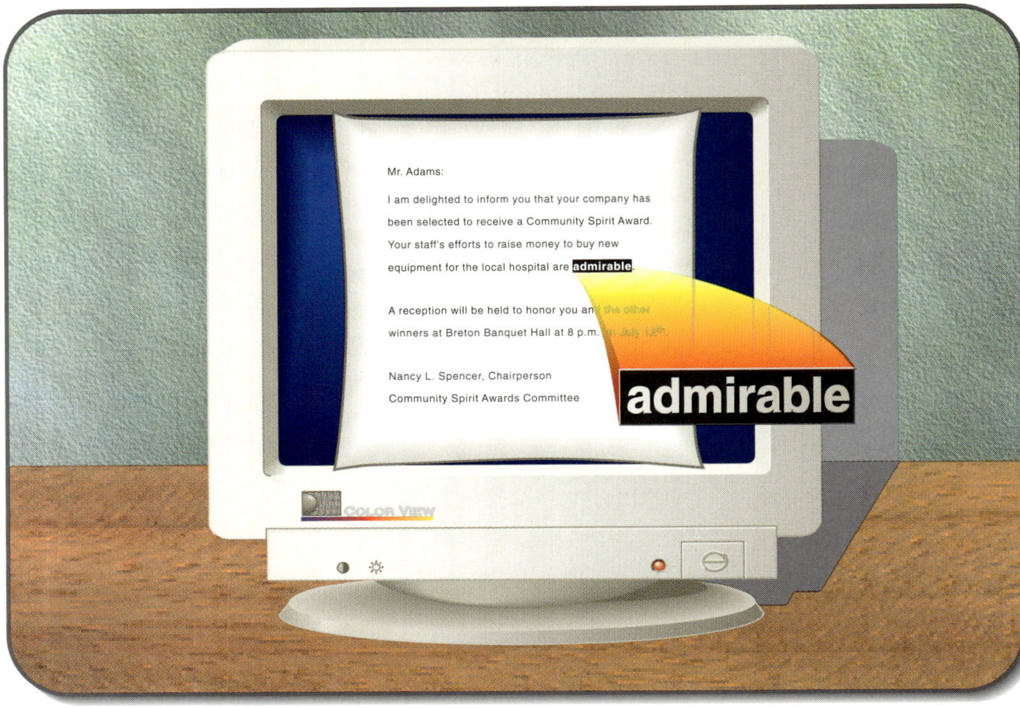

SELECT TEXT

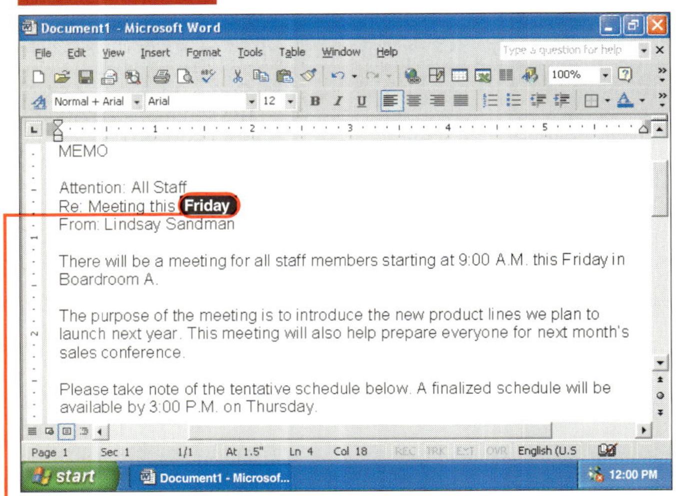

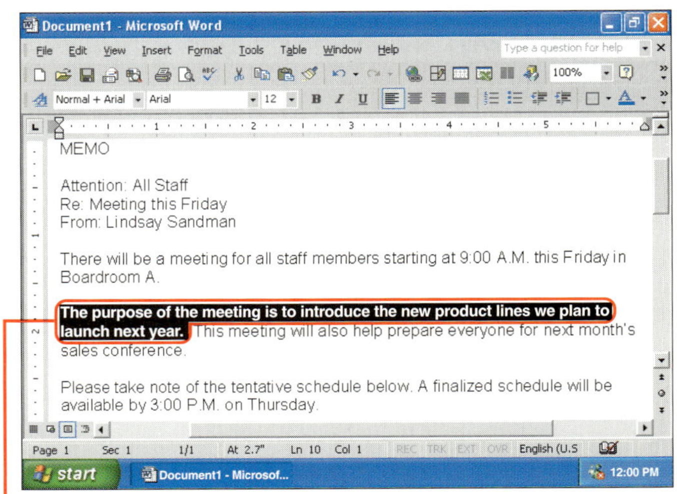

SELECT A WORD

1 Double-click the word you want to select. The word is highlighted.

■ To deselect text, click outside the selected area.

SELECT A SENTENCE

1 Press and hold down the Ctrl key as you click the sentence you want to select.

How do I select a paragraph or a large area of text?

To select a paragraph, position the mouse I over the paragraph you want to select and then quickly click **three** times.

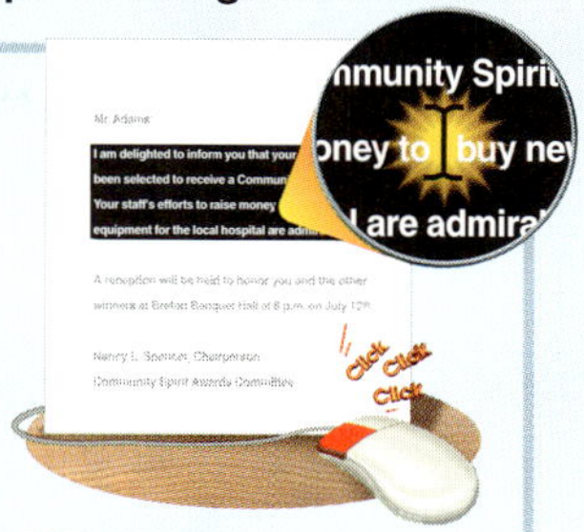

To select a large area of text, click at the beginning of the text. Then press and hold down the Shift key as you click at the end of the text.

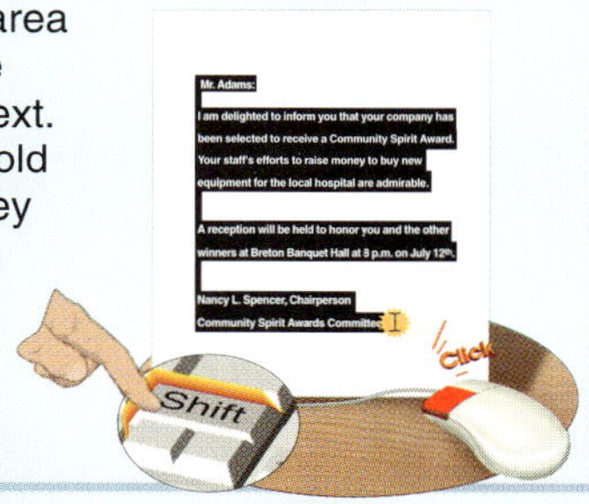

Can I select multiple areas of text in my document?

Yes. To select multiple areas of text, press and hold down the Ctrl key as you select each area.

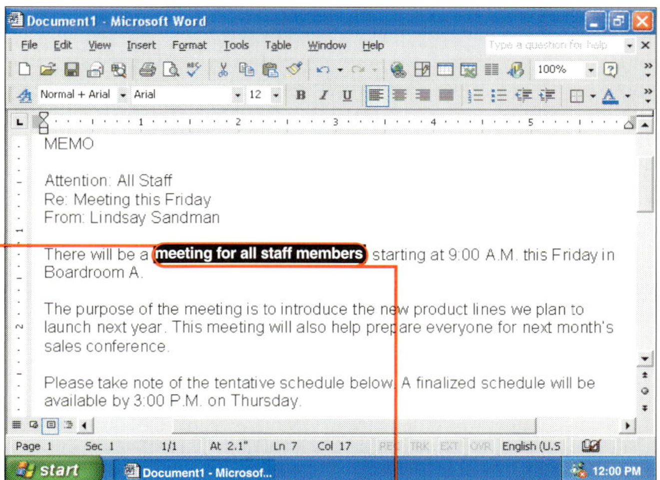

SELECT ANY AMOUNT OF TEXT

1 Position the mouse I over the first word you want to select.

2 Drag the mouse I over the text you want to select.

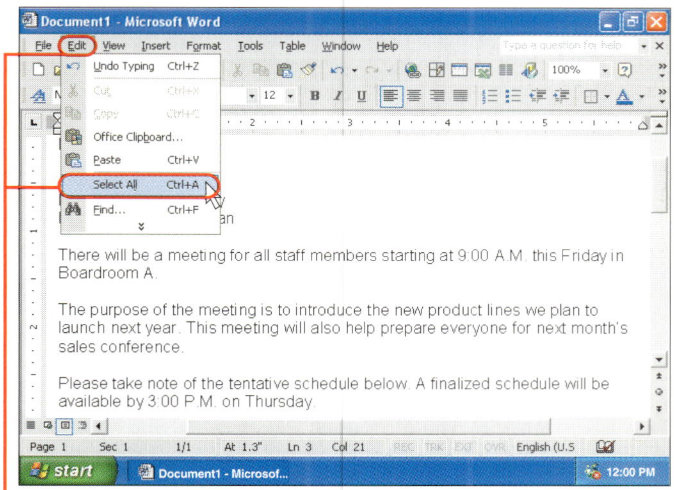

SELECT ENTIRE DOCUMENT

1 Click **Edit**.

2 Click **Select All** to select all the text in your document.

Note: You can also press and hold down the Ctrl key as you press the A key to select all the text in your document.

MOVE THROUGH A DOCUMENT

You can easily move to another location in your document.

If your document contains a lot of text, your computer screen may not be able to display all the text at once. You must scroll through your document to view other parts of the document.

MOVE THROUGH A DOCUMENT

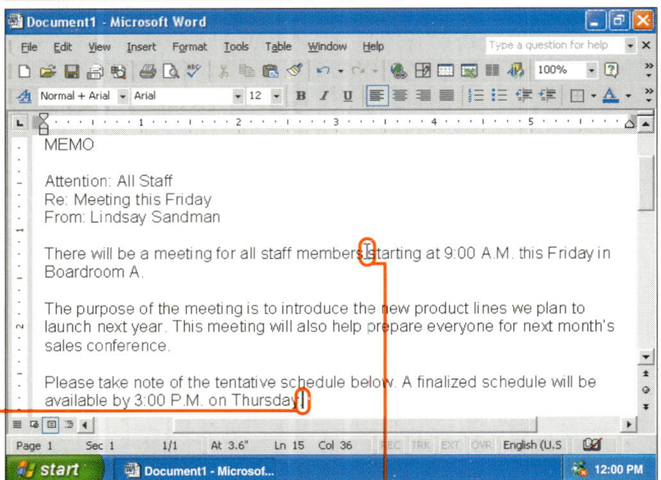

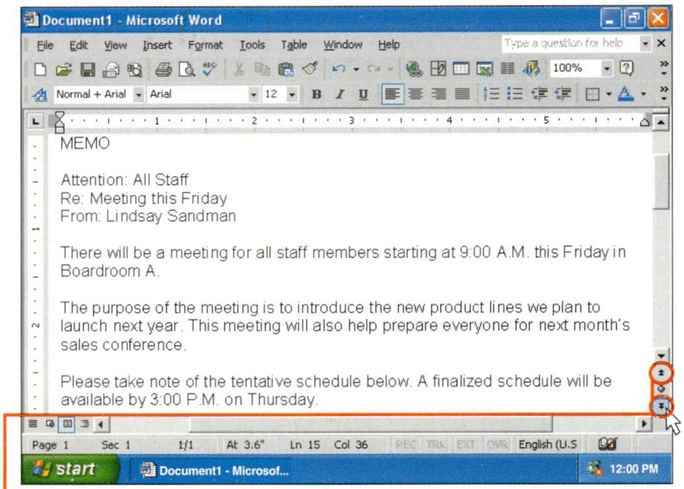

MOVE THE INSERTION POINT

■ The flashing line on your screen, called the insertion point, indicates where the text you type will appear.

1 Click the location in your document where you want to place the insertion point.

DISPLAY PREVIOUS OR NEXT PAGE

1 To display the previous or next page, click one of the following buttons.

- ⇞ Display previous page
- ⇟ Display next page

TEACH YOURSELF

How can I use my keyboard to move through a document?

You can press the ←, →, ↑ or ↓ key to move through a document one character or line at a time. You can press the Page Up or Page Down key to move through a document one screen at a time.

TEACH YOURSELF

How do I use the wheel on my mouse to scroll through a document?

You can purchase a mouse with a wheel between the left and right mouse buttons. Moving this wheel allows you to quickly scroll through a document.

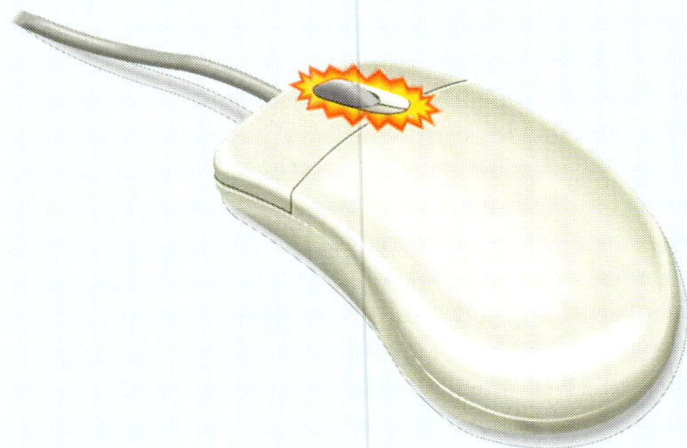

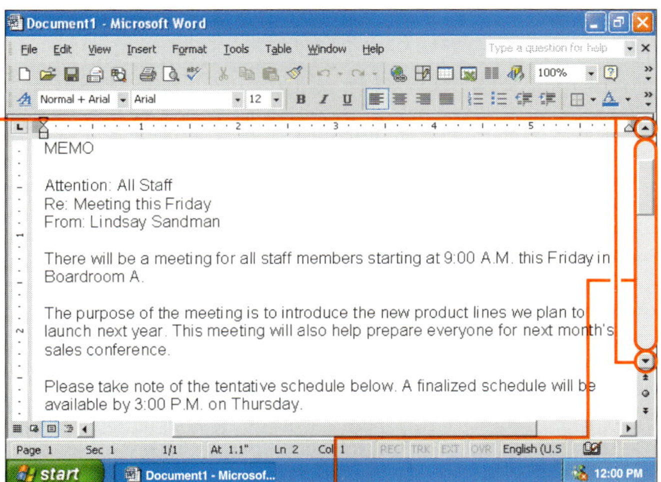

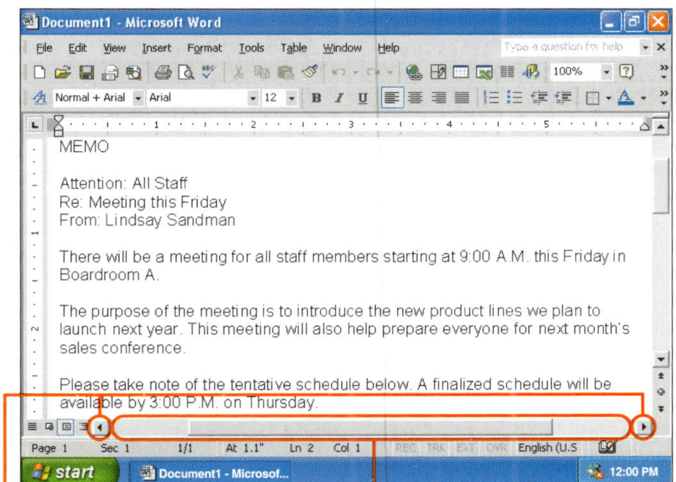

SCROLL UP OR DOWN

1 To scroll up or down, click ▲ or ▼.

■ To quickly scroll up or down, position the mouse over the scroll box and then drag the scroll box along the scroll bar.

Note: The location of the scroll box indicates which part of the document you are viewing. To view the middle of the document, drag the scroll box halfway down the scroll bar.

SCROLL LEFT OR RIGHT

1 To scroll left or right, click ◄ or ►.

■ To quickly scroll left or right, position the mouse over the scroll box and then drag the scroll box along the scroll bar.

SELECT A COMMAND

You can select a command from a menu or toolbar menu to perform a task in Word.

When you first start Word, the most commonly used commands and buttons appear on each menu and toolbar. As you work, Word customizes the menus and toolbars to display the commands and buttons you use most often.

SELECT A COMMAND

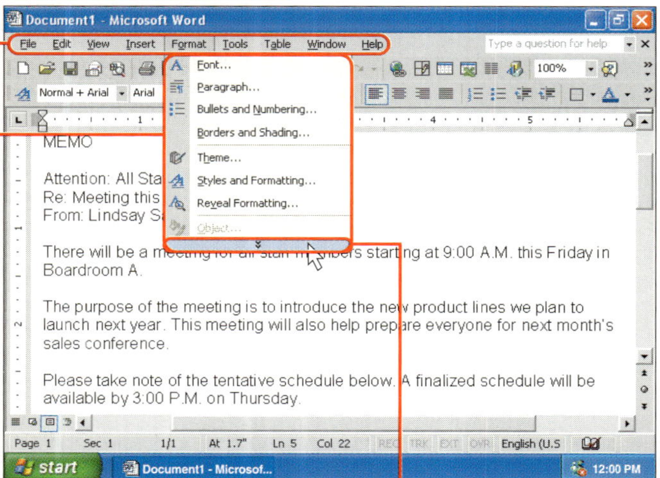

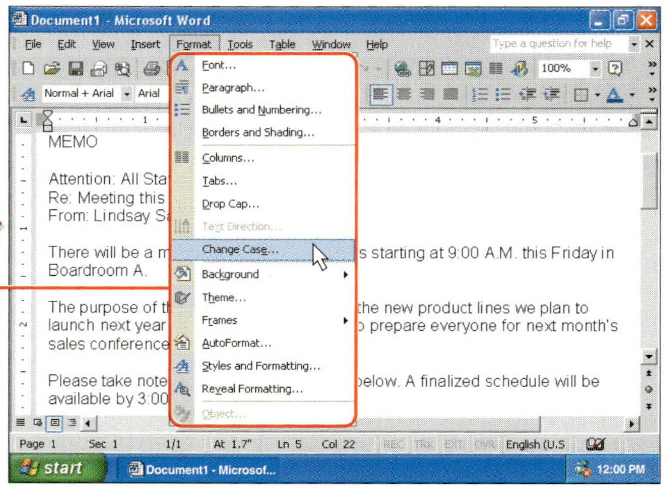

USING MENUS

1 Click the name of the menu you want to display.

■ A short version of the menu appears, displaying the most commonly used commands.

2 To expand the menu and display all the commands, position the mouse over ».

Note: If you do not perform step 2, the expanded menu will automatically appear after a few seconds.

■ The expanded menu appears, displaying all the commands.

3 Click the command you want to use.

Note: A dimmed command is currently not available.

■ To close a menu without selecting a command, click outside the menu.

How can I make a command appear on the short version of a menu?

When you select a command from an expanded menu, the command is automatically added to the short version of the menu. The next time you display the short version of the menu, the command you selected will appear.

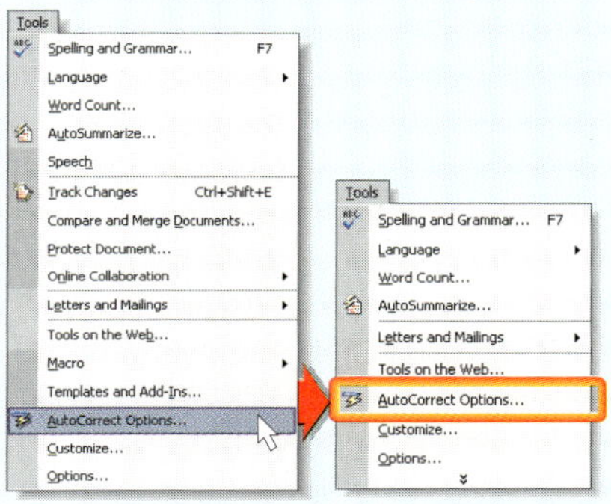

Expanded Menu **Short Menu**

How can I quickly select a command?

You can use a shortcut menu to quickly select a command.

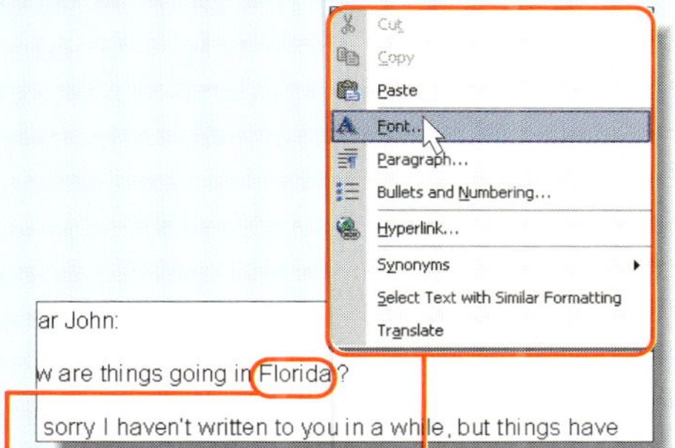

1 Right-click an item to display a shortcut menu. The shortcut menu displays the most frequently used commands for the item.

2 Click the command you want to use.

■ To close a shortcut menu without selecting a command, click outside the menu.

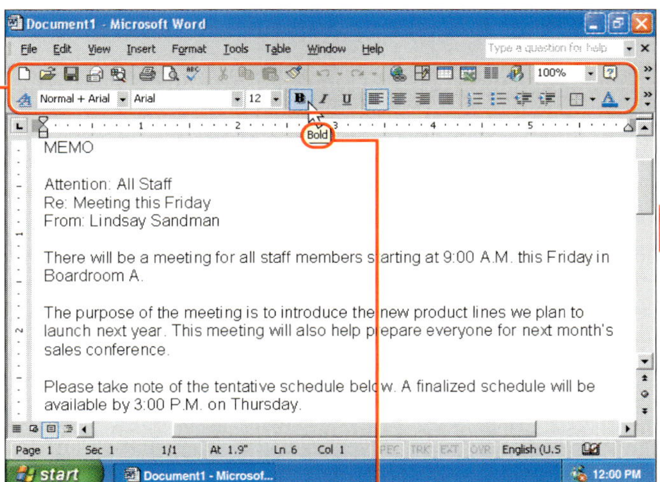

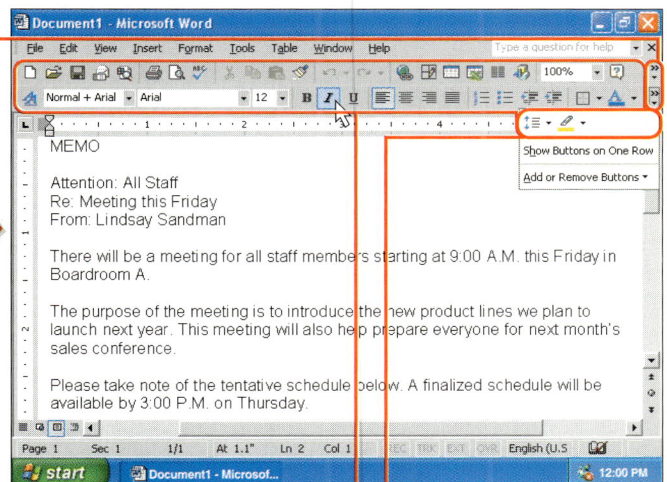

USING TOOLBARS

1 To display the name of a toolbar button, position the mouse over the button.

■ After a few seconds, the name of the button appears in a yellow box. The button name can help you determine the task the button performs.

2 A toolbar may not be able to display all of its buttons. Click » to display additional buttons for the toolbar.

■ Additional buttons for the toolbar appear.

3 To use a toolbar button to select a command, click the button.

USING THE TASK PANE

You can use the task pane to perform common tasks in Word. The task pane appears each time you start Word.

You can display or hide the task pane at any time. When you perform some tasks, such as searching for a document, the task pane will automatically appear.

USING THE TASK PANE

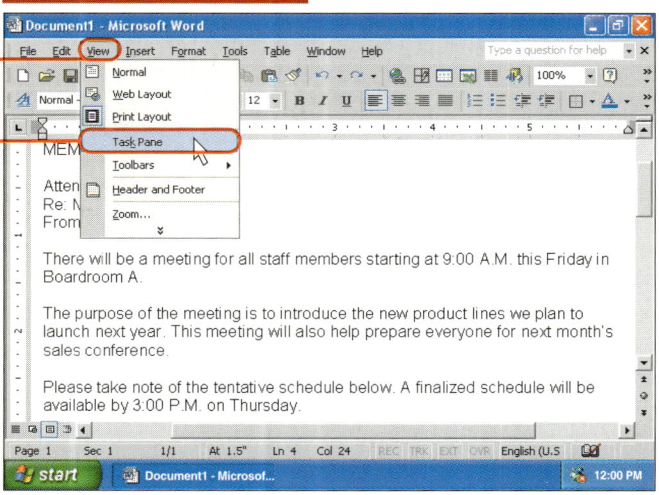

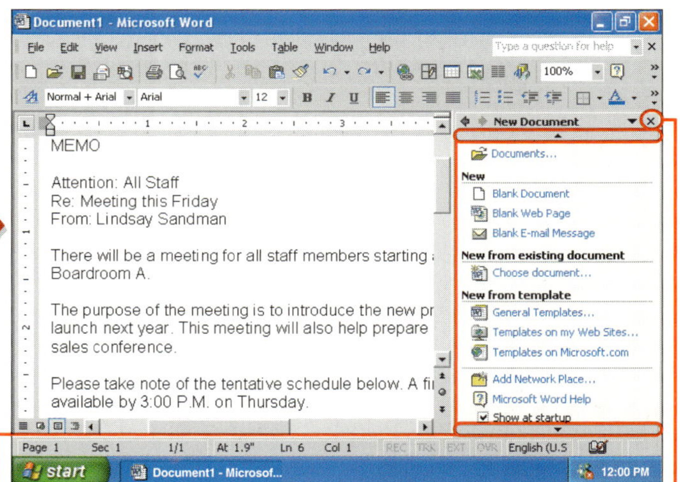

DISPLAY OR HIDE THE TASK PANE

1 Click **View**.

2 Click **Task Pane**.

Note: If Task Pane does not appear on the menu, position the mouse over the bottom of the menu to display all the menu options.

■ The task pane appears or disappears.

■ You can click ▲ or ▼ to browse through the information in the task pane.

■ To quickly hide the task pane at any time, click ☒.

What are some of the task panes available in Word?

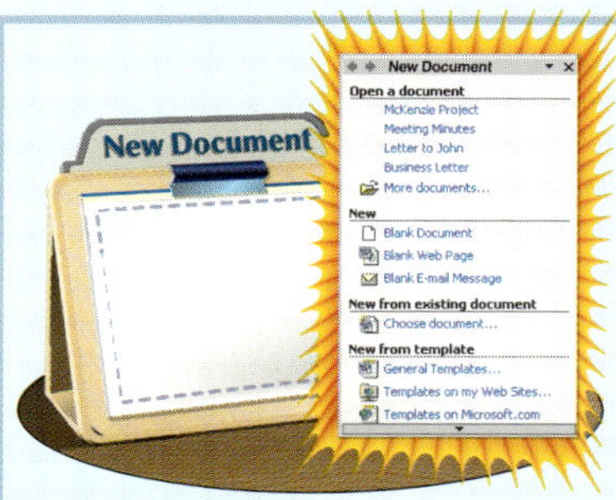

New Document

Allows you to open documents and create new documents. For information on opening a document, see page 28.

Clipboard

Displays each item you have selected to move or copy. For information on moving and copying text, see page 56.

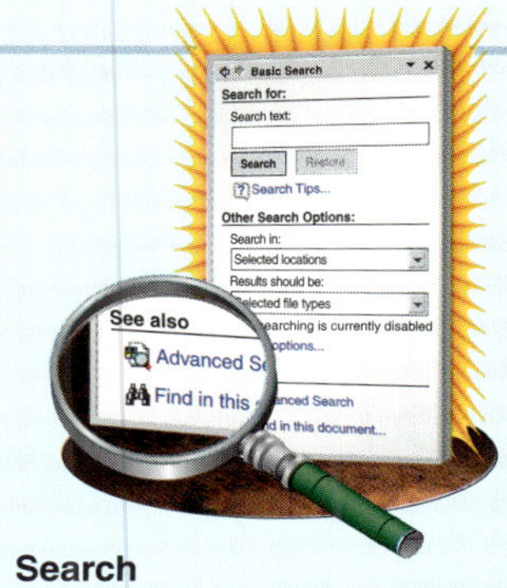

Search

Allows you to search for documents on your computer. For information on searching for documents, see page 32.

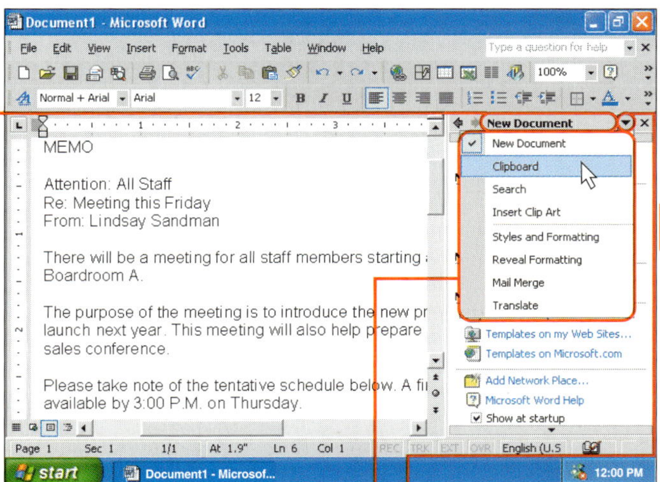

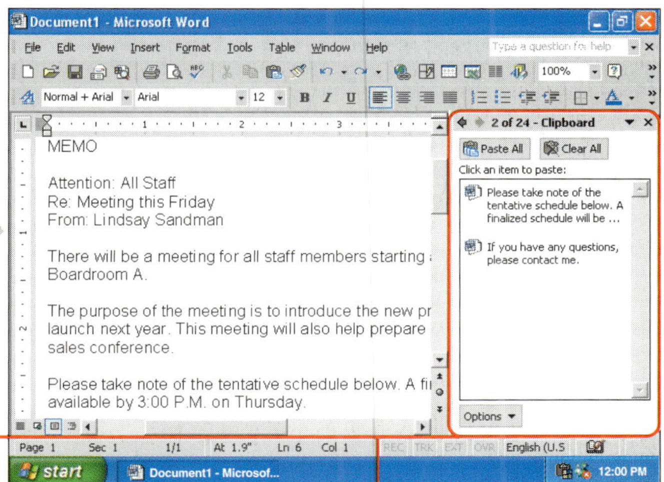

DISPLAY A DIFFERENT TASK PANE

- This area shows the name of the displayed task pane.

1. Click ▼ in this area to display a different task pane.
2. Click the task pane you want to display.

- The task pane you selected appears.

- In this example, the Clipboard task pane appears.

GETTING HELP

If you do not know how to perform a task in Word, you can ask a question to find help information for the task. Asking a question allows you to quickly find help information of interest.

GETTING HELP

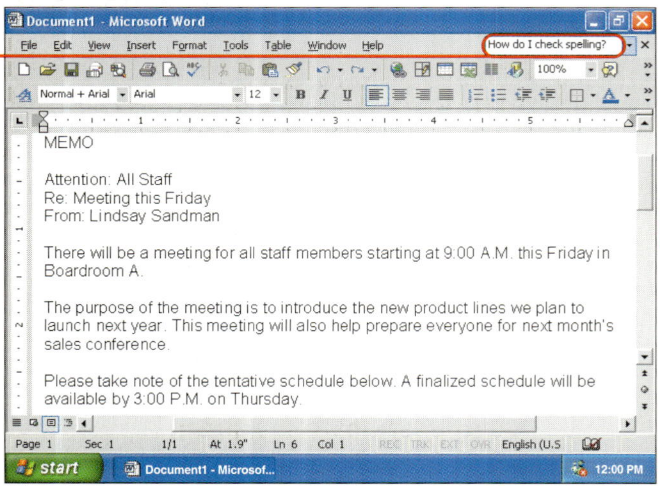

1 Click this area and type your question. Then press the Enter key.

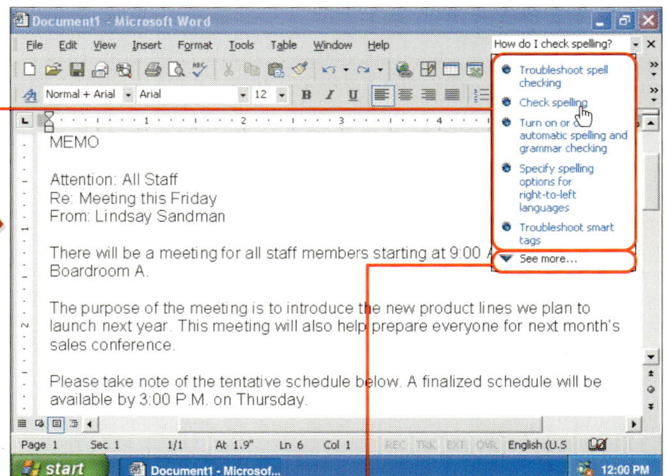

■ A list of help topics related to your question appears.

2 Click a help topic of interest.

■ If more help topics exist, you can click **See more** to view the additional topics.

What other ways can I obtain help?

In the Microsoft Word Help window, you can use the following tabs to obtain help information.

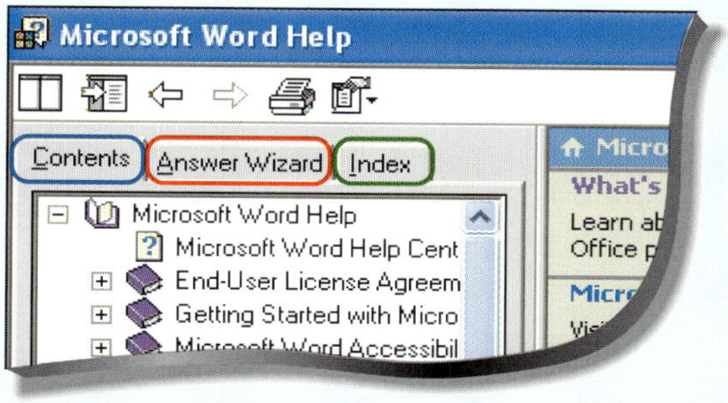

Index

You can double-click a word in the alphabetical list of keywords to display help topics related to the word.

Contents

You can double-click a book icon ( ) or click a page icon ( ) to browse through the contents of Microsoft Word Help.

Answer Wizard

You can type a question and then press the Enter key to display help topics related to the question.

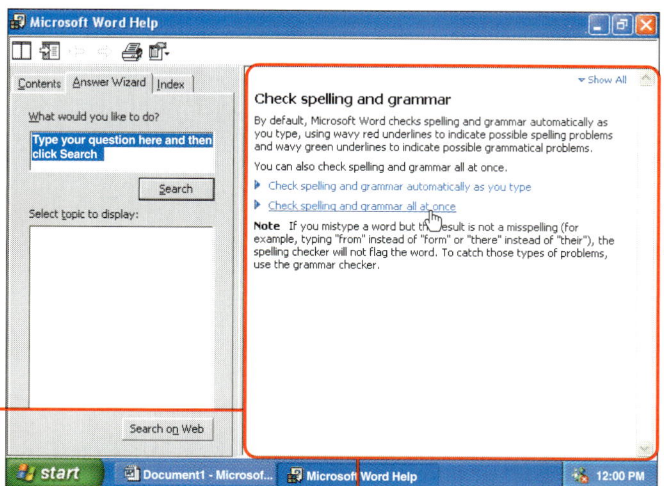

■ The Microsoft Word Help window appears.

Note: To maximize the Microsoft Word Help window to fill your screen, click in the top right corner of the window.

■ This area displays information about the help topic you selected.

3 You can display additional information for a word or phrase that appears in color. To display the additional information for a colored word or phrase, click the word or phrase.

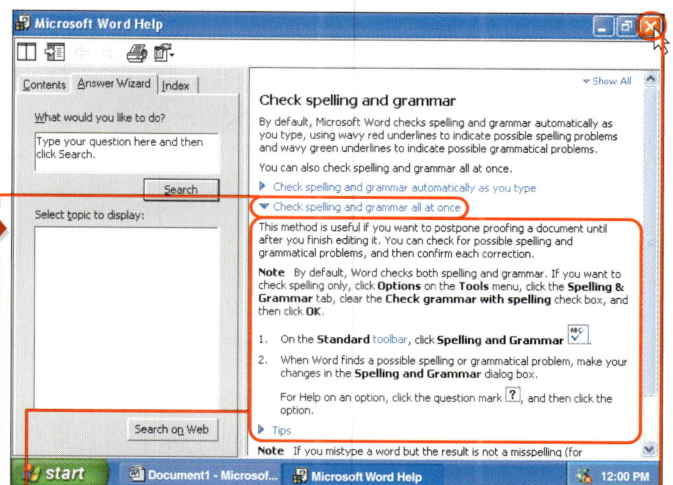

■ The additional information appears.

Note: The additional information may be a definition, series of steps or tips.

■ To once again hide the additional information, click the colored word or phrase.

4 When you finish reviewing the help information, click to close the Microsoft Word Help window.

EXIT

CHAPTER 2

Save and Open Documents

Are you wondering how to save, close or open a Word document? Learn how in this chapter.

Save a Document 22

Save a Document in a Different Format 24

Close a Document 26

Exit Word 27

Open a Document 28

Open a Document in a Different Format 30

Search for a Document 32

Protect a Document............................34

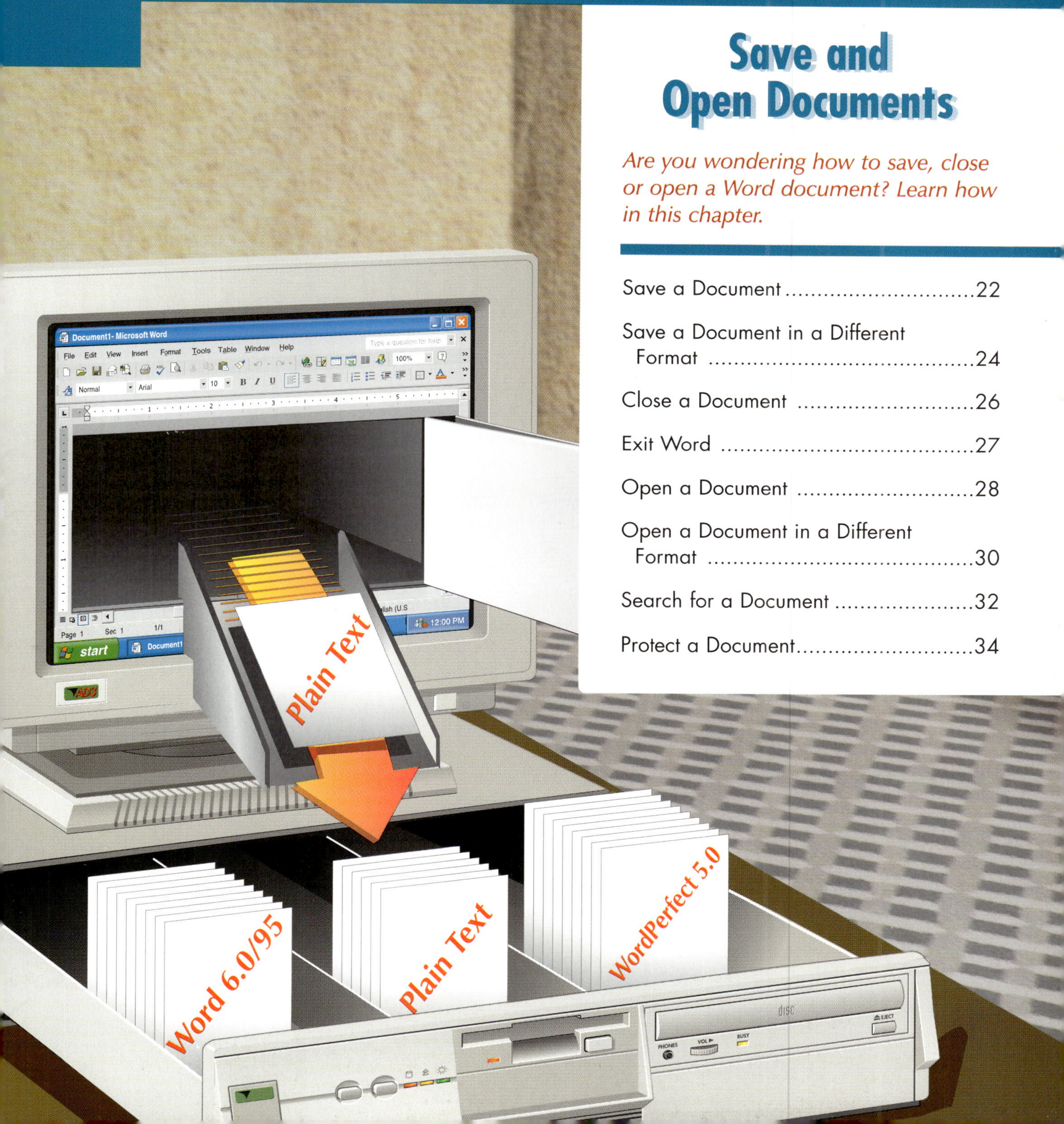

SAVE A DOCUMENT

You can save your document to store it for future use. Saving a document allows you to later review and edit the document.

SAVE A DOCUMENT

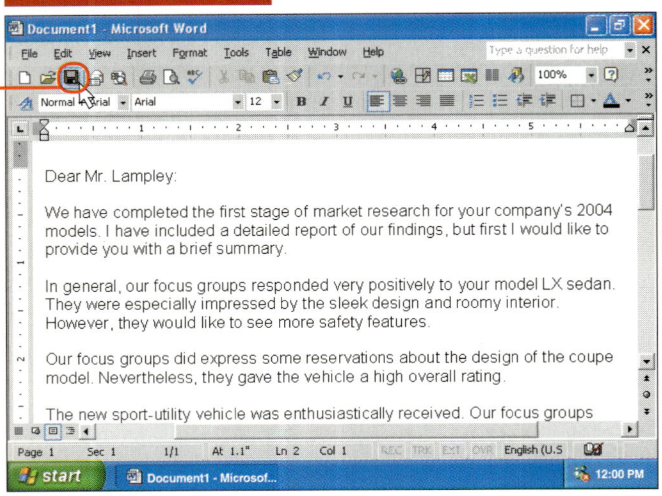

1 Click to save your document.

Note: If is not displayed, click on the Standard toolbar to display the button.

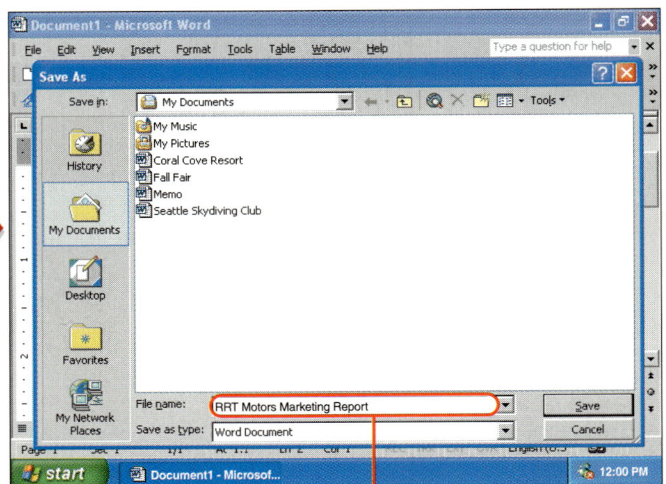

■ The Save As dialog box appears.

Note: If you previously saved your document, the Save As dialog box will not appear since you have already named the document.

2 Type a name for the document.

*Note: A document name cannot contain the * : ? > < | or " characters.*

What are the commonly used locations that I can access?

History

Provides access to folders and documents you recently worked with.

My Documents

Provides a convenient place to store a document.

Desktop

Allows you to store a document on the Windows desktop.

Favorites

Provides a place to store a document you will frequently use.

My Network Places

Allows you to store a document on your network.

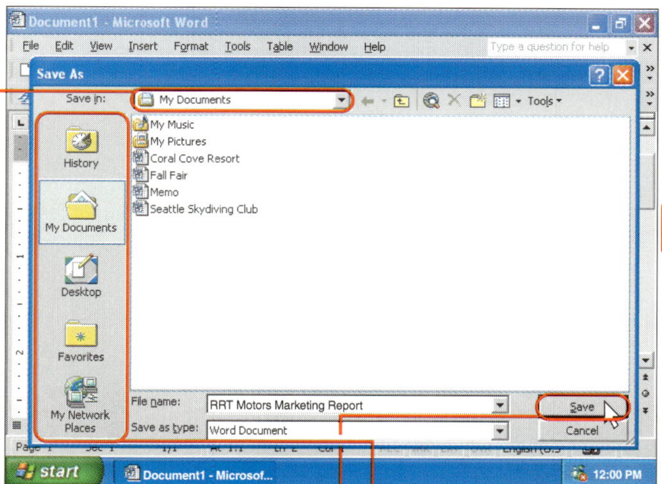

■ This area shows the location where Word will store your document. You can click this area to change the location.

■ This area allows you to access commonly used locations. You can click a location to save your document in the location.

3 Click **Save** to save your document.

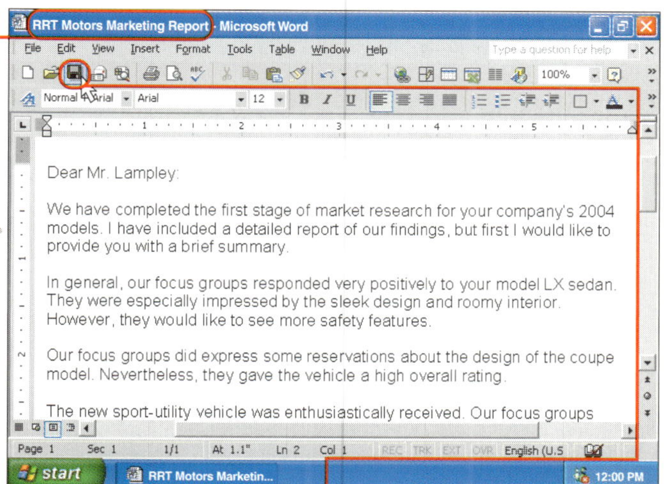

■ Word saves your document and displays the name of the document at the top of your screen.

SAVE CHANGES

You should regularly save changes you make to a document to avoid losing your work.

1 Click 💾 to save the changes you made to your document.

SAVE A DOCUMENT IN A DIFFERENT FORMAT

You can save a Word document in a different format. This is useful if you need to share a document with a colleague who does not use Word 2002.

SAVE A DOCUMENT IN A DIFFERENT FORMAT

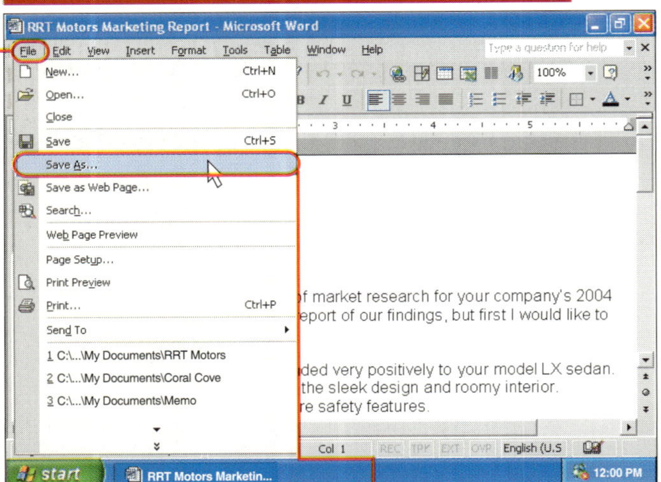

1 Click **File**.

2 Click **Save As**.

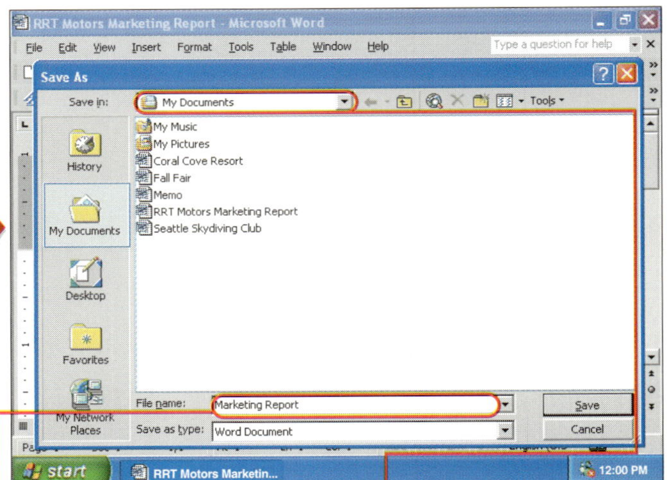

■ The Save As dialog box appears.

3 Type a name for the document.

*Note: A document name cannot contain the * : ? > < | or " characters.*

■ This area shows the location where Word will store your document. You can click this area to change the location.

Why does a dialog box appear when I save my document in a different format?

A dialog box appears if Word needs to install software before saving the document in the new format. Insert the CD-ROM disc you used to install Word into your computer's CD-ROM drive. Then click **Yes** to install the software.

Note: A window may appear on your screen. Click ☒ in the top right corner of the window to close the window.

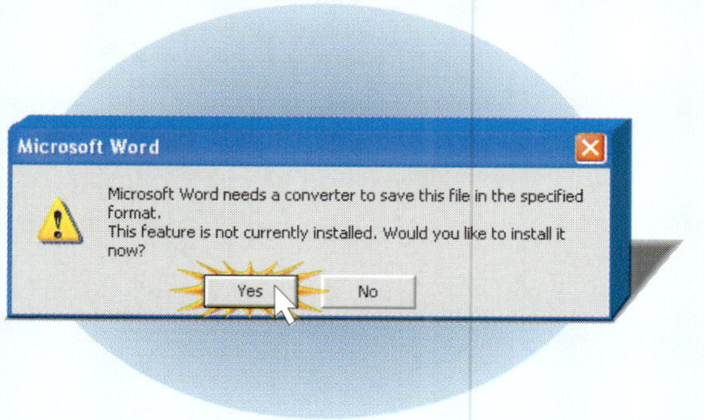

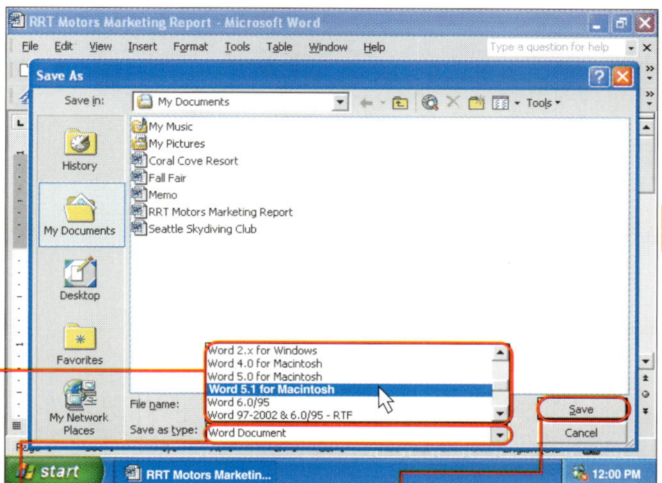

4 Click this area to select the format you want to use to save the document.

5 Click the format you want to use.

6 Click **Save** to save your document.

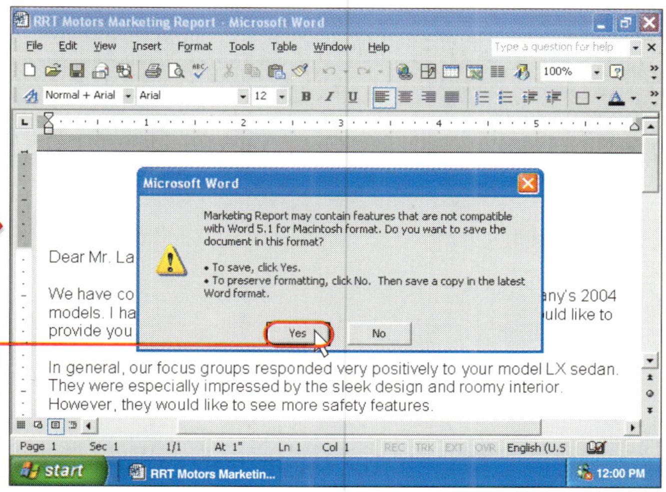

■ A dialog box may appear, indicating that some of the formatting in your document may be lost when you save the document in the new format.

7 Click **Yes** to continue.

Note: If a different dialog box appears, click ***Continue*** *or* ***OK*** *to save the document in the new format.*

■ Word saves your document in the new format. You can now open and work with the document in another program.

CLOSE A DOCUMENT

When you finish working with a document, you can close the document to remove it from your screen.

When you close a document, you do not exit the Word program. You can continue to work with other documents.

CLOSE A DOCUMENT

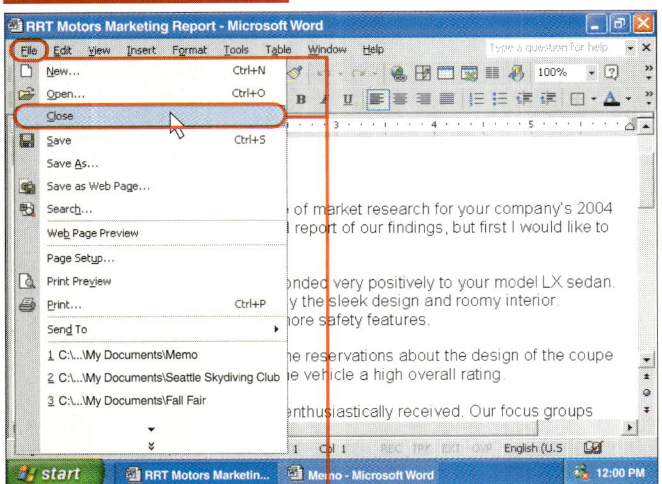

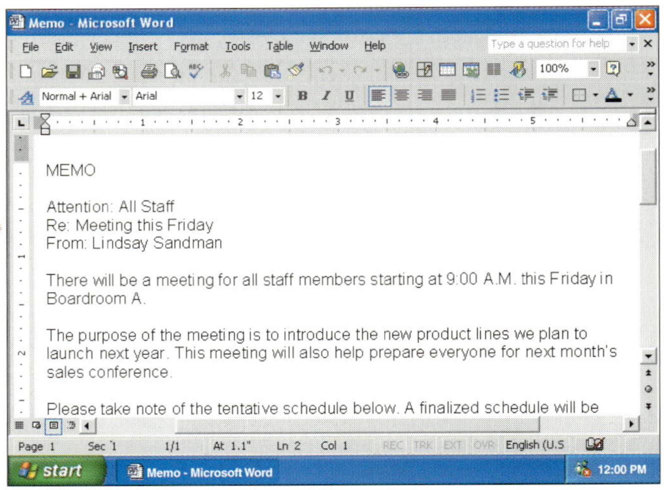

■ Before closing a document, you should save any changes you made to the document. To save a document, see page 22.

1 Click **File**.

2 Click **Close** to close the document.

■ The document disappears from your screen.

■ If you had more than one document open, the second last document you worked with appears on your screen.

EXIT WORD

When you finish using Word, you can exit the program.

You should always exit all open programs before turning off your computer.

EXIT WORD

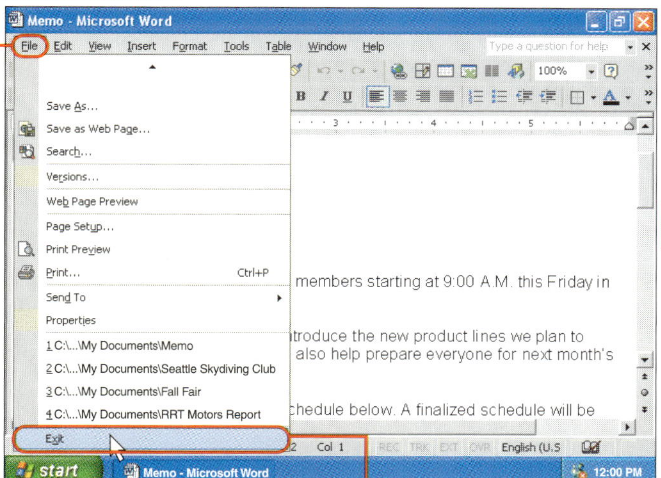

■ Before exiting Word, you should save all your open documents. To save a document, see page 22.

1 Click **File**.

2 Click **Exit**.

Note: If Exit does not appear on the menu, position the mouse over the bottom of the menu to display all the menu options.

■ The Microsoft Word window disappears from your screen.

■ The button for the Microsoft Word window disappears from the taskbar.

OPEN A DOCUMENT

You can open a saved document to view the document on your screen. Opening a document allows you to review and make changes to the document.

OPEN A DOCUMENT

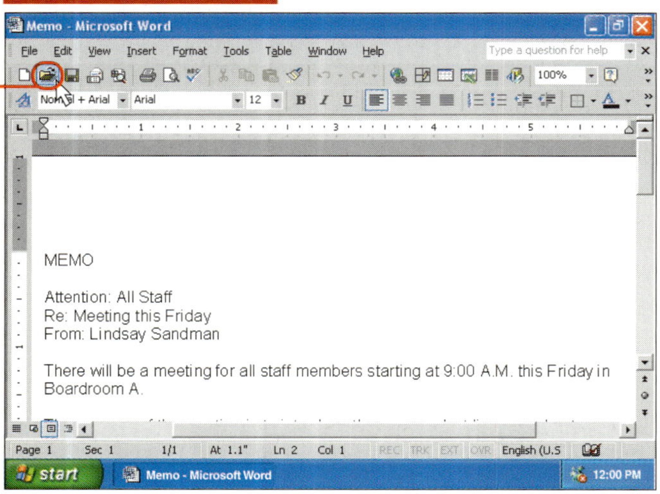

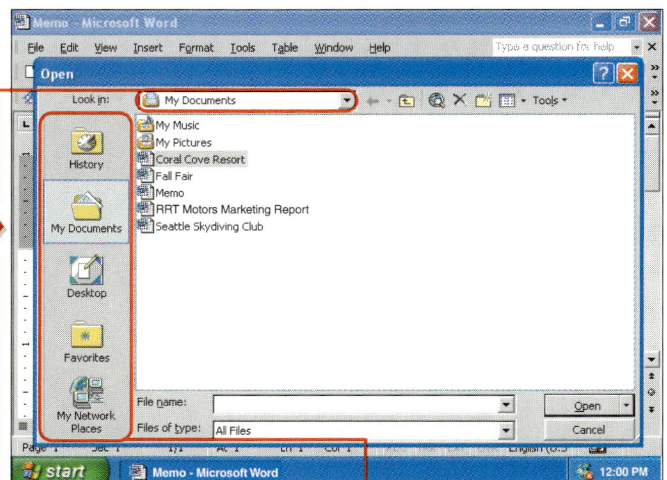

1 Click [open icon] to open a document.

Note: If [open icon] is not displayed, click [»] on the Standard toolbar to display the button.

■ The Open dialog box appears.

■ This area shows the location of the displayed documents. You can click this area to change the location.

■ This area allows you to access documents stored in commonly used locations. You can click a location to display the documents stored in the location.

Note: For information on the commonly used locations, see the top of page 23.

How can I quickly open a document I recently worked with?

Word remembers the names of the last four documents you worked with. You can use one of the following methods to quickly open one of these documents.

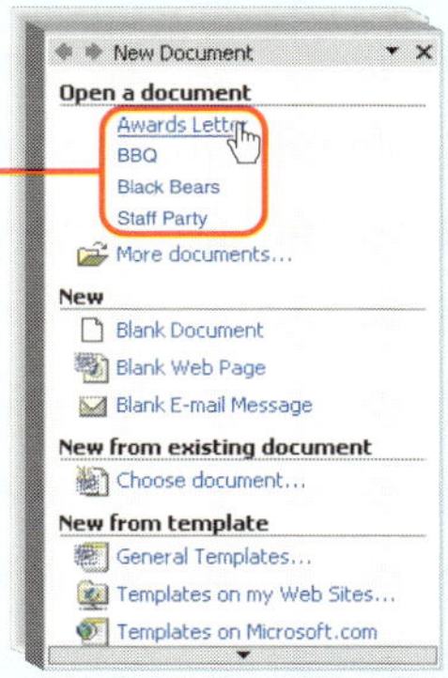

Use the Task Pane

The New Document task pane appears each time you start Word. To display the New Document task pane, see page 16.

1 Click the name of the document you want to open.

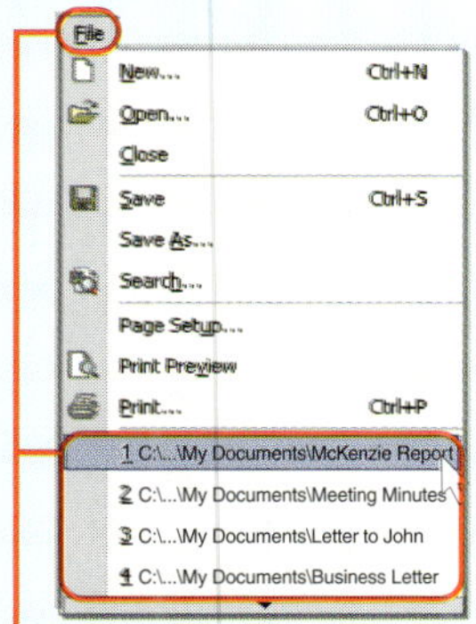

Use the File Menu

1 Click **File**.

2 Click the name of the document you want to open.

Note: If the names of the last four documents you worked with are not all displayed, position the mouse over the bottom of the menu to display all the names.

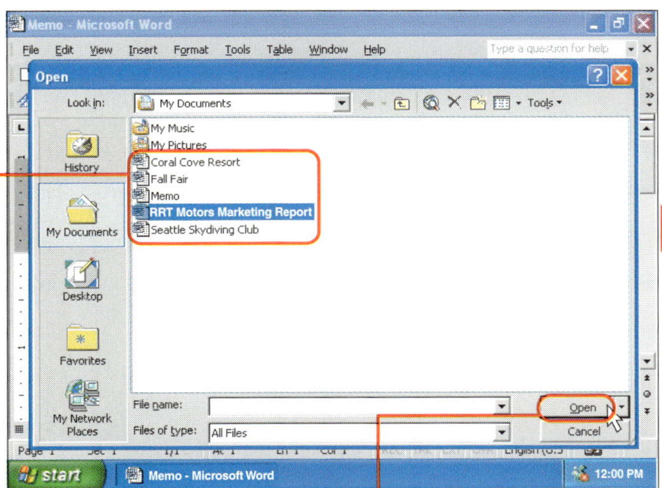

2 Click the name of the document you want to open.

3 Click **Open** to open the document.

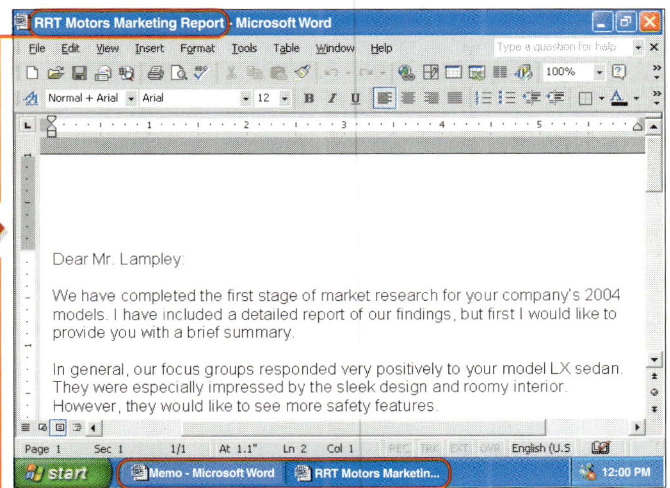

■ The document opens and appears on your screen. You can now review and make changes to the document.

■ This area displays the name of the document.

■ If you already had a document open, the new document appears in a new Microsoft Word window. You can click the buttons on the taskbar to switch between the open documents.

OPEN A DOCUMENT IN A DIFFERENT FORMAT

You can use Word to open and work with a document that was created in another program. This helps you work with documents from colleagues who use different word processing programs.

You can open documents created in many different programs, such as WordPerfect, Write, Word for Macintosh and older versions of Word for Windows.

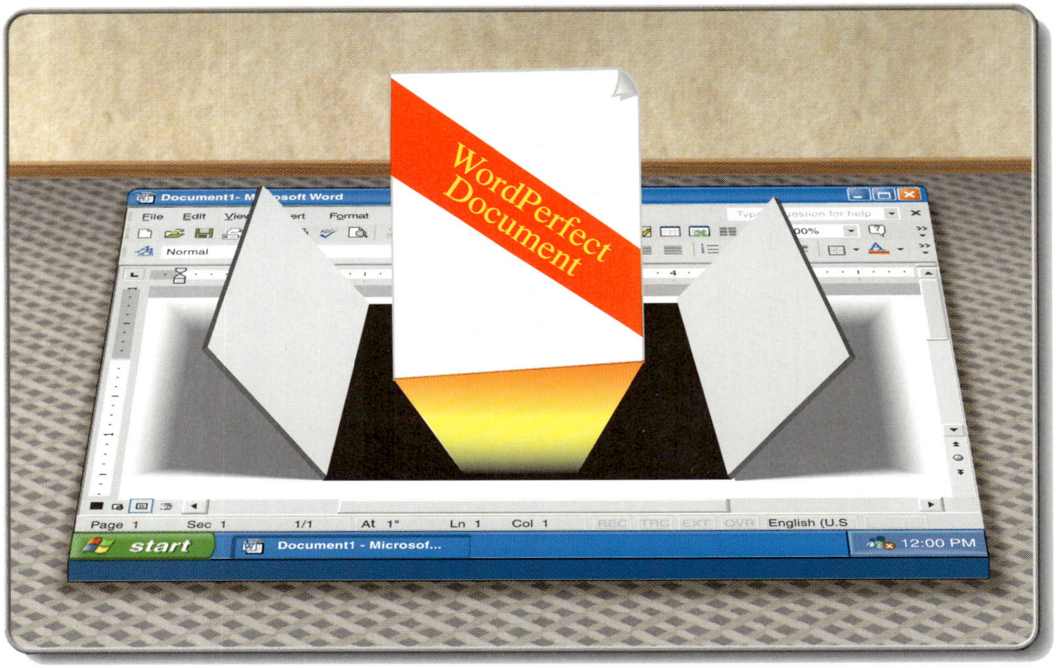

OPEN A DOCUMENT IN A DIFFERENT FORMAT

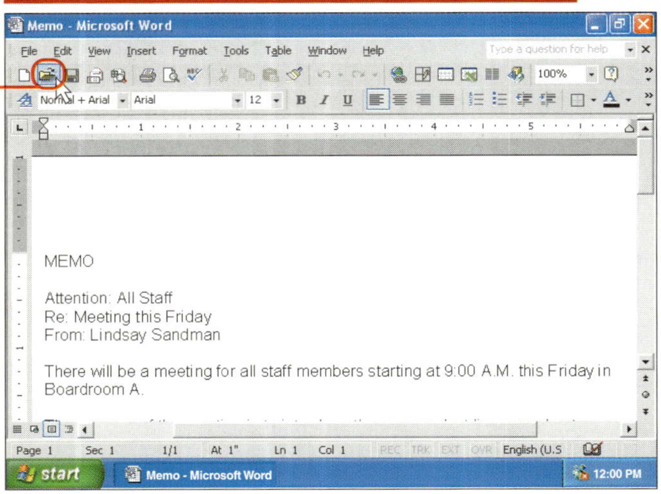

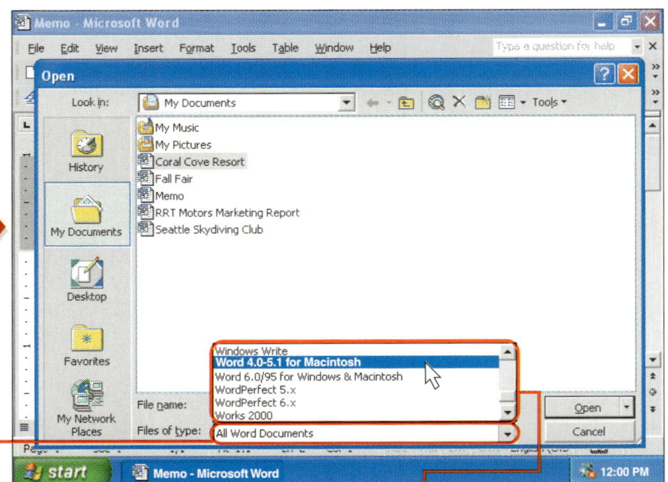

1 Click to open a document.

Note: If is not displayed, click on the Standard toolbar to display the button.

■ The Open dialog box appears.

2 Click this area to select the format of the document you want to open.

3 Click the format of the document you want to open.

*Note: If you do not know the format of the document you want to open, click **All Files**.*

Why does a dialog box appear when I try to open a document in a different format?

A dialog box appears if Word needs to install software before opening the document. Insert the CD-ROM disc you used to install Word into your computer's CD-ROM drive. Then click **Yes** to install the software.

Note: A window may appear on your screen. Click ✕ in the top right corner of the window to close the window.

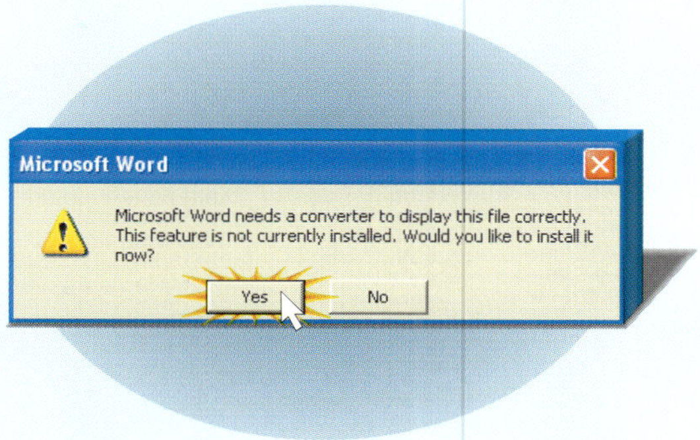

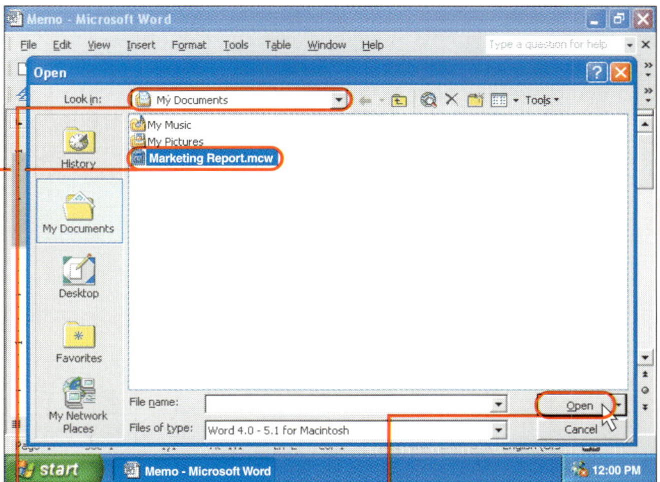

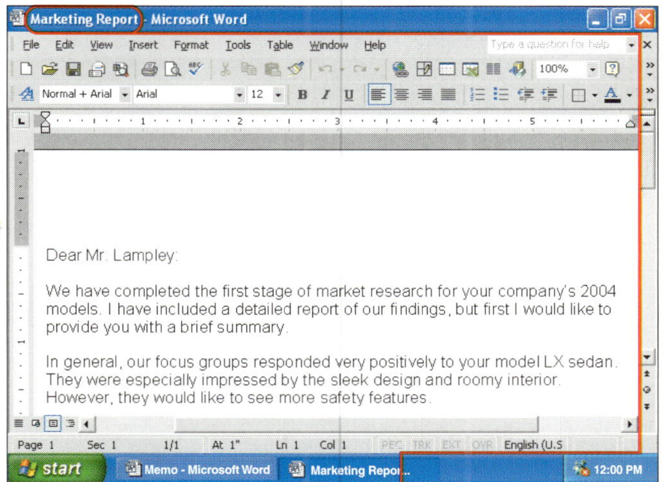

■ This area shows the location of the displayed documents. You can click this area to change the location.

4 Click the name of the document you want to open.

5 Click **Open** to open the document.

Note: If a dialog box appears on your screen, see the top of this page.

■ The document opens and appears on your screen. You can now review and make changes to the document.

■ This area displays the name of the document.

SEARCH FOR A DOCUMENT

If you cannot remember the name or location of a document you want to work with, you can search for the document.

SEARCH FOR A DOCUMENT

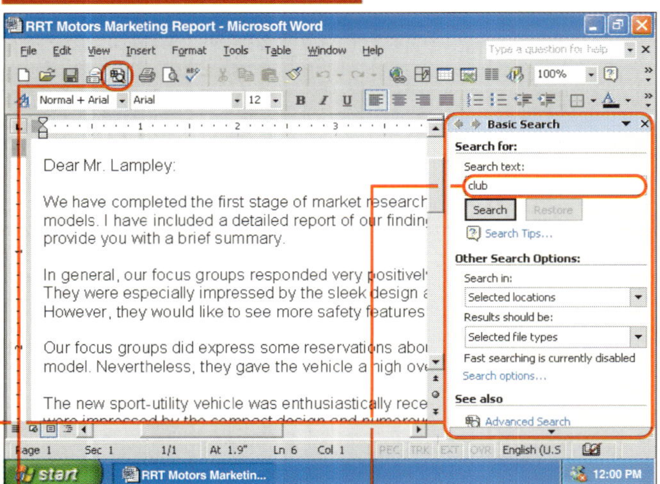

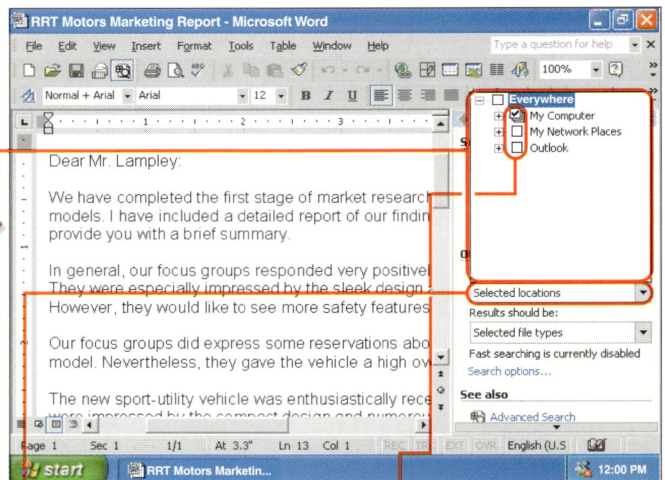

1 Click [icon] to search for a document.

Note: If [icon] is not displayed, click [icon] on the Standard toolbar to display the button.

■ The Search task pane appears.

2 Click this area and type one or more words you want to search for.

Note: If this area already contains text, drag the mouse I over the existing text and then press the **Delete** *key. Then perform step* ***2***.

3 Click [▼] in this area to select the locations you want to search.

■ A check mark (✔) appears beside each location Word will search.

Note: By default, Word will search all the drives and folders on your computer.

4 You can click the box beside a location to add (☑) or remove (☐) a check mark.

5 To close the list of locations, click outside the list.

How will Word use the words I specify to search for documents?

Word will search the contents of documents and the file names of documents for the words you specify. When searching the contents of documents, Word will search for various forms of the words. For example, searching for "run" will find "run," "running" and "ran."

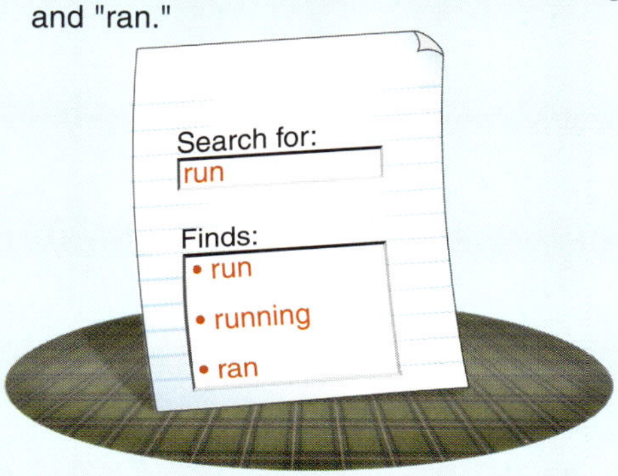

When selecting the locations and types of files I want to search for, how can I display more items?

Each item that displays a plus sign (⊞) contains hidden items. To display the hidden items, click the plus sign (⊞) beside the item (⊞ changes to ⊟). To once again hide the items, click the minus sign (⊟) beside the item.

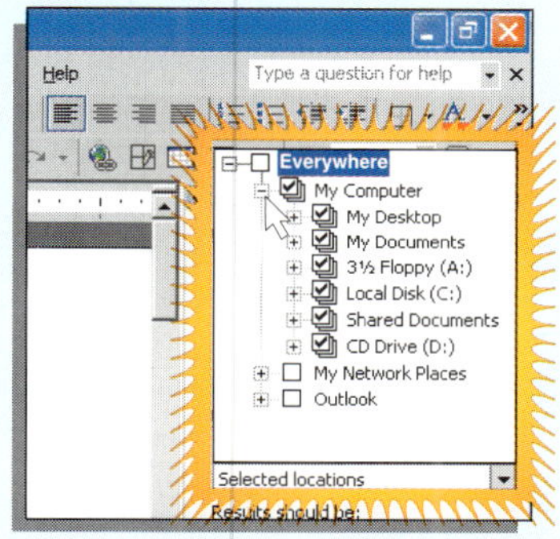

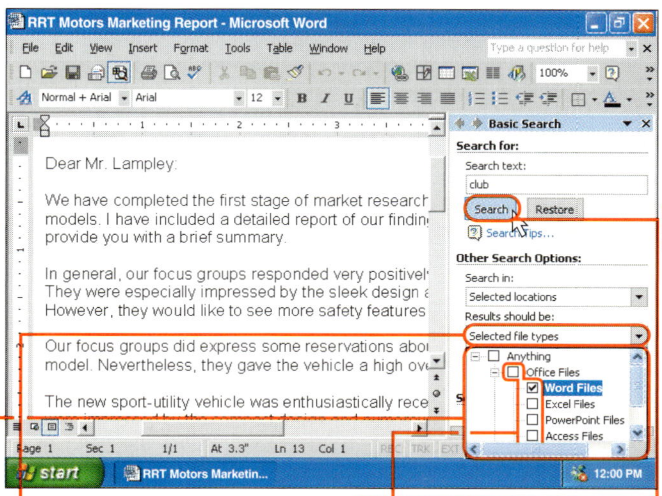

6 Click ▾ in this area to specify the types of files you want to search for.

■ A check mark (✔) appears beside each type of file Word will search for.

7 You can click the box beside a file type to add (✔) or remove (☐) a check mark.

8 To close the list of file types, click outside the list.

9 Click **Search** to start the search.

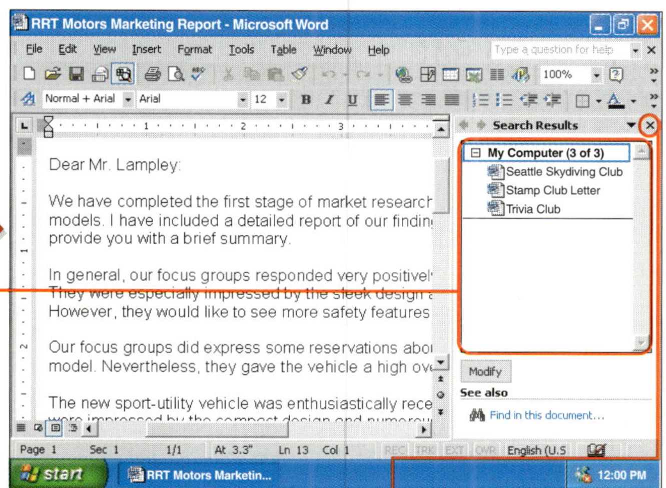

■ This area lists the documents that contain the words you specified.

■ To open a document in the list, click the document.

■ To hide the Search task pane at any time, click ☒.

PROTECT A DOCUMENT

You can prevent other people from opening or making changes to a document by protecting it with a password.

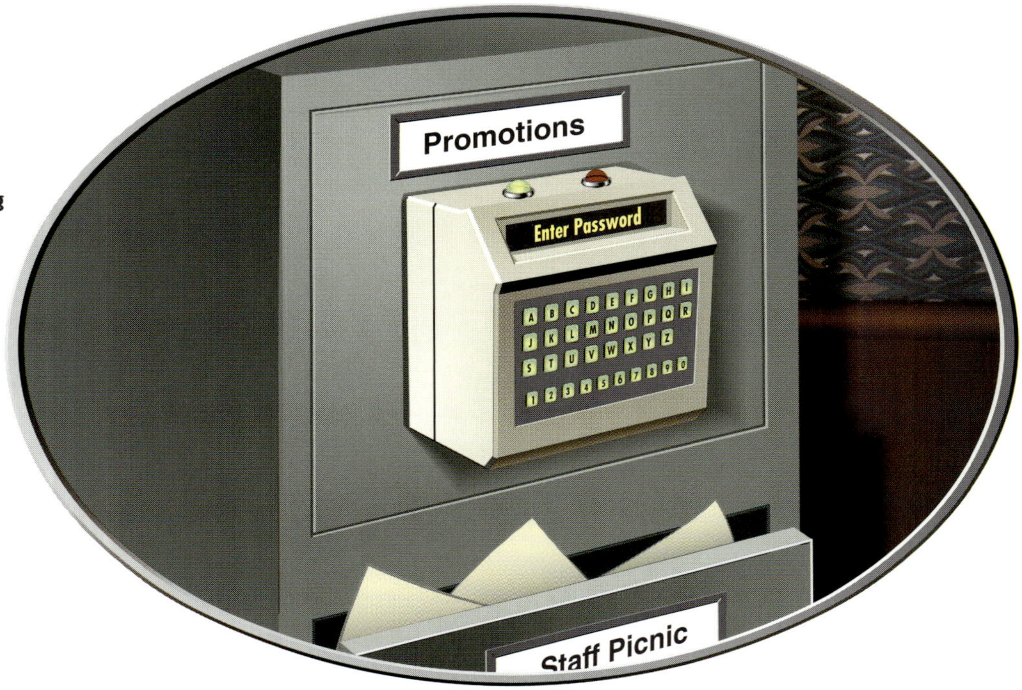

PROTECT A DOCUMENT

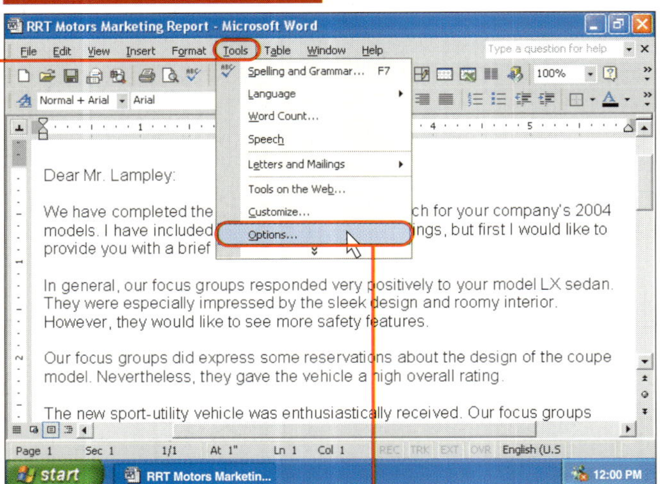

1 Click **Tools**.

2 Click **Options**.

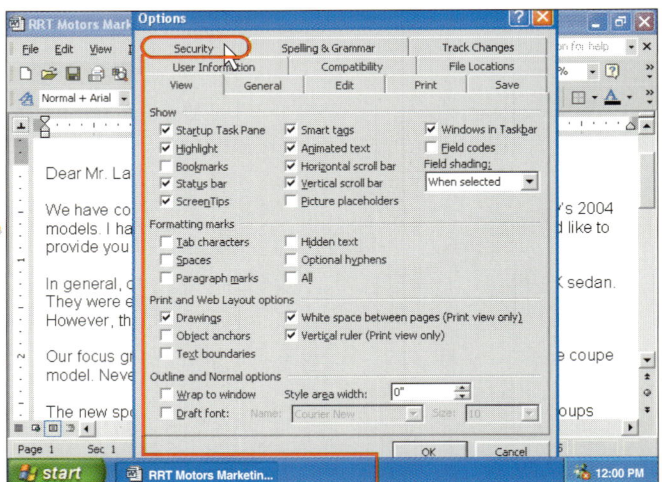

■ The Options dialog box appears.

3 Click the **Security** tab.

What password should I use to protect my document?

When choosing a password, you should not use words that people can easily associate with you, such as your name or favorite sport. The most effective passwords connect two words or numbers with a special character (example: **car#123**). A password can contain up to 15 characters and be any combination of letters, numbers and symbols.

Should I take any special precautions with my password?

You should write down your password and keep it in a safe place. If you forget the password, you may not be able to open the document.

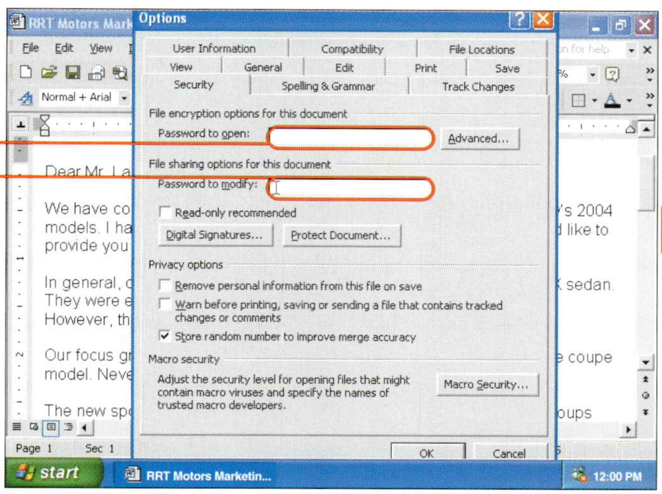

4 Click the box for the type of password you want to enter.

Password to open
Prevents people from opening the document without entering the correct password.

Password to modify
Prevents people from making changes to the document without entering the correct password.

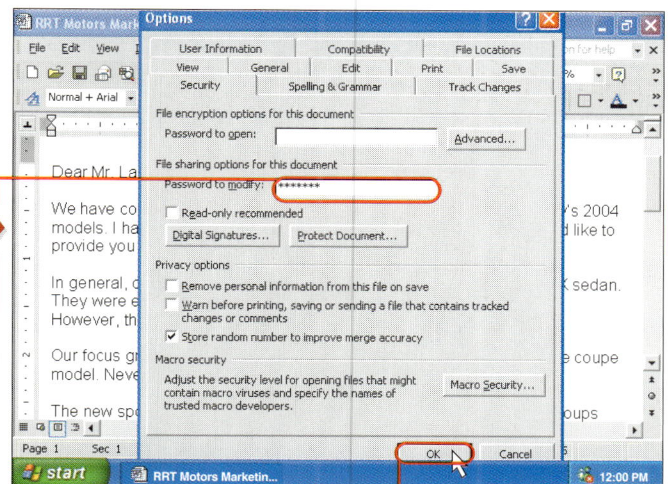

5 Type the password you want to use.

6 Click **OK** to continue.

CONTINUED

PROTECT A DOCUMENT

After you protect a document with a password, Word will ask you to enter the password each time you open the document.

PROTECT A DOCUMENT (CONTINUED)

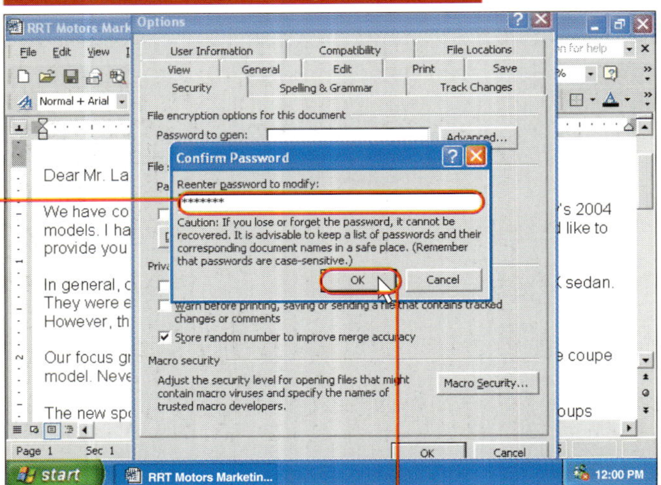

■ The Confirm Password dialog box appears, asking you to confirm the password you entered.

7 Type the password again to confirm the password.

8 Click **OK** to protect the document.

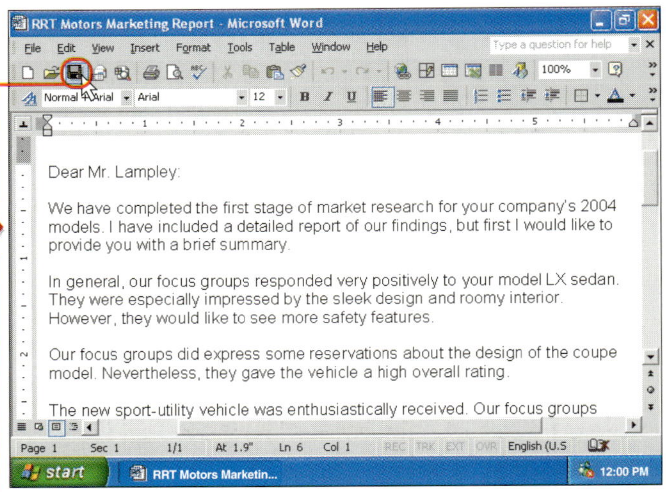

9 Click 💾 to save the changes you made to the document.

Note: If you have not previously saved the document, the Save As dialog box will appear. To save a document, see page 22.

I typed the correct password, but Word will not open my document. What is wrong?

Passwords in Word are case sensitive. If you do not enter the correct uppercase and lowercase letters, Word will not accept the password. For example, if your password is **car#123**, you cannot enter **Car#123** or **CAR#123** to open the document.

How do I unprotect a document?

To unprotect a document, perform steps **1** to **6** starting on page 34, except in step **5**, drag the mouse I over the existing password until you highlight the password and then press the **Delete** key. Then perform step **9** below.

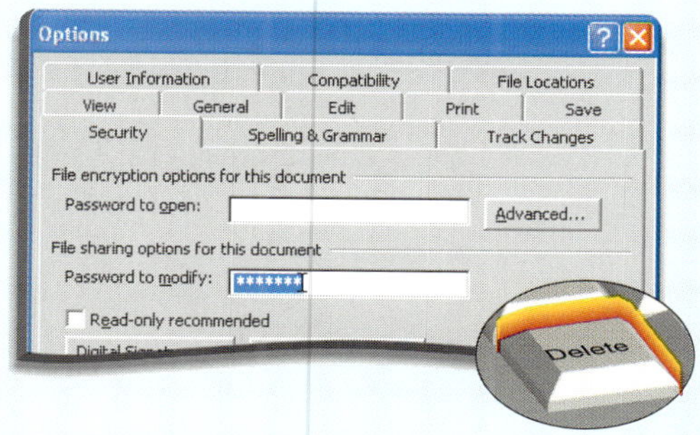

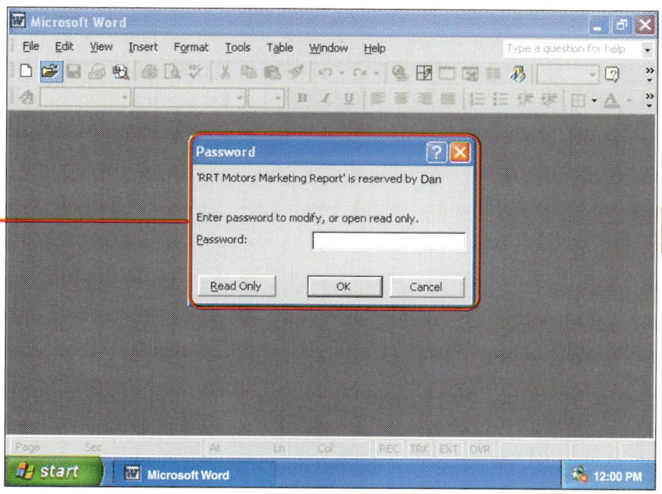

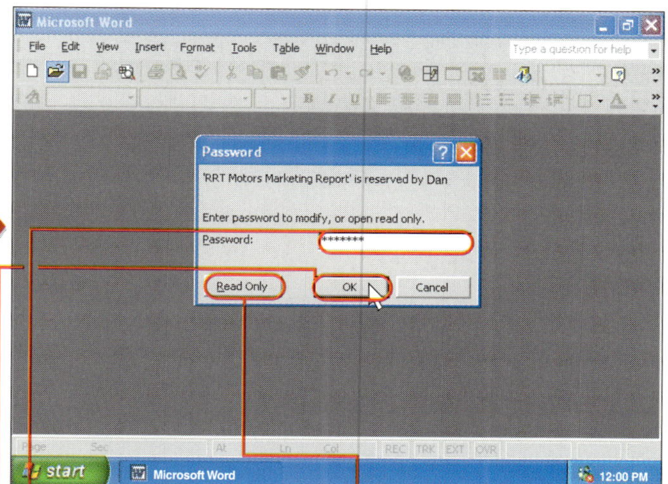

OPEN A PROTECTED DOCUMENT

■ A Password dialog box appears each time you open a protected document. To open a document, see page 28.

Note: The appearance of the dialog box depends on the type of password assigned to the document.

1 Type the correct password.

2 Click **OK**.

■ If the **Read Only** button is available, you can click the button to open the document without entering a password. You will not be able to save changes you make to the document.

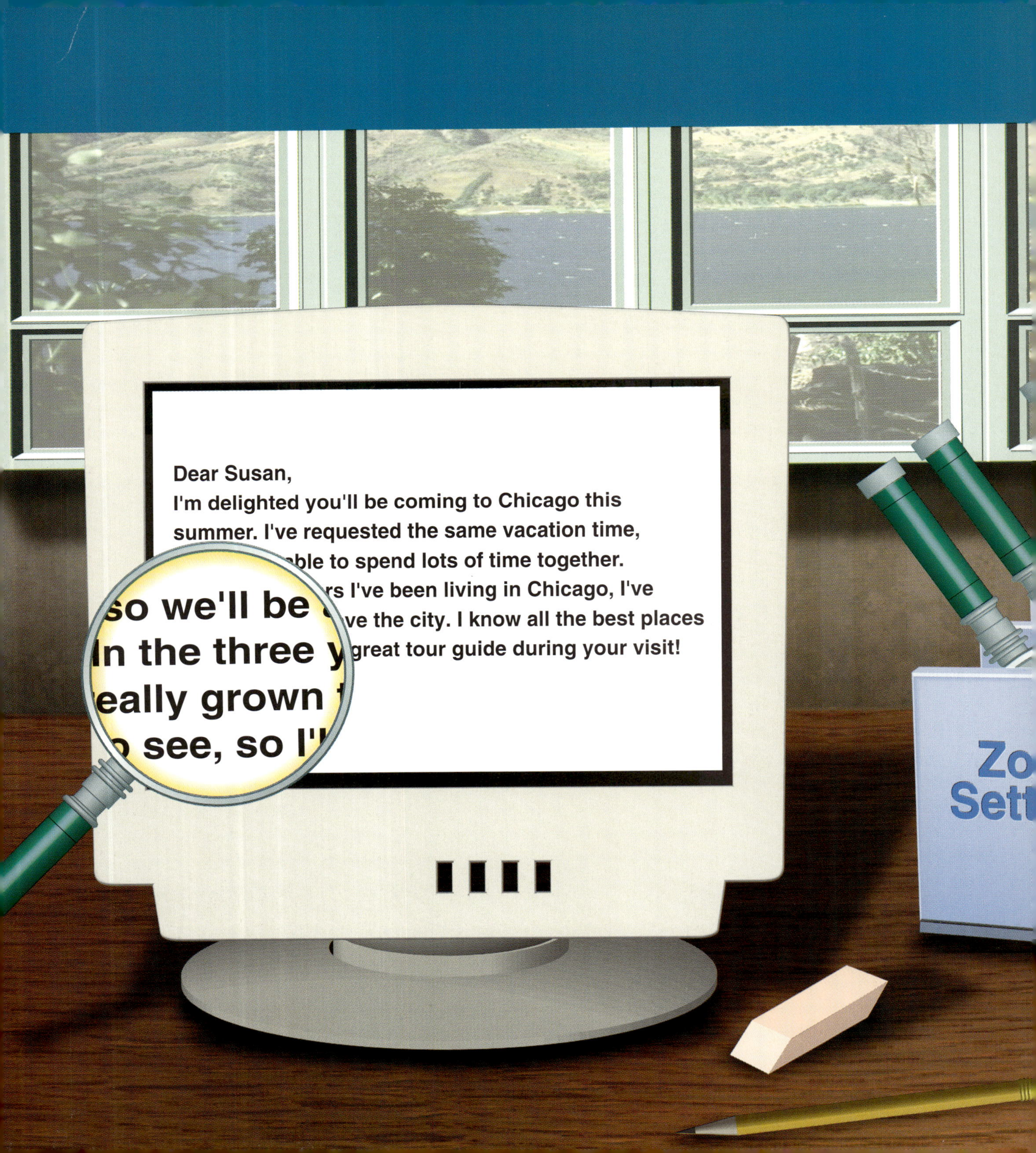

Dear Susan,
I'm delighted you'll be coming to Chicago this
summer. I've requested the same vacation time,
ble to spend lots of time together.
rs I've been living in Chicago, I've
ve the city. I know all the best places
great tour guide during your visit!
so we'll be
In the three y
eally grown
see, so I'
Zo
Sett

CHAPTER 3

Change Display of Documents

Are you interested in changing the way your document appears on your screen? In this chapter, you will learn how to display your document in a different view, display or hide a toolbar and more.

Change the View of a Document 40

Display or Hide the Ruler 42

Display or Hide a Toolbar 43

Move a Toolbar 44

Size a Toolbar 45

Zoom In or Out 46

Split a Document 47

Display or Hide White Space 48

Display or Hide Formatting Marks 49

Using the Document Map 50

CHANGE THE VIEW OF A DOCUMENT

Word offers four different views that you can use to display your document. You can choose the view that best suits your needs.

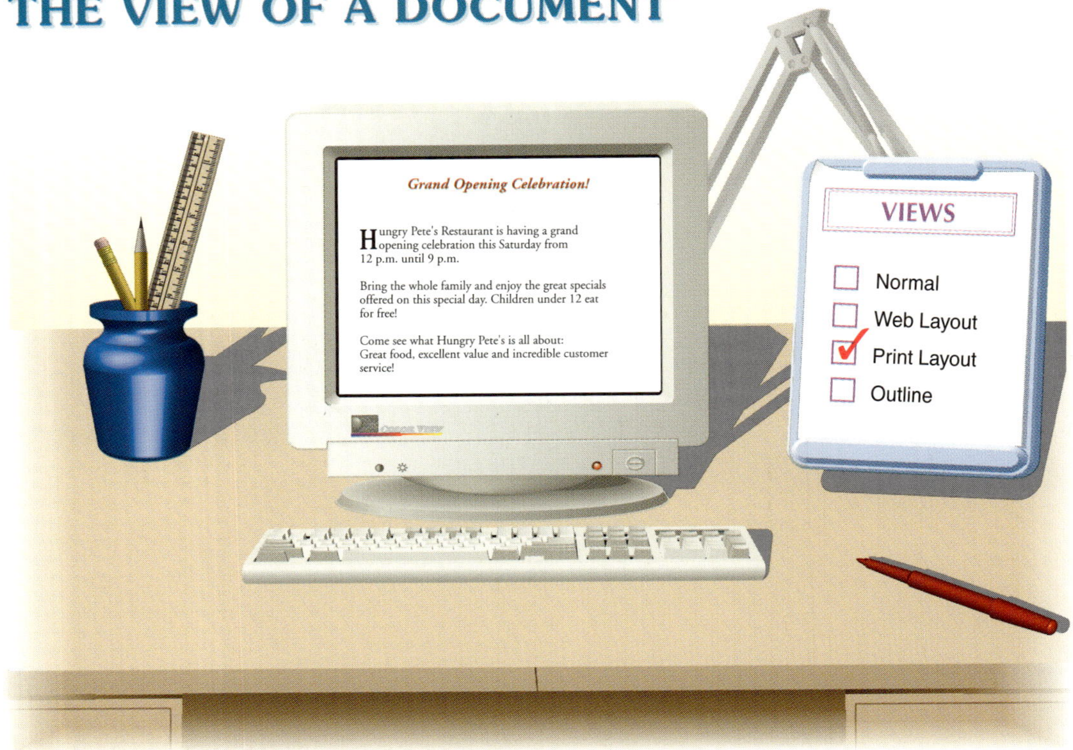

CHANGE THE VIEW OF A DOCUMENT

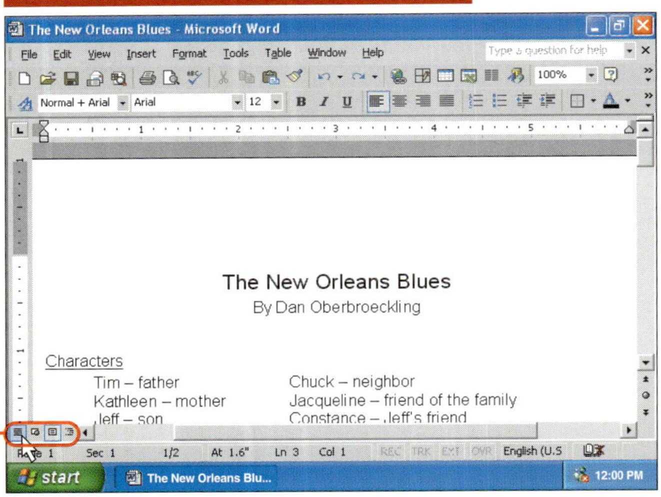

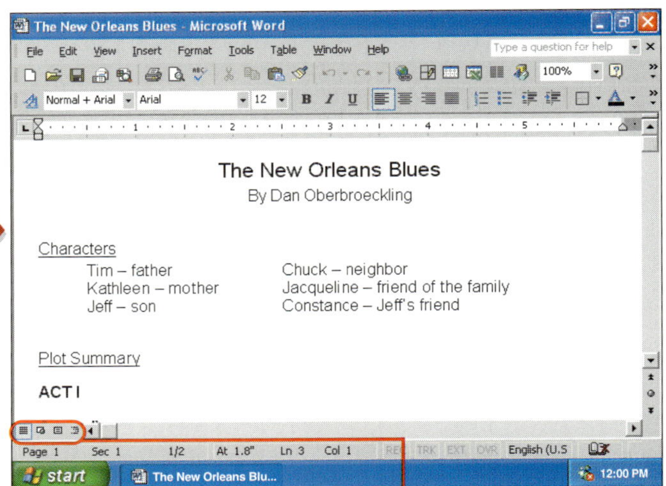

1 To change the view of your document, click one of the following buttons.

- Normal
- Web Layout
- Print Layout
- Outline

■ Your document appears in the view you selected.

■ A blue border appears around the button for the view you selected.

THE DOCUMENT VIEWS

Normal View

The Normal view simplifies the layout of your document so you can quickly enter, edit and format text. This view does not display certain elements in your document, such as margins, headers, footers, page numbers and some types of graphics.

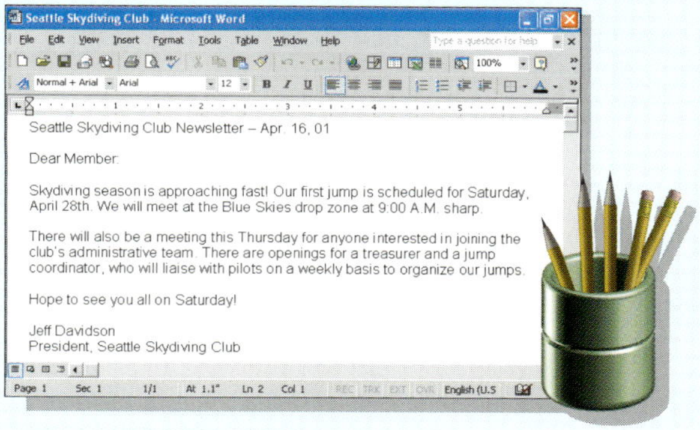

Web Layout View

Working in the Web Layout view is useful when you are creating a Web page or a document that you plan to view only on a computer screen.

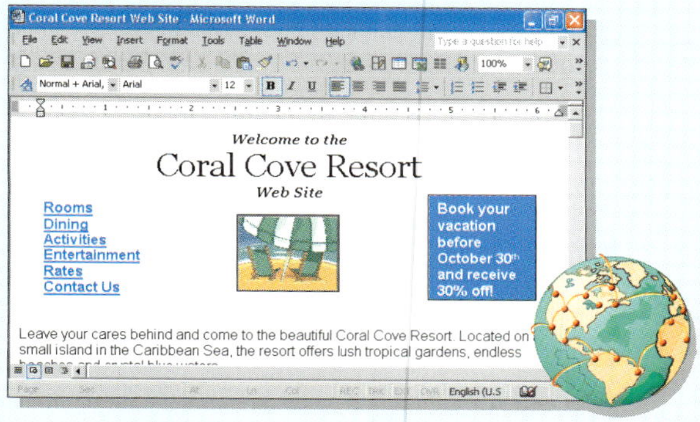

Print Layout View

You can work in the Print Layout view when you want to see how your document will appear on a printed page. This view displays all elements in your document, such as margins, headers, footers, page numbers and graphics.

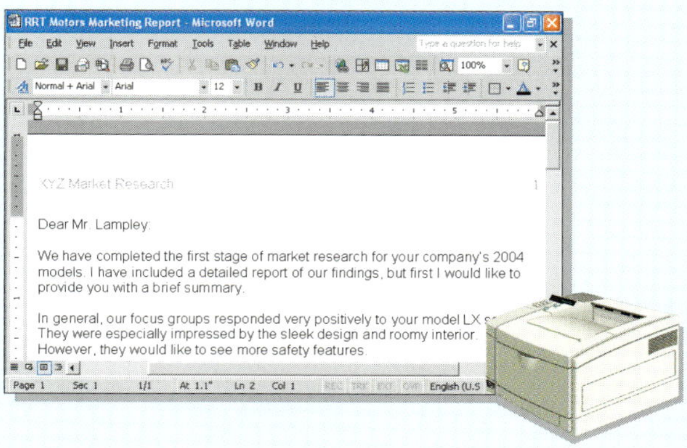

Outline View

The Outline view is useful when you want to review and work with the structure of your document. This view allows you to collapse a document to see only the headings or expand a document to see all the headings and text. The Outline view is useful when working with long documents.

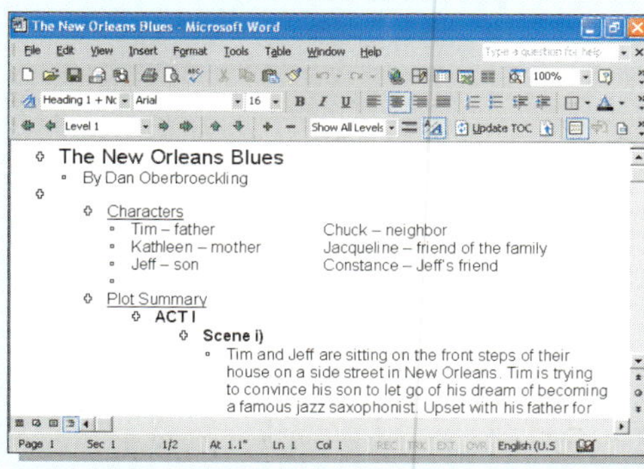

DISPLAY OR HIDE THE RULER

You can display or hide the ruler at any time. The ruler helps you position text in a document.

When you first start Word, the ruler appears on your screen.

You cannot display or hide the ruler in the Outline view. For information on the views, see page 40.

DISPLAY OR HIDE THE RULER

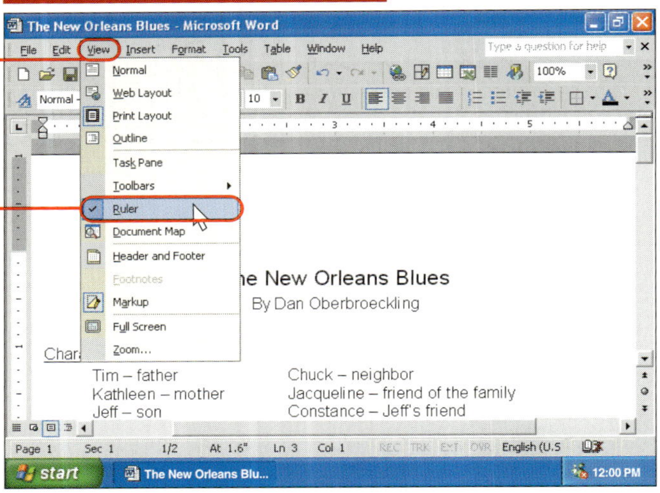

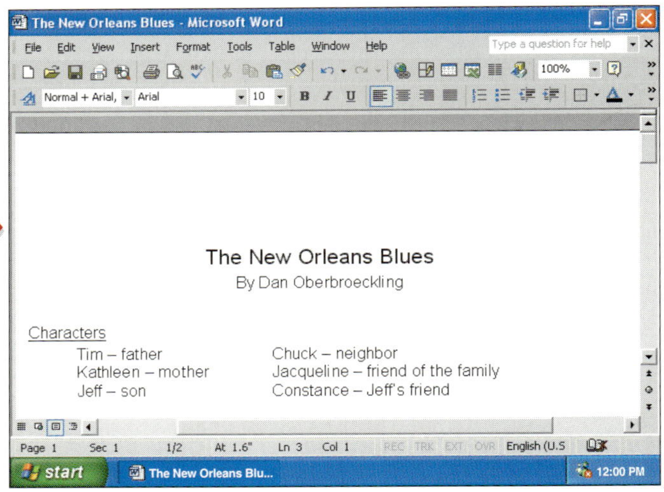

1 Click **View**.

2 Click **Ruler**. A check mark (✔) beside **Ruler** indicates the ruler is currently displayed.

Note: If Ruler does not appear on the menu, position the mouse over the bottom of the menu to display all the menu options.

■ Word displays or hides the ruler.

Note: Hiding the ruler provides a larger and less cluttered working area.

DISPLAY OR HIDE A TOOLBAR

Word offers several toolbars that you can display or hide to suit your needs. Toolbars contain buttons that you can select to quickly perform common tasks.

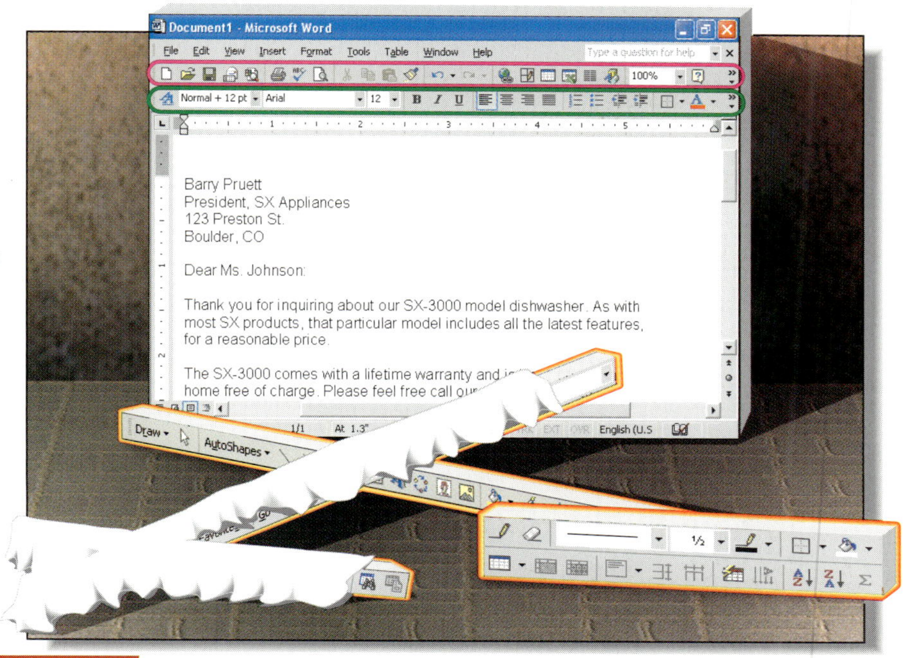

When you first start Word, the **Standard** and **Formatting** toolbars appear on your screen.

DISPLAY OR HIDE A TOOLBAR

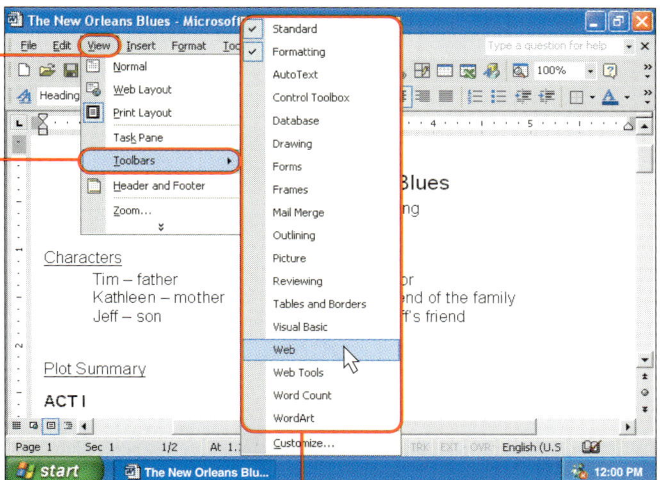

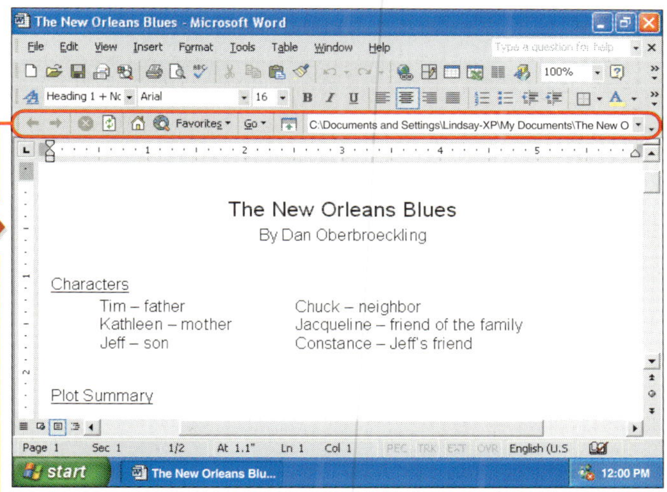

1. Click **View**.
2. Click **Toolbars**.

■ A list of toolbars appears. A check mark (✔) appears beside the name of each toolbar that is currently displayed.

3. Click the name of the toolbar you want to display or hide.

■ Word displays or hides the toolbar you selected.

Note: A screen displaying fewer toolbars provides a larger and less cluttered working area.

MOVE A TOOLBAR

You can move a toolbar to the top, bottom, right or left edge of your screen.

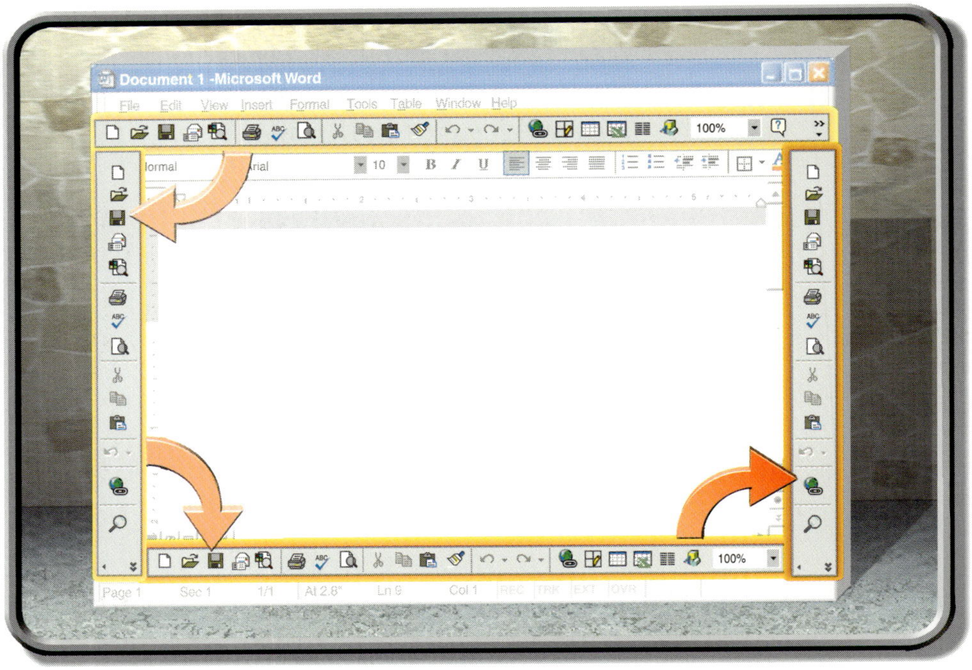

You can move a toolbar to the same row as another toolbar or to its own row.

MOVE A TOOLBAR

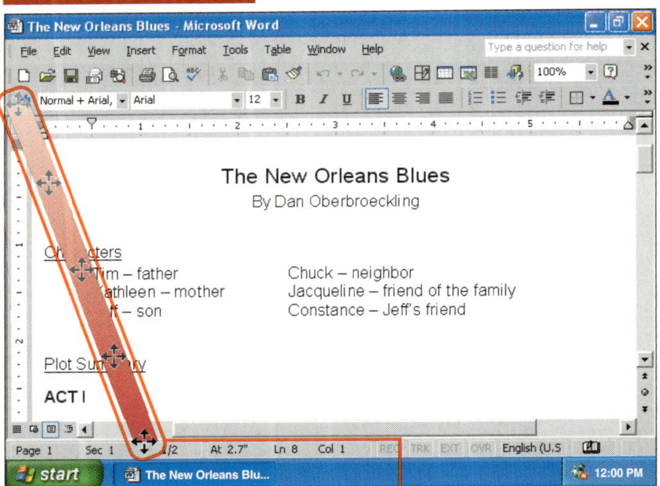

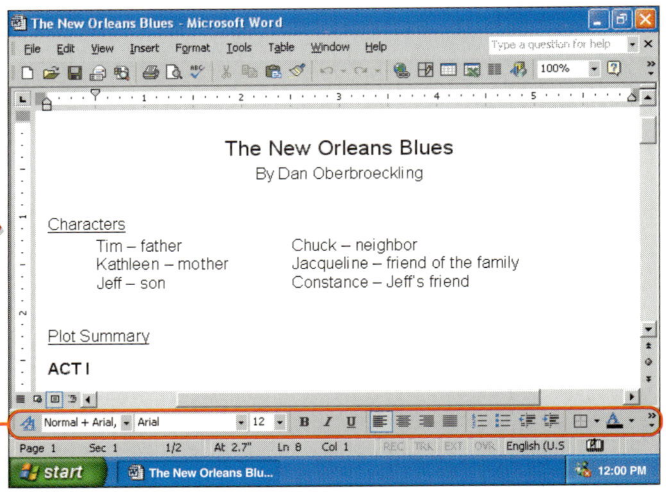

1 Position the mouse over the move handle ( ) of the toolbar you want to move (changes to).

2 Drag the toolbar to a new location.

■ The toolbar appears in the new location.

SIZE A TOOLBAR

You can increase the size of a toolbar to display more buttons on the toolbar. This is useful when a toolbar appears on the same row as another toolbar and cannot display all of its buttons.

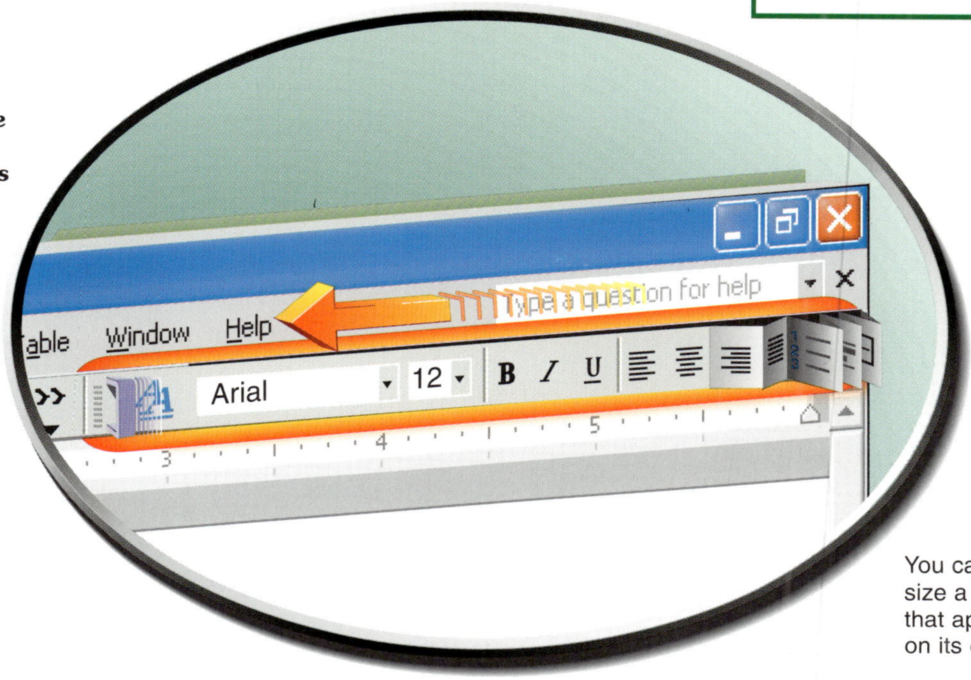

You cannot size a toolbar that appears on its own row.

SIZE A TOOLBAR

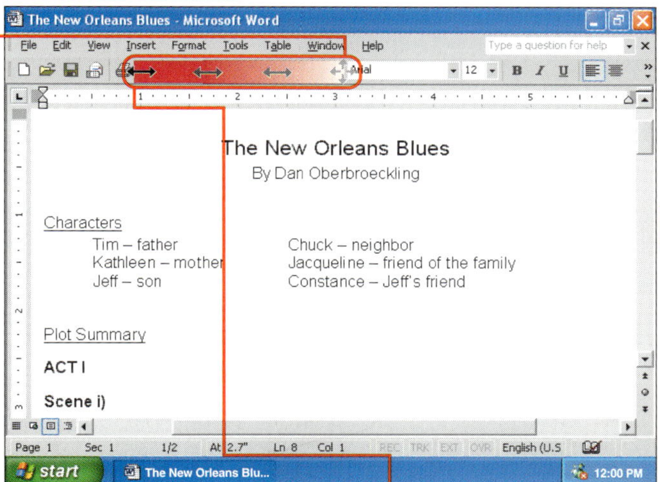

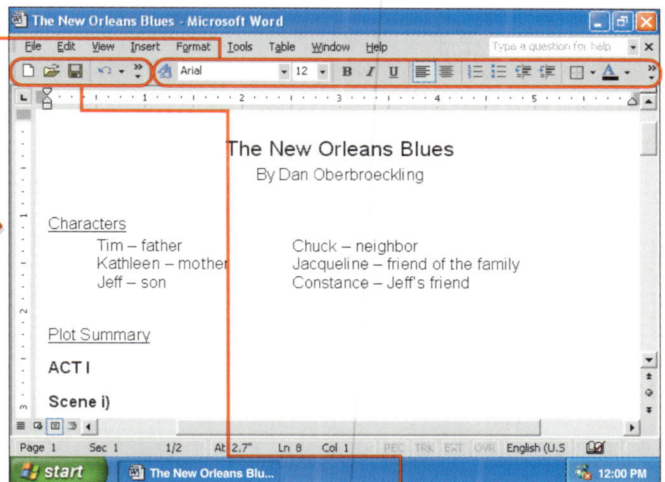

1 Position the mouse over the move handle ( ) of the toolbar you want to size (changes to ✥).

2 Drag the mouse ↔ until the toolbar is the size you want.

■ The toolbar displays the new size.

■ The new toolbar size affects the location and size of other toolbars on the same row.

ZOOM IN OR OUT

Word allows you to enlarge or reduce the display of text on your screen.

You can increase the zoom setting to view an area of your document in more detail or decrease the zoom setting to view more of your document at once.

The available zoom settings depend on the current view of your document. For information on the views, see page 40.

ZOOM IN OR OUT

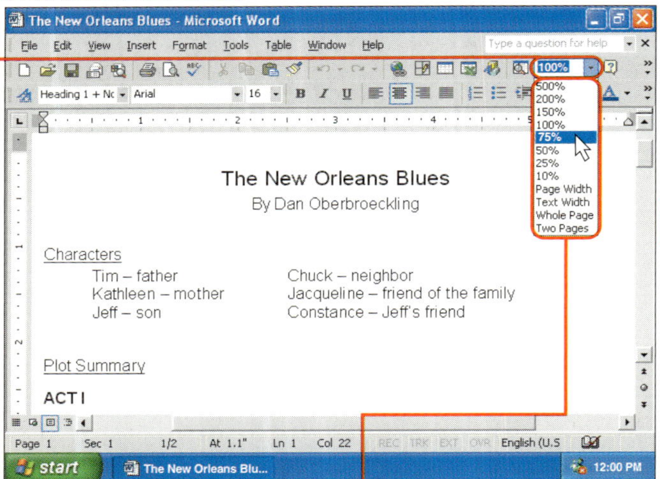

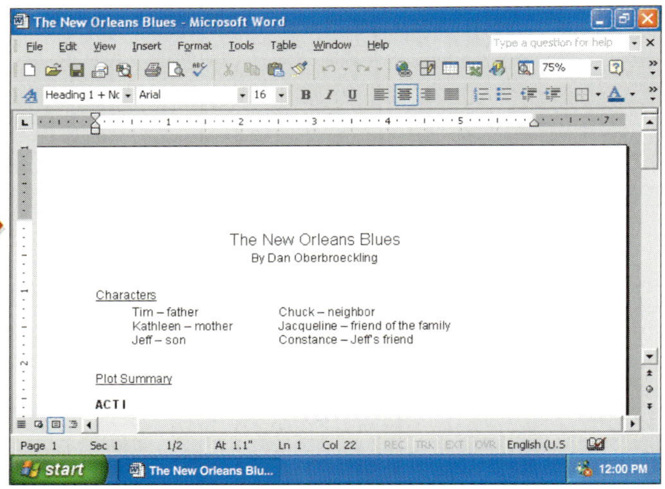

1 Click ▾ in this area to display a list of zoom settings.

Note: If the Zoom area is not displayed, click » on the Standard toolbar to display the area.

2 Click the zoom setting you want to use.

*Note: Select **Page Width** or **Text Width** to fit the page or the text across the width of your screen. Select **Whole Page** or **Two Pages** to display one or two full pages across your screen.*

■ The document appears in the new zoom setting. You can edit the document as usual.

■ Changing the zoom setting will not affect the way text appears on a printed page.

■ To return to the normal zoom setting, repeat steps **1** and **2**, selecting **100%** in step **2**.

SPLIT A DOCUMENT

You can split your document into separate sections. This allows you to display different areas of a long document at the same time.

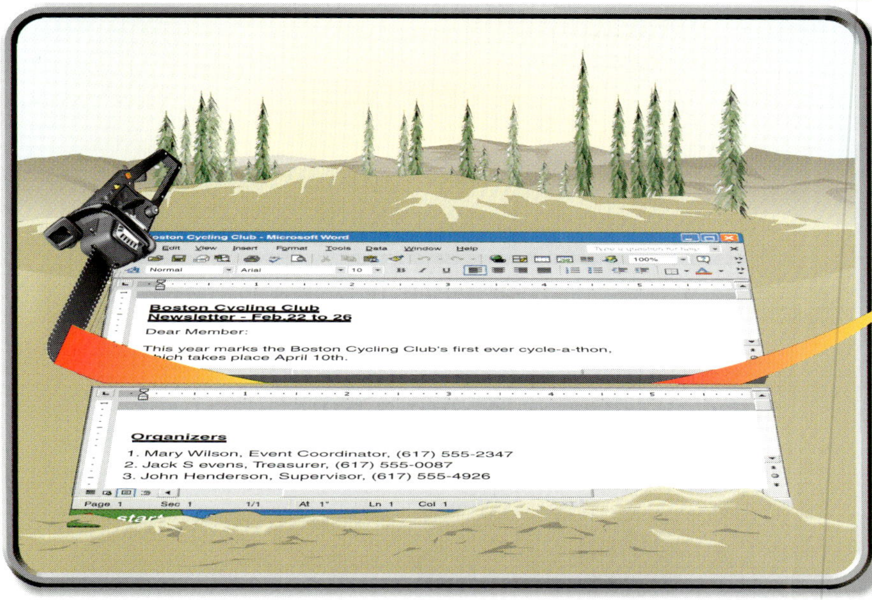

Each section of a split document contains a copy of the entire document.

SPLIT A DOCUMENT

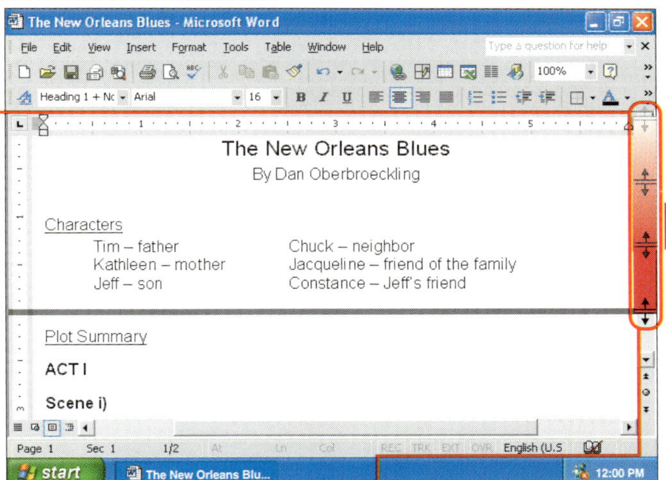

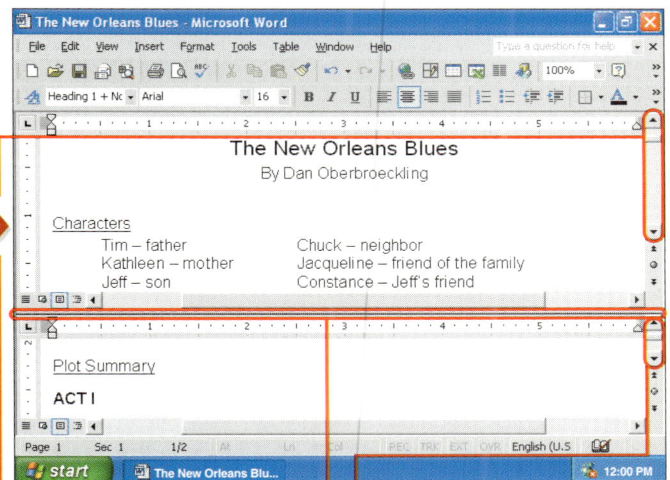

1 Position the mouse ↖ over this area (↖ changes to ⇕).

2 Drag the mouse ⇕ to where you want to split the document.

■ The document splits into two sections.

■ To move through the text above the dividing line, you can use this scroll bar.

■ To move through the text below the dividing line, you can use this scroll bar.

■ If you no longer want to split the document, position the mouse ↖ over the dividing line (↖ changes to ⇕). Then double-click the dividing line to remove the line from your screen.

DISPLAY OR HIDE WHITE SPACE

When your document is displayed in the Print Layout view, you can display or hide the white space that appears at the top and bottom of each page.

Hiding the white space allows you to display more text on your screen at once.

DISPLAY OR HIDE WHITE SPACE

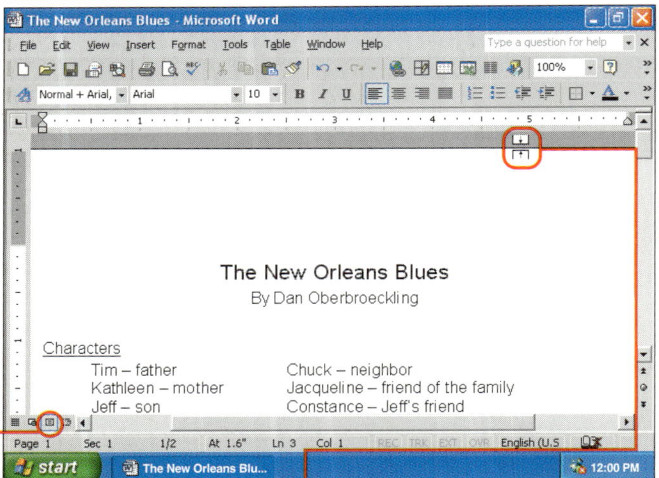

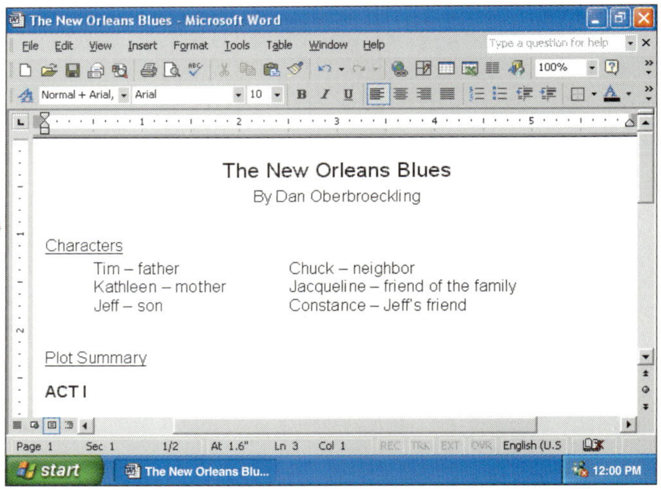

1 Click to display your document in the Print Layout view.

2 Position the mouse over the top or bottom edge of a page (changes to or).

3 Click the edge of the page to display or hide the white space.

■ Word displays or hides the white space on each page.

Note: If the document contains more than one page, Word also displays or hides the gray space between the pages.

DISPLAY OR HIDE FORMATTING MARKS

You can display formatting marks in your document. Formatting marks can help you edit your document and check for errors such as extra spaces between words.

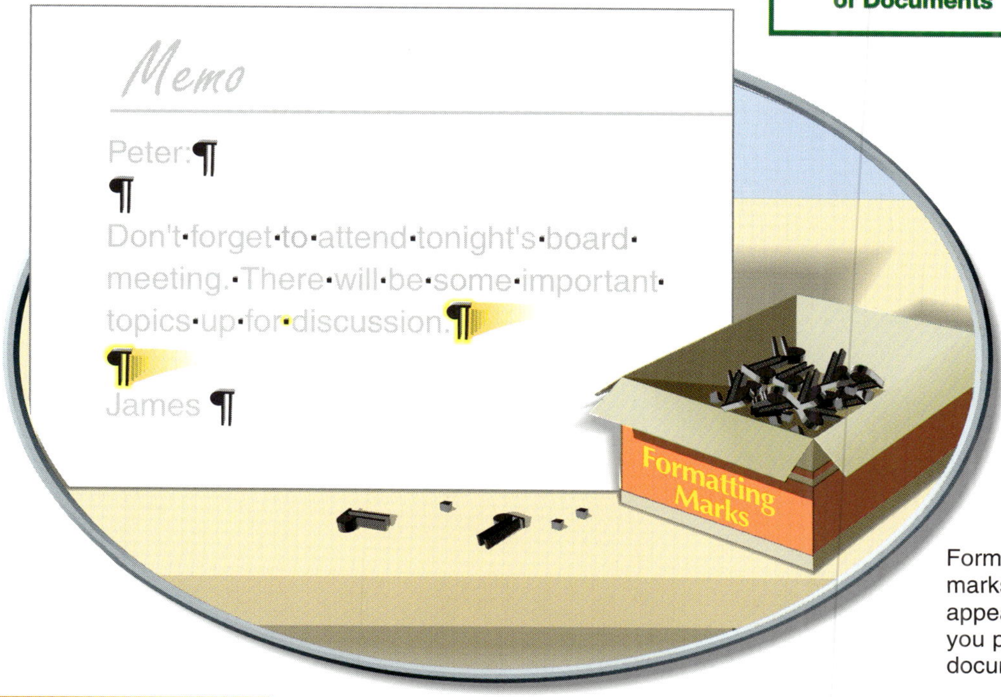

Formatting marks will not appear when you print your document.

DISPLAY OR HIDE FORMATTING MARKS

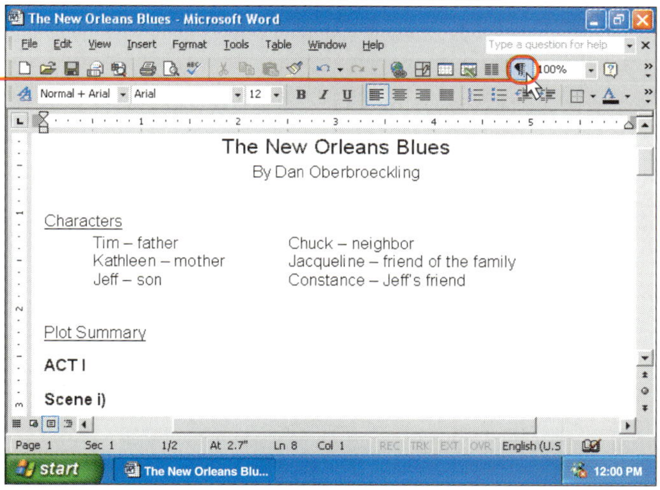

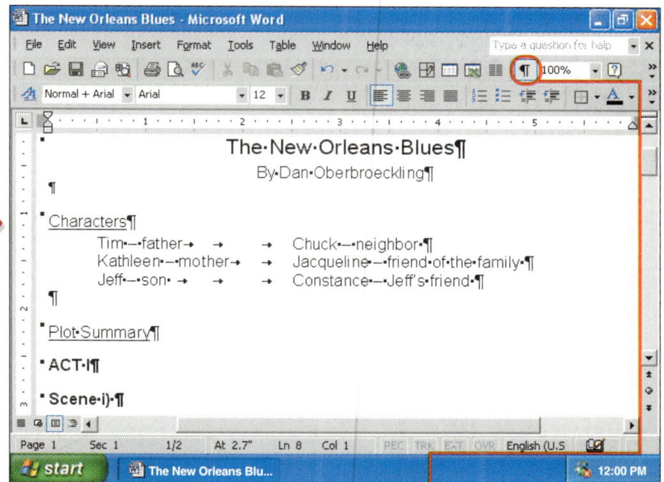

1 Click ¶ to display formatting marks in your document.

Note: If ¶ is not displayed, click » on the Standard toolbar to display the button.

■ Formatting marks, such as paragraph (¶), space (·) and tab (→), appear in your document.

■ To once again hide formatting marks, click ¶.

USING THE DOCUMENT MAP

You can use the Document Map to move through a long document. The Document Map displays an outline of the document on your screen.

USING THE DOCUMENT MAP

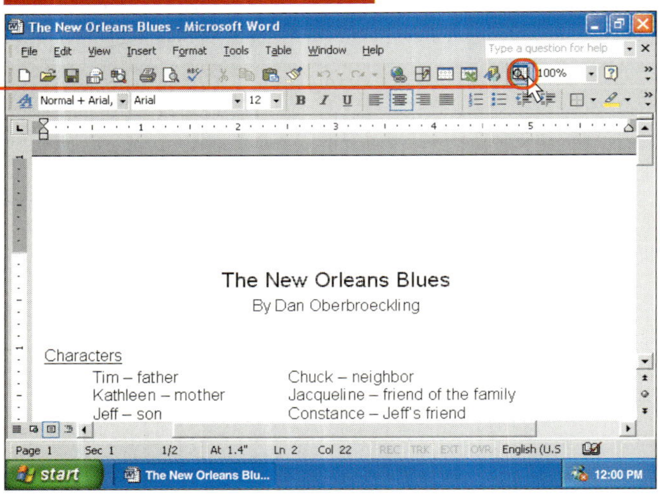

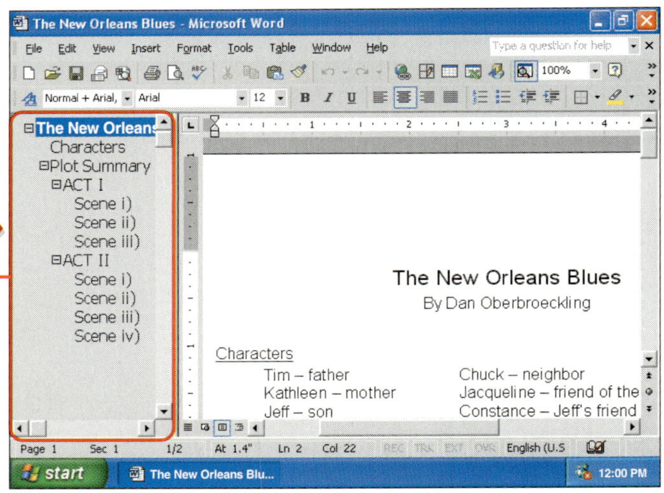

1 Click [icon] to display the Document Map.

Note: If [icon] is not displayed, click [icon] on the Standard toolbar to display the button.

■ The Document Map appears, showing the headings in your document.

Note: If the Document Map is blank, see the top of page 51.

Why doesn't the Document Map display any headings?

The Document Map appears blank if Word does not find any headings in your document. If you want to be able to use the Document Map to move through a document, you should format the headings in your document using one of the Heading styles included with Word. To apply a style included with Word, perform steps **1** to **3** starting on page 110, selecting a Heading style in step **3**.

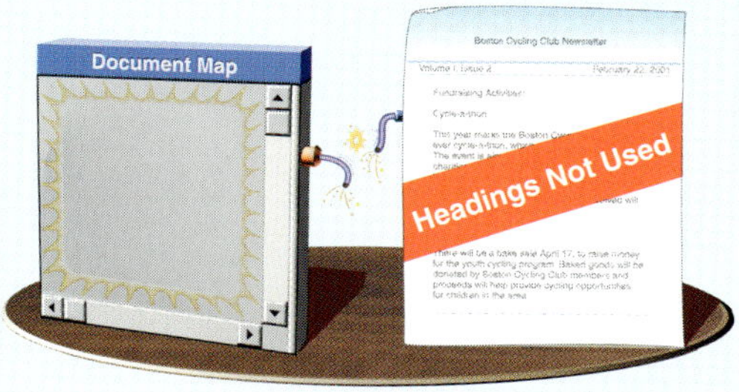

Part of a heading in the Document Map is hidden from view. How can I display the entire heading?

To display the entire heading, position the mouse over the heading. After a few seconds, the entire heading appears in a yellow box.

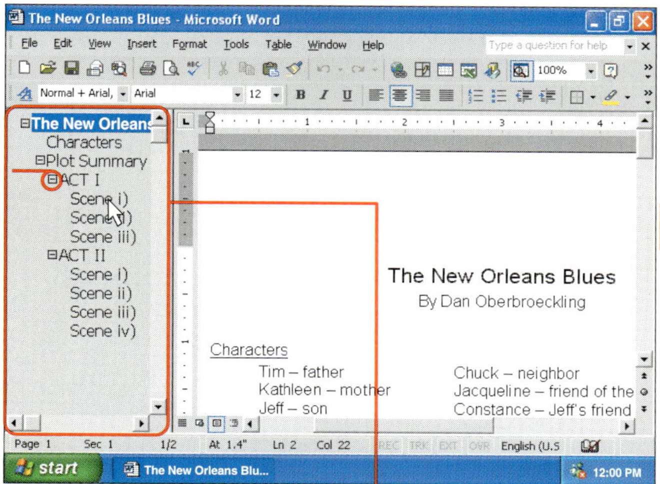

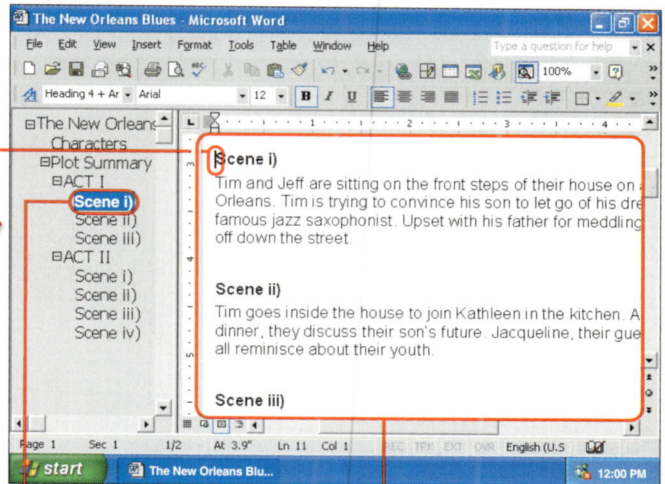

■ A minus sign (⊟) beside a heading indicates the heading has subheadings. To hide the subheadings, click the minus sign (⊟ changes to ⊞).

Note: To once again display the subheadings, click the plus sign (⊞).

2 Click a heading or subheading to instantly jump to a specific part of your document.

■ Word highlights the heading or subheading you selected.

■ The insertion point moves to the heading or subheading in your document.

■ This area displays the part of the document you selected.

■ To hide the Document Map, repeat step **1**.

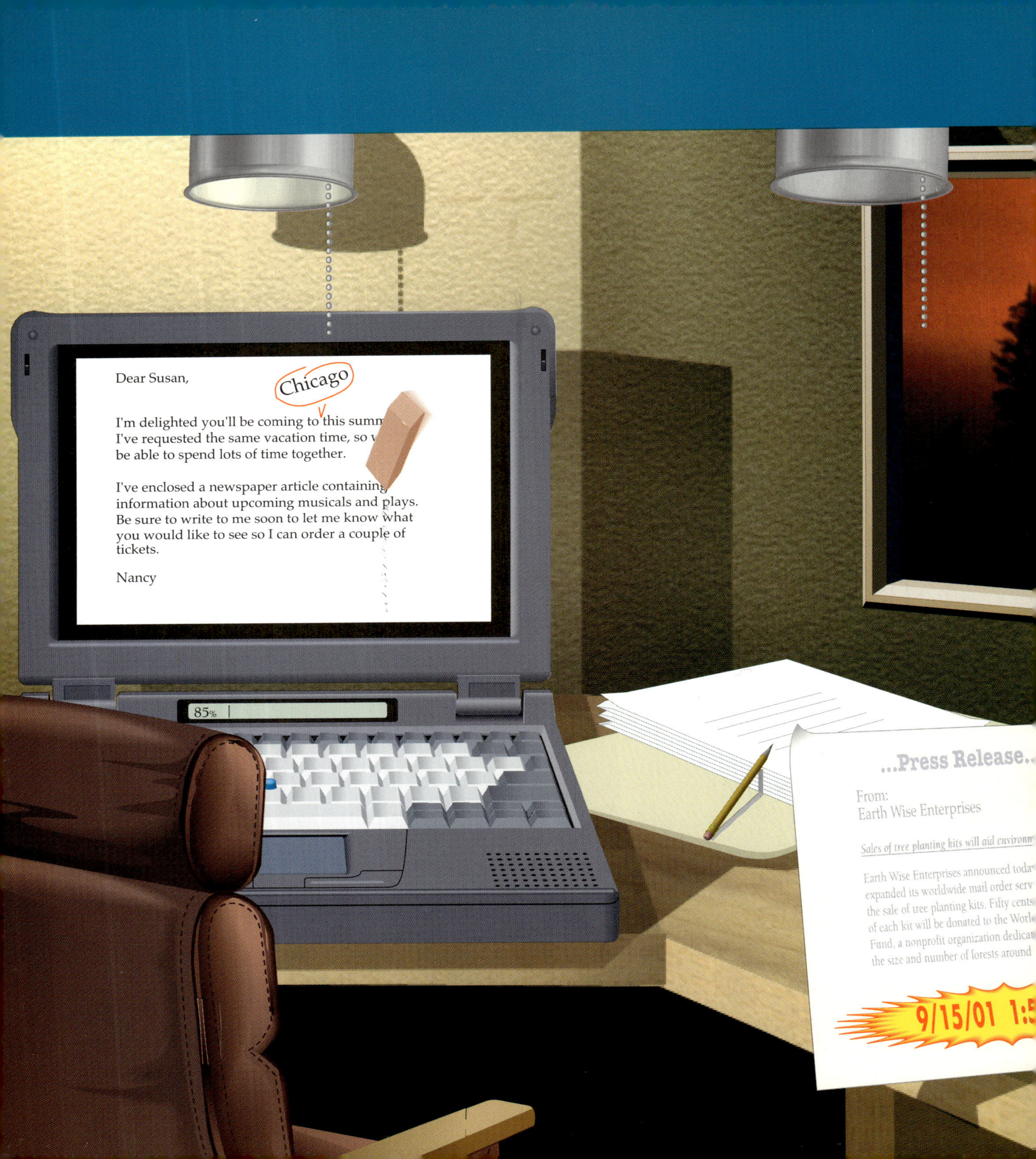

Dear Susan,
Chicago
I'm delighted you'll be coming to this summ
I've requested the same vacation time, so w
be able to spend lots of time together.
I've enclosed a newspaper article containing
information about upcoming musicals and plays.
Be sure to write to me soon to let me know what
you would like to see so I can order a couple of
tickets.
Nancy
85%
...Press Release...
From:
Earth Wise Enterprises
9/15/01

Edit Text

Do you want to edit the text in your document or check your document for spelling and grammar errors? This chapter teaches you how.

Insert and Delete Text 54

Move or Copy Text 56

Insert the Date and Time 58

Undo Changes 59

Count Words in a Document 60

Find Text 62

Replace Text 64

Check Spelling and Grammar 66

Turn Off Spelling and Grammar Check 68

Using the Thesaurus 70

Using AutoCorrect 72

Using AutoText 74

Insert Symbols 76

Add a Comment 78

Track Changes 80

Review Tracked Changes 82

Translate Text 84

INSERT AND DELETE TEXT

You can add new text to your document and remove text you no longer need.

INSERT TEXT

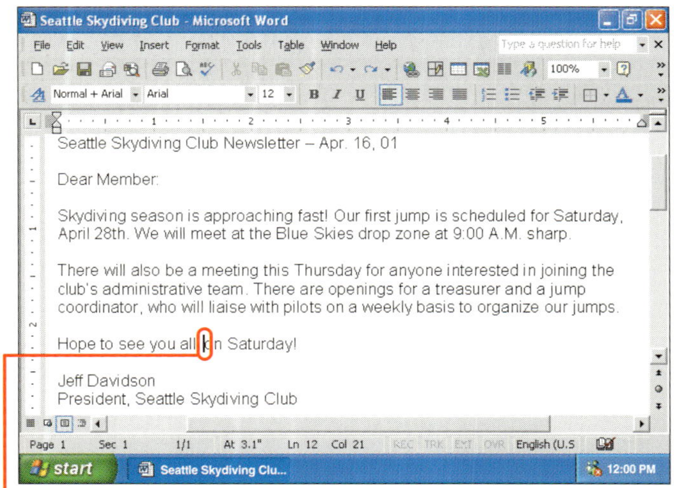

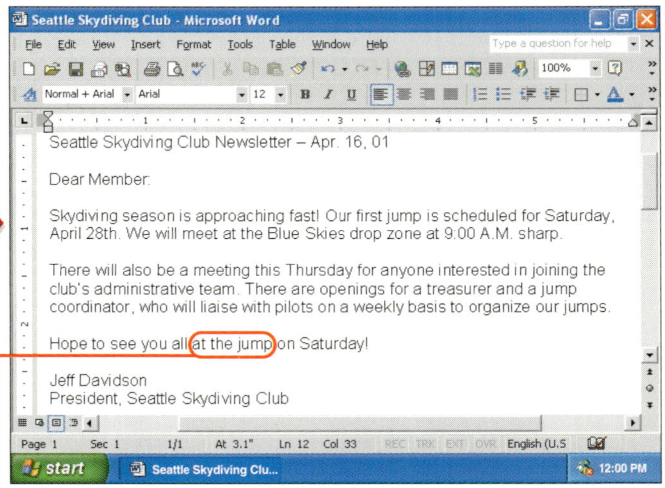

1 Click the location in your document where you want to insert new text.

■ The text you type will appear where the insertion point flashes on your screen.

Note: You can press the ←, →, ↑ or ↓ key to move the insertion point one character or line in any direction.

2 Type the text you want to insert.

■ To insert a blank space, press the **Spacebar**.

■ The words to the right of the new text move forward.

TEACH YOURSELF TY

Why does the existing text in my document disappear when I insert new text?

If the text you type replaces existing text in your document, you may have turned on the Overtype feature. When the Overtype feature is turned on, the **OVR** status indicator at the bottom of your screen is **bold**. To turn the Overtype feature on or off, press the Insert key.

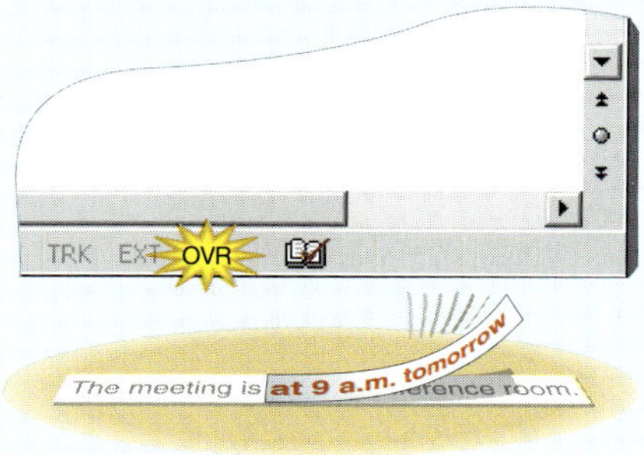

TEACH YOURSELF TY

Why did red and green underlines appear under the text I inserted?

Word automatically checks your document for spelling and grammar errors as you type. Misspelled words display a red underline and grammar errors display a green underline. For information on checking spelling and grammar in your document, see page 66.

DELETE TEXT

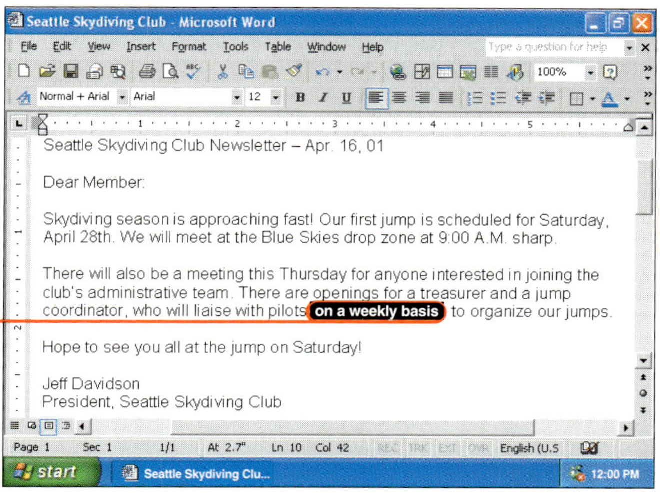

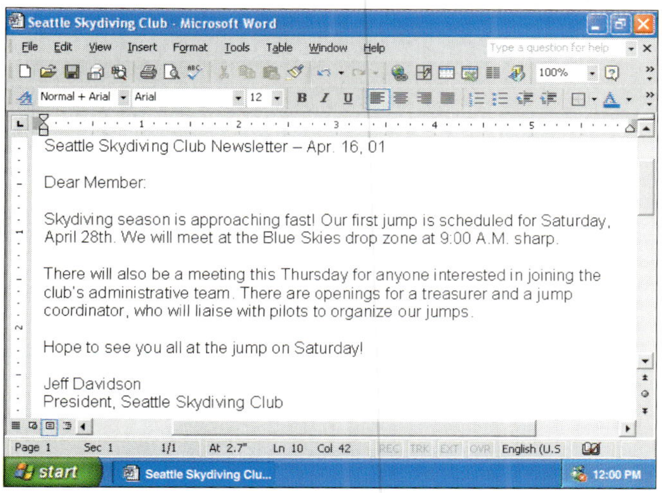

1 Select the text you want to delete. To select text, see page 10.

2 Press the Delete key to remove the text.

■ The text disappears. The remaining text in the line or paragraph moves to fill the empty space.

■ To delete a single character, click to the right of the character you want to delete and then press the ←Backspace key. Word deletes the character to the left of the flashing insertion point.

MOVE OR COPY TEXT

You can move or copy text to a new location in your document.

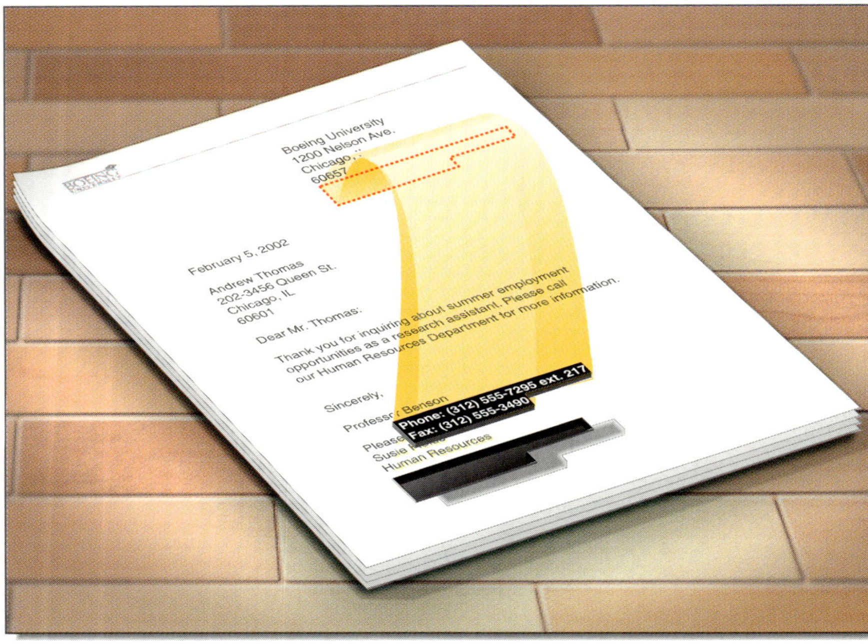

Moving text allows you to rearrange text in your document. When you move text, the text disappears from its original location.

Copying text allows you to repeat information in your document without having to retype the text. When you copy text, the text appears in both the original and new locations.

MOVE OR COPY TEXT

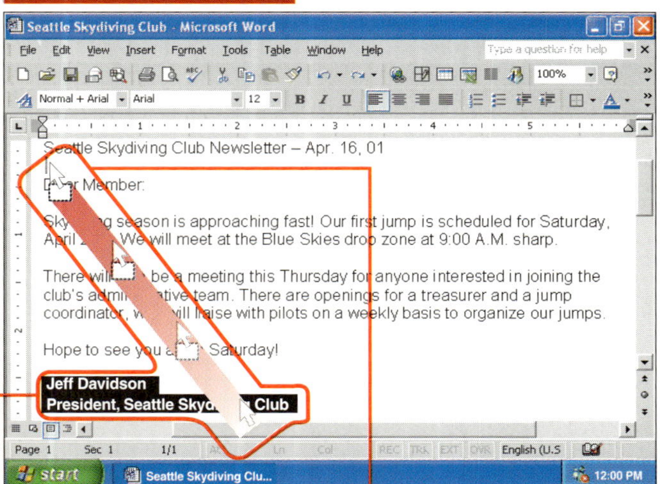

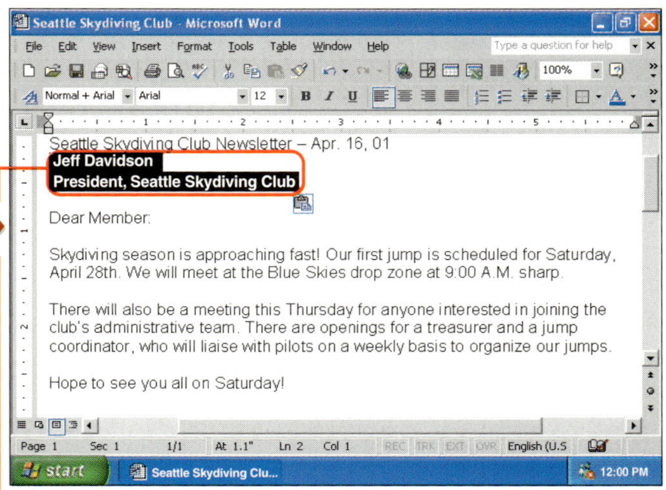

USING DRAG AND DROP

1 Select the text you want to move. To select text, see page 10.

2 Position the mouse I over the selected text (I changes to ↖).

3 To move the text, drag the mouse to the location where you want to place the text.

Note: The text will appear where you position the dotted insertion point on your screen.

■ The text moves to the new location.

■ To copy text, perform steps **1** to **3**, except press and hold down the **Ctrl** key as you perform step **3**.

How can I use the Clipboard task pane to move or copy text?

The Clipboard task pane displays up to the last 24 items you have selected to move or copy. To place a clipboard item in your document, click the location where you want the item to appear and then click the item in the task pane. For more information on the task pane, see page 16.

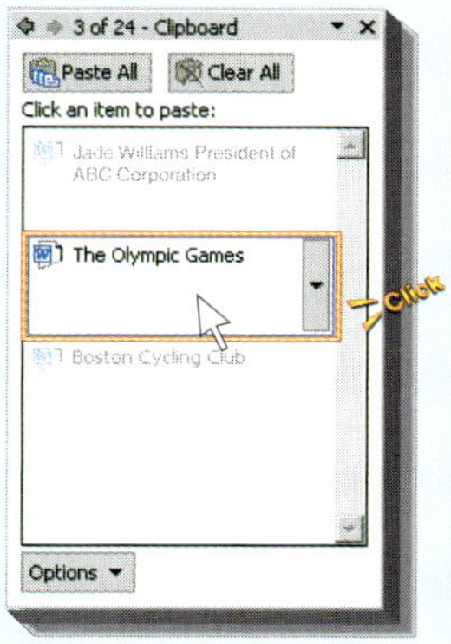

Why does the Paste Options button ( ) appear when I move or copy text?

You can use the Paste Options button ( ) to change the format of text you have moved or copied. For example, you can choose to keep the original formatting of the text or change the formatting of the text to match the text in the new location. Click the Paste Options button to display a list of options and then select the option you want to use. The Paste Options button is available only until you perform another task.

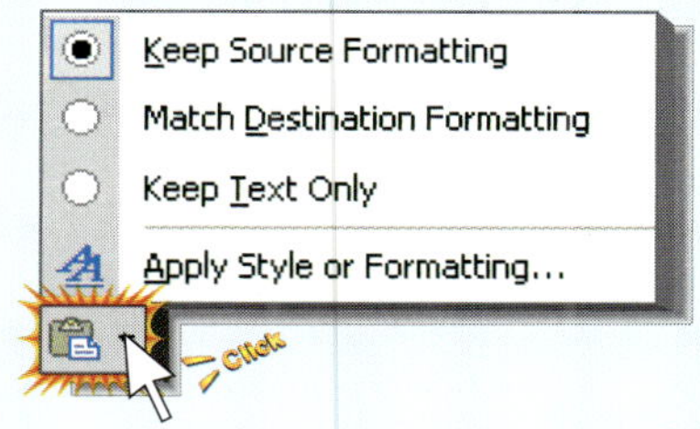

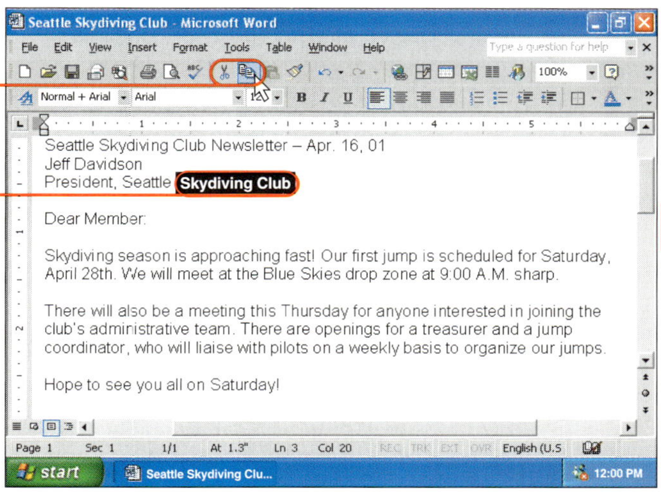

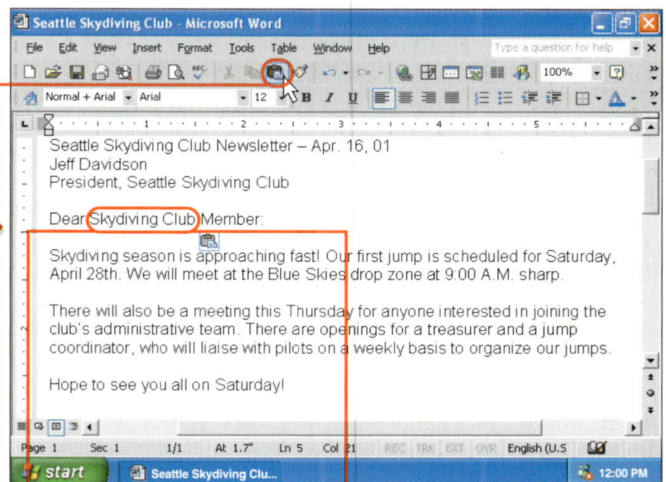

USING THE TOOLBAR BUTTONS

1 Select the text you want to move or copy. To select text, see page 10.

2 Click one of the following buttons.

Move text

Copy text

Note: If the button you want is not displayed, click on the Standard toolbar to display the button.

■ The Clipboard task pane may appear. To use the Clipboard task pane, see the top of this page.

3 Click the location where you want to place the text.

4 Click to place the text in the new location.

Note: If is not displayed, click on the Standard toolbar to display the button.

■ The text appears in the new location.

INSERT THE DATE AND TIME

You can insert the current date and time into your document. Word can automatically update the date and time each time you open or print the document.

Word uses your computer's built-in clock to determine the current date and time.

INSERT THE DATE AND TIME

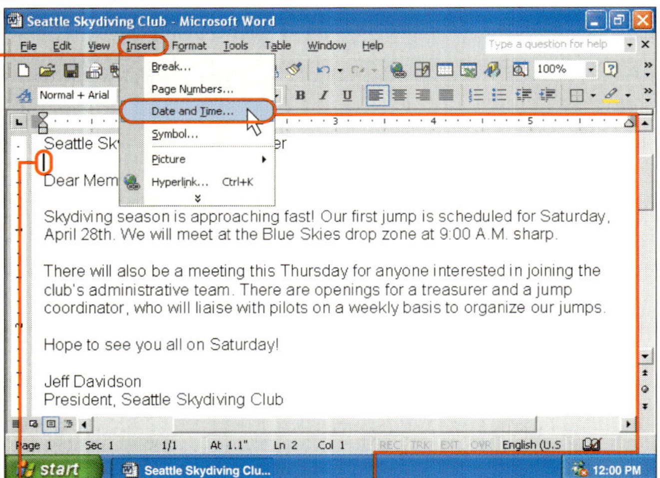

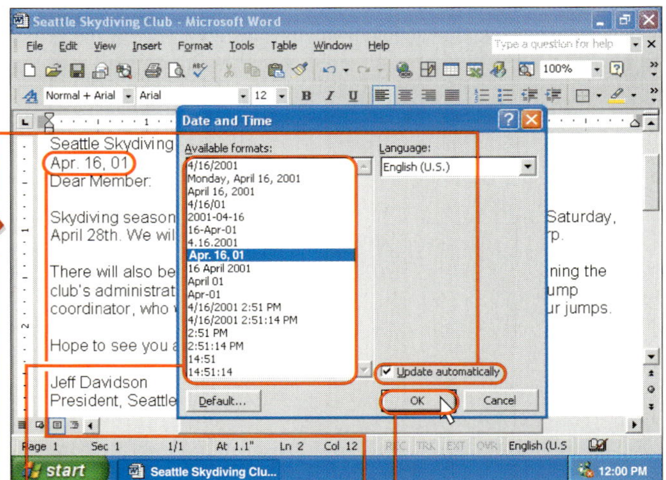

1 Click where you want the date and time to appear in your document.

2 Click **Insert**.

3 Click **Date and Time**.

■ The Date and Time dialog box appears.

4 Click the date and time format you want to use.

5 When this option displays a check mark (✔), Word will automatically update the date and time each time you open or print the document. You can click the option to add (☑) or remove (☐) the check mark.

6 Click **OK** to confirm your selections.

■ The date and time format you selected appears in your document.

UNDO CHANGES

Word remembers the last changes you made to your document. If you regret these changes, you can cancel them by using the Undo feature.

The Undo feature can cancel your last editing and formatting changes.

UNDO CHANGES

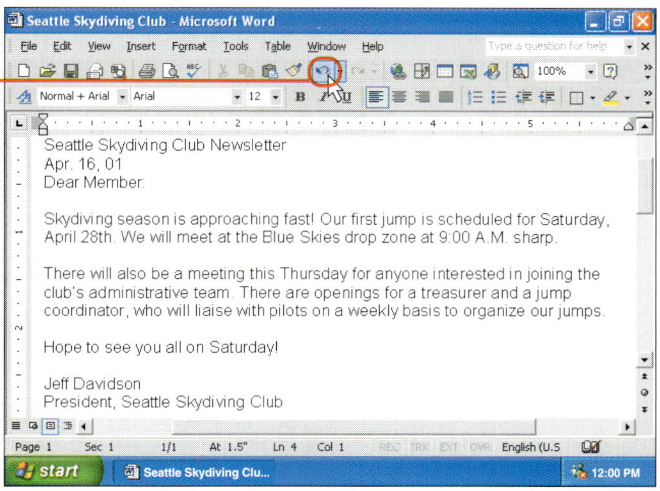

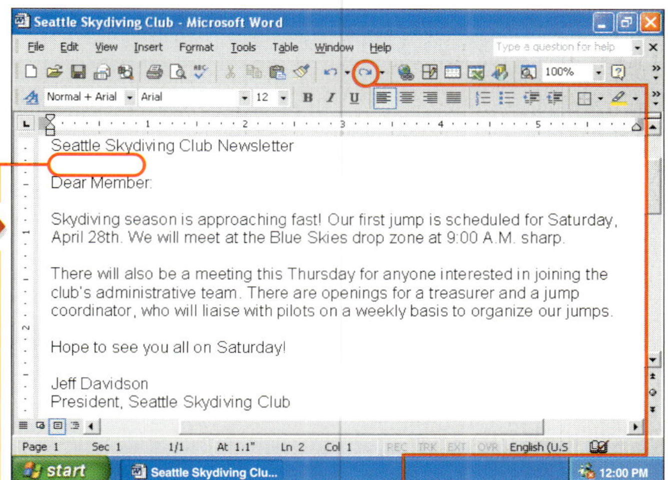

1 Click to undo the last change you made to your document.

Note: If is not displayed, click on the Standard toolbar to display the button.

■ Word cancels the last change you made to your document.

■ You can repeat step **1** to cancel previous changes you made.

■ To reverse the results of using the Undo feature, click .

Note: If is not displayed, click on the Standard toolbar to display the button.

COUNT WORDS IN A DOCUMENT

You can have Word count the number of words in your document.

When counting the number of words in your document, Word also counts the number of pages, characters, paragraphs and lines in your document.

COUNT WORDS IN A DOCUMENT

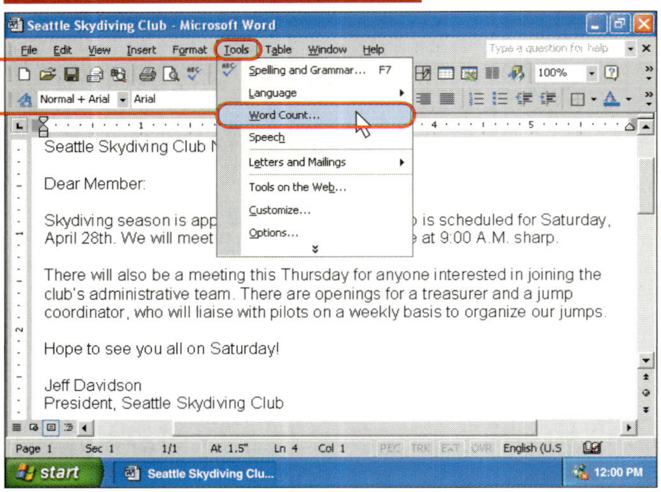

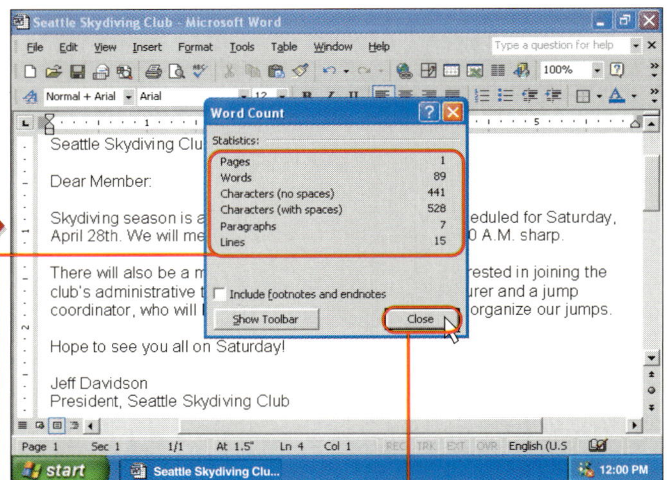

1 Click **Tools**.

2 Click **Word Count**.

■ The Word Count dialog box appears.

■ This area displays the total number of pages, words, characters, paragraphs and lines in your document.

3 When you finish reviewing the information, click **Close** to close the Word Count dialog box.

How can I count the number of words in only part of my document?

To count the number of words in only part of your document, select the text before performing the steps on page 60. To select text, see page 10.

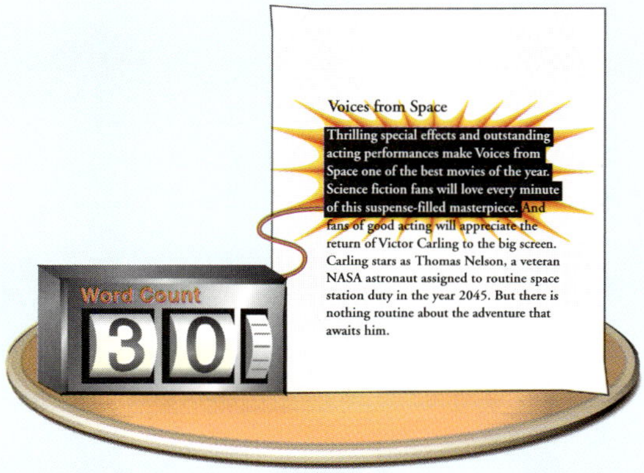

Is there another way to display the Word Count toolbar?

Yes. While reviewing the information in the Word Count dialog box, you can click the **Show Toolbar** button to display the Word Count toolbar.

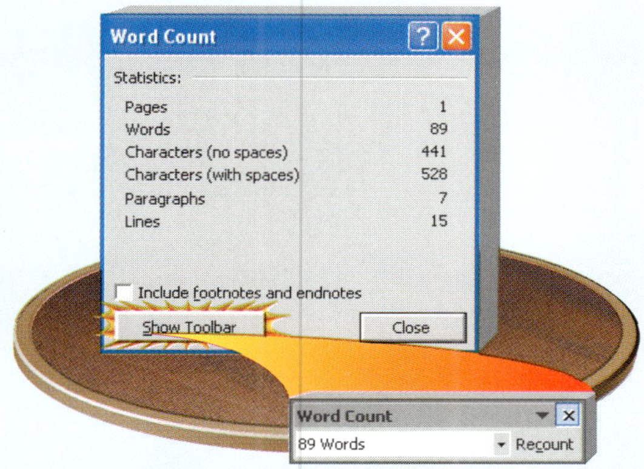

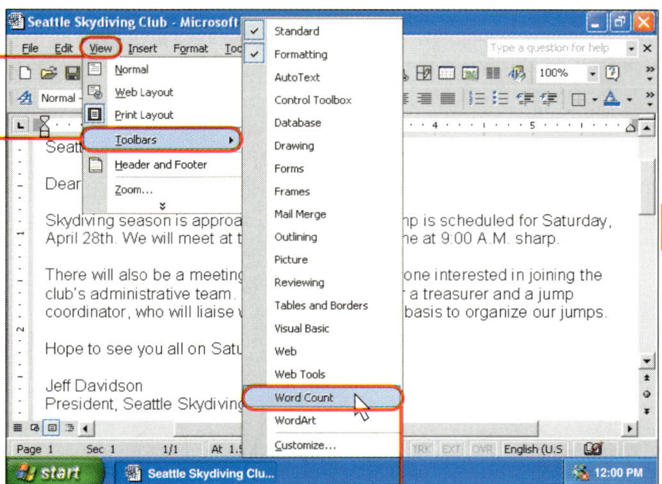

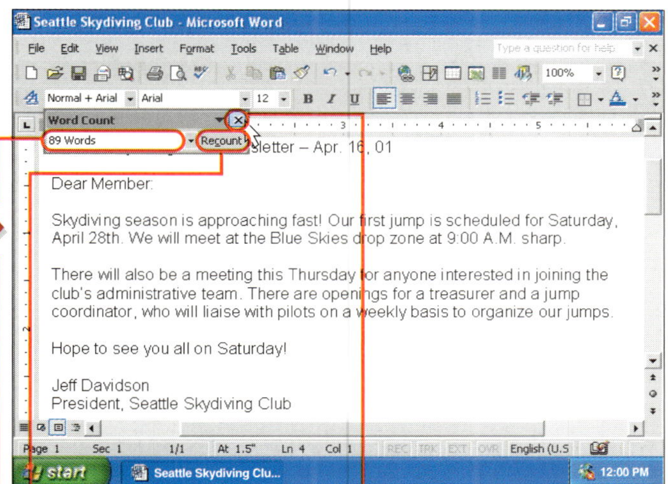

USING THE WORD COUNT TOOLBAR

The Word Count toolbar allows you to quickly recount the number of words in your document as you edit the document.

1. Click **View**.
2. Click **Toolbars**.
3. Click **Word Count**.
   - The Word Count toolbar appears.
4. Click **Recount**.
   - This area displays the total number of words in your document.
   - To display the number of characters, lines, pages or paragraphs, you can click this area to select the type of information you want to display.
5. To update the word count as you edit your document, repeat step **4**.
6. When you finish using the Word Count toolbar, click ☒ to hide the toolbar.

FIND TEXT

You can use the Find feature to quickly locate every occurrence of a word or phrase in your document.

FIND TEXT

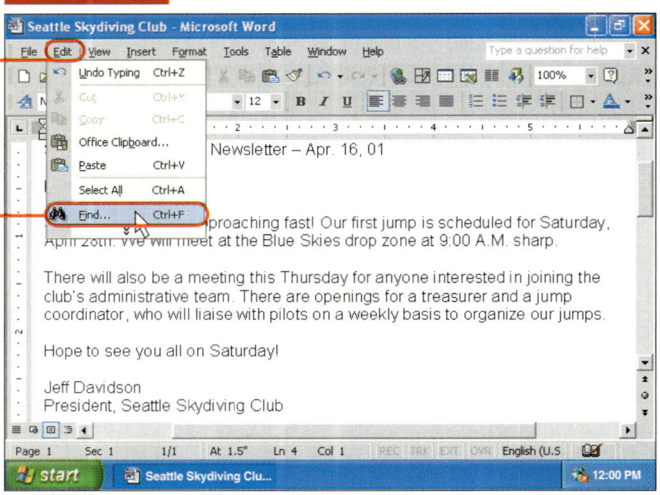

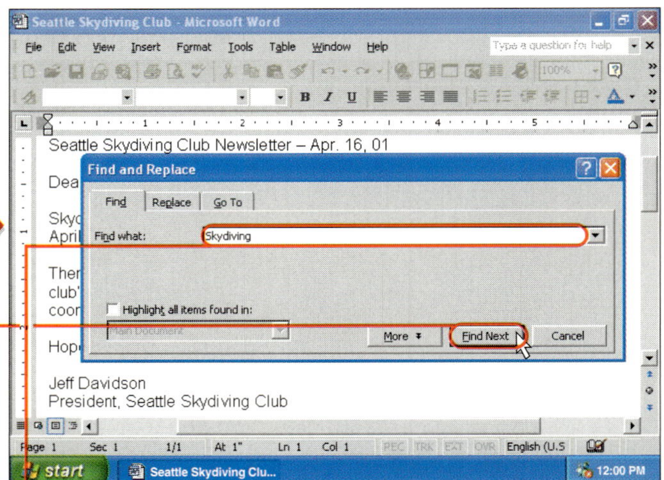

1 Click **Edit**.

2 Click **Find**.

■ The Find and Replace dialog box appears.

3 Type the text you want to find.

4 Click **Find Next** to start the search.

*Note: A dialog box appears if Word cannot find the text you specified. Click **OK** to close the dialog box and then skip to step **8**.*

Can I search for part of a word?

When you search for text in your document, Word will find the text even when the text is part of a larger word. For example, if you search for **place**, Word will also find **place**s, **place**ment and common**place**.

Can I search only a specific section of my document?

Yes. To search only a specific section of your document, select the text you want to search before starting the search. To select text, see page 10.

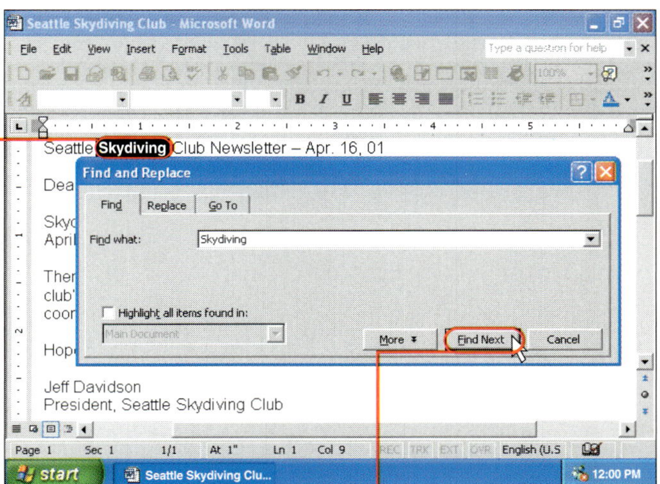

- Word highlights the first matching word it finds.

5 Click **Find Next** to find the next matching word.

*Note: To end the search at any time, click **Cancel**.*

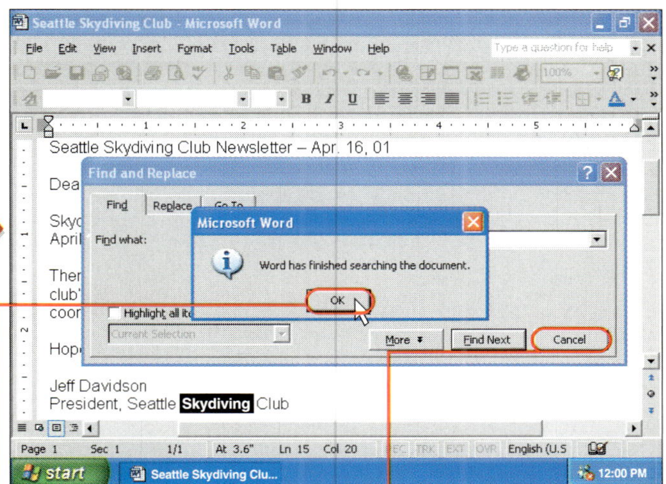

6 Repeat step **5** until a dialog box appears, telling you the search is complete.

7 Click **OK** to close the dialog box.

8 Click **Cancel** to close the Find and Replace dialog box.

REPLACE TEXT

You can find and replace every occurrence of a word or phrase in your document. This is useful if you have frequently misspelled a name.

REPLACE TEXT

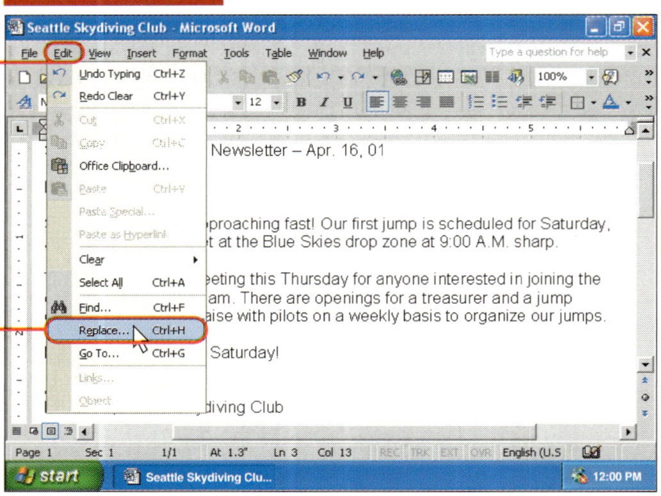

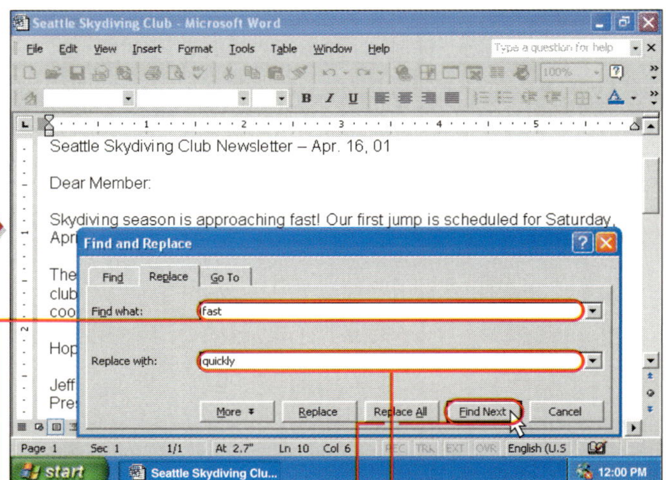

1 Click **Edit**.

2 Click **Replace**.

Note: If Replace does not appear on the menu, position the mouse over the bottom of the menu to display all the menu options.

■ The Find and Replace dialog box appears.

3 Type the text you want to find.

4 Click this area and type the text you want to replace the text you typed in step **3**.

5 Click **Find Next** to start the search.

Can the Replace feature help me quickly enter text?

Yes. When you need to type a long word or phrase, such as University of Massachusetts, many times in a document, you can use the Replace feature to simplify the task. You can type a short form of the word or phrase, such as UM, throughout your document and then have Word replace the short form with the full word or phrase.

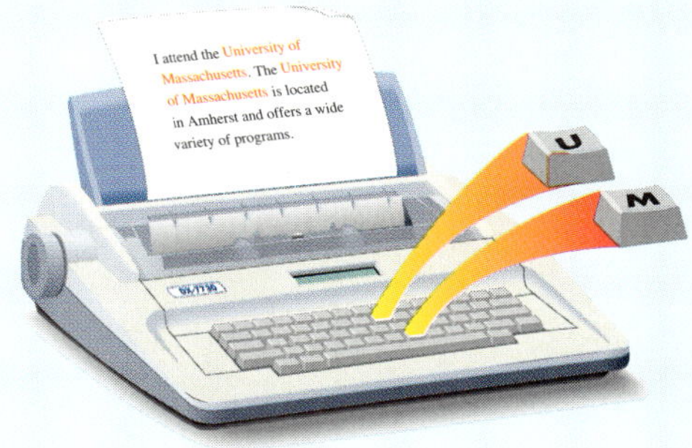

How can I quickly display the Find and Replace dialog box?

You can press and hold down the Ctrl key as you press the H key to quickly display the Find and Replace dialog box.

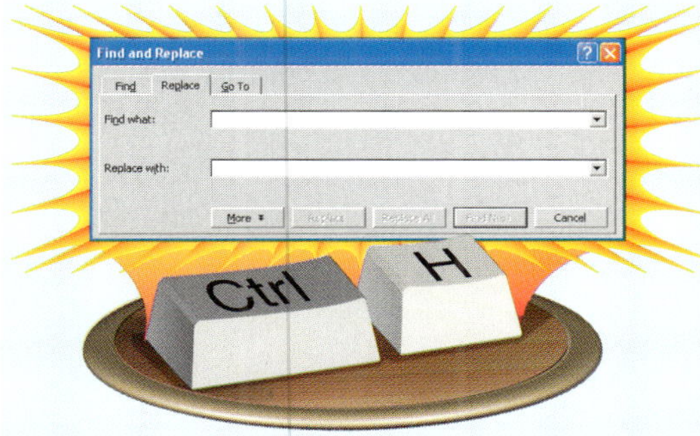

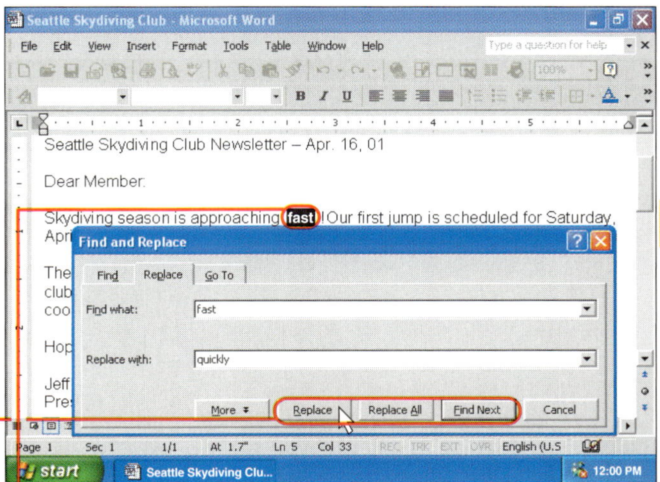

- Word highlights the first matching word it finds.

6 Click one of the following options.

Replace - Replace the word.

Replace All - Replace all occurrences of the word in the document.

Find Next - Ignore the word.

Note: To cancel the search at any time, press the Esc key.

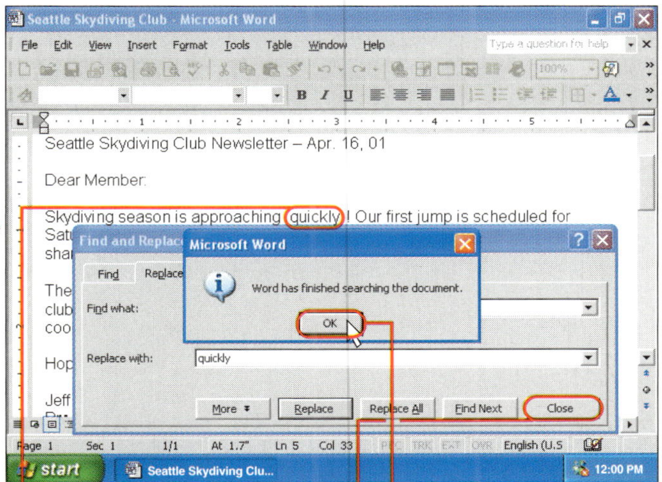

- In this example, Word replaces the word and searches for the next matching word.

7 Replace or ignore matching words until a dialog box appears, telling you the search is complete.

8 Click **OK** to close the dialog box.

9 Click **Close** or **Cancel** to close the Find and Replace dialog box.

CHECK SPELLING AND GRAMMAR

You can find and correct all the spelling and grammar errors in your document.

Word compares every word in your document to words in its dictionary. If a word does not exist in the dictionary, the word is considered misspelled.

Word will not find a correctly spelled word used in the wrong context, such as "My niece is **sit** years old." You should carefully review your document to find this type of error.

CHECK SPELLING AND GRAMMAR

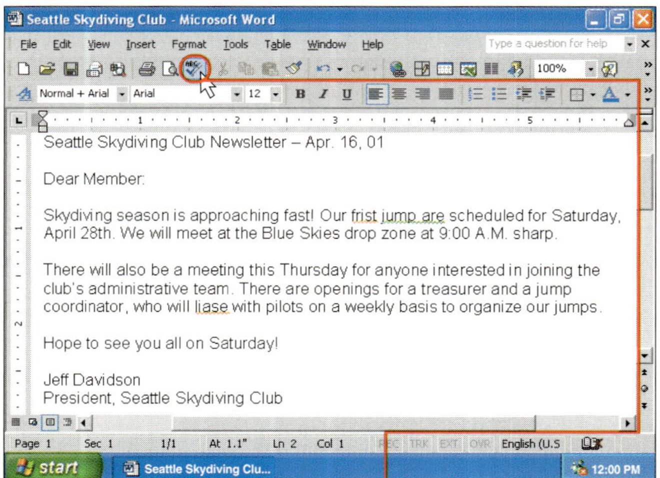

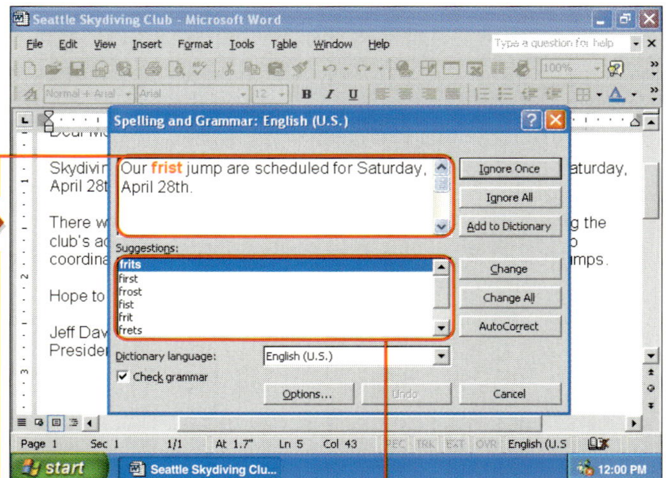

■ Word automatically underlines misspelled words in red and grammar errors in green. The underlines will not appear when you print your document.

1 Click to check your document for spelling and grammar errors.

Note: If is not displayed, click on the Standard toolbar to display the button.

■ The Spelling and Grammar dialog box appears if Word finds an error in your document.

■ This area displays the first misspelled word or grammar error.

■ This area displays suggestions for correcting the error.

Can Word automatically correct my typing mistakes?

Yes. Word automatically corrects common spelling errors as you type. To view a complete list of the spelling errors that Word will automatically correct, see page 72.

- adn → and
- alot → a lot
- comitte → committee
- don;t → don't
- nwe → new
- occurence → occurrence
- recieve → receive
- seperate → separate
- teh → the

How can I quickly correct a single misspelled word or grammar error in my document?

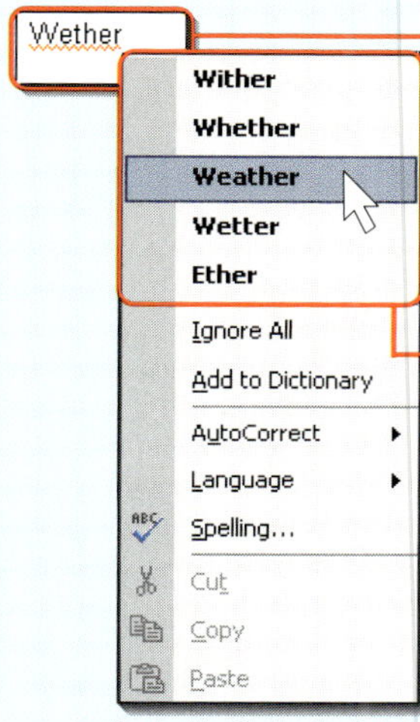

1 Right-click the misspelled word or grammar error in your document.

■ A menu appears with suggestions to correct the error.

2 Click the suggestion you want to use to correct the error.

Note: If you do not want to use any of the suggestions, click outside the menu to close the menu.

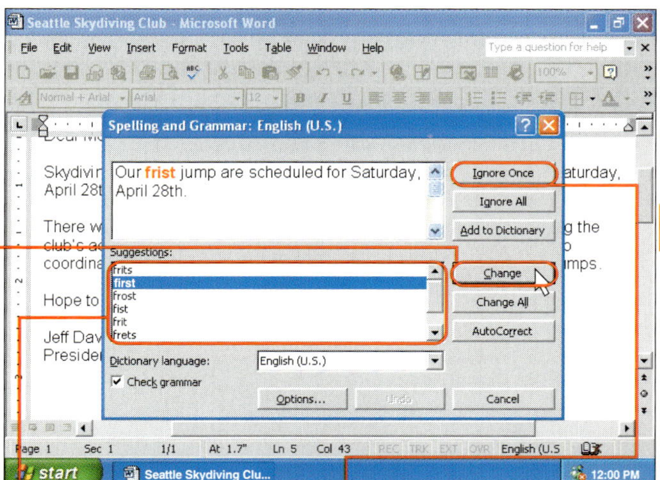

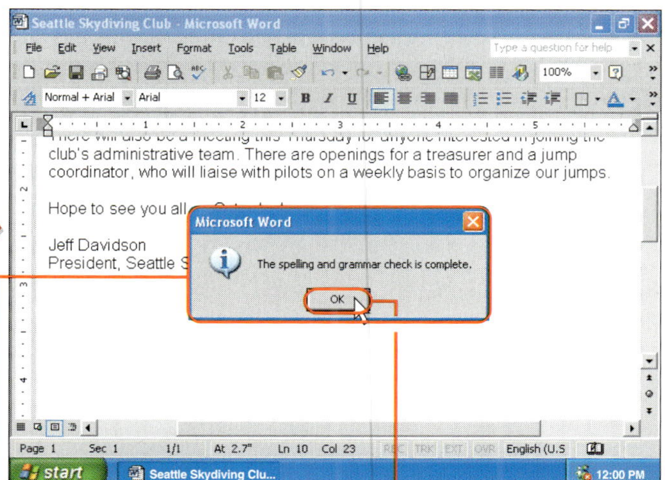

2 Click the suggestion you want to use to correct the error.

3 Click **Change** to correct the error in your document.

■ To skip the error and continue checking your document, click **Ignore Once**.

*Note: To skip the error and all other occurrences of the error in your document, click **Ignore All** or **Ignore Rule**. The name of the button depends on whether the error is a misspelled word or a grammar error.*

4 Correct or ignore misspelled words and grammar errors until this dialog box appears, telling you the spelling and grammar check is complete.

5 Click **OK** to close the dialog box.

TURN OFF SPELLING AND GRAMMAR CHECK

You can turn off Word's automatic spelling and grammar check features. This is useful if you are distracted by the red and green underlines Word uses to indicate errors in your documents.

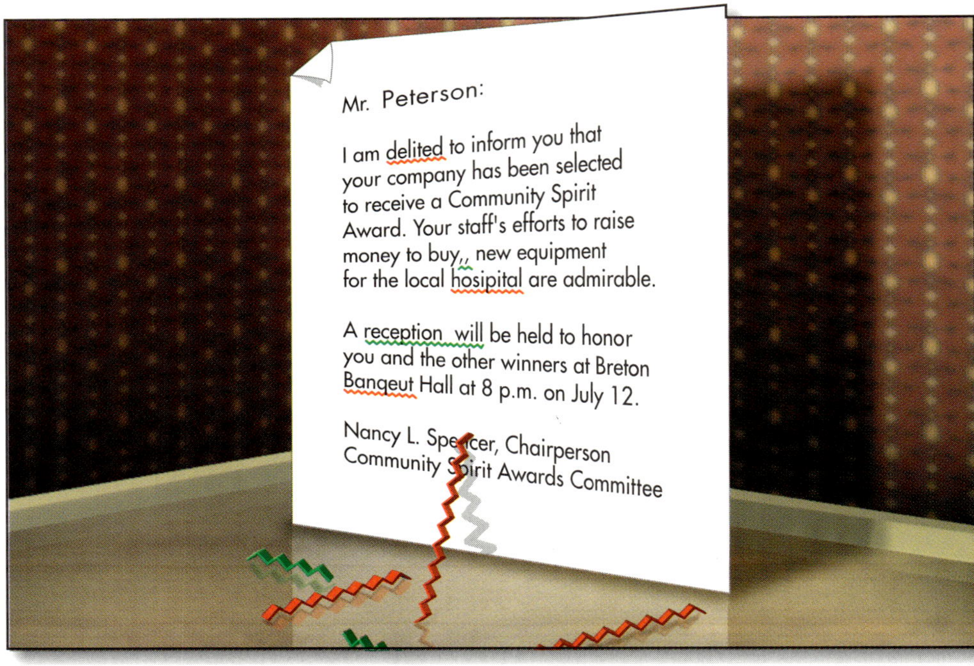

TURN OFF SPELLING AND GRAMMAR CHECK

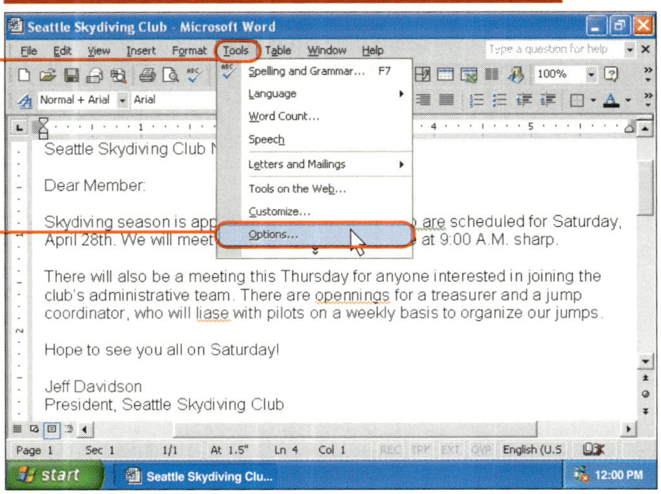

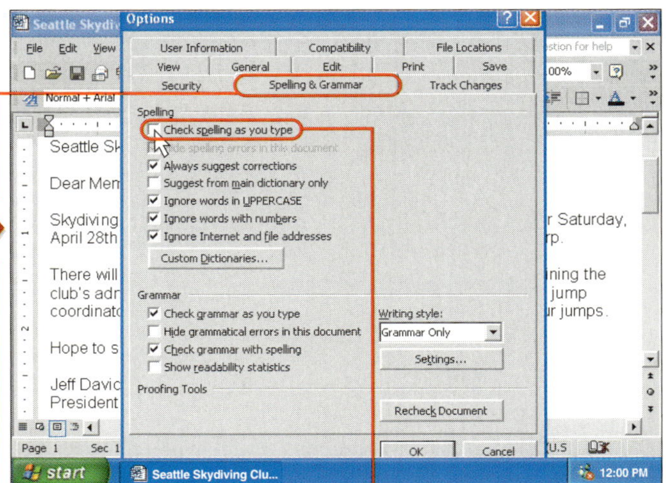

1 Click **Tools**.

2 Click **Options**.

■ The Options dialog box appears.

3 Click the **Spelling & Grammar** tab.

4 Click this option to turn off the automatic spelling check feature for all your documents (☑ changes to ☐).

TEACH YOURSELF

How can I find errors in my documents after I turn off the automatic spelling and grammar check features?

You can check for spelling and grammar errors in your documents at any time. For more information, see page 66.

TEACH YOURSELF

Can I hide the red and green underlines for only the current document?

You can hide the red and green underlines for the current document without turning off the automatic spelling and grammar check features for all your documents. Perform steps **1** to **6** below, selecting **Hide spelling errors in this document** in step **4** (☐ changes to ☑) and **Hide grammatical errors in this document** in step **5** (☐ changes to ☑).

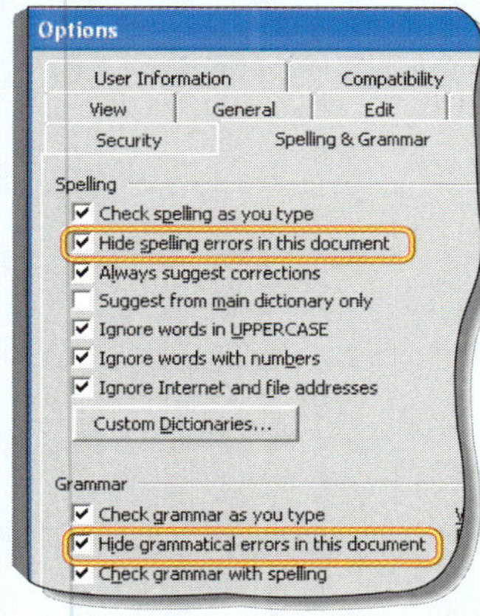

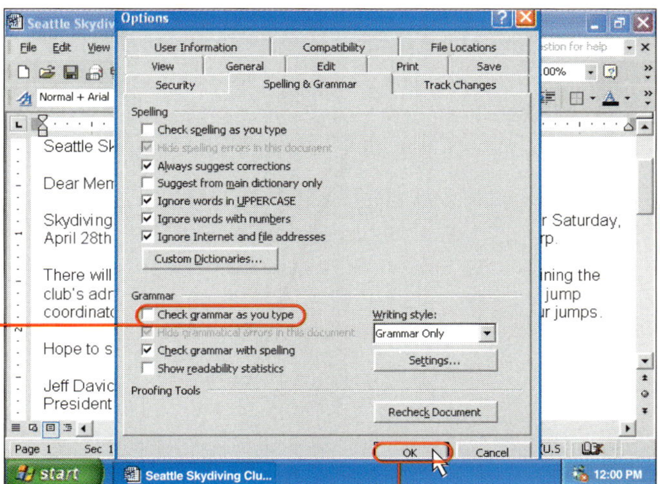

5 Click this option to turn off the automatic grammar check feature for all your documents (☑ changes to ☐).

6 Click **OK** to confirm your changes.

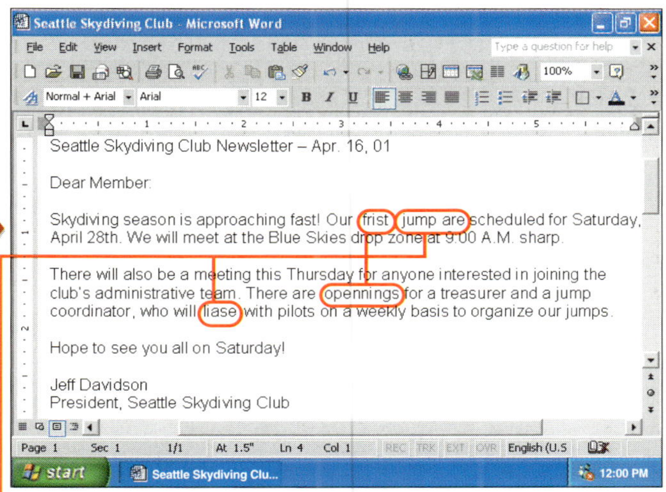

■ The spelling and grammar errors in your document are no longer underlined.

TURN ON SPELLING AND GRAMMAR CHECK

■ To turn on the automatic spelling and grammar check features, repeat steps **1** to **6** (☐ changes to ☑ in steps **4** and **5**).

USING THE THESAURUS

You can use the thesaurus to replace a word in your document with a more suitable word.

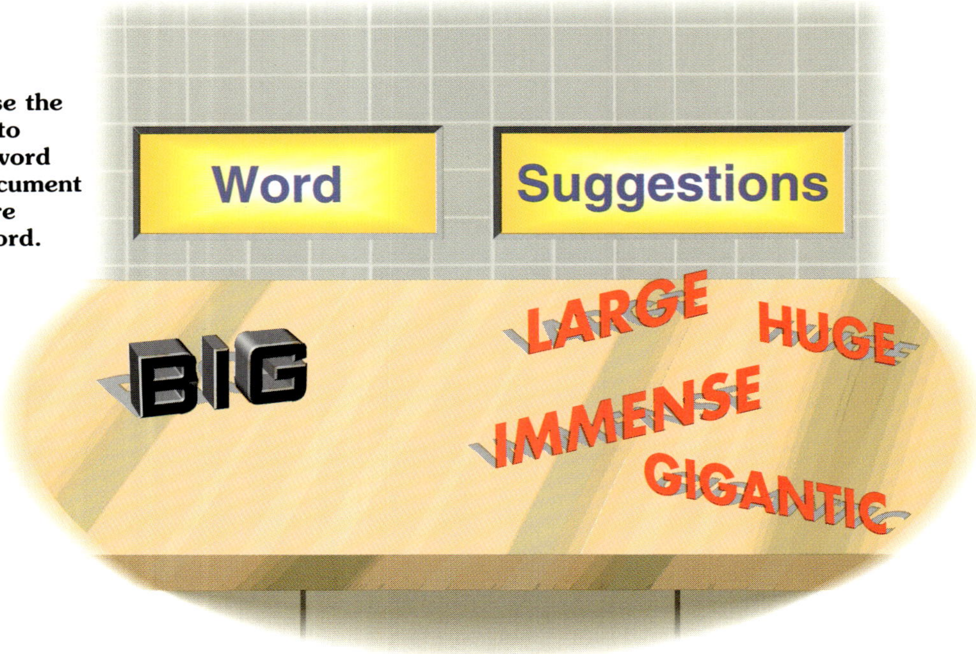

The thesaurus can replace a word in your document with a word that shares the same meaning, called a synonym.

Using the thesaurus included with Word is faster and more convenient than searching through a printed thesaurus.

USING THE THESAURUS

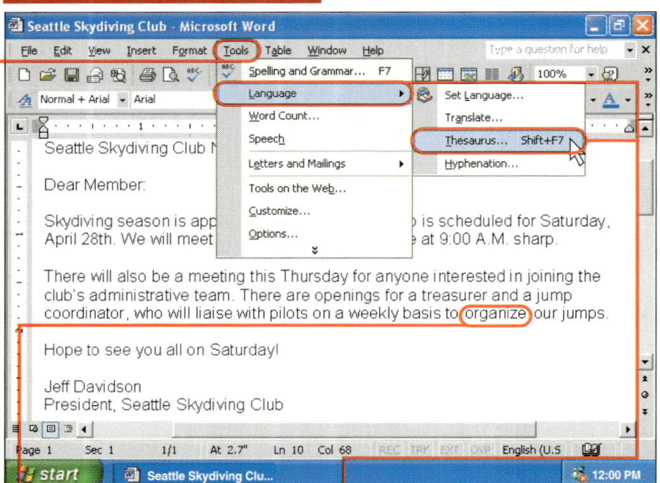

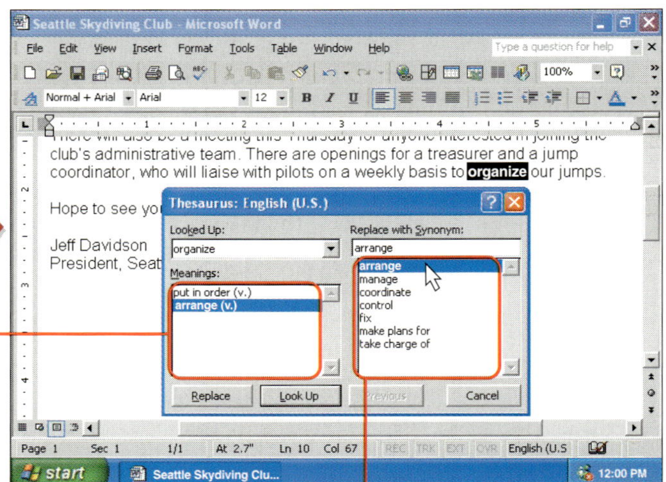

1 Click the word you want to replace with another word.

2 Click **Tools**.

3 Click **Language**.

4 Click **Thesaurus**.

■ The Thesaurus dialog box appears.

5 Click the most appropriate meaning of the word.

■ This area displays words that share the meaning you selected.

6 Click the word you want to use in your document.

Why would I use the thesaurus?

Many people use the thesaurus to replace a word that appears repeatedly in a document. Replacing repeatedly used words can help add variety to your writing and make your document appear more professional. You may also want to use the thesaurus to find a word that more clearly explains a concept.

What if the Thesaurus dialog box does not display a word I want to use?

You can look up synonyms for the words displayed in the Thesaurus dialog box to find a more suitable word.

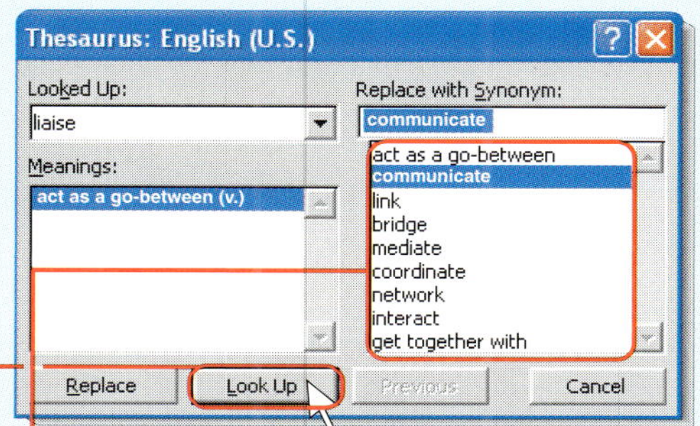

1 Click the word you want to find synonyms for.

2 Click **Look Up**.

3 When you find the word you want to use, perform steps 6 and 7 below.

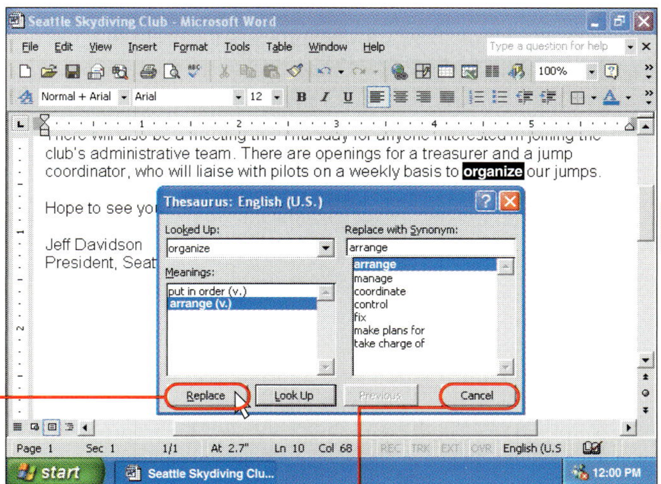

7 Click **Replace** to replace the word in your document with the word you selected.

■ If you do not want to use any of the words displayed in the Thesaurus dialog box, click **Cancel** to close the dialog box.

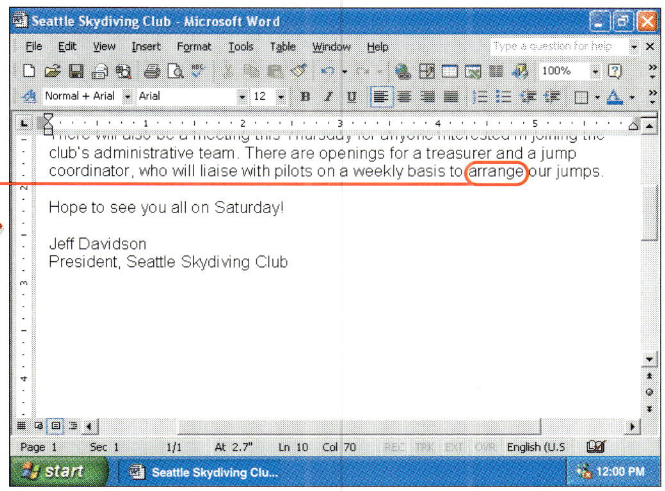

■ The word you selected replaces the word in your document.

USING AUTOCORRECT

Word automatically corrects hundreds of typing and spelling errors as you type. You can create an AutoCorrect entry to add your own word or phrase to the list of errors that Word corrects.

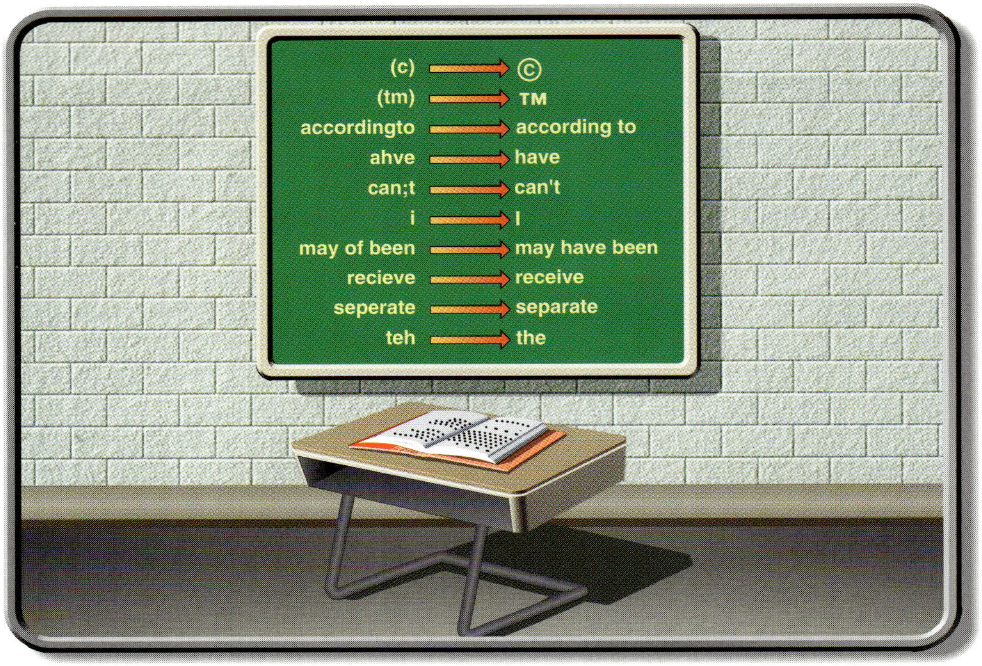

USING AUTOCORRECT

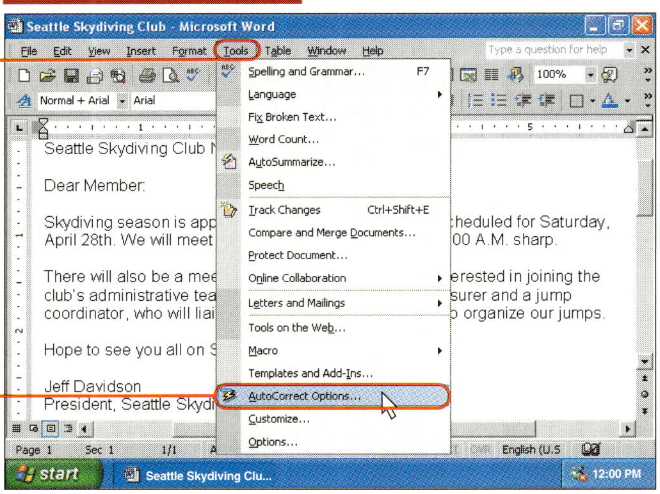

1 Click **Tools**.

2 Click **AutoCorrect Options**.

Note: If AutoCorrect Options does not appear on the menu, position the mouse ↖ over the bottom of the menu to display all the menu options.

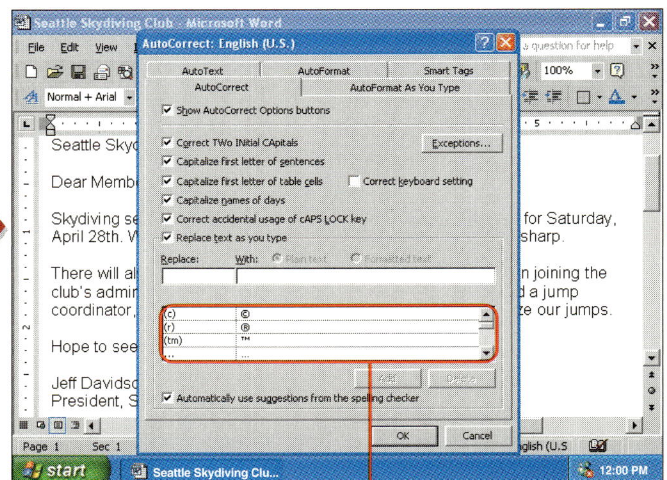

■ The AutoCorrect dialog box appears.

■ This area displays the list of AutoCorrect entries included with Word.

TEACH YOURSELF

What other types of errors does Word automatically correct?

When you type two consecutive uppercase letters, Word automatically converts the second letter to lowercase. When you type a lowercase letter for the first letter of a sentence or the name of a day, Word automatically converts the letter to uppercase.

Error		Correction
PRinter	→	Printer
friday	→	Friday
today I went to the dentist.	→	Today I went to the dentist.

TEACH YOURSELF

Why does a blue rectangle ( ) appear when I position the mouse over a word in my document?

A blue rectangle appears below a word that has been automatically corrected.

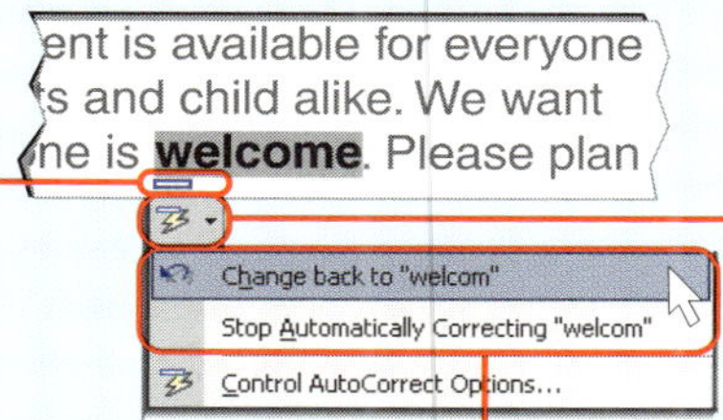

1 If you do not want to accept the correction, position the mouse over the blue rectangle to display the AutoCorrect Options button ( ).

2 Click the AutoCorrect Options button to display a list of options for the correction.

3 Click the option you want to use.

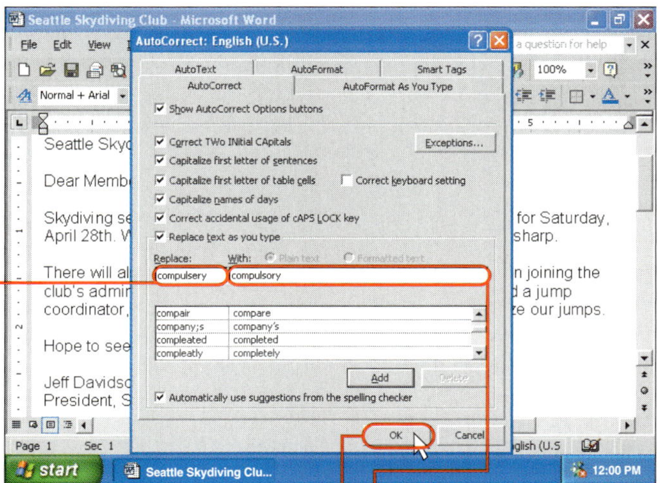

3 To add a new entry to the list, type the text you want Word to replace automatically. The text should not contain spaces and should not be a real word.

4 Click this area and type the text you want Word to automatically insert into your documents.

5 Click **OK** to confirm your change.

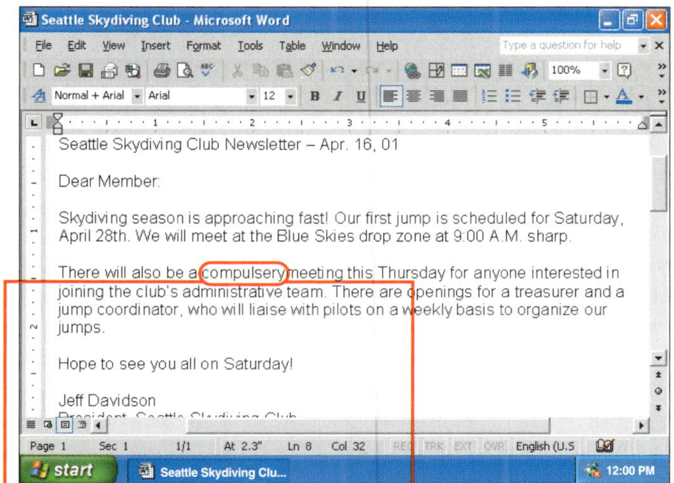

INSERT AN AUTOCORRECT ENTRY

■ After you create an AutoCorrect entry, Word will automatically insert the entry each time you type the corresponding text.

1 Click the location where you want the AutoCorrect entry to appear.

2 Type the text Word will automatically replace.

3 Press the **Spacebar** and Word automatically replaces the text with the AutoCorrect entry.

USING AUTOTEXT

You can use the AutoText feature to store text you frequently use, such as a mailing address, legal disclaimer or closing remark. You can then insert the text into your documents.

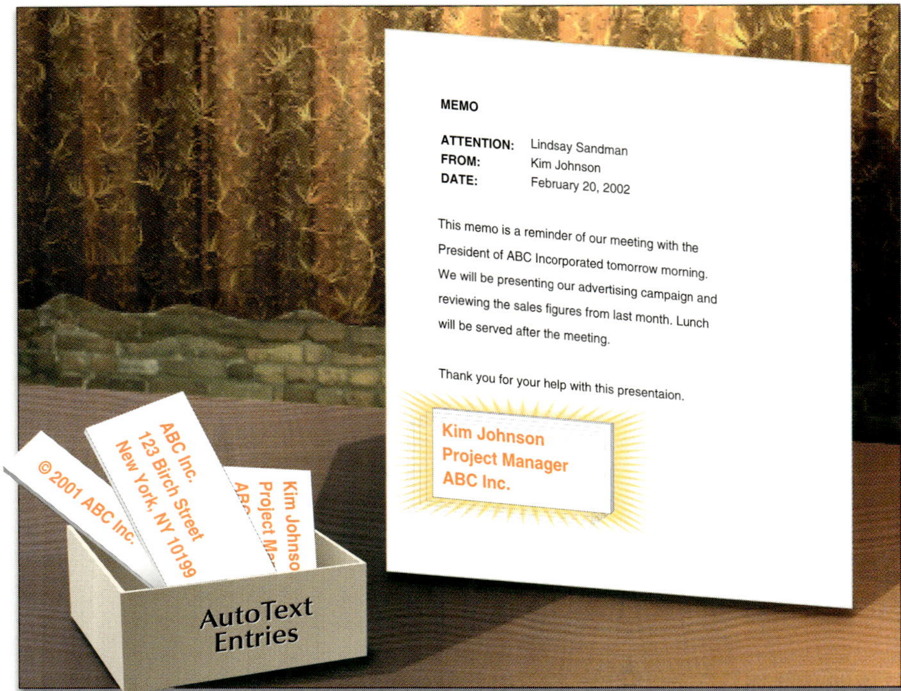

Using the AutoText feature saves you from having to type the same information over and over.

USING AUTOTEXT

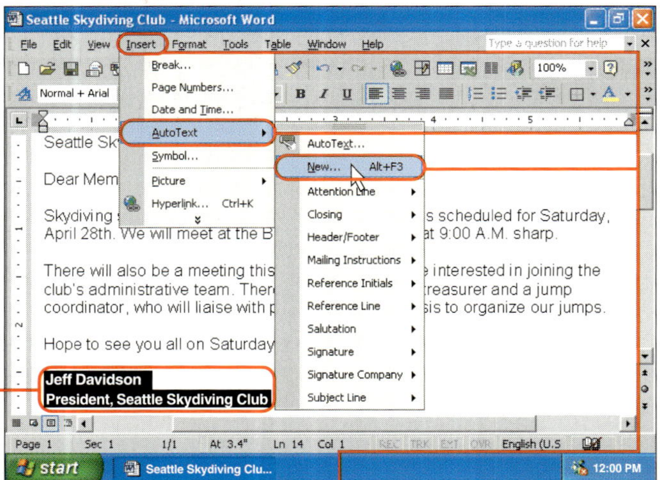

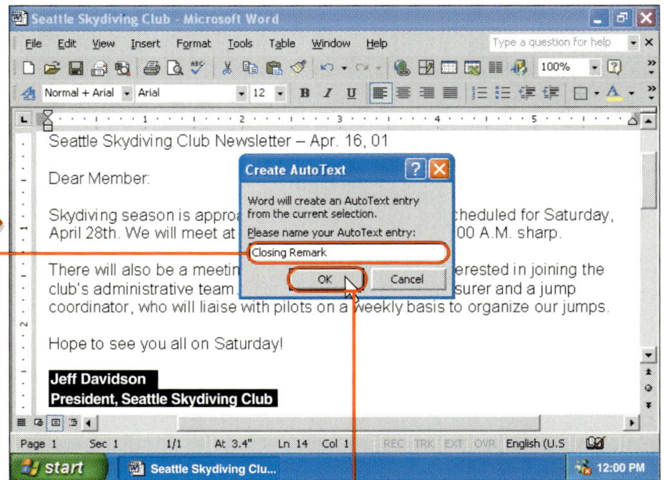

CREATE AN AUTOTEXT ENTRY

1 Type the text you want to store as an AutoText entry.

2 Select the text. To select text, see page 10.

3 Click **Insert**.

4 Click **AutoText**.

Note: If AutoText does not appear on the menu, position the mouse over the bottom of the menu to display all the menu options.

5 Click **New**.

■ The Create AutoText dialog box appears.

6 This area displays a name for the AutoText entry. To use a different name, type the name.

Note: The name of an AutoText entry should be at least four characters long.

7 Click **OK** to create the AutoText entry.

Does Word come with any AutoText entries?

Word comes with AutoText entries that can help you quickly create a letter.

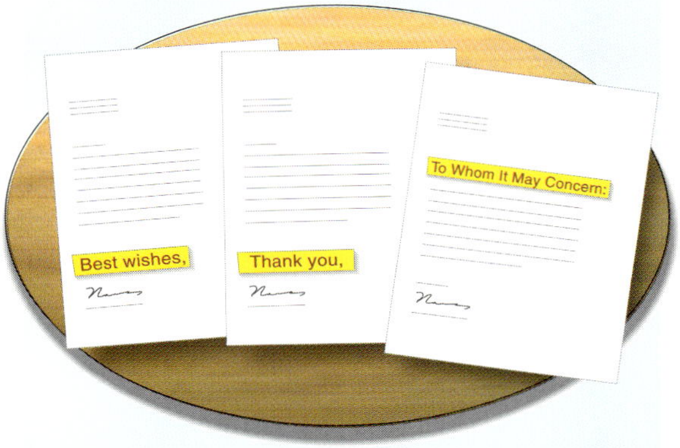

How can I quickly insert an AutoText entry into my document?

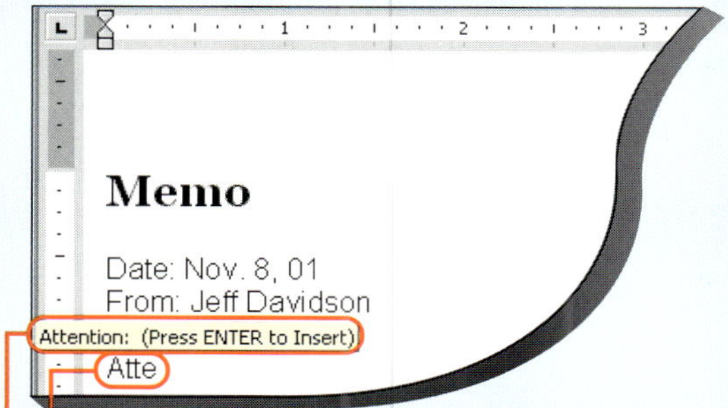

1 To quickly insert an AutoText entry, type the first few characters of the name of the AutoText entry.

■ A yellow box appears, displaying the AutoText entry for the text you typed.

2 To insert the AutoText entry, press the **Enter** key.

■ To ignore the AutoText entry, continue typing.

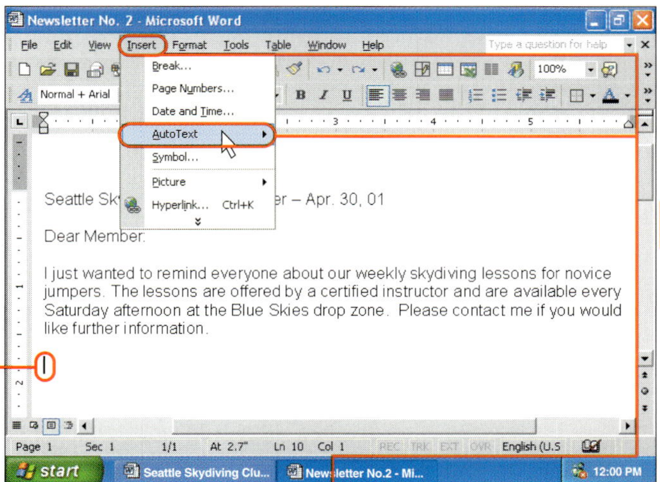

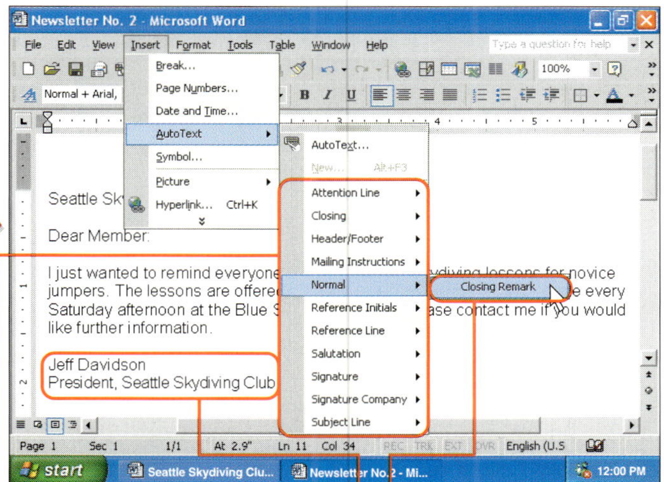

INSERT AN AUTOTEXT ENTRY

1 Click where you want the AutoText entry to appear in your document.

2 Click **Insert**.

3 Click **AutoText**.

Note: If AutoText does not appear on the menu, position the mouse over the bottom of the menu to display all the menu options.

4 Click the category that stores the AutoText entry you want to use.

Note: The Normal category stores most AutoText entries you have created.

5 Click the AutoText entry you want to use.

■ The text appears in your document.

INSERT SYMBOLS

You can insert symbols that do not appear on your keyboard into your document.

INSERT SYMBOLS

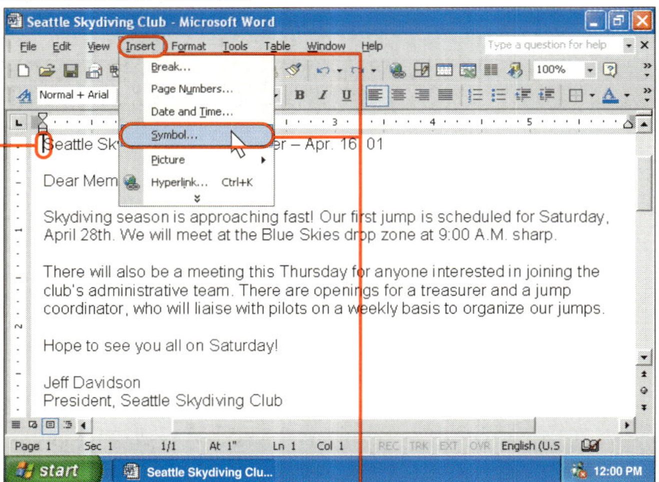

1 Click the location in your document where you want a symbol to appear.

2 Click **Insert**.

3 Click **Symbol**.

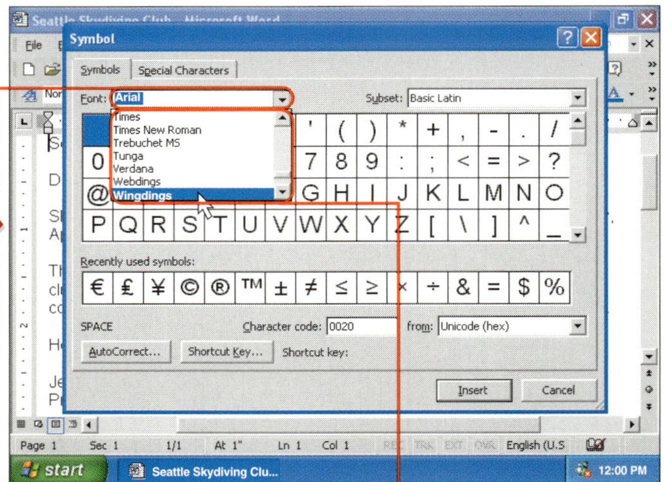

■ The Symbol dialog box appears, displaying the symbols for the current font.

4 To display the symbols for another font, click ▾ in this area.

5 Click the font that provides the symbols you want to display.

TEACH YOURSELF

How can I quickly insert a symbol I recently used?

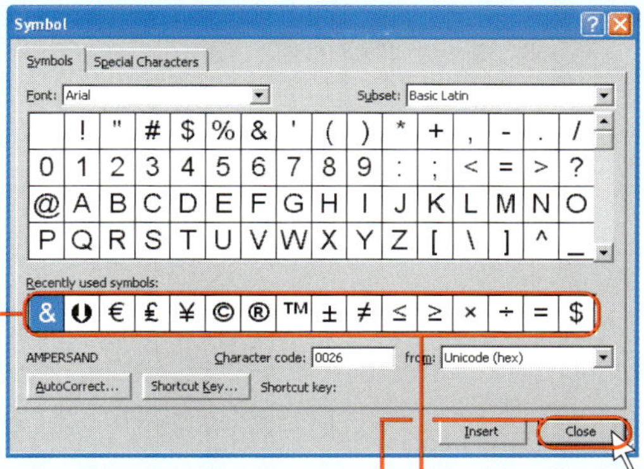

1 Perform steps **1** to **3** below to display the Symbol dialog box.

■ This area displays the most recently used symbols.

2 Double-click the symbol you want to place in your document.

3 Click **Close** to close the Symbol dialog box.

TEACH YOURSELF

Is there another way to enter symbols in my document?

When you type one of the following sets of characters, Word automatically replaces the characters with a symbol.

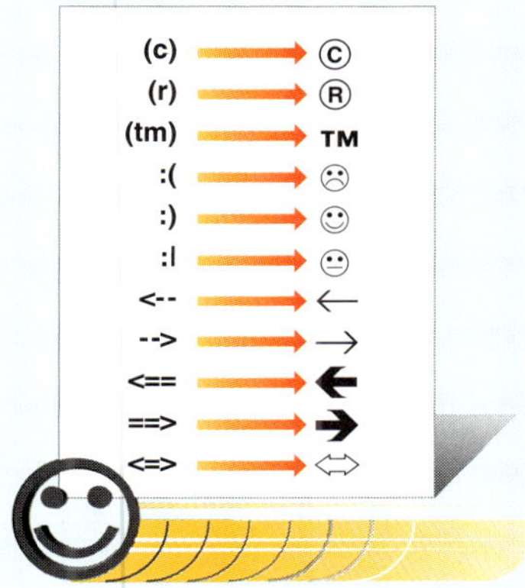

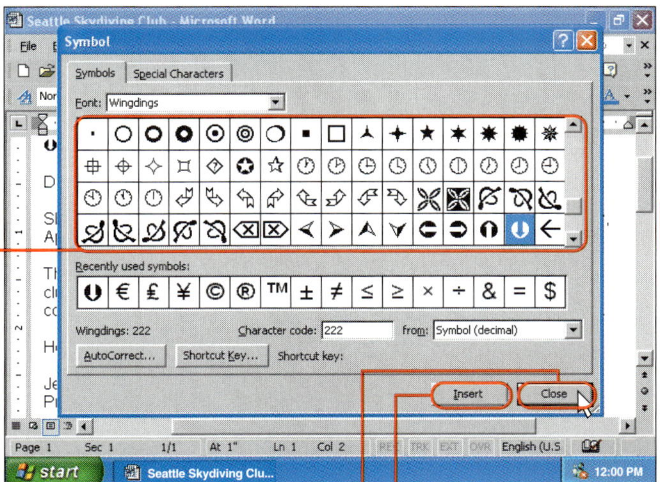

■ The symbols for the font you selected appear in this area.

6 Click the symbol you want to place in your document.

7 Click **Insert** to insert the symbol into your document.

8 Click **Close** to close the Symbol dialog box.

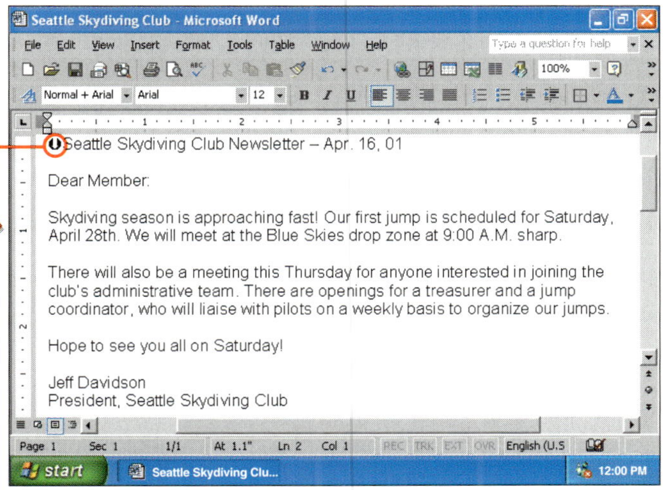

■ The symbol appears in your document.

■ To remove a symbol from your document, drag the mouse I over the symbol until you highlight the symbol and then press the Delete key.

ADD A COMMENT

You can add a comment to text in your document. A comment can be a note, explanation or reminder about information you need to verify later.

ADD A COMMENT

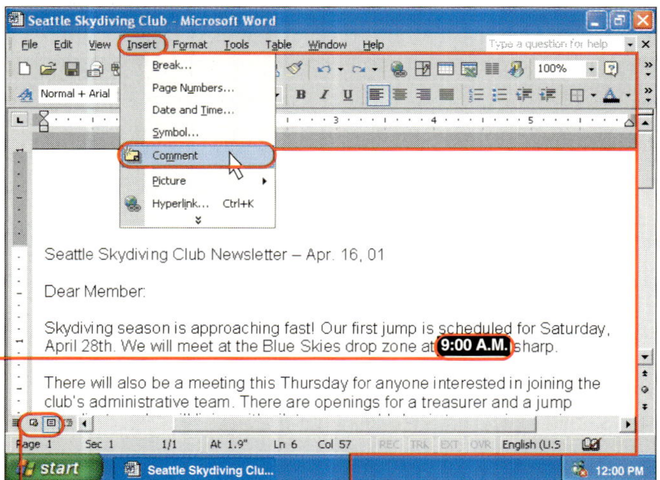

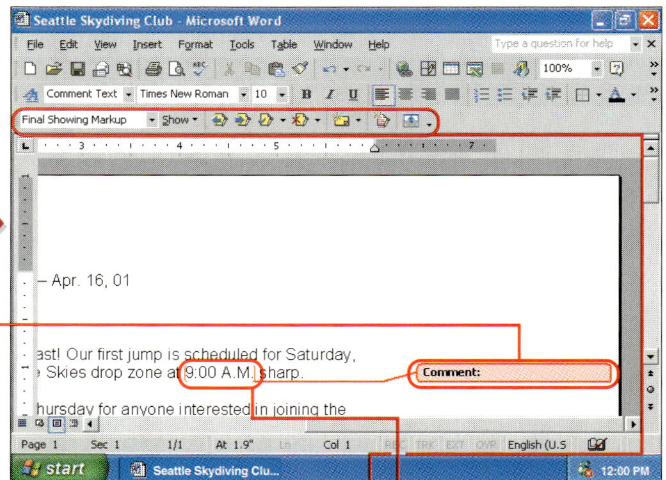

1 Click or to display your document in the Web Layout or Print Layout view.

2 Select the text you want to add a comment to. To select text, see page 10.

3 Click **Insert**.

4 Click **Comment**.

Note: If Comment does not appear on the menu, position the mouse over the bottom of the menu to display all the menu options.

■ A comment balloon appears in the right margin of your document.

Note: You may need to use the scroll bar to view the comment balloon.

■ Colored brackets appear around the text you selected.

■ The Reviewing toolbar appears.

Can I edit a comment?

You can edit a comment to update the information in the comment. Click the comment balloon containing the comment you want to edit. You can then edit the text as you would edit any text in a document. To edit text, see page 54.

How do I view a comment in the Normal or Outline view?

In the Normal and Outline view, colored brackets appear around text you have added a comment to. To view a comment, position the mouse I over the text for the comment. After a few seconds, the comment will appear in a colored box. For more information on the views, see page 40.

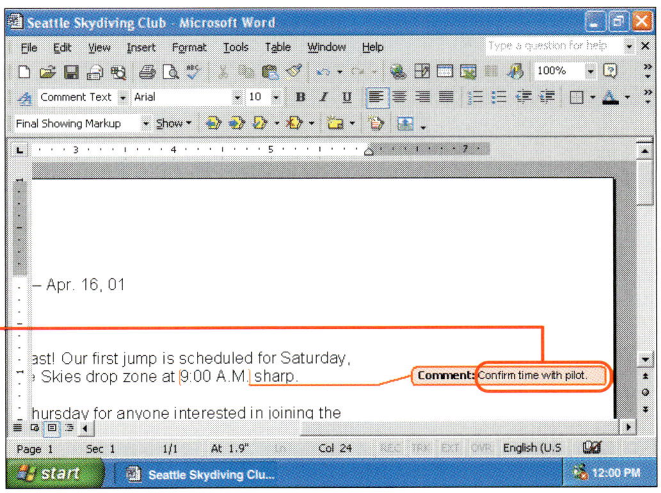

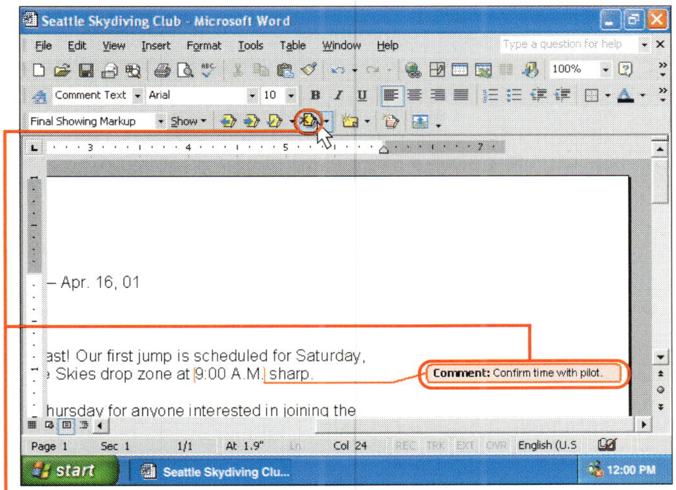

5 Type the comment you want to add.

6 When you finish typing the comment, click outside the comment balloon.

DELETE A COMMENT

1 Click the comment balloon containing the comment you want to delete.

2 Click to delete the comment.

■ Word deletes the comment and removes the comment balloon and colored brackets from your document.

■ When you finish working with your comments, you can hide the Reviewing toolbar. To hide a toolbar, see page 43.

TRACK CHANGES

Word can keep track of the editing and formatting changes that are made to your document. Tracking changes is useful when multiple people are working with the same document.

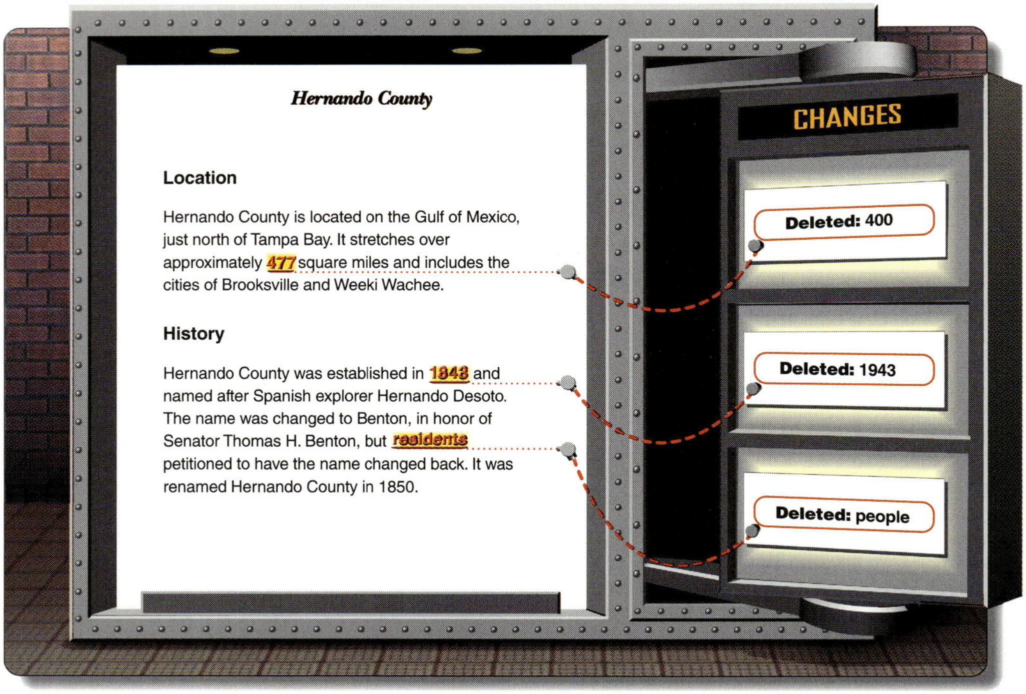

Multiple people can work with a document you store on your network. Word will keep track of the changes you make to the document, as well as the changes that other people make.

TRACK CHANGES

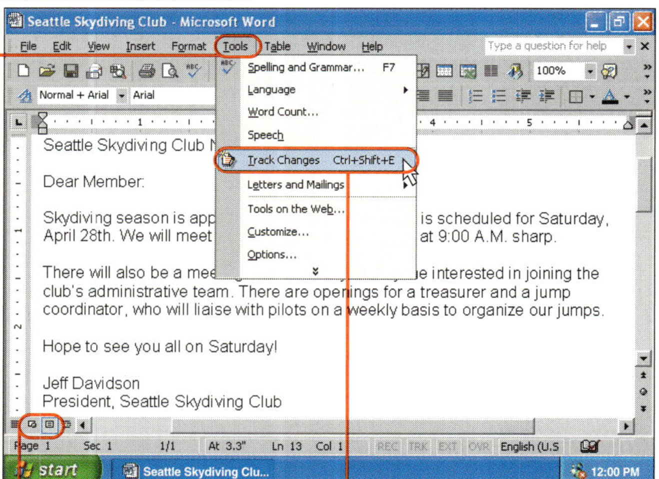

1 Click [Web Layout] or [Print Layout] to display the document in the Web Layout or Print Layout view.

2 Click **Tools**.

3 Click **Track Changes**.

Note: If Track Changes does not appear on the menu, position the mouse over the bottom of the menu to display all the menu options.

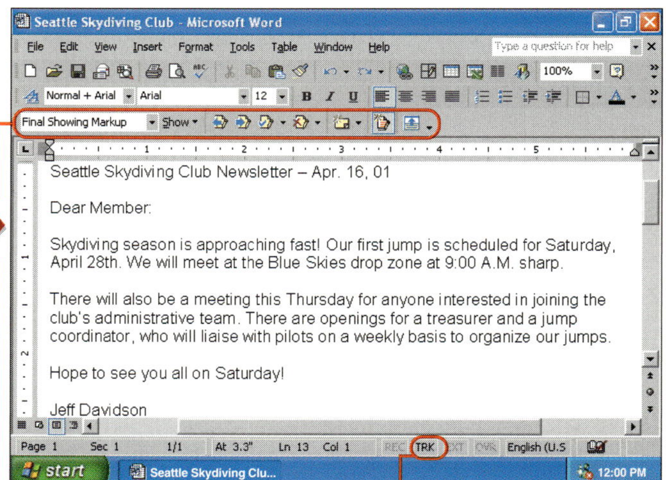

■ The Reviewing toolbar appears.

■ When Word tracks changes, this area displays **TRK** in bold.

4 You can now make changes to the document you want Word to track.

The balloons do not appear in the margin of the document. What is wrong?

The balloons only appear in the margin of a document when the document is displayed in the Print Layout or Web Layout view. When the document is displayed in the Normal or Outline view, deleted text appears in the body of the document, crossed out and in color. Formatted text displays the formatting. For information on the views, see page 40.

Will the tracked changes appear on a printed page?

Yes. When you print a document that displays tracked changes, Word may automatically shrink the text in the document to fit the tracked changes on the printed page.

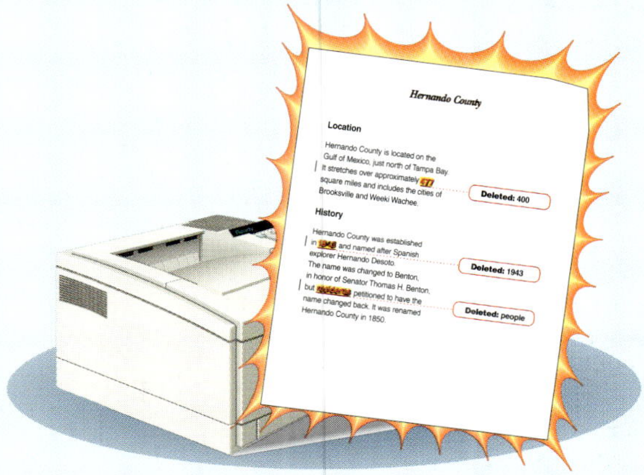

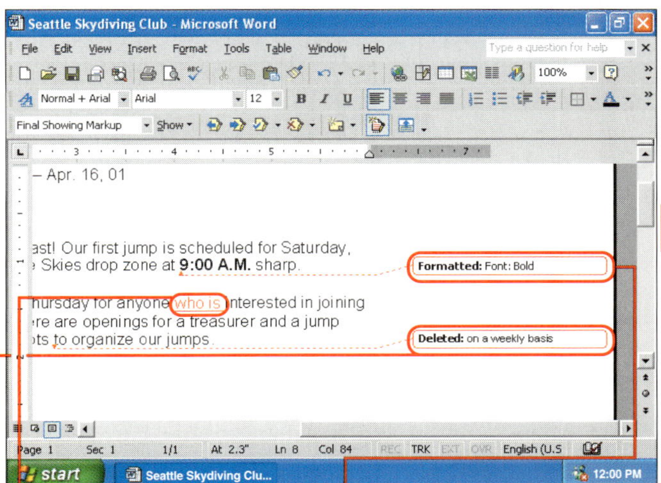

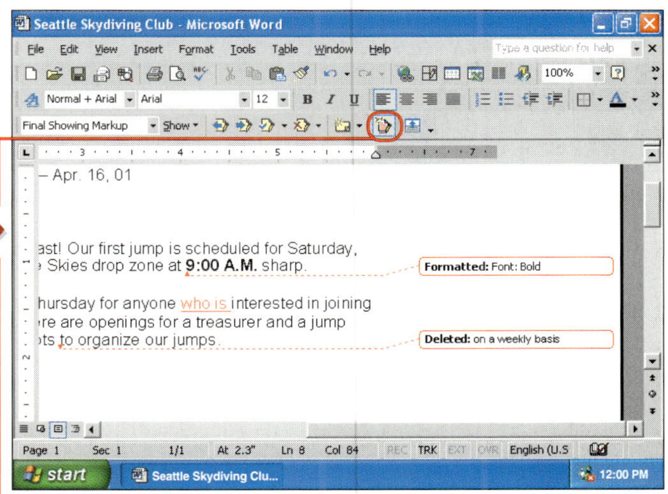

- Text you add to the document appears underlined and in color.
- Text you delete from the document appears in a balloon in the right margin of the document.
- Formatting changes you make appear in a balloon in the right margin of the document.

Note: You may need to use the scroll bar to view the balloons.

- A vertical line appears in the left margin beside text that contains a tracked change.
- To stop tracking changes in the document, click .
- You can now review the tracked changes in the document. To review tracked changes, see page 82.

REVIEW TRACKED CHANGES

You can review the tracked changes in a document and choose whether to accept or reject each change.

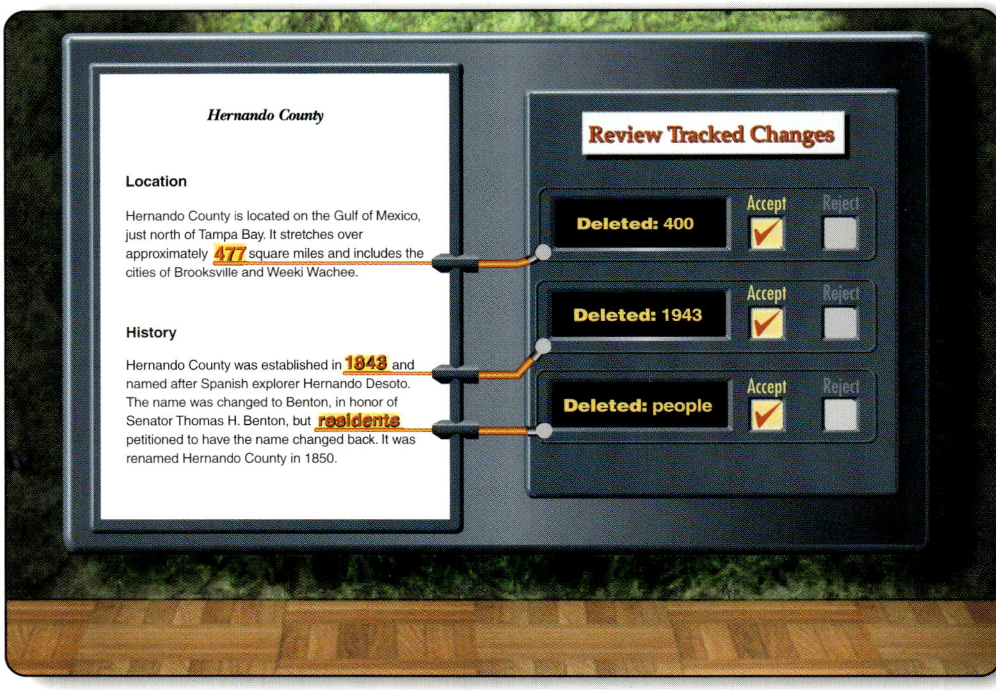

REVIEW TRACKED CHANGES

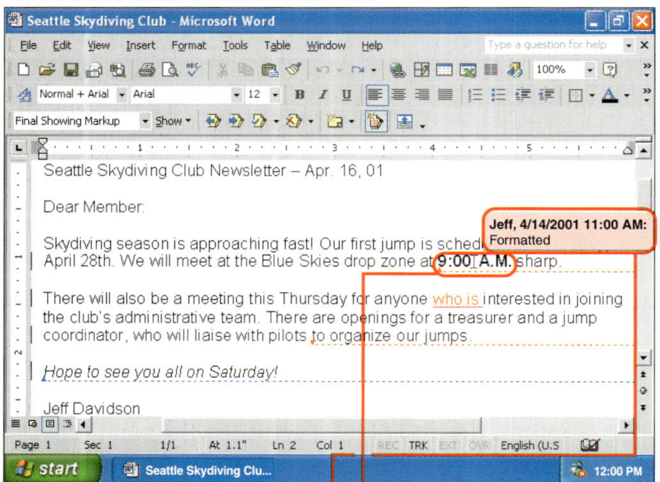

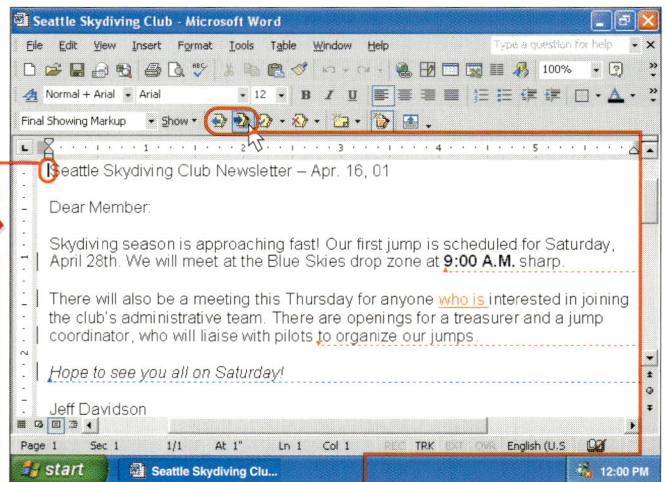

1 Open the document you want to review tracked changes for. To open a document, see page 28.

■ Word displays the changes that each person made in a different color.

2 To display information about a change, position the mouse I over the change.

■ After a few seconds, a colored box appears, displaying the name of the person who made the change and the date and time the change was made.

3 Click at the beginning of the document.

4 Click one of the following buttons to move to a tracked change in the document.

Previous

Next

TEACH YOURSELF

How can I accept all the changes in a document at once?

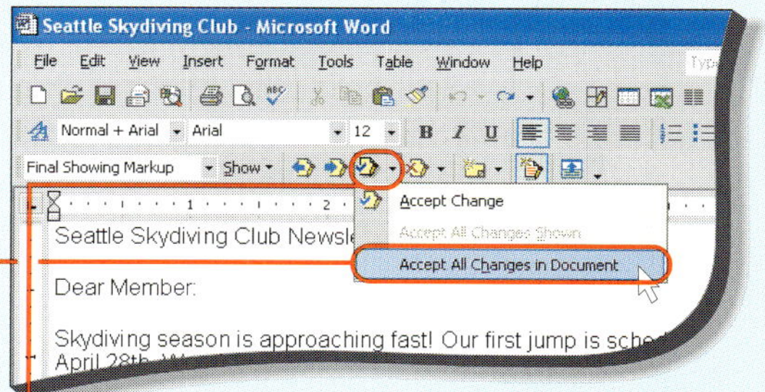

1 Click ▾ in this area.

2 Click **Accept All Changes in Document.**

■ Word will accept all the changes in the document and stop tracking the changes.

*Note: To reject all the changes in a document, click ▾ beside the Reject Change button ( ) and then click **Reject All Changes in Document**.*

TEACH YOURSELF

How do I hide the Reviewing toolbar?

You can hide or display the Reviewing toolbar as you would hide or display any toolbar. To hide or display a toolbar, see page 43.

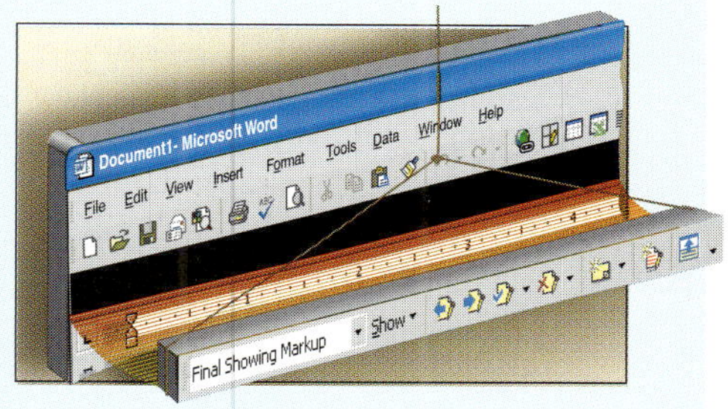

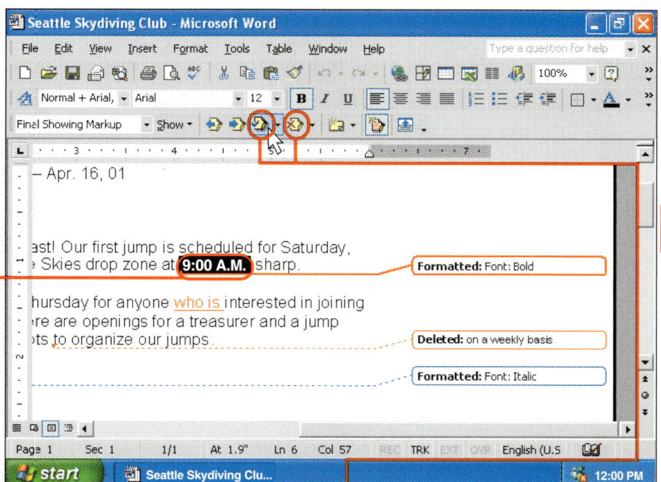

■ Word highlights the tracked change.

5 Click one of the following buttons to accept or reject the change.

- Accept Change
- Reject Change

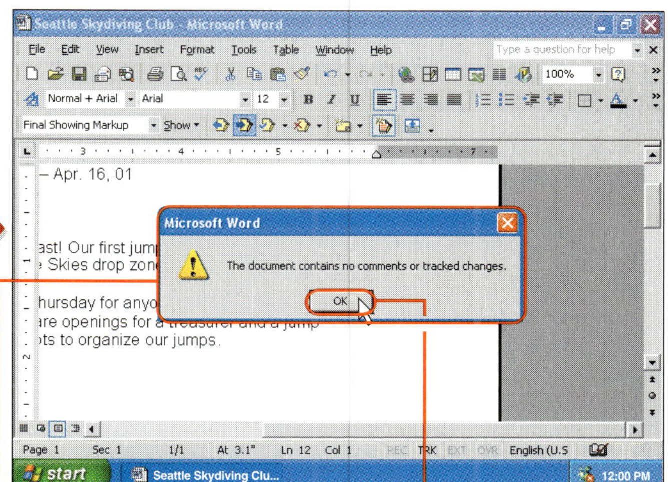

■ Word accepts or rejects the change and stops tracking the change.

6 Repeat steps **4** and **5** until this dialog box appears.

7 Click **OK** to close the dialog box.

TRANSLATE TEXT

You can translate a word in your document from one language to another.

Word's translation feature offers only basic translation services. If you need to translate important information or a large amount of text, you may want to hire a professional translator.

TRANSLATE TEXT

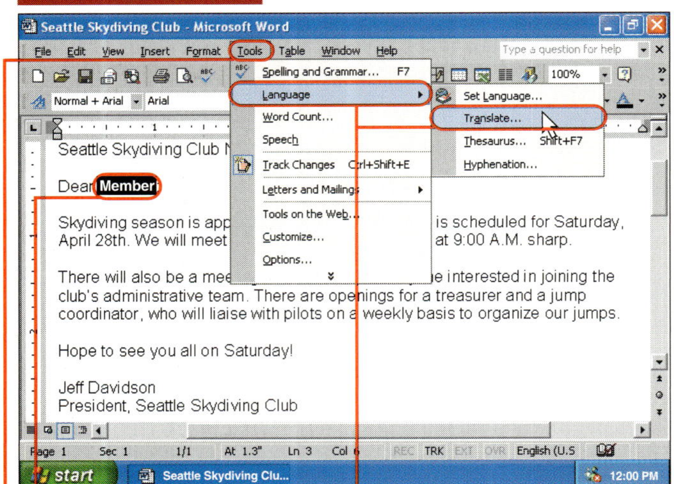

1 Select the word you want to translate. To select text, see page 10.

2 Click **Tools**.

3 Click **Language**.

4 Click **Translate**.

■ The Translate task pane appears.

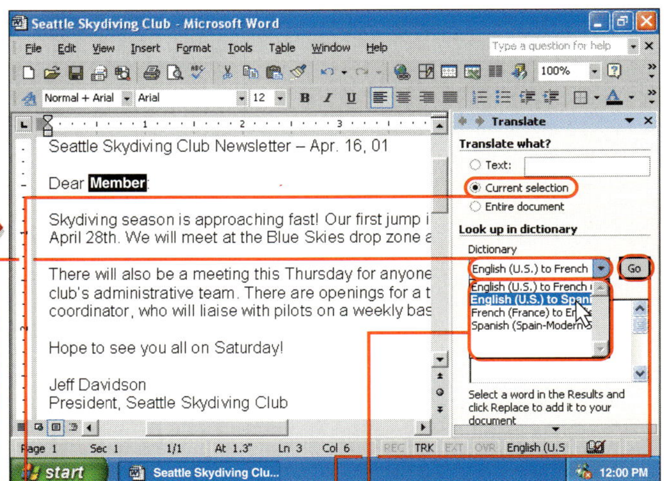

5 Click **Current selection** to translate the word you selected (○ changes to ⊙).

6 Click this area to specify the languages you want to use in the translation.

7 Click the option that specifies the language of the word you selected and the language you want to translate the word to.

8 Click **Go** to translate the word.

Note: If a dialog box appears, see the top of page 85.

TEACH YOURSELF TY

Why does a dialog box appear when I try to translate a word?

A dialog box appears if the appropriate dictionary is not installed on your computer. Insert the CD-ROM disc you used to install Word into your computer's CD-ROM drive. Then click **Yes** to install the dictionary.

Note: A window may appear on your screen. Click ✕ in the top right corner of the window to close the window.

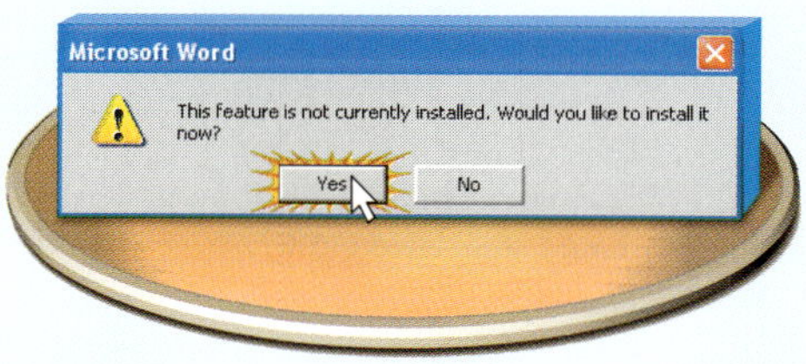

TEACH YOURSELF TY

How can I translate a word that is not in my document?

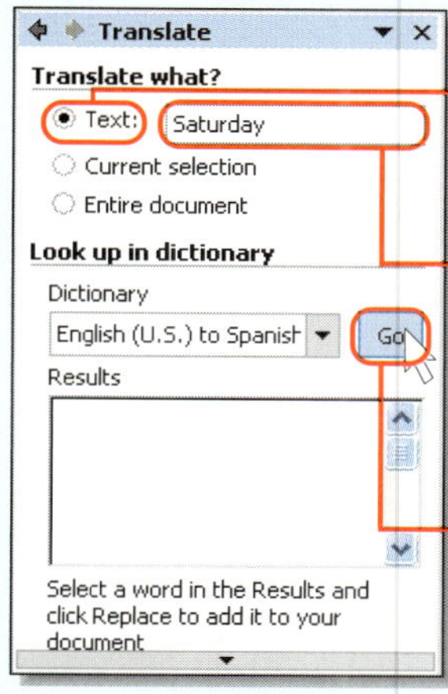

1 Perform steps **2** to **4** below to display the Translate task pane.

2 Click **Text** (○ changes to ⦿).

3 Click this area and then type the word you want to translate.

4 Click **Go** to translate the word.

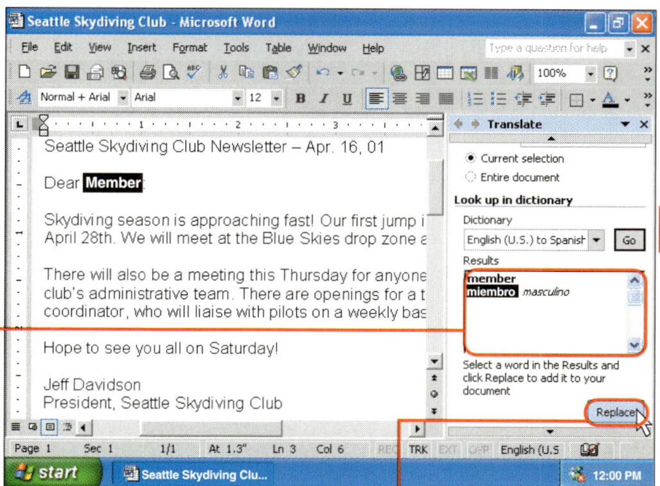

■ This area displays the results of the translation.

9 To replace the word in your document with a translated word, drag the mouse I over the translated word until you highlight the word.

10 Click **Replace**.

Note: If you cannot see the Replace button, click ▼ to scroll down through the Translate task pane.

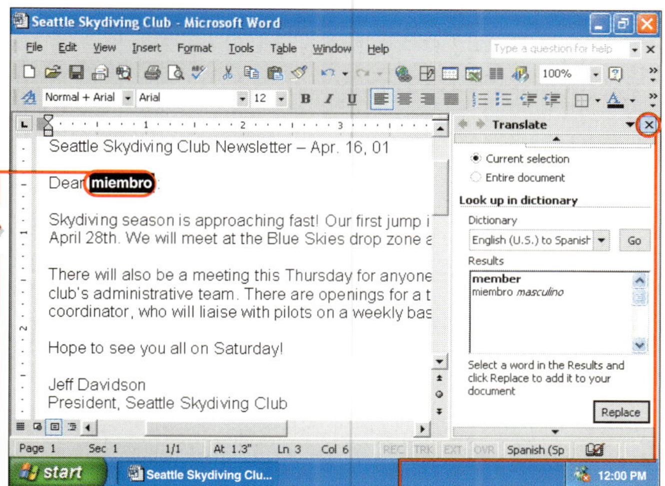

■ The translated word appears in your document.

■ To hide the Translate task pane, click ✕.

Bold
Italic
Underline
TEXT
Ultra Gloss

Format Text

Would you like to emphasize information in your document and enhance the appearance of text? Read this chapter to learn how.

Change Font of Text 88

Change Size of Text 89

Bold, Italicize or Underline Text 90

Change Case of Text 91

Change Color of Text 92

Highlight Text...................................93

Change Alignment of Text 94

Change Appearance of Text 96

Change Font for All New Documents ..98

Animate Text 100

Copy Formatting 102

Change Line Spacing 104

Remove Formatting From Text...........105

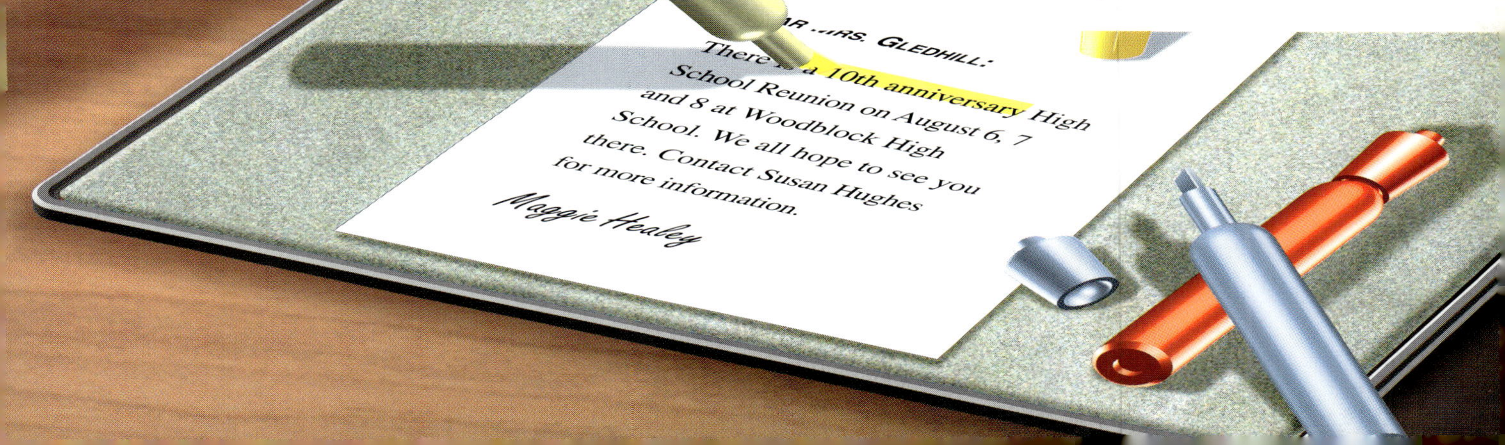

CHANGE FONT OF TEXT

You can change the font of text to enhance the appearance of your document.

CHANGE FONT OF TEXT

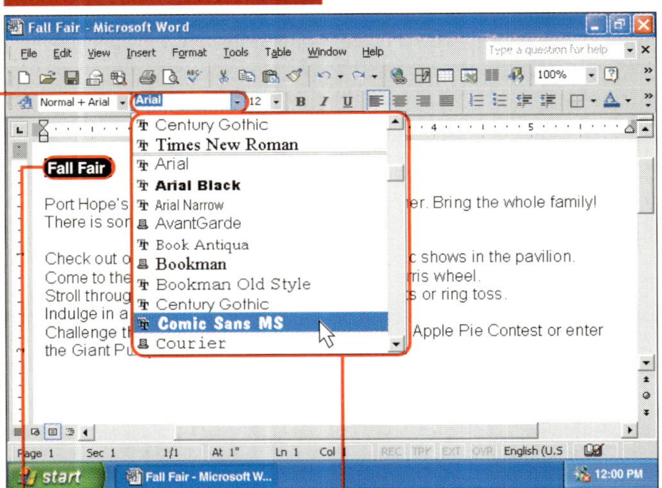

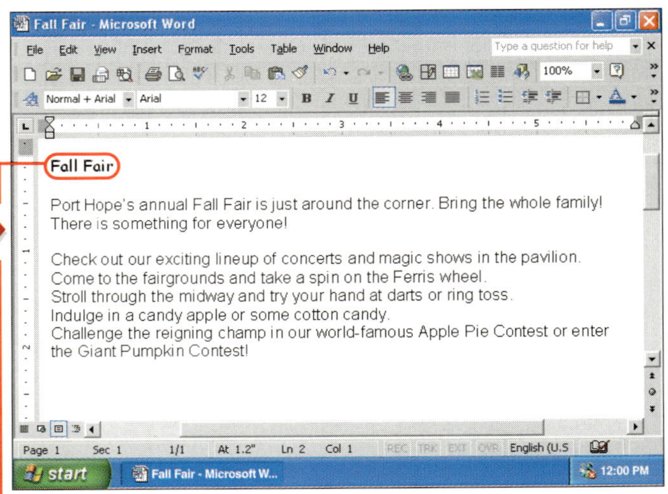

1 Select the text you want to change to a different font. To select text, see page 10.

2 Click ▾ in this area to display a list of the available fonts.

Note: If the Font area is not displayed, click » on the Formatting toolbar to display the area.

3 Click the font you want to use.

Note: Word displays the fonts you have recently used at the top of the list.

■ The text you selected changes to the new font.

■ To deselect text, click outside the selected area.

CHANGE SIZE OF TEXT

You can increase or decrease the size of text in your document.

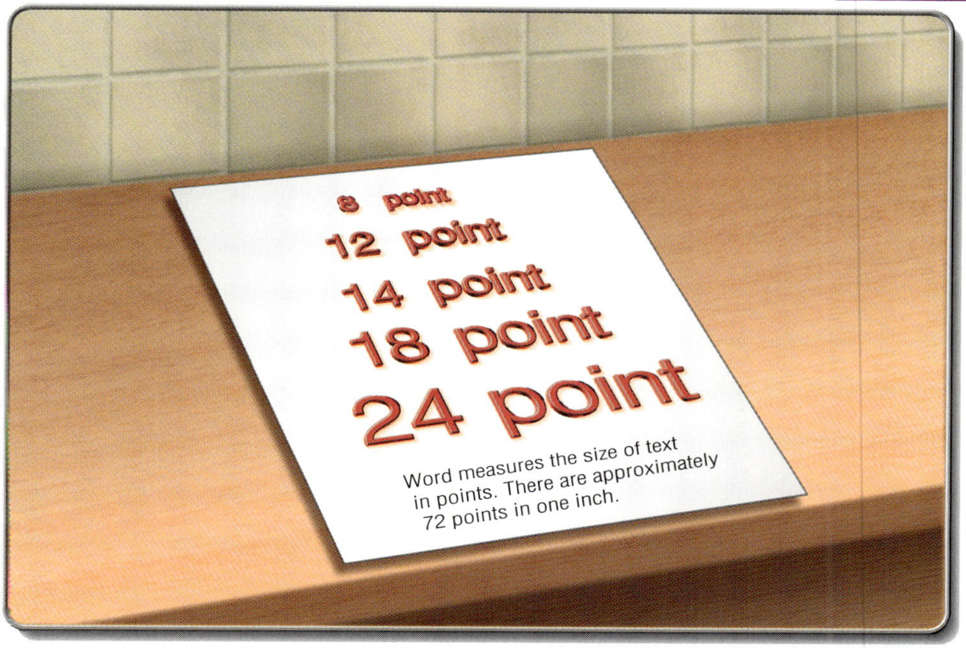

Larger text is easier to read, but smaller text allows you to fit more information on a page.

CHANGE SIZE OF TEXT

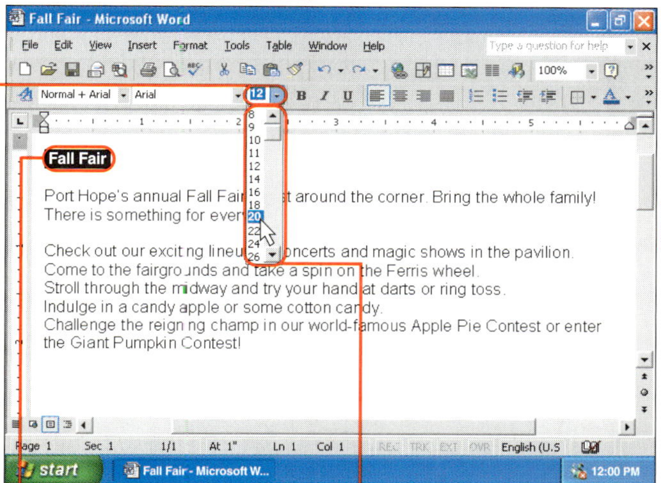

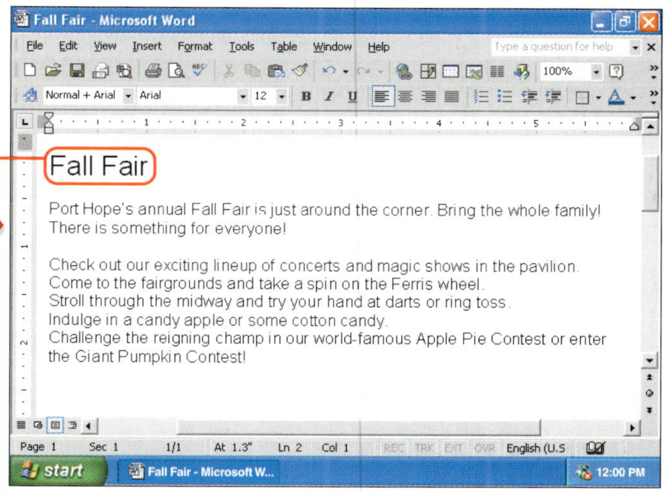

1 Select the text you want to change to a new size.

To select text, see page 10.

2 Click ▼ in this area to display a list of the available sizes.

Note: If the Font Size area is not displayed, click » on the Formatting toolbar to display the area.

3 Click the size you want to use.

■ The text you selected changes to the new size.

■ To deselect text, click outside the selected area.

BOLD, ITALICIZE OR UNDERLINE TEXT

You can bold, italicize or underline text to emphasize information in your document.

BOLD, ITALICIZE OR UNDERLINE TEXT

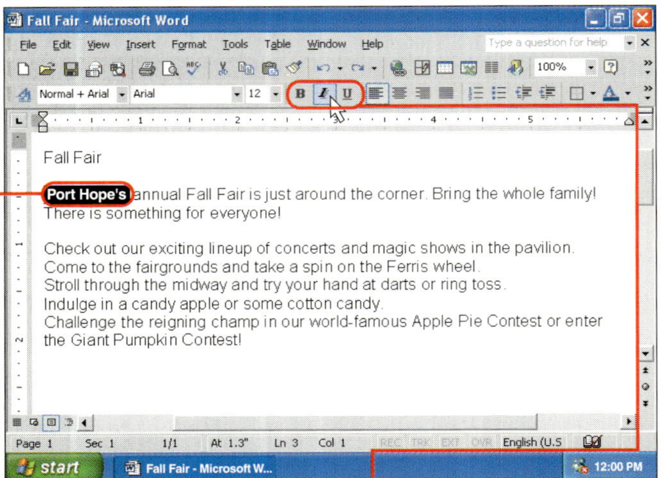

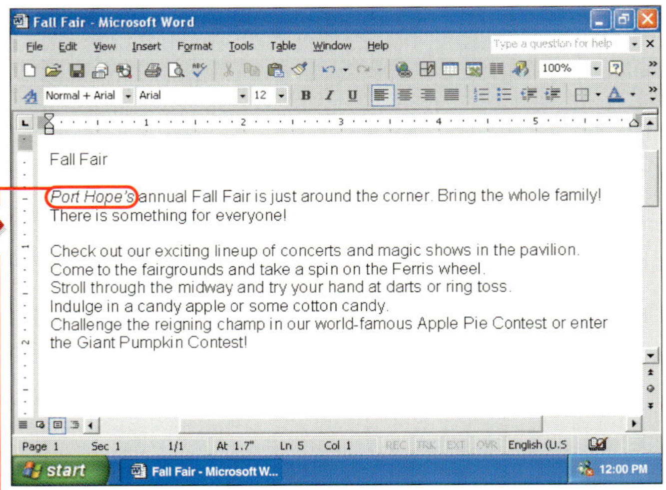

1 Select the text you want to bold, italicize or underline. To select text, see page 10.

2 Click one of the following buttons.

- **B** Bold
- *I* Italic
- U Underline

Note: If the button you want is not displayed, click » on the Formatting toolbar to display the button.

- The text you selected appears in the new style.

- To deselect text, click outside the selected area.

- To remove a bold, italic or underline style, repeat steps **1** and **2**.

CHANGE CASE OF TEXT

You can change the case of text in your document without retyping the text. Word offers five case styles for you to choose from.

CHANGE CASE OF TEXT

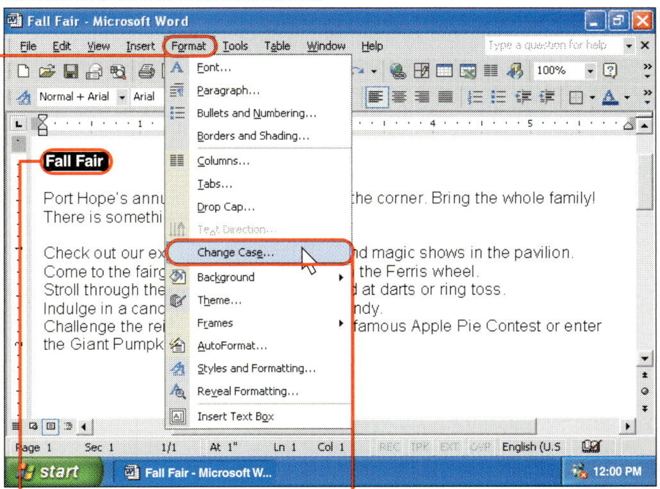

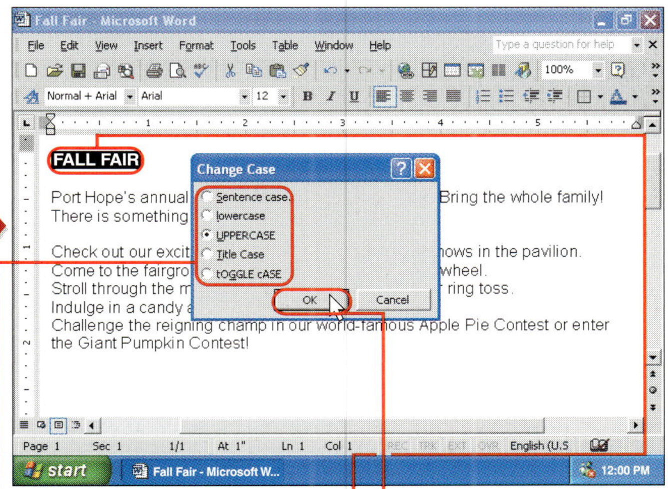

1 Select the text you want to change to a new case style. To select text, see page 10.

2 Click **Format**.

3 Click **Change Case**.

Note: If Change Case does not appear on the menu, position the mouse over the bottom of the menu to display all the menu options.

■ The Change Case dialog box appears.

4 Click the case style you want to use (○ changes to ⊙).

5 Click **OK** to confirm your selection.

■ The text you selected changes to the new case style.

■ To deselect text, click outside the selected area.

CHANGE COLOR OF TEXT

You can change the color of text to draw attention to headings or important information in your document.

CHANGE COLOR OF TEXT

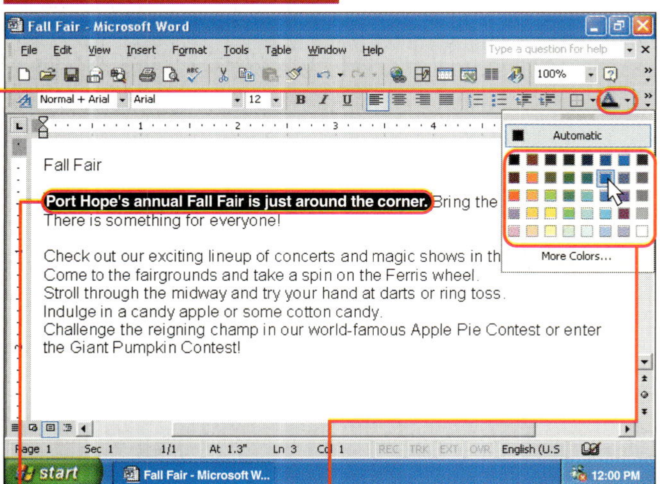

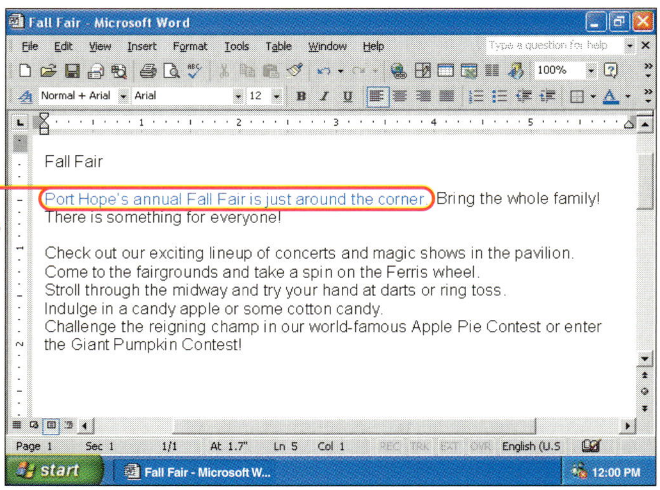

1 Select the text you want to change to a different color. To select text, see page 10.

2 Click ▾ in this area to display the available colors.

Note: If A▾ *is not displayed, click* » *on the Formatting toolbar to display the button.*

3 Click the color you want to use.

■ The text you selected appears in the new color.

■ To deselect text, click outside the selected area.

■ To return text to its original color, repeat steps **1** to **3**, selecting **Automatic** in step **3**.

HIGHLIGHT TEXT

You can highlight text that you want to stand out in your document. Highlighting text is useful for marking information you want to review or verify later.

If you plan to print your document on a black-and-white printer, use a light highlight color so you will be able to easily read the printed text.

HIGHLIGHT TEXT

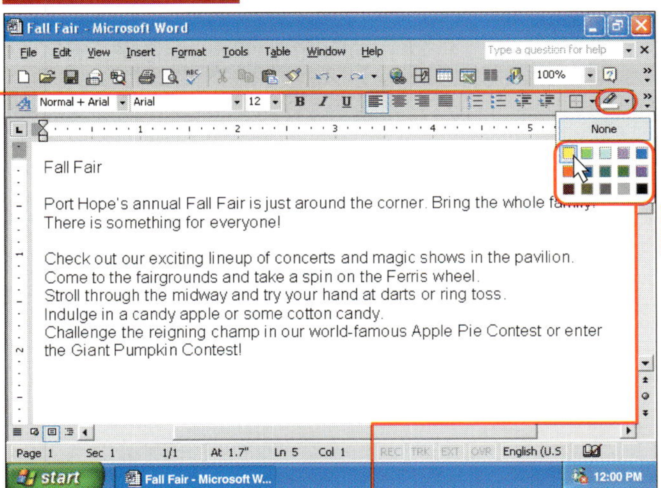

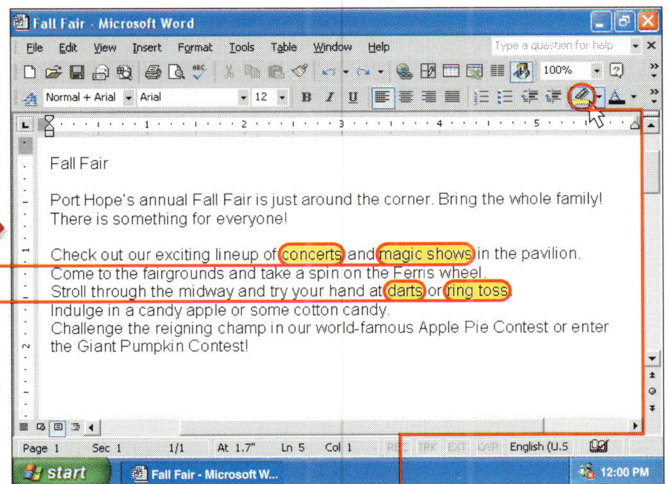

1 Click ▾ in this area to display the available highlight colors.

Note: If [highlight ▾] *is not displayed, click* » *on the Formatting toolbar to display the button.*

2 Click the highlight color you want to use.

■ The mouse I changes to [highlight pointer] when over your document.

3 Select each area of text you want to highlight. To select text, see page 10.

■ The text you selected appears highlighted.

4 When you finish highlighting text, click [highlight] or press the Esc key.

■ To remove a highlight from text, repeat steps **1** to **4**, selecting **None** in step **2**.

CHANGE ALIGNMENT OF TEXT

You can enhance the appearance of your document by aligning text in different ways.

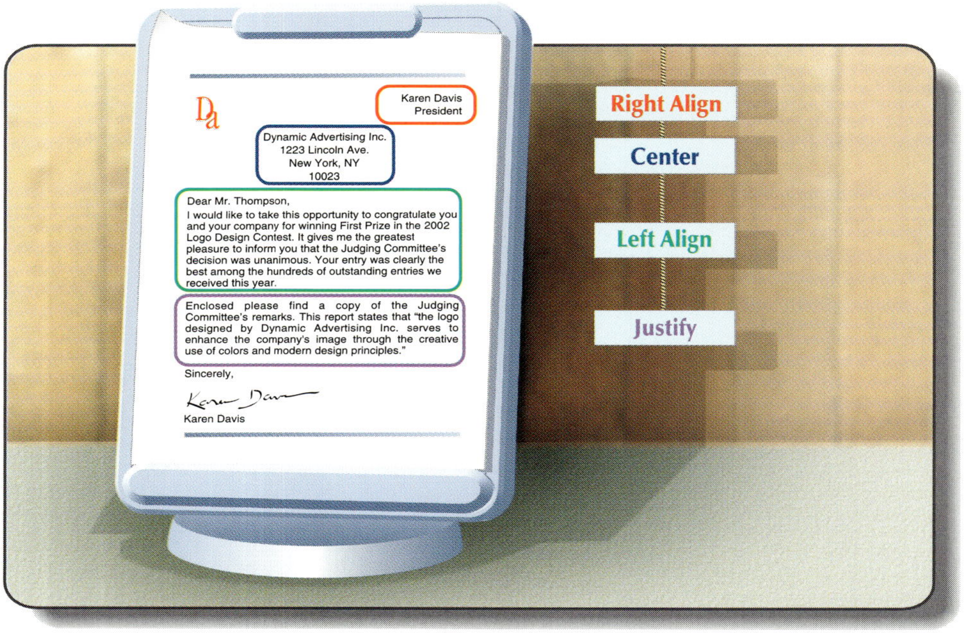

CHANGE ALIGNMENT OF TEXT

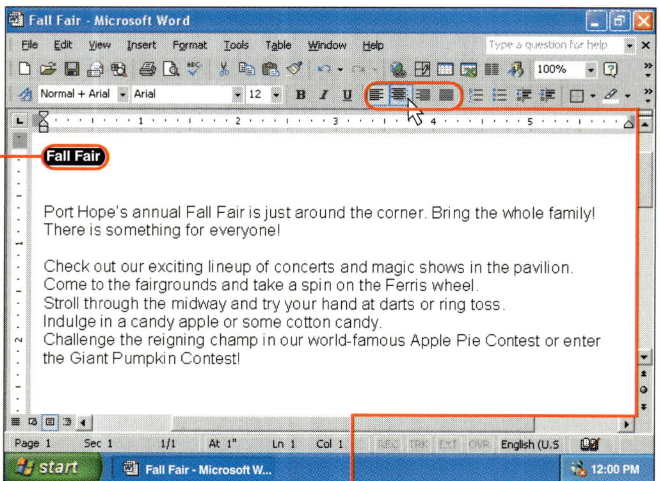

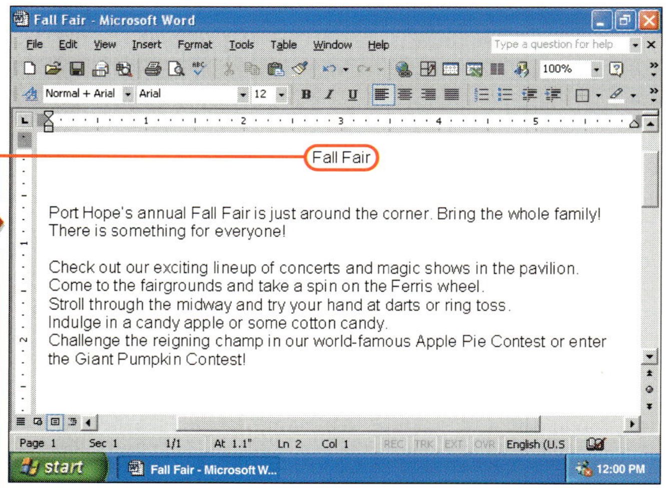

USING TOOLBAR BUTTONS

1 Select the text you want to align differently. To select text, see page 10.

2 Click one of the following buttons.

- Left align
- Center
- Right align
- Justify

Note: If the button you want is not displayed, click on the Formatting toolbar to display the button.

■ The text displays the new alignment.

■ To deselect text, click outside the selected area.

Can I use different alignments within a single line of text?

You can use the Click and Type feature to vary the alignment within a line of text. For example, you can left align your name and right align the date on the same line.

I cannot use the Click and Type feature to align text. What is wrong?

The Click and Type feature is only available in the Web Layout and Print Layout views. To change the view of a document, see page 40.

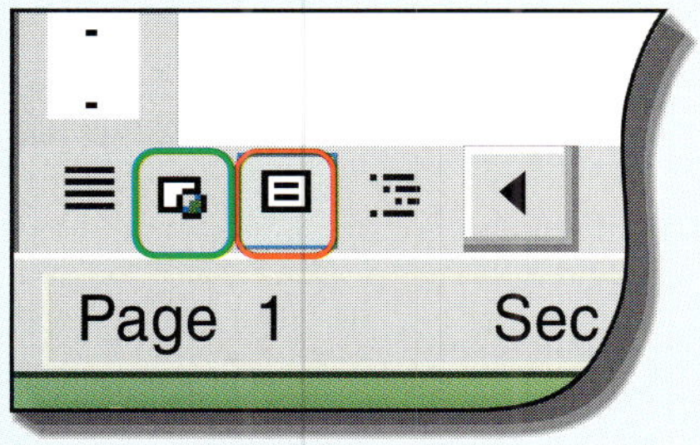

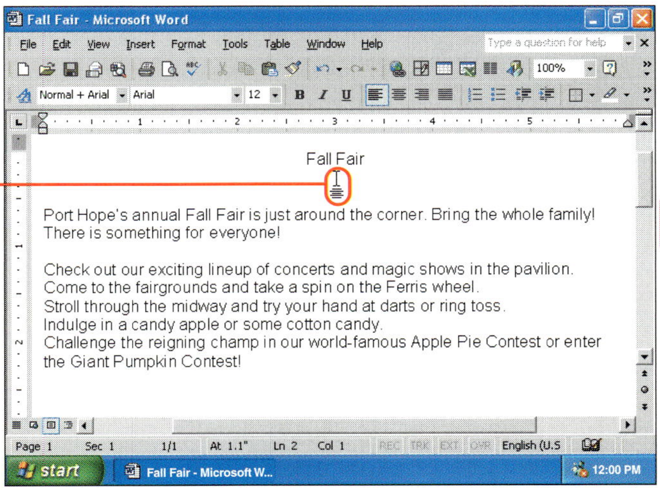

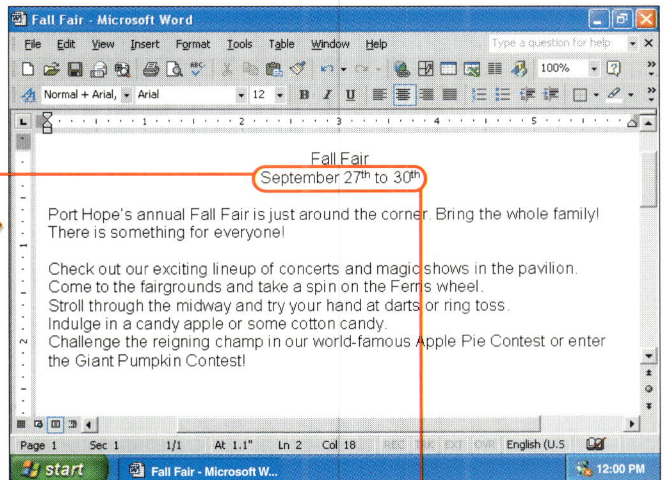

USING CLICK AND TYPE

1 Position the mouse I where you want text to appear. The appearance of the mouse I indicates how Word will align the text.

- Left align
- Center
- Right align

Note: If the appearance of the mouse I does not change, click where you want to add text.

2 Double-click the location to position the insertion point.

3 Type the text you want to add.

CHANGE APPEARANCE OF TEXT

You can make text in your document look more attractive by using various fonts, styles, sizes, effects and colors.

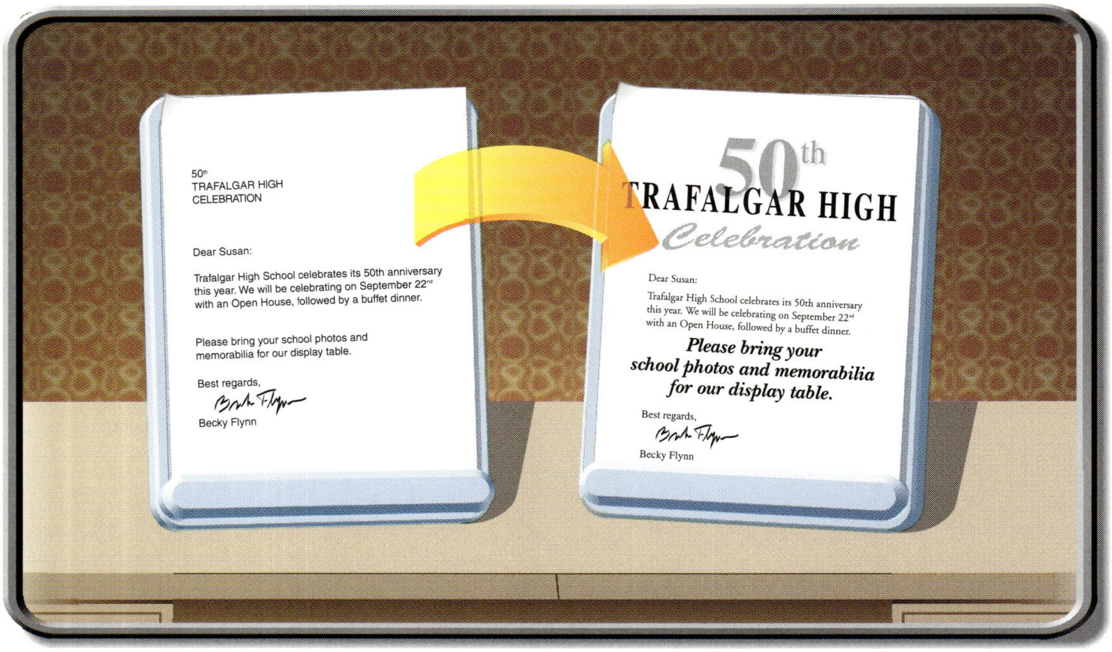

CHANGE APPEARANCE OF TEXT

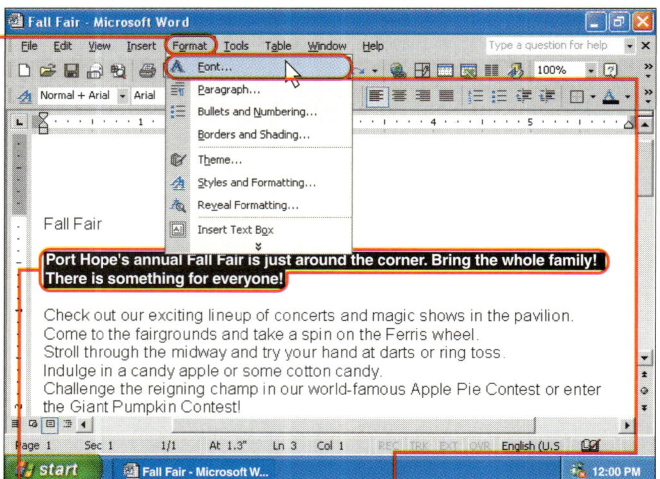

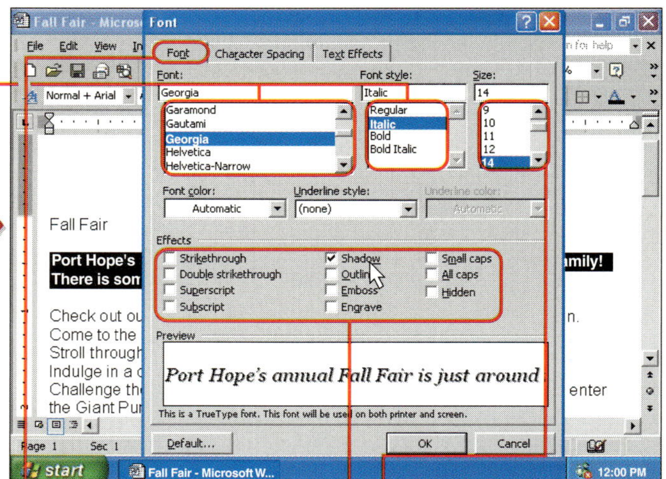

1 Select the text you want to change. To select text, see page 10.

2 Click **Format**.

3 Click **Font**.

■ The Font dialog box appears.

4 Click the **Font** tab.

5 To select a font for the text, click the font you want to use.

6 To select a style for the text, click the style you want to use.

7 To select a size for the text, click the size you want to use.

8 To select effects for the text, click each effect you want to use (☐ changes to ☑).

What determines which fonts are available on my computer?

The fonts available on your computer depend on the programs installed on your computer, the setup of your computer and your printer. You can obtain additional fonts at computer stores and on the Internet.

What effects can I add to text in my document?

Word offers many effects that you can use to change the appearance of text in your document.

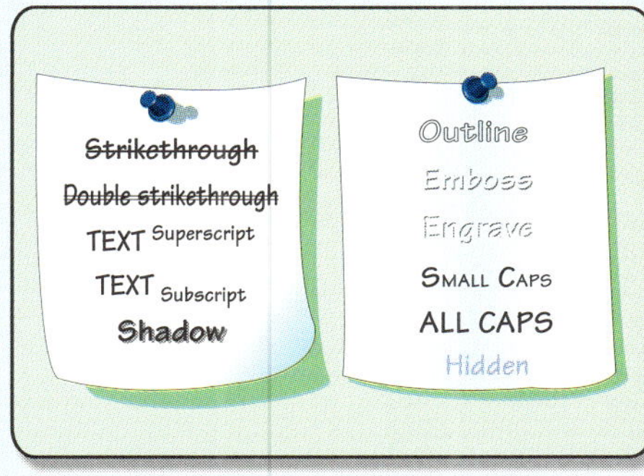

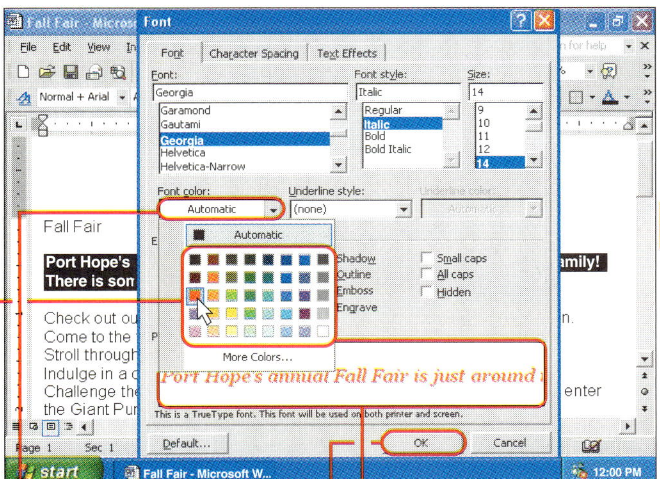

9 To select a color for the text, click this area.

10 Click the color you want to use.

■ This area displays a preview of how the text will appear in your document.

11 Click **OK** to apply your changes.

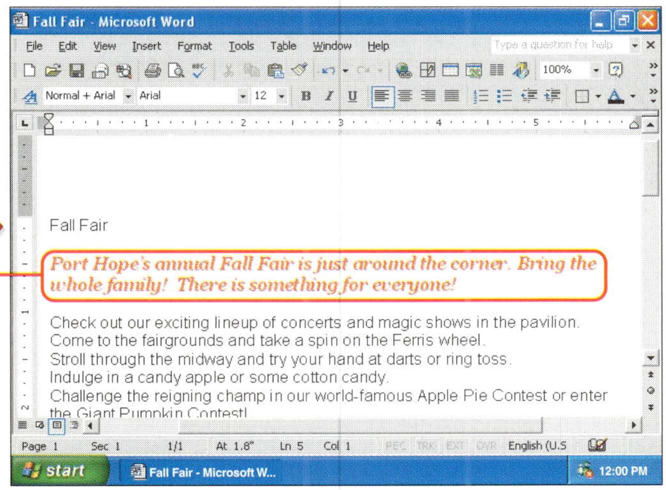

■ The text you selected displays the changes.

■ To deselect text, click outside the selected area.

CHANGE FONT FOR ALL NEW DOCUMENTS

You can change the font that Word uses for all new documents you create. This is useful when you want all your future documents to appear in a specific font.

The font that Word uses for all new documents is called the default font.

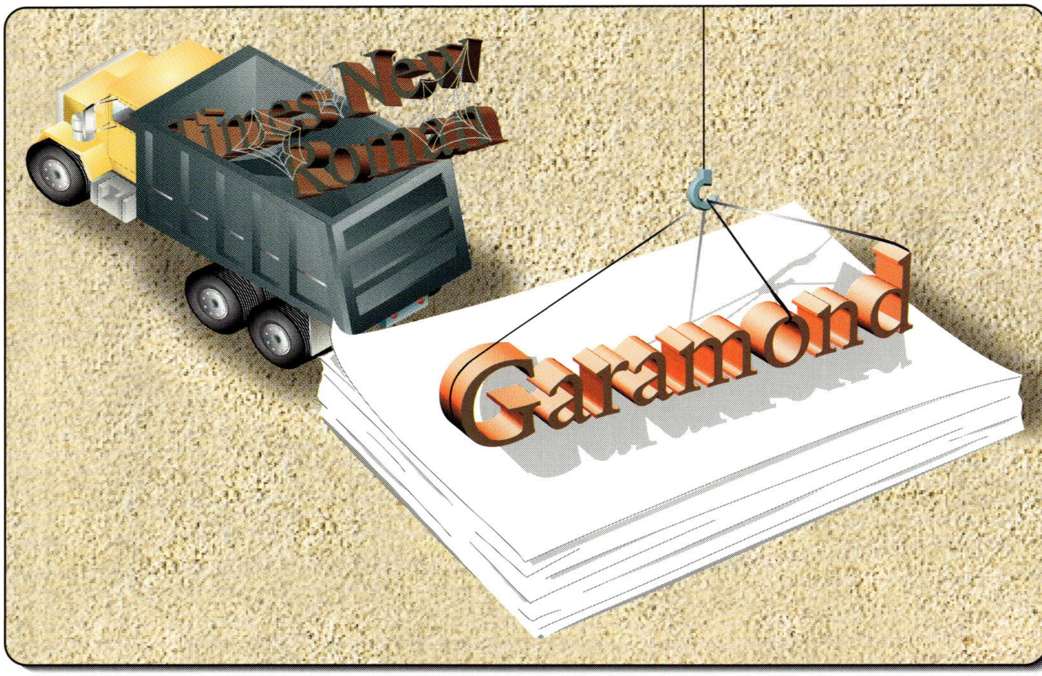

CHANGE FONT FOR ALL NEW DOCUMENTS

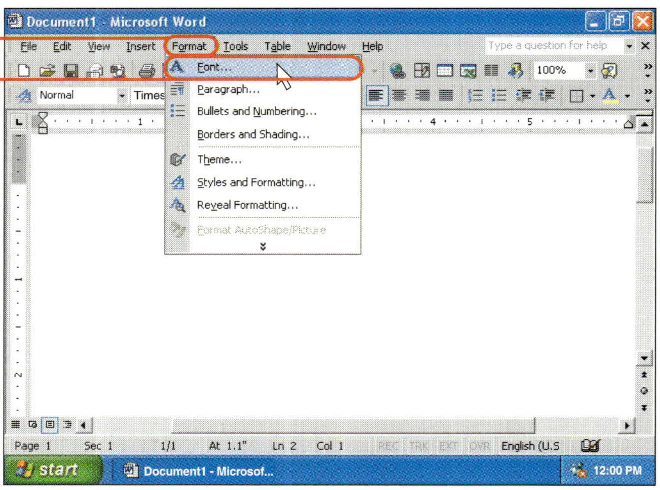

1 Click **Format**.

2 Click **Font**.

■ The Font dialog box appears.

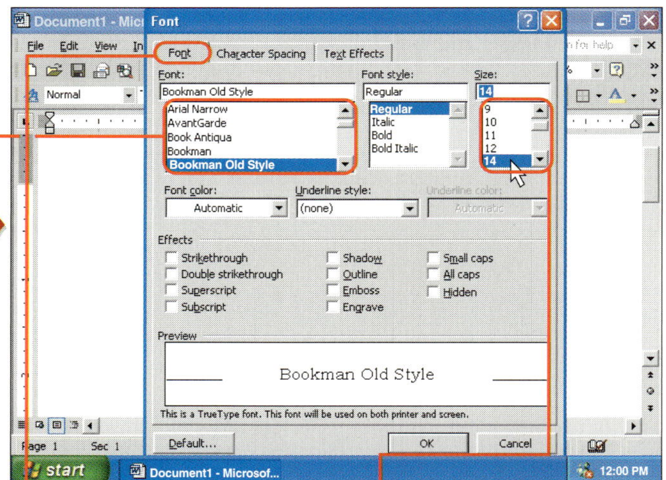

3 Click the **Font** tab.

4 To select a font for all your new documents, click the font you want to use.

5 To select a font size for all your new documents, click the font size you want to use.

Will changing the font for all new documents affect the text in the documents I have already created?

No. Word will not change the font or size of text in documents you have already created. To change the font or size of text in existing documents, see page 96.

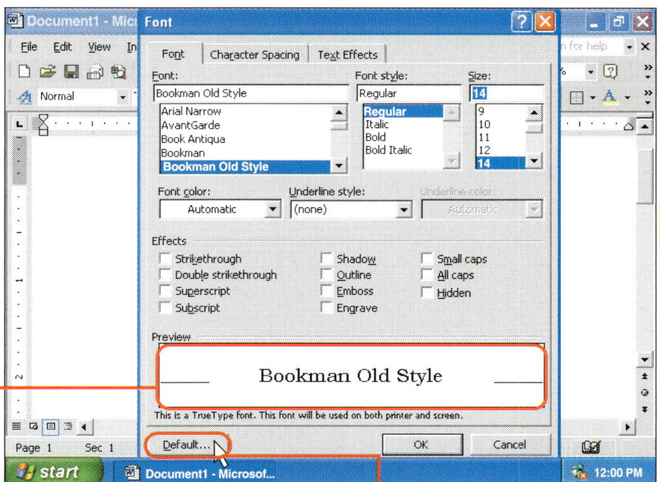

■ This area displays a preview of how the font will appear in all your new documents.

6 Click **Default** to use the font for all your new documents.

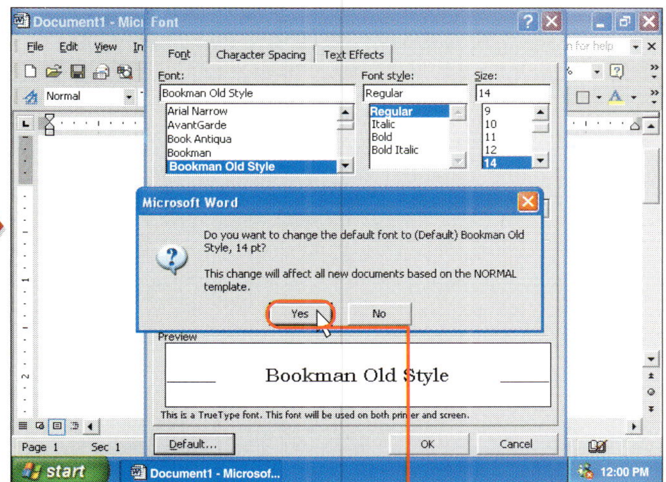

■ A dialog box appears, asking you to confirm the change.

7 Click **Yes** to confirm the change.

ANIMATE TEXT

You can animate text in your document to make the text stand out. Animation effects are ideal for emphasizing text in a document that will be viewed on a computer screen.

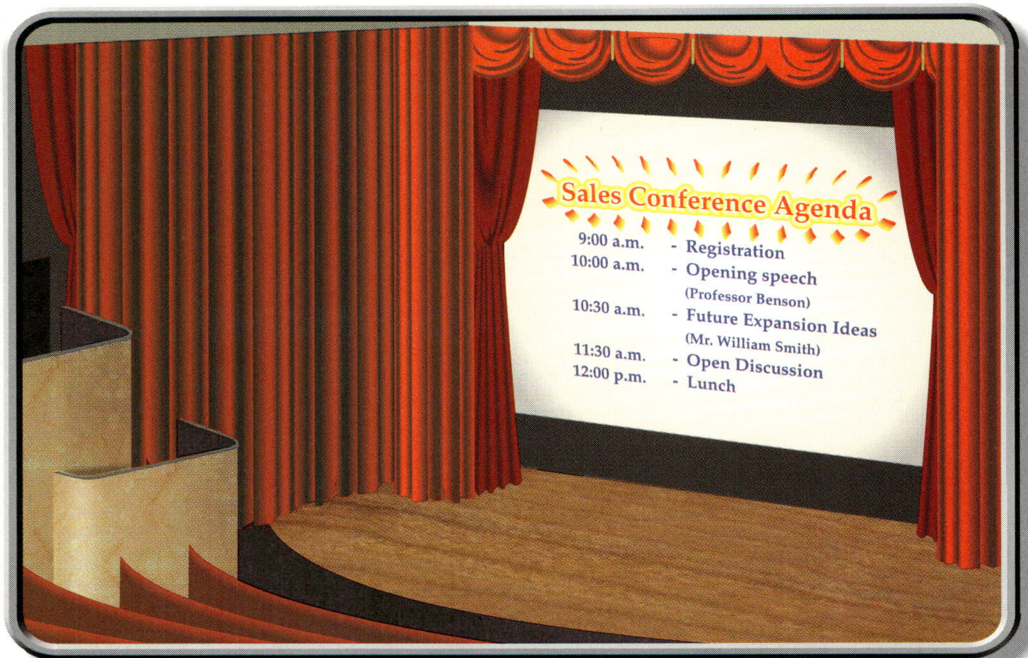

ANIMATE TEXT

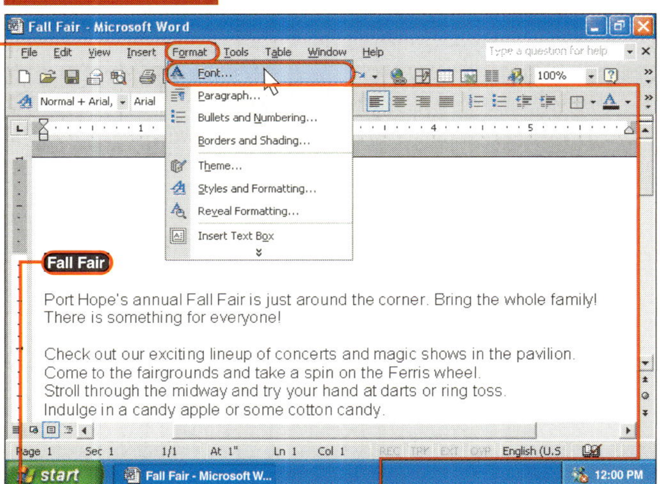

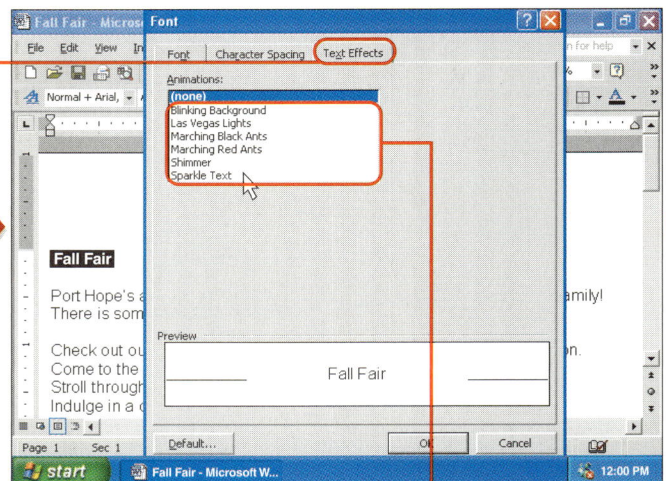

1 Select the text you want to animate. To select text, see page 10.

2 Click **Format**.

3 Click **Font**.

■ The Font dialog box appears.

4 Click the **Text Effects** tab.

5 Click the animation effect you want to use.

What types of animation effects does Word offer?

Word offers several animation effects that you can use to draw attention to text in your document.

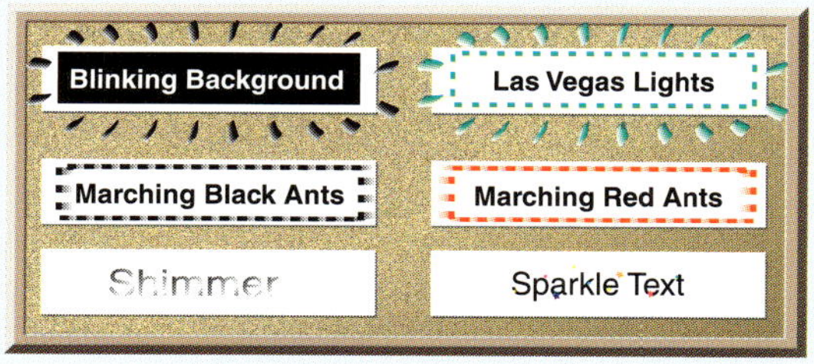

Will the animation effect appear when I print my document?

The animation effect will not appear when you print your document. For information on printing a document, see page 172.

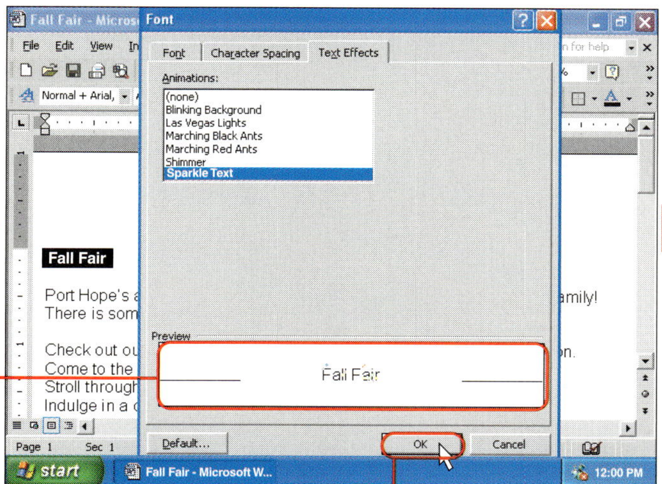

■ This area displays a preview of the animation effect.

6 Click **OK** to confirm your change.

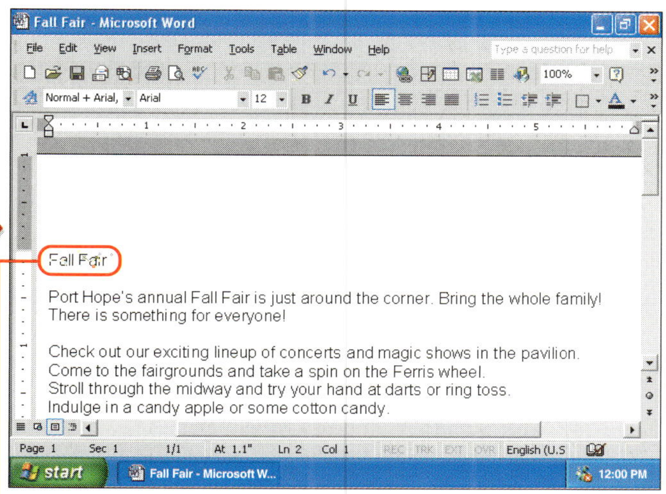

■ The text you selected displays the animation effect.

■ To deselect text, click outside the selected area.

■ To remove an animation effect, repeat steps **1** to **6**, selecting **(none)** in step **5**.

COPY FORMATTING

You can copy the formatting of text to make one area of text in your document look exactly like another.

You may want to copy the formatting of text to make all the headings or important words in your document look the same. This will give the text in your document a consistent appearance.

COPY FORMATTING

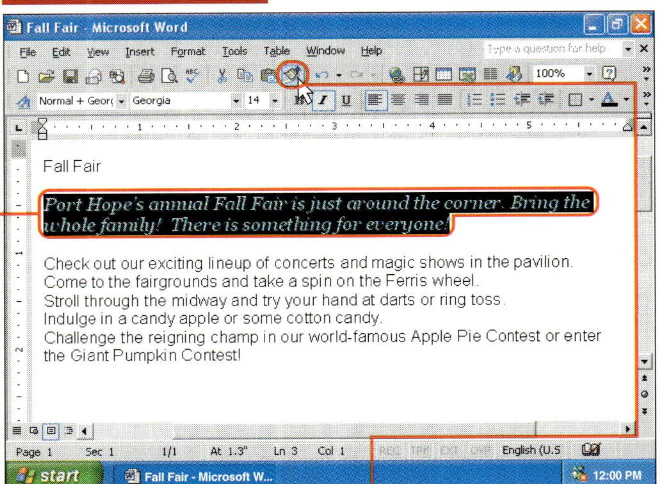

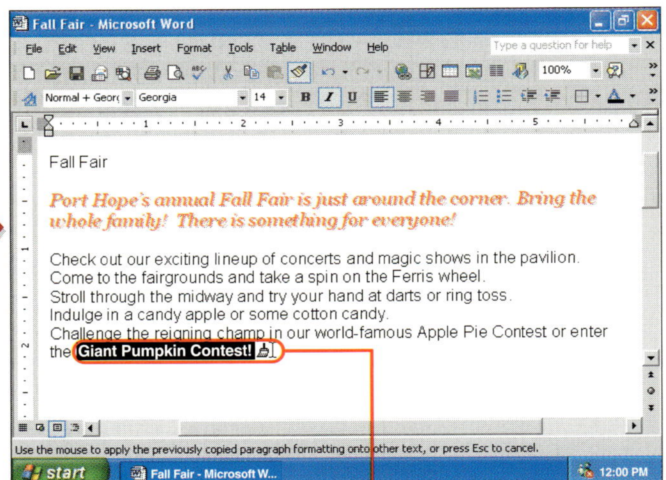

1 Select the text that displays the formatting you want to copy. To select text, see page 10.

2 Click to copy the formatting of the text.

Note: If is not displayed, click on the Standard toolbar to display the button.

■ The mouse changes to when over your document.

3 Select the text you want to display the formatting.

Will Word copy all the formatting of the original text?

If you copy the formatting of text that contains more than one type of the same formatting, such as multiple fonts, Word will copy only the formatting that appears first. For example, if you select text that contains the Arial font followed by the Monotype Corsiva font, Word will copy only the Arial font.

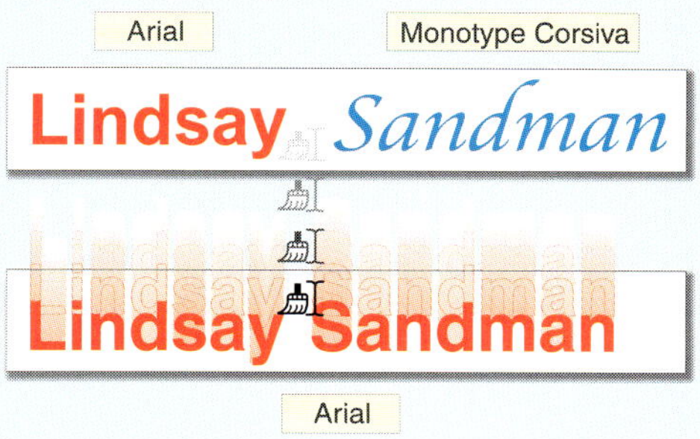

Is there another way that I can copy the formatting of text?

Yes. You can use the Styles and Formatting task pane to copy the formatting of text in your document. This task pane lists all the formatting you have applied to text in your document.

To use the Styles and Formatting task pane, see page 110.

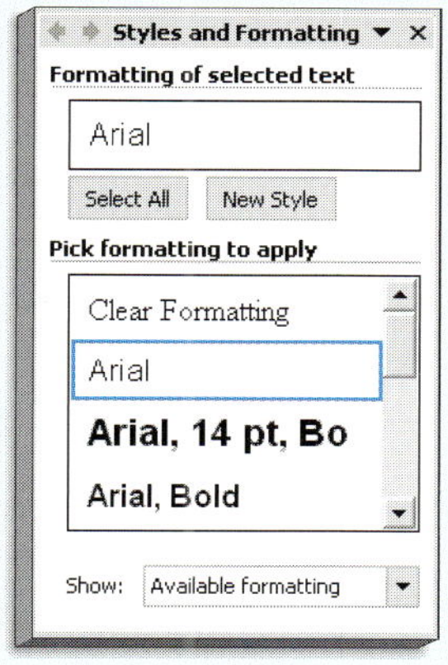

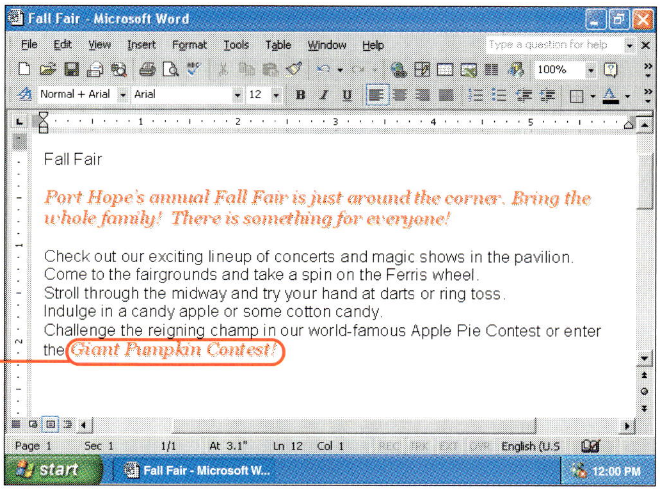

■ The text you selected displays the formatting.

■ To deselect text, click outside the selected area.

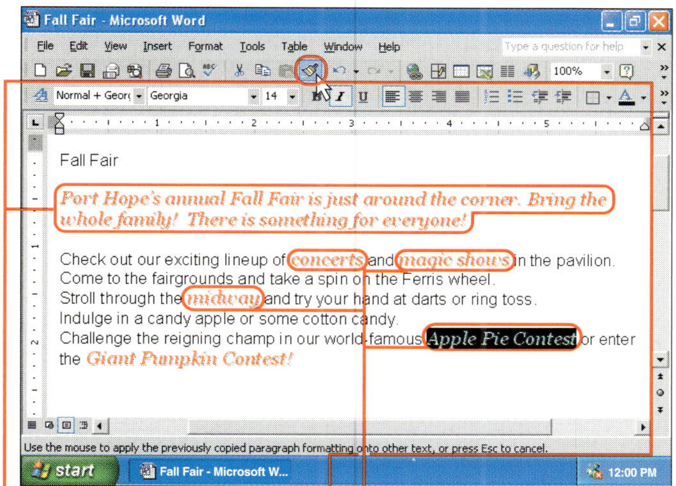

COPY FORMATTING TO SEVERAL AREAS

1 Select the text that displays the formatting you want to copy.

2 Double-click [format painter] to copy the formatting of the text.

3 Select each area of text you want to display the formatting.

4 When you finish selecting all the text you want to display the formatting, click [format painter] or press the Esc key.

CHANGE LINE SPACING

You can change the amount of space between the lines of text in your document.

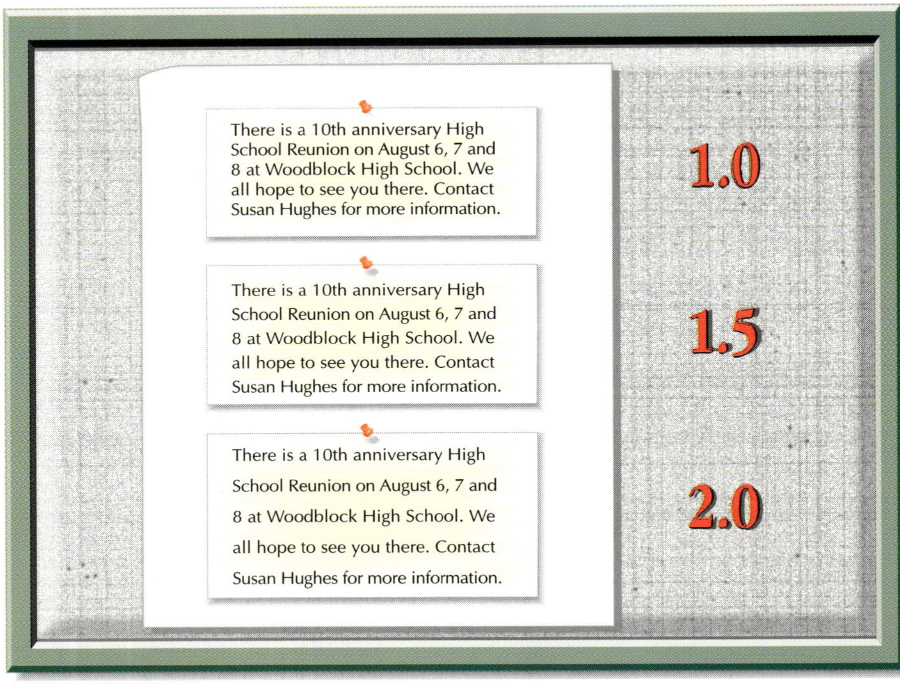

Changing the line spacing can make a document easier to review and edit.

CHANGE LINE SPACING

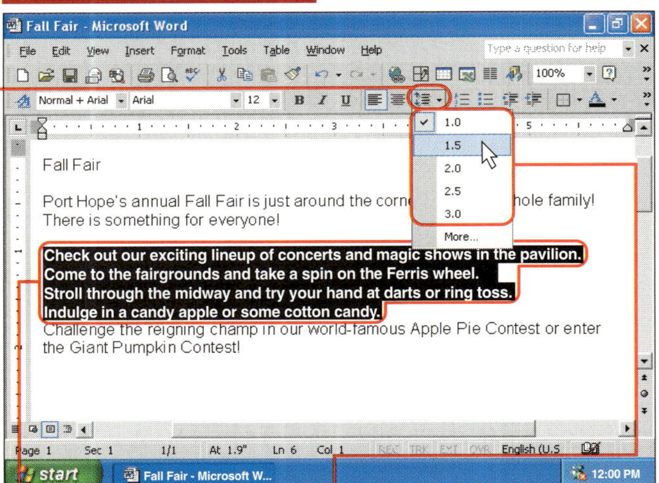

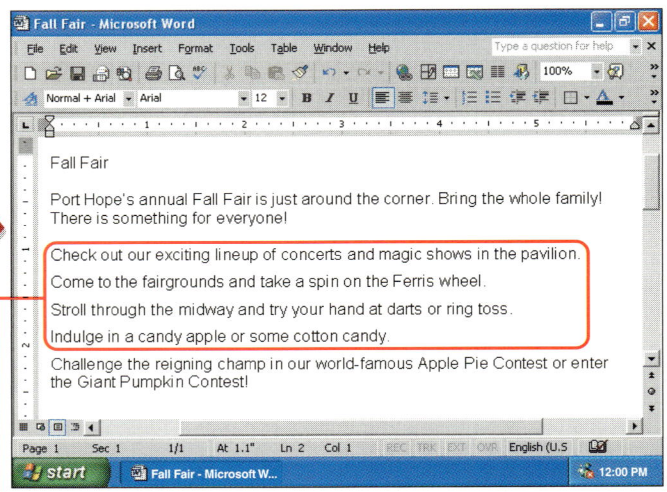

1 Select the text you want to use a different line spacing. To select text, see page 10.

2 Click ▾ in this area to display the available line spacing options.

Note: If ☰▾ is not displayed, click » on the Formatting toolbar to display the button.

3 Click the line spacing option you want to use.

■ The text appears in the line spacing you selected.

■ To deselect text, click outside the selected area.

REMOVE FORMATTING FROM TEXT

You can remove all the formatting you have applied to text in your document.

REMOVE FORMATTING FROM TEXT

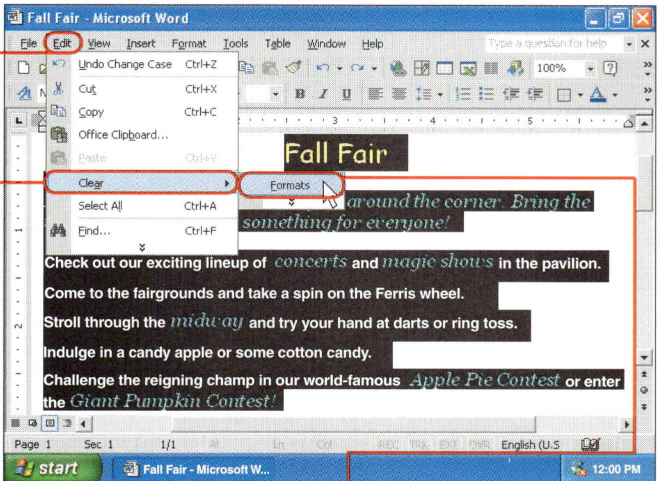

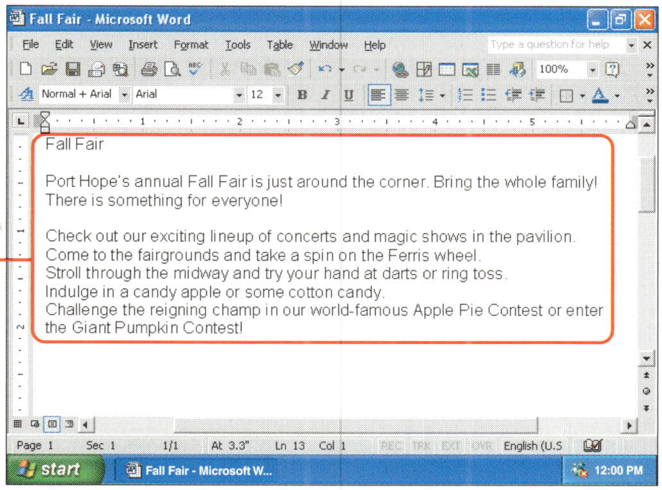

1 Select the text that displays the formatting you want to remove. To select text, see page 10.

2 Click **Edit**.

3 Click **Clear**.

Note: If Clear does not appear on the menu, position the mouse over the bottom of the menu to display all the menu options.

4 Click **Formats**.

■ The formatting disappears from the text.

■ To deselect text, click outside the selected area.

CHECKING FORMATTING
The New Orleans Blues
ACT 1
Scene i)
Tim and Jeff are sitting on the front steps of their house on a side street in New Orleans. Tim is trying to convince his son to let go of his dream of becoming a famous jazz saxophonist. Upset with his father for meddling in his life, Jeff storms off down the street.
Scene ii)
Tim goes inside the house to join Kathleen in the kitchen. As Kathleen prepares dinner, they discuss their son's future. Jacqueline, their guest, arrives and they all reminisce about their youth.

CHAPTER 6

Work With Formatting and Styles

Do you want to learn how to quickly apply formatting to text in a document? This chapter shows you how.

Check Formatting 108

Apply Formatting 110

Create a Style 114

Change a Style 116

Review Formatting 118

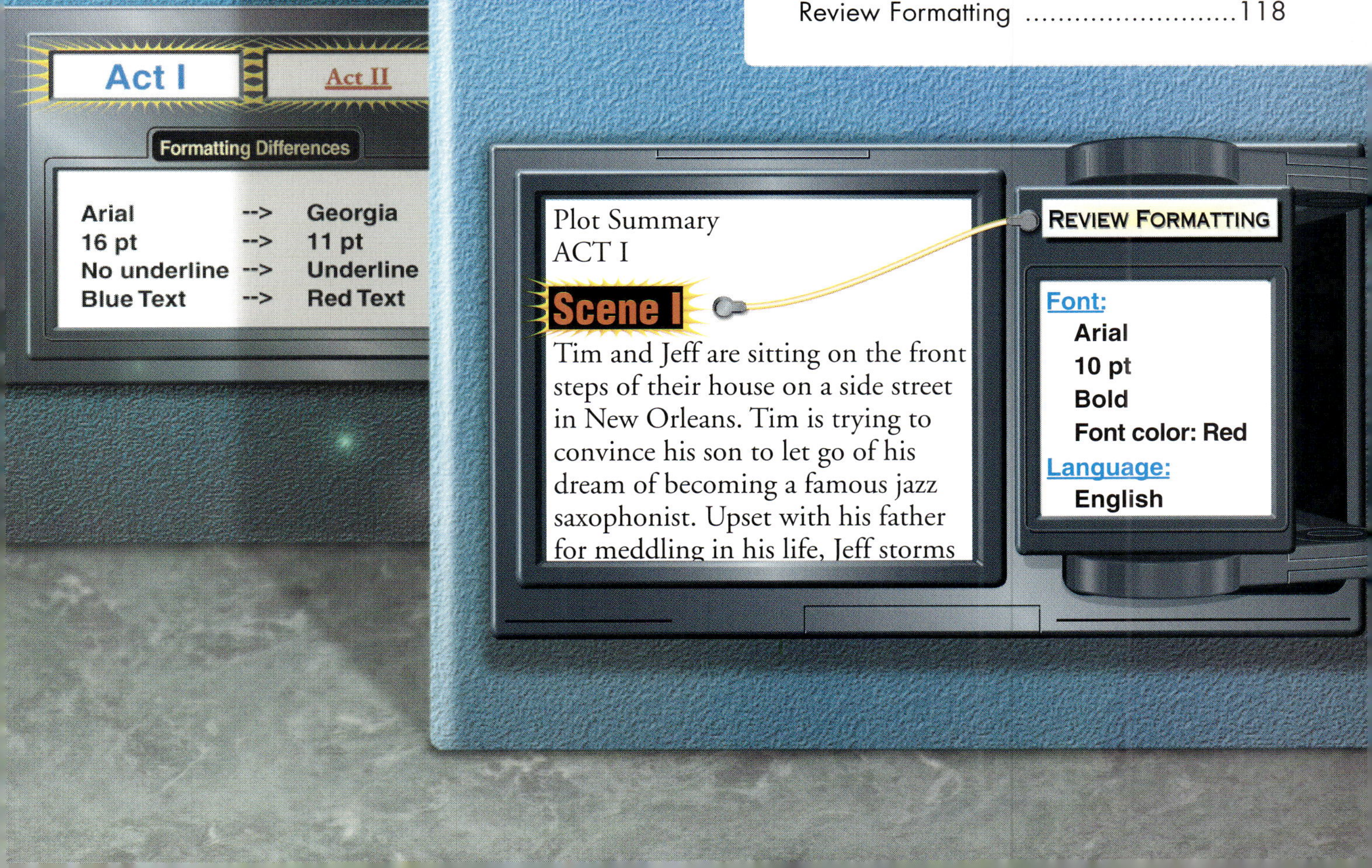

CHECK FORMATTING

You can have Word underline formatting inconsistencies in your document. You can then correct the inconsistencies to give the document a professional appearance.

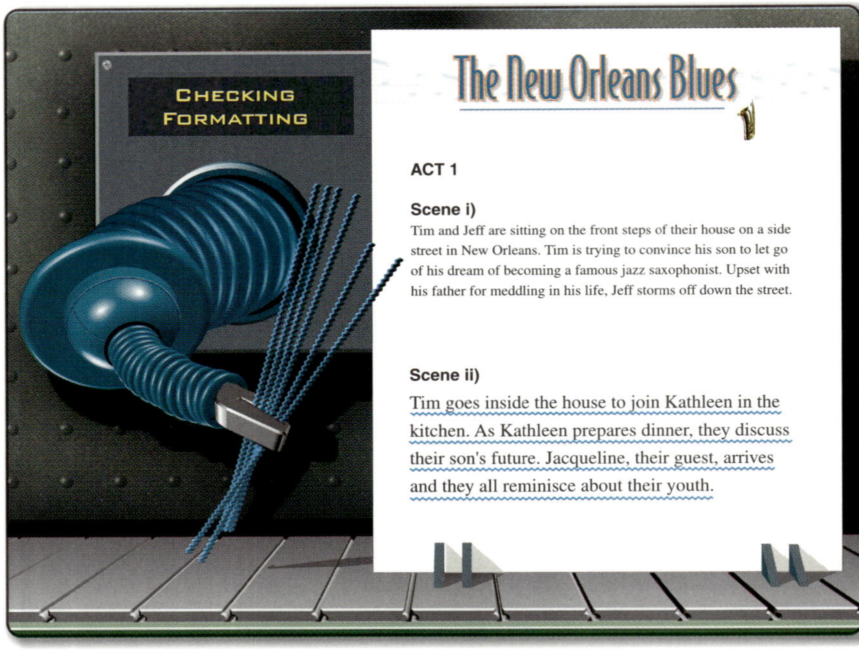

Word underlines formatting inconsistencies in blue.

CHECK FORMATTING

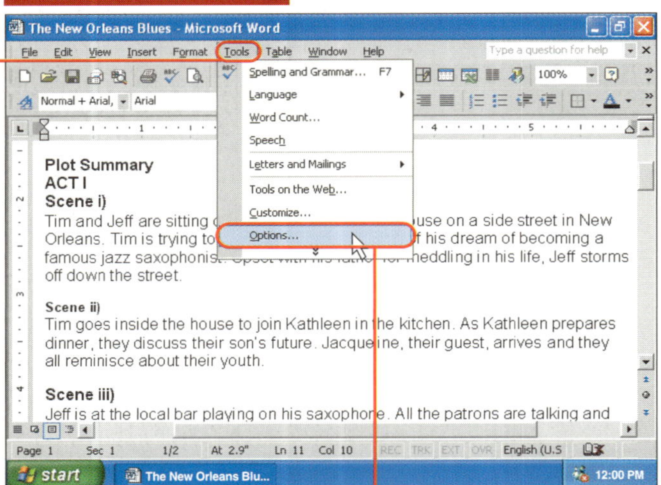

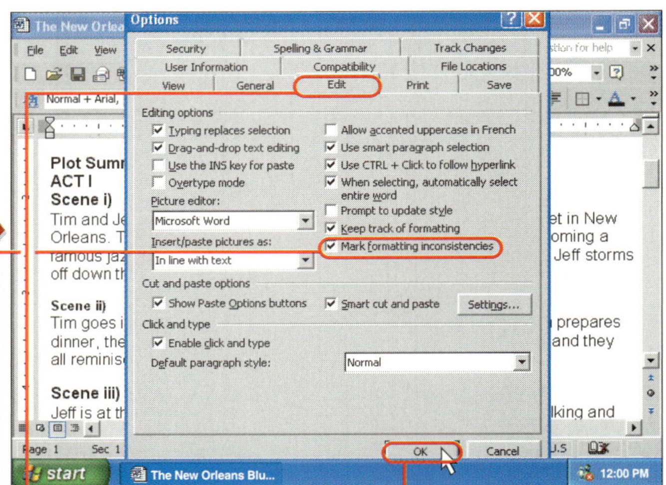

TURN ON FORMAT CHECKING

1 Click **Tools**.

2 Click **Options**.

■ The Options dialog box appears.

3 Click the **Edit** tab.

4 Click **Mark formatting inconsistencies** (☐ changes to ☑).

5 Click **OK** to confirm your change.

■ To turn off format checking, repeat steps **1** to **5** (☑ changes to ☐ in step **4**).

Why didn't Word underline all the formatting inconsistencies in my document?

Word only underlines inconsistent formatting that appears accidental, such as a heading that is slightly smaller than other headings in your document.

Is there another way I can check for inconsistent formatting in my document?

You can use the Reveal Formatting task pane to review details about the formatting applied to text in your document and compare the formatting of two areas of text. For more information on the Reveal Formatting task pane, see page 118.

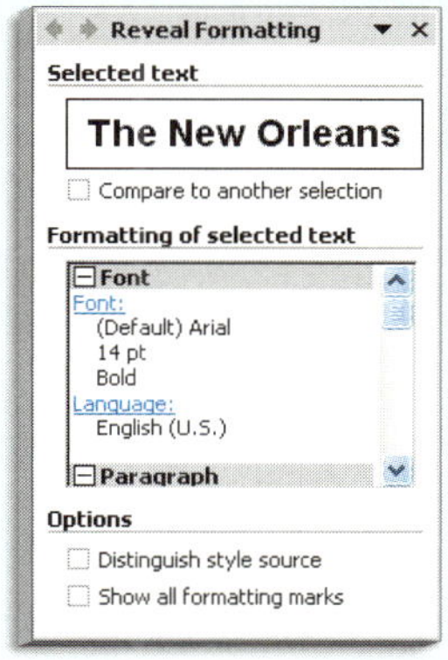

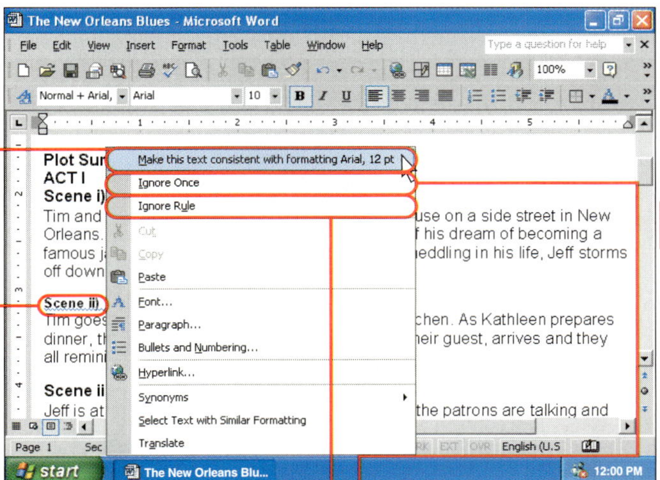

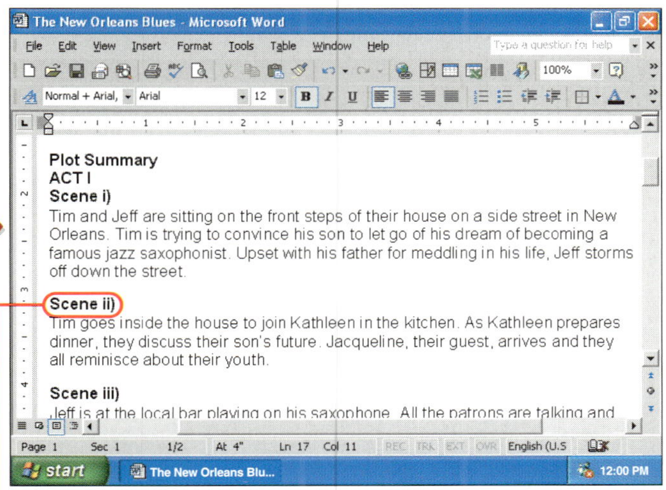

CHECK FORMATTING

1 Right-click a formatting inconsistency underlined in blue. A menu appears.

2 Click the option at the top of the menu to correct the inconsistency.

Note: The name of the option depends on the formatting inconsistency you selected.

- To skip the inconsistency, click **Ignore Once**.
- To skip all occurrences of the inconsistency in your document, click **Ignore Rule**.

- Word corrects or ignores the formatting inconsistency.
- The blue underline disappears from the text.

- You can repeat steps 1 and 2 for each formatting inconsistency in your document.

APPLY FORMATTING

Word keeps track of the formatting you have applied to text in your document. You can apply the formatting to another area of text.

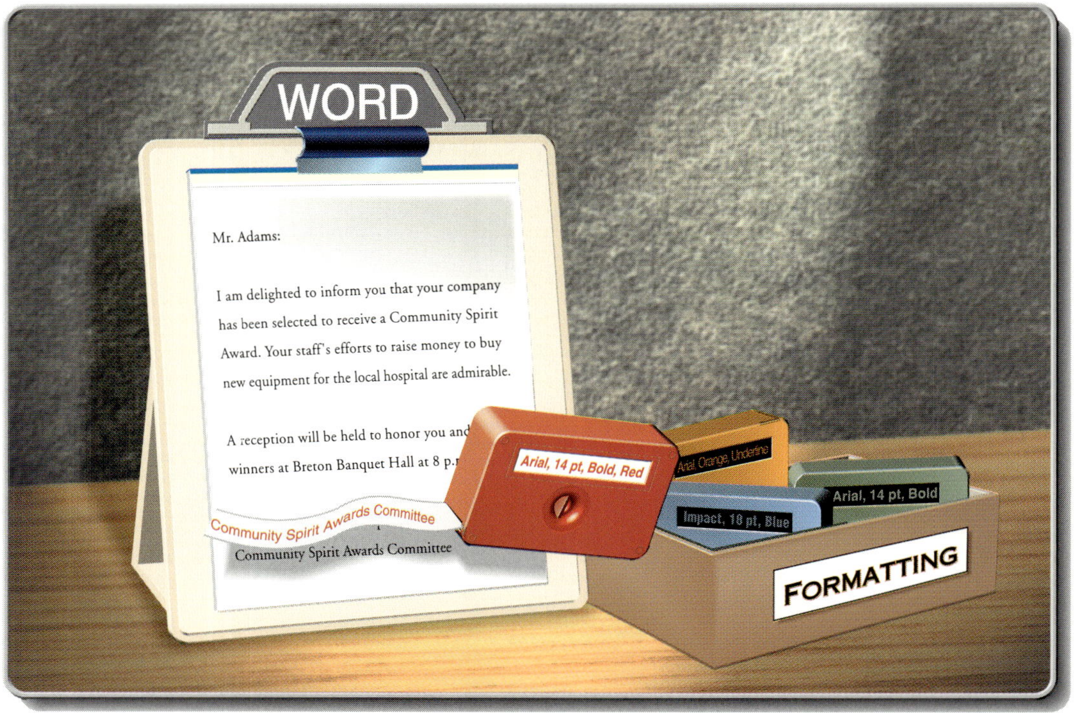

APPLY FORMATTING TO ONE AREA OF TEXT

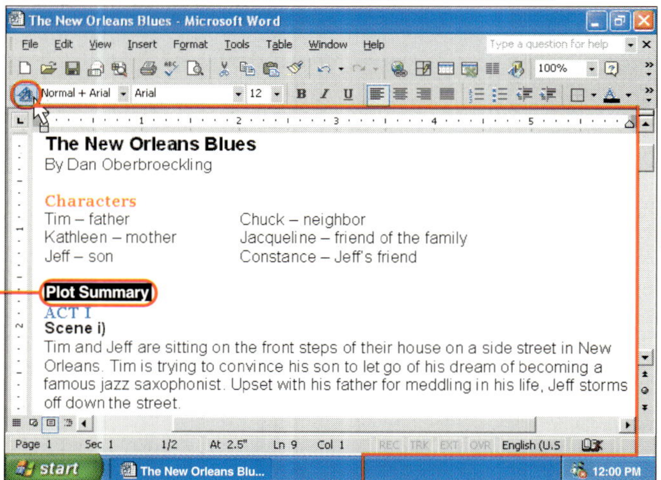

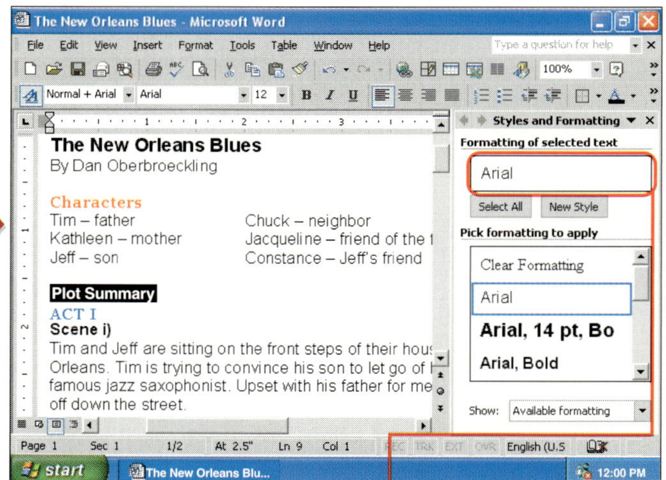

1 Select the text you want to apply formatting to. To select text, see page 10.

2 Click [icon] to display the Styles and Formatting task pane.

Note: If [icon] is not displayed, click [icon] on the Formatting toolbar to display the button.

■ The Styles and Formatting task pane appears.

■ This area describes the current formatting of the text you selected.

Is there another way to apply formatting to text in my document?

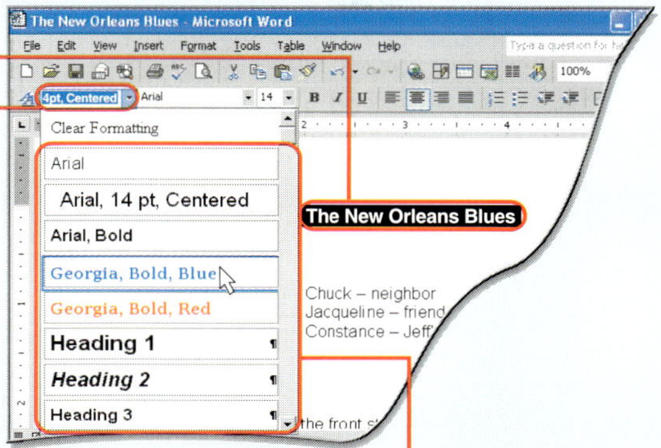

1 Select the text you want to apply formatting to. To select text, see page 10.

2 Click ▾ in this area to display a list of available formatting.

Note: If the Style area is not displayed, click » on the Formatting toolbar to display the area.

3 Click the formatting you want to use.

Can I remove formatting I have applied to text?

You can remove formatting you have applied to text in your document. Perform steps **1** to **3** below, selecting **Clear Formatting** in step **3**.

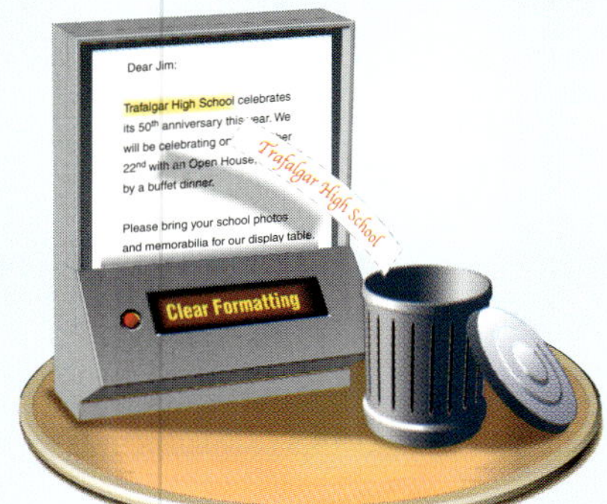

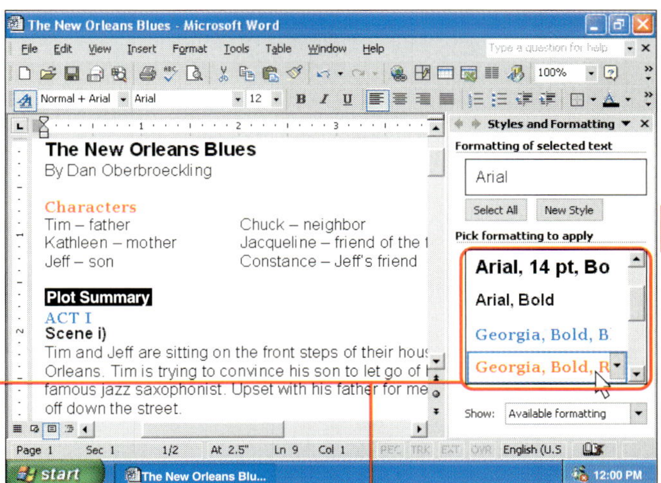

■ This area displays formatting you have used in your document.

Note: The area also displays styles included with Word and styles you have created. For information on styles, see pages 114 to 117.

3 Click the formatting you want to apply to the text.

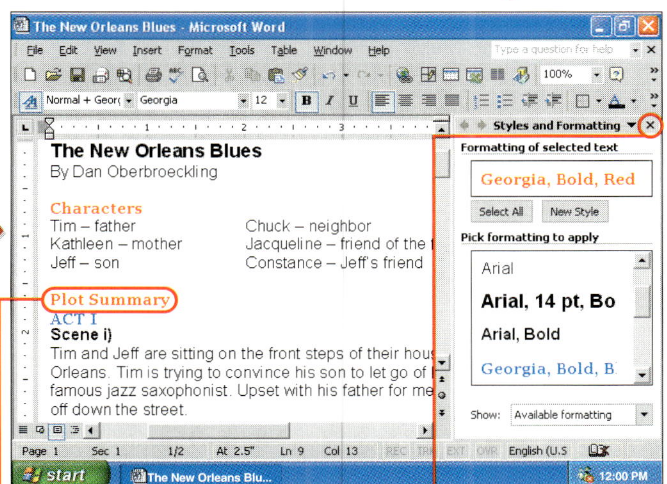

■ The text you selected displays the new formatting.

■ To deselect text, click outside the selected area.

■ To hide the Styles and Formatting task pane, click ✕.

CONTINUED

APPLY FORMATTING

You can instantly change the appearance of all the text in a document that displays the same formatting. This saves you time and keeps the appearance of text in your document consistent.

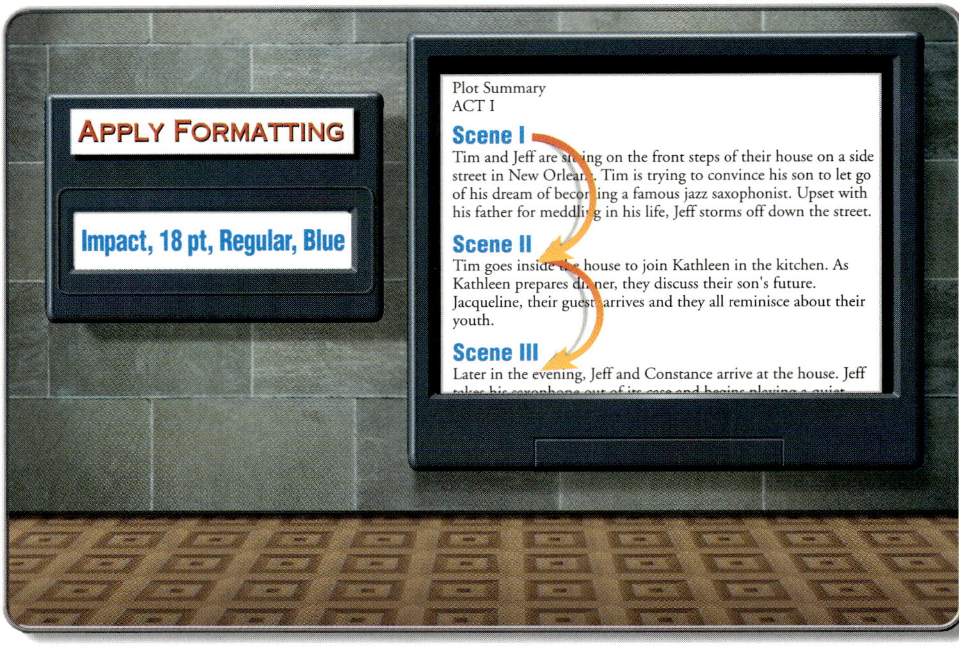

APPLY FORMATTING TO MANY AREAS OF TEXT

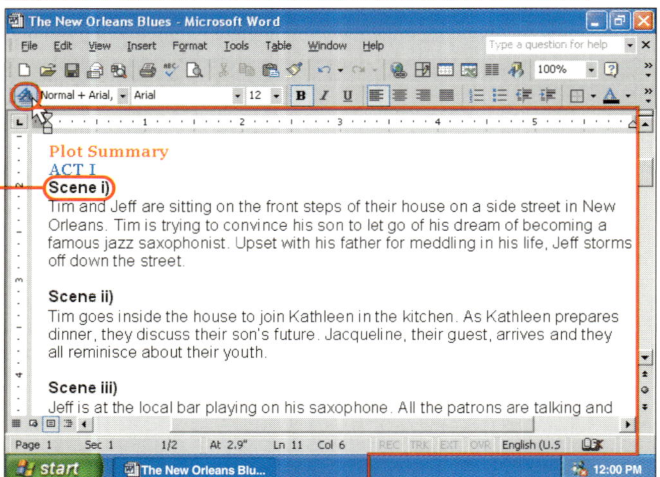

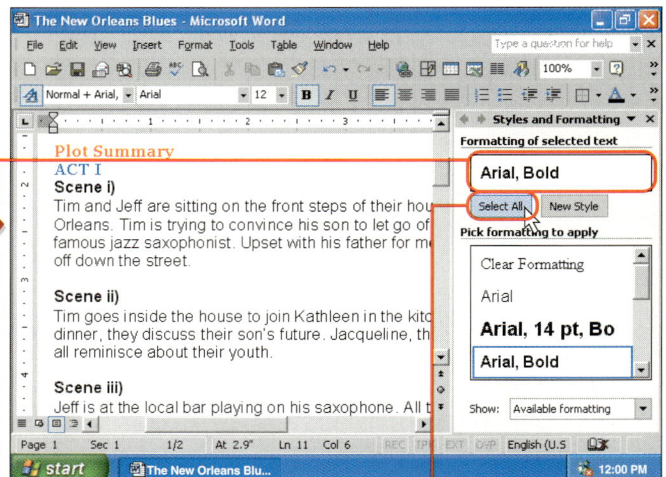

1 Click an area of text that displays the formatting you want to change throughout your document.

2 Click [icon] to display the Styles and Formatting task pane.

Note: If [icon] is not displayed, click [»] on the Formatting toolbar to display the button.

■ The Styles and Formatting task pane appears.

■ This area describes the current formatting of the text you selected.

3 Click **Select All**.

The Styles and Formatting task pane does not display the formatting I want to apply. What can I do?

Perform steps 1 to 3 below to select the areas of text you want to format. You can then format the text as you would format any text in a document. For example, you can change the font, size, color or alignment of the text. To format text, see pages 88 to 97.

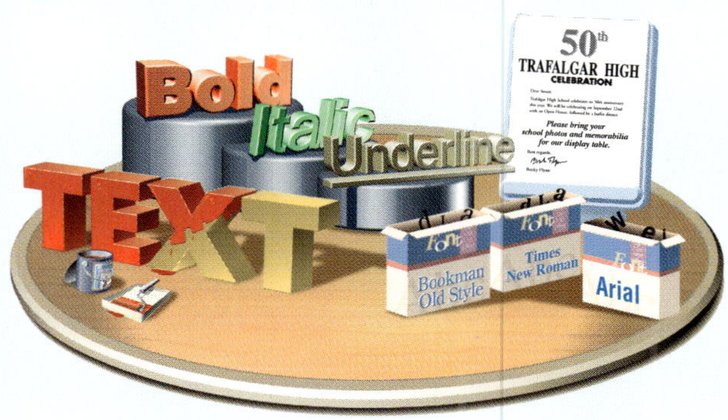

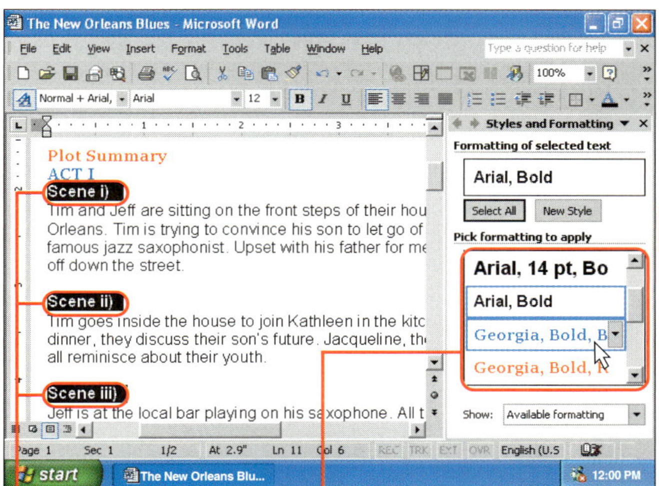

■ Word selects all the text in your document that displays the same formatting.

■ This area displays formatting you have used in your document.

Note: The area also displays styles included with Word and styles you have created. For information on styles, see pages 114 to 117.

4 Click the formatting you want to apply to the selected text.

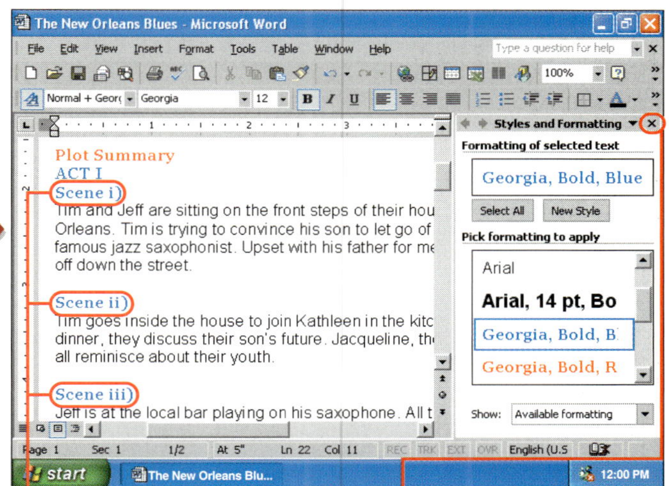

■ The selected text displays the new formatting.

■ To deselect text, click outside a selected area.

■ To hide the Styles and Formatting task pane, click ☒.

CREATE A STYLE

You can create a style to store formatting you like. You can then use the style to quickly apply formatting to text in your documents.

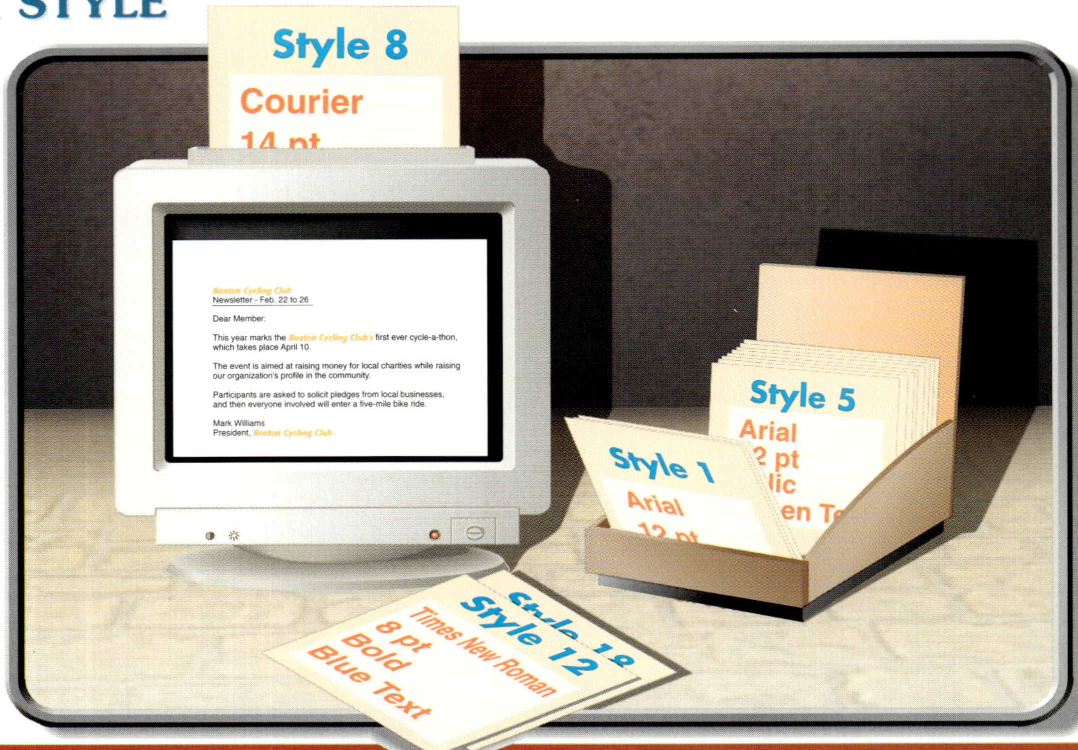

CREATE A STYLE

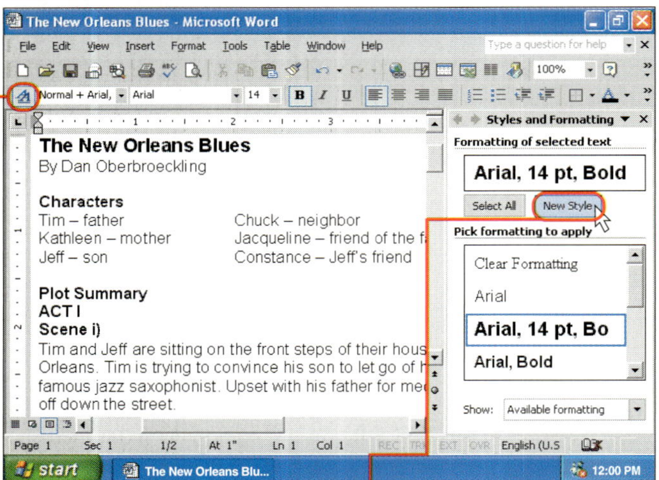

1 Click to display the Styles and Formatting task pane.

Note: If is not displayed, click on the Formatting toolbar to display the button.

2 Click **New Style** to create a new style.

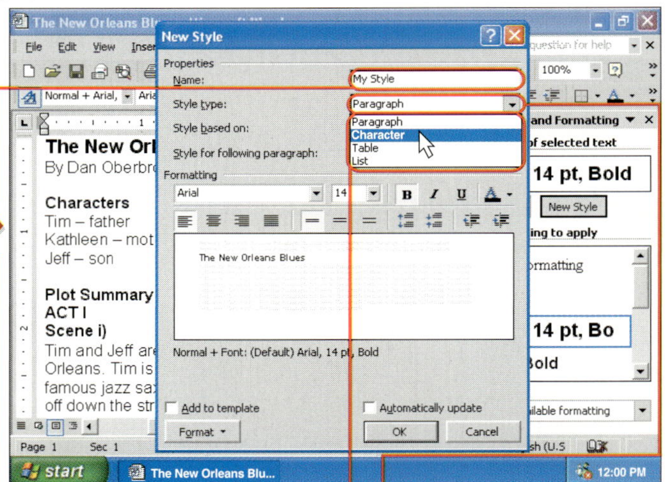

■ The New Style dialog box appears.

3 Type a name for the new style.

4 Click this area to select the type of style you want to create.

5 Click the type of style you want to create.

Note: For information on the types of styles, see the top of page 115.

TEACH YOURSELF

What types of styles can I create?

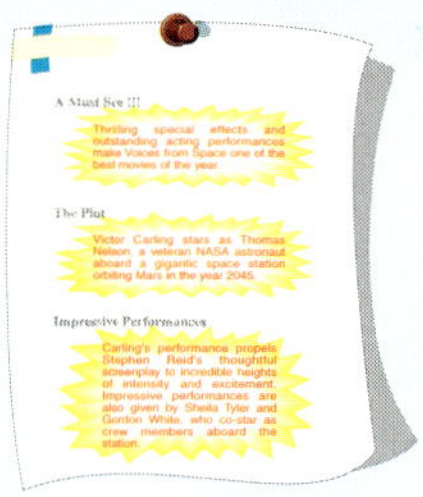

Paragraph (¶)

A paragraph style includes formatting that changes the appearance of individual characters and entire paragraphs, such as text alignment and line spacing.

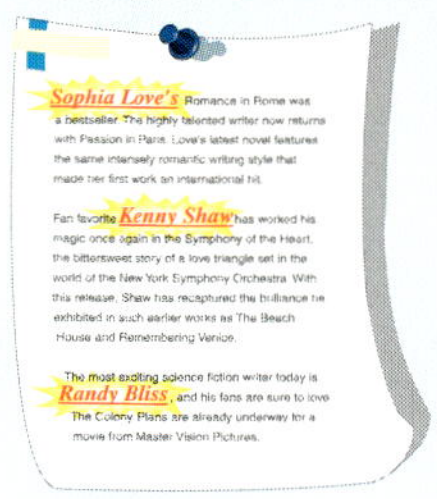

Character (a)

A character style includes formatting that changes the appearance of individual characters, such as font and text color.

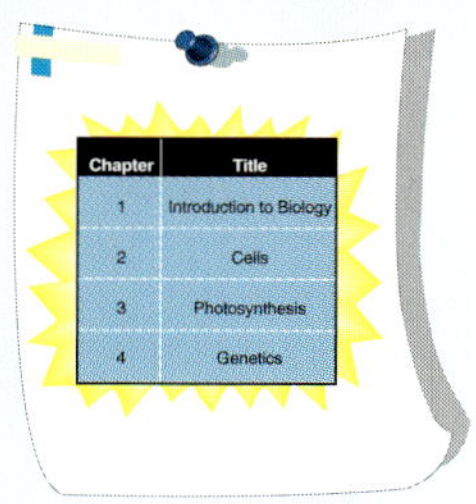

Table (⊞)

A table style includes formatting that changes the appearance of tables, such as borders and shading. For information on tables, see pages 192 to 209.

List (☰)

A list style includes formatting that changes the appearance of numbers or bullets in a list, such as number or bullet styles and indenting. For information on lists, see pages 124 to 127.

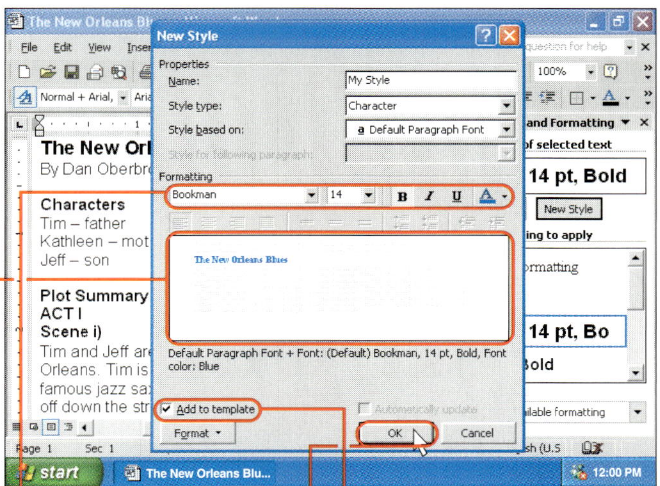

6 Select the formatting options you want to use for the style.

Note: The available formatting options depend on the type of style you selected.

■ This area displays a preview of the style.

7 If you want to use the style in new documents you create, click **Add to template** (☐ changes to ☑).

8 Click **OK** to create the style.

Note: To hide the Styles and Formatting task pane, repeat step 1.

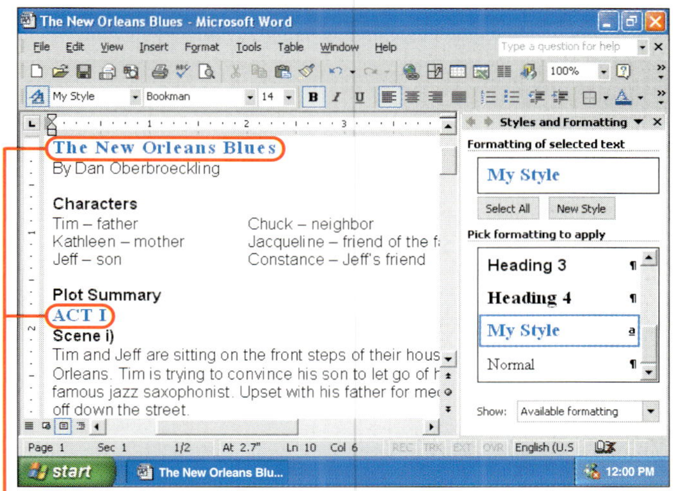

APPLY A STYLE

1 Select the text or list you want to apply a style to. To select text, see page 10.

■ To apply a style to a table, click the table.

2 Perform steps **2** and **3** starting on page 110 to apply the style.

CHANGE A STYLE

You can change a style you created. When you change a style, Word automatically changes all the text you formatted with the style.

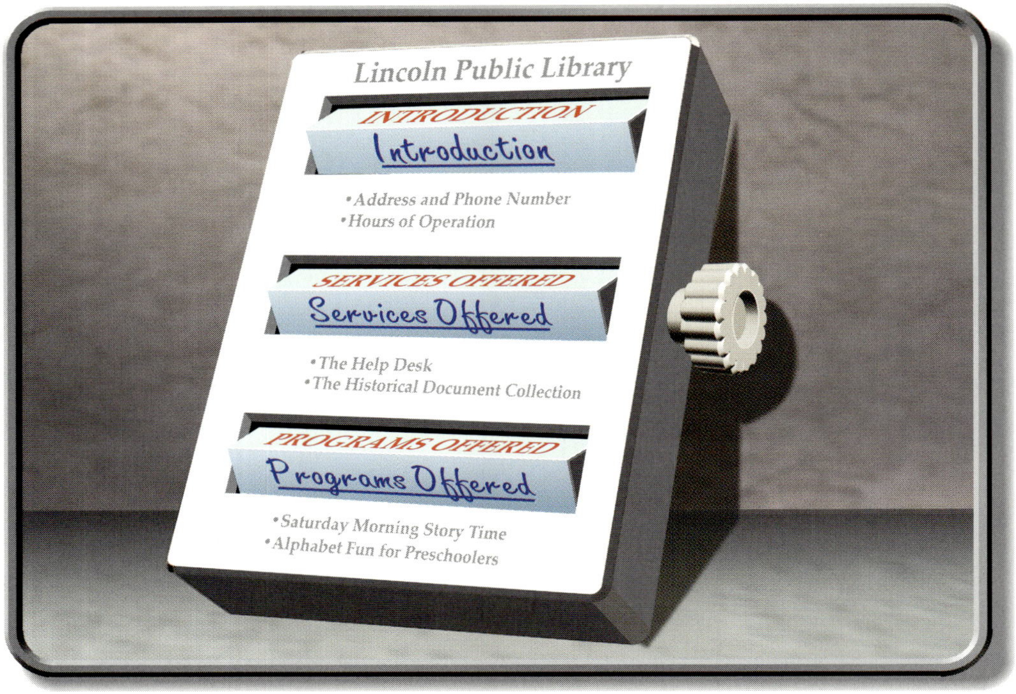

CHANGE A STYLE

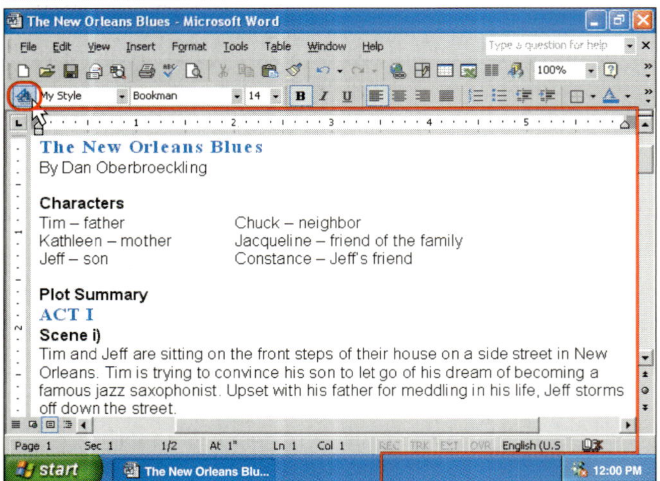

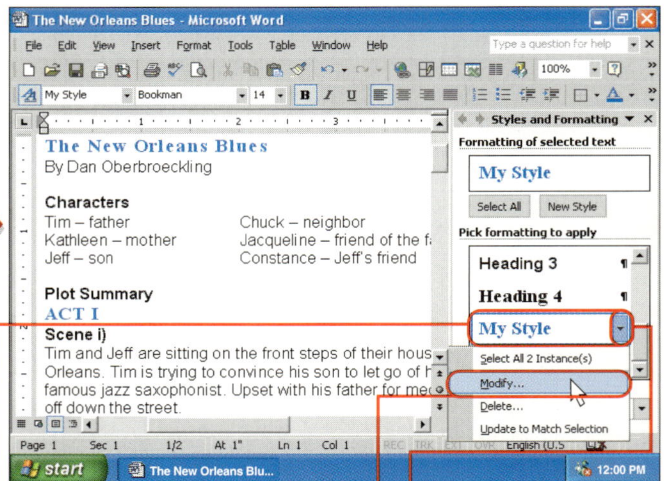

1 Open a document containing the style you want to change. To open a document, see page 28.

2 Click to display the Styles and Formatting task pane.

Note: If is not displayed, click on the Formatting toolbar to display the button.

■ The Styles and Formatting task pane appears.

3 Position the mouse over the style you want to change. An arrow ( ) appears.

4 Click the arrow to display a list of options.

5 Click **Modify**.

■ The Modify Style dialog box appears.

When would I want to change a style?

You may want to change an existing style to quickly change the appearance of a document. You can try several formats until the document appears the way you want.

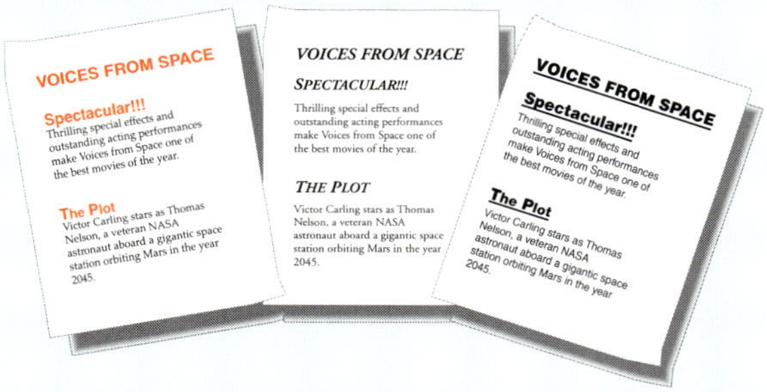

Will changing a style affect documents I have already created?

No. When you change a style, Word will not change the appearance of text, lists or tables formatted with the style in documents you have already created.

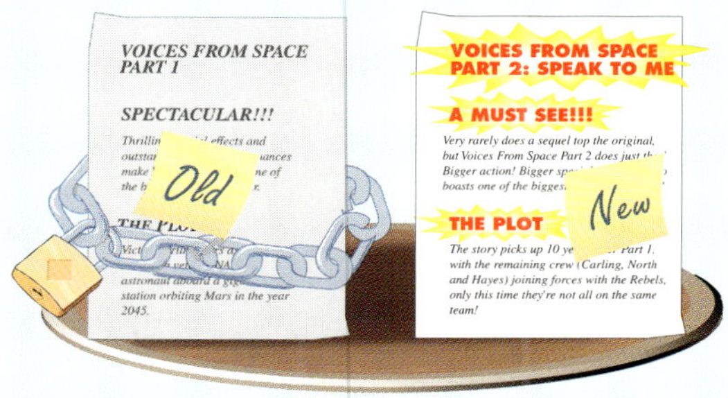

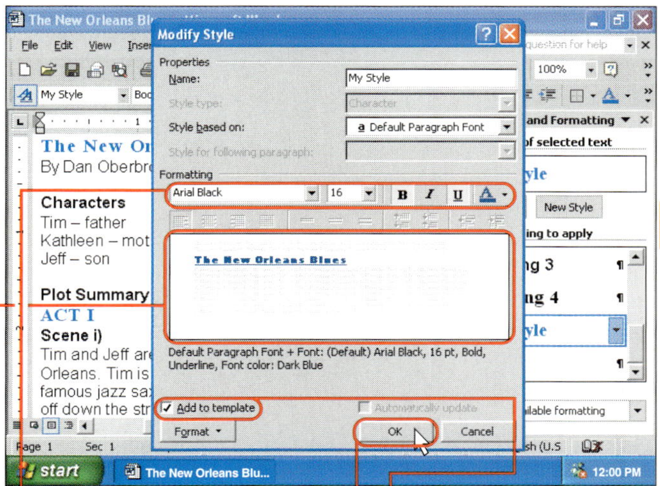

6 Select the formatting options you want to use for the style.

Note: The available formatting options depend on the type of style you are changing.

■ This area displays a preview of the style.

7 If you want to use the changed style in new documents you create, click **Add to template** (☐ changes to ☑).

8 Click **OK** to change the style.

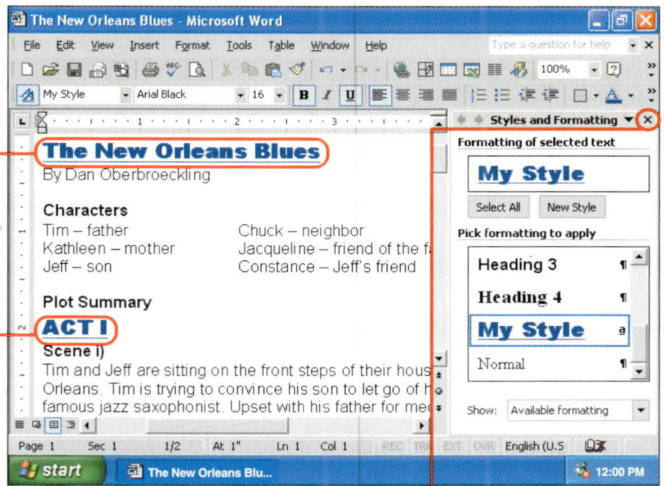

■ All the text, lists or tables formatted with the style display the changes.

■ To hide the Styles and Formatting task pane, click ☒.

REVIEW FORMATTING

You can review details about the formatting applied to text in a document. This is useful when you want to determine exactly what formatting was applied to the text.

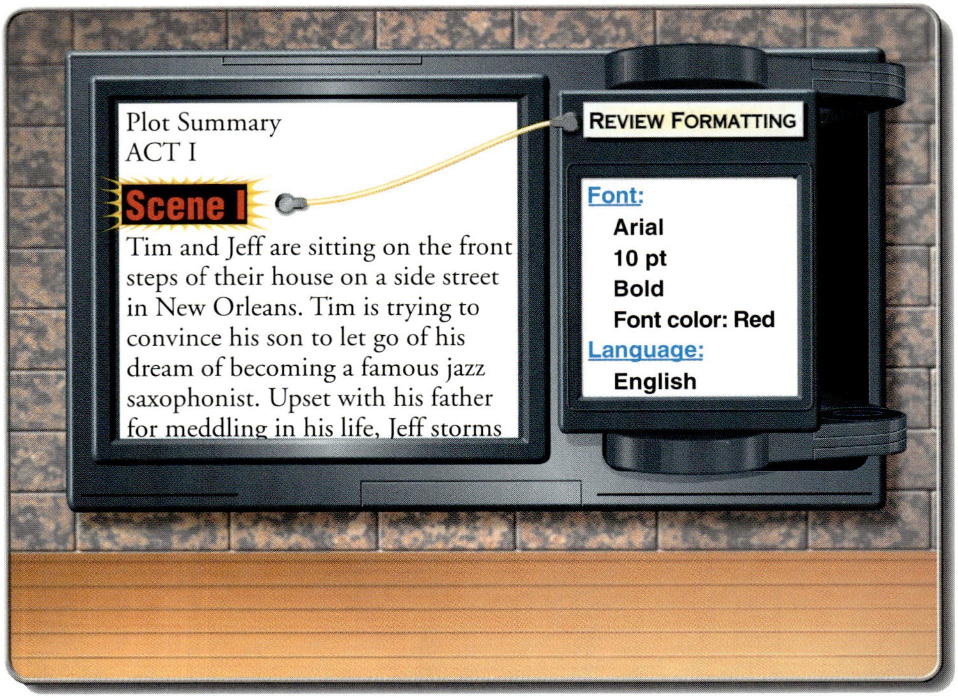

REVIEW FORMATTING

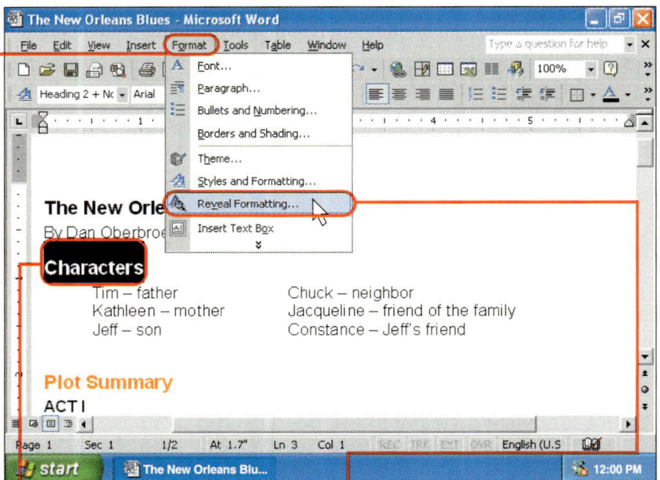

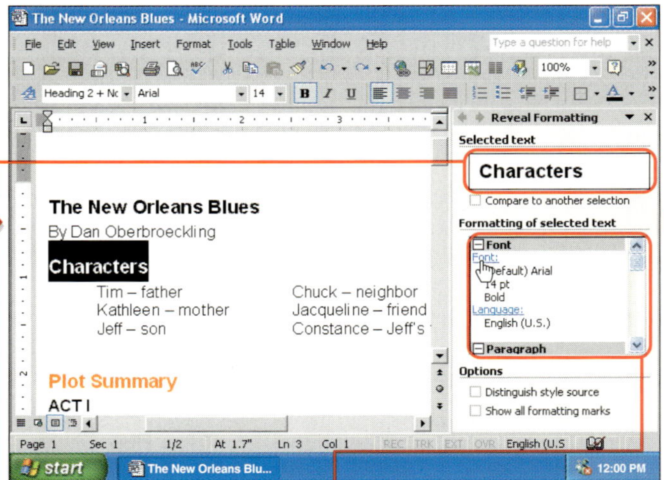

1 Select the text displaying the formatting you want to review. To select text, see page 10.

2 Click **Format**.

3 Click **Reveal Formatting**.

■ The Reveal Formatting task pane appears.

■ This area displays a sample of the text you selected.

■ This area displays the formatting details for the text.

4 To change the formatting of the text you selected, click the blue, underlined heading for the type of formatting you want to change.

What types of formatting can I review using the Reveal Formatting task pane?

The Reveal Formatting task pane allows you to review several types of formatting including font, paragraph and section formatting. For example, you can review paragraph formatting to determine the alignment of the paragraph or review section formatting to determine the margin settings for the section.

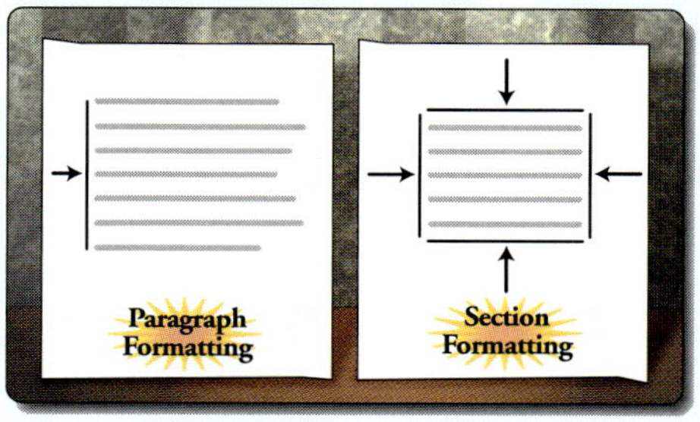

When reviewing formatting, how can I display more details?

Each item that displays a plus sign (⊞) contains hidden details. To display the hidden details, click the plus sign (⊞) beside the item (⊞ changes to ⊟). To once again hide the details, click the minus sign (⊟) beside the item.

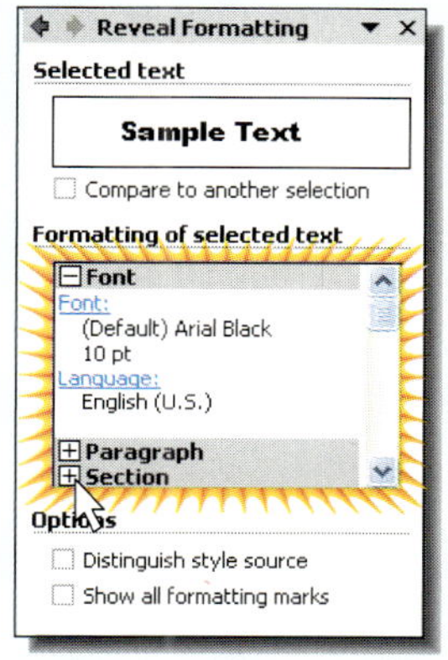

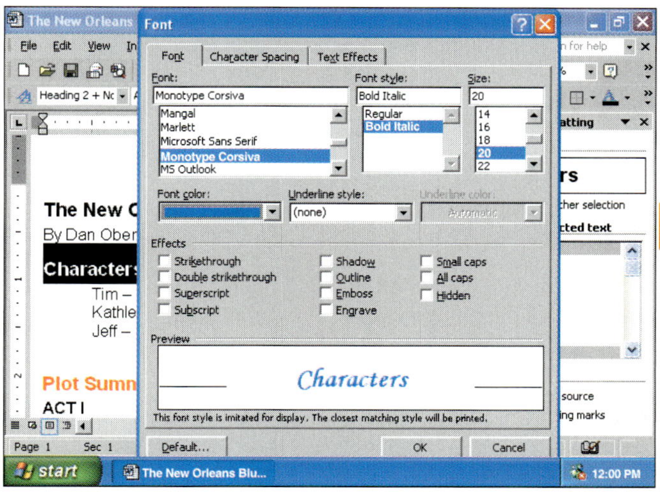

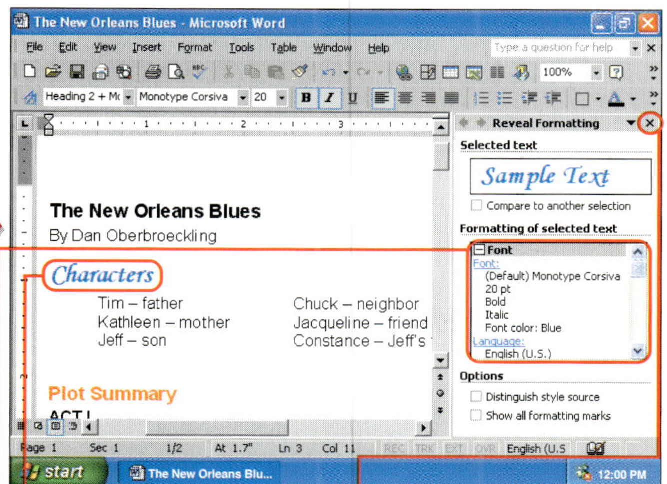

■ In this example, the Font dialog box appears.

Note: The dialog box that appears depends on the blue, underlined heading you selected.

5 Perform steps **5** to **11** starting on page 96 to change the font.

■ The text you selected displays the formatting changes.

■ This area displays the new formatting details.

■ To deselect text, click outside the selected area.

■ To hide the Reveal Formatting task pane, click ☒.

CONTINUED

REVIEW FORMATTING

Word allows you to compare the formatting of two areas of text in a document. You can then match the formatting of the areas so they display the same formatting.

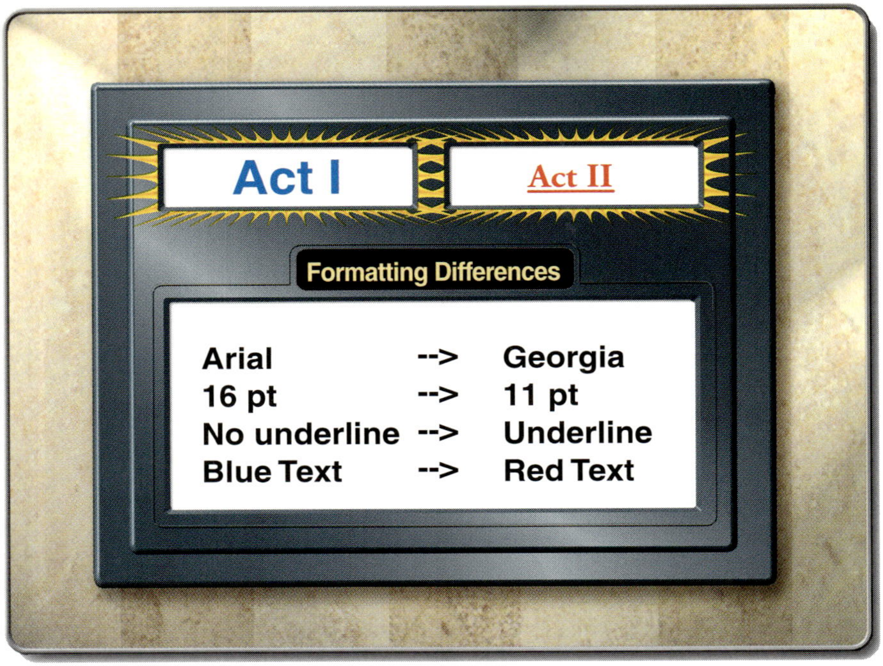

COMPARE FORMATTING

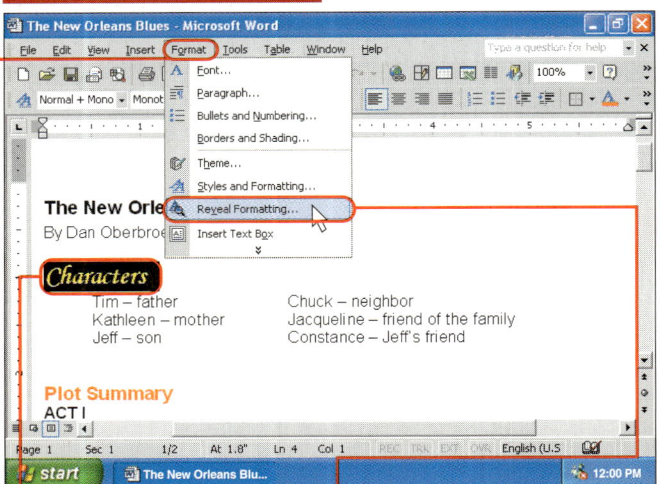

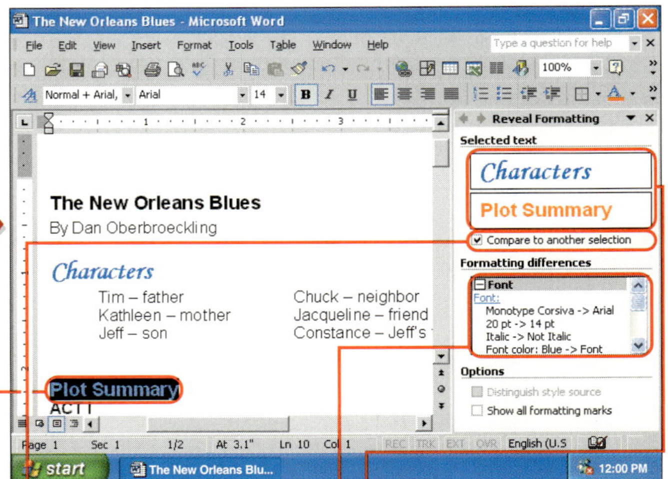

1 Select the text you want to compare to another area of text in your document. To select text, see page 10.

2 Click **Format**.

3 Click **Reveal Formatting**.

■ The Reveal Formatting task pane appears.

4 Click **Compare to another selection** (☐ changes to ☑).

5 Select the text you want to compare to the text you selected in step **1**.

■ These areas display samples of the two areas of text you selected.

■ This area indicates the formatting differences between the two areas of text.

Note: If there are no differences, the area displays the text ***No formatting differences****.*

When would I need to compare formatting?

You should compare formatting in a document that may contain inconsistent formatting. For example, when formatting a long document, you may have applied different formatting to different areas of the document. If you created a new document by copying text from other documents, the new document may display several different types of formatting.

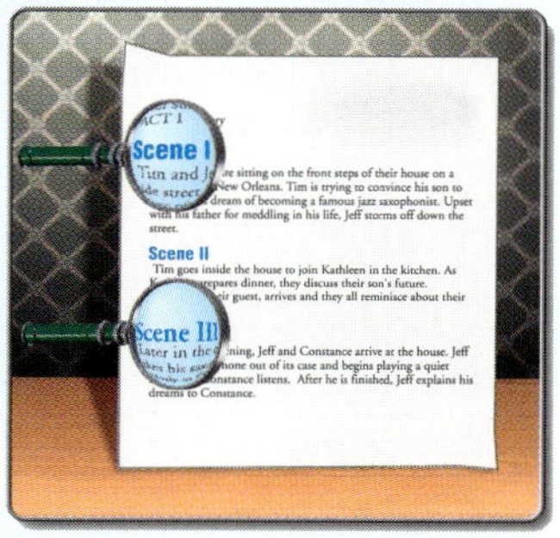

How can I ensure the formatting in my documents is consistent?

You can use the Styles and Formatting task pane to apply consistent formatting to text in your documents. For information on using the Styles and Formatting task pane, see pages 110 to 113.

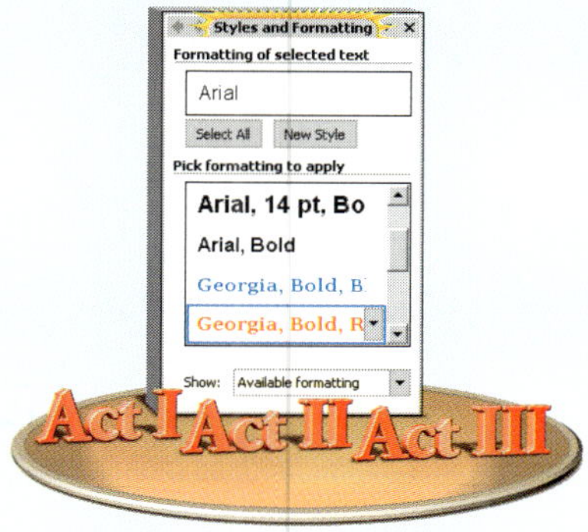

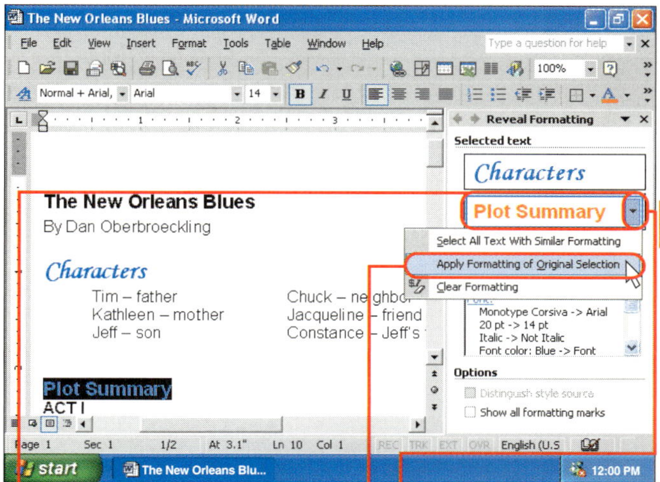

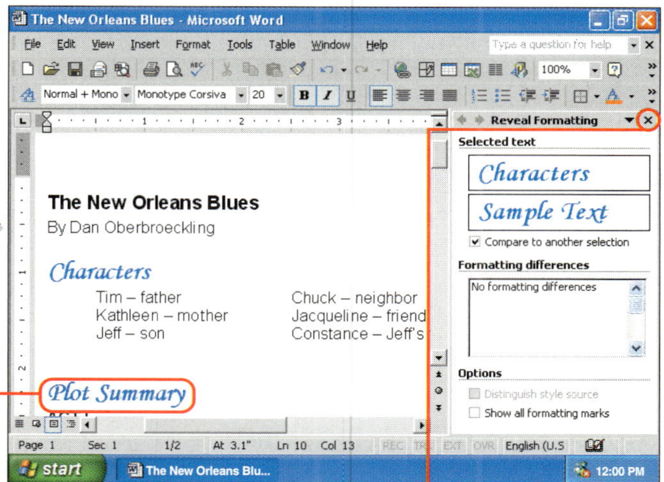

6 To match the formatting of the second area of text to the first area of text, position the mouse over this area. An arrow (▾) appears.

7 Click the arrow to display a list of options.

8 Click **Apply Formatting of Original Selection**.

■ Word changes the formatting of the second area of text to match the formatting of the first area of text.

■ To deselect text, click outside the selected area.

■ To hide the Reveal Formatting task pane, click ✕.

Trafalgar High School celebrates its 50th anniversary this year. We will be celebrating on September 22nd with an open house, followed by a buffet dinner.
Trafalgar High School celebrates its 50th anniversary this year. We will be celebrating on September 22nd with an open house, followed by a buffet dinner.
Trafalgar High School celebrates its 50th anniversary this year. We will be celebrating on September 22nd with an open house, followed by a buffet dinner.
Trafalgar High School celebrates its 50th anniversary this year. We will be celebrating on September 22nd with an open house, followed by a buffet dinner.
1

CHAPTER 7

Format Paragraphs

Do you want to create bulleted or numbered lists, indent paragraphs and add shading to text in your document? Learn how in this chapter.

Create a Bulleted or Numbered List ..124

Indent Paragraphs 128

Change Tab Settings........................130

Create a Drop Cap 134

Add a Border 136

Add Shading 138

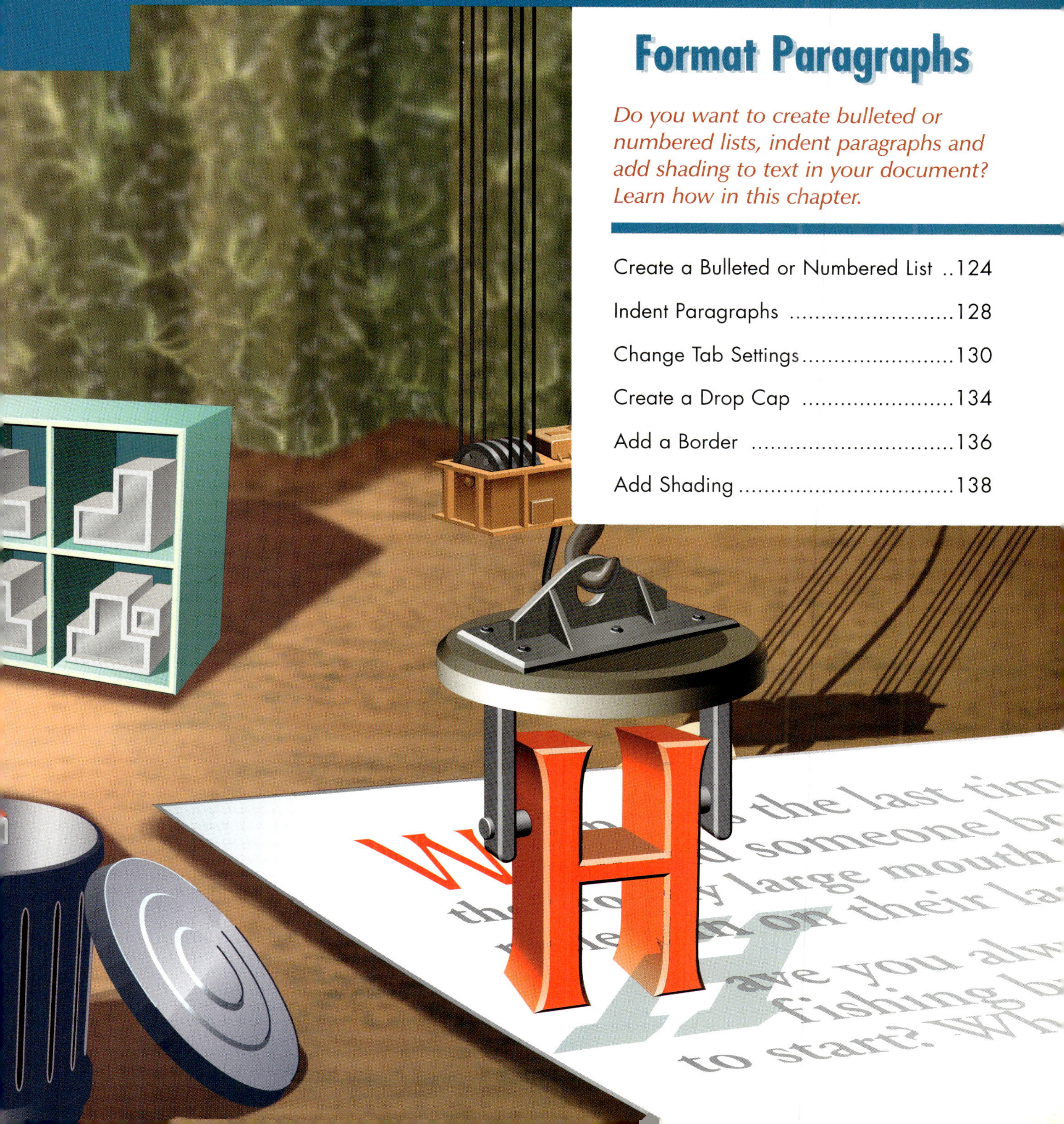

CREATE A BULLETED OR NUMBERED LIST

You can separate items in a list by beginning each item with a bullet or number.

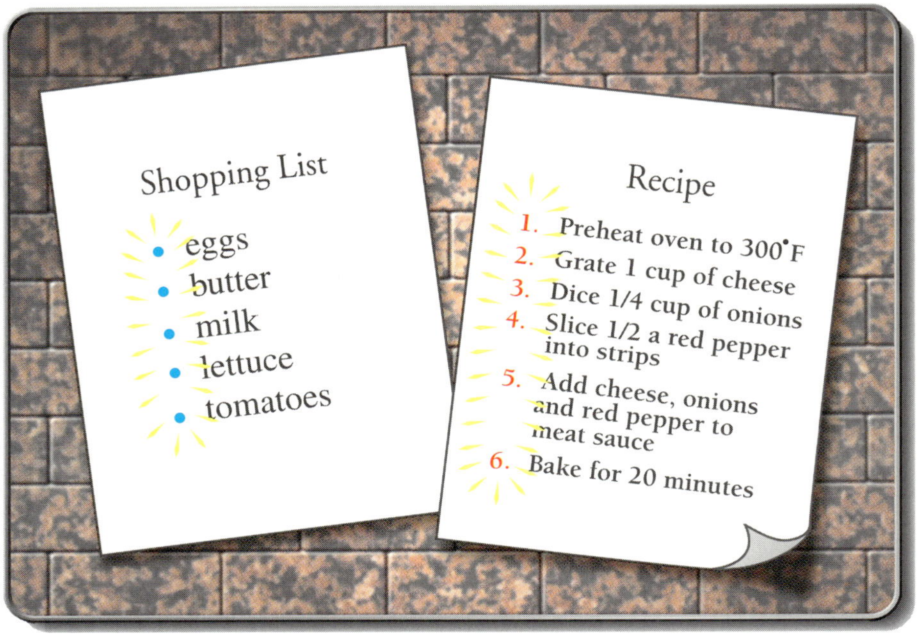

Bulleted lists are useful for items in no particular order, such as items in a shopping list.

Numbered lists are useful for items in a specific order, such as instructions in a recipe.

CREATE A BULLETED OR NUMBERED LIST

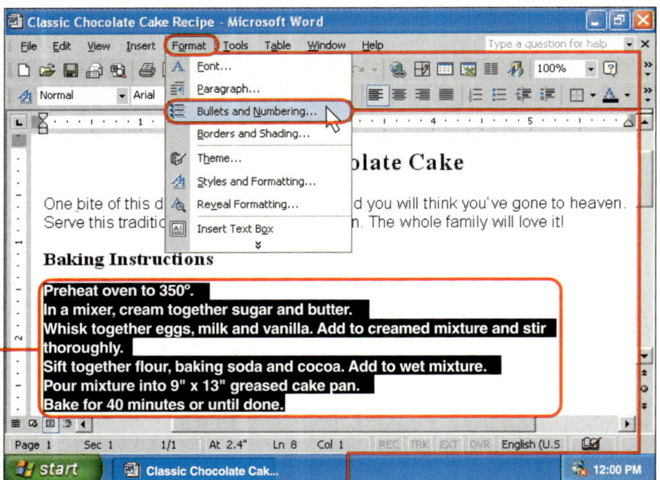

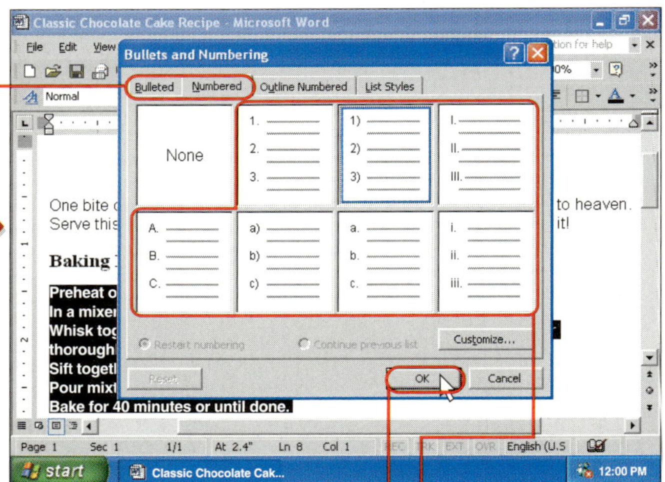

1 Select the text you want to display as a bulleted or numbered list. To select text, see page 10.

2 Click **Format**.

3 Click **Bullets and Numbering**.

■ The Bullets and Numbering dialog box appears.

4 Click the tab for the type of list you want to create.

5 Click the style you want to use.

6 Click **OK** to confirm your selection.

How can I create a bulleted or numbered list as I type?

1 Type * to create a bulleted list or type **1**. to create a numbered list. Then press the **Spacebar**.

2 Type the first item in the list and then press the Enter key. Word automatically adds a bullet or number for the next item.

3 Repeat step **2** for each item in the list.

4 To finish the list, press the Enter key twice.

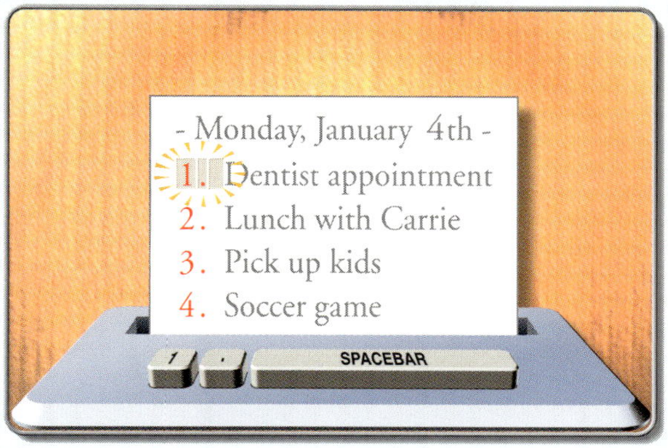

Note: When you create a bulleted or numbered list as you type, the AutoCorrect Options button ( ) appears. You can click this button to specify that you do not want Word to create a bulleted or numbered list as you type.

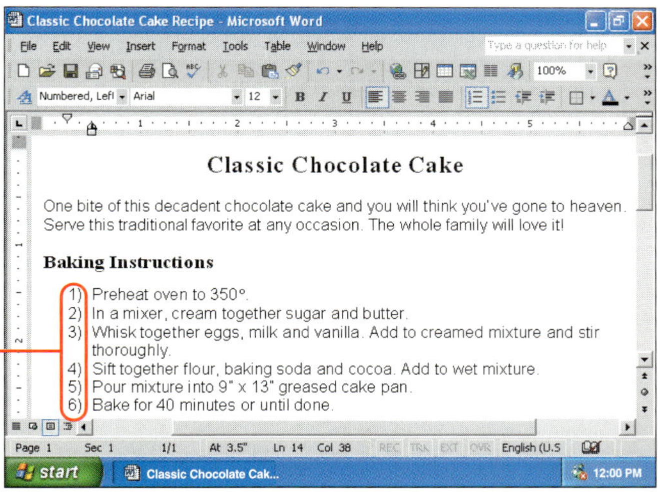

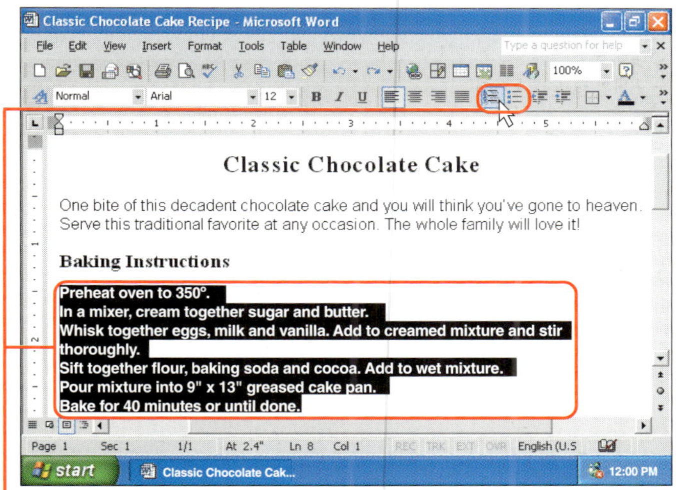

■ A bullet or number appears in front of each item in the list.

■ To deselect the text in the list, click outside the selected area.

■ To remove bullets or numbers from a list, repeat steps **1** to **6**, selecting **None** in step **5**.

QUICKLY CREATE A LIST

1 Select the text you want to display as a bulleted or numbered list. To select text, see page 10.

2 Click one of the following buttons.

- Add numbers
- Add bullets

Note: If the button you want is not displayed, click on the Formatting toolbar to display the button.

CONTINUED

CREATE A BULLETED OR NUMBERED LIST

You can use picture bullets to enhance the appearance of a list in your document.

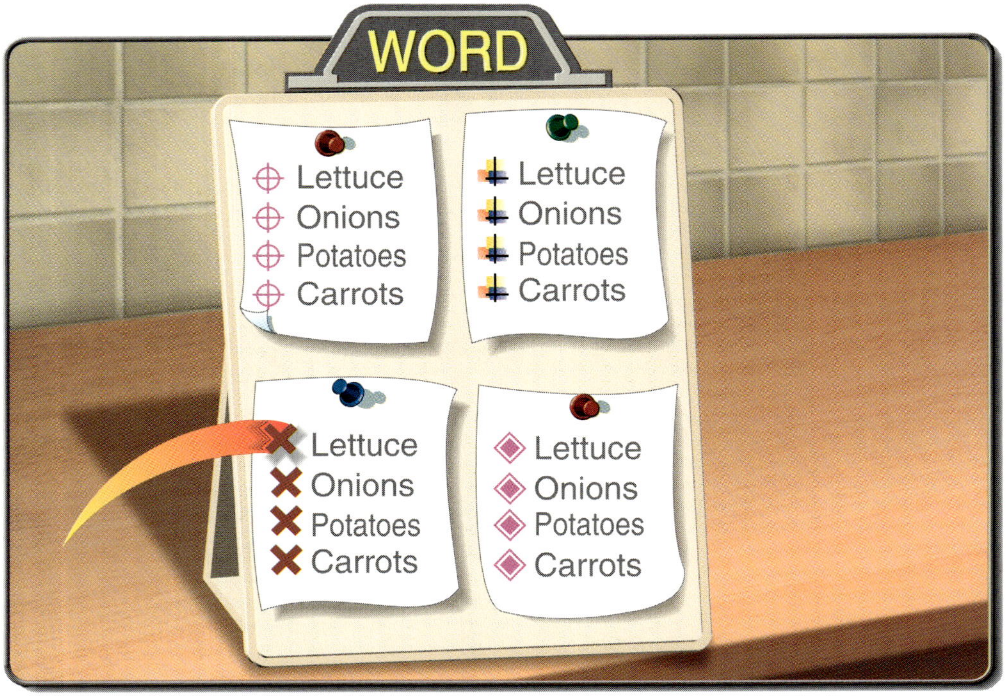

CREATE A BULLETED OR NUMBERED LIST (CONTINUED)

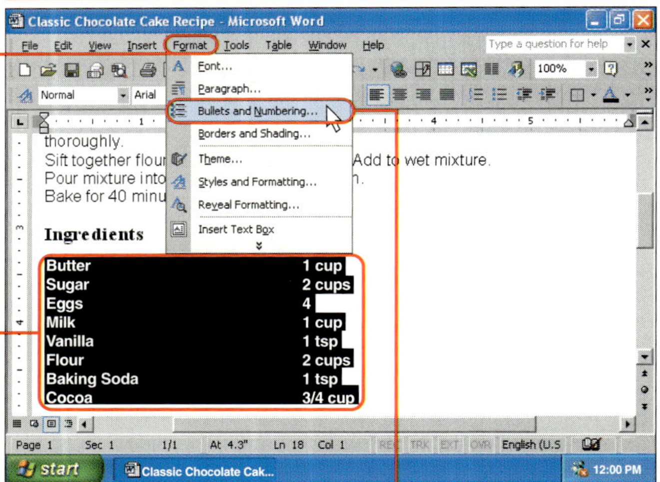

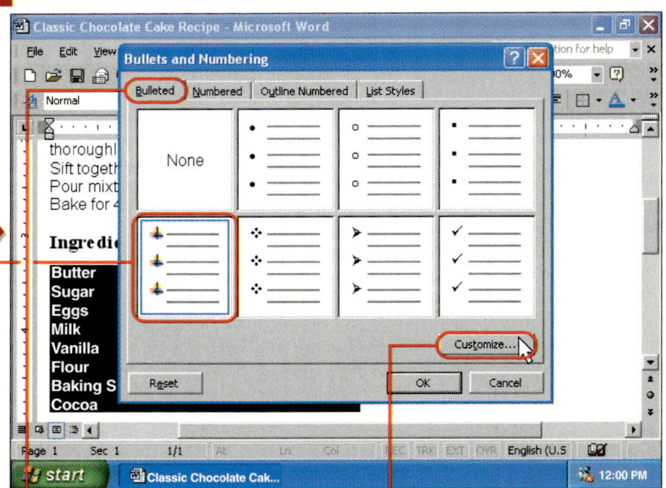

ADD PICTURE BULLETS

1 Select the text you want to display as a picture bulleted list. To select text, see page 10.

2 Click **Format**.

3 Click **Bullets and Numbering**.

■ The Bullets and Numbering dialog box appears.

4 Click the **Bulleted** tab.

5 Click the bullet style displayed in this area.

6 Click **Customize**.

■ The Customize Bulleted List dialog box appears.

How can I quickly add the picture bullet I selected to another list in my document?

Word remembers the last picture bullet you added to your document. To add the picture bullet to another list, drag the mouse I over the list until you highlight the list and then click the Bullets button ( ) on the Formatting toolbar.

Note: If is not displayed, click on the Formatting toolbar to display the button.

How do I remove picture bullets from a list in my document?

To remove picture bullets from a list, perform steps **1** to **6** on page 124, selecting **None** in step **5**.

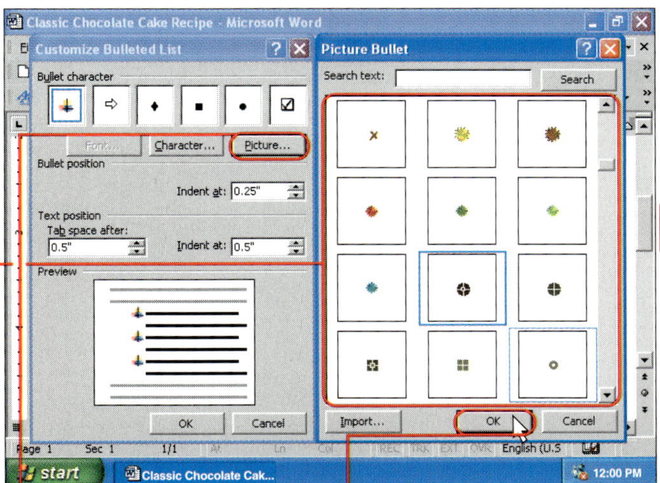

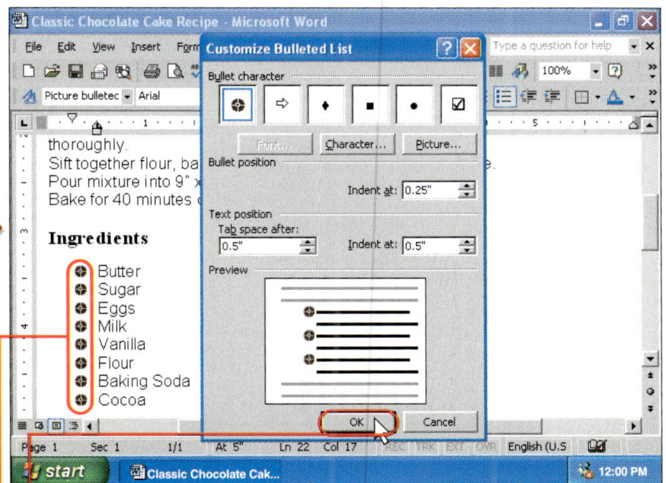

7 Click **Picture**.

■ The Picture Bullet dialog box appears.

8 Click the picture bullet you want to use.

Note: You can use the scroll bar to browse through the available picture bullets.

9 Click **OK** to confirm your selection.

10 Click **OK** in the Customize Bulleted List dialog box to add the picture bullet to your document.

■ A picture bullet appears in front of each item in the list.

■ To deselect the text in the list, click outside the selected area.

INDENT PARAGRAPHS

You can indent text to make paragraphs in your document stand out.

INDENT PARAGRAPHS

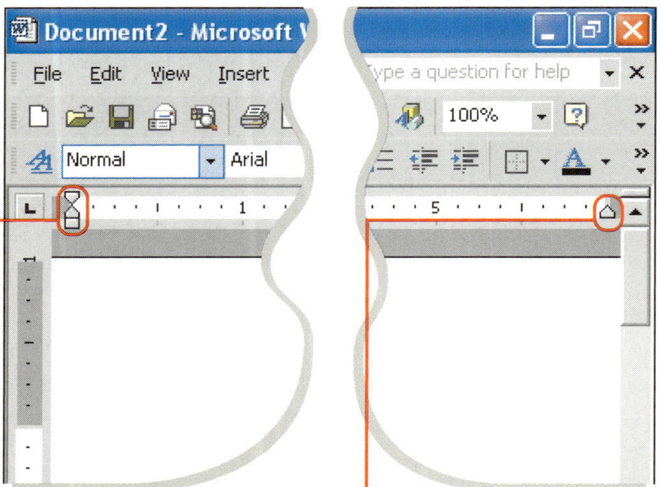

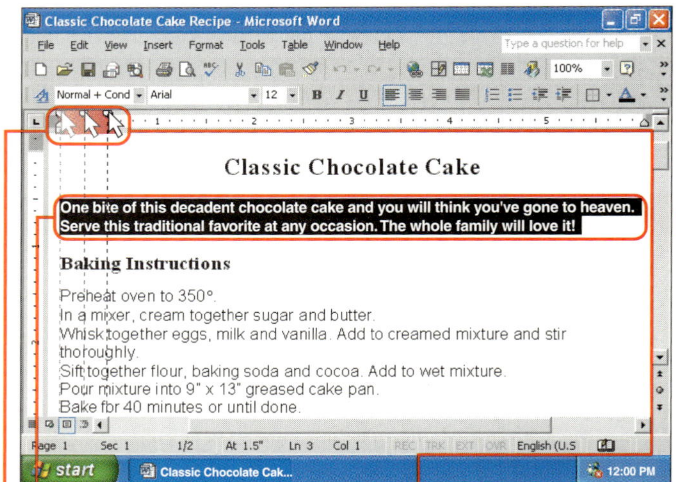

■ These symbols allow you to indent the left edge of a paragraph.

▽ Indent first line.

△ Indent all but the first line.

□ Indent all lines.

■ This symbol (△) allows you to indent the right edge of a paragraph.

Note: If the ruler is not displayed, see page 42 to display the ruler.

1 Select the paragraph(s) you want to indent. To select text, see page 10.

2 Position the mouse over the indent symbol you want to use to indent the text.

3 Drag the indent symbol to a new position on the ruler.

■ A dotted line shows the new indent position.

What types of indents can I create?

First Line Indent

Indents only the first line of a paragraph. First line indents are often used to mark the beginning of paragraphs in letters and professional documents.

Hanging Indent

Indents all but the first line of a paragraph. Hanging indents are useful when you are creating a glossary or bibliography.

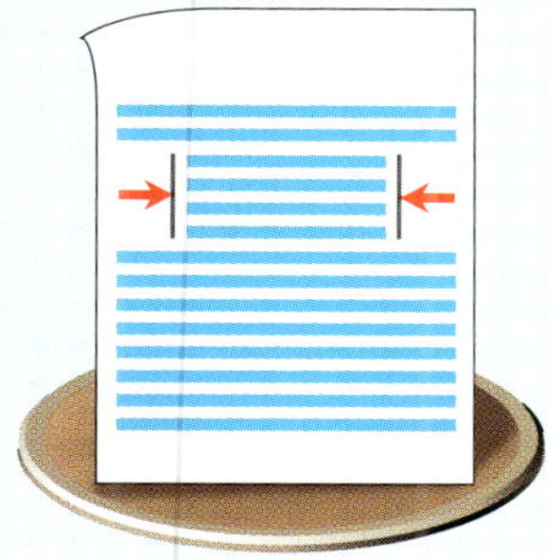

Indent Both Sides

Indenting both the left and right sides of a paragraph is useful when you want to set text, such as a quotation, apart from the rest of the text in your document.

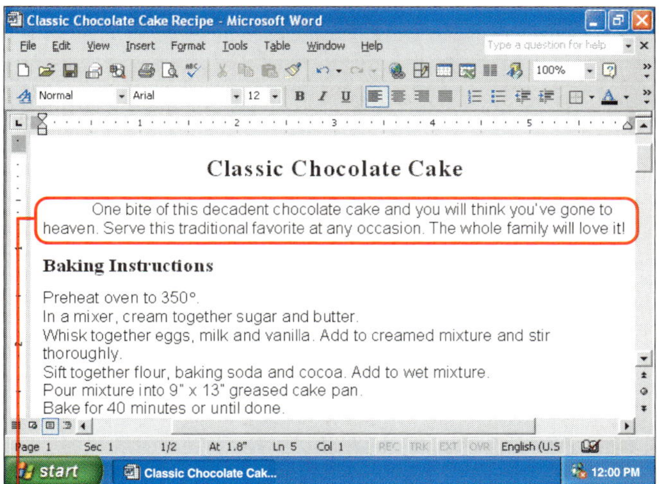

■ Word indents the paragraph(s) you selected.

■ To deselect text, click outside the selected area.

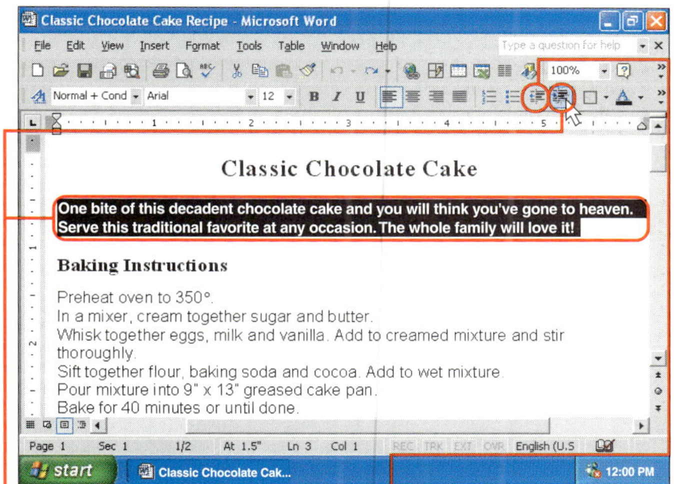

QUICKLY INDENT PARAGRAPHS

1 Select the paragraph(s) you want to indent. To select text, see page 10.

2 Click to indent the left edge of the paragraph(s).

Note: If is not displayed, click on the Formatting toolbar to display the button.

■ You can repeat step 2 to further indent the text.

■ To decrease the indent, click .

CHANGE TAB SETTINGS

You can use tabs to line up information in your document. Word offers several types of tabs for you to choose from.

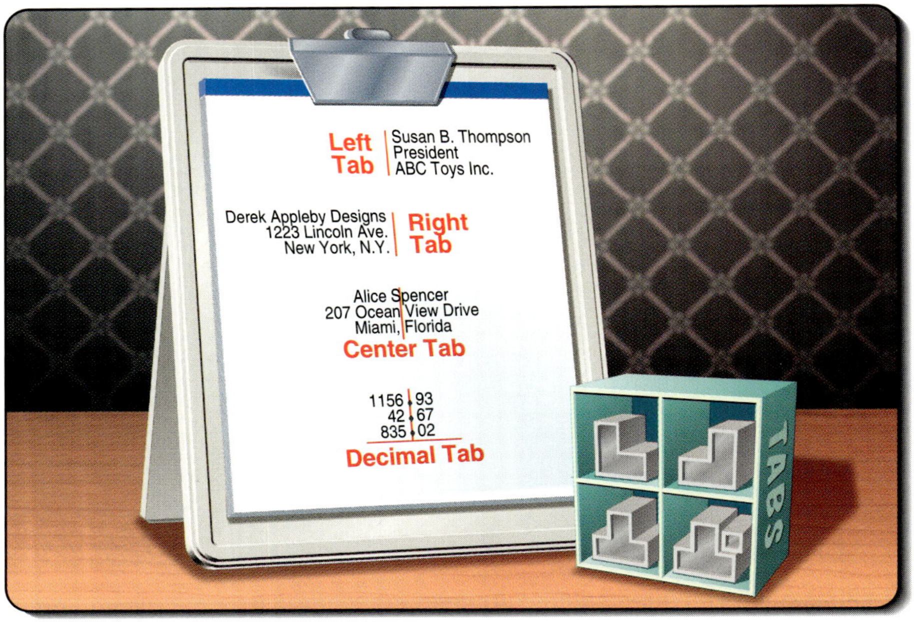

Word automatically places a tab every 0.5 inches across a page.

CHANGE TAB SETTINGS

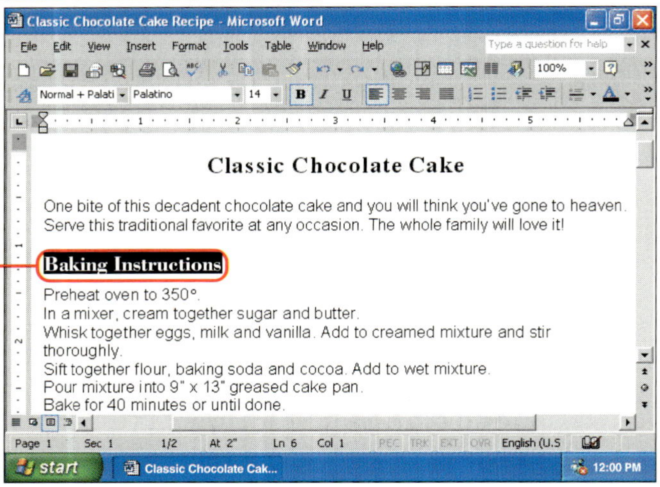

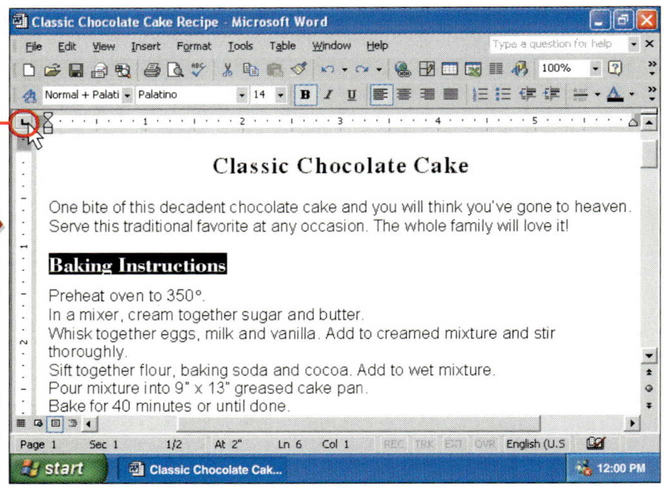

ADD A TAB

1 Select the text you want to use a new tab. To select text, see page 10.

■ To add a tab to text you are about to type, click the location in your document where you want to type the text.

2 Click this area until the type of tab you want to add appears.

- Left tab
- Center tab
- Right tab
- Decimal tab

Note: If the ruler is not displayed, see page 42 to display the ruler.

TEACH YOURSELF

How do I move a tab?

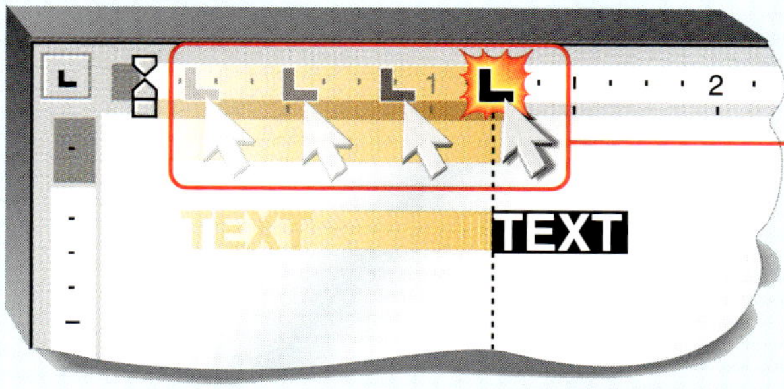

1 Select the text that uses the tab you want to move. To select text, see page 10.

2 Position the mouse over the tab you want to move and then drag the tab to a new location on the ruler. A dotted line shows the new location.

■ The text that uses the tab moves to the new location.

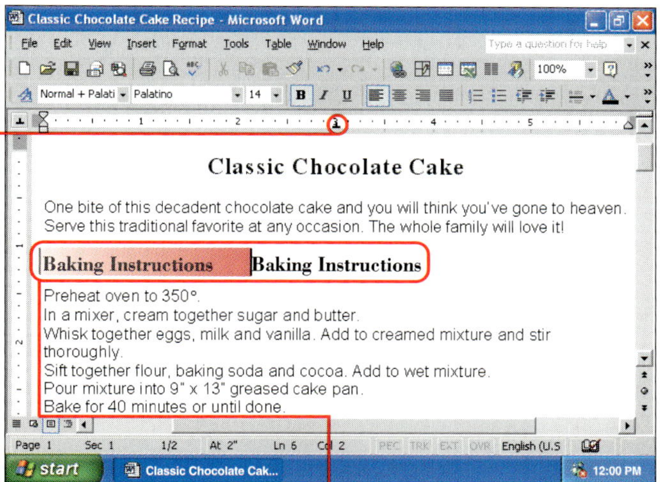

3 Click the bottom half of the ruler where you want to add the tab.

■ The new tab appears on the ruler.

USE A TAB

1 Click to the left of the first character in the line you want to move to the tab. Then press the Tab key.

■ The insertion point and the text that follows move to the tab you set.

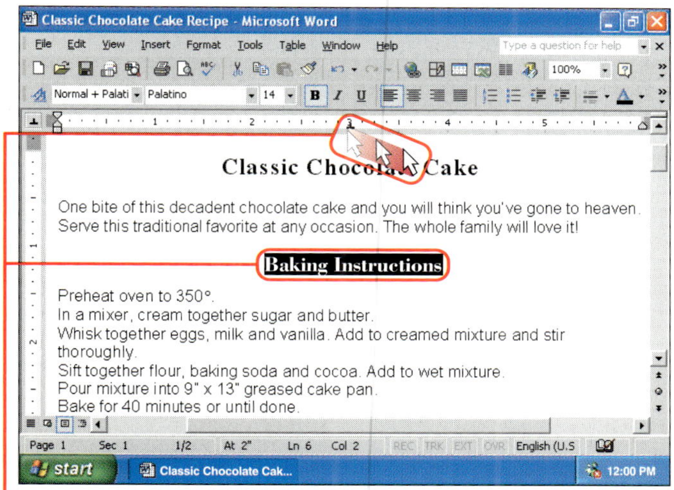

REMOVE A TAB

1 Select the text that uses the tab you want to remove. To select text, see page 10.

2 Position the mouse over the tab you want to remove and then drag the tab downward off the ruler.

■ The tab disappears from the ruler.

■ To move the text back to the left margin, click to the left of the first character. Then press the ←Backspace key.

CONTINUED

CHANGE TAB SETTINGS

You can insert a line or row of dots, called leader characters, before a tab to help lead the eye from one column of information to another.

ADD A TAB WITH LEADER CHARACTERS

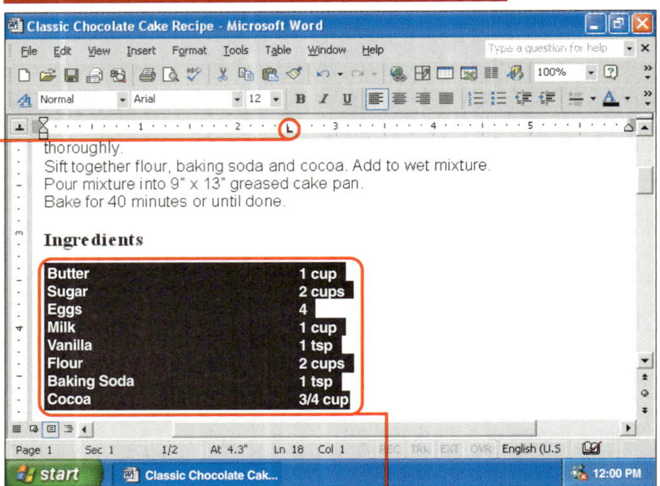

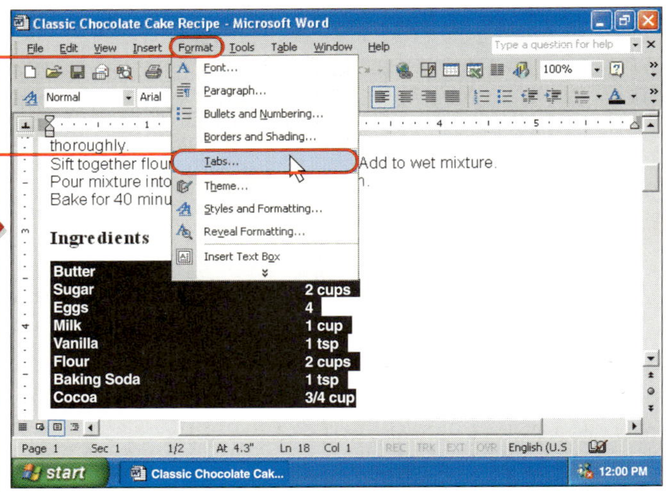

1 Add a tab to the text you want to display leader characters. To add a tab, see page 130.

2 Select the text containing the tab. To select text, see page 10.

3 Click **Format**.

4 Click **Tabs**.

Note: If Tabs does not appear on the menu, position the mouse over the bottom of the menu to display all the menu options.

■ The Tabs dialog box appears.

Why would I use leader characters?

Leader characters make information such as a table of contents or a list of telephone numbers easier to read.

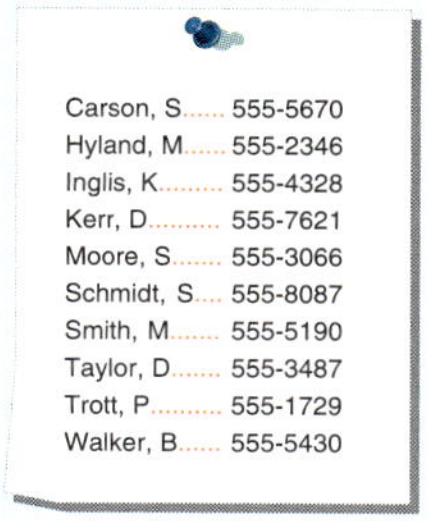

Leader characters are also used in forms to create areas where people can enter information.

How do I remove the leader characters from my document?

To remove the leader characters, perform steps **2** to **7** below, selecting **None** in step **6**.

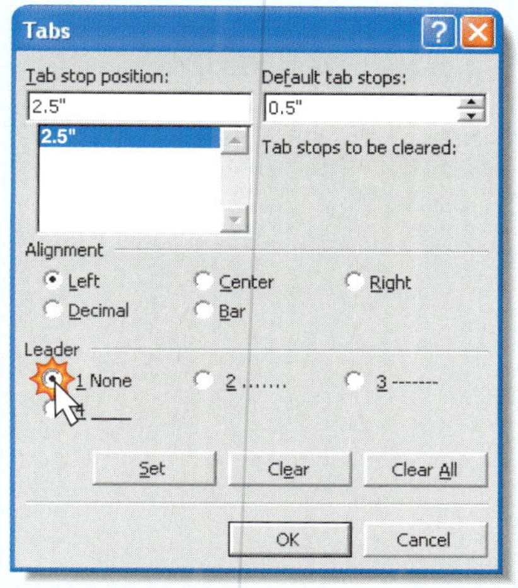

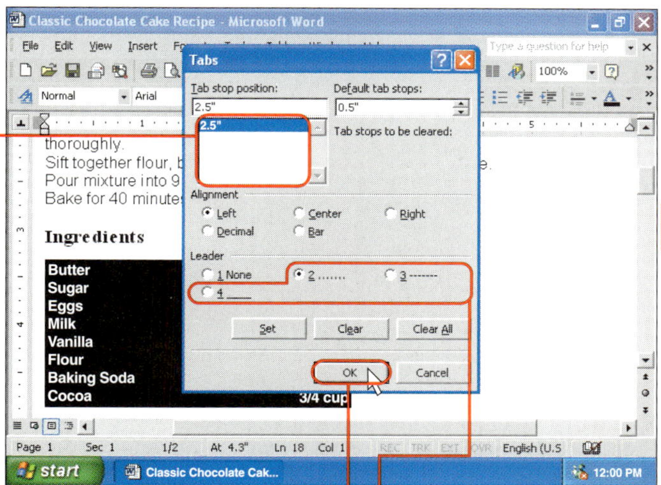

■ This area displays the positions of all the tabs for the text you selected.

5 Click the tab you want to display leader characters.

6 Click the type of leader character you want to use (○ changes to ⊙).

7 Click **OK** to confirm your selections.

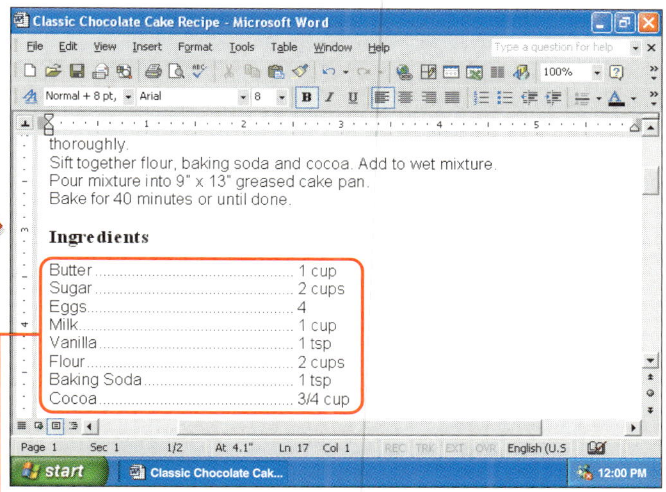

■ The text you selected displays the leader characters.

■ To deselect text, click outside the selected area.

CREATE A DROP CAP

You can create a large capital letter at the beginning of a paragraph to enhance the appearance of the paragraph.

Word can properly display a drop cap only in the Print Layout and Web Layout views. To change the view of a document, see page 40.

CREATE A DROP CAP

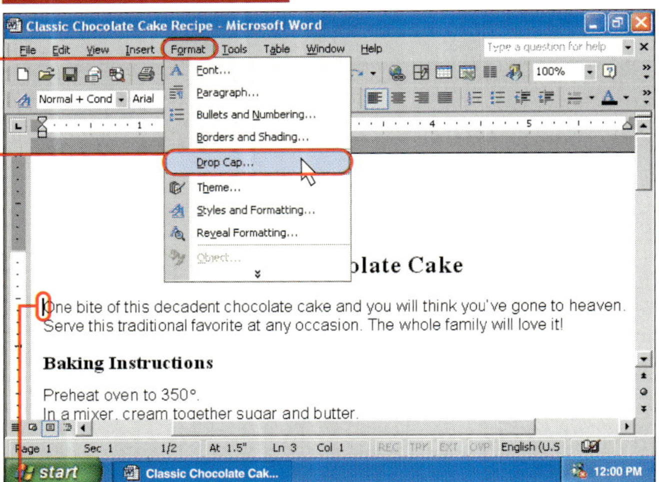

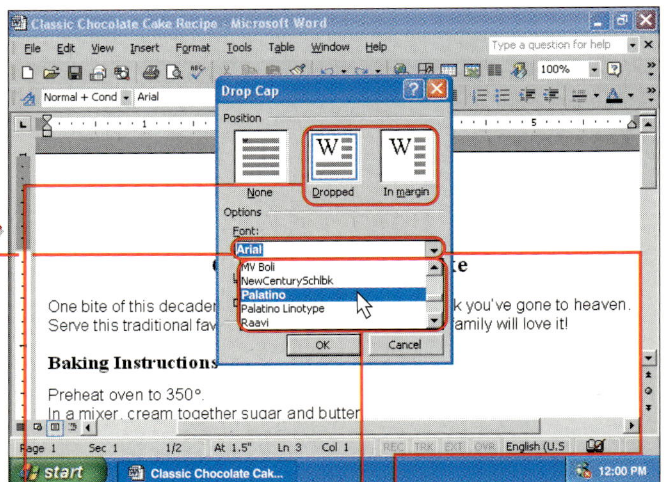

1 Click the paragraph you want to display a drop cap.

2 Click **Format**.

3 Click **Drop Cap**.

Note: If Drop Cap does not appear on the menu, position the mouse over the bottom of the menu to display all the menu options.

■ The Drop Cap dialog box appears.

4 Click the type of drop cap you want to create.

Note: For information on the types of drop caps you can create, see the top of page 135.

■ This area displays the font the drop cap will display.

5 To select another font for the drop cap, click ▾ in this area.

6 Click the font you want the drop cap to display.

What types of drop caps can I create?

Dropped

Wraps text in the paragraph around the drop cap.

In margin

Moves the drop cap into the left margin of the document. For information on margins, see page 156.

Can I create a drop cap using more than one letter?

You can create a drop cap using several letters or an entire word at the beginning of a paragraph. Drag the mouse I over the letters or word you want to make a drop cap until you highlight the text. Then perform steps **2** to **8** below.

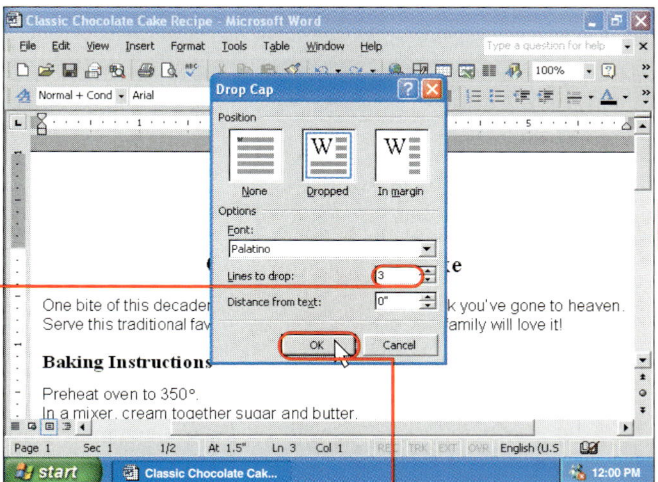

■ This area displays the number of lines that the drop cap will extend down from the first line of the paragraph.

7 To change the number of lines, double-click the number in this area and then type a new number.

8 Click **OK** to create the drop cap.

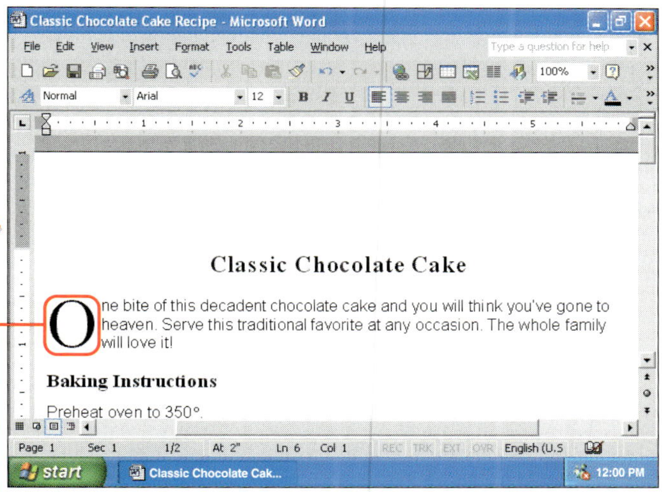

■ The drop cap appears in your document.

■ To deselect the drop cap, click outside the drop cap.

■ To remove a drop cap, repeat steps **1** to **4**, selecting **None** in step **4**. Then perform step **8**.

ADD A BORDER

You can add a border to text in your document to draw attention to important information.

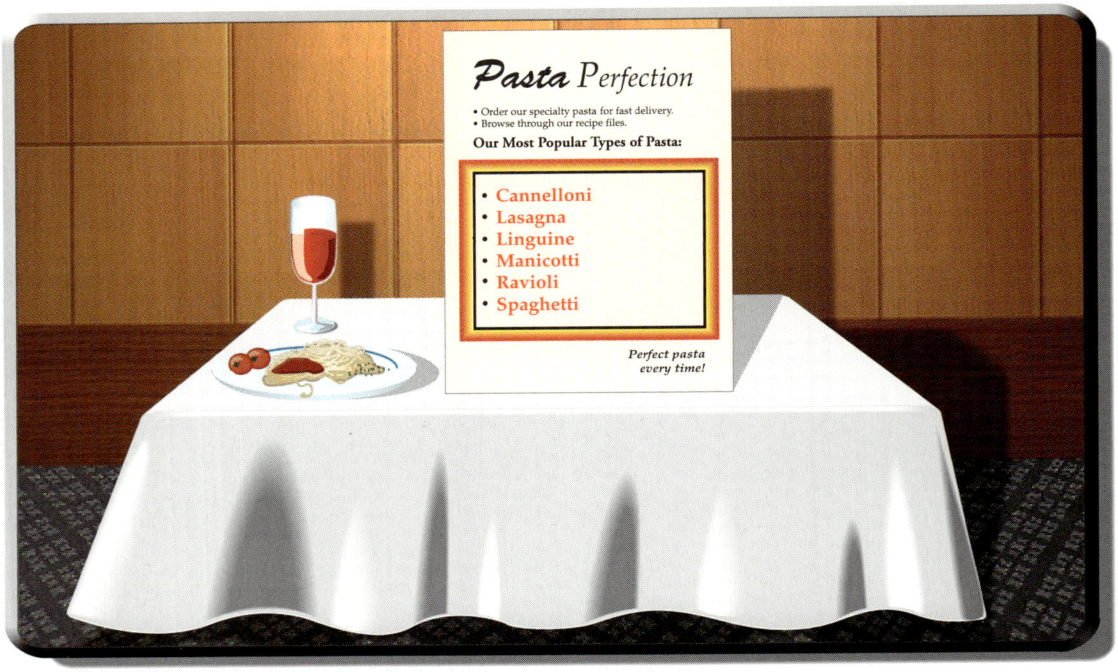

ADD A BORDER

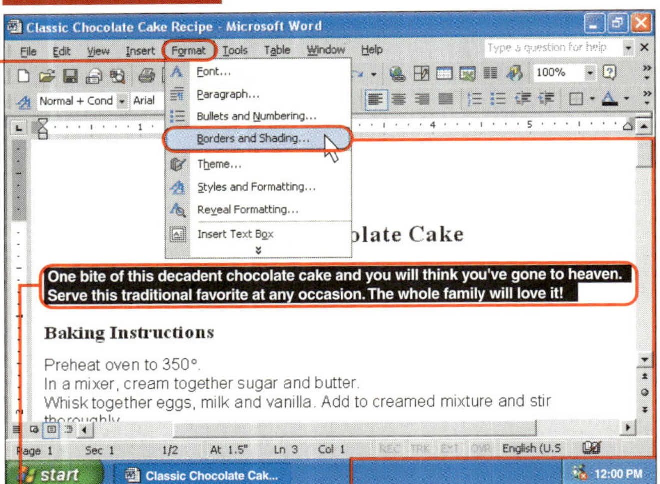

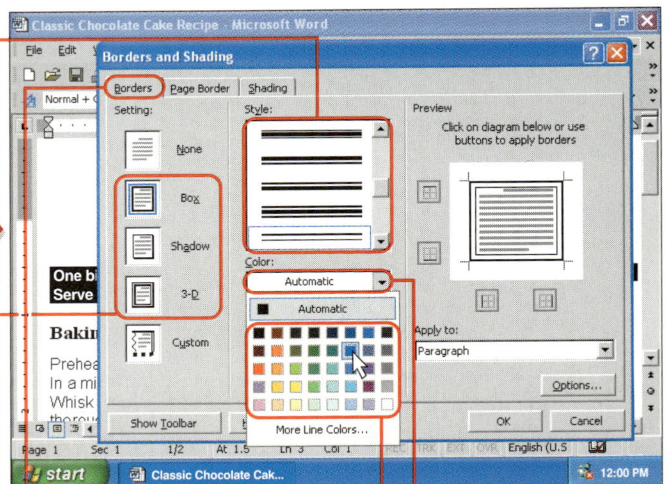

1 Select the text you want to display a border. To select text, see page 10.

2 Click **Format**.

3 Click **Borders and Shading**.

■ The Borders and Shading dialog box appears.

4 Click the **Borders** tab.

5 Click the type of border you want to add.

6 Click the line style you want to use for the border.

7 To select a color for the border, click this area.

8 Click the color you want to use.

How can I quickly add a border to text in my document?

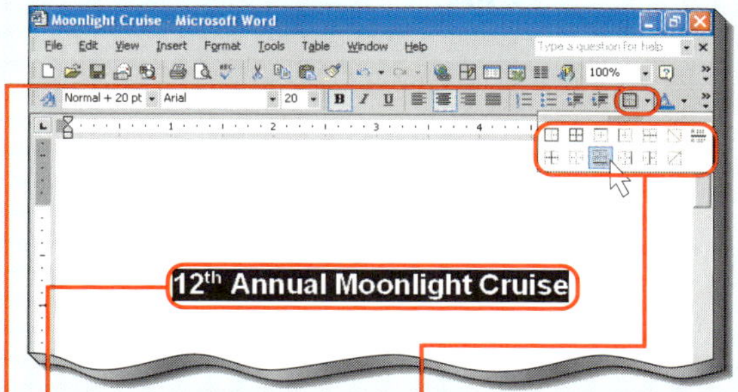

1 Select the text you want to display a border. To select text, see page 10.

2 Click ▾ in this area to display the available types of borders.

Note: If the border button is not displayed, click » on the Formatting toolbar to display the button.

3 Click the type of border you want to add.

How can I quickly add a line across my page?

Type a set of characters shown in the chart below and then press the **Enter** key. Word will automatically add a line across your page.

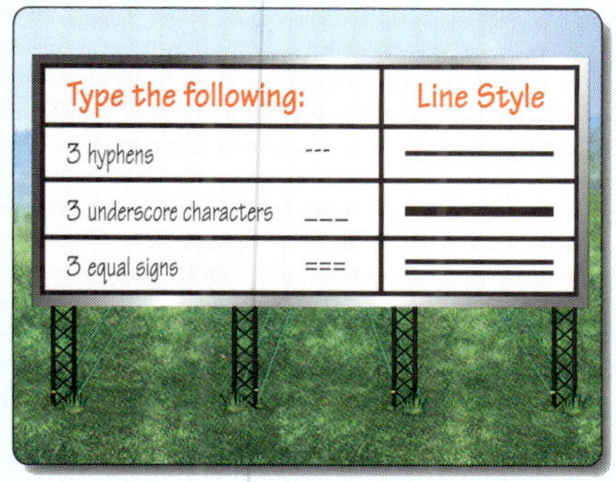

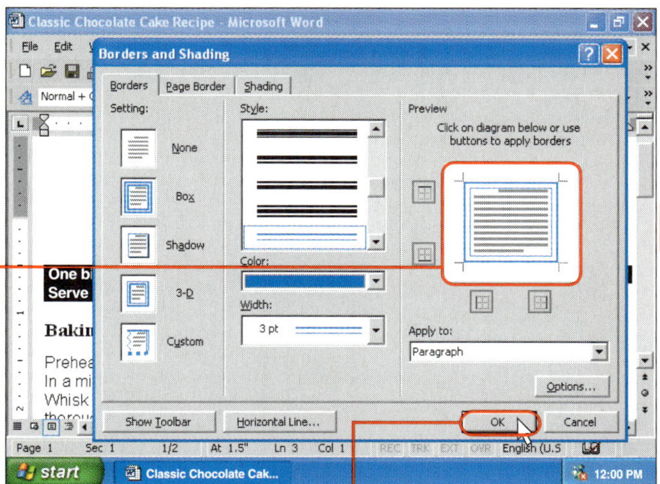

■ This area displays a preview of the border you selected.

9 Click **OK** to add the border to your document.

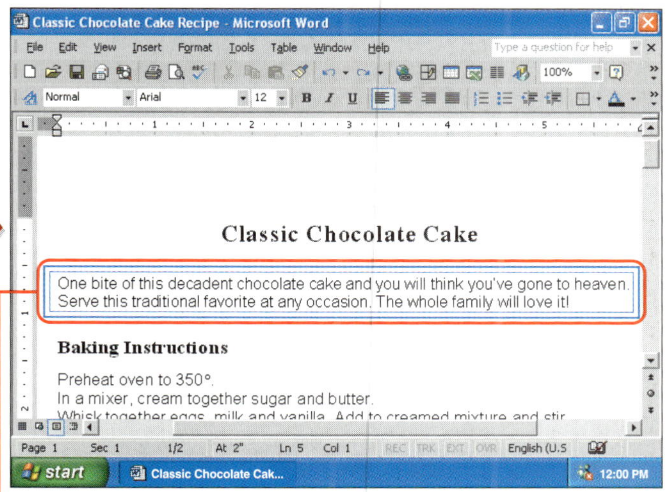

■ The text you selected displays the border.

■ To deselect text, click outside the selected area.

■ To remove a border, repeat steps **1** to **5**, selecting **None** in step **5**. Then perform step **9**.

ADD SHADING

You can add shading to your document to emphasize an area of text.

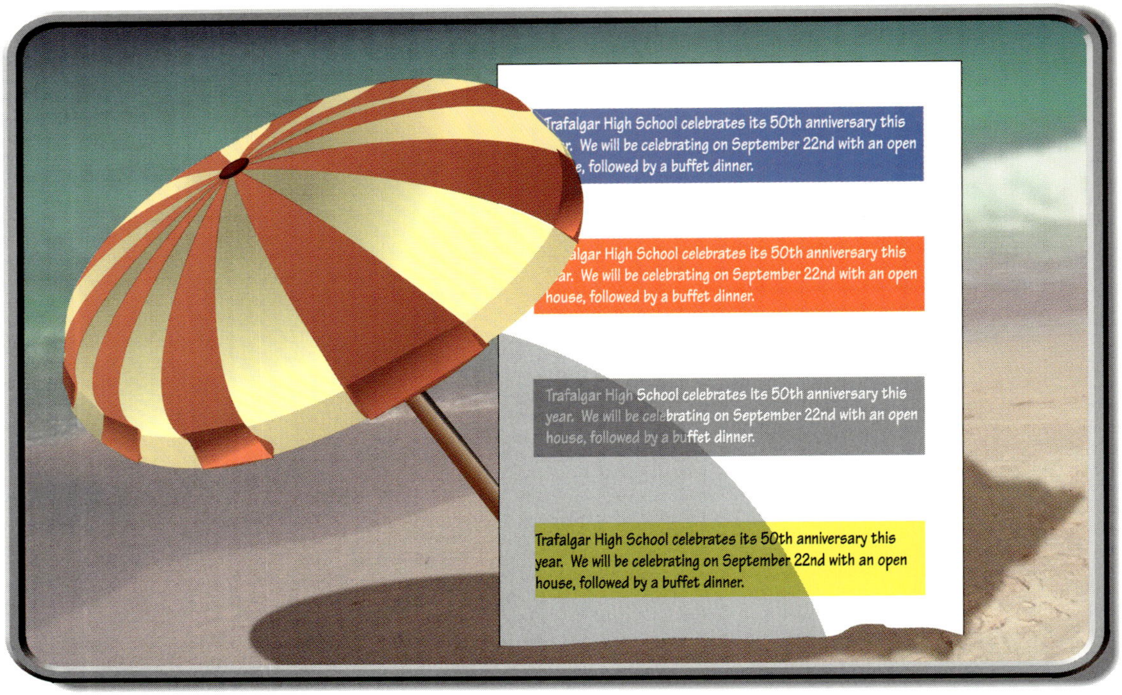

ADD SHADING

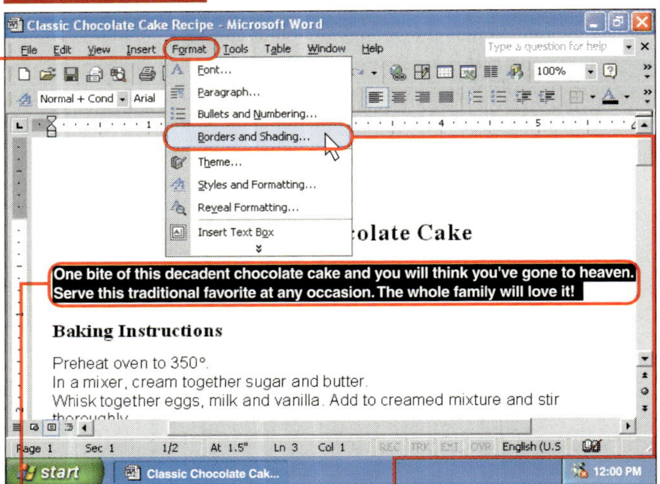

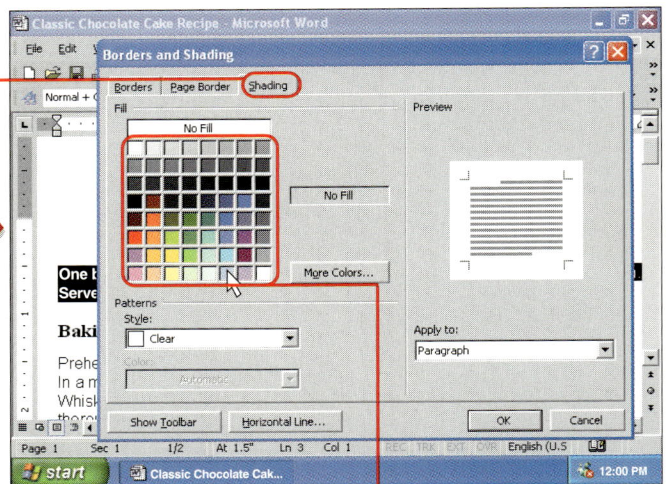

1 Select the text you want to display shading. To select text, see page 10.

2 Click **Format**.

3 Click **Borders and Shading**.

■ The Borders and Shading dialog box appears.

4 Click the **Shading** tab.

■ This area displays the available colors for the shading.

5 Click the color you want to use.

How will the shading I add to my document appear when I print the document?

When you print your document on a color printer, the shading will appear on the printed page as it appears on your screen. When you print your document on a black-and-white printer, any colored shading you added will appear as a shade of gray on the printed page.

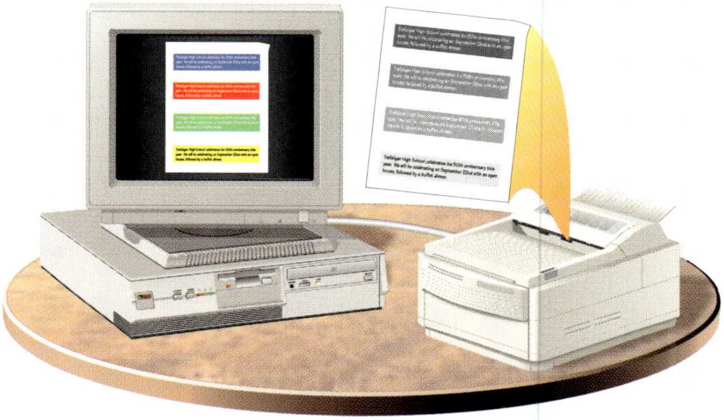

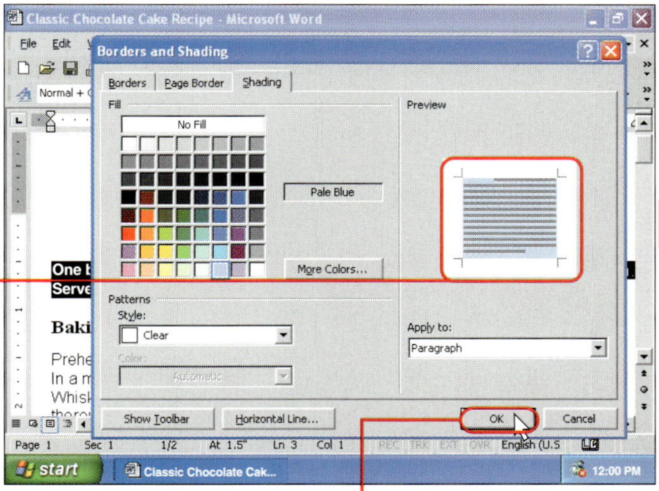

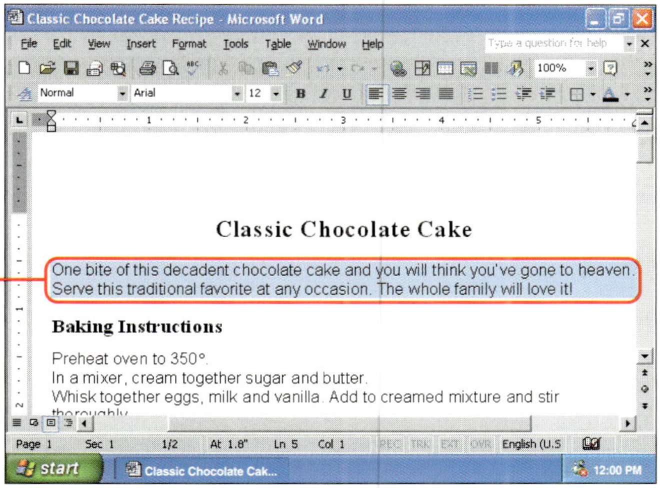

■ This area displays a preview of the shading you selected.

6 Click **OK** to add the shading to your document.

■ The text you selected displays the shading.

■ To deselect text, click outside the selected area.

■ To remove shading from your document, repeat steps 1 to 6, selecting **No Fill** in step 5.

The Olympic Flame
One constant that remains from ancient times, is the Olympic flame. It has remained since the beginning.
In ancient times the Olympic games took on a very religious significance. Olympia, the grounds on which the first games were played, was considered sacred.
The ancient Greeks believed very deeply in a relationship between life and death and the connection that existed between
time the ancient Olympic games were held, the Olympic flame was lit to symbolize the re-birth of the spirit of their dead heroes.
Today, that tradition continues. In 1936, for the first time in modern Olympic history, the sacred Olympic flame was carried to Berlin, Germany where the 11th Olympiad took place.
torch which burns throughout the games until it is extinguished during the closing ceremony.
ATTENTION: Lindsay Sandr
FROM: Kim Johnson
DATE: August 6, 20
This memo is a rem
ABC Incorporated
advertising camp
last month.
Please meet in
1
2
3
4
5

CHAPTER 8

Format Pages

Are you wondering how to change the appearance of pages in your document? In this chapter, you will learn how to add page numbers, change margins, create newspaper columns and more.

Insert a Page Break 142

Insert a Section Break 144

Add Page Numbers 146

Add a Header or Footer 148

Add Footnotes or Endnotes 152

Change Margins 156

Center Text on a Page 158

Change Page Orientation 159

Control Page Breaks 160

Add a Watermark 162

Add a Page Border 164

Create Newspaper Columns 166

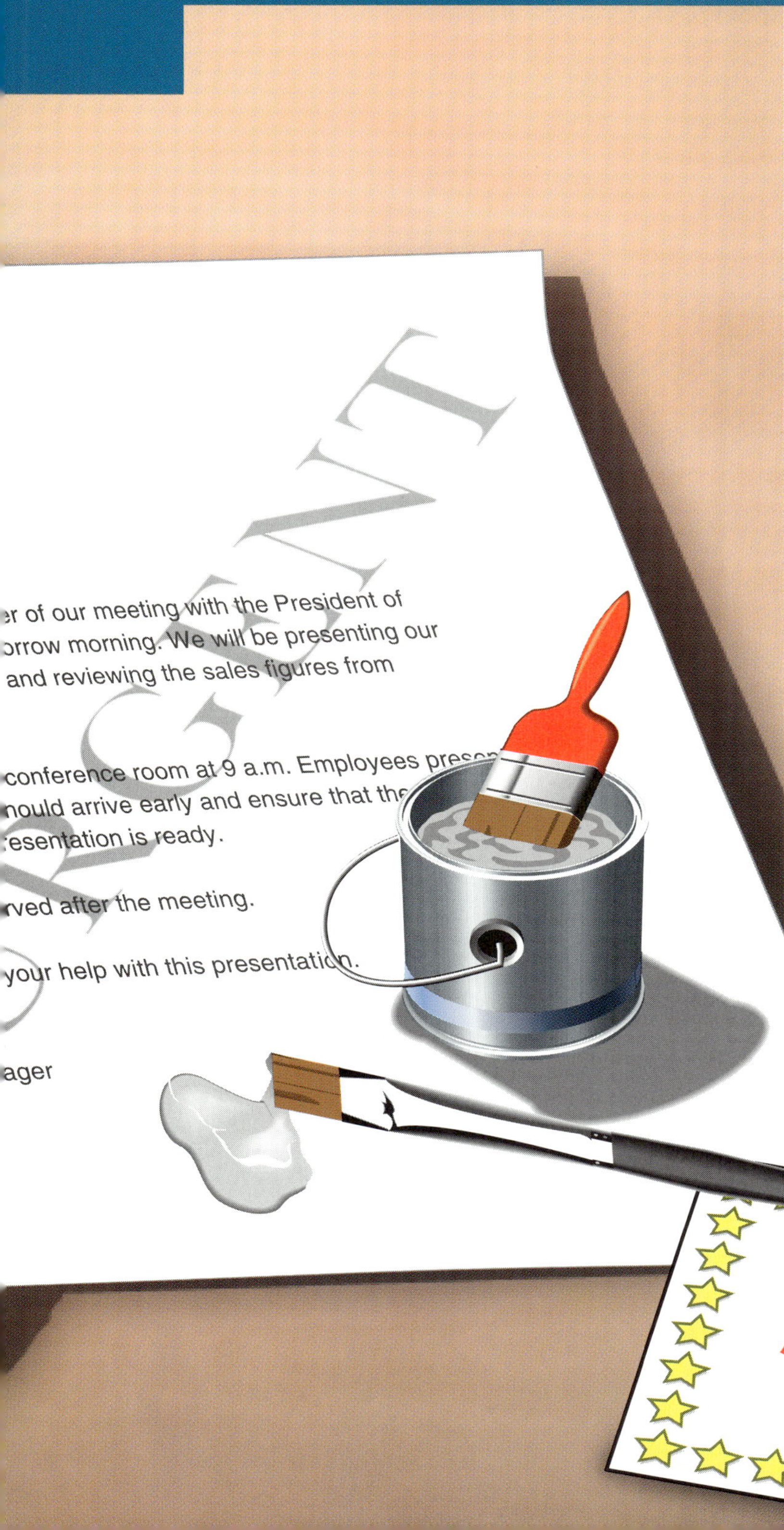

INSERT A PAGE BREAK

You can insert a page break to start a new page at a specific location in your document. A page break indicates where one page ends and another begins.

Inserting a page break is useful when you want a heading to appear at the top of a new page.

INSERT A PAGE BREAK

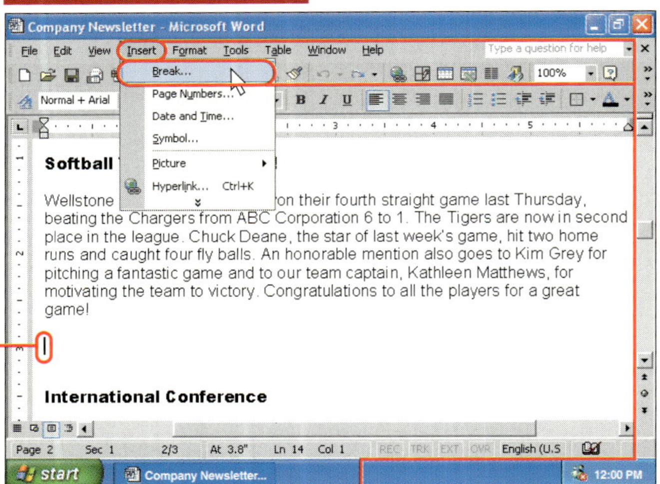

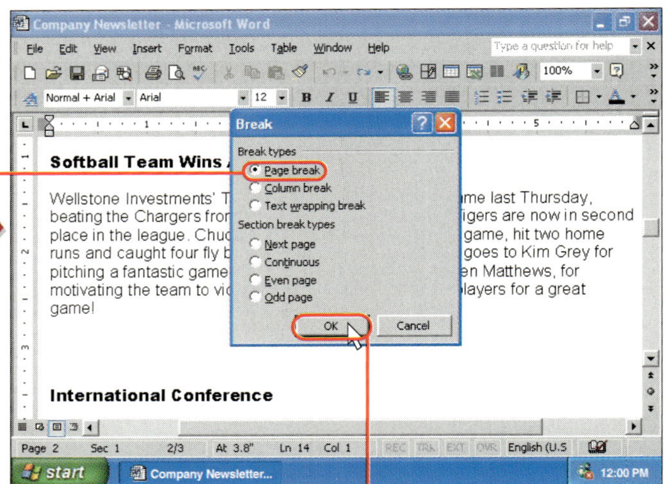

1 Click the location in your document where you want to start a new page.

2 Click **Insert**.

3 Click **Break**.

■ The Break dialog box appears.

4 Click this option to add a page break to your document (○ changes to ◉).

5 Click **OK** to confirm your selection.

■ Word adds the page break to your document.

Will Word ever insert a page break automatically?

When you fill a page with information, Word automatically inserts a page break to start a new page.

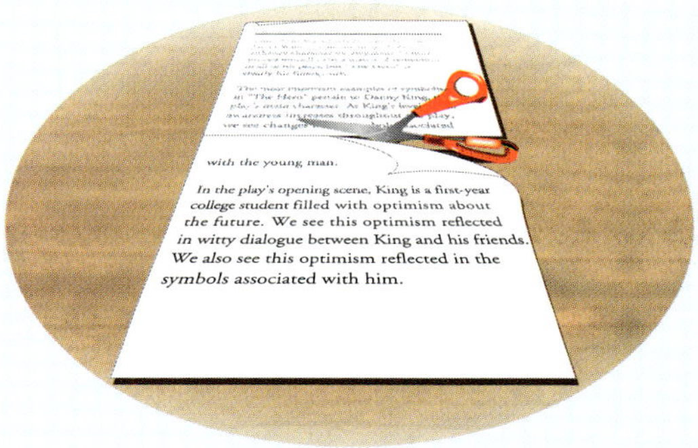

How can I quickly insert a page break?

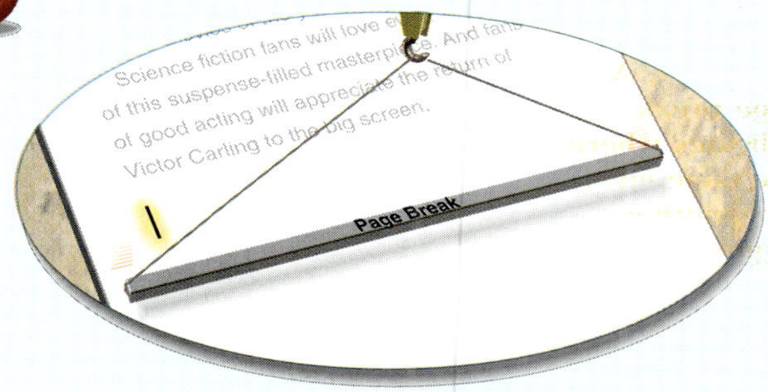

1 Click the location in your document where you want to insert a page break.

2 Press and hold down the **Ctrl** key as you press the **Enter** key.

DELETE A PAGE BREAK

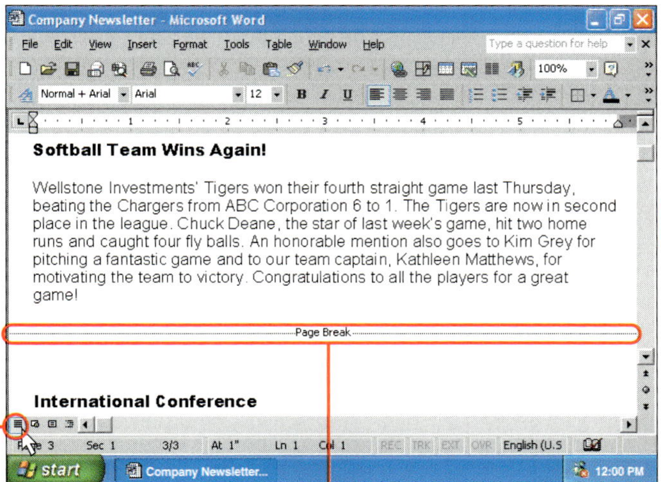

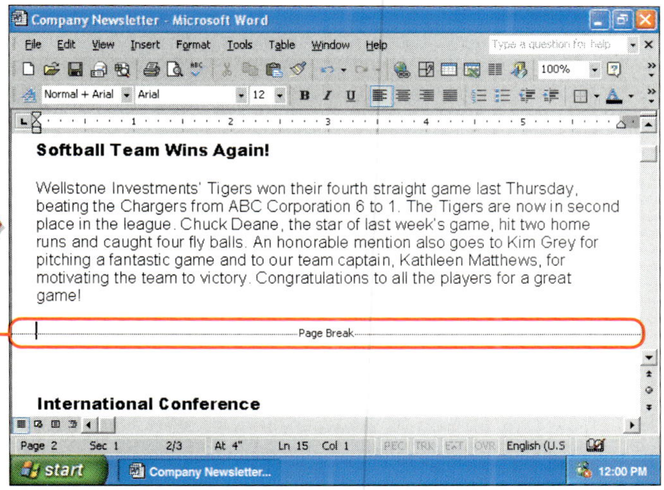

1 Click ▤ to display your document in the Normal view.

■ The **Page Break** line shows where one page ends and another begins. The line will not appear when you print your document.

Note: You may need to scroll through your document to view the line.

2 Click the **Page Break** line.

3 Press the **Delete** key to remove the page break.

INSERT A SECTION BREAK

You can insert section breaks to divide your document into sections.

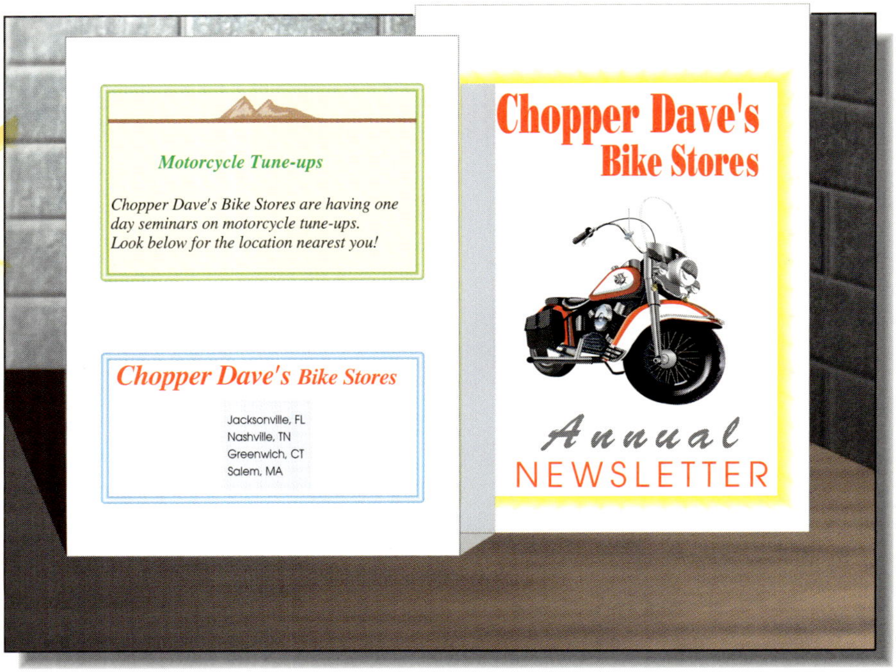

Dividing your document into sections allows you to apply different formatting to each section. For example, you may want to add newspaper columns or change the margins for only part of your document.

INSERT A SECTION BREAK

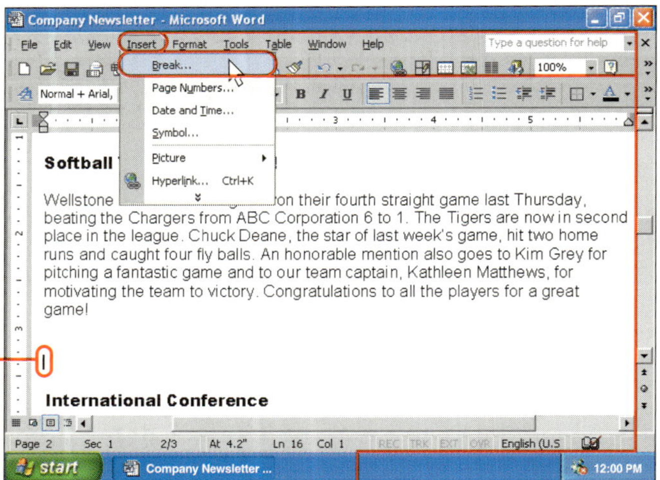

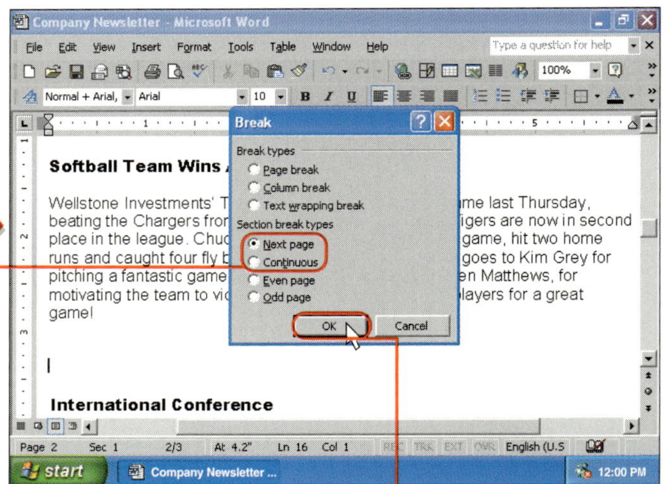

1 Click the location in your document where you want to start a new section.

2 Click **Insert**.

3 Click **Break**.

■ The Break dialog box appears.

4 Click the type of section break you want to add (○ changes to ⊙).

Next page - Starts a new section on a new page.

Continuous - Starts a new section on the current page.

5 Click **OK** to confirm your selection.

■ Word adds the section break to your document.

Will the appearance of my document change when I delete a section break?

When you delete a section break, the text above the break assumes the appearance of the text below the break. For example, if the text below a section break appears in newspaper columns, the text above the break will also appear in newspaper columns when you delete the break.

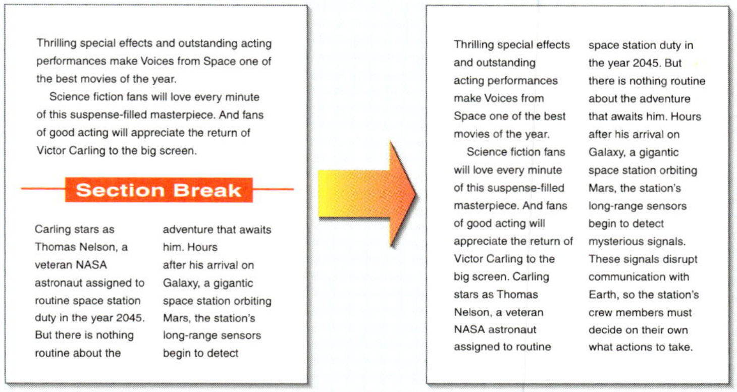

DELETE A SECTION BREAK

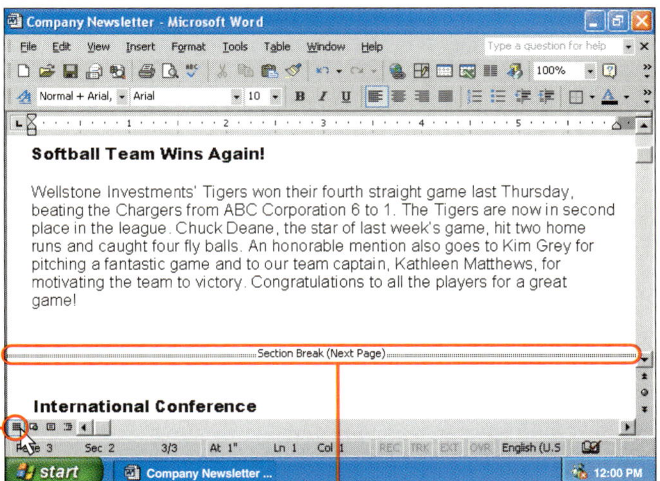

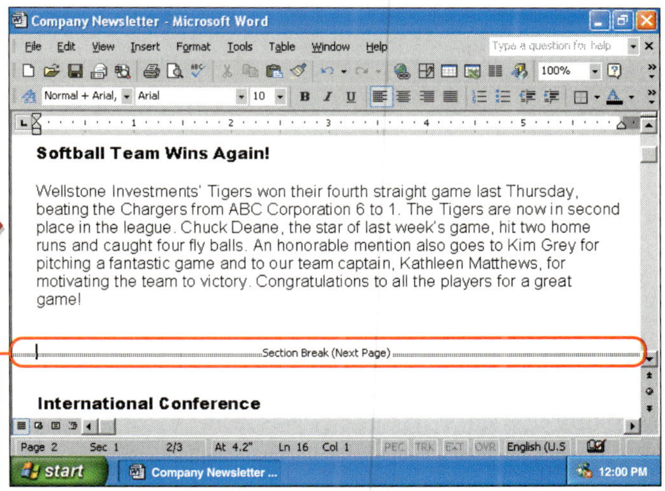

1 Click ▤ to display your document in the Normal view.

■ The **Section Break** line shows where one section ends and another begins. The line will not appear when you print your document.

Note: You may need to scroll through your document to view the line.

2 Click the **Section Break** line.

3 Press the Delete key to remove the section break.

ADD PAGE NUMBERS

You can have Word number the pages in your document.

Word can display page numbers only in the Print Layout view. To change the view of a document, see page 40.

ADD PAGE NUMBERS

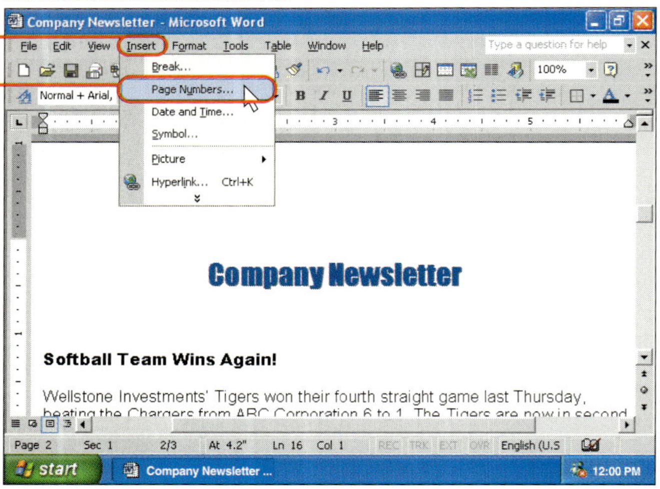

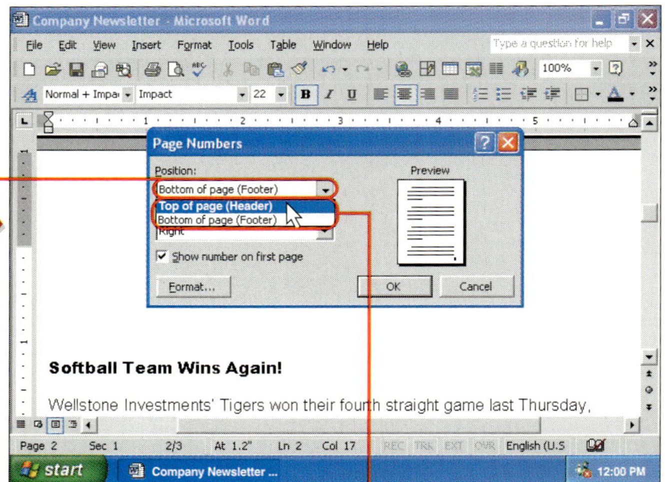

1 Click **Insert**.

2 Click **Page Numbers**.

■ The Page Numbers dialog box appears.

3 Click this area to select a position for the page numbers.

4 Click the position where you want the page numbers to appear.

How do I remove page numbers from my document?

Deleting a page number from your document's header or footer will remove all the page numbers from your document.

1 Double-click a page number to display the Header or Footer area.

2 Double-click the page number to select the number.

3 Press the **Delete** key to delete the page number.

Note: To close the Header or Footer area, click the ***Close*** *button on the Header and Footer toolbar.*

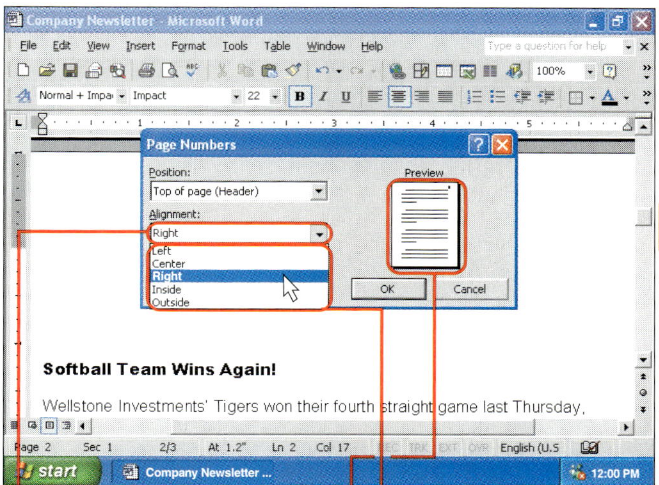

5 Click this area to select an alignment for the page numbers.

6 Click the alignment you want to use.

■ This area displays a preview of the position and alignment you selected for the page numbers.

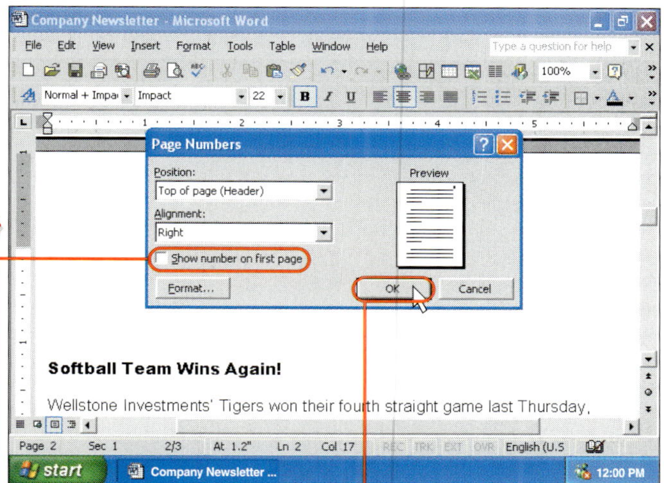

7 If you want to hide the page number on the first page of your document, click this option (☑ changes to ☐).

Note: Turning off this option is useful if the first page in your document is a title page.

8 Click **OK** to add the page numbers to your document.

■ If you later make changes that affect the pages in your document, such as adding or removing text, Word will automatically adjust the page numbers for you.

ADD A HEADER OR FOOTER

You can add a header or footer to display additional information on each page of your document. A header or footer can contain information such as a chapter title, a page number or the current date.

A **header** appears at the top of each printed page.

A **footer** appears at the bottom of each printed page.

Word can display headers and footers only in the Print Layout view. To change the view of a document, see page 40.

ADD A HEADER OR FOOTER

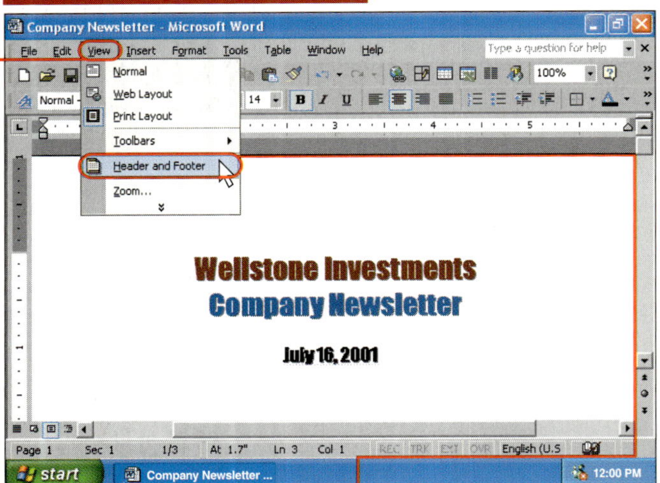

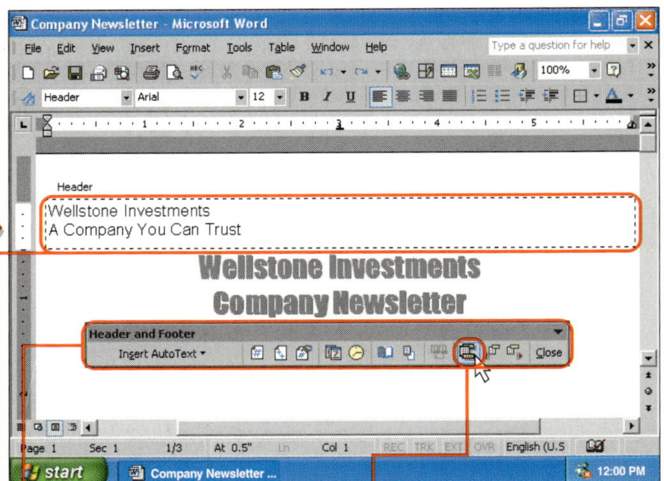

1 Click **View**.

2 Click **Header and Footer**.

■ The Header and Footer toolbar appears.

■ The text in your document is dimmed.

3 To add a header, type the header text.

Note: You can format header text as you would format any text in a document. To format text, see pages 88 to 97.

4 Click ▣ to display the Footer area.

Can I edit a header or footer?

Yes. Double-click the dimmed text for the header or footer you want to edit. You can then edit the header or footer text as you would edit any text in a document. To edit text, see page 54. When you finish editing header or footer text, perform step **6** below.

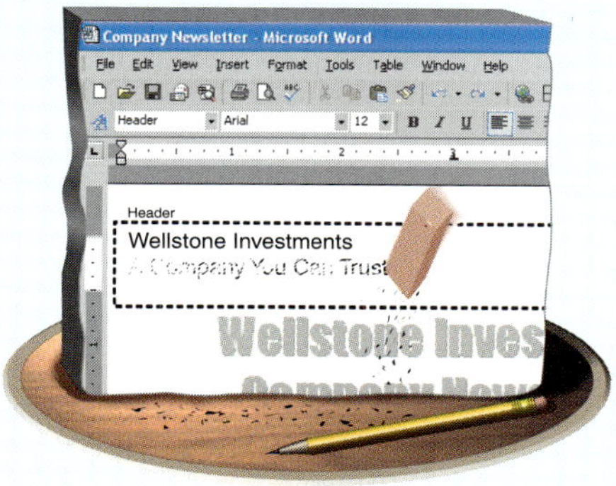

How do I remove a header or footer from my document?

Double-click the dimmed text for the header or footer you want to remove. Drag the mouse over the header or footer text until you highlight all the text. Then press the Delete key to remove the header or footer from your document. When you finish deleting header or footer text, perform step **6** below.

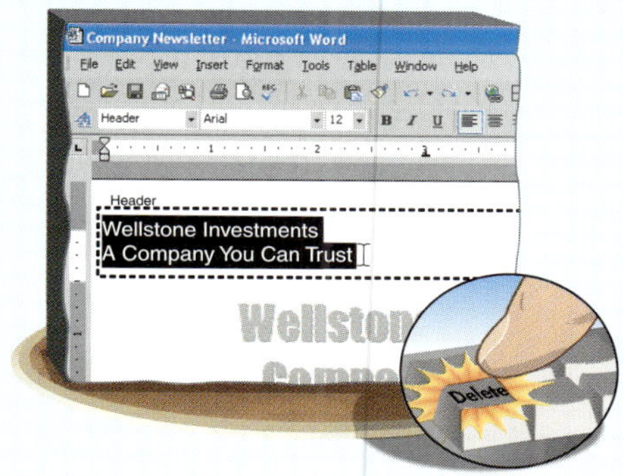

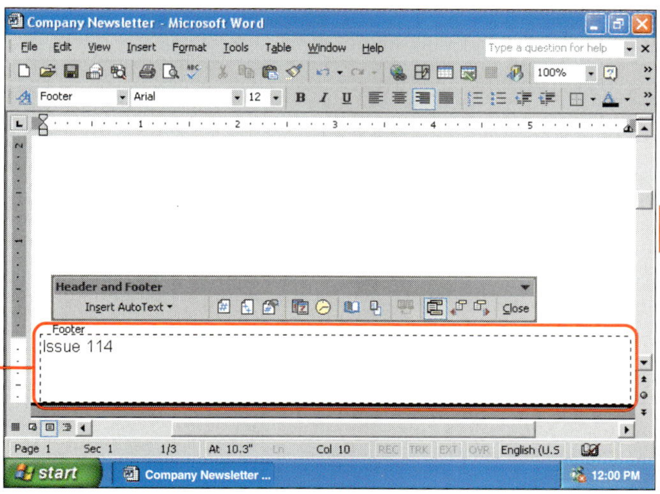

- The Footer area appears.

Note: You can repeat step ***4*** *to return to the Header area at any time.*

5 To add a footer, type the footer text.

Note: You can format footer text as you would format any text in a document. To format text, see pages 88 to 97.

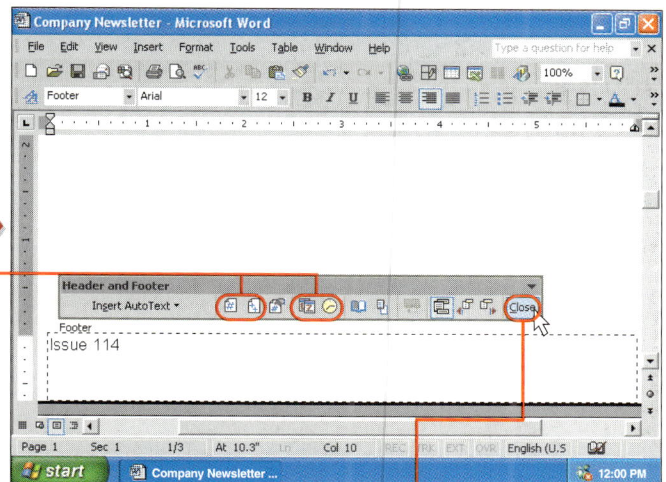

- You can click one of the following buttons to quickly insert information into a header or footer.

  - Page number
  - Total number of pages
  - Date
  - Time

6 When you finish adding the header and footer to your document, click **Close**.

CONTINUED

ADD A HEADER OR FOOTER

You can add different headers and footers to different pages in your document.

VARY HEADERS OR FOOTERS WITHIN A DOCUMENT

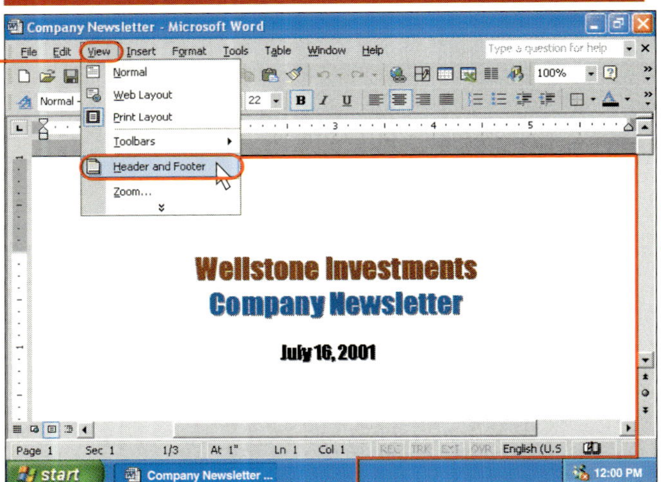

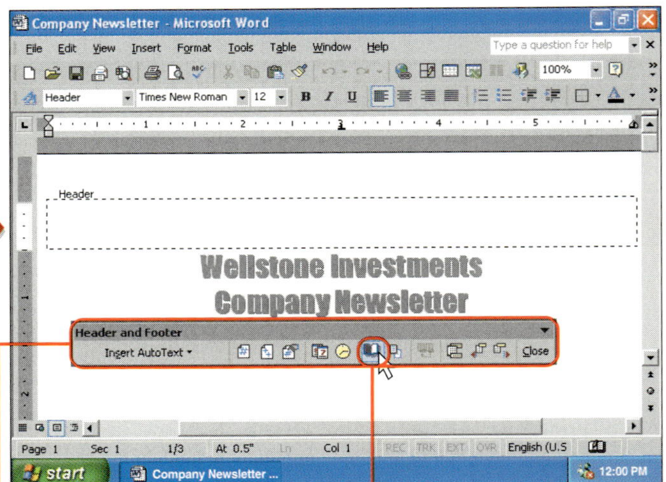

1 Click **View**.

2 Click **Header and Footer**.

■ The Header and Footer toolbar appears.

■ The text in your document is dimmed.

3 Click to set up different headers and footers for different pages in your document.

■ The Page Setup dialog box appears.

TEACH YOURSELF TY

What Header and Footer areas does Word provide?

Word offers the following Header and Footer areas. The Header and Footer areas available in your document depend on the options you select in steps **4** and **5** below.

First Page Header/Footer

The text you type in this area only appears on the first page of the document.

Note: If you do not want a header or footer on the first page, leave this area blank.

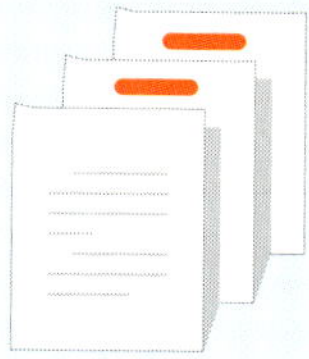

Header/Footer

The text you type in this area appears on all but the first page of the document.

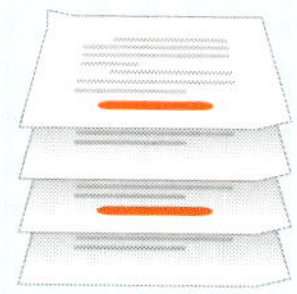

Odd Page Header/Footer

The text you type in this area appears on each odd-numbered page in the document.

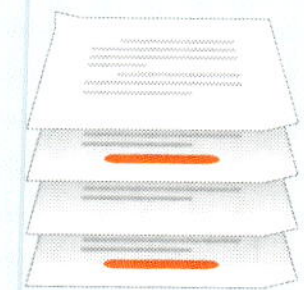

Even Page Header/Footer

The text you type in this area appears on each even-numbered page in the document.

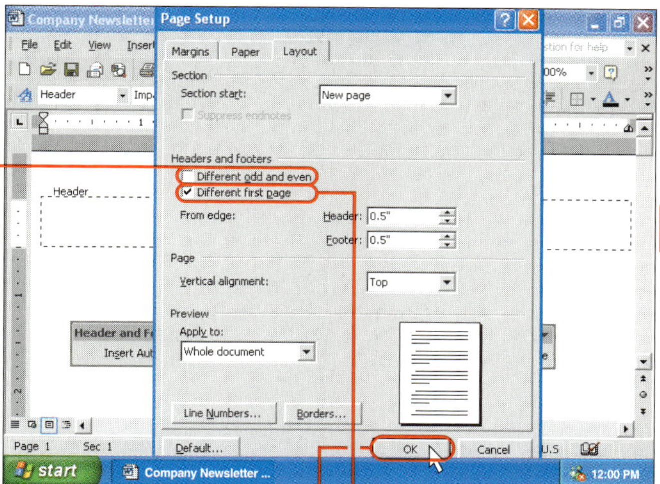

4 To display one header and footer on odd-numbered pages and a different header and footer on even-numbered pages, click this option (☐ changes to ☑).

5 To display one header and footer on the first page and a different header and footer on all the other pages, click this option (☐ changes to ☑).

6 Click **OK** to confirm your changes.

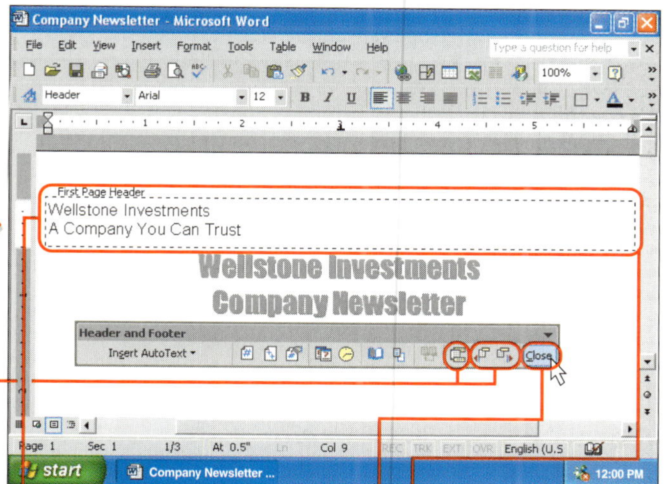

■ The first Header area appears.

■ You can click [icon] to switch between the Header and Footer areas on the current page.

■ You can click [icon] or [icon] to display the previous or next Header or Footer area.

7 Type the header or footer text for each area.

8 When you have finished adding headers and footers to your document, click **Close**.

ADD FOOTNOTES OR ENDNOTES

You can add a footnote or endnote to provide additional information about text in your document. Footnotes and endnotes can provide information such as an explanation, comment or reference.

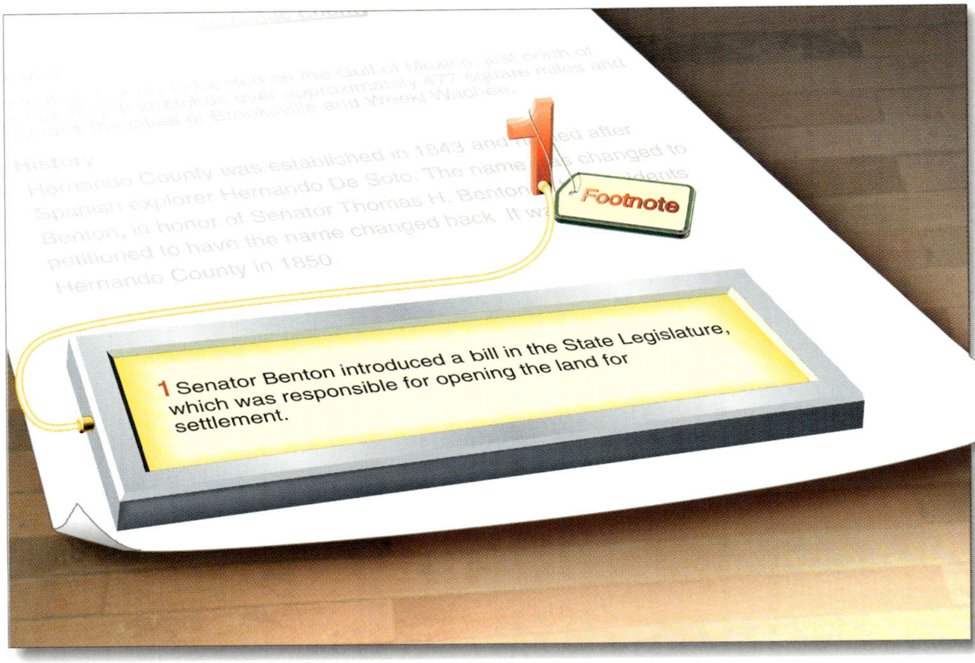

Word displays footnotes and endnotes as they will appear on a printed page in the Print Layout view. For information on the views, see page 40.

ADD FOOTNOTES OR ENDNOTES

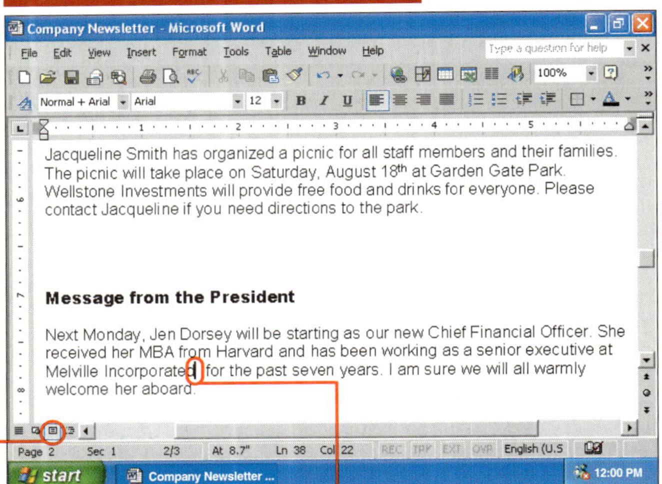

1 Click ▤ to display your document in the Print Layout view.

2 Click the location in your document where you want the number for the footnote or endnote to appear.

Note: The footnote or endnote number will appear where the insertion point flashes on your screen.

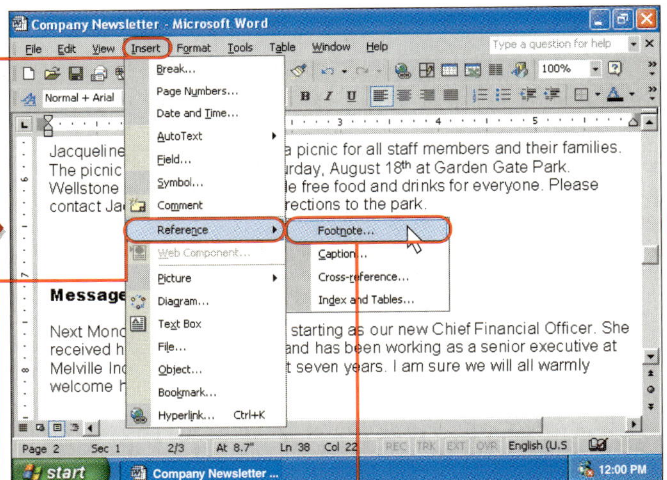

3 Click **Insert**.

4 Click **Reference**.

Note: If Reference does not appear on the menu, position the mouse ↖ over the bottom of the menu to display all the menu options.

5 Click **Footnote**.

What is the difference between footnotes and endnotes?

Footnotes

By default, Footnotes appear at the bottom of a page. Word ensures that the text for a footnote appears on the same page as the footnote number.

Endnotes

By default, Endnotes appear at the end of a document.

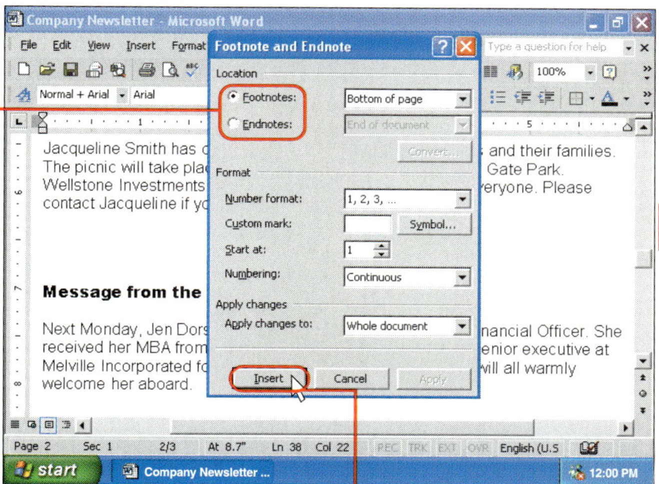

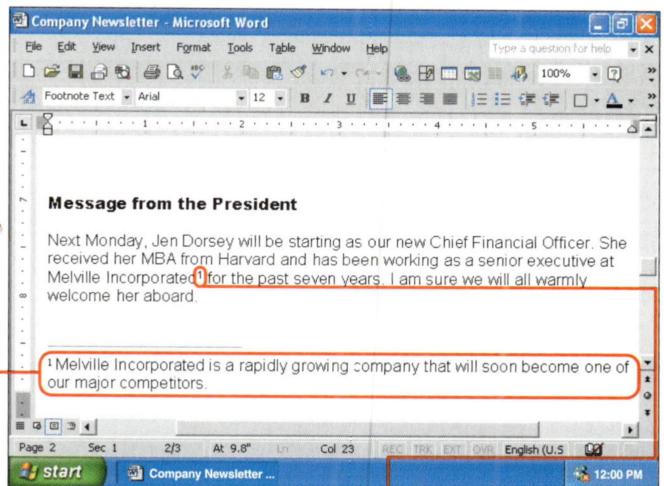

■ The Footnote and Endnote dialog box appears.

6 Click **Footnotes** or **Endnotes** to specify the type of note you want to add (○ changes to ⊙).

7 Click **Insert** to add the note to your document.

■ Word displays the footnote or endnote area.

8 Type the text for the footnote or endnote. You can format the text as you would format any text in a document. To format text, see pages 88 to 97.

■ The number for the footnote or endnote appears in your document.

Note: You may need to scroll through your document to view the number.

CONTINUED

ADD FOOTNOTES OR ENDNOTES

You can view and edit a footnote or endnote you added to your document. You can also delete a footnote or endnote you no longer need.

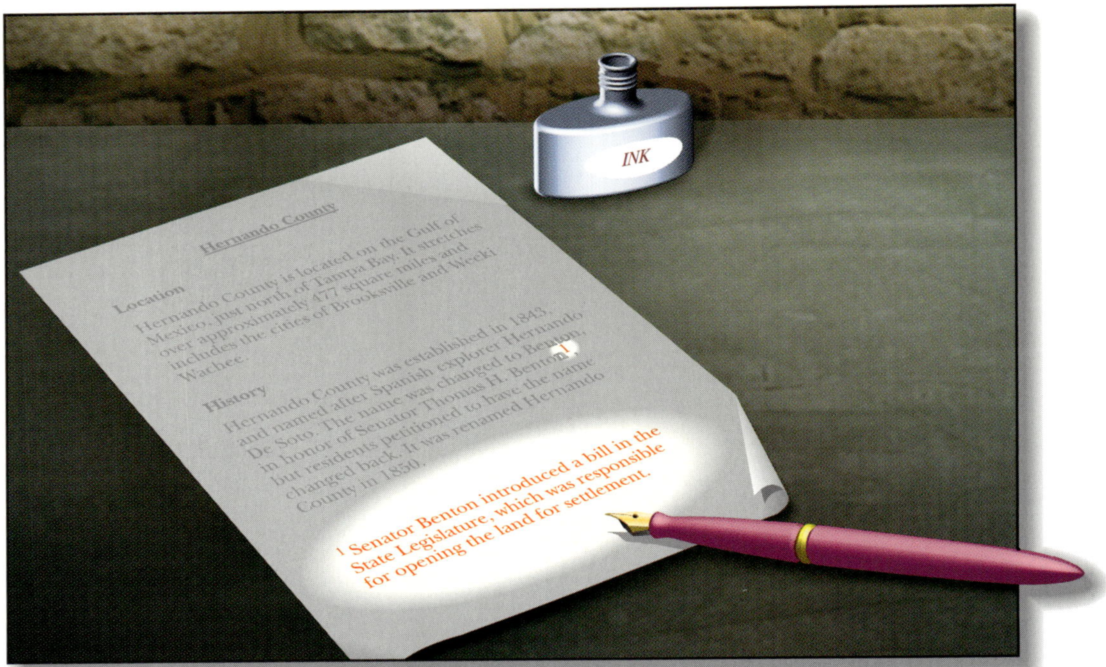

VIEW FOOTNOTES OR ENDNOTES

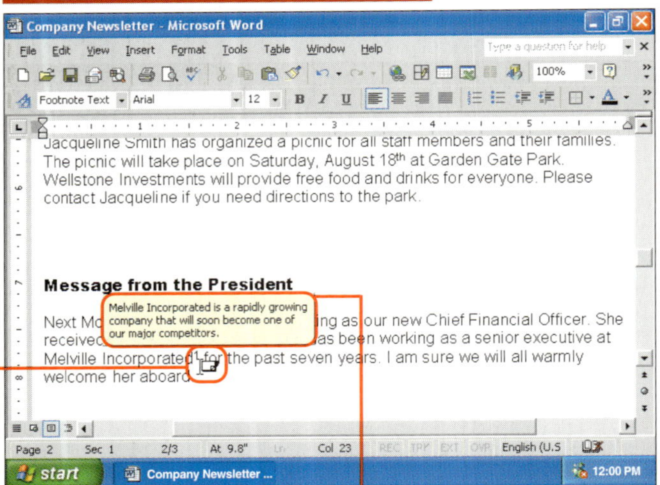

1 To view the text for a footnote or endnote, position the mouse [I-beam] over the footnote or endnote number in your document ([I-beam] changes to [footnote pointer]).

■ A yellow box appears, displaying the text for the footnote or endnote.

EDIT FOOTNOTES OR ENDNOTES

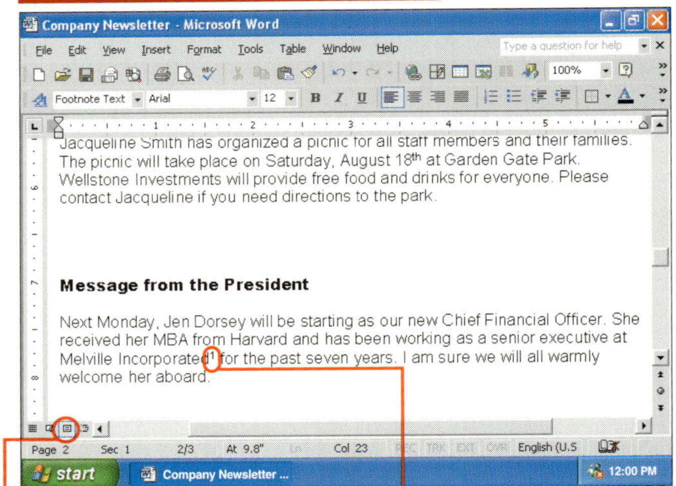

1 Click [Print Layout button] to display your document in the Print Layout view.

2 To edit the text for a footnote or endnote, double-click the footnote or endnote number in your document.

How can I print endnotes on a separate page?

Word automatically prints endnotes after the last line in your document. To print endnotes on a separate page, you need to insert a page break directly above the endnote area. To insert a page break, see page 142.

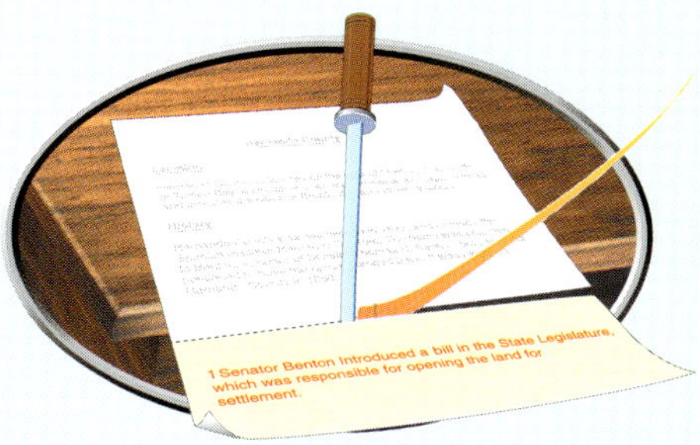

Can I copy a footnote or endnote?

Yes. Copying a footnote or endnote is useful when you want to provide the same comment or reference for several areas of text.

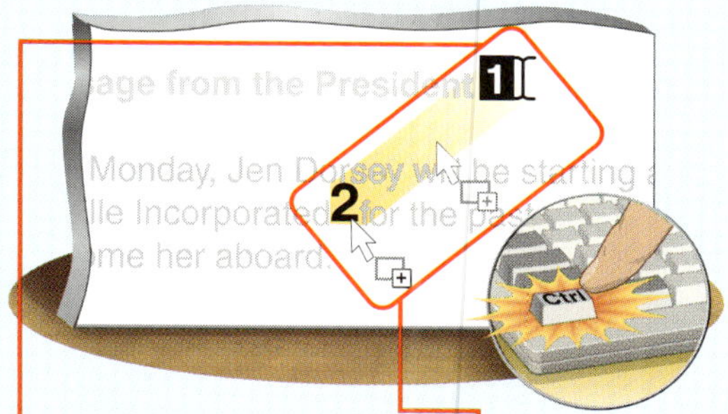

1 To copy a note, drag the mouse I over the footnote or endnote number until you highlight the number.

2 Press and hold down the Ctrl key as you drag the number to a new location.

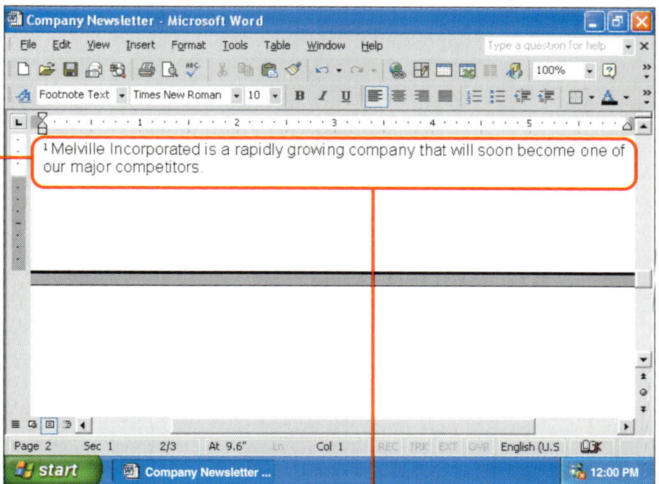

■ The corresponding footnote or endnote area appears.

■ You can edit the text for a footnote or endnote as you would edit any text in a document. To edit text, see page 54.

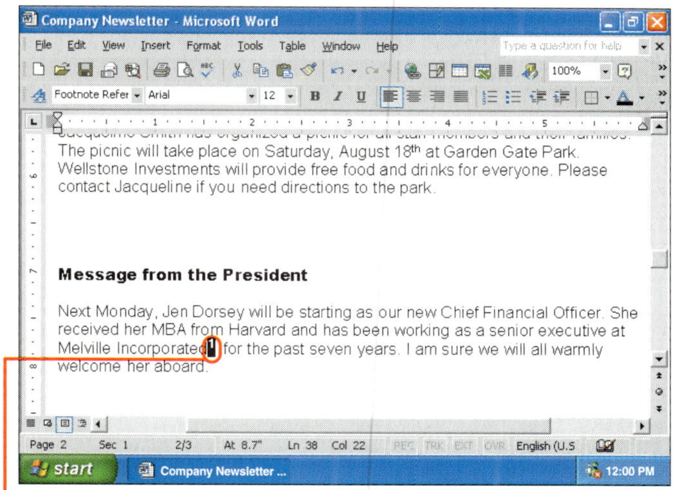

DELETE FOOTNOTES OR ENDNOTES

1 Drag the mouse I over the number for the footnote or endnote you want to delete until you highlight the number.

2 Press the Delete key.

■ The footnote or endnote disappears from your document.

■ Word automatically renumbers the remaining footnotes or endnotes in your document.

CHANGE MARGINS

You can change the margins in your document to suit your needs. A margin is the space between the text in your document and the edge of your paper.

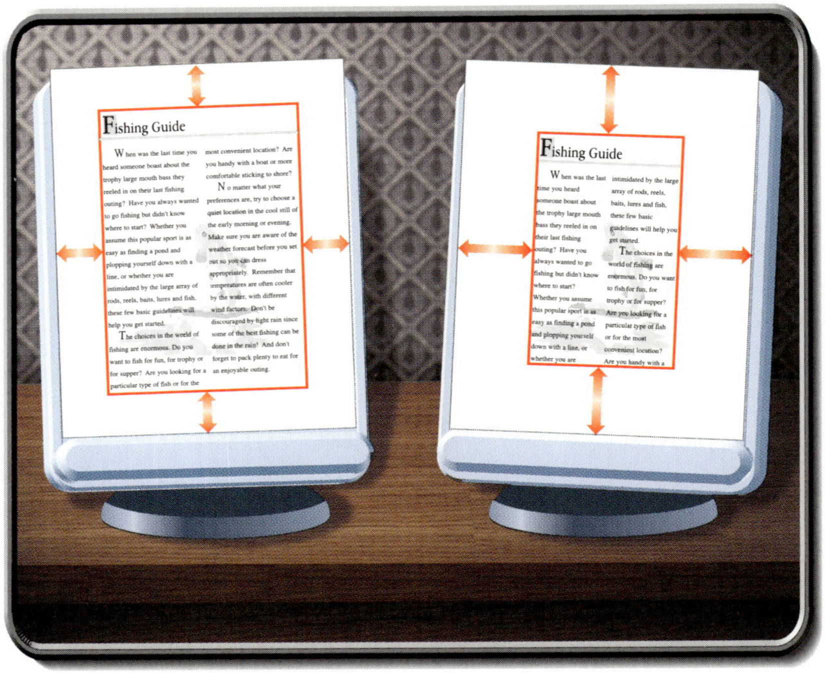

Word automatically sets the top and bottom margins to 1 inch and the left and right margins to 1.25 inches.

Changing the margins allows you to fit more or less information on a page and can help you accommodate letterhead and other specialty paper.

CHANGE MARGINS

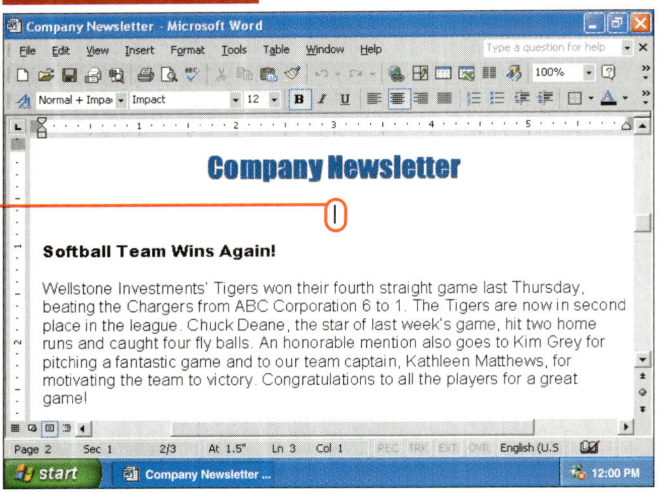

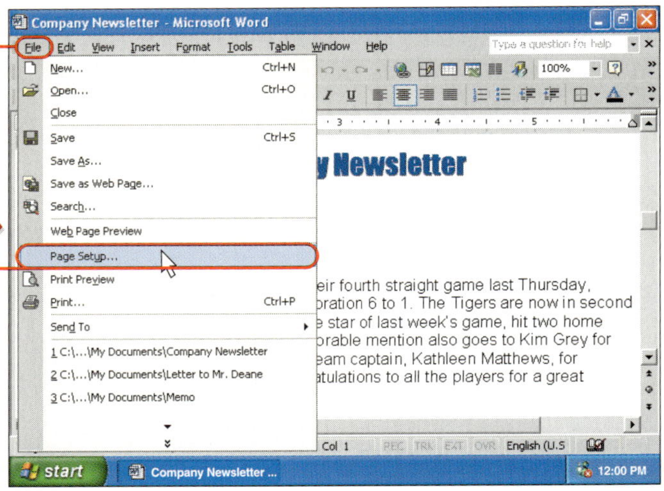

1 Click anywhere in the document or section where you want to change the margins.

Note: To change the margins for only part of your document, you must divide the document into sections. To divide a document into sections, see page 144.

2 Click **File**.

3 Click **Page Setup**.

■ The Page Setup dialog box appears.

Is there another way to change the margins for my document?

Yes. In the Print Layout view, margins are shown in gray on the ruler. To change a margin, position the mouse ↖ over the edge of the margin (↖ changes to ↔ or ↕) and then drag the margin to a new location on the ruler.

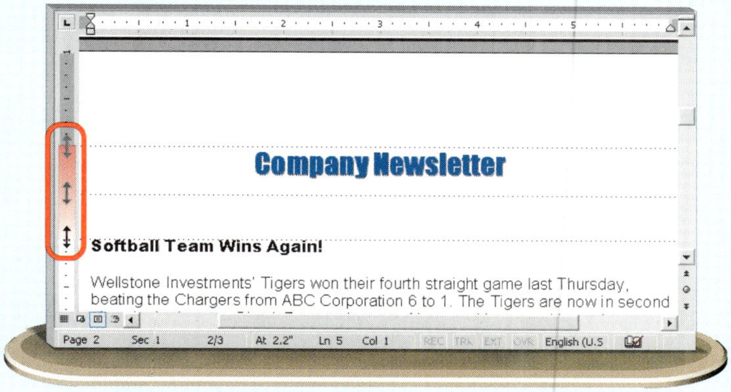

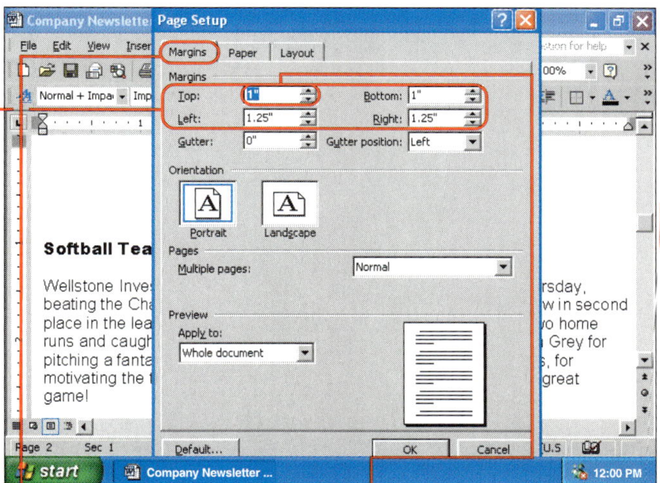

4 Click the **Margins** tab.

■ This area displays the current margins for the document or section.

5 To change a margin, drag the mouse I over the number for the margin you want to change until you highlight the number.

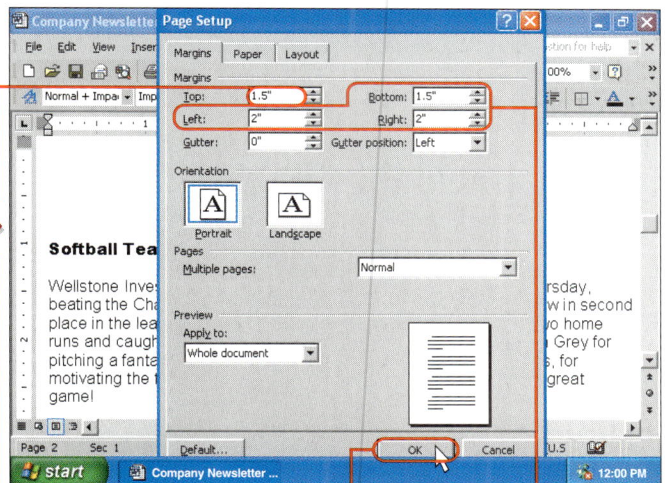

6 Type a new number for the margin.

Note: Margins are measured in inches.

7 Repeat steps **5** and **6** for each margin you want to change.

8 Click **OK** to confirm your changes.

CENTER TEXT ON A PAGE

You can vertically center the text on each page in your document. Vertically centering text is useful when creating title pages and short memos.

When you vertically center text on a page, Word centers the text between the top and bottom margins of the page. For information on margins, see page 156.

Word can display text vertically centered on a page only in the Print Layout view. To change the view of a document, see page 40.

CENTER TEXT ON A PAGE

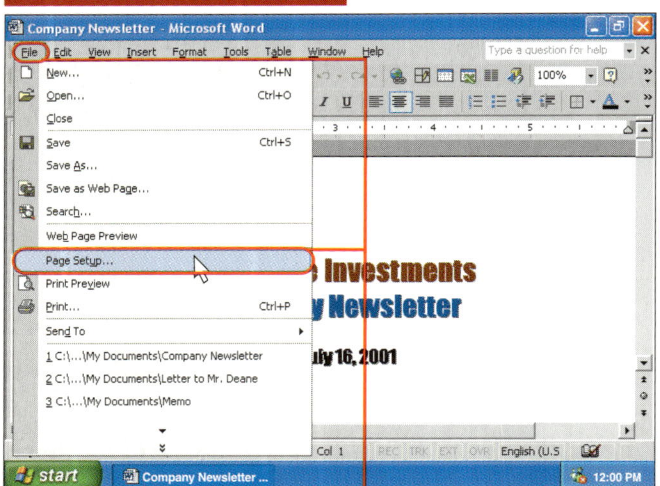

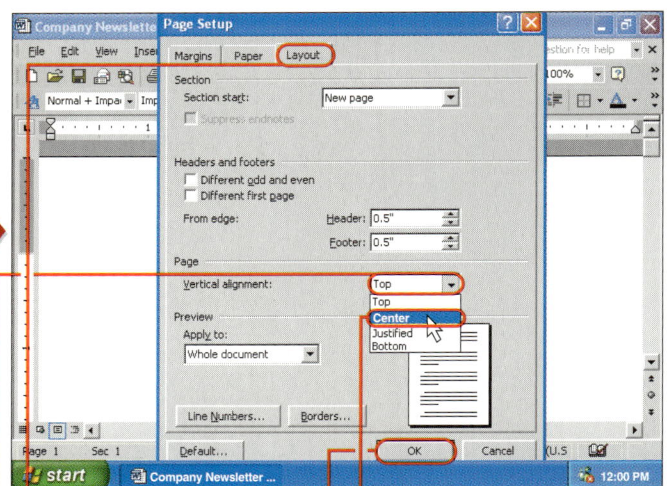

1 Click anywhere in the document or section you want to vertically center.

Note: To vertically center only part of your document, you must divide the document into sections. To divide a document into sections, see page 144.

2 Click **File**.

3 Click **Page Setup**.

■ The Page Setup dialog box appears.

4 Click the **Layout** tab.

5 Click this area to display the vertical alignment options.

6 Click **Center** to vertically center the text.

7 Click **OK** to confirm your change.

■ To remove the centering, repeat steps **1** to **7**, selecting **Top** in step **6**.

CHANGE PAGE ORIENTATION

You can change the orientation of pages in your document. The page orientation determines the direction information prints on a page.

Portrait

Portrait is the standard page orientation and is used to print most documents, such as letters, memos and reports.

Landscape

Landscape prints information across the long side of a page and is often used to print certificates and tables.

CHANGE PAGE ORIENTATION

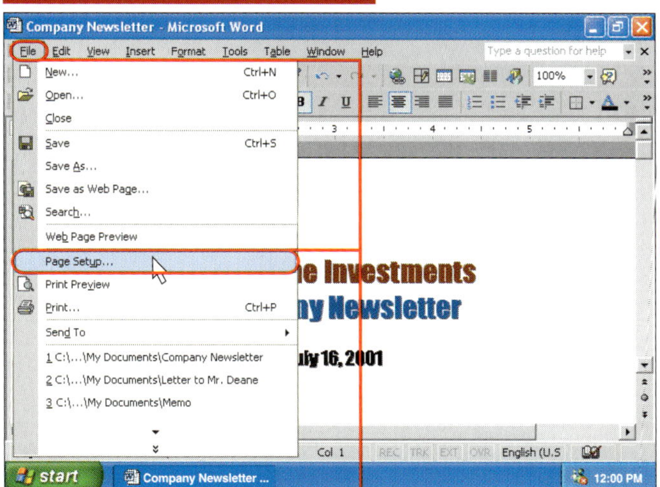

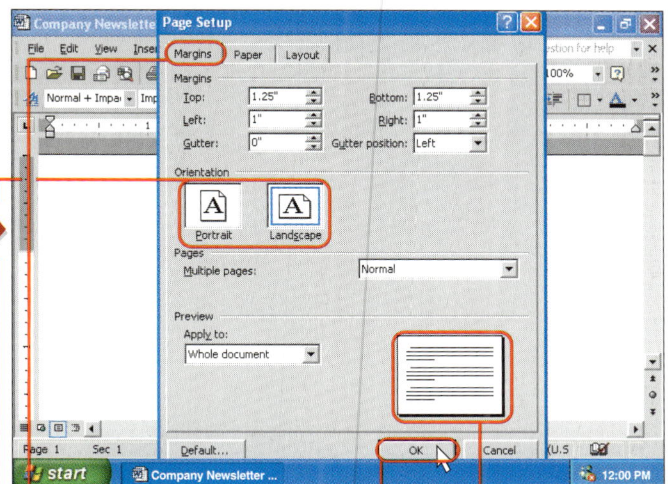

1 Click anywhere in the document or section you want to change to a different page orientation.

Note: To change the page orientation for only part of your document, you must divide the document into sections. To divide a document into sections, see page 144.

2 Click **File**.

3 Click **Page Setup**.

■ The Page Setup dialog box appears.

4 Click the **Margins** tab.

5 Click the page orientation you want to use.

■ This area displays a preview of how your document will appear.

6 Click **OK** to confirm your change.

CONTROL PAGE BREAKS

You can control the page breaks in a long document to tell Word how you want text to flow from one page to the next.

When you fill a page with information, Word automatically inserts a page break to start a new page.

CONTROL PAGE BREAKS

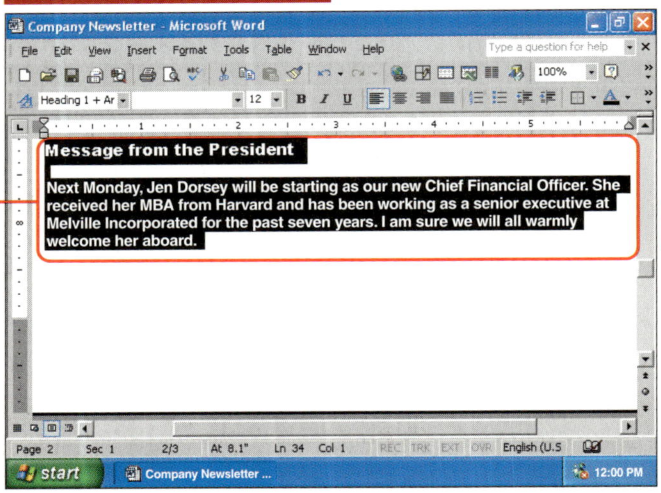

1 Select the paragraphs you want to control page breaks for. To select text, see page 10.

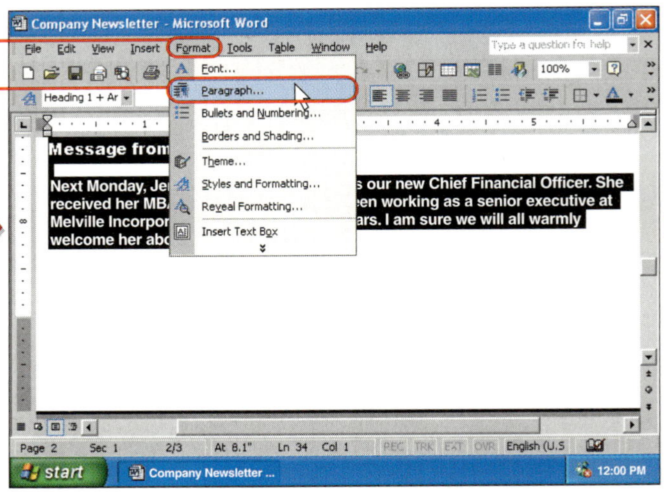

2 Click **Format**.

3 Click **Paragraph**.

■ The Paragraph dialog box appears.

What page break options can I choose?

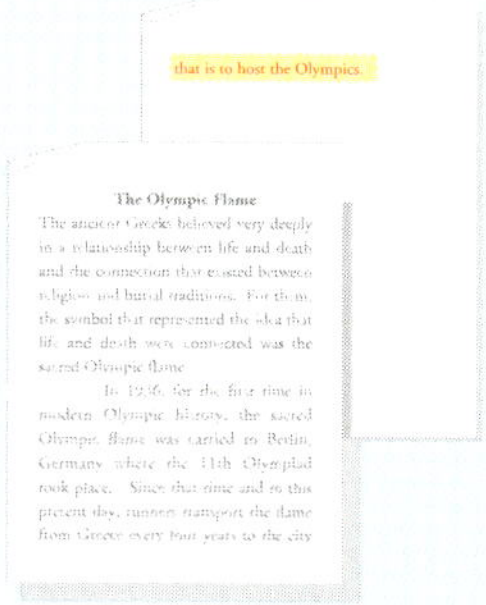

Widow/Orphan control

Prevents a single line from appearing at the top or bottom of a page.

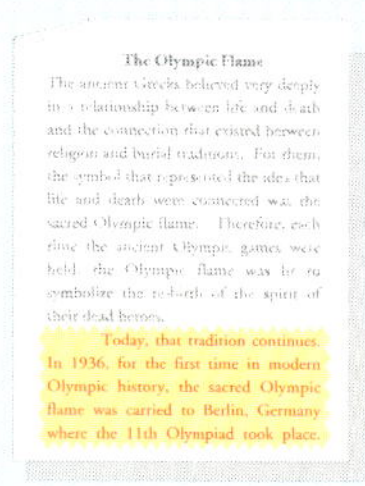

Keep lines together

Keeps all the lines of a paragraph on the same page.

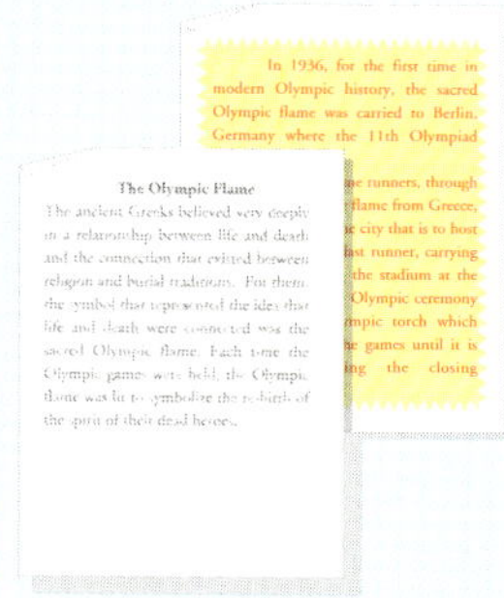

Keep with next

Keeps a paragraph on the same page as the next paragraph.

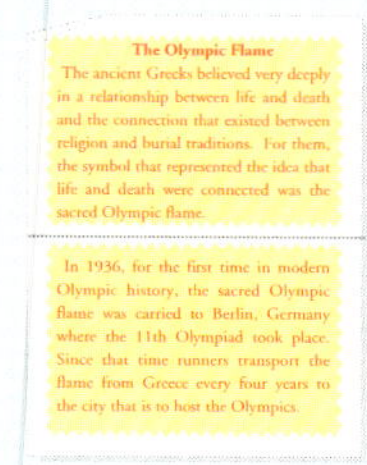

Page break before

Places a page break before a paragraph.

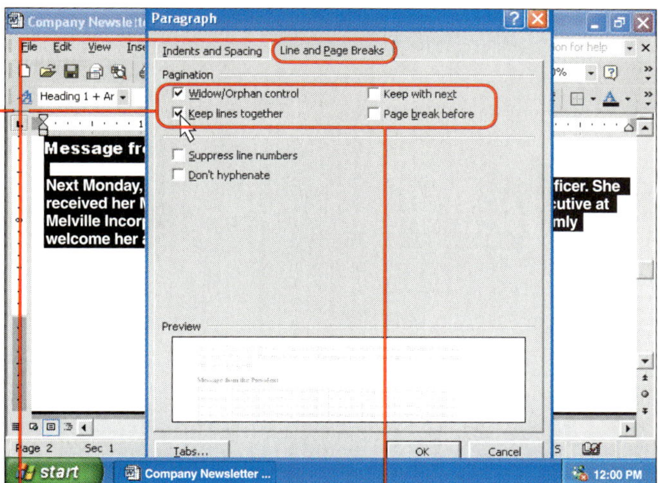

4 Click the **Line and Page Breaks** tab.

■ This area displays the options you can use to control page breaks for the paragraphs you selected.

5 Click an option to turn the option on (☑) or off (☐).

Note: For information on the page break options, see the top of this page.

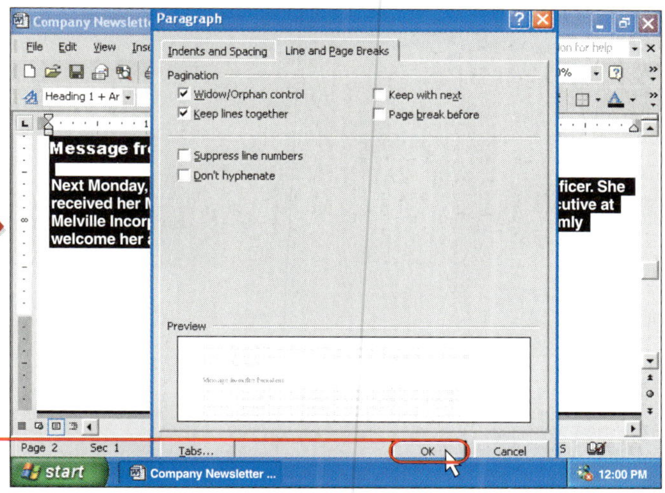

6 Click **OK** to confirm your changes.

■ To deselect text, click outside the selected area.

ADD A WATERMARK

You can add a watermark to your document to display a faint picture or text behind the information in the document. A watermark can add interest to or identify the status of a document.

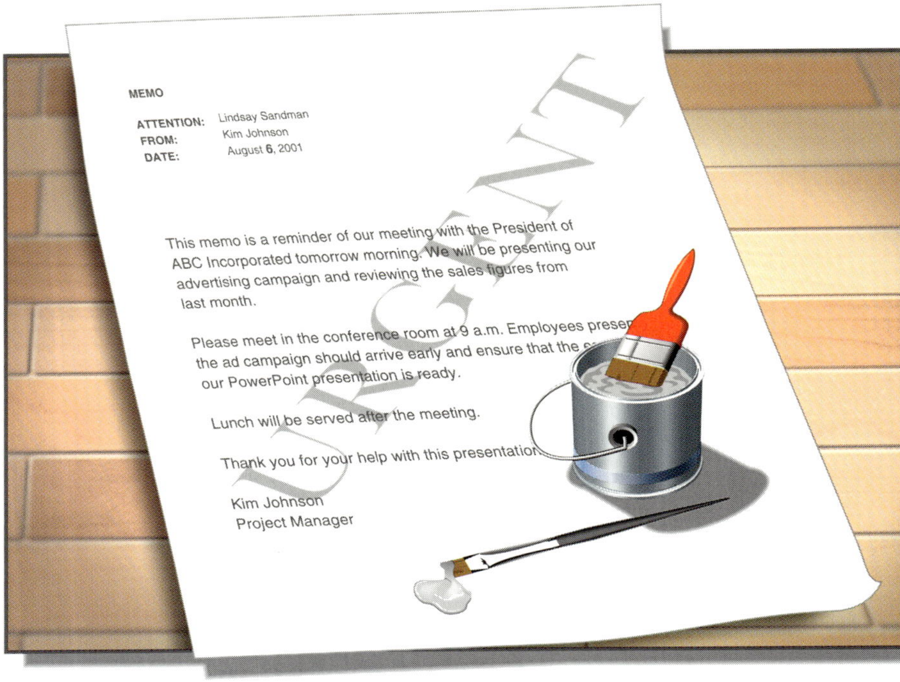

Word can display watermarks only in the Print Layout view. To change the view of a document, see page 40.

ADD A WATERMARK

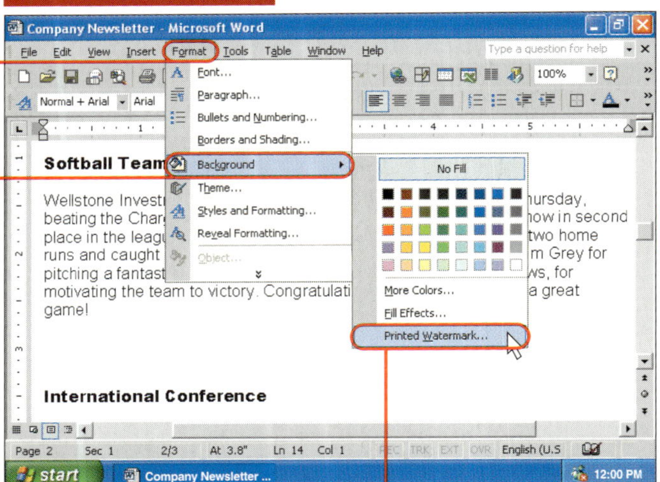

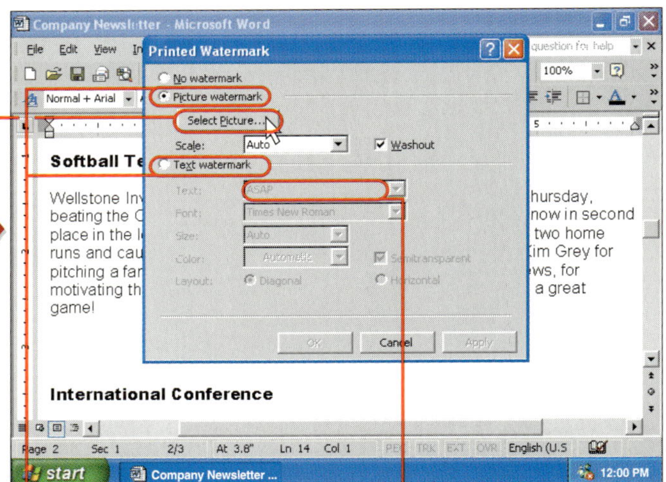

1 Click **Format**.

2 Click **Background**.

Note: If Background does not appear on the menu, position the mouse over the bottom of the menu to display all the menu options.

3 Click **Printed Watermark**.

■ The Printed Watermark dialog box appears.

4 Click an option to specify the type of watermark you want to add (○ changes to ⦿).

5 If you selected **Picture watermark** in step **4**, click **Select Picture** to locate the picture you want to use.

■ If you selected **Text watermark** in step **4**, double-click the text in this area and then type the text you want to use. Then skip to step **8**.

Does Word provide any text watermarks that I can use?

Yes. Word provides several text watermarks including ASAP, CONFIDENTIAL, PERSONAL and URGENT, that you can add to your document.

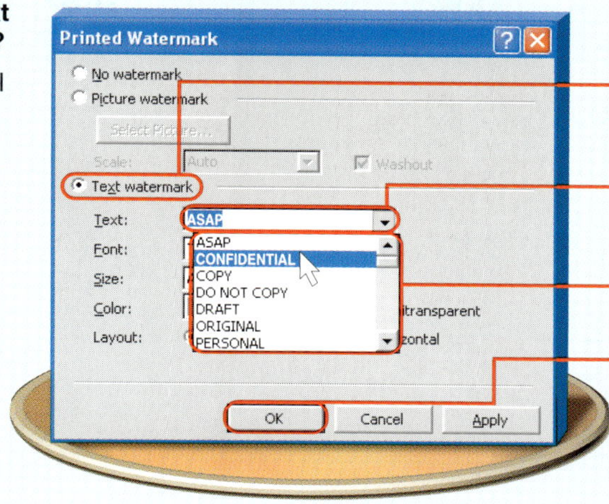

1 Perform steps **1** to **4** below, selecting **Text watermark** in step **4**.

2 Click ▾ in this area to display a list of the available text watermarks.

3 Click the text watermark you want to use.

4 Click **OK** to confirm your change.

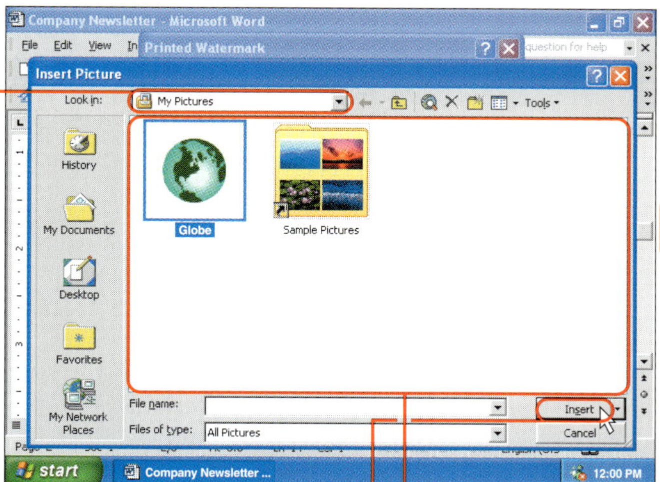

■ The Insert Picture dialog box appears.

■ This area shows the location of the displayed pictures. You can click this area to change the location.

6 Click the picture you want to use for the watermark.

7 Click **Insert**.

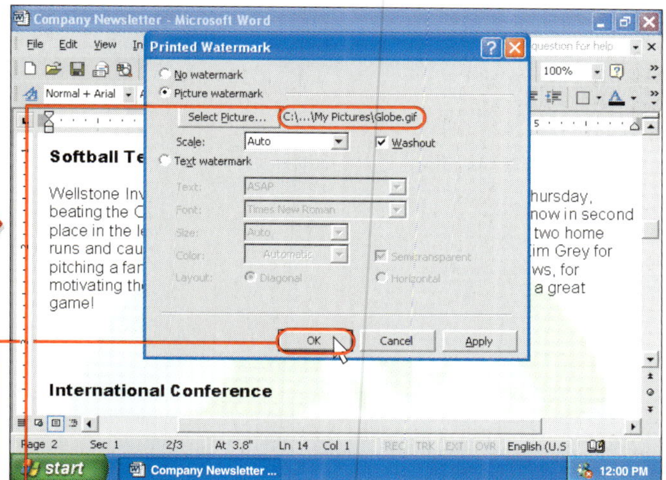

■ This area shows the location and name of the picture you selected.

8 Click **OK** to confirm your change.

■ The watermark appears in your document.

■ To remove a watermark, repeat steps **1** to **4**, selecting **No watermark** in step **4**. Then press the Enter key.

ADD A PAGE BORDER

You can place a border around each page of your document to enhance the appearance of the document.

Word can display page borders only in the Print Layout view. To change the view of a document, see page 40.

Line Borders

You can use a line border for certificates and title pages.

Art Borders

You can use a colorful art border to enhance invitations and newsletters.

ADD A PAGE BORDER

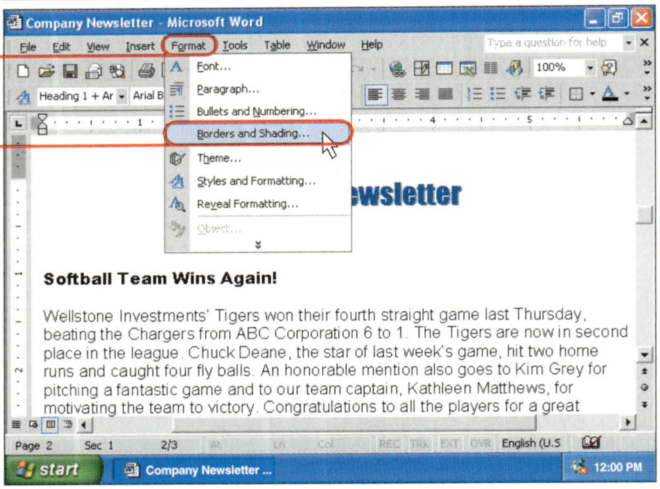

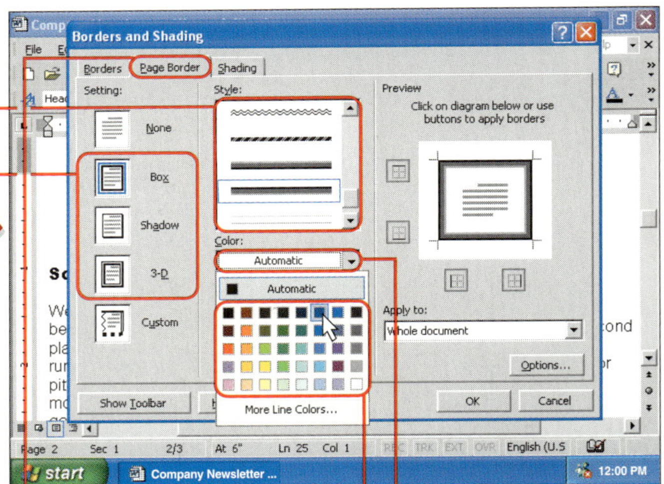

ADD A LINE BORDER

1 Click **Format**.

2 Click **Borders and Shading**.

■ The Borders and Shading dialog box appears.

3 Click the **Page Border** tab.

4 Click the type of line border you want to add.

5 Click the line style you want to use for the border.

6 To select a color for the border, click this area.

7 Click the color you want to use.

Why does a dialog box appear when I try to add an art border to my document?

A dialog box appears if the art borders are not installed on your computer. Insert the CD-ROM disc you used to install Word into your computer's CD-ROM drive. Then click **Yes** to install the art borders.

Note: A window may appear on your screen. Click ✕ in the top right corner of the window to close the window.

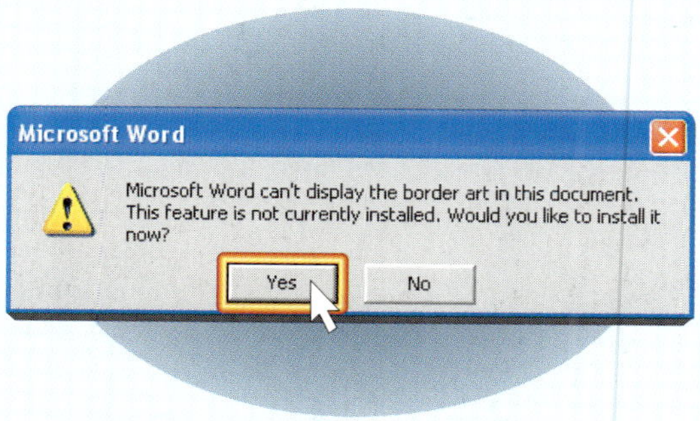

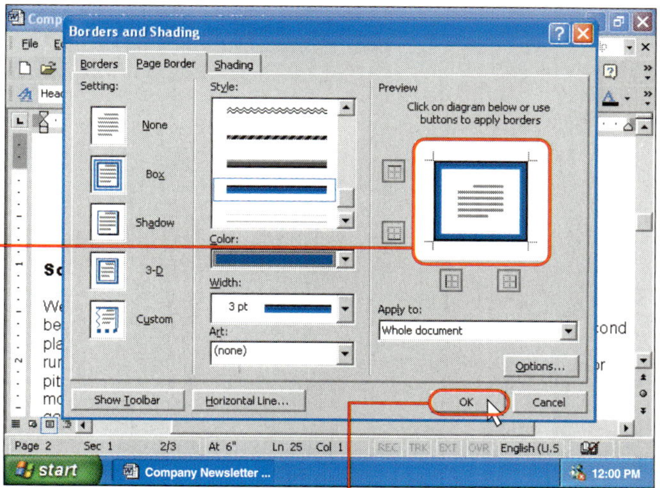

■ This area displays a preview of the border you selected.

8 Click **OK** to add the border to your document.

■ To remove a line border, repeat steps **1** to **4**, selecting **None** in step **4**. Then perform step **8**.

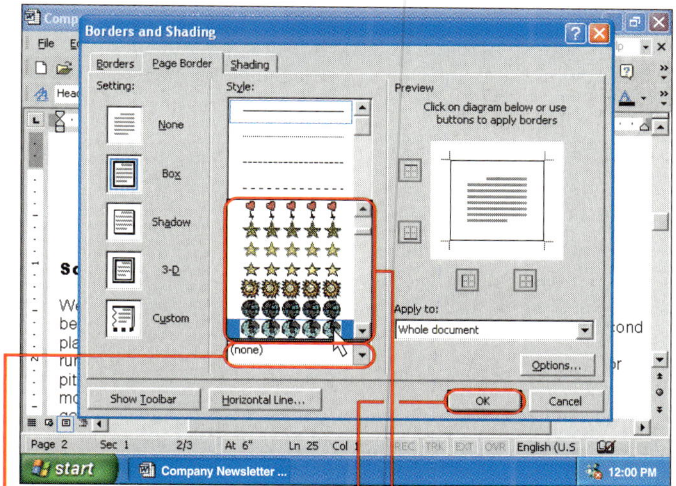

ADD AN ART BORDER

1 Perform steps **1** to **3** on page 164.

2 Click this area to display the available art borders.

Note: If a dialog box appears, see the top of this page.

3 Click the art border you want to use.

4 Click **OK**.

■ To remove an art border, perform steps **1** to **4** on page 164, selecting **None** in step **4**. Then perform step **8**.

CREATE NEWSPAPER COLUMNS

You can display text in columns like those found in a newspaper. Creating columns is useful in documents such as newsletters and brochures.

CREATE NEWSPAPER COLUMNS

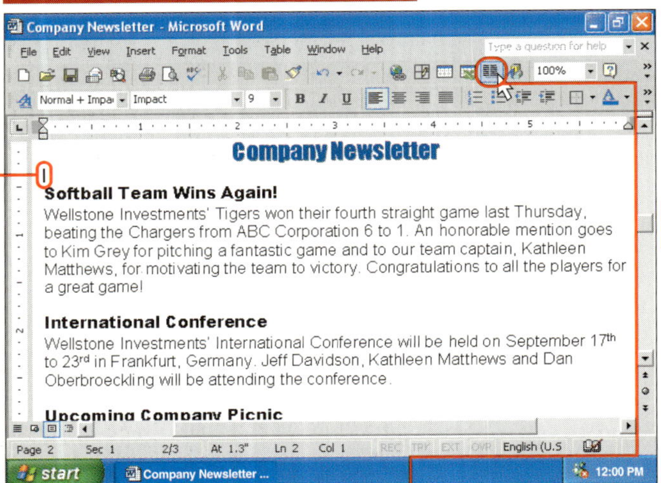

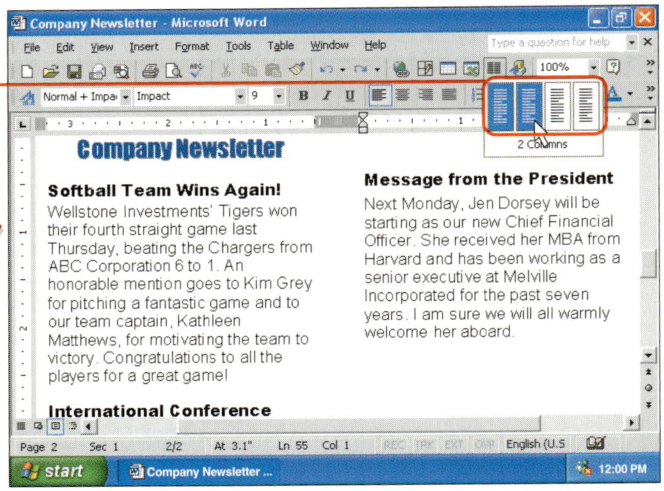

1 Click anywhere in the document or section you want to display in newspaper columns.

Note: To create newspaper columns for only part of your document, you must divide the document into sections. To divide a document into sections, see page 144.

2 Click ▤ to create newspaper columns.

Note: If ▤ is not displayed, click » on the Standard toolbar to display the button.

3 Drag the mouse ↖ until you highlight the number of columns you want to create.

■ The text in the document or section appears in newspaper columns.

■ Word will fill one column with text before starting a new column.

■ To remove newspaper columns, repeat steps **1** to **3**, selecting one column in step **3**.

Why do the newspaper columns disappear when I change the view of my document?

Word can display newspaper columns side by side only in the Print Layout view. To change the view of a document, see page 40.

How do I remove a column break?

If you want to move text back to the previous column, you can remove a column break.

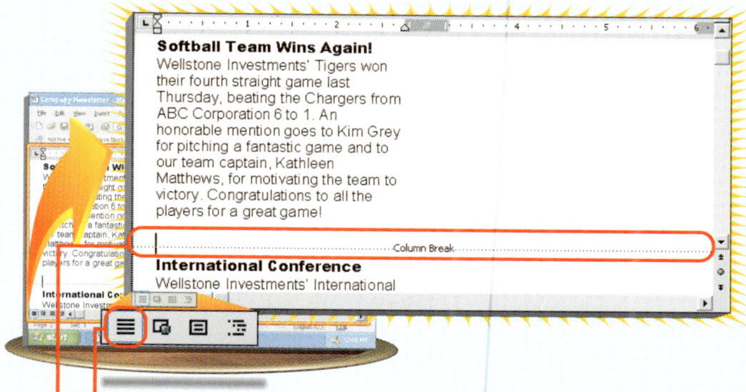

1 Click ☰ to display your document in the Normal view.

2 Click the **Column Break** line.

3 Press the Delete key to remove the column break.

INSERT A COLUMN BREAK

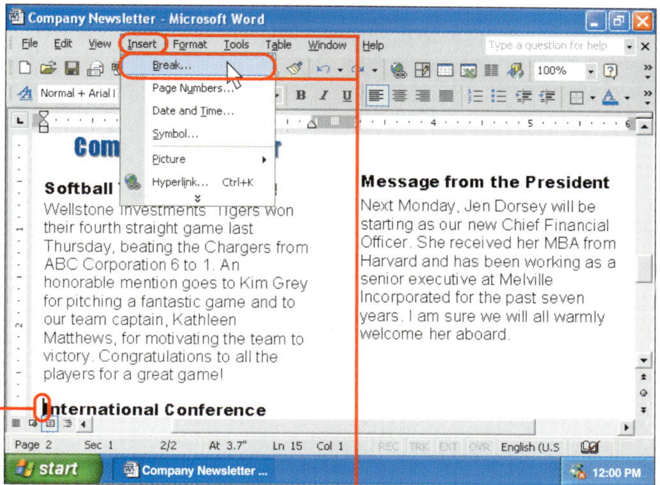

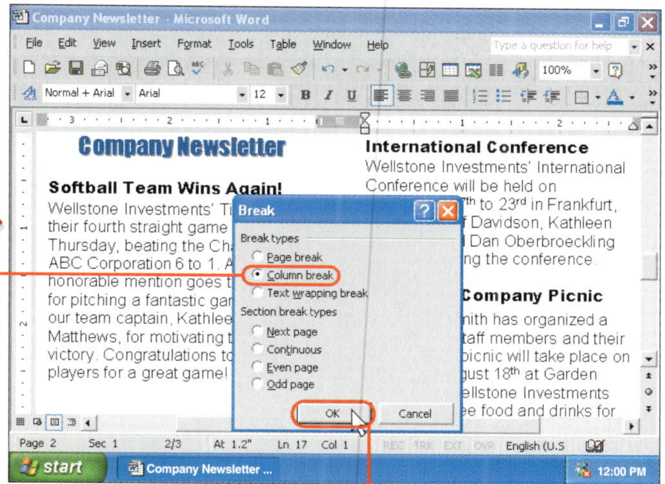

You can insert a column break to move text from one column to the top of the next column.

1 Click to the left of the text you want to move to the next column.

2 Click **Insert**.

3 Click **Break**.

■ The Break dialog box appears.

4 Click this option to add a column break (○ changes to ⦿).

5 Click **OK** to confirm your selection.

■ Word moves the text after the insertion point to the top of the next column.

Grand Opening Celebration!
Hungry Pete's Restaurant is having a grand opening celebration this Saturday from 12 p.m. until 9 p.m.
Bring the whole family and enjoy the great specials offered on this special day. Children under 12 eat for free!
Come see what Hungry Pete's is all about: Great food, excellent value and incredible customer service!
Pete Parker
Pete Parker
Gwen Yates
16 Maple Drive
Baltimore, Maryland
21201
David C. Thompson
President
Dynamic Advertising Inc.
1223 Lincoln Ave.
New York, NY
10023
Dear Mr. Thompson,
I would like to take this opportunity to congratulate you and your company for winning First Prize in the 2001 Logo Design Contest. It gives me the greatest pleasure to inform you that the Judging Committee's decision was unanimous. Your entry was clearly the best among the hundreds of outstanding entries we received this year.
Enclosed please find a copy of the Judging Committee's remarks. This report states that "the logo designed by Dynamic Advertising Inc. serves to enhance the company's image through the creative use of colors and modern design principles."
The award will be presented on August 20 at the International Design Institute's annual banquet. We hope to see you there.
Once again, please accept my congratulations.
Sincerely,
Karen Davis
Chairperson
Judging Committee
Helping the Third World Countries
By: Michelle Millington, MBA
University of Washington

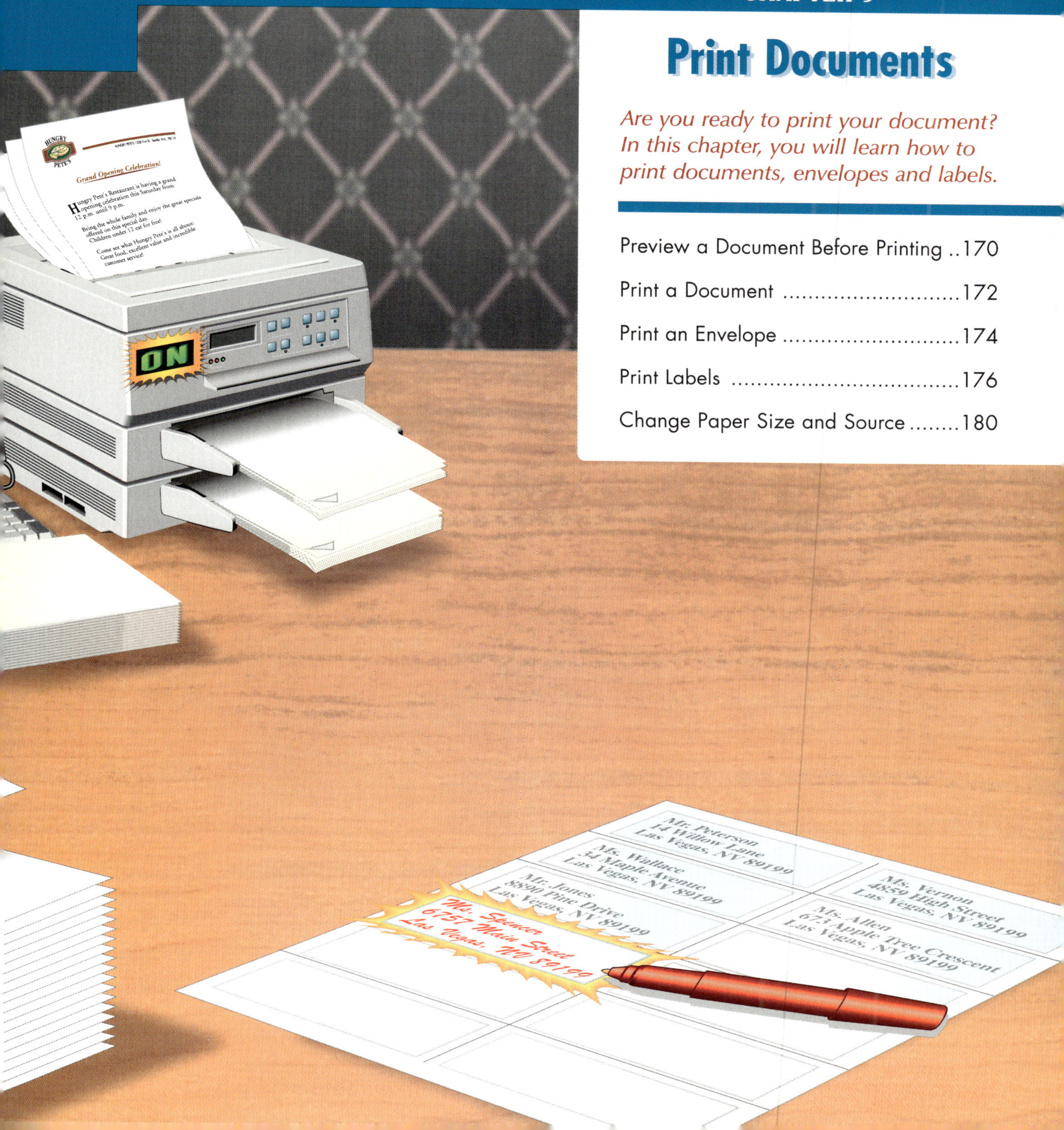

CHAPTER 9

Print Documents

Are you ready to print your document? In this chapter, you will learn how to print documents, envelopes and labels.

Preview a Document Before Printing ..170

Print a Document 172

Print an Envelope 174

Print Labels 176

Change Paper Size and Source 180

PREVIEW A DOCUMENT BEFORE PRINTING

You can use the Print Preview feature to see how your document will look when printed.

This allows you to confirm that the document will print the way you expect.

PREVIEW A DOCUMENT BEFORE PRINTING

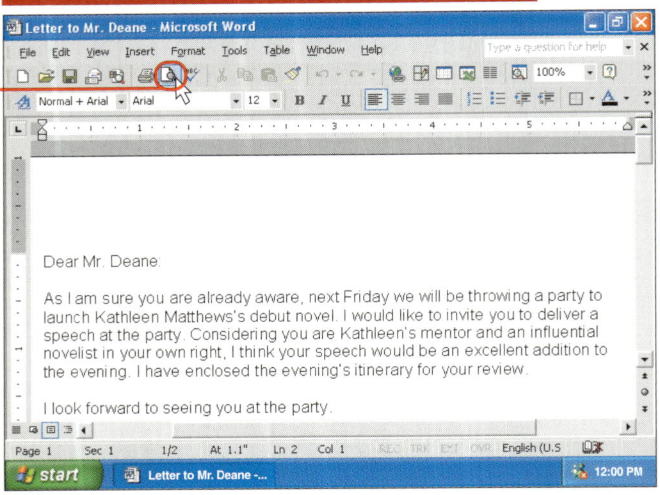

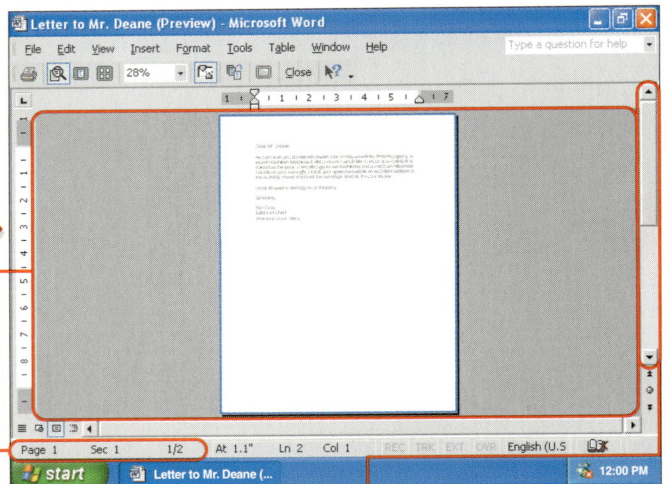

1 Click [icon] to preview your document before printing.

Note: If [icon] is not displayed, click [icon] on the Standard toolbar to display the button.

■ The Print Preview window appears.

■ This area displays a page from your document.

■ This area indicates which page is displayed and the total number of pages in your document.

■ If your document contains more than one page, you can use the scroll bar to view the other pages.

Can I edit my document in the Print Preview window?

Yes. If the mouse pointer looks like I when over your document, you can edit the document. If the mouse pointer looks like or when over your document, you can enlarge or reduce the size of the page displayed on your screen. To change the appearance of the mouse pointer, click the Magnifier button ( ).

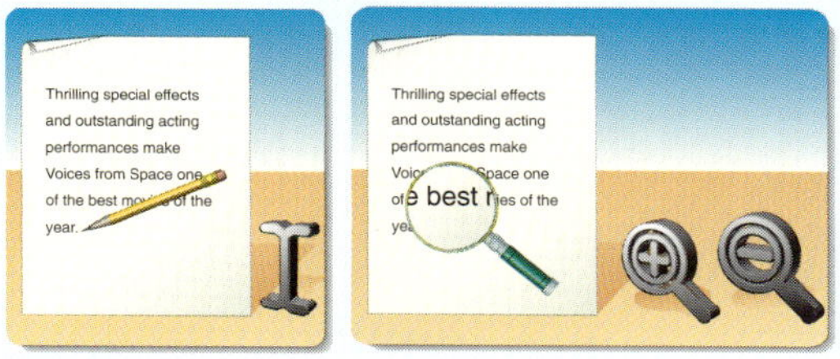

Can I shrink the text in my document to fit on one less page?

If the last page in your document contains only a few lines of text, Word can shrink the text in your document to fit on one less page. In the Print Preview window, click the Shrink to Fit button ( ) to shrink the text in your document.

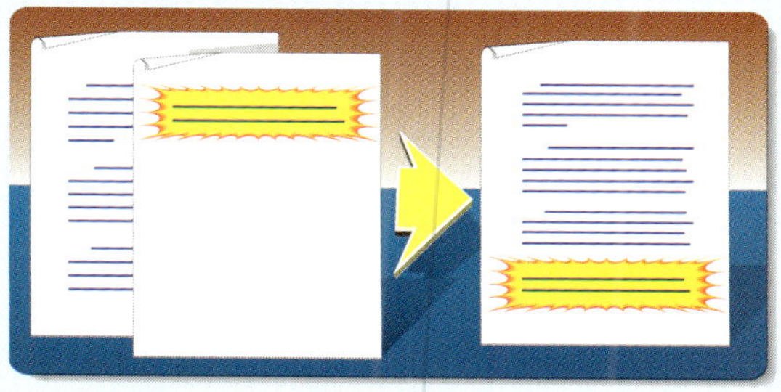

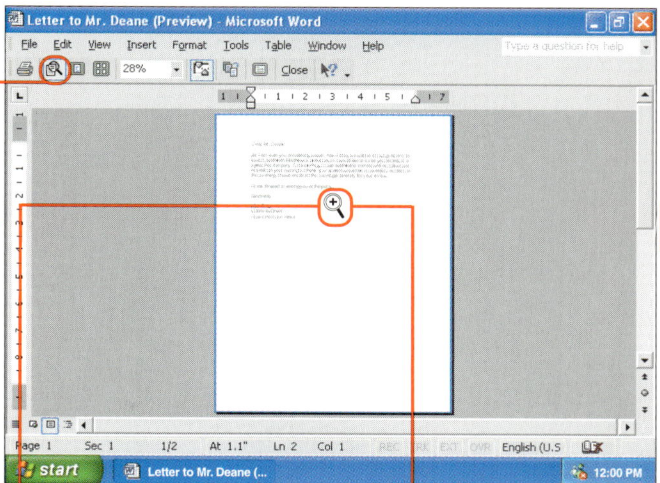

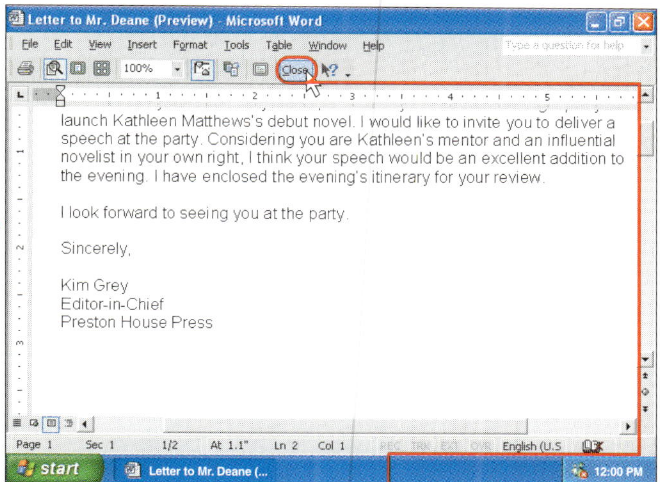

2 To magnify an area of the page, position the mouse over the area you want to magnify (changes to).

■ If the mouse pointer looks like I when over the page, click .

3 Click the area to magnify the area.

■ A magnified view of the area appears.

4 To once again display the entire page, click anywhere on the page.

5 When you finish previewing your document, click **Close** to close the Print Preview window.

PRINT A DOCUMENT

You can produce a paper copy of the document displayed on your screen.

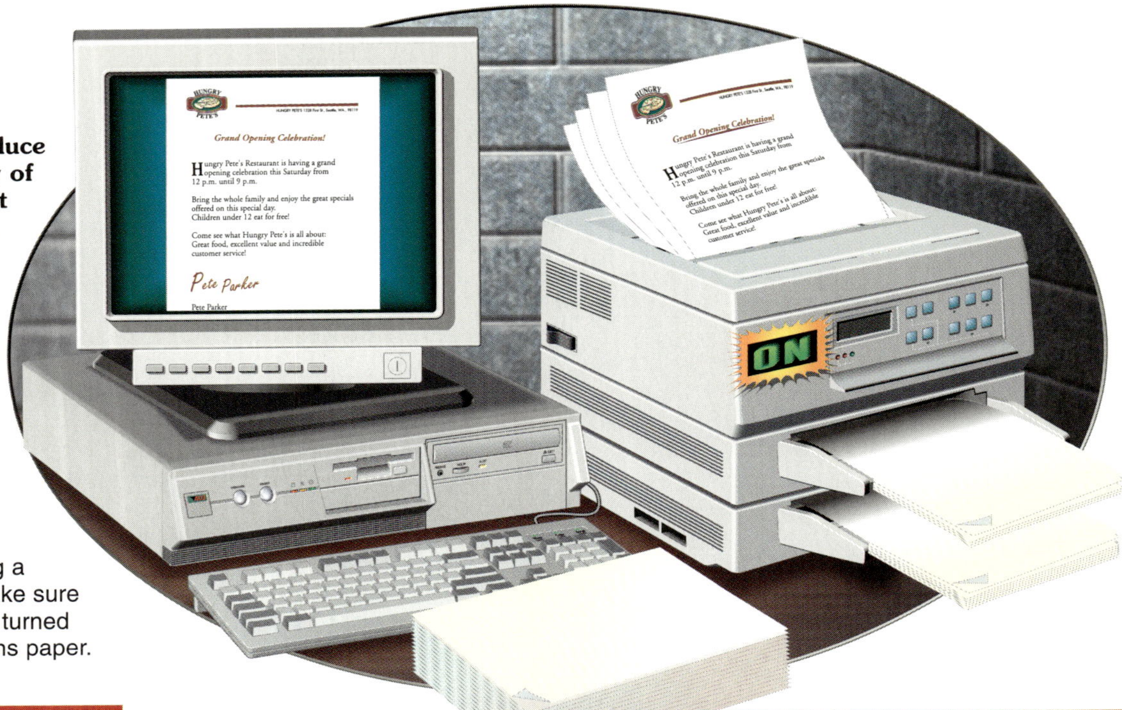

Before printing a document, make sure your printer is turned on and contains paper.

PRINT A DOCUMENT

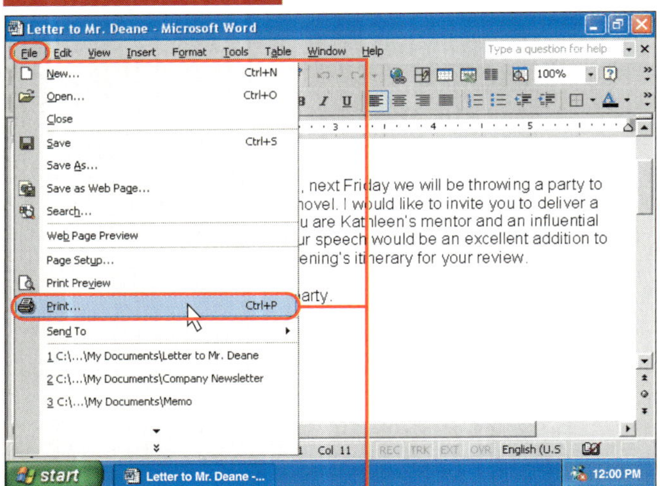

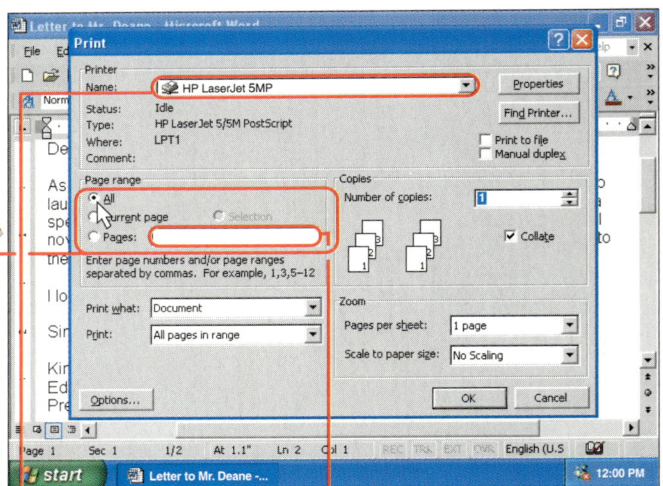

1 Click anywhere in the document or page you want to print.

■ To print only some of the text in the document, select the text you want to print. To select text, see page 10.

2 Click **File**.

3 Click **Print**.

■ The Print dialog box appears.

■ This area displays the printer that will print your document. You can click this area to select a different printer.

4 Click the print option you want to use (○ changes to ⦿).

Note: For information on the print options, see the top of page 173.

■ If you selected **Pages** in step **4**, type the pages you want to print in this area (example: 1,3,5 or 2-4).

Which print option should I use?

All

Prints every page in the document.

Current page

Prints the page containing the insertion point.

Pages

Prints the pages you specify.

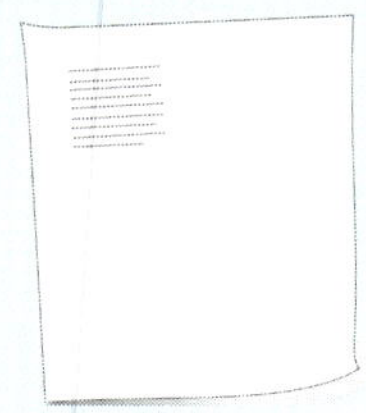

Selection

Prints the text you selected.

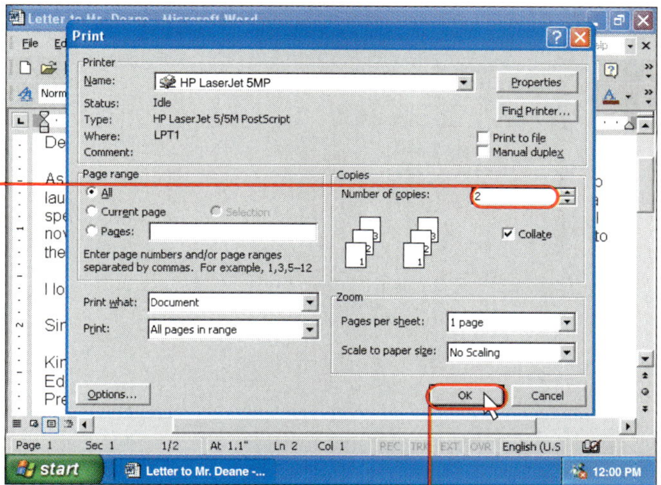

5 To print more than one copy of the document, double-click the number in this area and then type the number of copies you want to print.

6 Click **OK**.

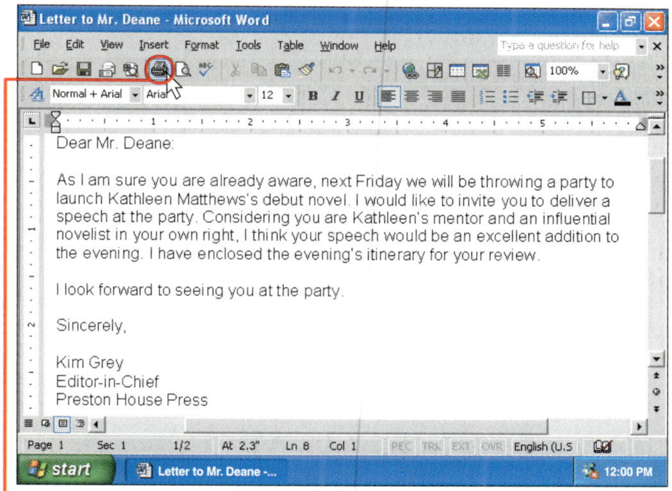

QUICKLY PRINT ENTIRE DOCUMENT

1 Click 🖶 to quickly print your entire document.

Note: If 🖶 is not displayed, click » on the Standard toolbar to display the button.

PRINT AN ENVELOPE

You can use Word to print a delivery address and return address on an envelope.

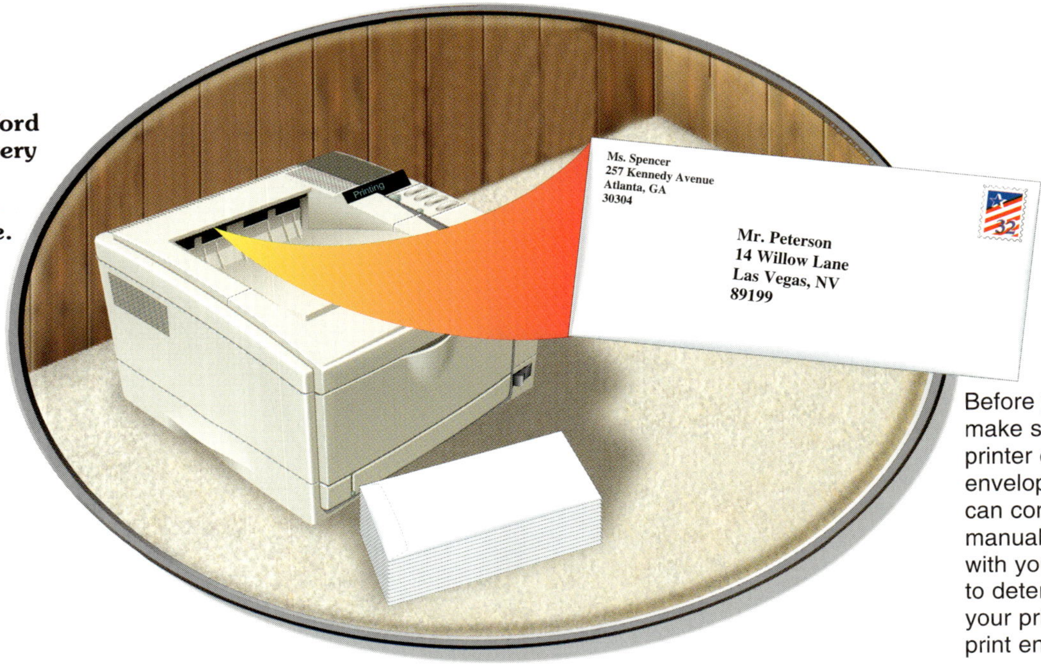

Before you begin, make sure your printer can print envelopes. You can consult the manual that came with your printer to determine if your printer can print envelopes.

PRINT AN ENVELOPE

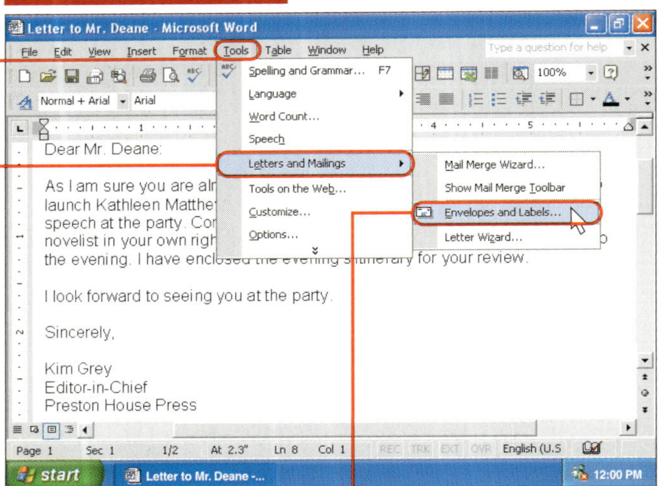

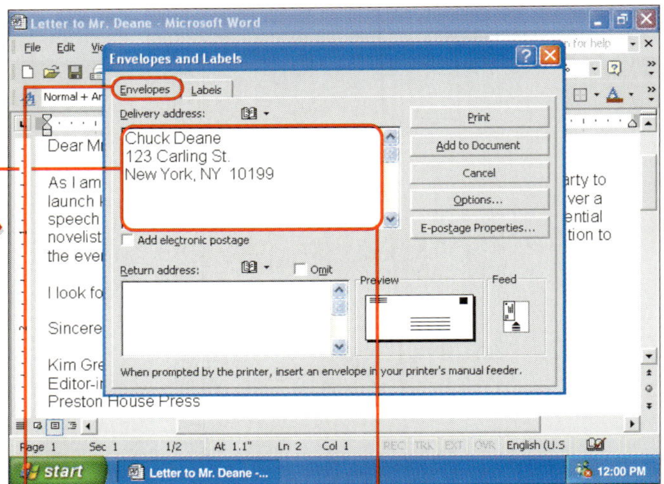

1 Click **Tools**.

2 Click **Letters and Mailings**.

3 Click **Envelopes and Labels**.

■ The Envelopes and Labels dialog box appears.

4 Click the **Envelopes** tab.

■ This area displays the delivery address. If Word finds an address in your document, Word will enter the address for you.

5 To enter a delivery address, click this area. Then type the delivery address.

Note: To remove any existing text before typing a delivery address, drag the mouse I over the text until you highlight the text. Then press the **Delete** *key.*

When would I omit the return address from an envelope?

You would omit the return address if your envelope already displays a return address. Company stationery often displays a return address.

Can I make an envelope part of my document?

Yes. To make an envelope part of your document, perform steps **1** to **9** below, except click the **Add to Document** button in step **8**. The envelope appears before the first page in your document. You can edit, format, save and print the envelope as part of your document.

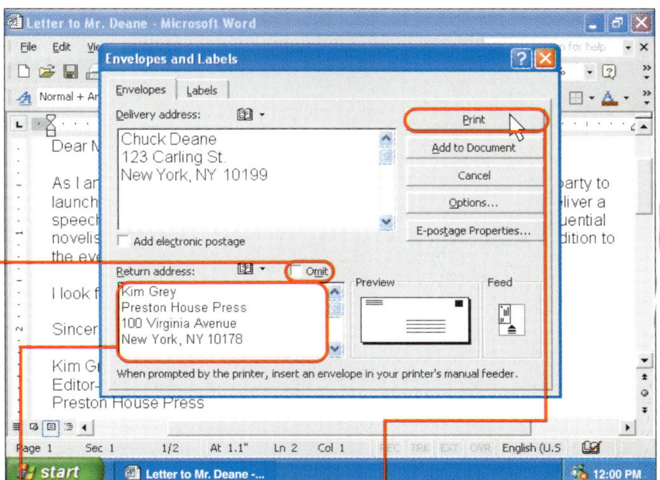

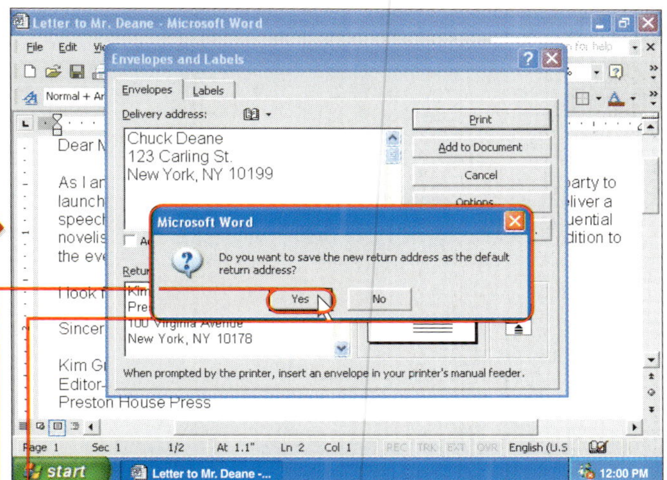

6 To enter a return address, click this area. Then type the return address.

7 If you do not want to print a return address, click **Omit** (☐ changes to ☑).

8 Click **Print** to print the envelope.

■ This dialog box appears if you entered a return address.

9 To save the return address, click **Yes**.

■ If you save the return address, the address will appear as the return address each time you print an envelope. This saves you from having to retype the address.

PRINT LABELS

You can use Word to print labels. Labels are useful for addressing envelopes, creating name tags, labeling file folders and more.

PRINT LABELS

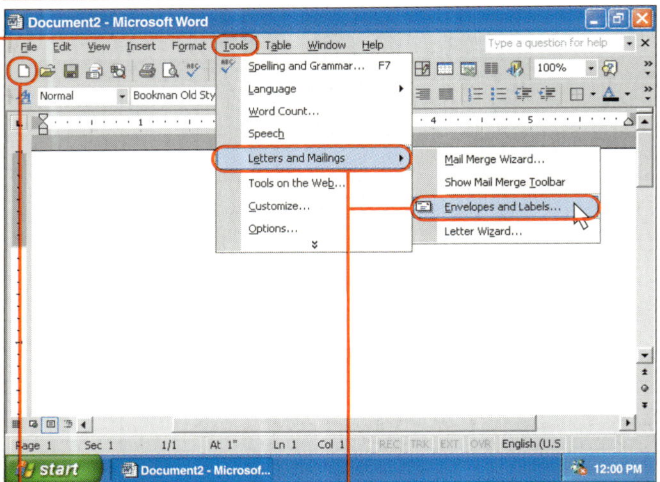

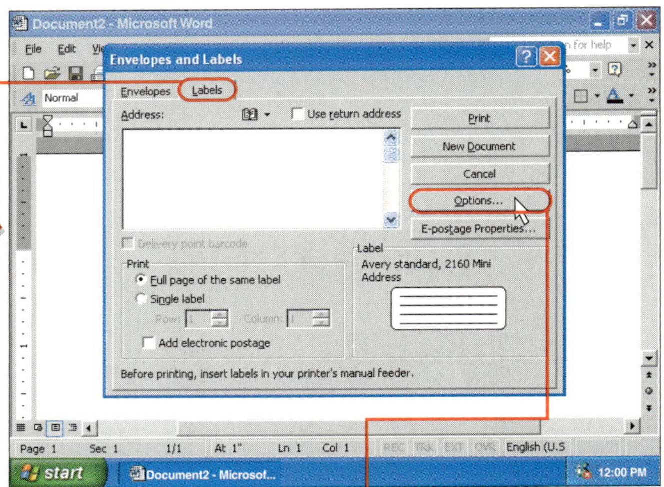

1 Click ▢ to create a new document.

Note: If ▢ is not displayed, click ▾ on the Standard toolbar to display the button.

2 Click **Tools**.

3 Click **Letters and Mailings**.

4 Click **Envelopes and Labels**.

■ The Envelopes and Labels dialog box appears.

5 Click the **Labels** tab.

6 Click **Options** to select the type of label you will use.

■ The Label Options dialog box appears.

What types of printers can I use to print labels?

Word can set up labels to print on dot matrix, laser and ink jet printers. If you are not sure which type of printer you have, you can consult the documentation included with the printer.

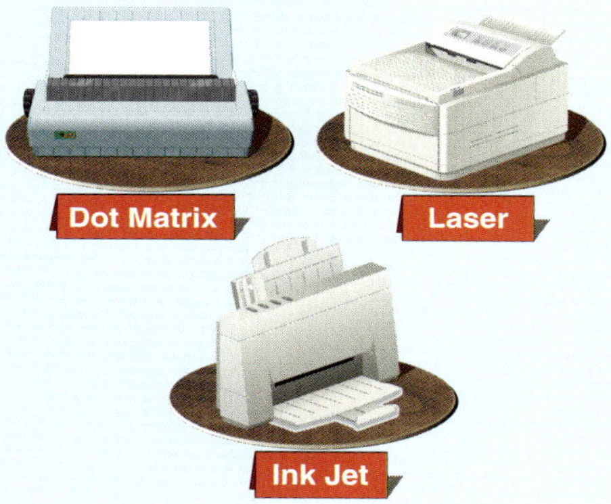

Which label product and type should I choose?

You can check your label packaging to determine which label product and type you should choose when printing labels.

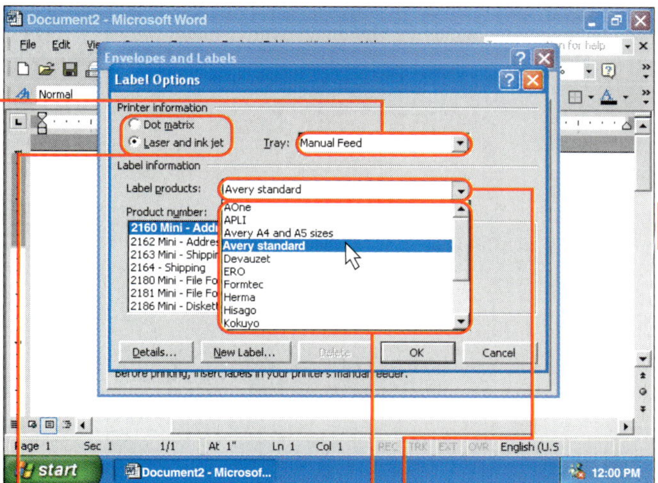

7 Click an option to specify the type of printer you will use to print the labels (○ changes to ⊙).

■ This area displays the printer tray that will contain the labels. You can click this area to specify a different tray.

8 Click this area to display a list of the available label products.

9 Click the label product you will use.

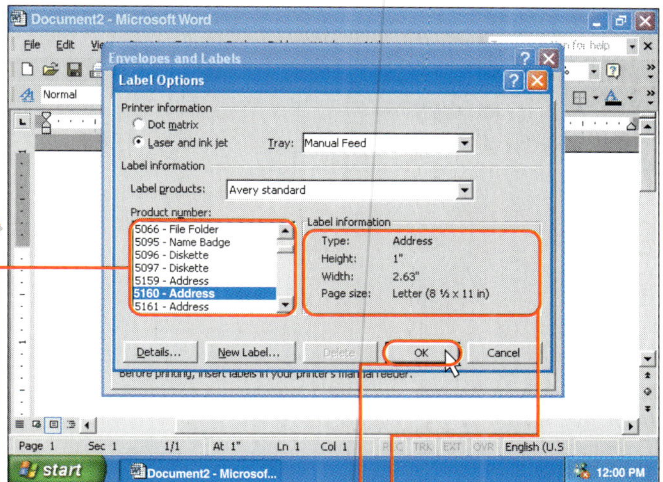

■ This area displays the types of labels available for the label product you selected.

10 Click the type of label you will use.

■ This area displays information about the type of label you selected.

11 Click **OK** to confirm your selections.

CONTINUED

After you specify the type of label you will use, Word can add the labels to a new document. You can then enter the information you want to appear on each label.

PRINT LABELS (CONTINUED)

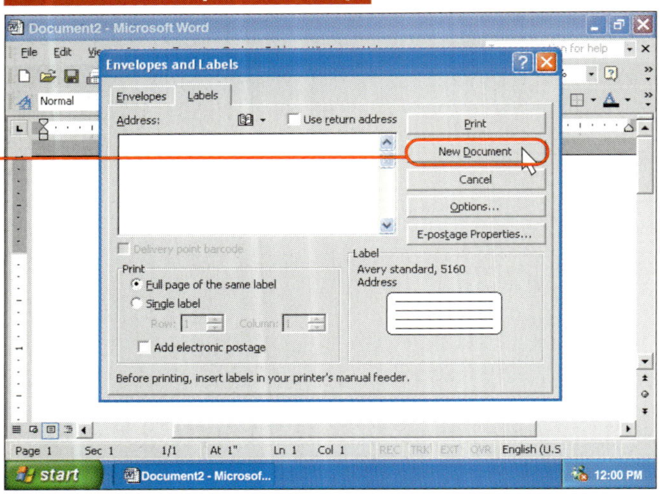

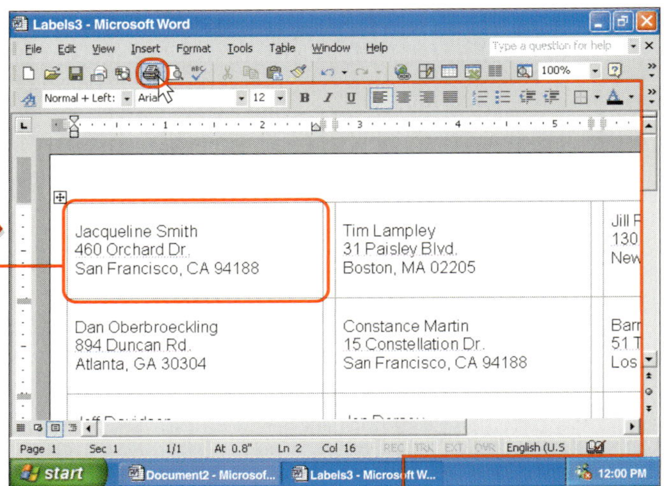

12 Click **New Document** to add the labels to a new document.

■ The labels appear in a new document.

13 Click a label where you want to enter text and then type the text. Repeat this step for each label.

Note: You can format the text on the labels as you would format any text in a document. To format text, see pages 88 to 97.

14 Click [print icon] to print the labels.

Note: If [print icon] is not displayed, click [»] on the Standard toolbar to display the button.

Should I save the labels I created?

If you want to be able to edit and print the labels in the future, you should save the labels you created. To save the document containing the labels, see page 22.

Can I quickly create a label for each person on my mailing list?

You can use the Mail Merge Wizard included with Word to quickly create a label for each person on your mailing list. For information on using the Mail Merge Wizard to create labels, see page 270.

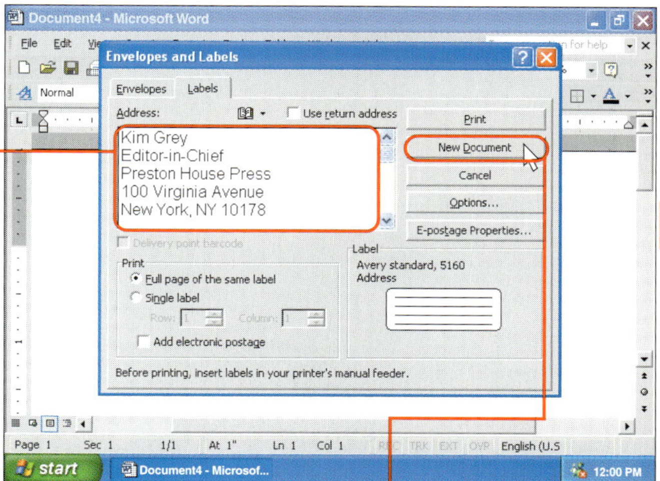

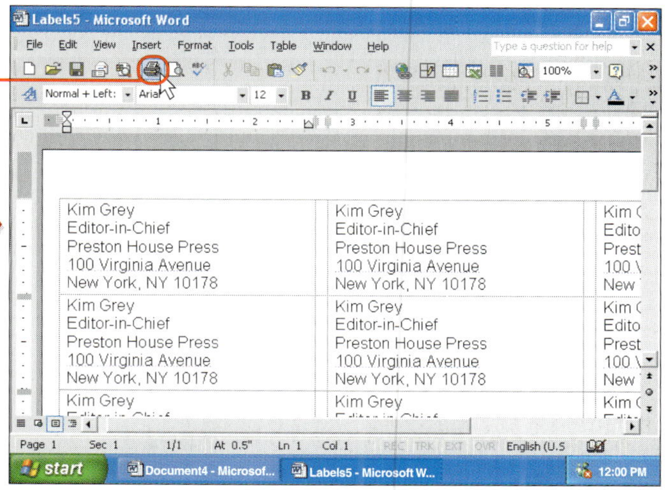

PRINT THE SAME INFORMATION ON EVERY LABEL

1 Perform steps **1** to **11**, starting on page 176.

2 Click this area and then type the information you want to appear on every label.

3 Click **New Document** to add the labels to a new document.

■ The labels appear in a new document. Each label displays the same information.

4 Click 🖨 to print the labels.

Note: If 🖨 is not displayed, click » on the Standard toolbar to display the button.

CHANGE PAPER SIZE AND SOURCE

Word sets each page in your document to print on letter-sized paper. If you want to use a different paper size, you can change this setting. You can also change the location where Word will look for the paper to print your document.

CHANGE PAPER SIZE AND SOURCE

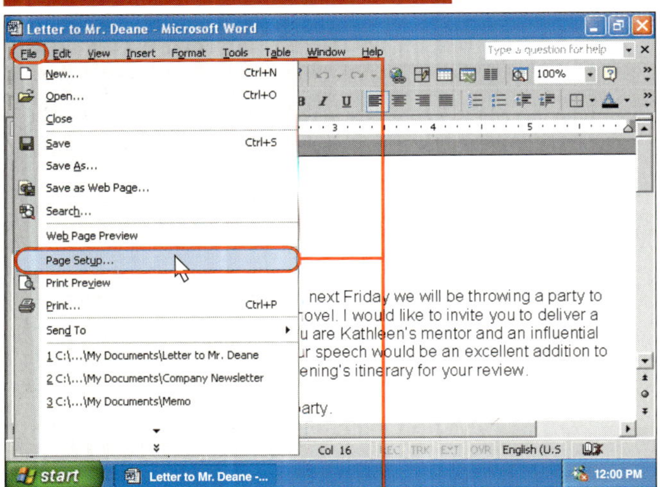

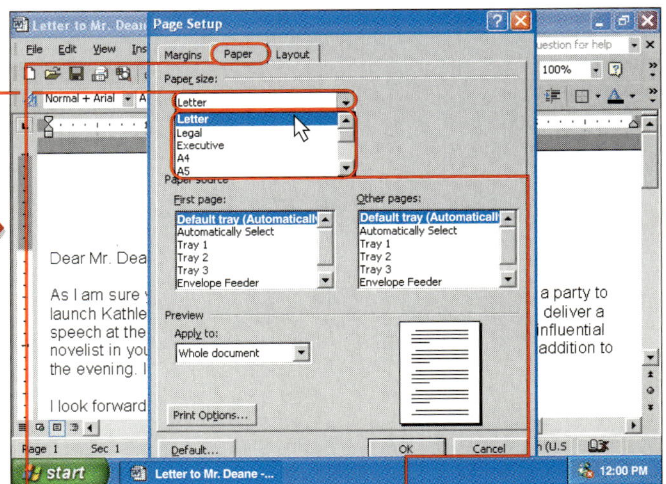

1 Click anywhere in the document or section you want to print using a different paper size or source.

Note: To change the paper size or source for only part of your document, you must divide the document into sections. To divide a document into sections, see page 144.

2 Click **File**.

3 Click **Page Setup**.

■ The Page Setup dialog box appears.

4 Click the **Paper** tab.

5 To change the paper size, click this area to display a list of the paper sizes your printer supports.

6 Click the paper size you want to use.

TEACH YOURSELF

What paper sizes can I use?

The available paper sizes depend on the printer you are using. Most printers can print on letter-sized and legal-sized paper. You can consult the manual that came with your printer to determine which paper sizes the printer can use.

TEACH YOURSELF

Why would I change the paper source?

Changing the paper source is useful if your printer stores letterhead in one location and plain paper in another location. You can print the first page of your document on letterhead and print the rest of the document on plain paper.

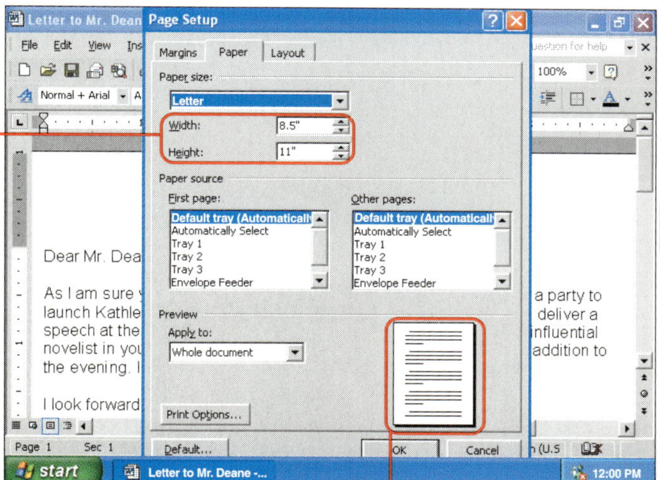

■ This area displays the width and height of the paper size you selected.

■ This area displays a preview of the paper size you selected.

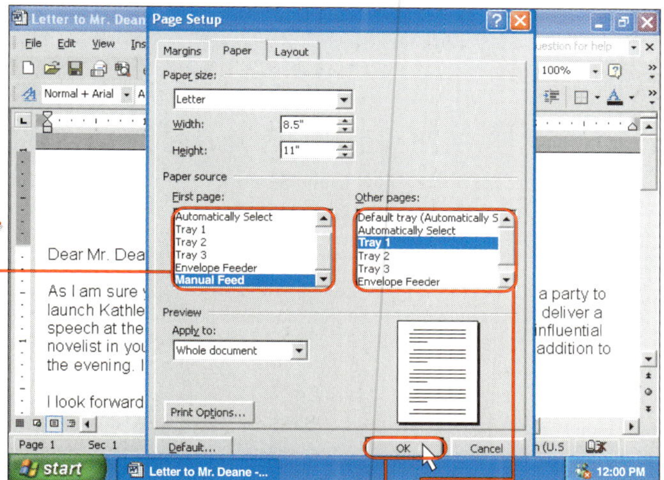

7 To change the paper source, click the location of the paper you want to use for the first page of the document or section in this area.

Note: The available paper source options depend on your printer.

8 Click the location of the paper you want to use for the other pages of the document or section in this area.

9 Click **OK** to confirm your changes.

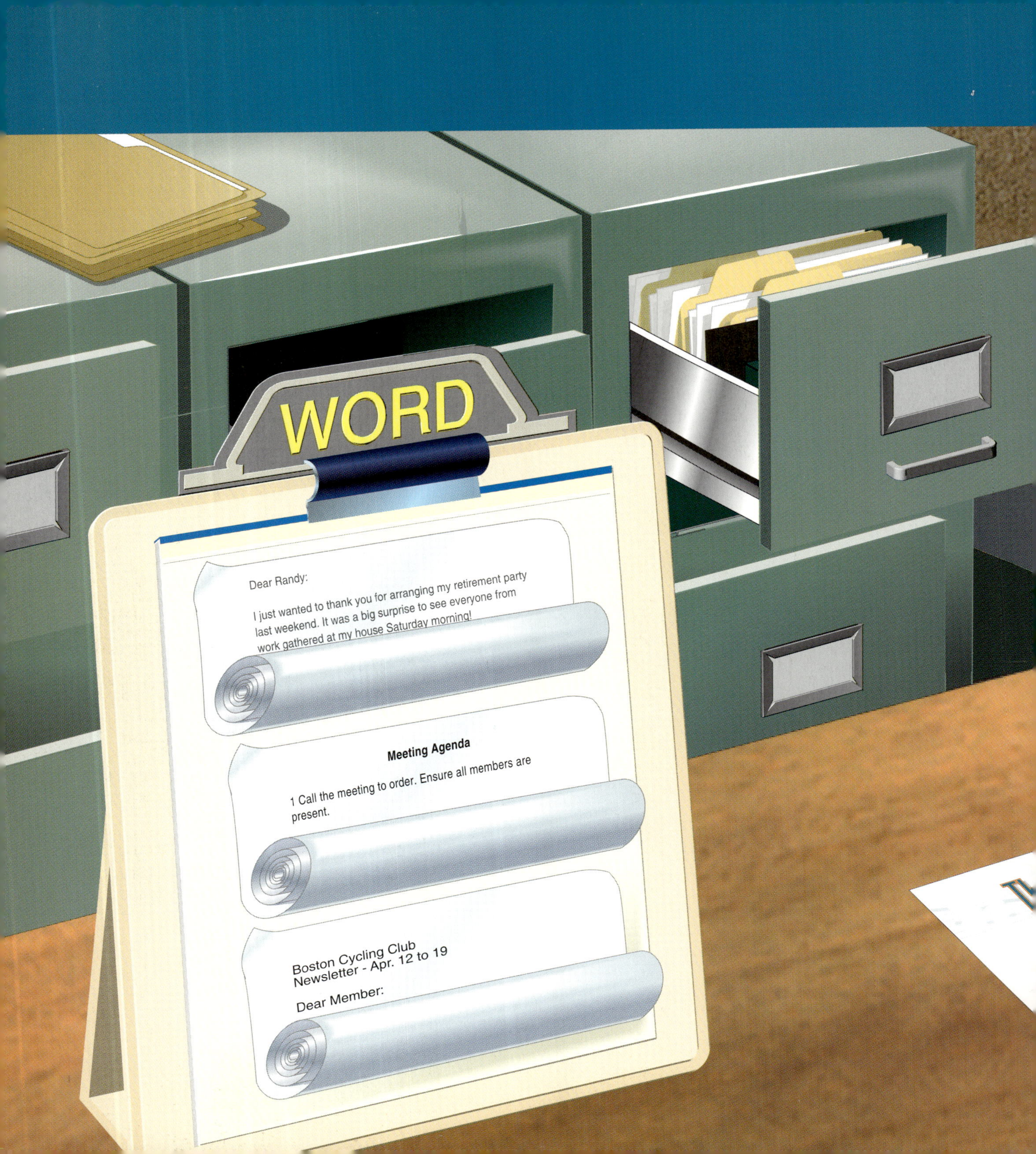
WORD
Dear Randy:
I just wanted to thank you for arranging my retirement party last weekend. It was a big surprise to see everyone from work gathered at my house Saturday morning!
Meeting Agenda
1 Call the meeting to order. Ensure all members are present.
Boston Cycling Club
Newsletter - Apr. 12 to 19
Dear Member:

CHAPTER 10

Work With Multiple Documents

Do you want to work with more than one document at a time? This chapter teaches you how to switch between documents, move or copy text between documents and more.

Create a New Document..................184

Switch Between Documents 185

Arrange Open Documents................186

Move or Copy Text Between Documents...................................188

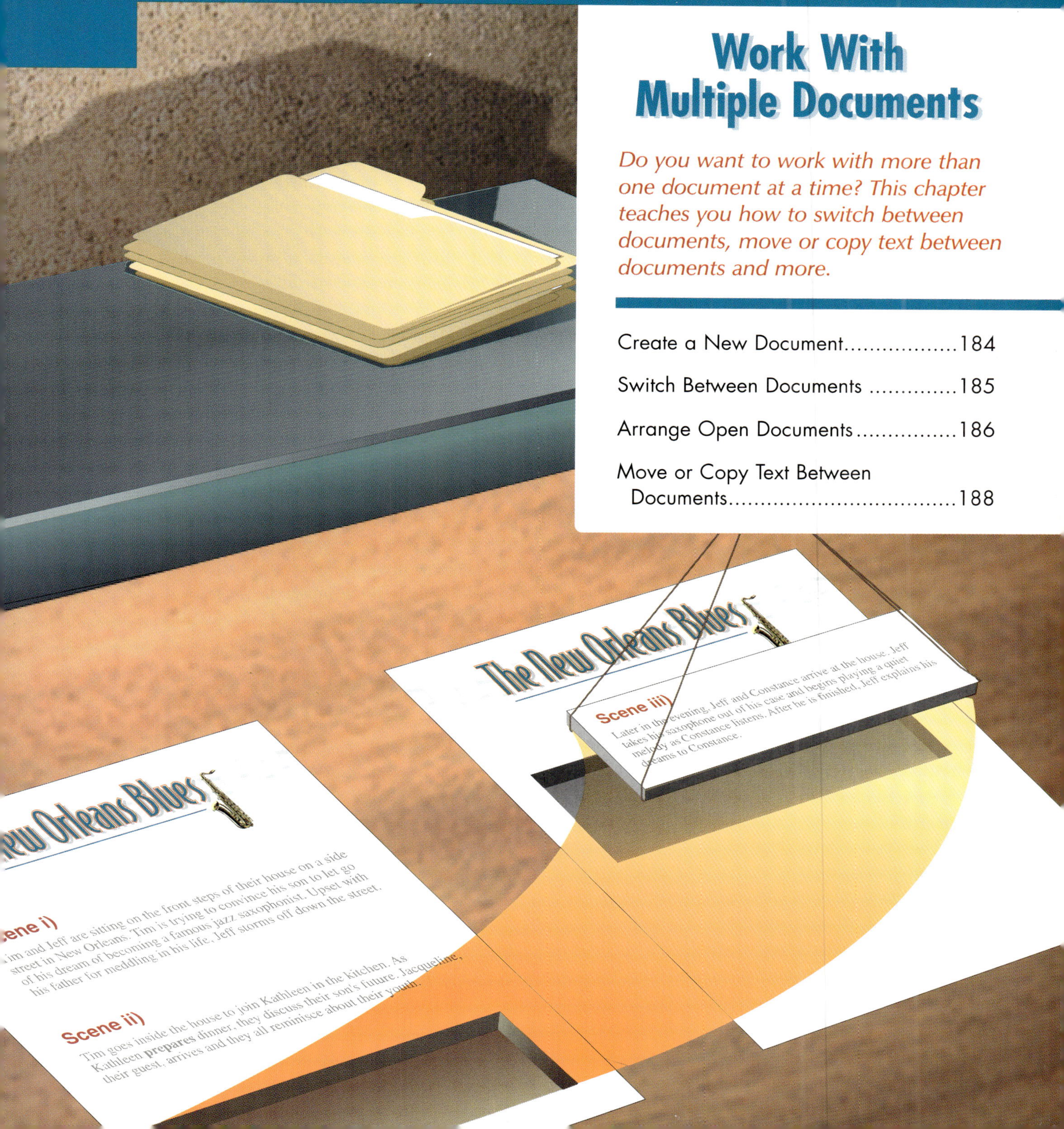

CREATE A NEW DOCUMENT

You can create a new document to start writing a new letter, memo or report.

CREATE A NEW DOCUMENT

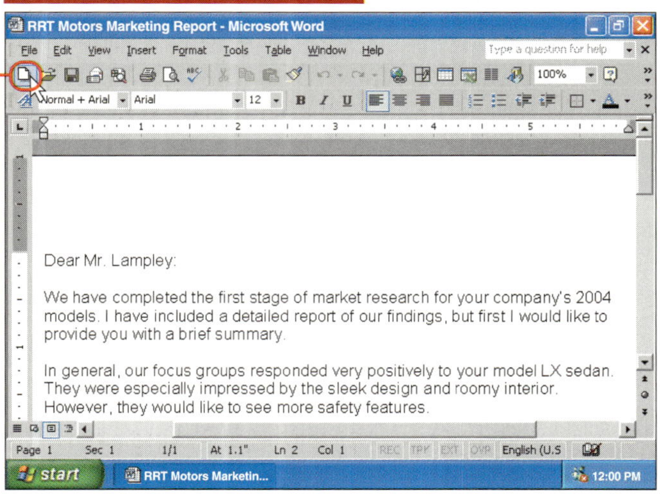

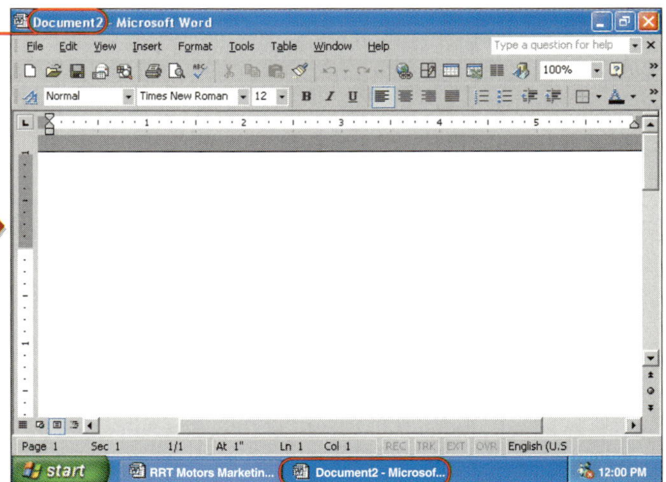

1 Click to create a new document.

Note: If is not displayed, click on the Standard toolbar to display the button.

■ A new document appears. The previous document is now hidden behind the new document.

■ Word gives the new document a temporary name, such as Document2, until you save the document. To save a document, see page 22.

■ A button for the new document appears on the taskbar.

SWITCH BETWEEN DOCUMENTS

You can have several documents open at once. Word allows you to easily switch from one open document to another.

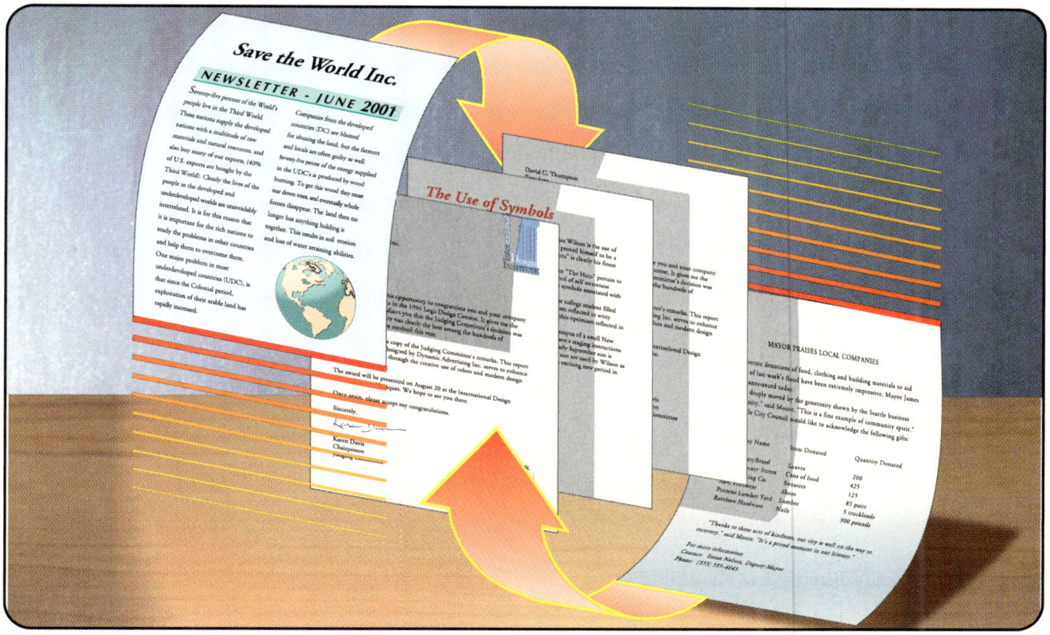

SWITCH BETWEEN DOCUMENTS

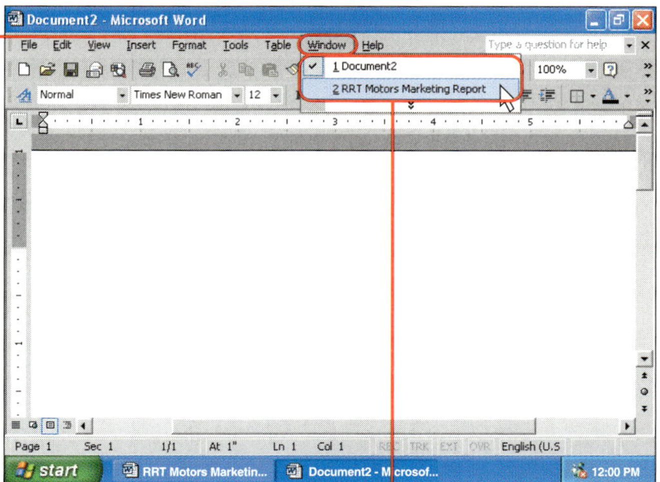

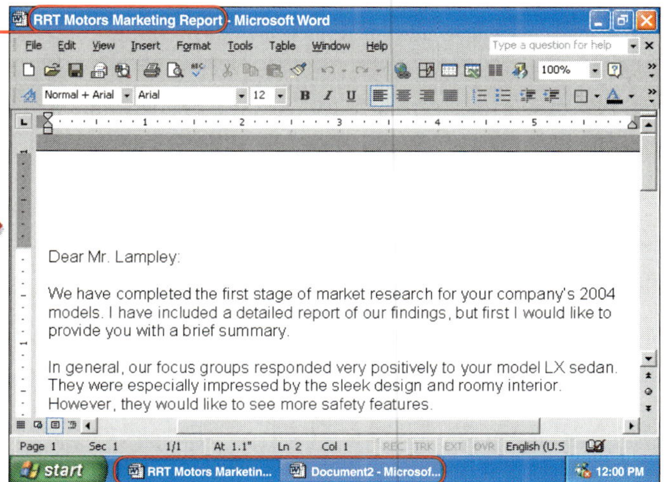

1 Click **Window** to display a list of all the documents you have open.

2 Click the name of the document you want to switch to.

- The document appears.
- This area shows the name of the displayed document.
- The taskbar displays a button for each open document. You can also click the buttons on the taskbar to switch between the open documents.

ARRANGE OPEN DOCUMENTS

If you have several documents open, some of them may be hidden from view. You can display the contents of all your open documents at once.

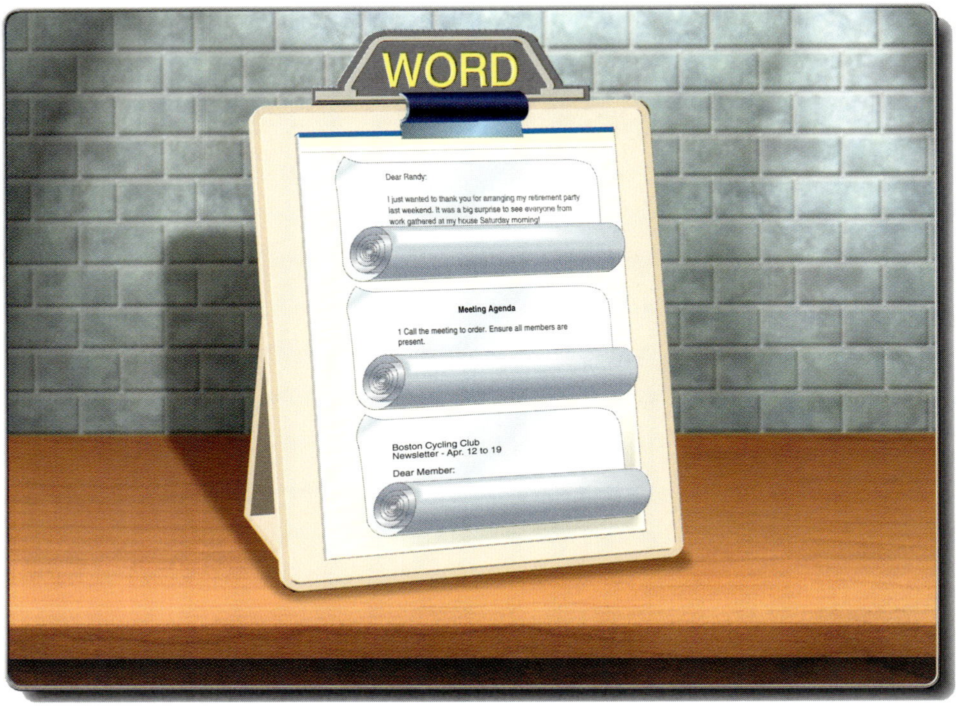

ARRANGE OPEN DOCUMENTS

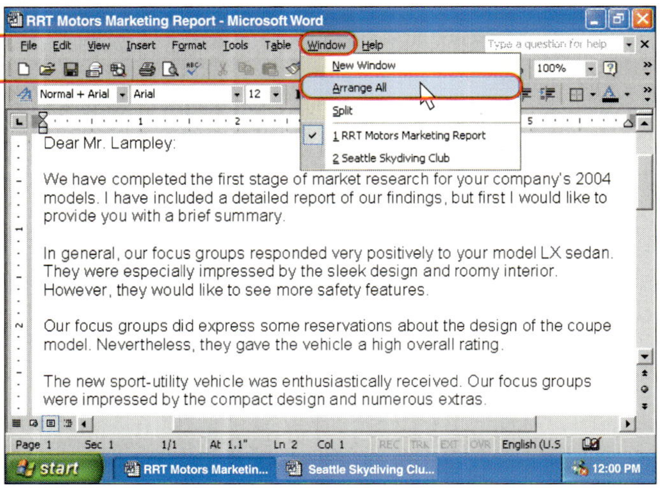

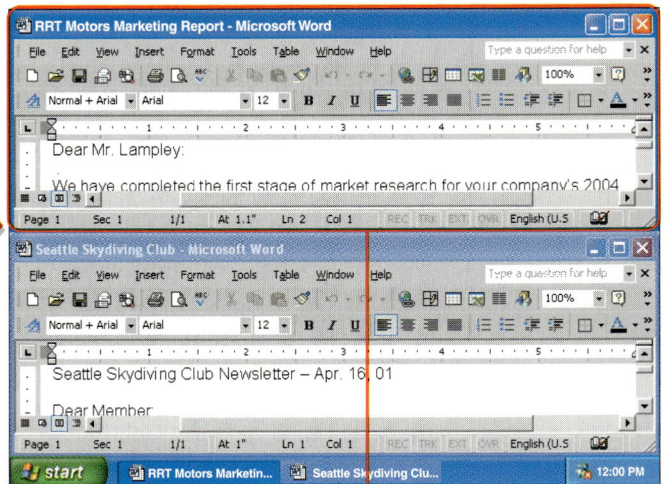

1 Click **Window**.

2 Click **Arrange All**.

Note: If Arrange All does not appear on the menu, position the mouse over the bottom of the menu to display all the menu options.

■ The documents appear neatly arranged.

■ You can work with only one document at a time. The current document displays a dark title bar.

How can I display more of the arranged documents on my screen?

You can remove items, such as the ruler or a toolbar, from a document to display more of the document on your screen. To hide the ruler, see page 42. To hide a toolbar, see page 43.

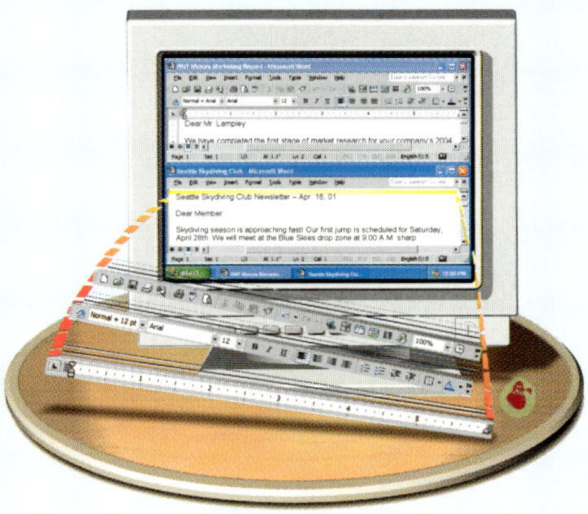

Why didn't Word arrange all my open documents?

Word will not arrange an open document that is minimized to its button on the taskbar. You minimize a document when you click ▬ in the top right corner of a Microsoft Word window. To display a minimized document, click the button for the document on the taskbar. You can then repeat steps **1** and **2** below to arrange all your open documents.

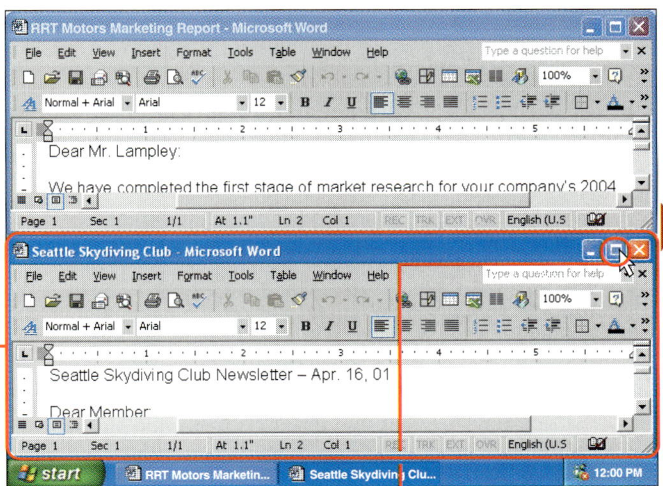

3 To make another document current, click anywhere in the document.

4 To maximize the current document to fill your screen, click ▢.

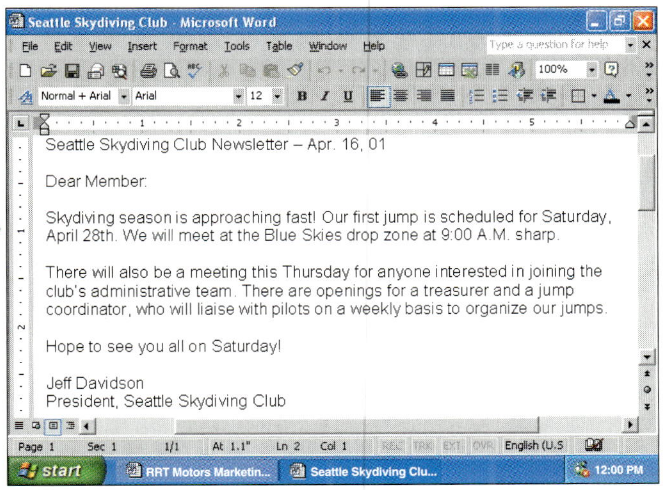

■ The document fills your screen.

■ The other document(s) are hidden behind the maximized document.

MOVE OR COPY TEXT BETWEEN DOCUMENTS

You can move or copy text from one document to another. This saves you time when you want to use text from another document.

When you move text, the text disappears from the original document.

When you copy text, the text appears in both the original and new documents.

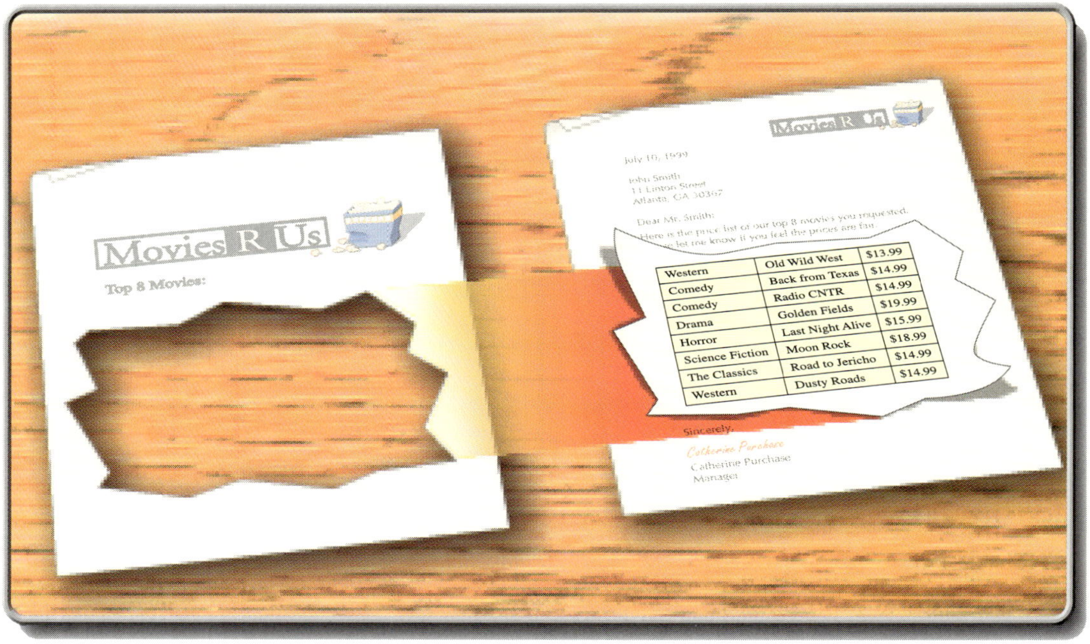

MOVE OR COPY TEXT BETWEEN DOCUMENTS

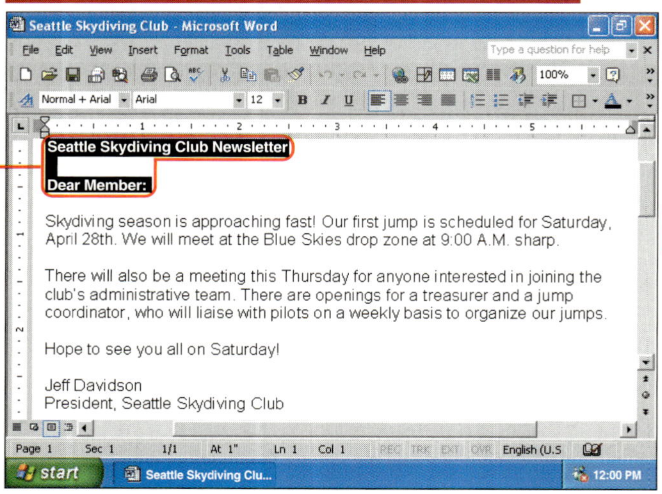

1 Select the text you want to move or copy to another document. To select text, see page 10.

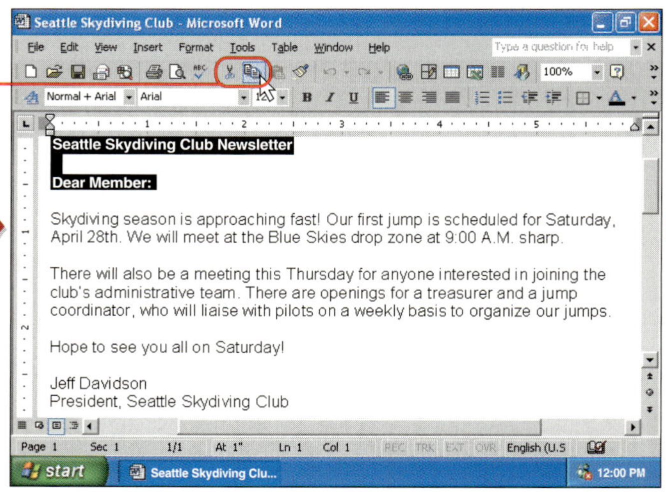

2 Click one of the following buttons.

- Move text
- Copy text

Note: If the button you want is not displayed, click » on the Standard toolbar to display the button.

■ The Clipboard task pane may appear, displaying items you have selected to move or copy. To use the Clipboard task pane, see the top of page 189.

How can I use the Clipboard task pane to move or copy text?

The Clipboard task pane displays up to the last 24 items you have selected to move or copy. To place a clipboard item in your document, click the location where you want the item to appear and then click the item in the task pane. For more information on the task pane, see page 16.

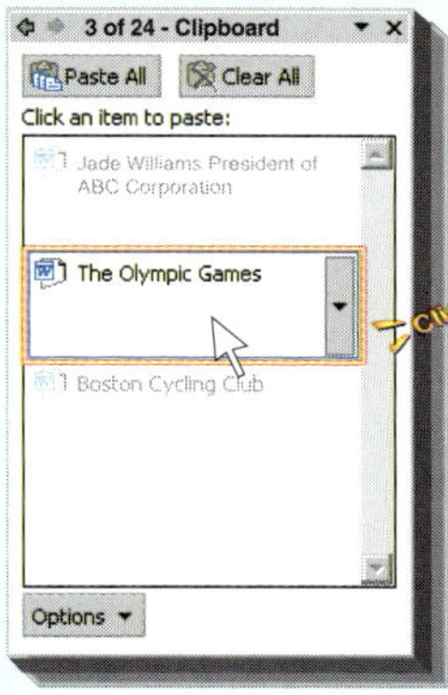

Why does the Paste Options button ( ) appear when I move or copy text?

You can use the Paste Options button ( ) to change the format of text you have moved or copied. For example, you can choose to keep the original formatting of the text or change the formatting of the text to match the text in the new location. Click the Paste Options button to display a list of options and then select the option you want to use. The Paste Options button is available only until you perform another task.

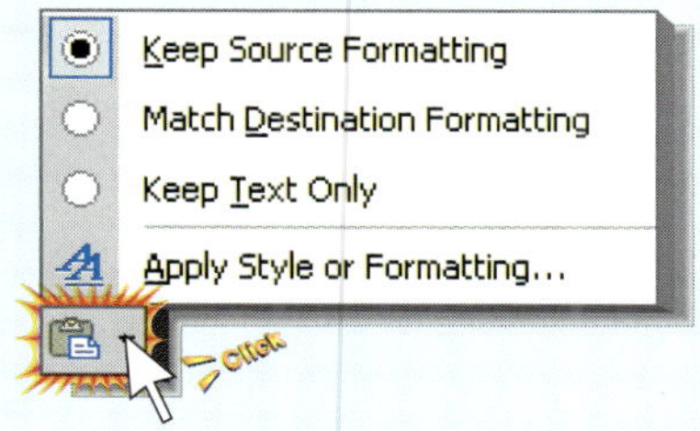

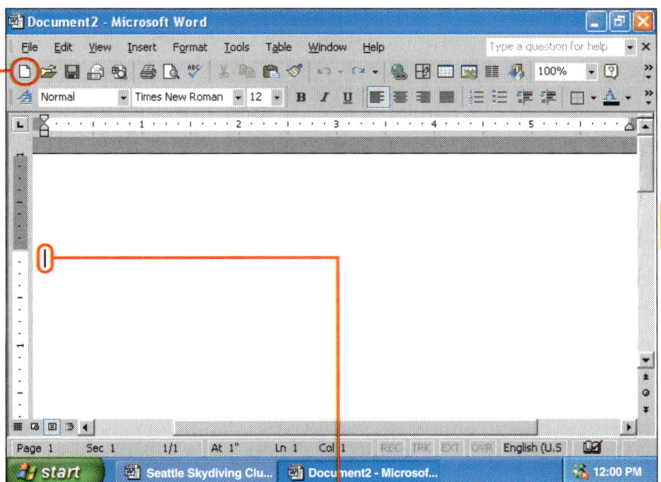

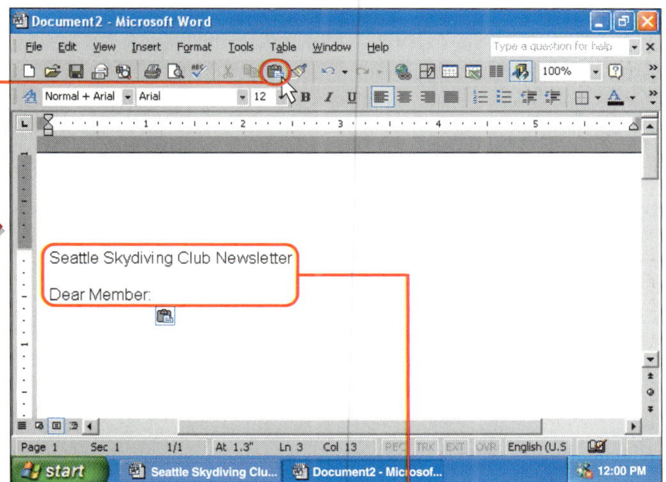

3 To place the text in a new document, click to create a new document.

Note: If is not displayed, click on the Standard toolbar to display the button.

■ To place the text in an existing document, open the document. To open a document, see page 28.

4 Click the location where you want to place the text.

5 Click to place the text in the new location.

Note: If is not displayed, click on the Standard toolbar to display the button.

■ The text appears in the new location.

Work With Tables

Do you want to learn how to display information in a table? This chapter teaches you how to create and work with tables.

Create a Table 192

Add a Row or Column 194

Delete a Row or Column 196

Change Row Height or Column Width 198

Move a Table....................200

Resize a Table 201

Combine Cells 202

Split Cells 203

Align Text in Cells....................204

Add Shading to Cells 205

Change Table Borders 206

Format a Table....................208

CREATE A TABLE

You can create a table to neatly display information in your document.

CREATE A TABLE

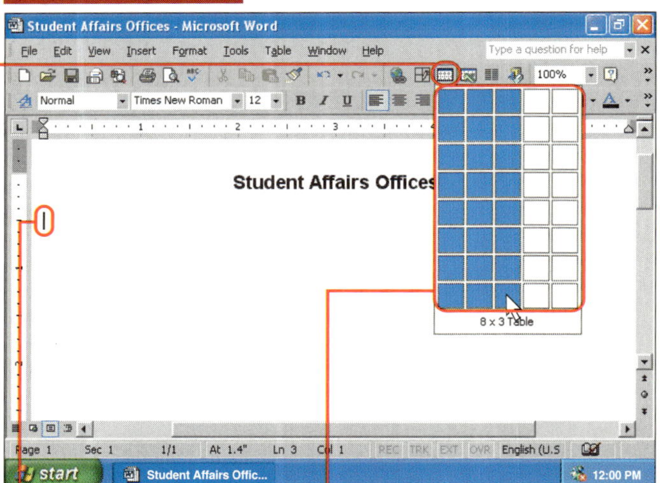

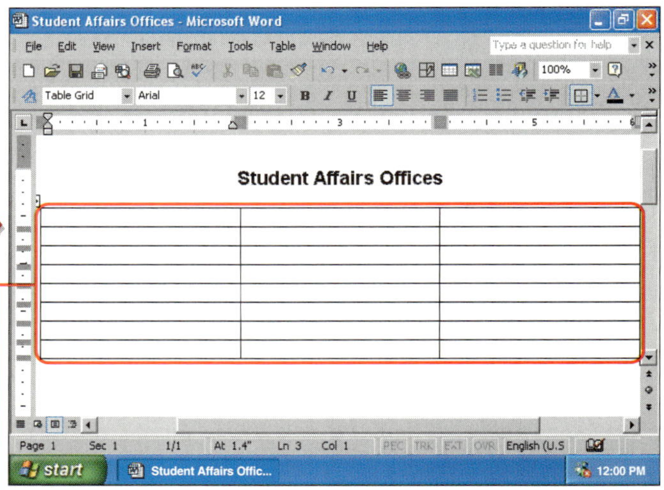

1 Click the location in your document where you want a table to appear.

2 Click to create a table.

Note: If is not displayed, click on the Standard toolbar to display the button.

3 Drag the mouse until you highlight the number of rows and columns you want the table to contain.

■ The table appears in your document.

What are the parts of a table?

A table consists of rows, columns and cells.

Row

Column

Cell

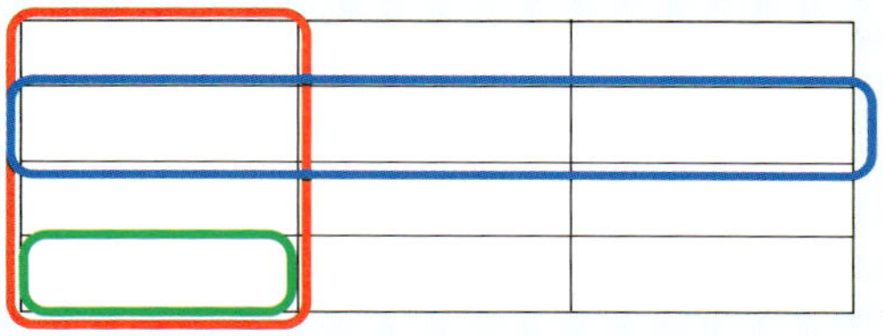

Can I change the appearance of text in a table?

Yes. You can format text in a table as you would format any text in your document. For example, you can change the font, size, color and alignment of text in a table. To format text, see pages 88 to 97.

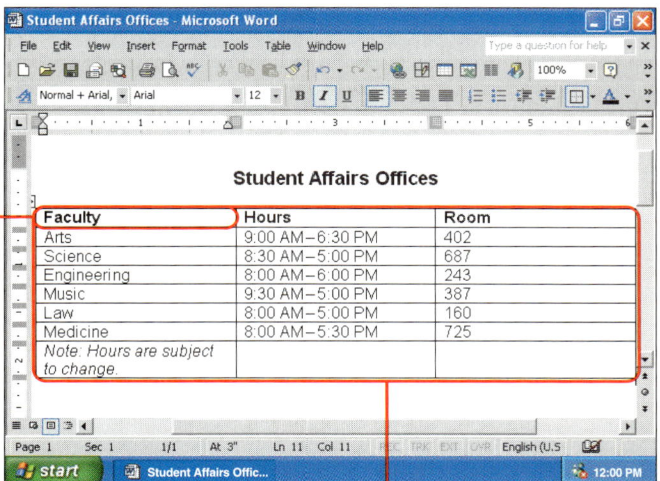

ENTER TEXT INTO A TABLE

1 Click the cell in the table where you want to enter text. Then type the text.

2 Repeat step **1** until you finish entering all the text you want the table to display.

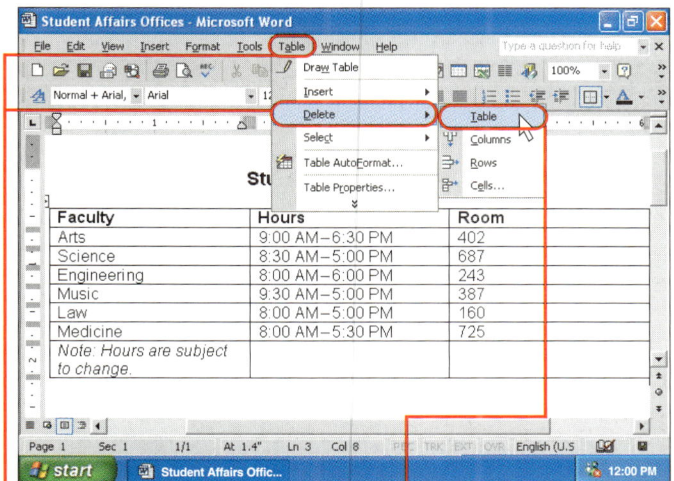

DELETE A TABLE

1 Click anywhere in the table you want to delete.

2 Click **Table**.

3 Click **Delete**.

4 Click **Table**.

■ The table disappears from your document.

ADD A ROW OR COLUMN

You can add a row or column to your table to insert additional information.

ADD A ROW

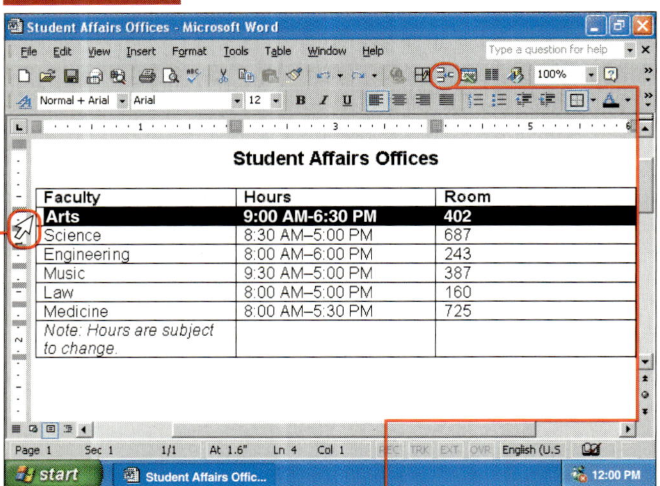

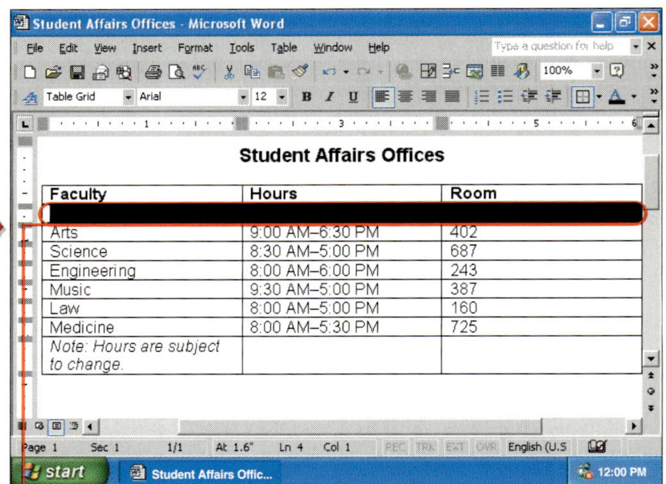

Word will insert a row above the row you select.

1 To select a row, position the mouse I to the left of the row (I changes to). Then click to select the row.

2 Click to add a row to the table.

Note: If is not displayed, click on the Standard toolbar to display the button.

■ The new row appears in your table.

■ To deselect a row, click outside the selected area.

How do I add a row to the bottom of a table?

To add a row to the bottom of a table, click the bottom right cell in the table. Then press the Tab key.

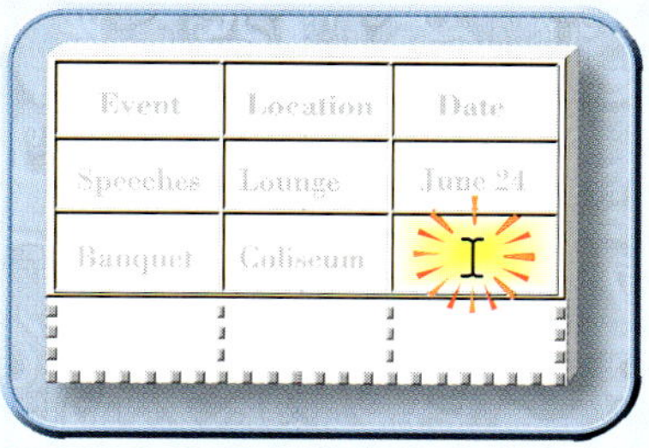

How do I add a column to the right of the last column in a table?

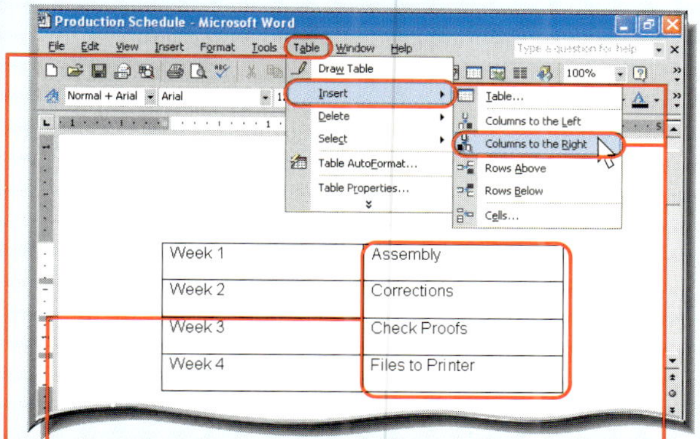

1 Click a cell in the last column.

2 Click **Table**.

3 Click **Insert**.

4 Click **Columns to the Right**.

ADD A COLUMN

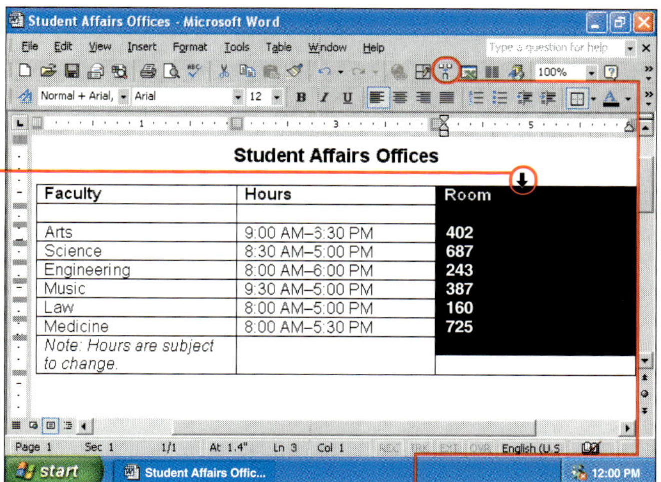

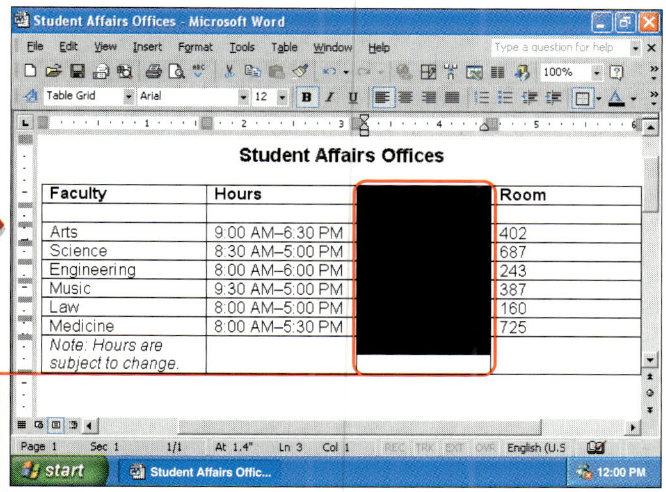

Word will insert a column to the left of the column you select.

1 To select a column, position the mouse I above the column (I changes to ⬇). Then click to select the column.

2 Click [icon] to add a column.

Note: If [icon] is not displayed, click [icon] on the Standard toolbar to display the button.

■ The new column appears in your table.

■ To deselect a column, click outside the selected area.

DELETE A ROW OR COLUMN

You can delete a row or column you no longer need from your table.

Deleting a row or column will also delete all the information in the row or column.

DELETE A ROW

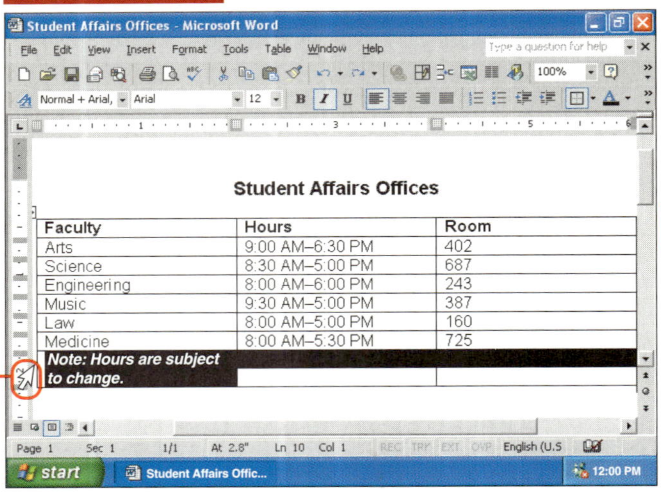

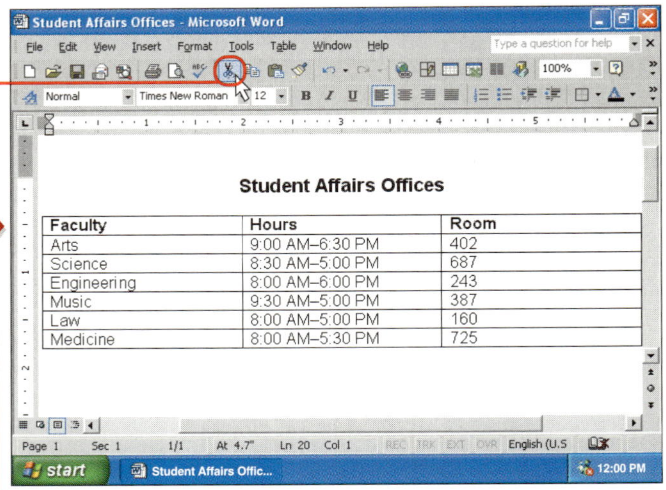

1 To select the row you want to delete, position the mouse to the left of the row (changes to). Then click to select the row.

2 Click to delete the row.

Note: If is not displayed, click on the Standard toolbar to display the button.

■ The row disappears from your table.

Can I delete the information in a row or column without removing the row or column from my table?

Yes. To select the cells in your table that contain the information you want to delete, drag the mouse I over the cells until you highlight the cells. Then press the Delete key to remove the information.

How can I restore a row or column I accidentally deleted?

If you accidentally delete a row or column, you can click the Undo button (↶) to immediately restore the row or column to your table. For more information on the Undo feature, see page 59.

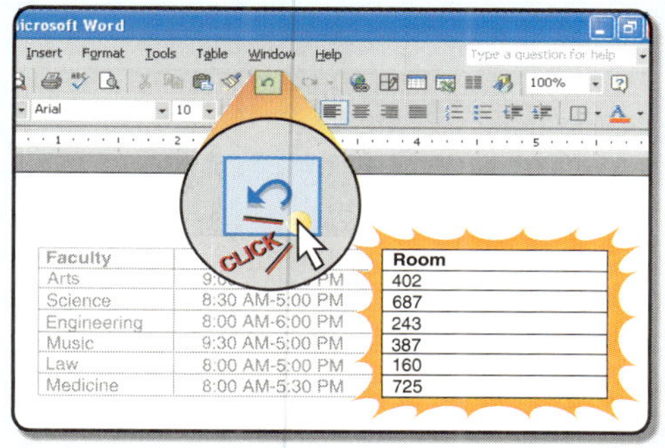

DELETE A COLUMN

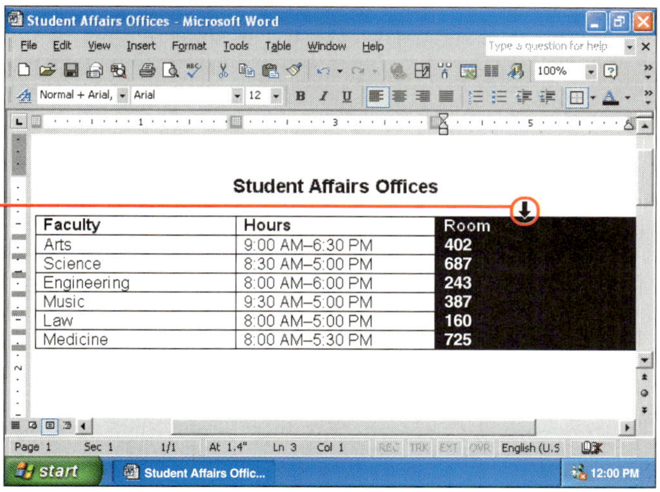

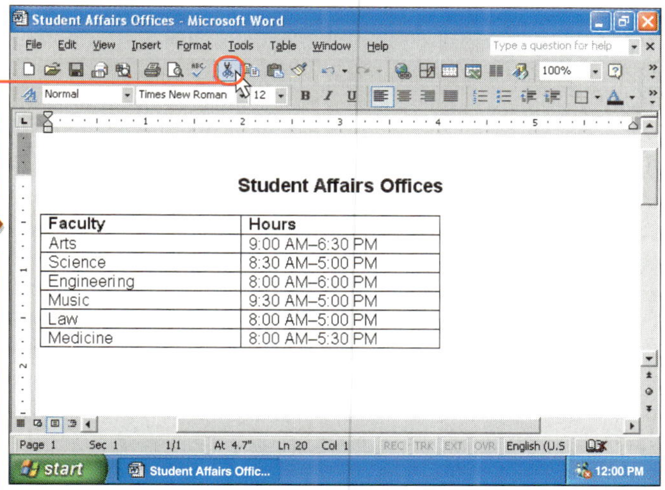

1 To select the column you want to delete, position the mouse I above the column (I changes to ⬇). Then click to select the column.

2 Click ✂ to delete the column.

Note: If ✂ is not displayed, click » on the Standard toolbar to display the button.

■ The column disappears from your table.

CHANGE ROW HEIGHT OR COLUMN WIDTH

You can change the height of rows and the width of columns to improve the layout of your table.

CHANGE ROW HEIGHT

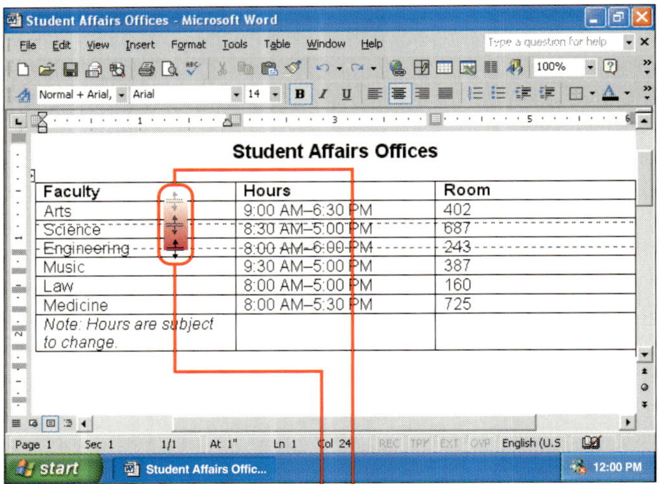

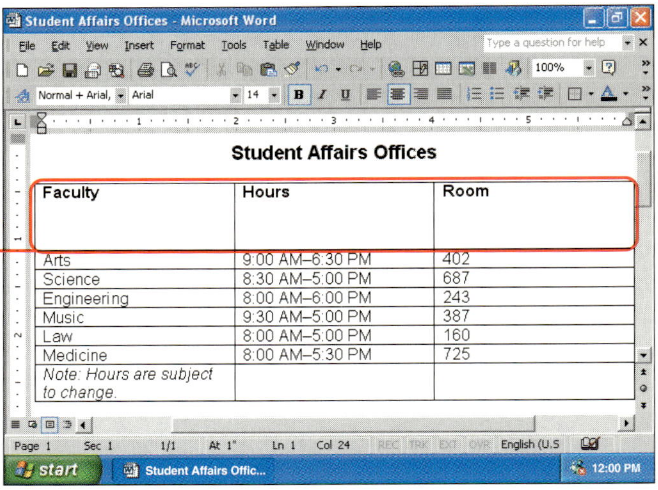

■ You can change a row height only when your document is displayed in the Print Layout or Web Layout view. To change the view of a document, see page 40.

1 Position the mouse I over the bottom edge of the row you want to change to a new height (I changes to ‡).

2 Drag the row edge to a new position.

■ A dotted line shows the new position.

■ The row displays the new height.

Note: When you change the height of a row, the height of the entire table changes.

Can Word automatically adjust a row height or column width?

Yes. When you enter text into a table, Word automatically increases the row height or column width to accommodate the text you type.

Can I change the column width for only a few cells in a column?

Yes. To select the cells you want to change, position the mouse I over the first cell and then drag the mouse until you highlight all the cells you want to change in the column. To change the width of the selected cells, perform steps **1** and **2** on page 199.

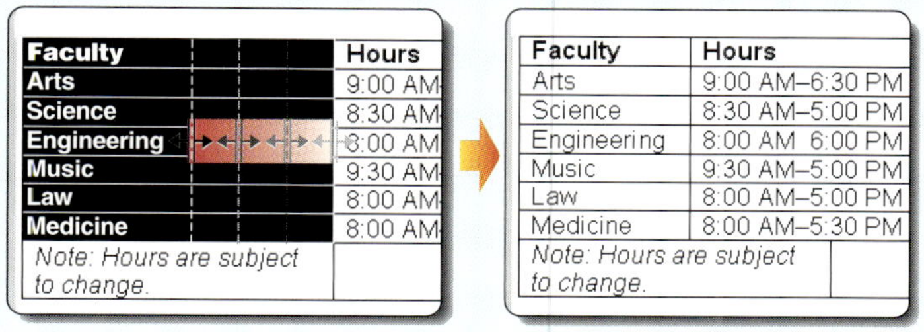

CHANGE COLUMN WIDTH

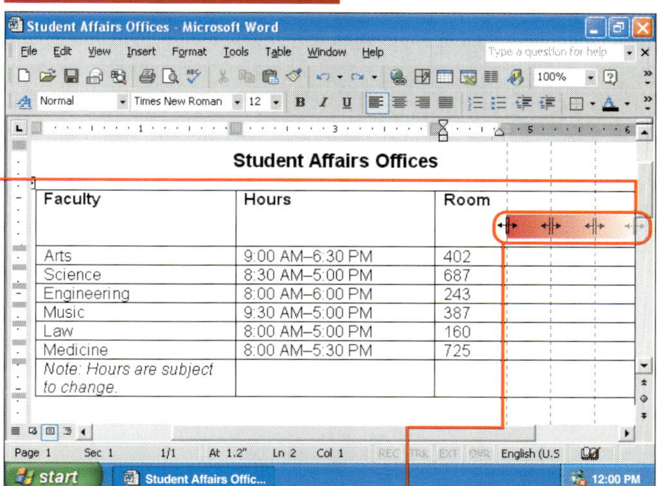

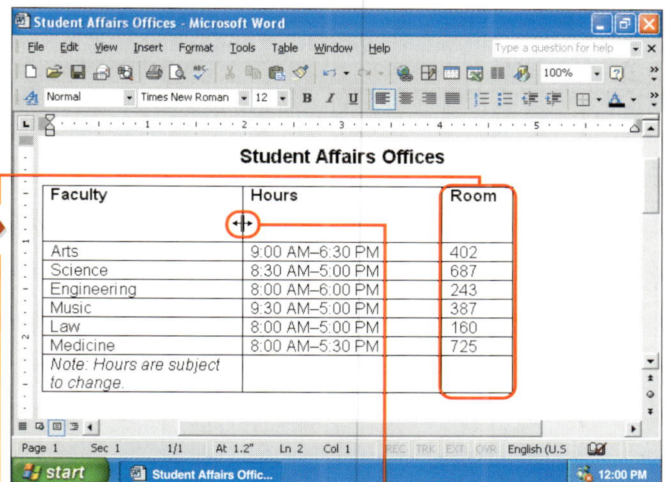

1 Position the mouse I over the right edge of the column you want to change to a new width (I changes to ⇹).

2 Drag the column edge to a new position.

■ A dotted line shows the new position.

■ The column displays the new width.

Note: When you change the width of a column, the width of the neighboring column also changes. When you change the width of the last column, the width of the entire table changes.

FIT LONGEST ITEM

1 To quickly change a column width to fit the longest item in the column, double-click the right edge of the column.

MOVE A TABLE

You can move a table from one location in your document to another.

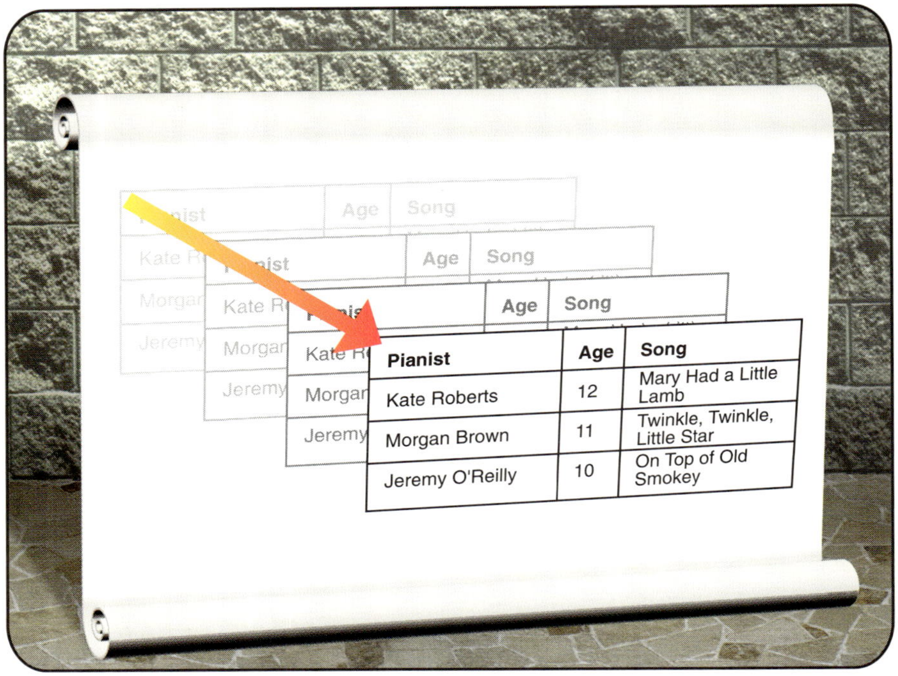

You can move a table only in the Print Layout or Web Layout view. To change the view of a document, see page 40.

MOVE A TABLE

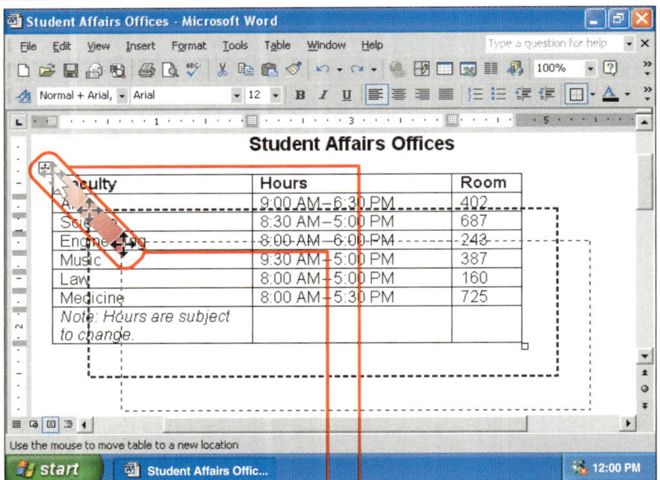

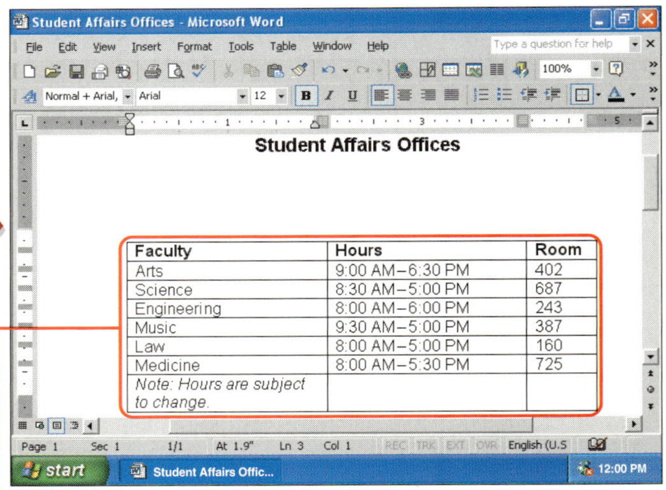

1 Position the mouse I over the table you want to move. A handle (⊞) appears.

Note: You may have to scroll to the left to view the handle.

2 Position the mouse I over the handle (I changes to ✥).

3 Drag the table to a new location.

■ A dashed outline indicates the new location.

■ The table appears in the new location.

■ To copy a table, perform steps **1** to **3**, except press and hold down the **Ctrl** key as you perform step **3**.

RESIZE A TABLE

You can change the size of a table to improve the layout of the table.

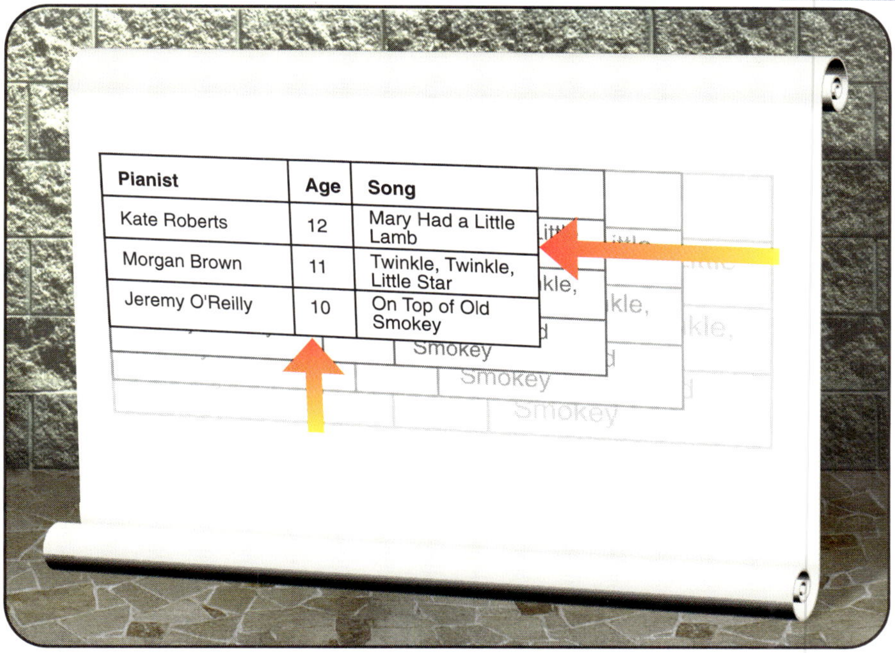

You can resize a table only in the Print Layout or Web Layout view. To change the view of a document, see page 40.

RESIZE A TABLE

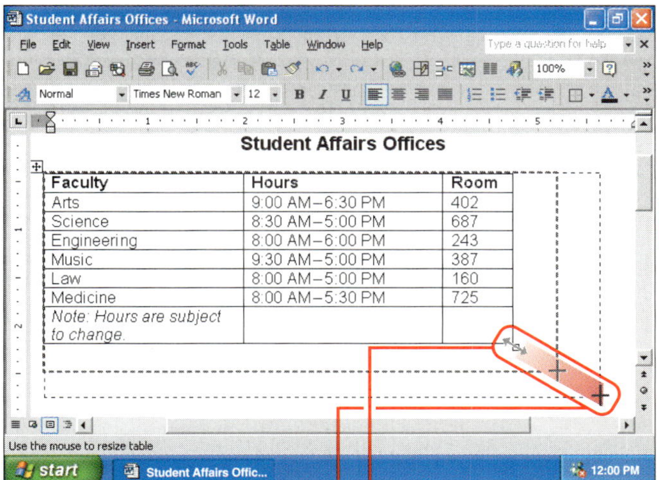

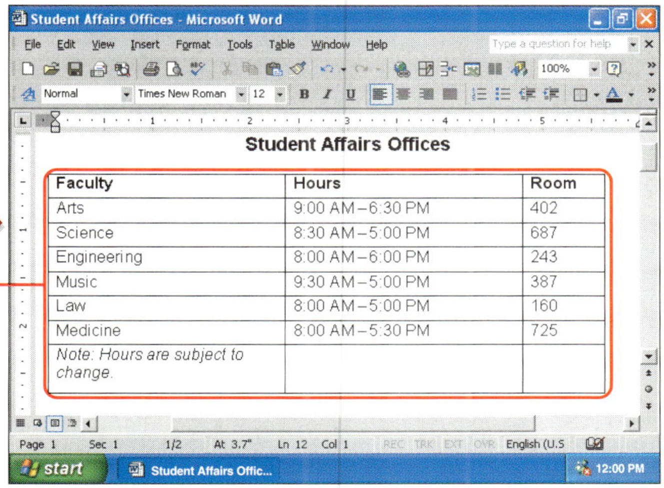

1 Position the mouse I over the table you want to resize. A handle (□) appears.

Note: You may have to scroll to the right to view the handle.

2 Position the mouse I over the handle (I changes to ↘).

3 Drag the handle until the table is the size you want.

■ A dashed outline indicates the new size.

■ The table appears in the new size.

COMBINE CELLS

You can combine two or more cells in your table to create one large cell. Combining cells is useful when you want to display a title across the top or down the side of your table.

COMBINE CELLS

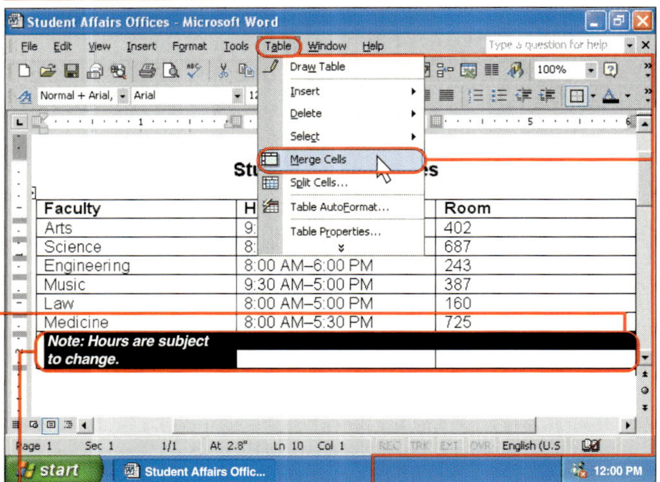

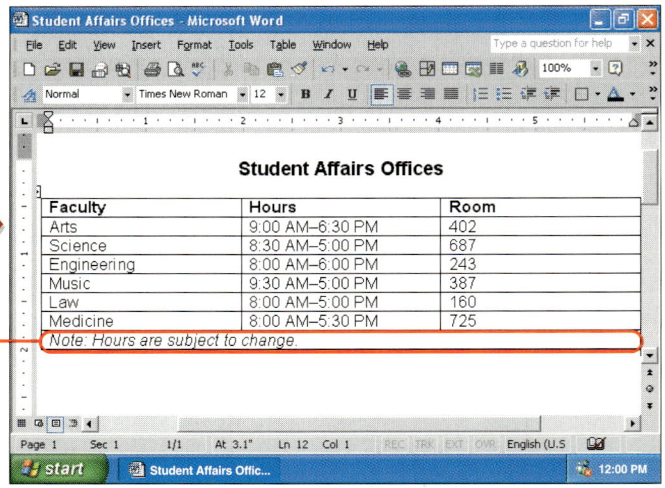

1 Position the mouse I over the first cell you want to combine with other cells.

2 Drag the mouse I until you highlight all the cells you want to combine.

3 Click **Table**.

4 Click **Merge Cells**.

Note: If Merge Cells does not appear on the menu, position the mouse over the bottom of the menu to display all the menu options.

■ The cells combine to create one large cell.

■ To deselect cells, click outside the selected area.

SPLIT CELLS

You can split one cell in your table into two or more cells.

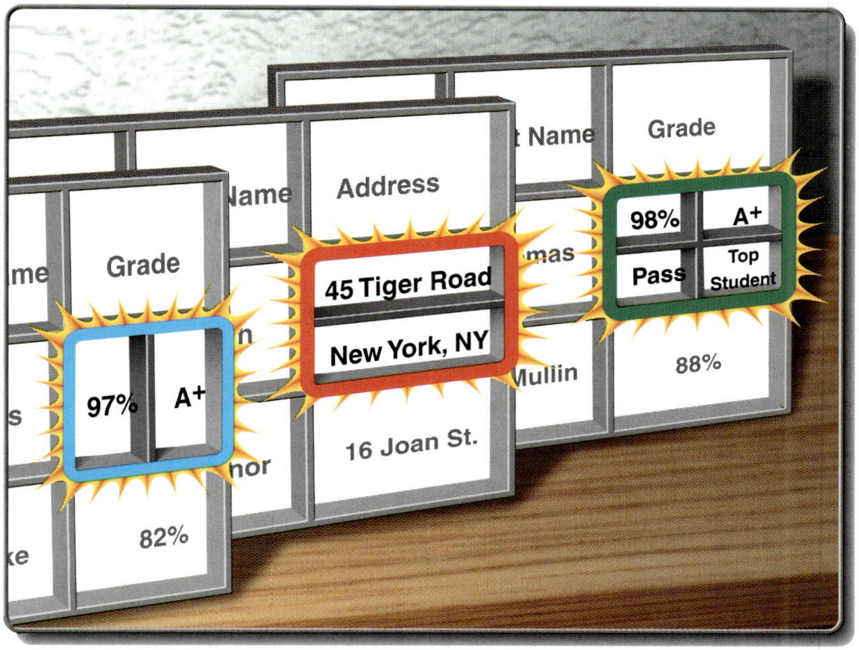

You can split a cell into columns, rows or both columns and rows.

Split Cell into Columns

Split Cell into Rows

Split Cell into Columns and Rows

SPLIT CELLS

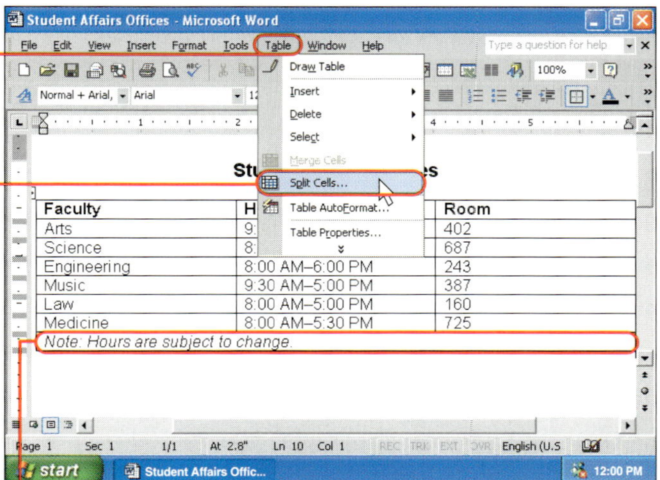

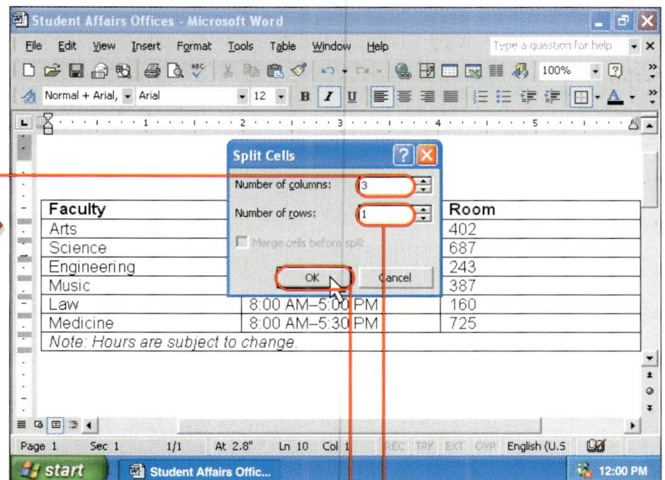

1 Click in the cell you want to split into two or more cells.

2 Click **Table**.

3 Click **Split Cells**.

Note: If Split Cells does not appear on the menu, position the mouse over the bottom of the menu to display all the menu options.

■ The Split Cells dialog box appears.

4 Double-click the number in this area and type the number of columns you want to split the cell into.

5 Double-click the number in this area and type the number of rows you want to split the cell into.

6 Click **OK** to split the cell.

ALIGN TEXT IN CELLS

You can enhance the appearance of your table by changing the position of text in cells.

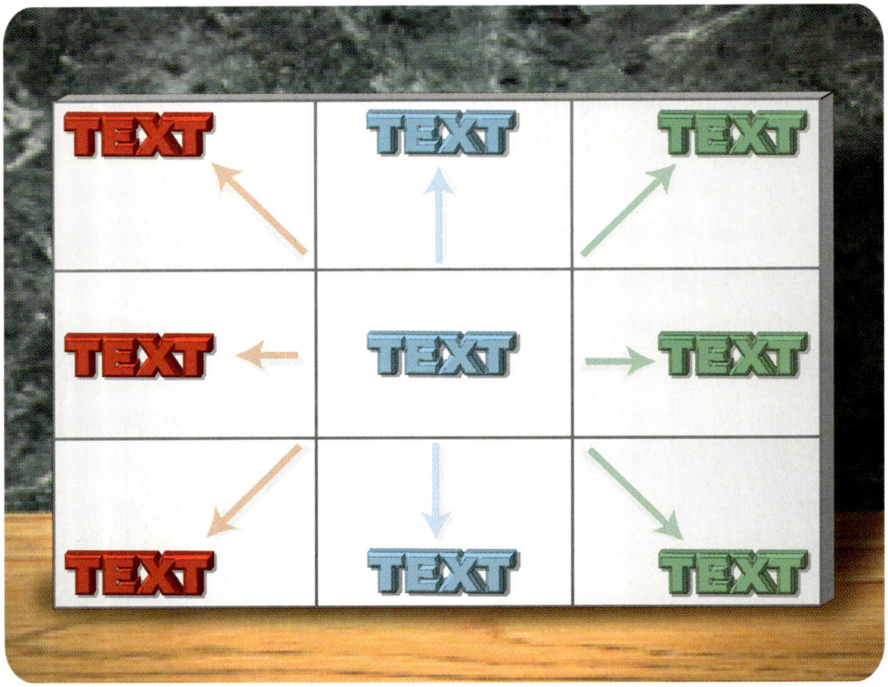

When you enter text into a cell, Word automatically aligns the text at the top left of the cell.

ALIGN TEXT IN CELLS

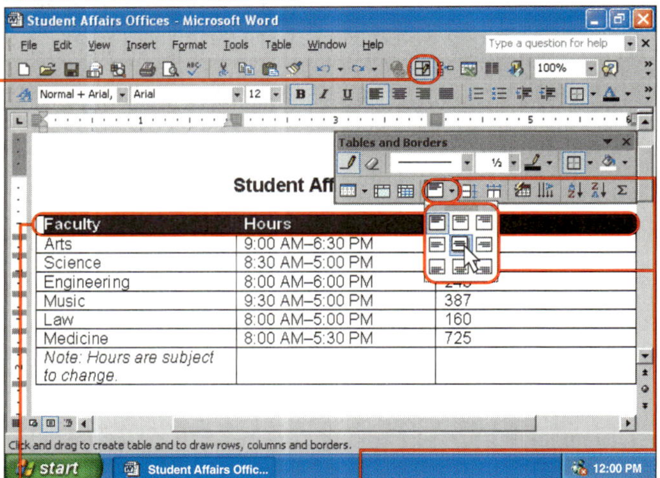

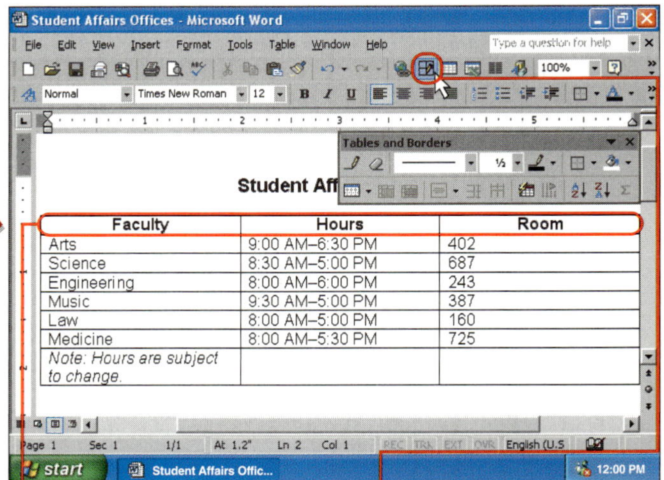

1 To select the cells containing the text you want to align differently, drag the mouse I over the cells.

2 Click [icon] to display the Tables and Borders toolbar.

Note: If [icon] is not displayed, click [icon] on the Standard toolbar to display the button.

3 Click [icon] in this area.

4 Click the alignment you want to use.

■ The text displays the new alignment.

■ To deselect cells, click outside the selected area.

5 To hide the Tables and Borders toolbar, click [icon].

ADD SHADING TO CELLS

You can add shading to cells to make the cells stand out in your table.

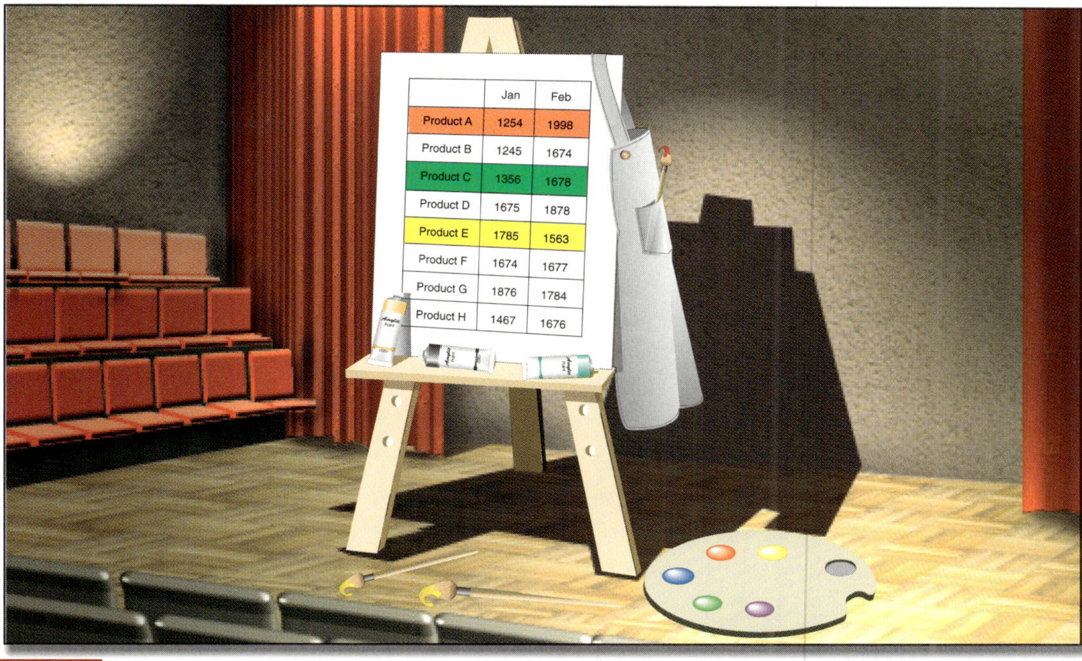

ADD SHADING TO CELLS

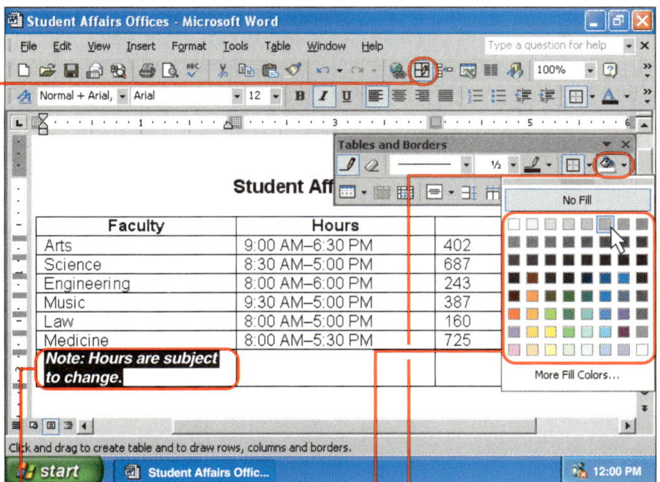

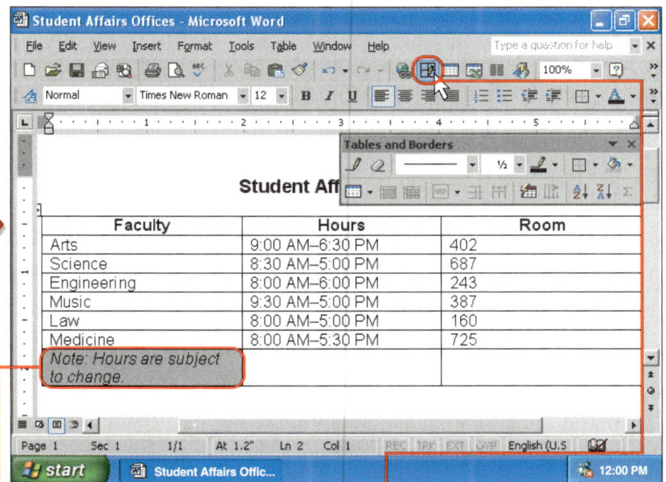

1 To select the cells you want to display shading, drag the mouse I over the cells.

2 Click ▣ to display the Tables and Borders toolbar.

Note: If ▣ is not displayed, click » on the Standard toolbar to display the button.

3 Click ▾ in this area to select a color for the shading.

4 Click the color you want to use.

■ The cells you selected display the shading.

■ To deselect cells, click outside the selected area.

5 To hide the Tables and Borders toolbar, click ▣.

■ To remove shading from cells, repeat steps 1 to 5, selecting **No Fill** in step 4.

CHANGE TABLE BORDERS

You can change the borders in your table to enhance the appearance of the table.

CHANGE TABLE BORDERS

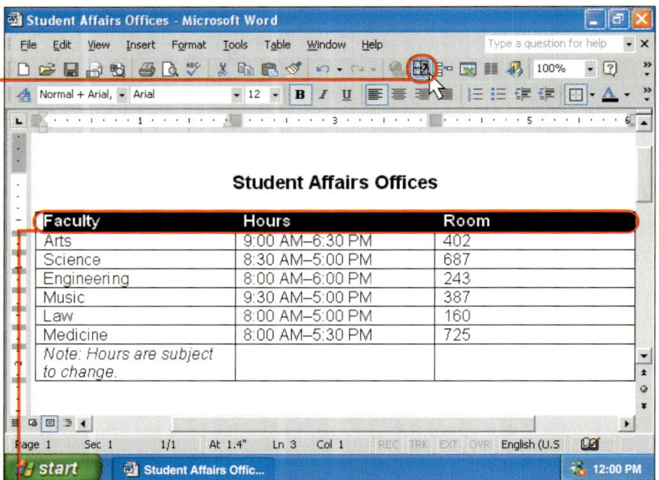

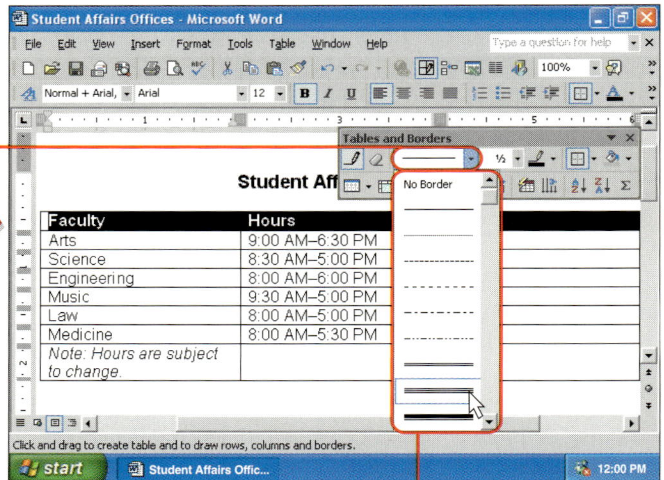

1 To select the cells where you want to change the border, drag the mouse I over the cells.

2 Click ▦ to display the Tables and Borders toolbar.

Note: If ▦ is not displayed, click » on the Standard toolbar to display the button.

■ The Tables and Borders toolbar appears.

3 Click this area to display a list of the available line styles for the border.

4 Click the line style you want to use.

Why would I change the border for only some of the cells in my table?

Changing the border for specific cells in your table can help you emphasize important information or divide your table into sections.

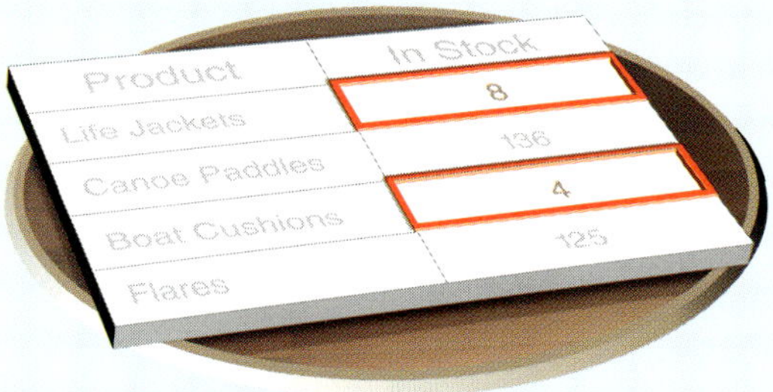

Can I remove a border from my table?

Yes. When you remove a border from your table, the border appears in gray in your document, but will not appear on a printed page. To remove a border from your table, perform steps **1** and **2** below. Then perform steps **5** to **7**, selecting in step **6**.

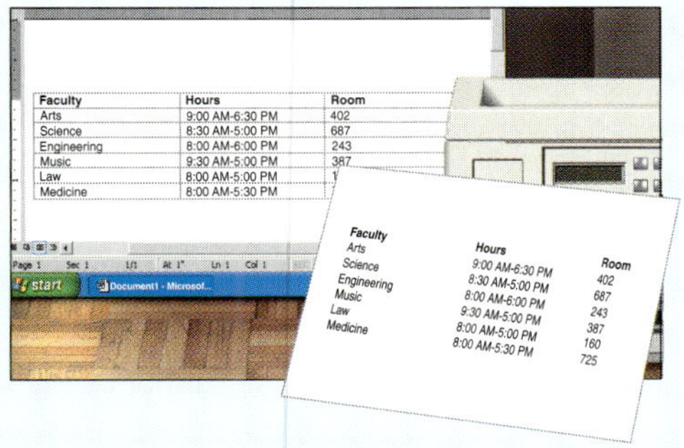

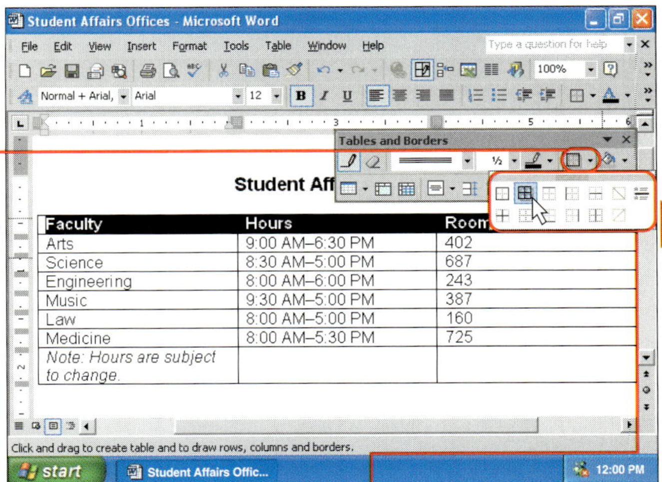

5 Click in this area to display the borders you can change.

6 Click the border you want to change.

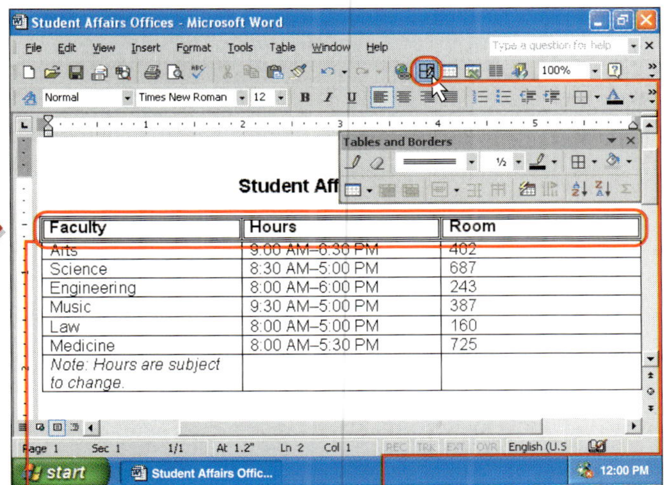

- The cells you selected display the new border.
- To deselect cells, click outside the selected area.

7 To hide the Tables and Borders toolbar, click .

FORMAT A TABLE

Word offers many ready-to-use designs that you can choose from to quickly give your table a professional appearance.

FORMAT A TABLE

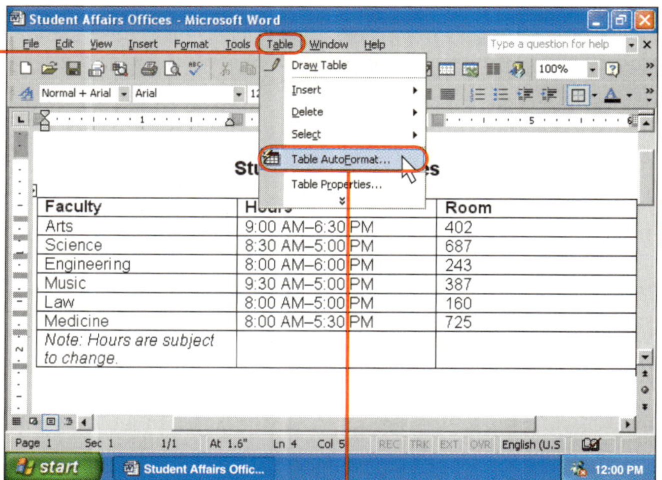

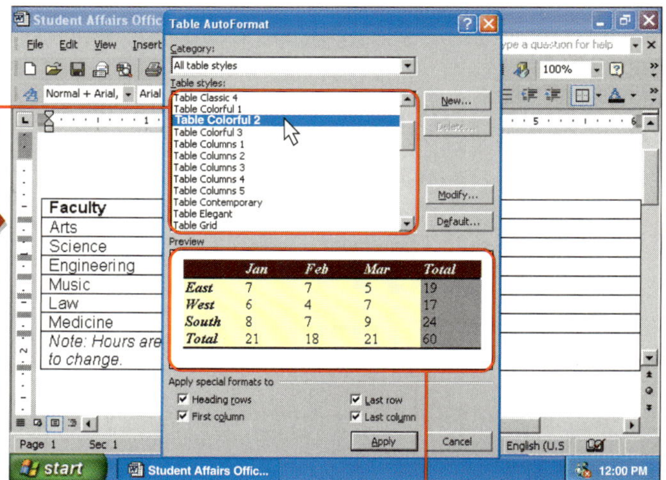

1 Click anywhere in the table you want to format.

2 Click **Table**.

3 Click **Table AutoFormat**.

■ The Table AutoFormat dialog box appears.

■ This area displays a list of the available table designs.

4 Click the table design you want to use.

■ This area displays a sample of the table design you selected.

Note: To display a sample of a different table design, repeat step 4.

What parts of a table can Word apply special formats to?

Word can apply special formats to the heading rows, the first column, the last row and the last column of a table. For example, Word can **bold text** in the heading rows of a table or apply borders to the last row of a table.

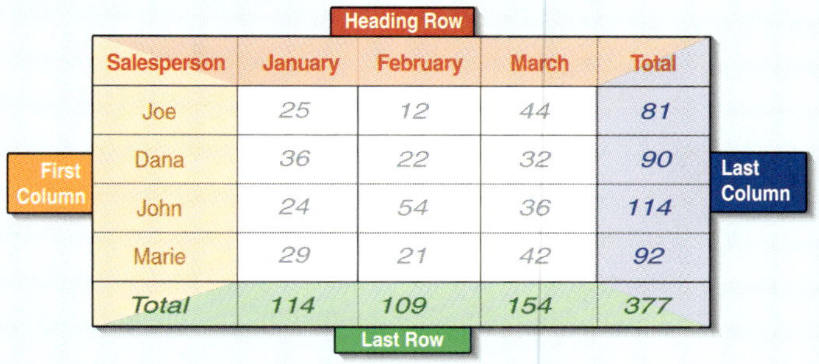

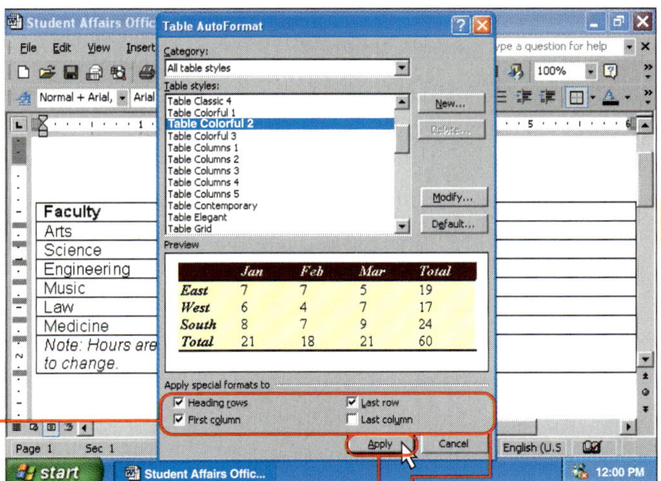

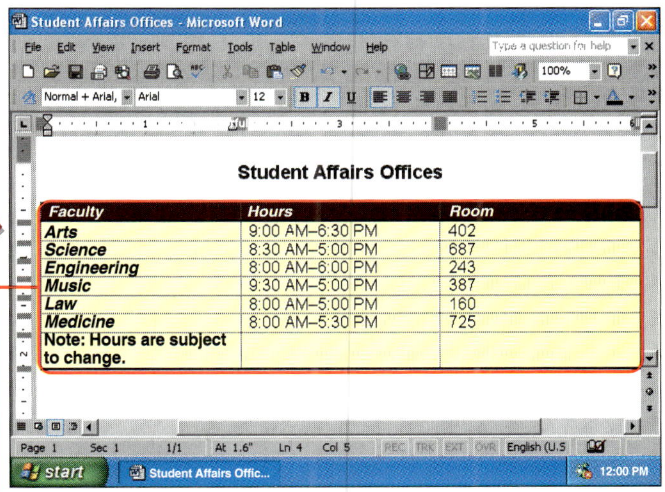

- This area displays the parts of the table that Word can apply special formats to.
- A check mark (✔) beside an option indicates that Word will apply special formats to that part of the table.

5 To add (✔) or remove (☐) a check mark beside an option, click the option.

6 Click **Apply** or press the Enter key to apply the design to your table.

- The table displays the design you selected.
- To remove a table design from a table, repeat steps 1 to 4, selecting **Table Grid** in step 4. Then press the Enter key.

color
Paint

CHAPTER 12

Work With Graphics

Are you interested in using graphics to enhance the appearance of your document? This chapter shows you how.

Add an AutoShape....212

Add WordArt....214

Add a Text Box....216

Add a Picture....218

Add a Clip Art Image....220

Move a Graphic....224

Resize a Graphic....225

Change Color of a Graphic....226

Rotate a Graphic....227

Create a Drawing Canvas....228

Wrap Text Around a Graphic....230

Add a Diagram....232

ADD AN AUTOSHAPE

Word provides a group of ready-made shapes, called AutoShapes, that you can add to your document.

Word offers several types of AutoShapes such as lines, arrows, stars and banners.

Word can display AutoShapes only in the Print Layout and Web Layout views. To change the view of a document, see page 40.

ADD AN AUTOSHAPE

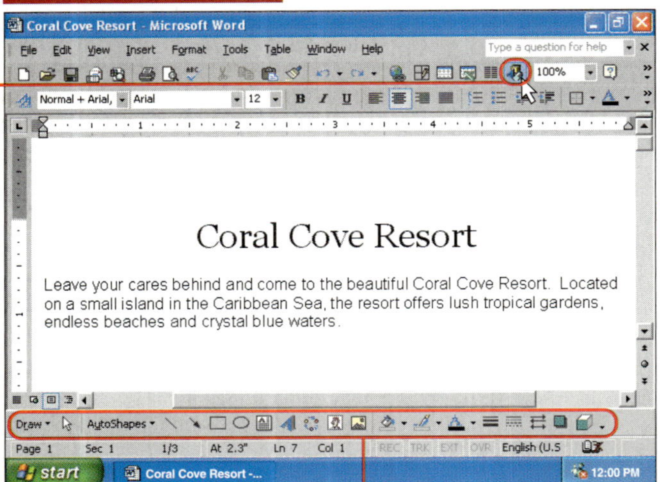

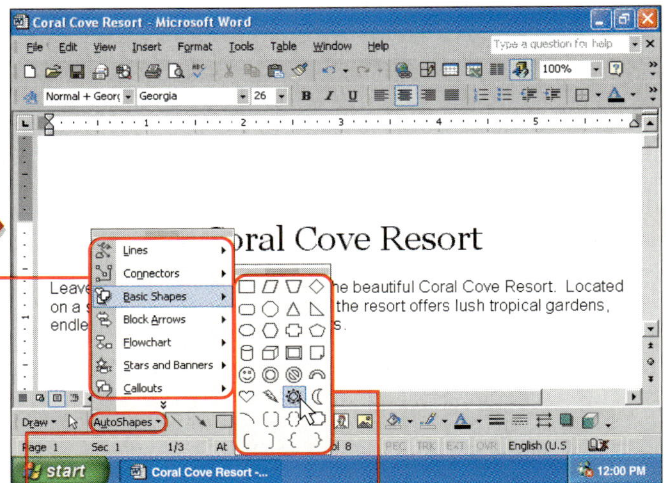

1 Click to display the Drawing toolbar.

Note: If is not displayed, click on the Standard toolbar to display the button.

■ The Drawing toolbar appears.

2 Click **AutoShapes**.

3 Click the type of AutoShape you want to add.

4 Click the AutoShape you want to add.

How can I add text to an AutoShape?

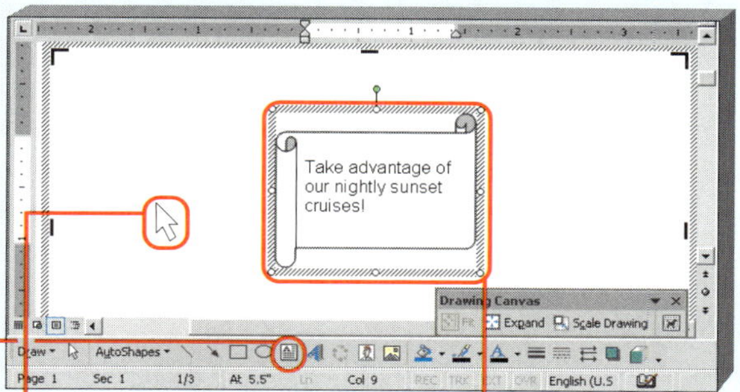

1 Click a blank area beside the AutoShape to display the drawing canvas.

2 Click on the Drawing toolbar.

*Note: If you are adding text to an AutoShape from the Callouts category, do not perform steps **1** and **2**.*

3 Click the AutoShape you want to display text and then type the text.

4 When you finish typing the text, click outside the AutoShape.

How do I delete an AutoShape?

To delete an AutoShape, click an edge of the AutoShape and then press the **Delete** key.

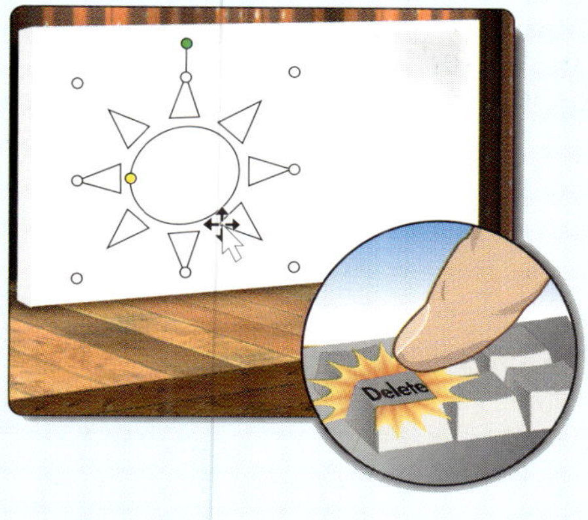

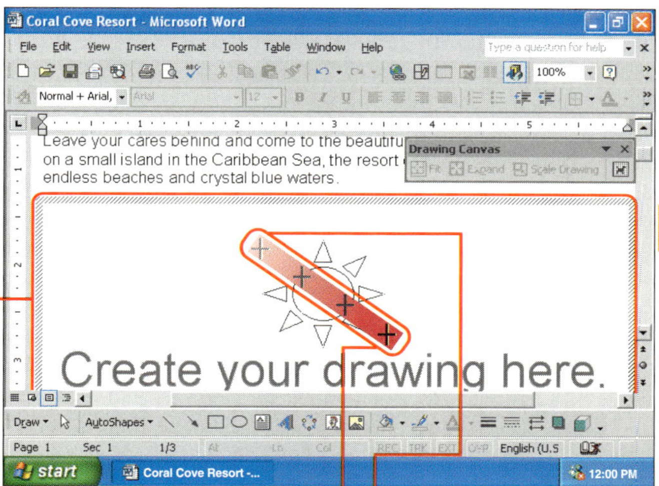

■ Word adds a drawing canvas to your document. A drawing canvas provides an area that allows you to arrange graphics and move several graphics at once.

Note: For more information on using a drawing canvas, see page 228.

5 Position the mouse + where you want to begin drawing the AutoShape.

6 Drag the mouse + until the AutoShape is the size you want.

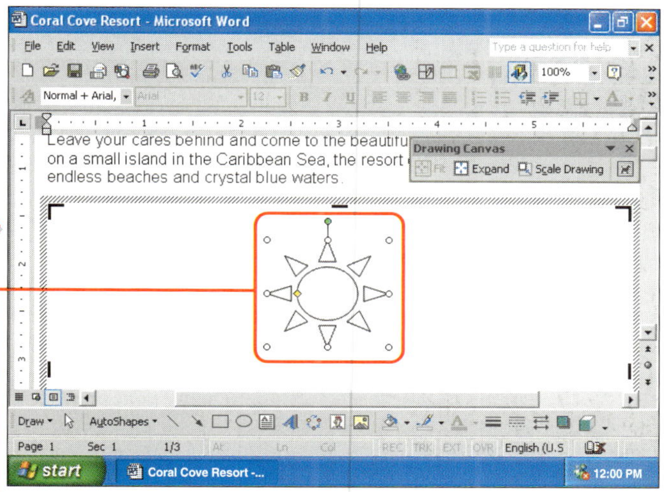

■ The AutoShape appears. The handles (o) around the AutoShape allow you to change the size of the AutoShape. To move or resize an AutoShape, see page 224 or 225.

■ To deselect an AutoShape, click outside the AutoShape.

■ To hide the drawing canvas, click outside the drawing canvas or press the **Esc** key.

*Note: To hide the Drawing toolbar, repeat step **1**.*

ADD WORDART

You can add WordArt to your document to display a decorative title or draw attention to important information.

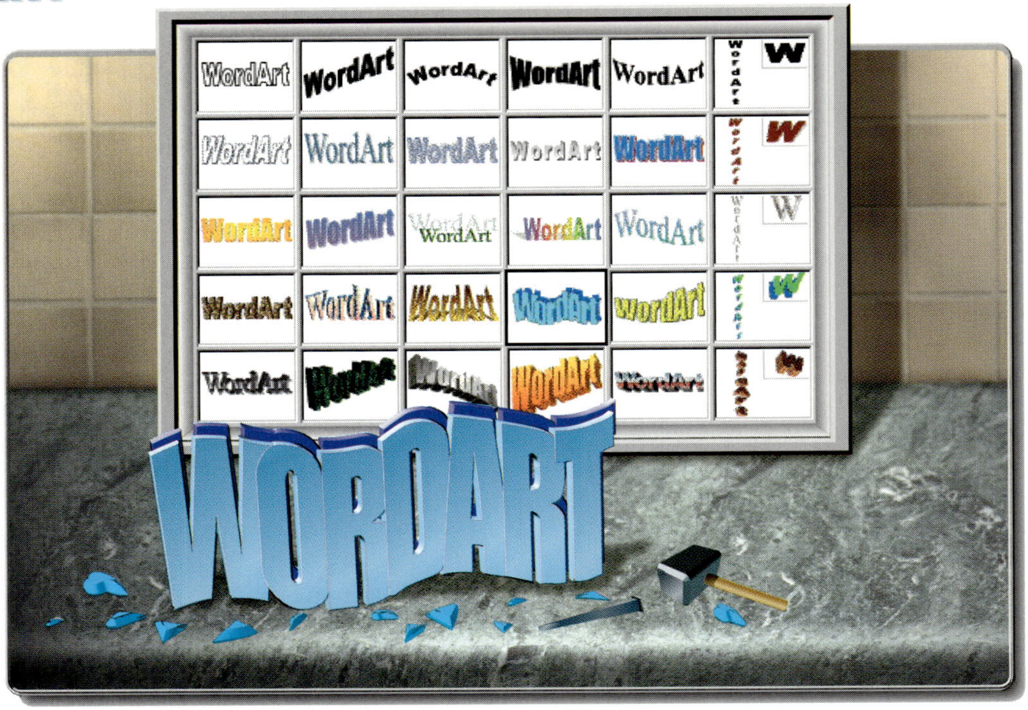

ADD WORDART

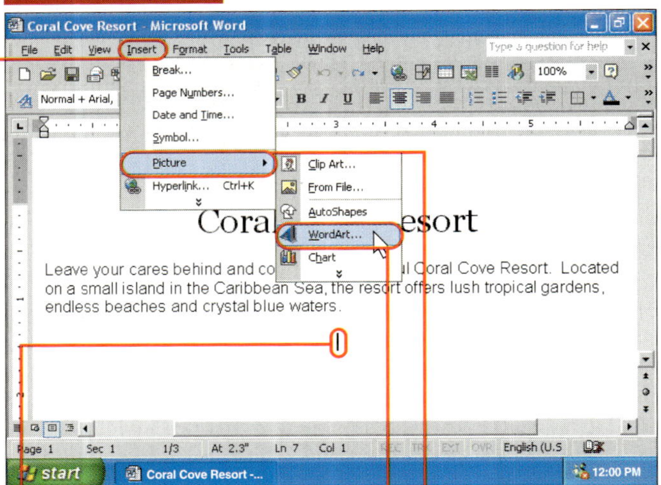

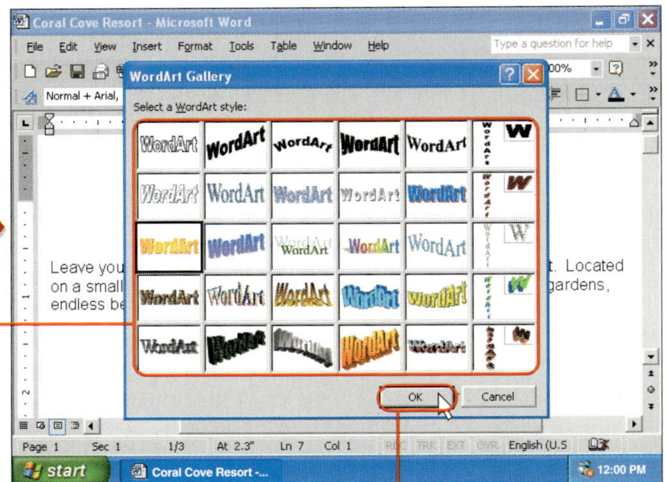

1 Click the location in your document where you want to add WordArt.

2 Click **Insert**.

3 Click **Picture**.

4 Click **WordArt**.

■ The WordArt Gallery dialog box appears.

5 Click the WordArt style you want to use.

6 Click **OK** to confirm your selection.

How do I edit WordArt text?

To edit WordArt text, double-click the WordArt to redisplay the Edit WordArt Text dialog box. Then perform steps **7** and **8** below to specify the new text you want the WordArt to display.

How can I change the appearance of WordArt?

When you click WordArt, the WordArt toolbar appears, displaying buttons that allow you to change the appearance of the WordArt. For example, you can click [Aa] to display all the letters in the WordArt at the same height.

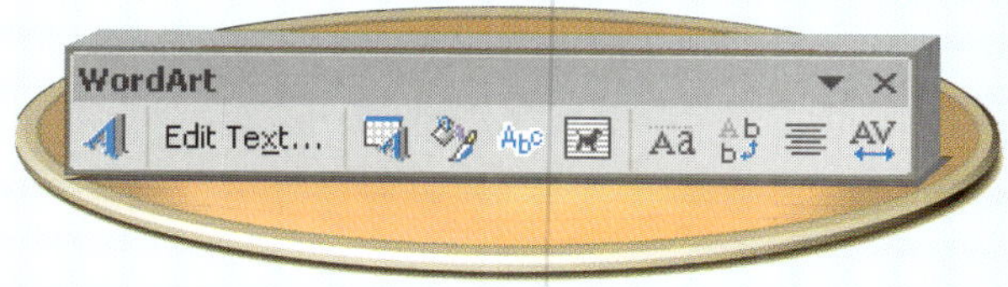

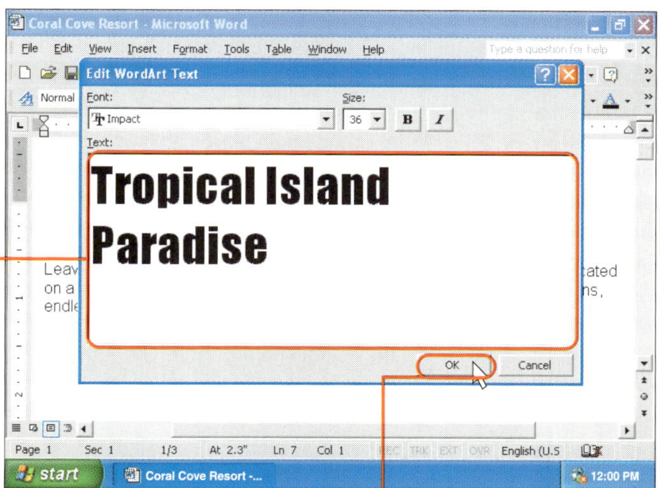

■ The Edit WordArt Text dialog box appears.

7 Type the text you want the WordArt to display.

8 Click **OK** to add the WordArt to your document.

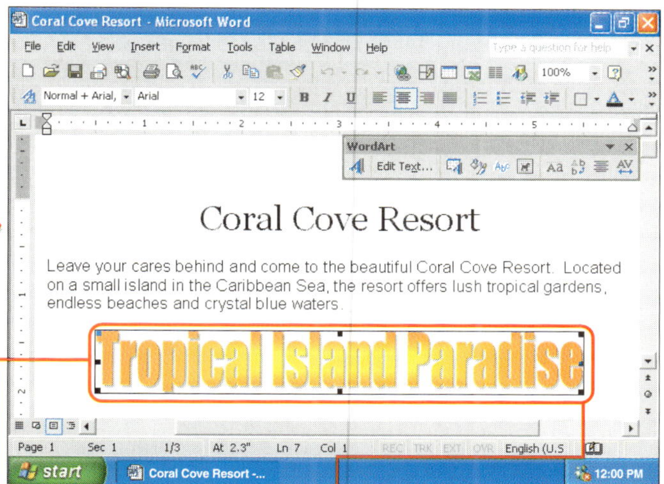

■ The WordArt appears in your document.

Note: To move or resize WordArt, see page 224 or 225.

DELETE WORDART

1 Click the WordArt you want to delete. Handles (■) appear around the WordArt.

2 Press the Delete key to delete the WordArt.

ADD A TEXT BOX

You can add a text box to your document. Text boxes are useful for controlling the placement of text in a document.

Word can display text boxes only in the Print Layout and Web Layout views. To change the view of a document, see page 40.

ADD A TEXT BOX

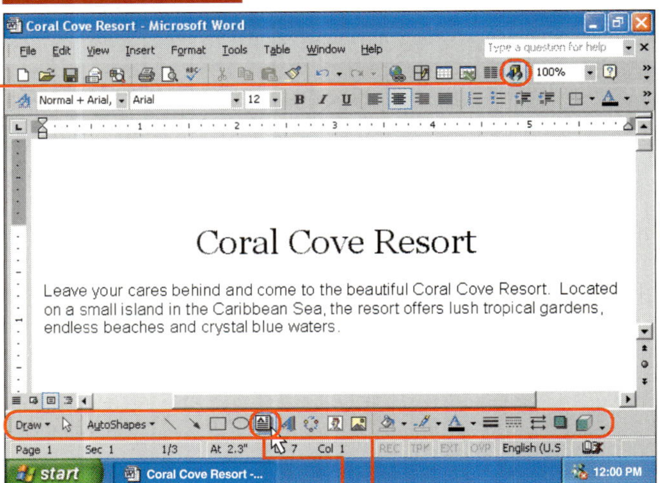

1 Click to display the Drawing toolbar.

Note: If is not displayed, click on the Standard toolbar to display the button.

■ The Drawing toolbar appears.

2 Click to add a text box.

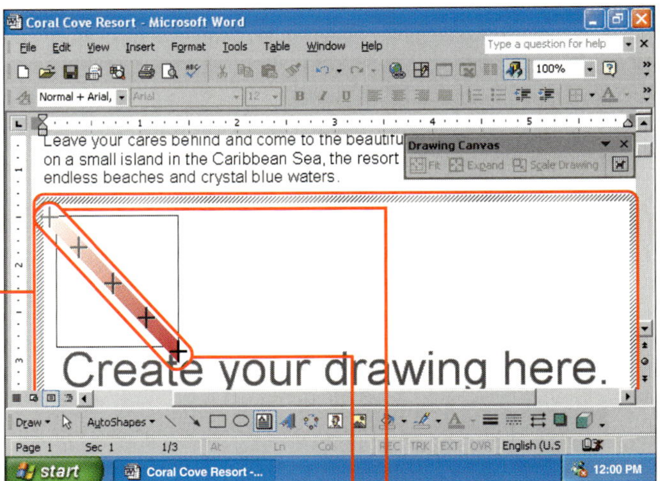

■ Word adds a drawing canvas to your document. A drawing canvas provides an area that allows you to arrange graphics and move several graphics at once.

Note: For more information on using a drawing canvas, see page 228.

3 Position the mouse + where you want to begin drawing the text box.

4 Drag the mouse + until the text box is the size you want.

How do I edit the text in a text box?

To edit the text in a text box, click the text box and then edit the text as you would edit any text in a document. To edit text, see page 54. When you finish editing the text, click outside the text box.

Can I format the text in a text box?

Yes. You can format the text in a text box as you would format any text in a document. For example, you can bold, italicize and change the font of text in a text box. To format text, see pages 88 to 97.

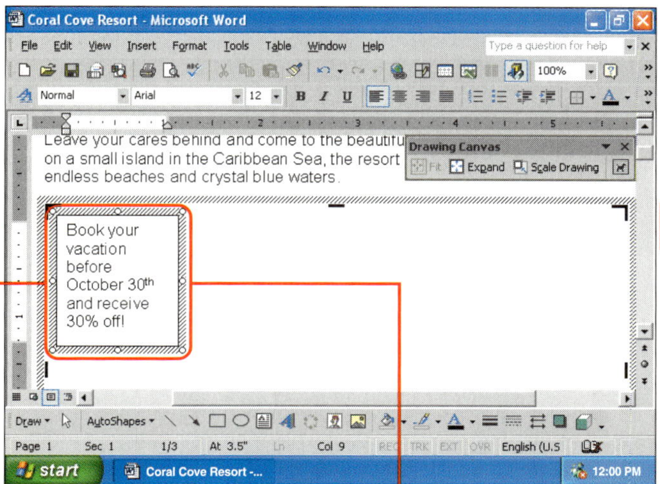

■ The text box appears. The handles (o) around the text box allow you to change the size of the text box. To move or resize a text box, see page 224 or 225.

5 Type the text you want the text box to display.

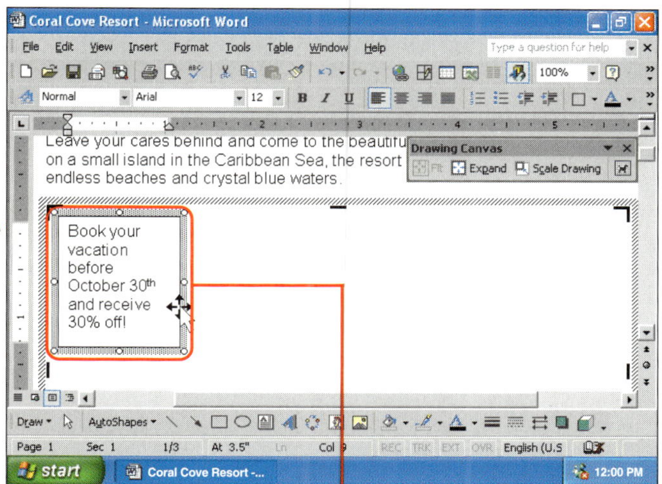

■ To deselect a text box, click outside the text box.

■ To hide the drawing canvas, click outside the drawing canvas or press the **Esc** key.

Note: To hide the Drawing toolbar, repeat step 1.

DELETE A TEXT BOX

1 Click an edge of the text box you want to delete. Handles (o) appear around the text box.

2 Press the **Delete** key to delete the text box.

ADD A PICTURE

You can add a picture to your document to illustrate a concept or enhance the appearance of the document.

Word can display pictures only in the Print Layout and Web Layout views. To change the view of a document, see page 40.

ADD A PICTURE

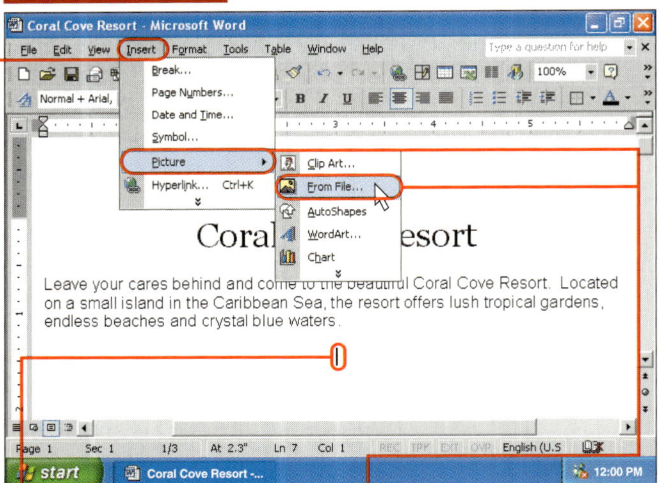

1 Click the location in your document where you want to add a picture.

2 Click **Insert**.

3 Click **Picture**.

4 Click **From File**.

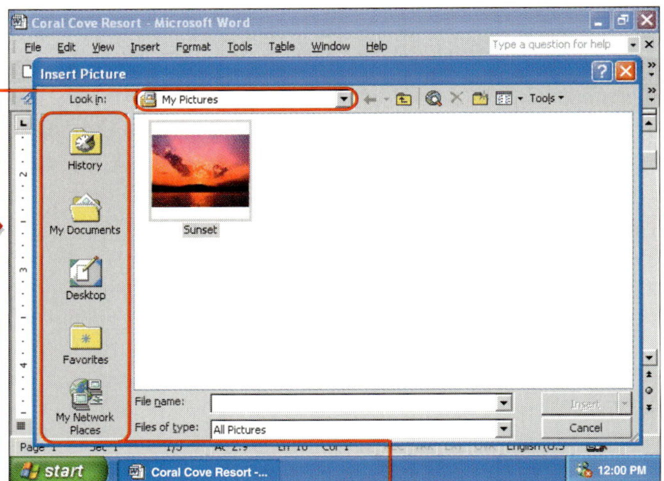

■ The Insert Picture dialog box appears.

■ This area shows the location of the displayed pictures. You can click this area to change the location.

■ This area allows you to access pictures stored in commonly used locations. You can click a location to display the pictures stored in the location.

Note: For information on the commonly used locations, see the top of page 23.

Where can I get pictures that I can add to my documents?

You can purchase collections of pictures at computer stores or obtain pictures on the Internet. You can also use a scanner to scan pictures into your computer or create your own pictures using an image editing program, such as Jasc Paint Shop Pro.

How can I change the appearance of a picture?

When you click a picture, the Picture toolbar appears, displaying buttons that allow you to change the appearance of the picture. For example, you can click [icon] or [icon] to increase or decrease the brightness of the picture.

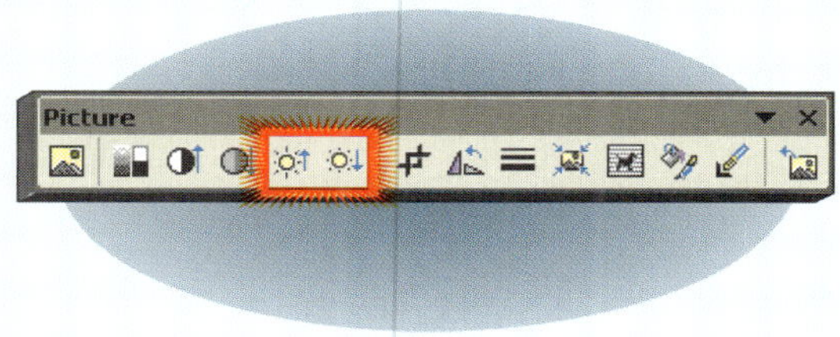

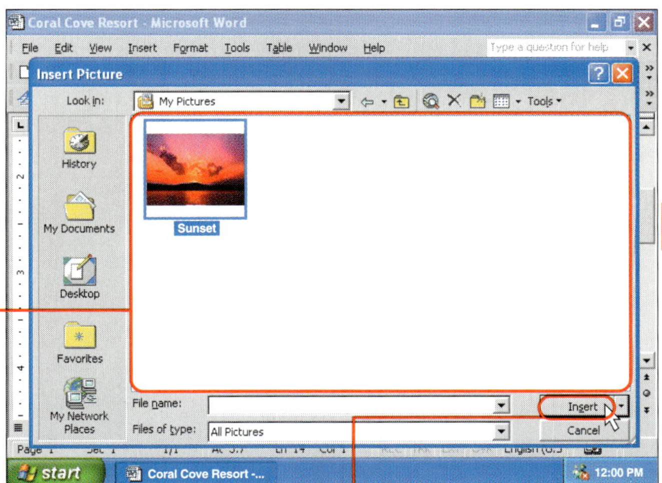

5 Click the picture you want to add to your document.

6 Click **Insert** to add the picture to your document.

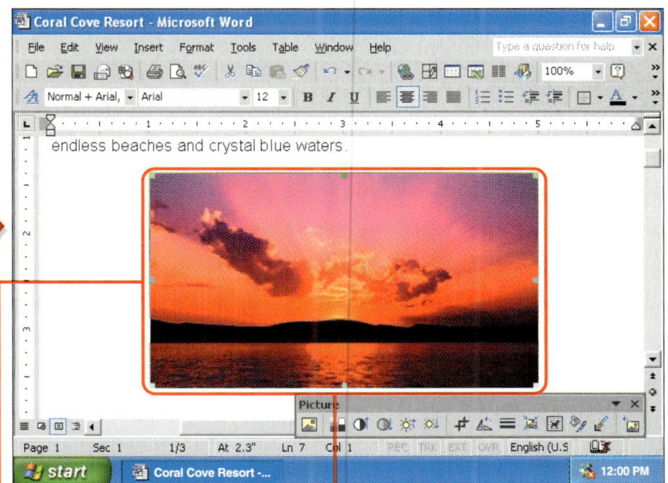

■ The picture appears in your document.

Note: To move or resize a picture, see page 224 or 225.

DELETE A PICTURE

1 Click the picture you want to delete. Handles (■) appear around the picture.

2 Press the Delete key to delete the picture.

ADD A CLIP ART IMAGE

You can add professionally-designed clip art images to your document. Clip art images can help illustrate concepts and make your document more interesting.

ADD A CLIP ART IMAGE

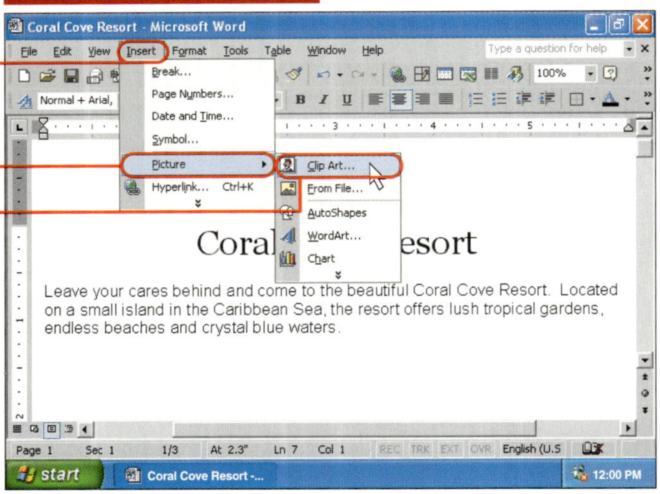

1 Click **Insert**.

2 Click **Picture**.

3 Click **Clip Art**.

*Note: The first time you add a clip art image to a document, the Add Clips to Organizer dialog box appears. Click **Now** in the dialog box to catalog the image, sound and video files on your computer.*

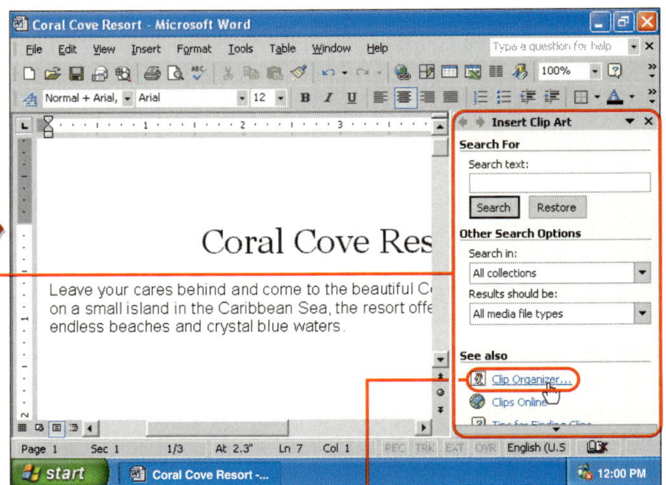

■ The Insert Clip Art task pane appears.

4 Click **Clip Organizer** to view the image, sound and video files in the Clip Organizer.

■ The Microsoft Clip Organizer window appears.

How does the Clip Organizer arrange image, sound and video files?

The Clip Organizer arranges media files into three main folders.

My Collections

Displays the media files you have specified as your favorites and media files that came with Microsoft Windows.

Office Collections

Displays the media files that came with Microsoft Office.

Web Collections

Displays the media files that are available at Microsoft's Web site and Web sites in partnership with Microsoft.

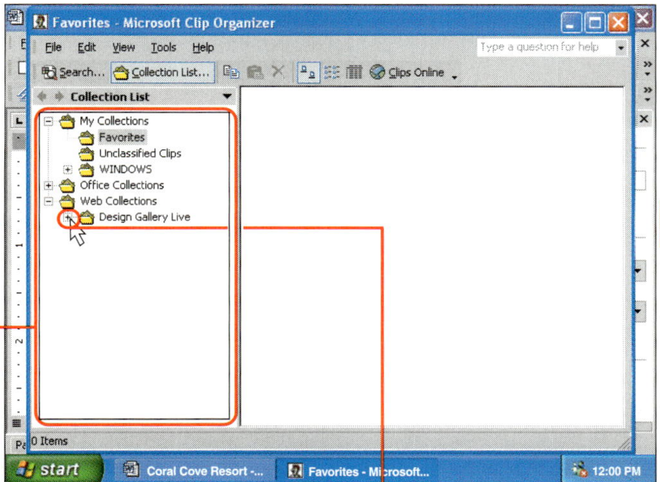

■ This area lists the folders containing image, sound and video files that you can add to your document.

■ A folder displaying a plus sign (⊞) contains hidden folders.

5 To display the hidden folders within a folder, click a plus sign (⊞) beside a folder (⊞ changes to ⊟).

Note: You must be connected to the Internet to view the contents of the Web Collections folder.

■ The hidden folders appear.

Note: To once again hide the folders within a folder, click a minus sign (⊟) beside a folder.

6 Click a folder of interest.

■ This area displays the contents of the folder you selected.

7 Click the image you want to add to your document.

CONTINUED

ADD A CLIP ART IMAGE

After you locate an image you want to add to your document, you can copy the image and then place the image in your document.

ADD A CLIP ART IMAGE (CONTINUED)

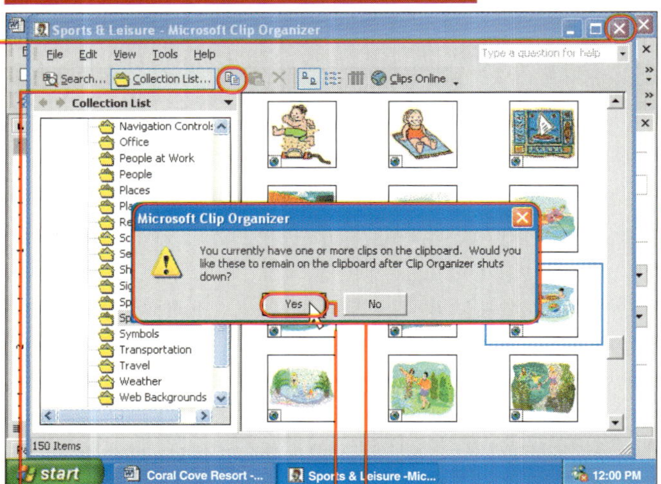

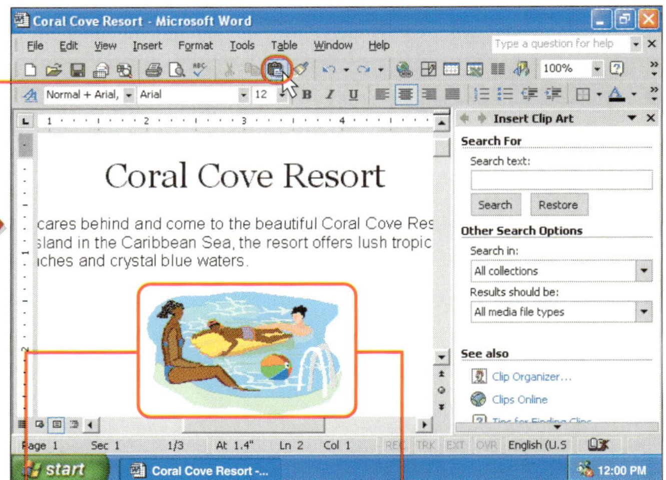

8 Click to copy the image you selected.

9 Click to close the Microsoft Clip Organizer window.

■ A dialog box appears, stating that you have one or more clip art images on the clipboard.

Note: The clipboard temporarily stores information you have selected to move or copy.

10 Click **Yes** to keep the image on the clipboard.

11 Click the location in your document where you want to add the image.

12 Click to place the image in your document.

■ The image appears in your document.

Note: To move or resize an image, see page 224 or 225.

Where can I obtain more clip art images?

You can buy collections of clip art images at computer stores. Many Web sites, such as www.allfree-clipart.com and www.noeticart.com, also offer clip art images you can use in your documents.

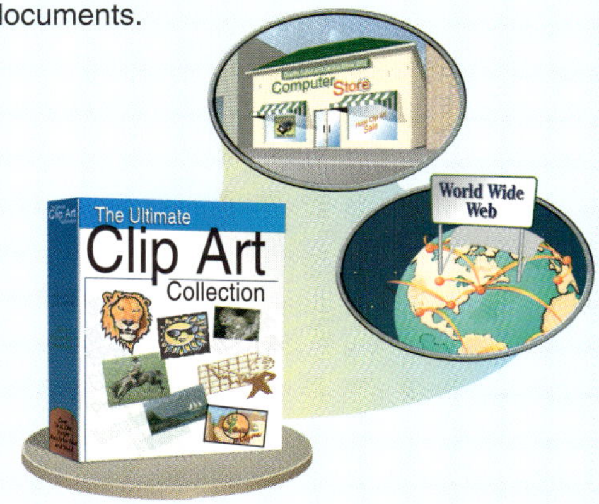

How do I delete a clip art image?

To delete a clip art image, click the clip art image and then press the Delete key.

SEARCH FOR A CLIP ART IMAGE

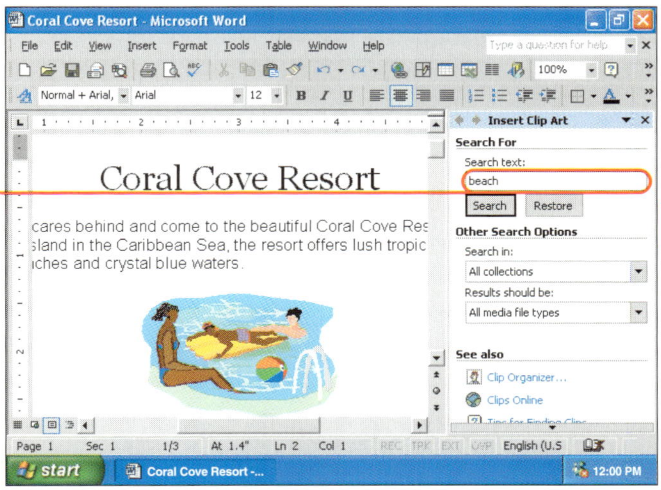

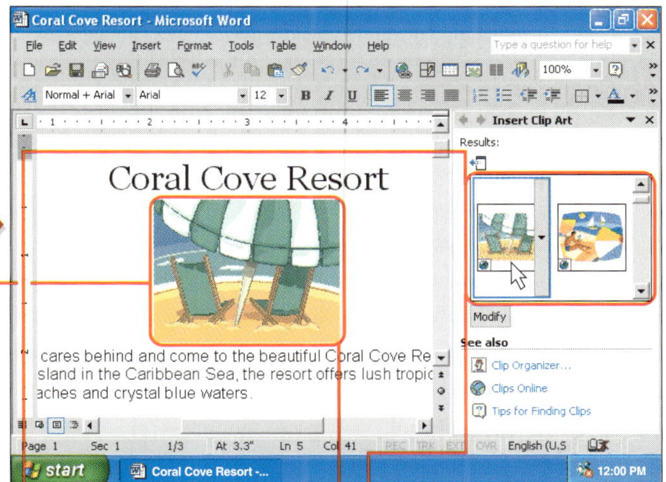

You can search for clip art images by specifying one or more words of interest.

1 Click this area and then type one or more words that describe the clip art image you want to find. Then press the Enter key.

Note: If the Insert Clip Art task pane is not displayed, perform steps 1 to 3 on page 220 to display the task pane.

■ This area displays the images that match the words you specified.

2 Click the location in your document where you want to add an image.

3 Click the image you want to add to your document.

■ The image appears in your document.

Note: To move or resize an image, see page 224 or 225.

MOVE A GRAPHIC

You can change the location of a graphic in your document.

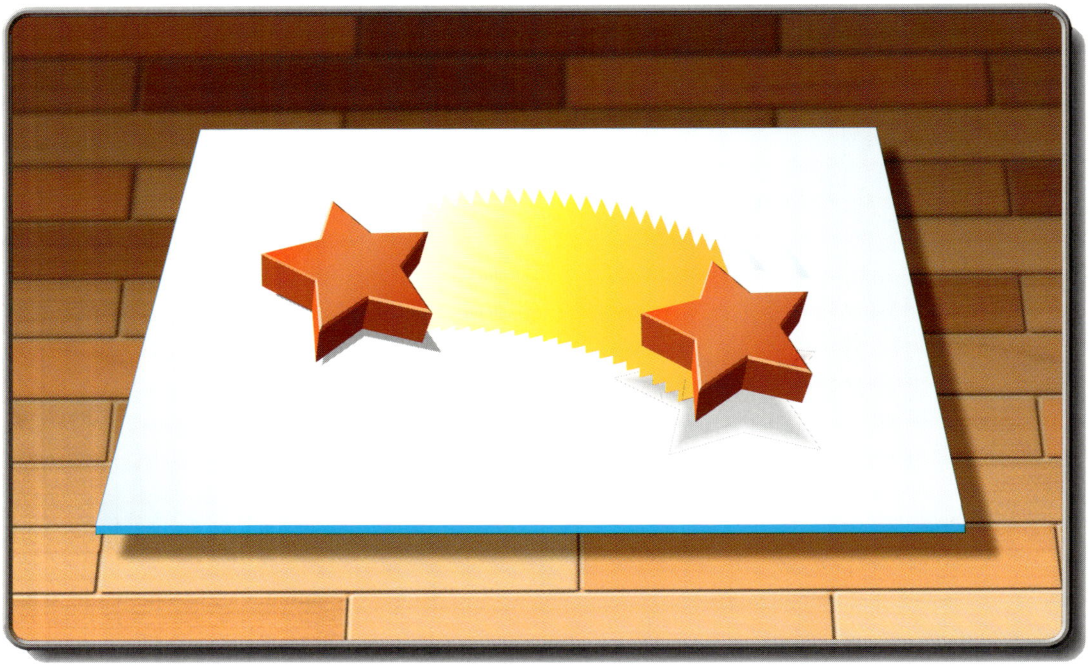

Word can display all types of graphics in the Print Layout and Web Layout views. To change the view of a document, see page 40.

MOVE A GRAPHIC

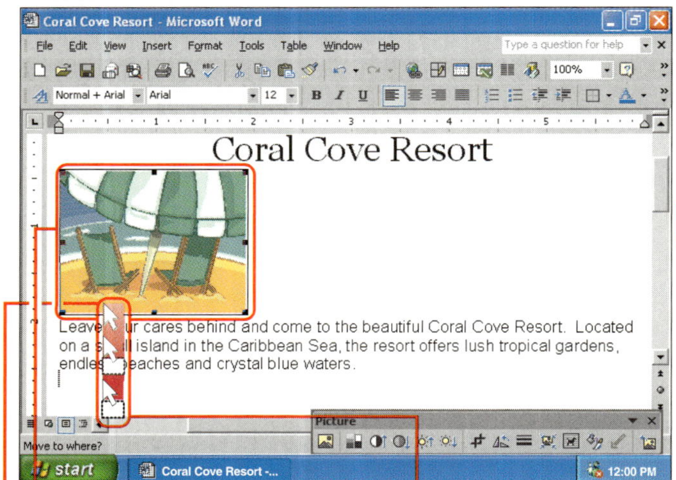

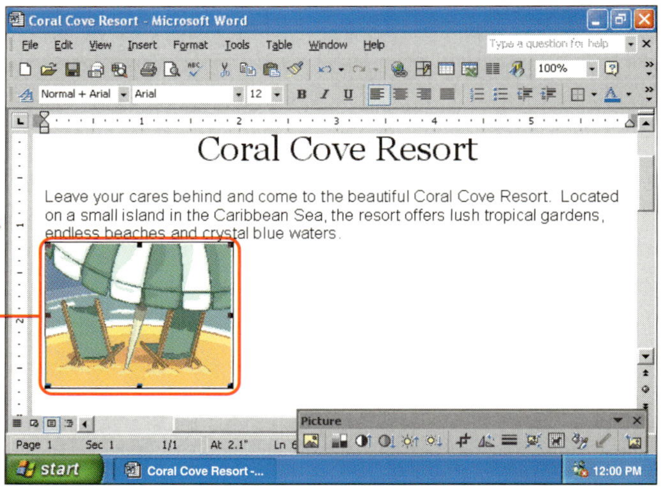

1 Click the graphic you want to move. Handles (o or ■) appear around the graphic.

2 Position the mouse I over an edge of the graphic (I changes to ✥ or ↖).

3 Drag the graphic to a new location in your document.

■ The graphic appears in the new location.

■ To deselect the graphic, click outside the graphic.

RESIZE A GRAPHIC

You can change the size of a graphic in your document.

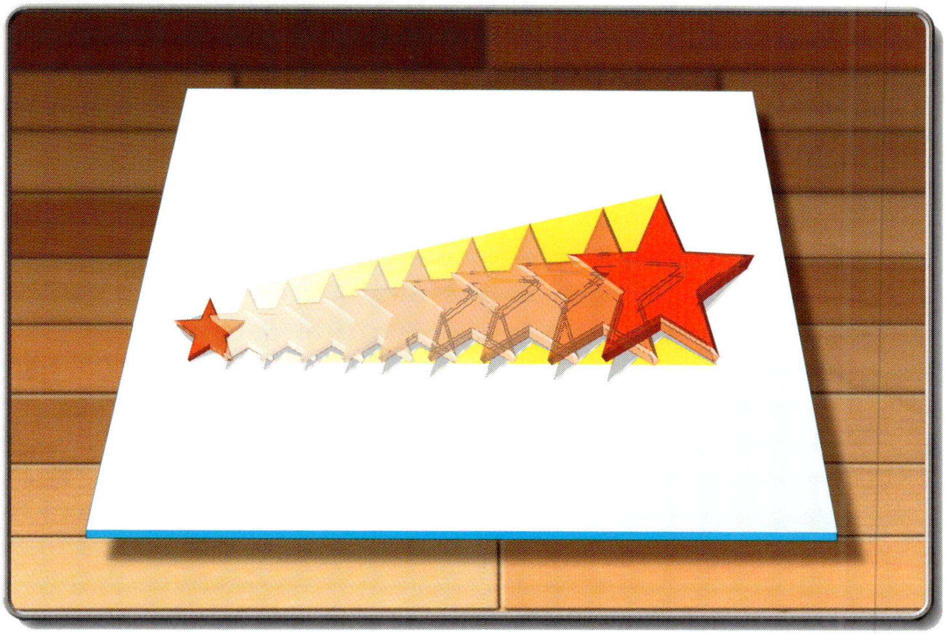

Word can display all types of graphics in the Print Layout and Web Layout views. To change the view of a document, see page 40.

RESIZE A GRAPHIC

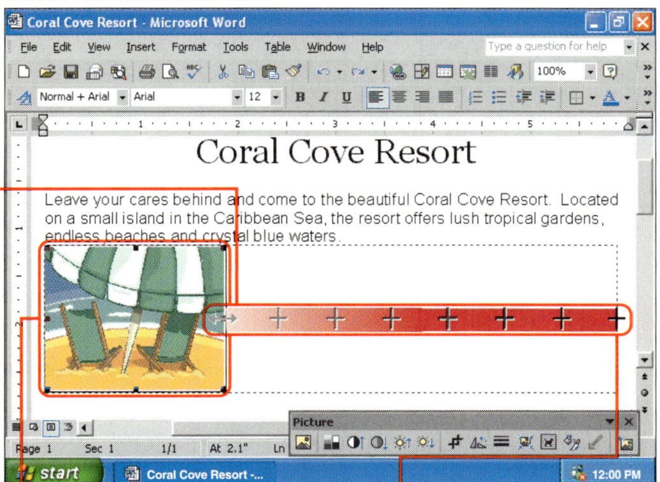

1 Click the graphic you want to resize. Handles (o or ■) appear around the graphic.

2 Position the mouse I over one of the handles (I changes to ↔, ↕, ⤢ or ⤡).

3 Drag the handle until the graphic is the size you want.

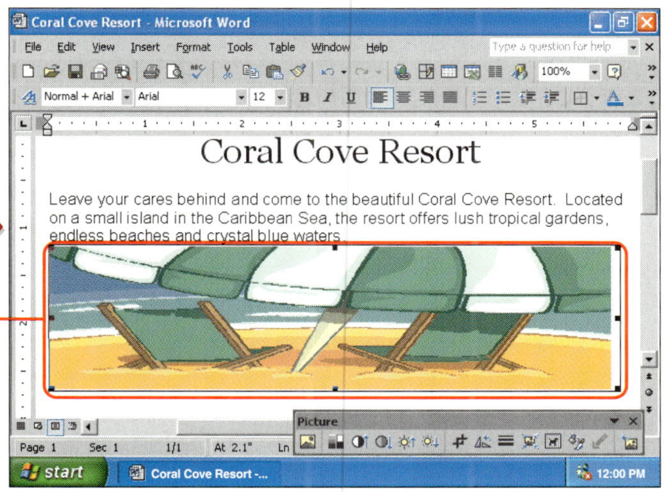

■ The graphic appears in the new size.

■ To deselect the graphic, click outside the graphic.

CHANGE COLOR OF A GRAPHIC

You can change the color of a graphic in your document.

You cannot change the color of some clip art images and pictures.

CHANGE COLOR OF A GRAPHIC

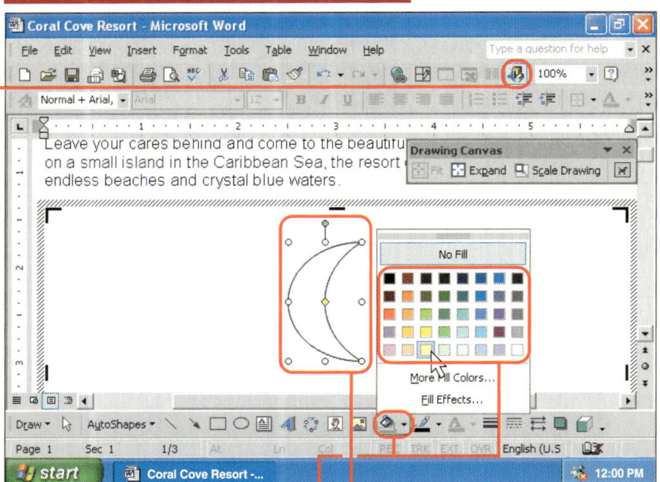

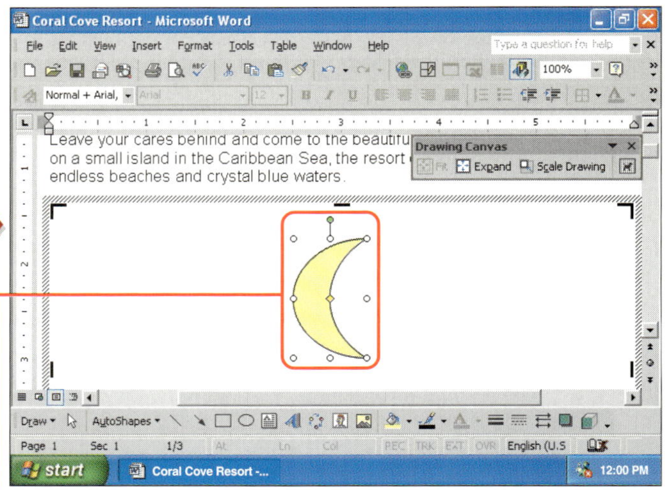

1 Click to display the Drawing toolbar.

Note: If is not displayed, click on the Standard toolbar to display the button.

2 Click the graphic you want to change to a different color. Handles (○ or ■) appear around the graphic.

3 Click in this area to display the available colors.

4 Click the color you want to use.

■ The graphic appears in the color you selected.

■ To deselect a graphic, click outside the graphic.

*Note: To hide the Drawing toolbar, repeat step **1**.*

ROTATE A GRAPHIC

You can rotate a graphic in your document.

You cannot rotate text boxes and some AutoShapes.

ROTATE A GRAPHIC

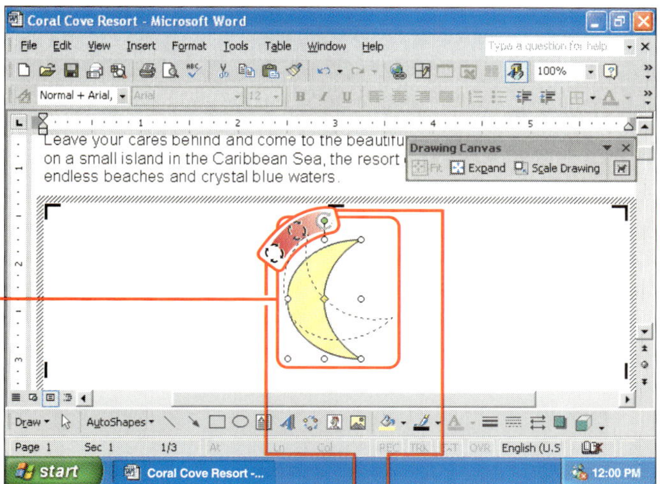

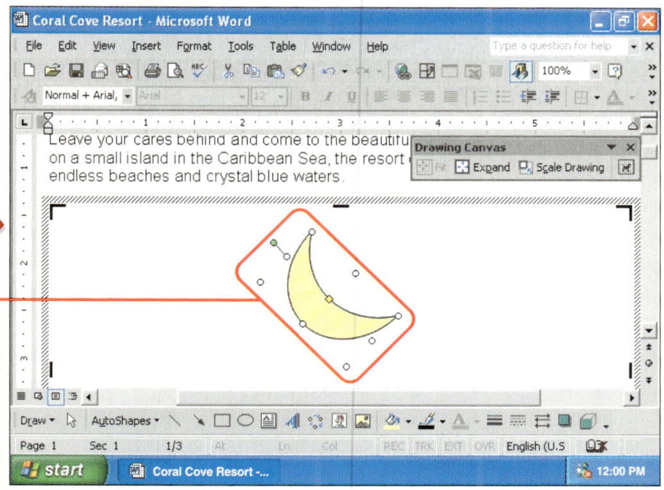

1 Click the graphic you want to rotate. Handles (o) appear around the graphic.

Note: If ■ handles appear around the graphic, you cannot rotate the graphic.

2 Position the mouse over the green dot (changes to ↻).

3 Drag the mouse in the direction you want to rotate the graphic.

■ The graphic appears in the new position.

■ To deselect a graphic, click outside the graphic.

CREATE A DRAWING CANVAS

You can add a drawing canvas to your document. A drawing canvas provides an area that allows you to arrange graphics and move several graphics at once.

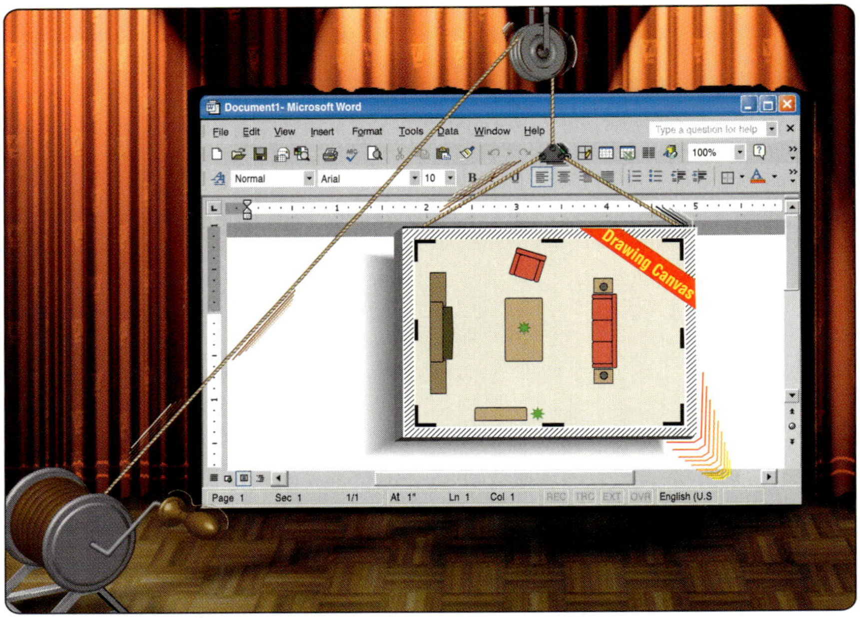

Word can display a drawing canvas only in the Print Layout and Web Layout views. To change the view of a document, see page 40.

Word automatically creates a drawing canvas when you add some types of graphics to your document, such as AutoShapes and text boxes.

CREATE A DRAWING CANVAS

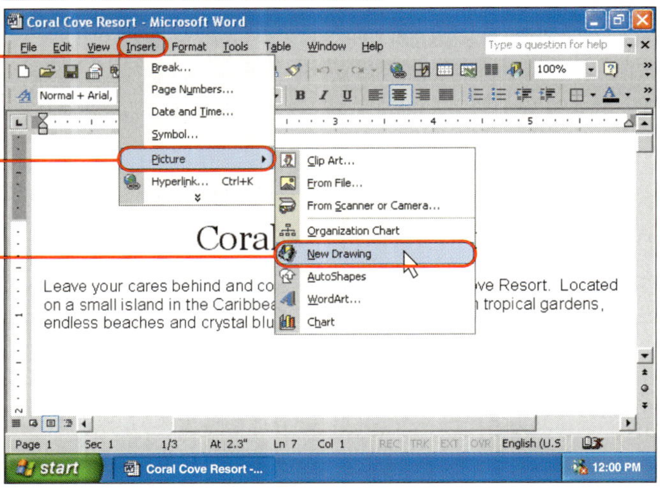

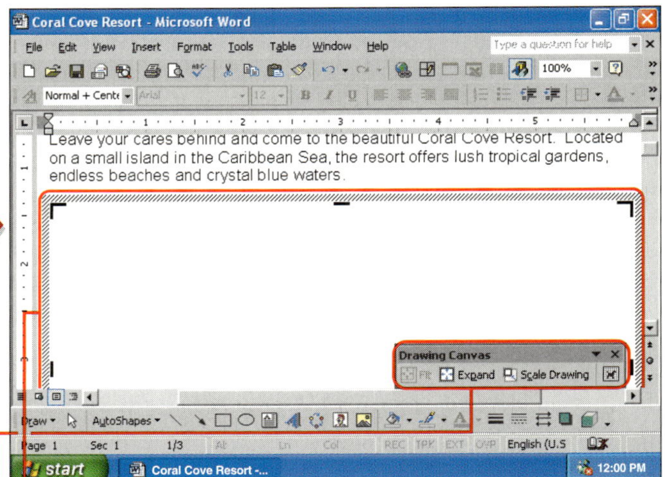

1 Click **Insert**.

2 Click **Picture**.

3 Click **New Drawing**.

Note: If New Drawing does not appear on the menu, position the mouse over the bottom of the menu to display all the menu options.

■ A drawing canvas appears in your document.

■ The Drawing Canvas toolbar also appears, displaying buttons you can use to work with the drawing canvas.

*Note: If the Drawing Canvas toolbar does not appear, right-click the drawing canvas and then select **Show Drawing Canvas Toolbar**.*

■ You can add graphics, such as an AutoShape, text box or picture, to the drawing canvas.

■ To deselect the drawing canvas, click outside the drawing canvas or press the Esc key.

How do I delete a drawing canvas?

To delete a drawing canvas, click a blank area inside the canvas and then press the Delete key. Deleting a drawing canvas will delete all the graphics on the canvas. If you want to keep the graphics, you must move the graphics off the drawing canvas before deleting the canvas. To move a graphic, see page 224.

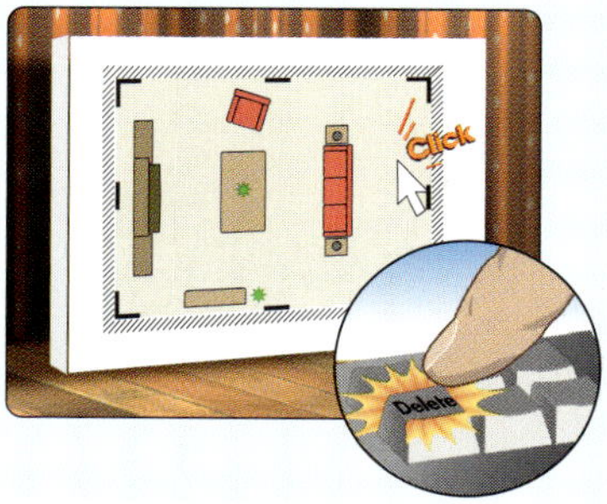

How can I change the size of a drawing canvas and the graphics on the canvas at the same time?

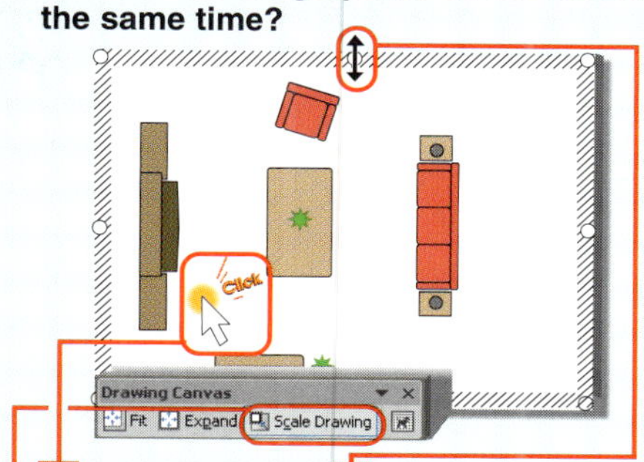

1 Click inside the drawing canvas you want to resize.

2 Click **Scale Drawing**.

3 Position the mouse over a handle (○) on the drawing canvas border and then drag the handle until the canvas and the graphics are the size you want.

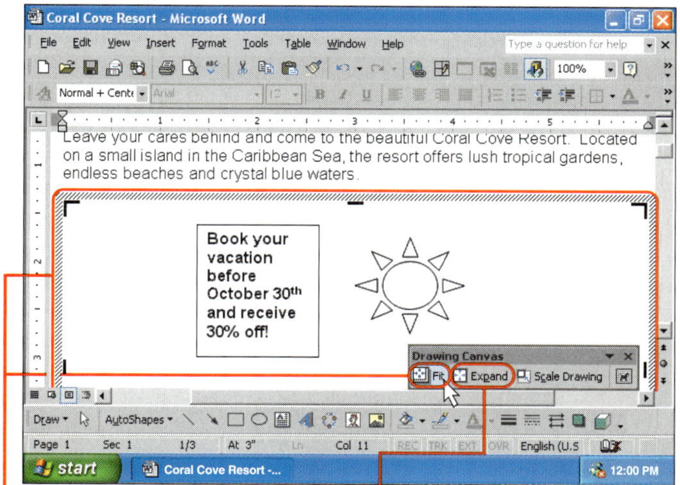

RESIZE A DRAWING CANVAS

1 Click inside the drawing canvas you want to resize.

2 Click **Fit** to make the drawing canvas border fit tightly around the graphics.

Note: The Fit button is only available if you have two or more graphics on the drawing canvas.

■ To enlarge the drawing canvas, click **Expand** until the drawing canvas is the size you want.

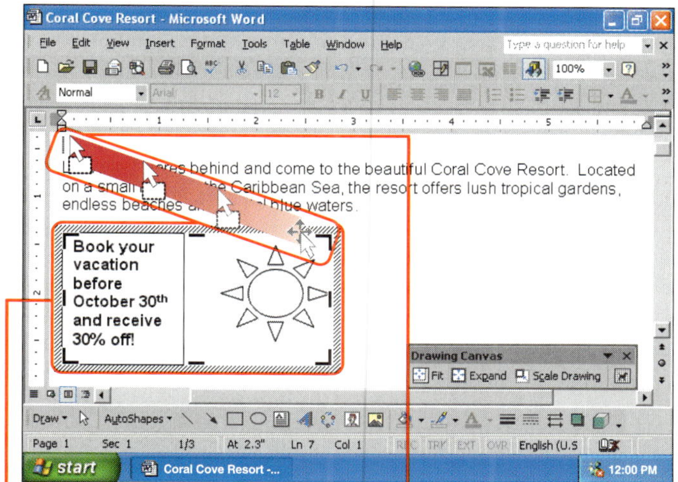

MOVE A DRAWING CANVAS

1 Click inside the drawing canvas you want to move.

2 Position the mouse over the border of the drawing canvas (changes to ✥).

3 Drag the drawing canvas to a new location.

Note: The drawing canvas will appear where you position the dotted insertion point on your screen.

WRAP TEXT AROUND A GRAPHIC

After you add a graphic to your document, you can choose how you want to wrap text around the graphic.

WRAP TEXT AROUND A GRAPHIC

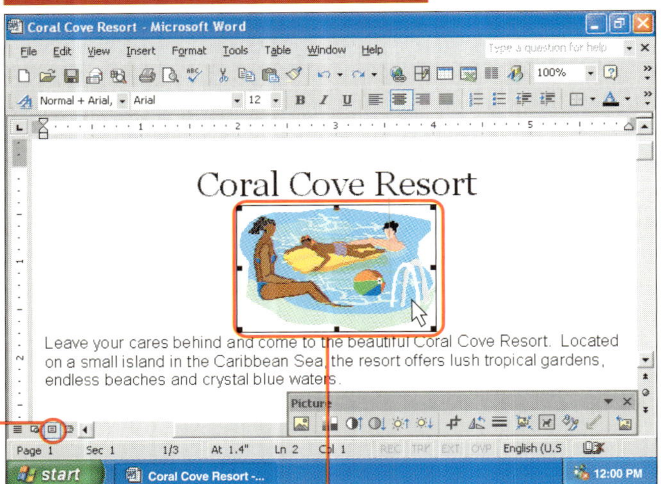

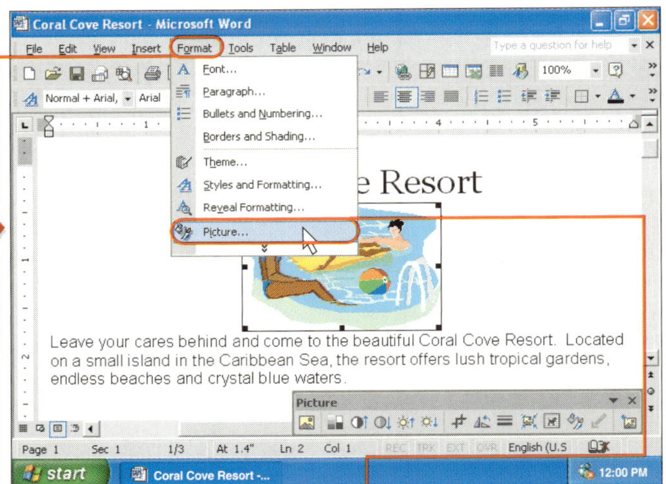

1 Click ▤ to display your document in the Print Layout view.

2 Click the graphic in your document you want to wrap text around. Handles (○ or ■) appear around the graphic.

Note: For information on wrapping text around a graphic on a drawing canvas, see the top of page 231.

3 Click **Format**.

4 Click the command for the type of graphic you selected, such as **AutoShape**, **Picture** or **WordArt**.

■ The Format dialog box appears.

How can Word align a graphic with text?

Word can align a graphic to the left, center or right of text.

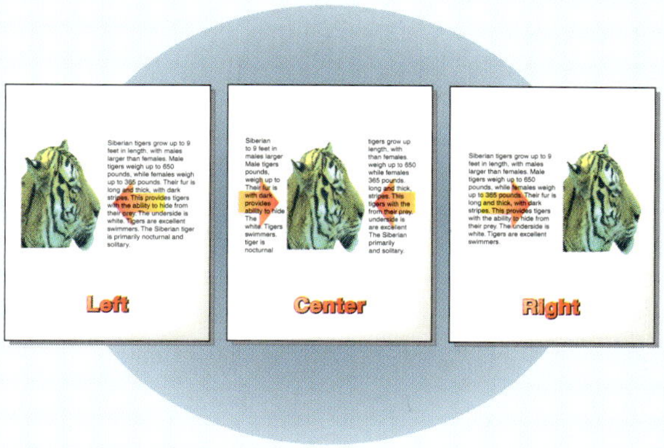

Can I wrap text around a graphic on a drawing canvas?

Yes. To wrap text around a graphic on a drawing canvas, perform steps **1** to **8** below, except click a blank area on the drawing canvas in step **2** and select **Drawing Canvas** in step **4**. For information on using a drawing canvas, see page 228.

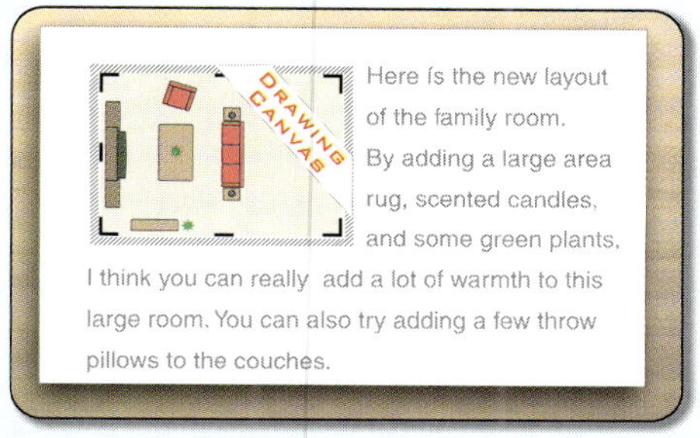

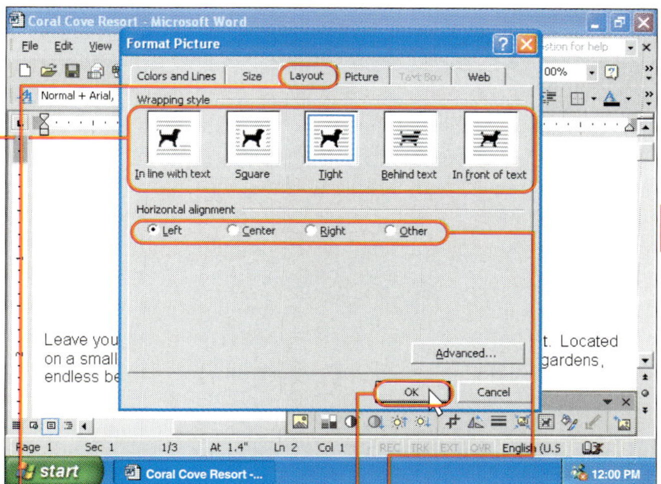

5 Click the **Layout** tab.

6 Click the way you want to wrap text around the graphic.

7 Click the way you want to align the graphic with the text.

8 Click **OK** to confirm your changes.

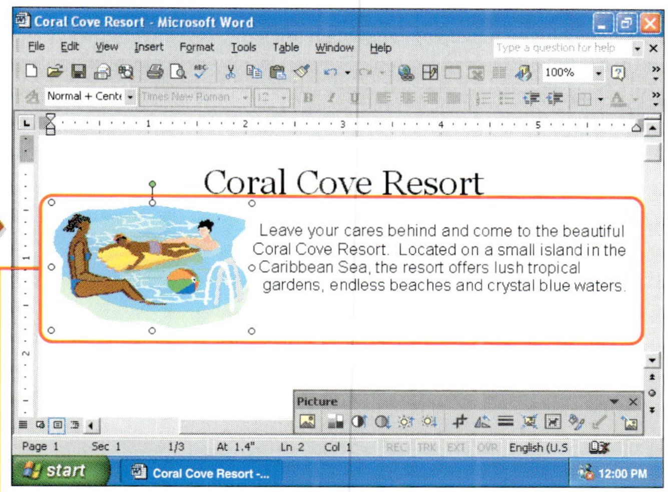

■ The text wraps around the graphic.

■ To deselect a graphic, click outside the graphic.

ADD A DIAGRAM

You can add a diagram to a document to illustrate a concept or idea. Word provides several types of diagrams for you to choose from.

Word can display diagrams only in the Print Layout and Web Layout views. To change the view of a document, see page 40.

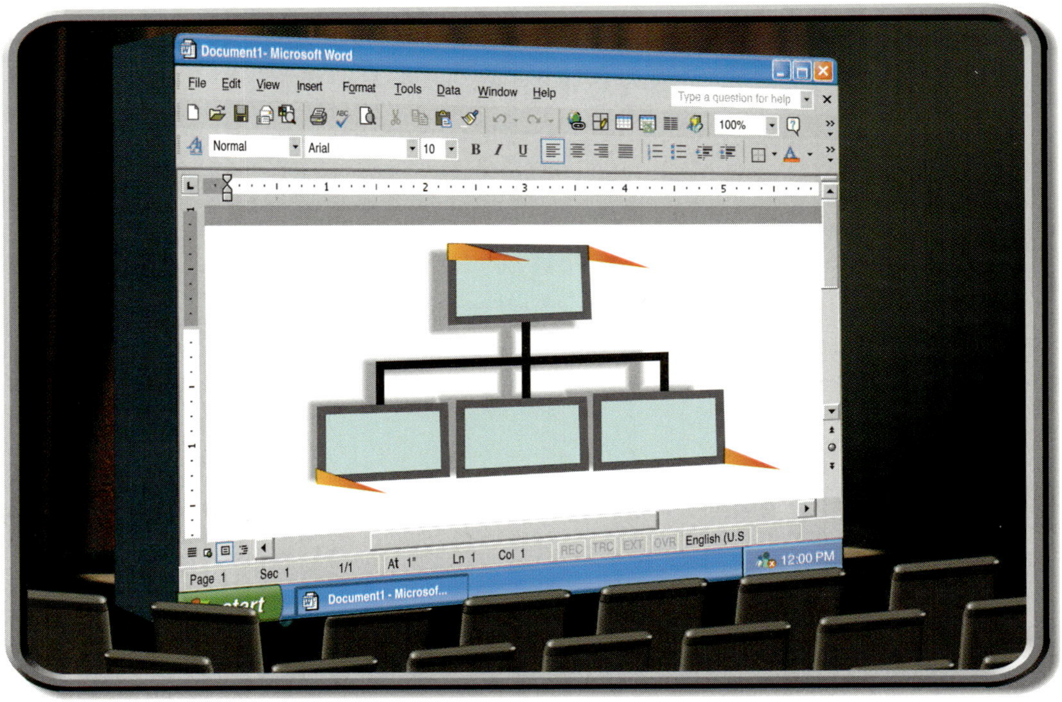

ADD A DIAGRAM

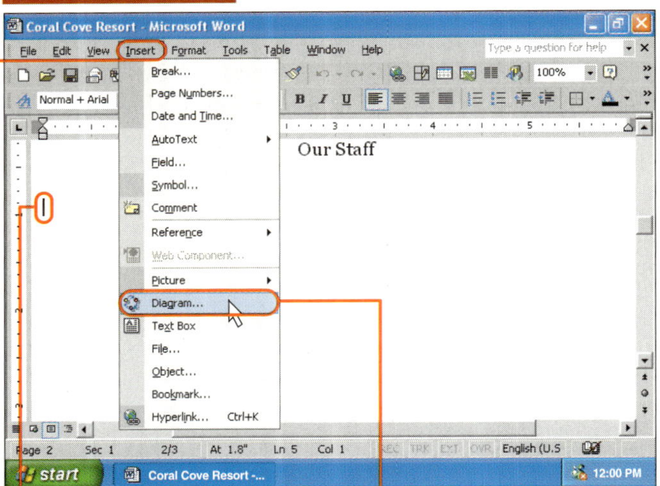

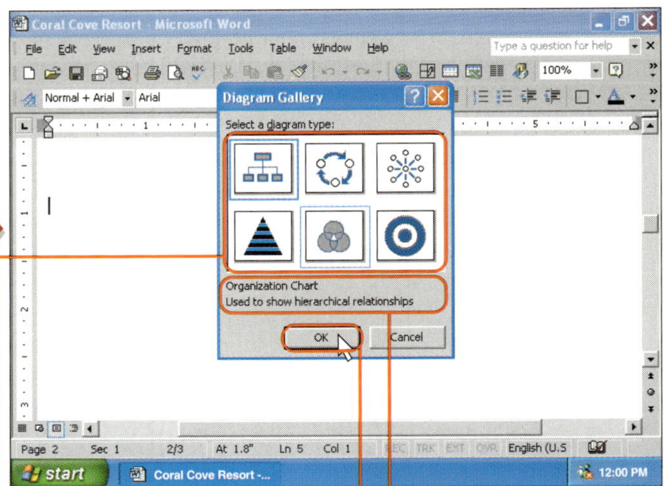

1 Click the location in your document where you want to add a diagram.

2 Click **Insert**.

3 Click **Diagram**.

Note: If Diagram does not appear on the menu, position the mouse over the bottom of the menu to display all the menu options.

■ The Diagram Gallery dialog box appears.

4 Click the type of diagram you want to add to your document.

Note: For information on the types of diagrams, see the top of page 233.

■ This area displays a description of the diagram you selected.

5 Click **OK** to add the diagram to your document.

What types of diagrams can I add to my document?

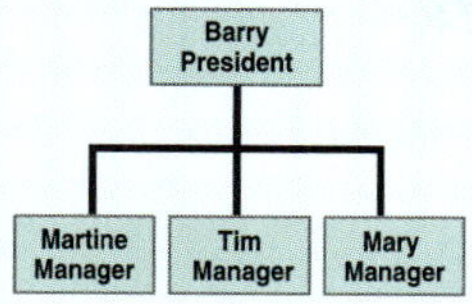

Organization Chart
Shows how items are related and ranked.

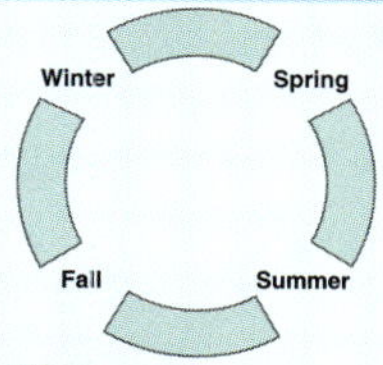

Cycle Diagram
Shows a procedure that has an uninterrupted cycle.

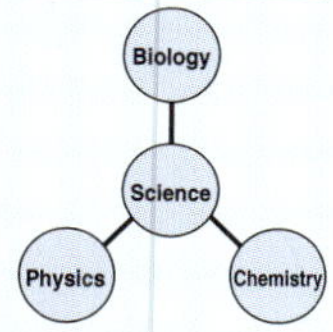

Radial Diagram
Shows how items relate to a central item.

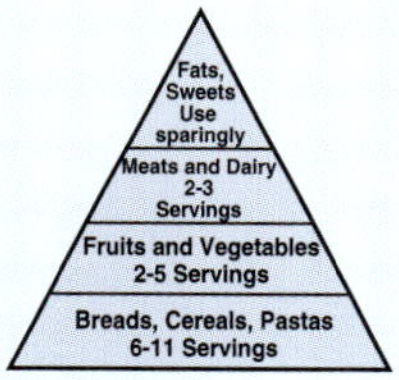

Pyramid Diagram
Shows how items build on one another.

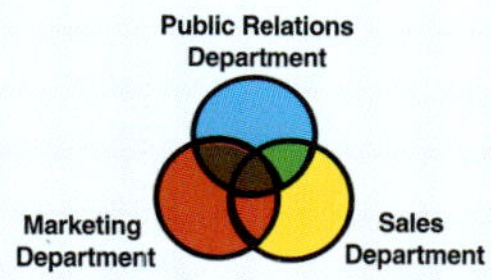

Venn Diagram
Shows areas of similarity between items.

Target Diagram
Shows a progression towards a goal.

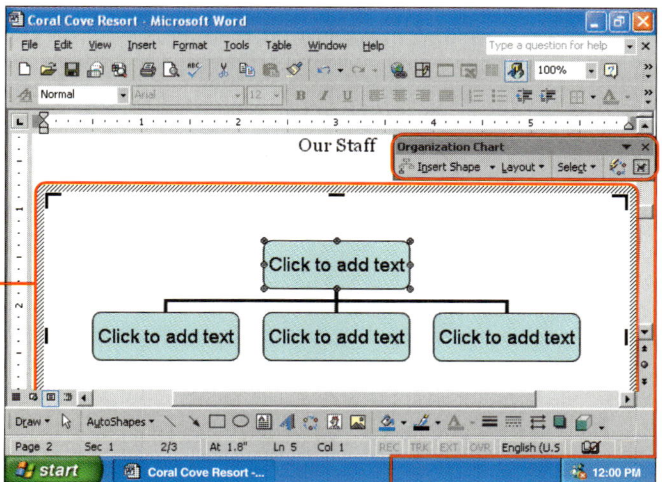

■ The diagram appears in your document.

Note: To customize the diagram, see pages 234 to 237.

■ A border appears around the diagram. The border will not appear when you print your document.

■ A toolbar also appears, displaying buttons that allow you to change the diagram.

■ To deselect a diagram, click outside the diagram or press the **Esc** key.

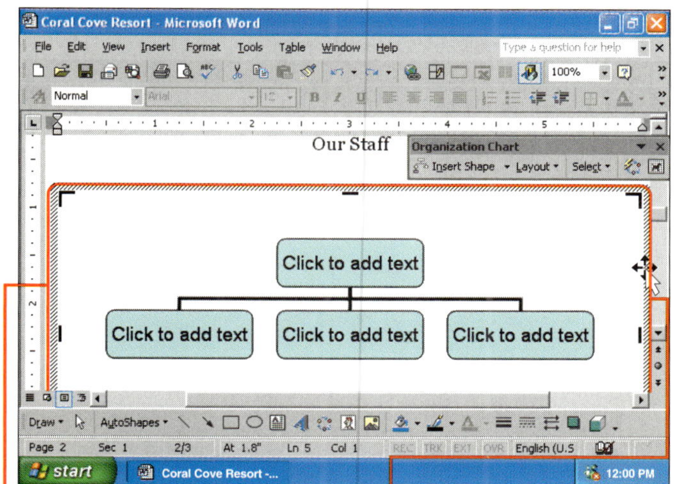

DELETE A DIAGRAM

1 Click the diagram you want to delete. A border appears around the diagram.

2 Click the border and then press the **Delete** key.

■ The diagram disappears from your document.

CONTINUED

ADD A DIAGRAM

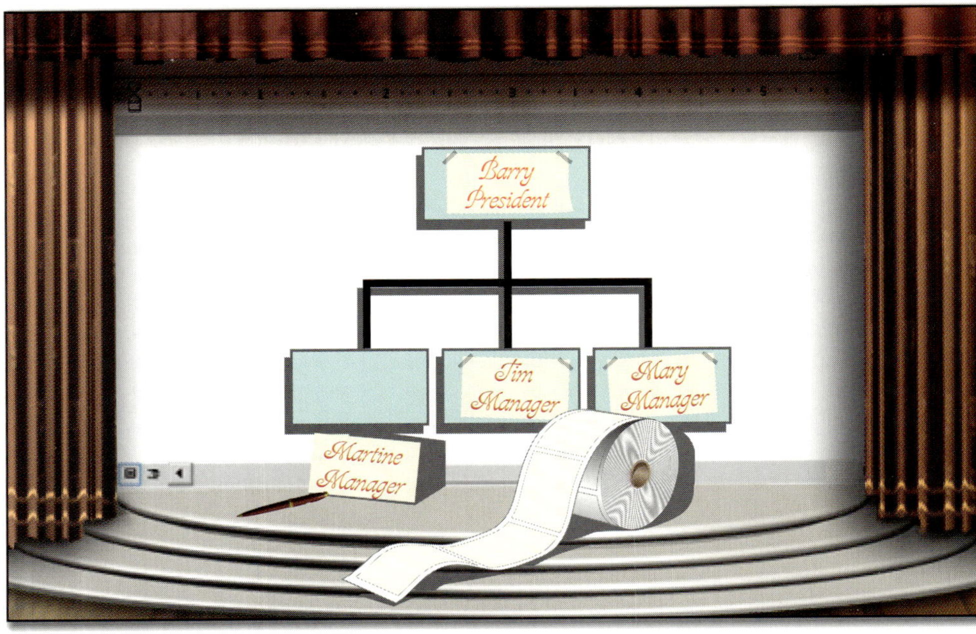

You can add text to a diagram to provide descriptions for the shapes in the diagram.

ADD TEXT TO A DIAGRAM

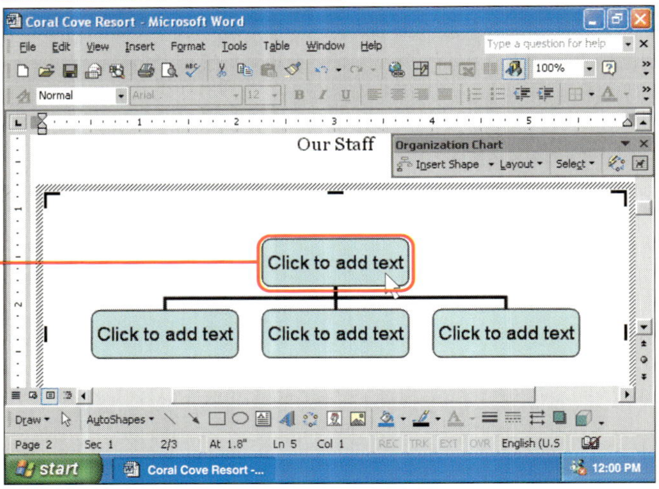

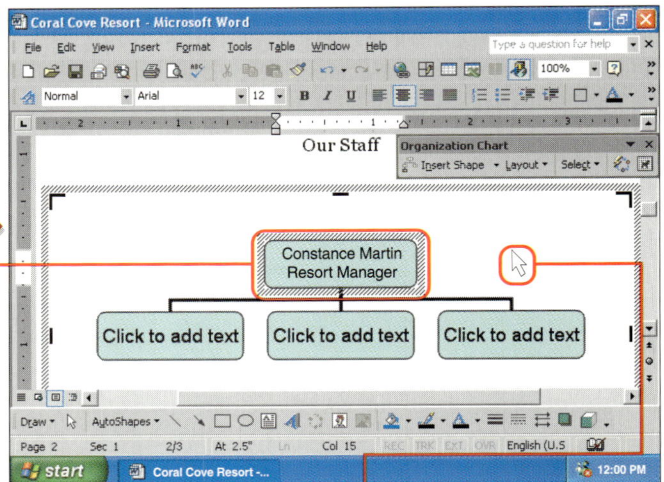

1 To add text to a diagram, click an area that displays the phrase **Click to add text**.

■ A border appears around the area.

2 Type the text you want to add.

3 When you finish typing the text, click outside the text area.

■ You can repeat steps **1** to **3** to add text to another text area in the diagram.

You can add a new shape to a diagram to include additional information in the diagram.

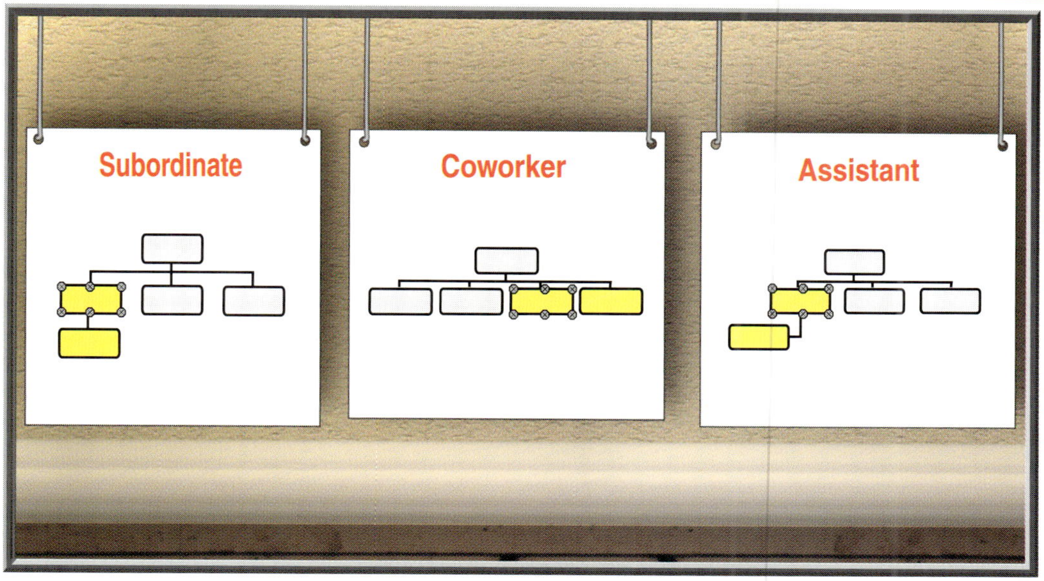

When adding a new shape to an organization chart, there are three types of shapes you can choose from—subordinate, coworker or assistant.

ADD A SHAPE

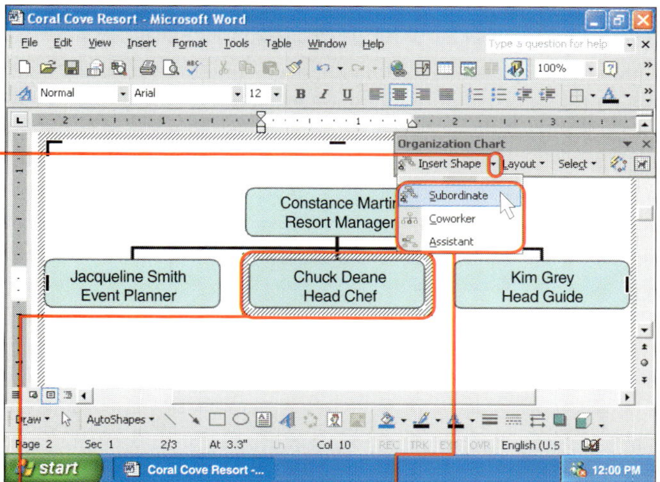

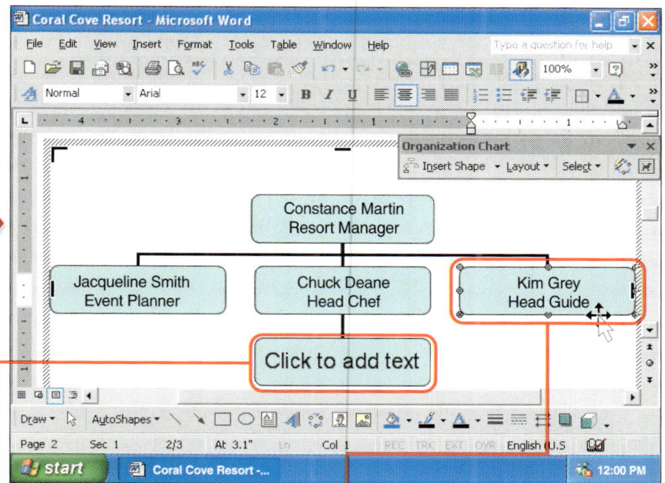

1 Click the shape above or beside where you want the new shape to appear.

2 To add a shape to an organization chart, click ▾ beside **Insert Shape**.

3 Click the type of shape you want to add.

■ To add a shape to all other types of diagrams, click **Insert Shape**.

■ A new shape appears in the diagram.

■ You can add text to the text area for new shape.

DELETE A SHAPE

1 Click an edge of the shape you want to delete. Handles (⊗) appear around the shape.

2 Press the Delete key to delete the shape.

CONTINUED

ADD A DIAGRAM

Word offers many ready-to-use styles that you can choose from to give a diagram a new appearance.

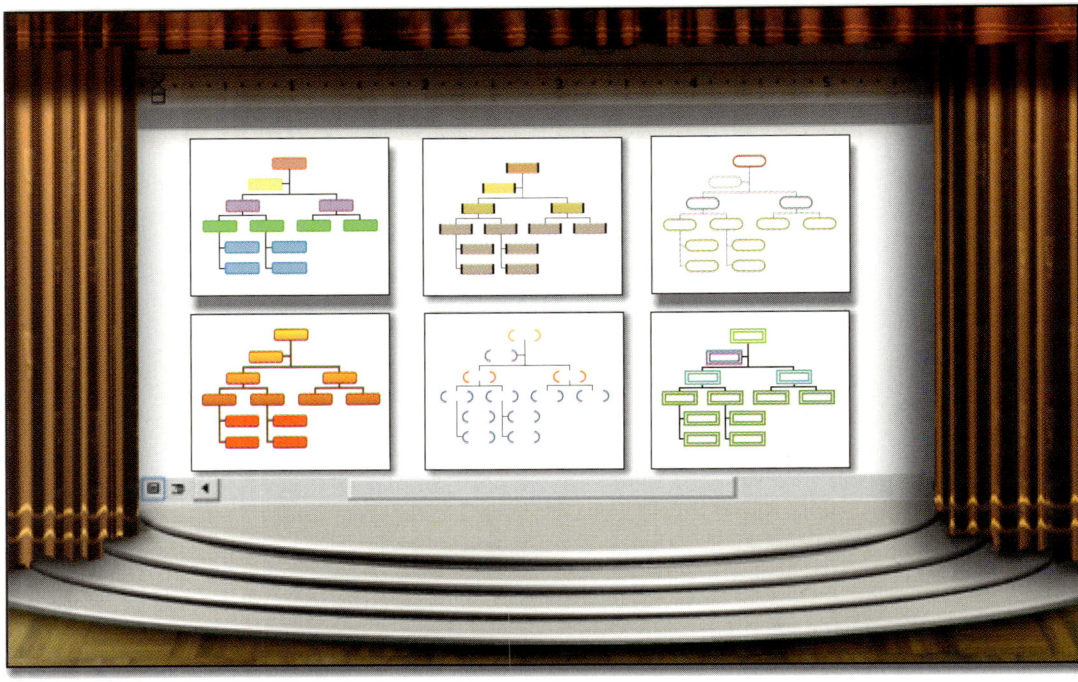

APPLY A DIAGRAM STYLE

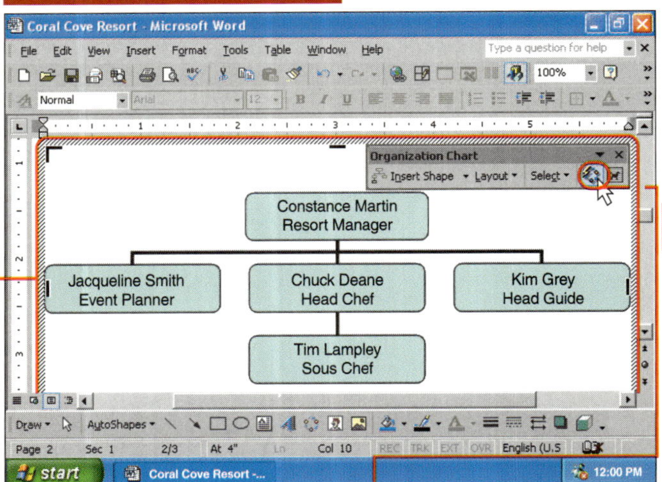

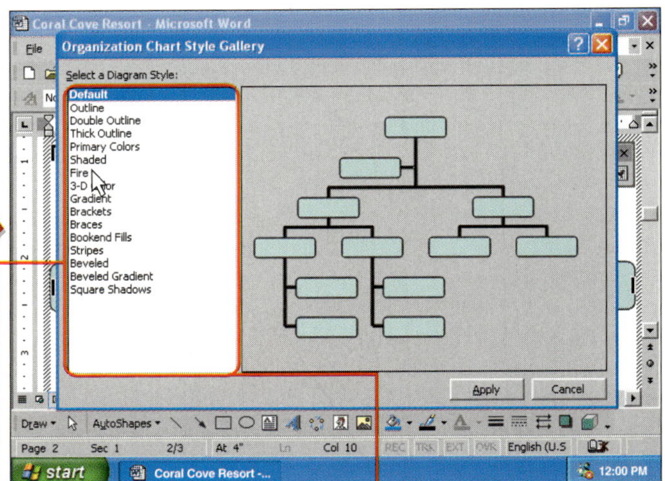

1 Click the diagram you want to apply a style to.

A border appears around the diagram.

2 Click (icon) to apply a style to the diagram.

■ The Style Gallery dialog box appears.

■ This area displays a list of the available styles.

*Note: The available styles depend on the type of diagram you selected in step **1**.*

3 Click the style you want to use.

Instead of applying a style to a diagram, how can I change the color of only one shape?

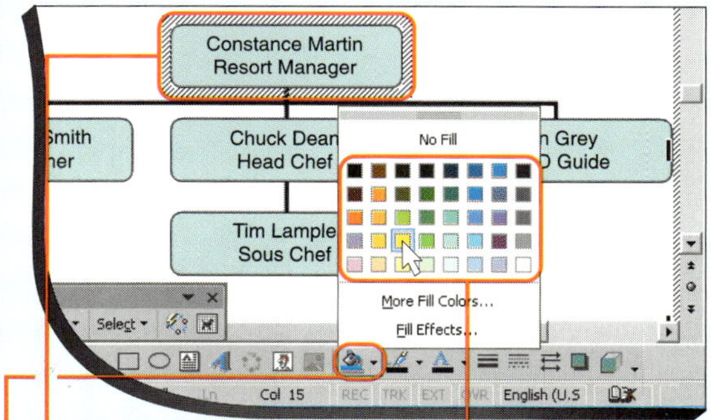

1 Click the shape you want to change to a different color.

2 Click ▾ in this area to display the available colors.

3 Click the color you want to use.

■ The shape will change to the new color.

How can I change the color of the text in a diagram?

You can change the color of text in a diagram as you would change the color of any text in your document. To change the color of text, see page 92.

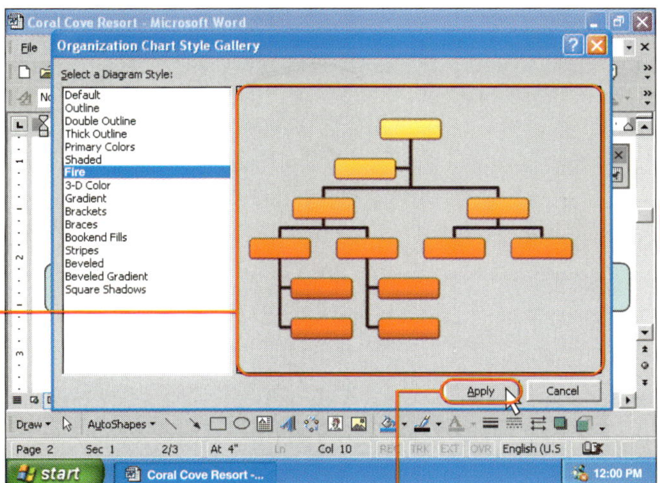

■ This area displays a preview of the style you selected.

Note: You can repeat step 3 to view a preview of a different style.

4 Click **Apply** to apply the style to the diagram.

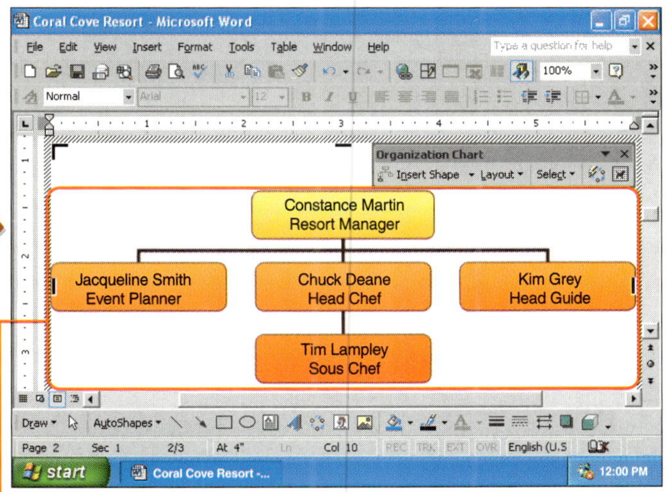

■ The diagram displays the new style.

■ To return to the original diagram style, repeat steps **1** to **4**, selecting **Default** in step **3**.

My AutoShapes
Alt + J
Click Insert
Click Picture
Click From File
Select the file you want to insert
Click Insert

CHAPTER 13

Time-Saving Features

Do you want to learn how to save time when creating documents? In this chapter, you will learn how to perform tasks using smart tags, create a document using a template and more.

Using Smart Tags 240

Using Templates and Wizards 242

Create a Template 244

Customize a Toolbar........................246

Create a New Toolbar 250

Record a Macro..............................252

Run a Macro 256

USING SMART TAGS

Word labels certain types of information, such as dates and addresses, with smart tags. You can use a smart tag to perform an action, such as scheduling a meeting on a specific date or displaying a map for an address.

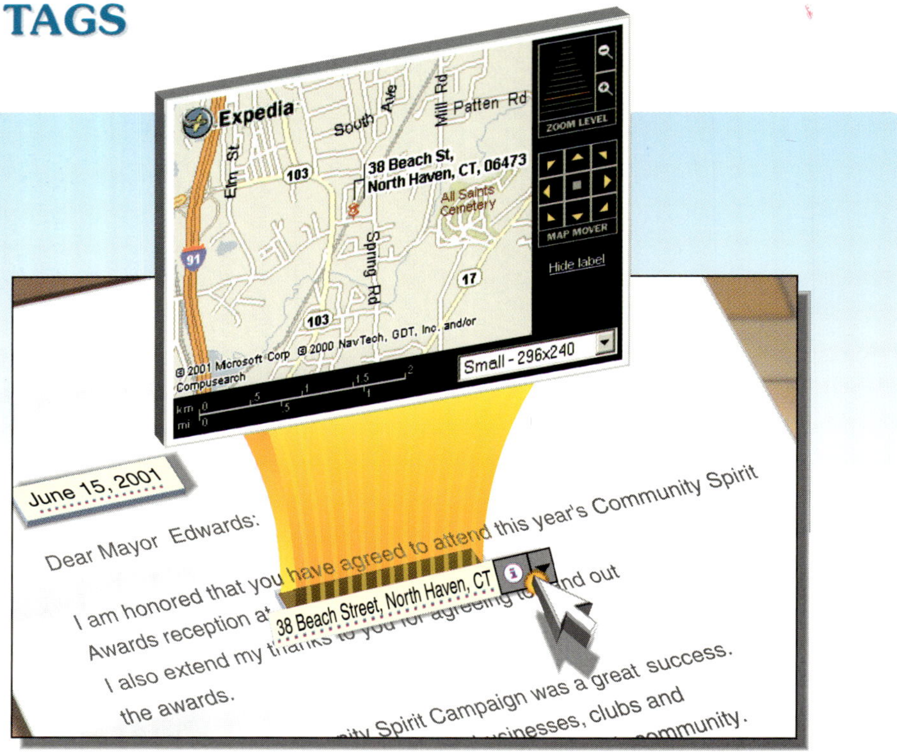

USING SMART TAGS

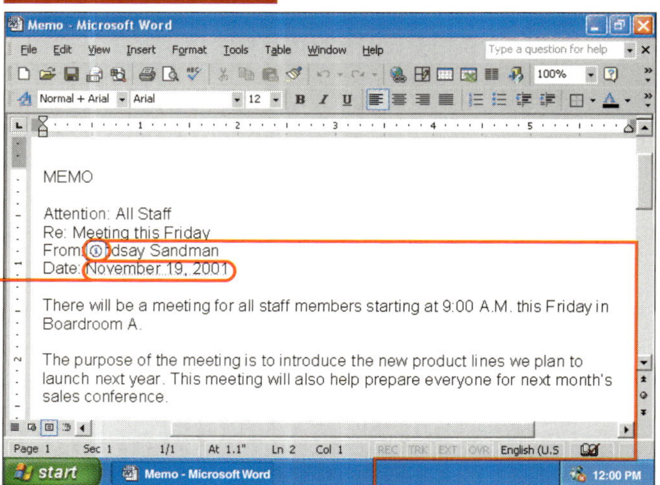

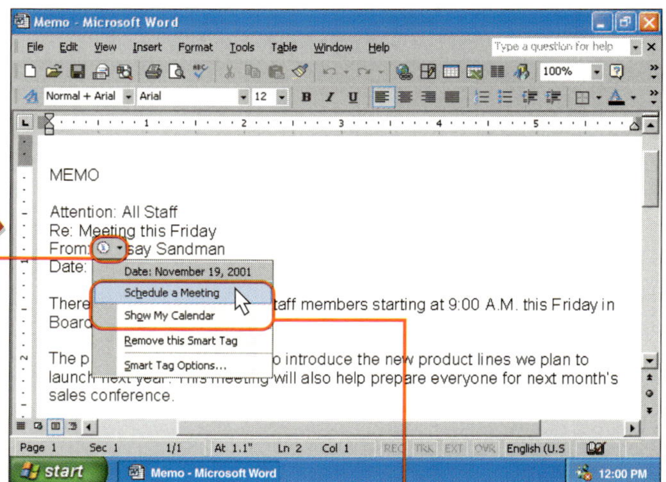

■ A purple dotted underline appears below text Word labels with a smart tag.

1 To perform an action using a smart tag, position the mouse I over the text labeled with a smart tag.

■ The Smart Tag Actions button appears.

2 Click the Smart Tag Actions button to display a list of actions you can perform using the smart tag.

3 Click the action you want to perform.

■ The program that allows you to perform the action will appear on your screen.

Can I remove a smart tag from my document?

Yes. To remove a smart tag from text in your document, perform steps **1** to **3** on page 240, selecting **Remove this Smart Tag** in step **3**.

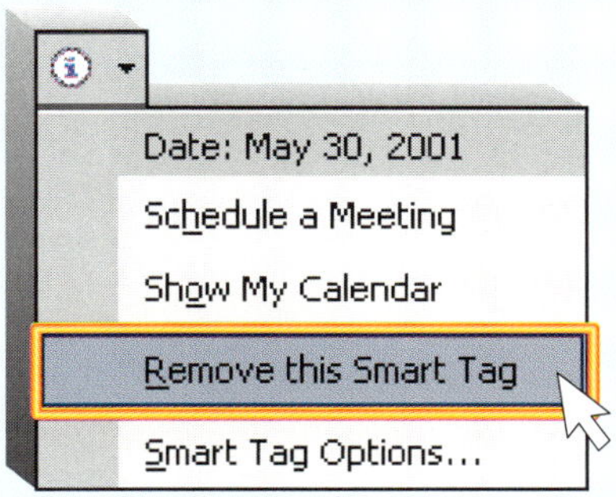

What types of information can Word label with smart tags?

Word can label people's names, dates, times, addresses, places and telephone numbers with smart tags. Word can also label e-mail addresses of people you recently sent messages to using Microsoft Outlook and financial symbols you type in capital letters, such as MSFT.

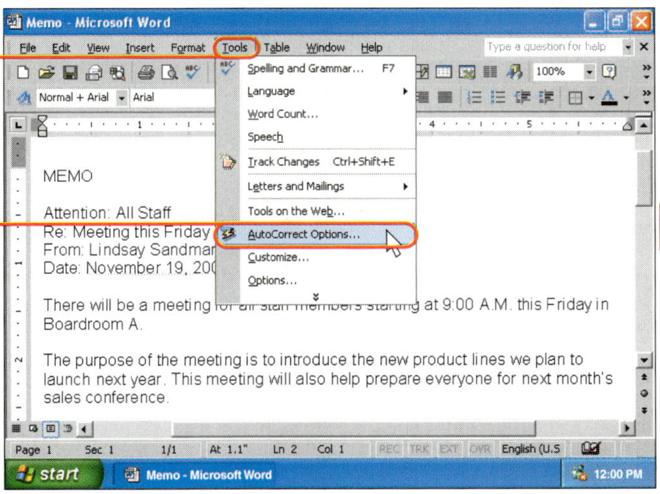

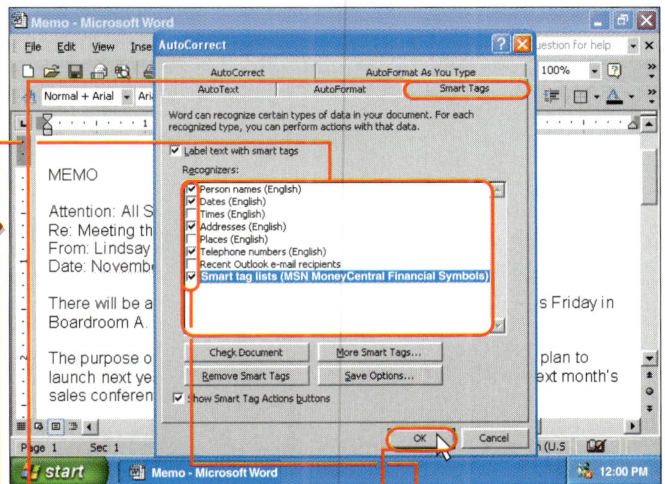

CHANGE SMART TAG OPTIONS

1 Click **Tools**.

2 Click **AutoCorrect Options**.

Note: If AutoCorrect Options does not appear on the menu, position the mouse over the bottom of the menu to display all the menu options.

■ The AutoCorrect dialog box appears.

3 Click the **Smart Tags** tab.

■ This area displays the types of information Word can label with smart tags. Smart tags are turned on for each type of information that displays a check mark (✔).

4 You can click the box beside a type of information to turn smart tags on (☑) or off (☐) for the information.

5 Click **OK** to confirm your changes.

USING TEMPLATES AND WIZARDS

You can use templates and wizards to save time when creating common types of documents, such as letters, memos and reports.

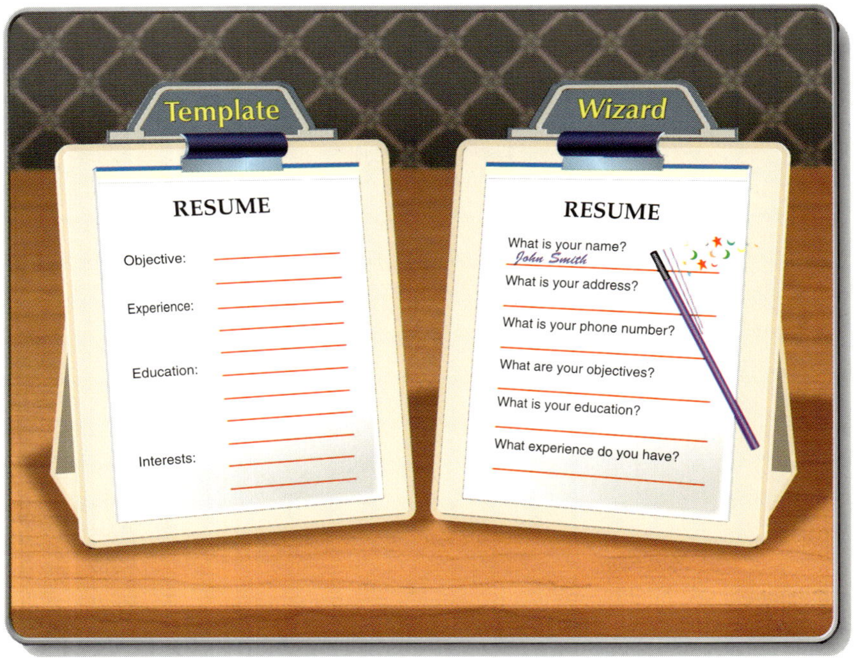

Template

A template is a document that provides areas for you to fill in your personalized information.

Wizard

A wizard asks you a series of questions and then uses your answers to create a document.

USING TEMPLATES AND WIZARDS

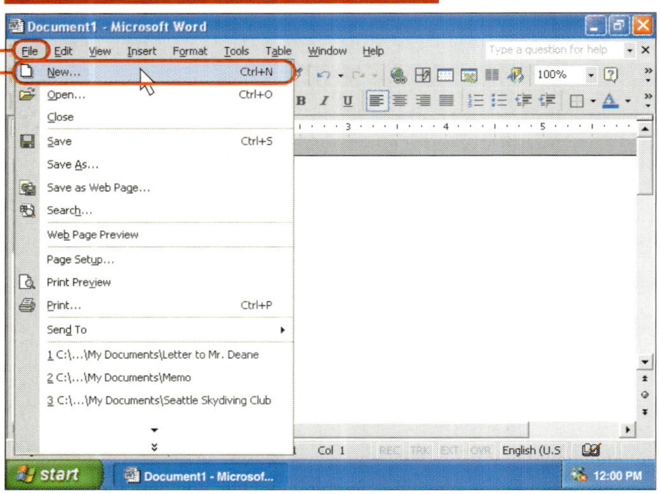

1 Click **File**.

2 Click **New**.

■ The New Document task pane appears.

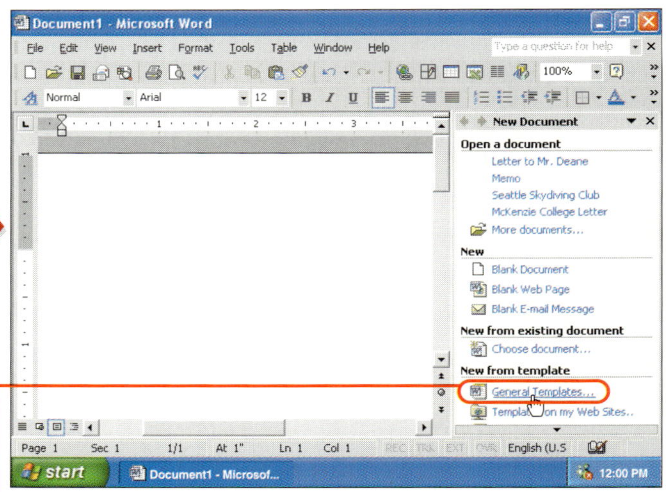

3 Click **General Templates**.

*Note: If you cannot see the **General Templates** option, click ▼ to scroll down through the New Document task pane.*

■ The Templates dialog box appears.

Why does a dialog box appear when I select a template or wizard?

A dialog box appears if the template or wizard you selected is not installed on your computer. Insert the CD-ROM disc you used to install Word into your computer's CD-ROM drive. Then click **OK** to install the template or wizard.

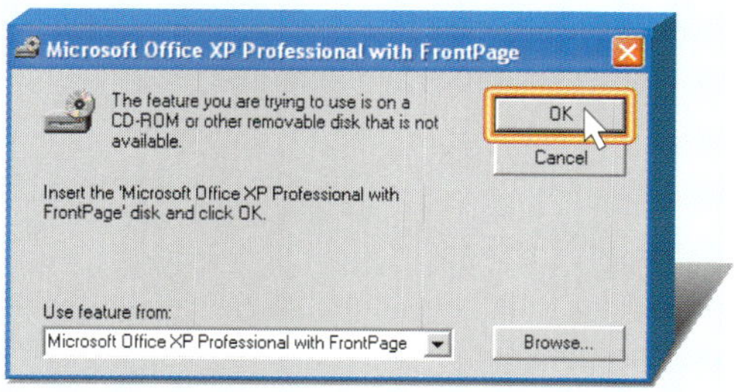

How can I quickly begin using a template or wizard I recently worked with?

The New Document task pane displays the names of the last two templates or wizards you worked with. To display the New Document task pane, perform steps **1** and **2** on page 242.

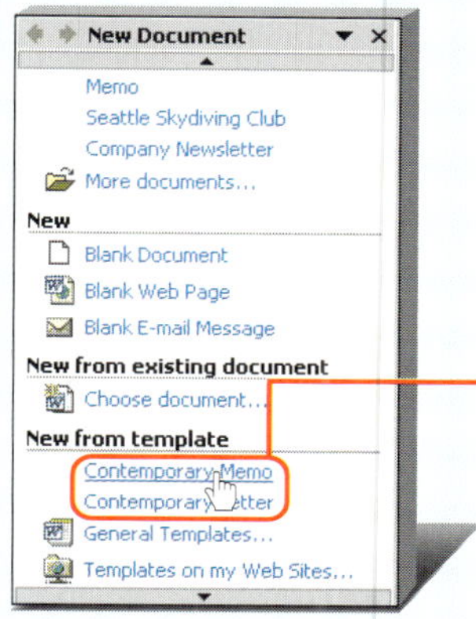

1 To quickly begin using a template or wizard, click the name of the template or wizard you want to use.

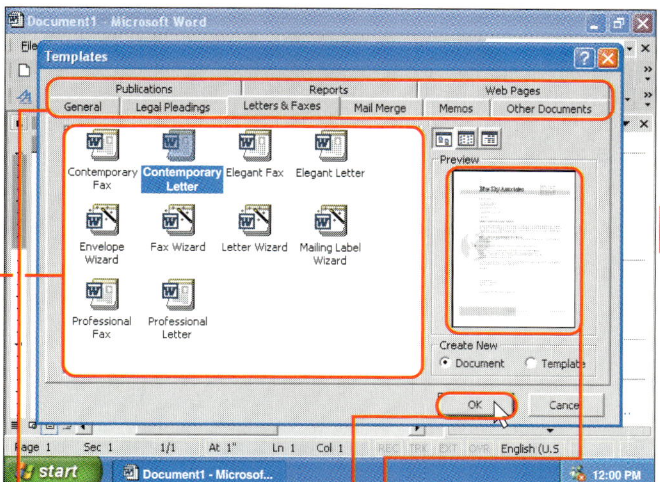

4 Click the tab for the type of document you want to create.

5 Click the template or wizard for the document you want to create.

Note: The icon for a wizard displays a magic wand ( ).

■ If a preview of the document you selected is available, the preview appears in this area.

6 Click **OK** to create the document.

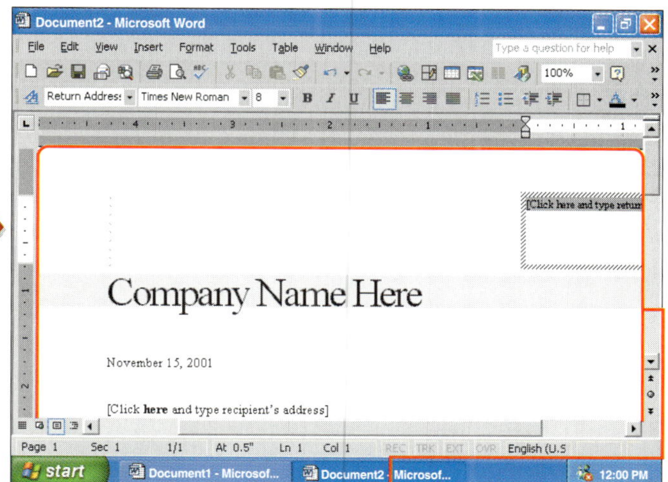

■ The document appears on your screen.

*Note: If you selected a wizard in step **5**, Word will ask you a series of questions before creating the document.*

7 Type your personalized information in the appropriate areas to complete the document.

CREATE A TEMPLATE

You can create a template from any document. You can then use the template to quickly create other documents that use the same graphics, text, formatting and page settings.

A template provides the basic structure of a document and can contain formatting, such as fonts, text alignment, line spacing and borders. A template can also contain page settings, such as margins and page orientation.

CREATE A TEMPLATE

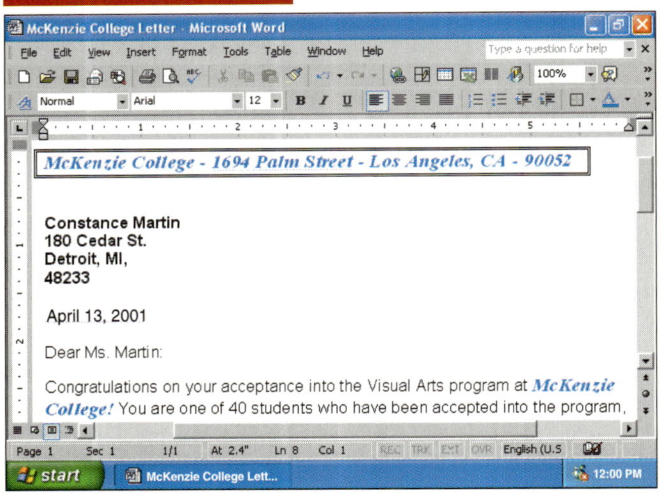

1 Open the document you want to use as the basis for the template. To open a document, see page 28.

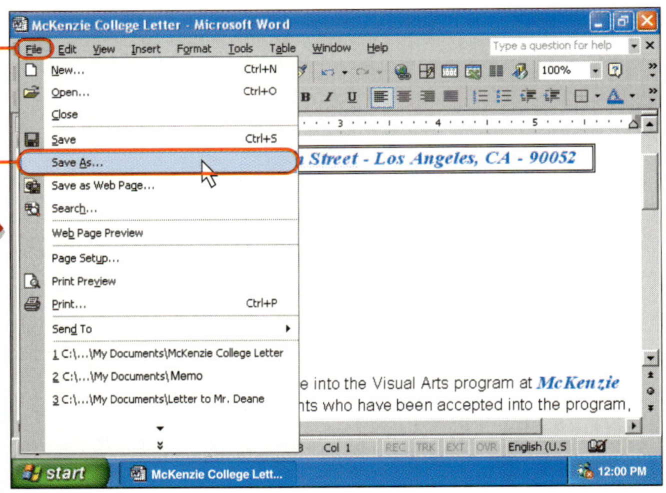

2 Click **File**.

3 Click **Save As**.

■ The Save As dialog box appears.

How do I use a template I created?

Word stores templates you create in the Templates folder. To use a template stored in the Templates folder, perform steps **1** to **7** starting on page 242, selecting the **General** tab in step **4**.

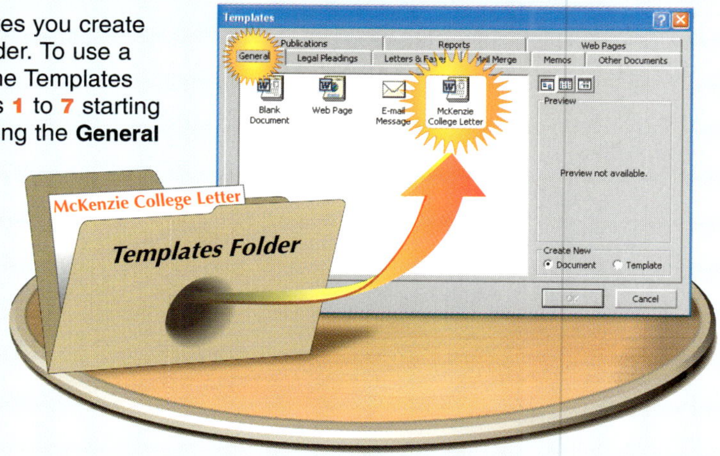

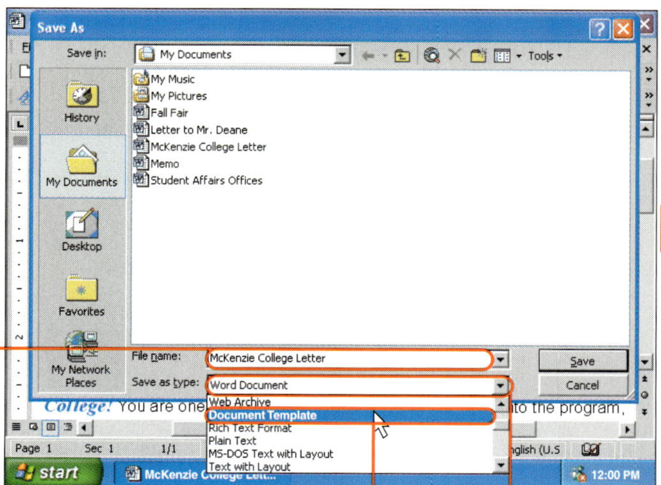

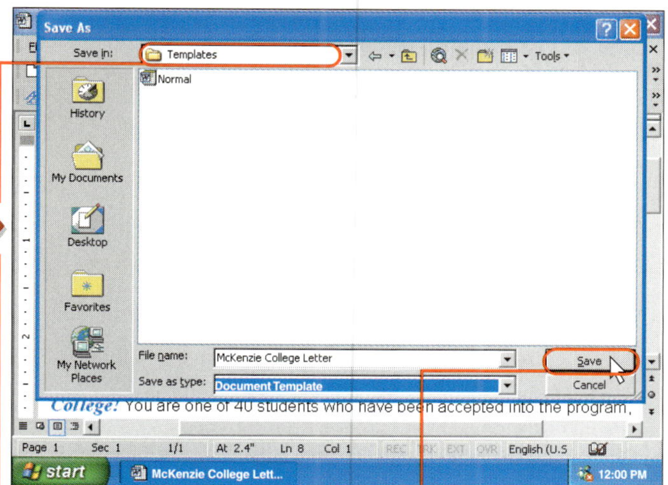

4 Type a name for your template.

*Note: A template name cannot contain the * : ? > < | or " characters.*

5 Click this area to specify you want to save your document as a template.

6 Click **Document Template**.

■ This area indicates Word will store your template in the Templates folder.

7 Click **Save** to save your document as a template.

CUSTOMIZE A TOOLBAR

You can add buttons to a toolbar to provide quick access to the commands you use most often. This can help you work more efficiently.

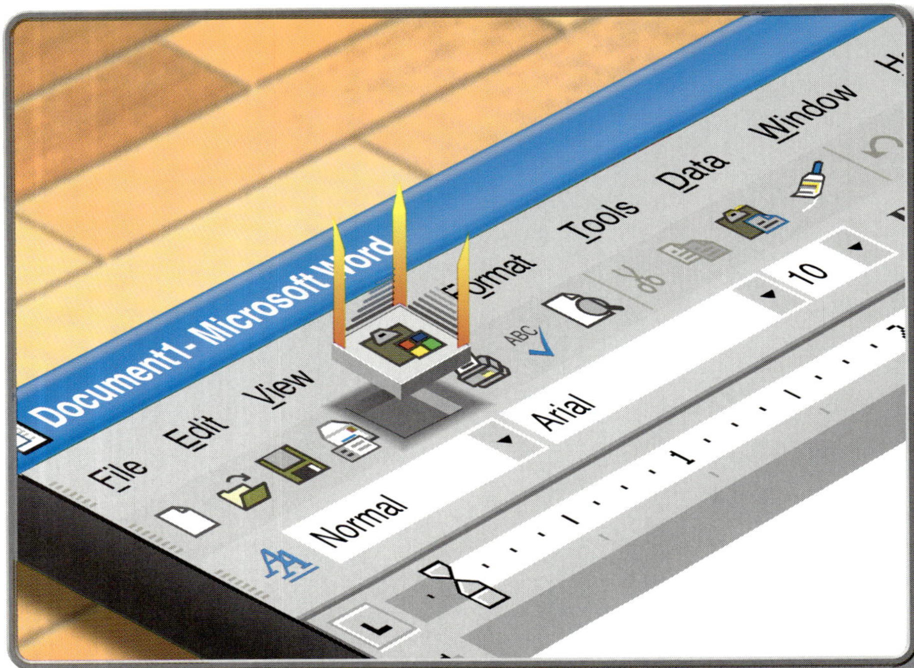

Word offers hundreds of buttons for you to choose from.

ADD A BUTTON

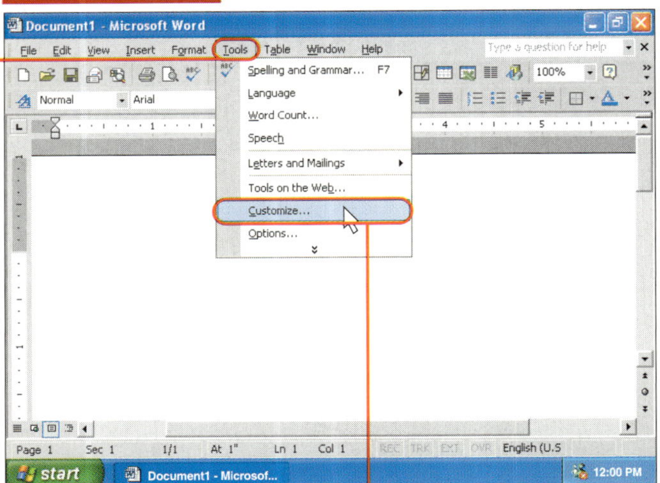

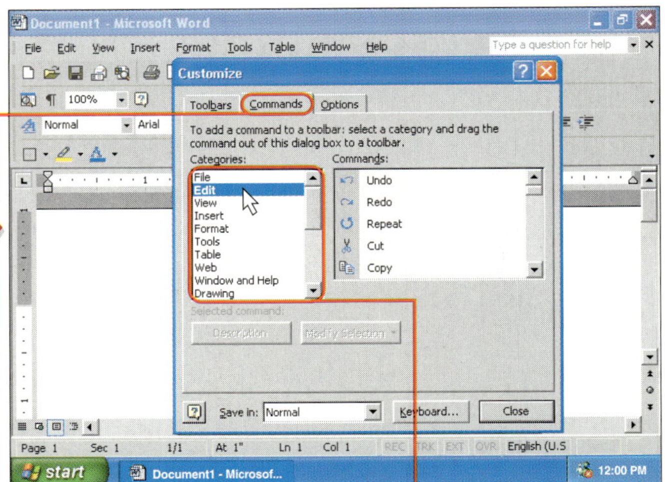

1 Display the toolbar you want to customize. To display a toolbar, see page 43.

2 Click **Tools**.

3 Click **Customize**.

■ The Customize dialog box appears.

4 Click the **Commands** tab.

5 Click the category that contains the button you want to add to the toolbar.

How can I learn more about a button I want to add to a toolbar?

When adding buttons to a toolbar, click the button you want to learn more about and then click the **Description** button. A yellow box appears, displaying information about the button. To remove the yellow box from your screen, click the box.

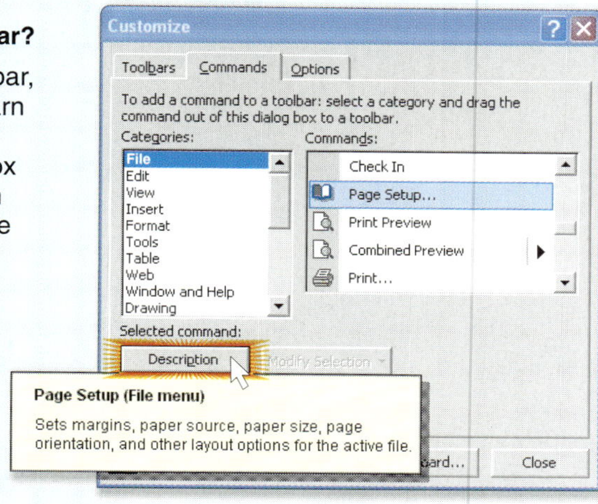

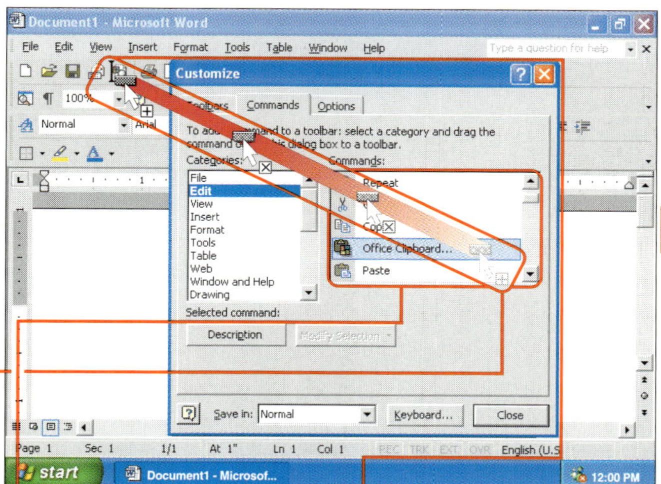

■ This area displays the buttons in the category you selected.

6 Position the mouse over the button you want to add to the toolbar.

7 Drag the button to the toolbar. A line (I) indicates where the button will appear.

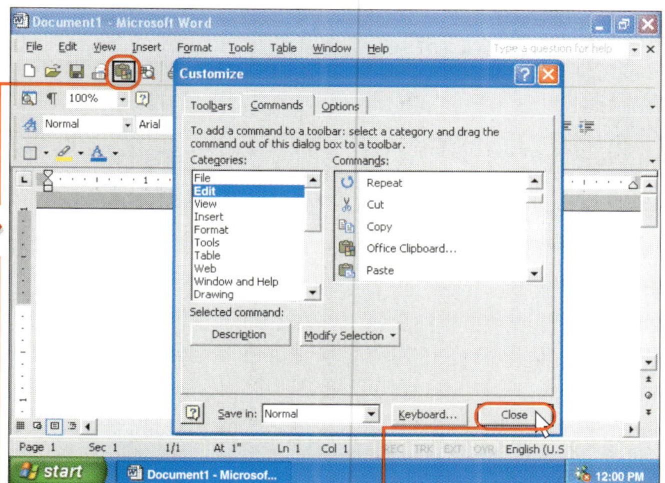

■ The button appears on the toolbar.

■ You can repeat steps **5** to **7** for each button you want to add to the toolbar.

8 When you finish adding buttons to the toolbar, click **Close** to close the Customize dialog box.

CONTINUED

CUSTOMIZE A TOOLBAR

You can move buttons on a toolbar to place buttons for related tasks together. This can make it easier to find the buttons you need.

MOVE A BUTTON

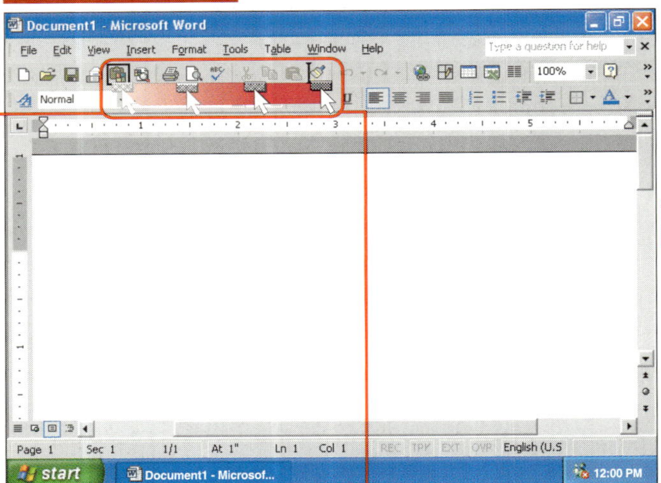

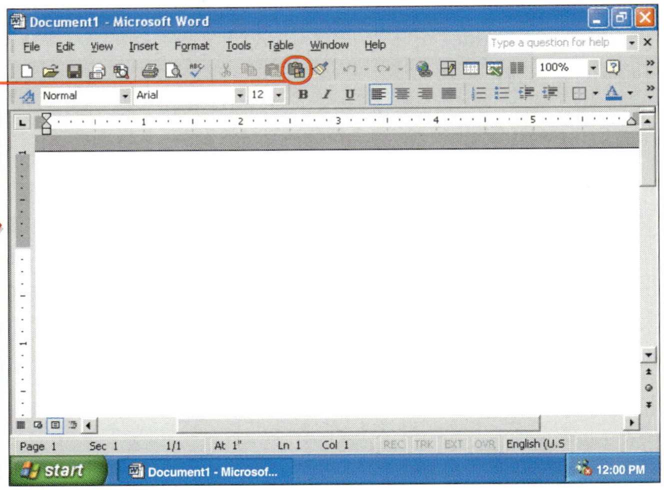

1 Display the toolbar you want to customize. To display a toolbar, see page 43.

2 Position the mouse over the button you want to move to a new location.

3 Press and hold down the Alt key as you drag the button to a new location. A line (I) indicates where the button will appear.

■ The button appears in the new location on the toolbar.

You can remove buttons you do not use from a toolbar.

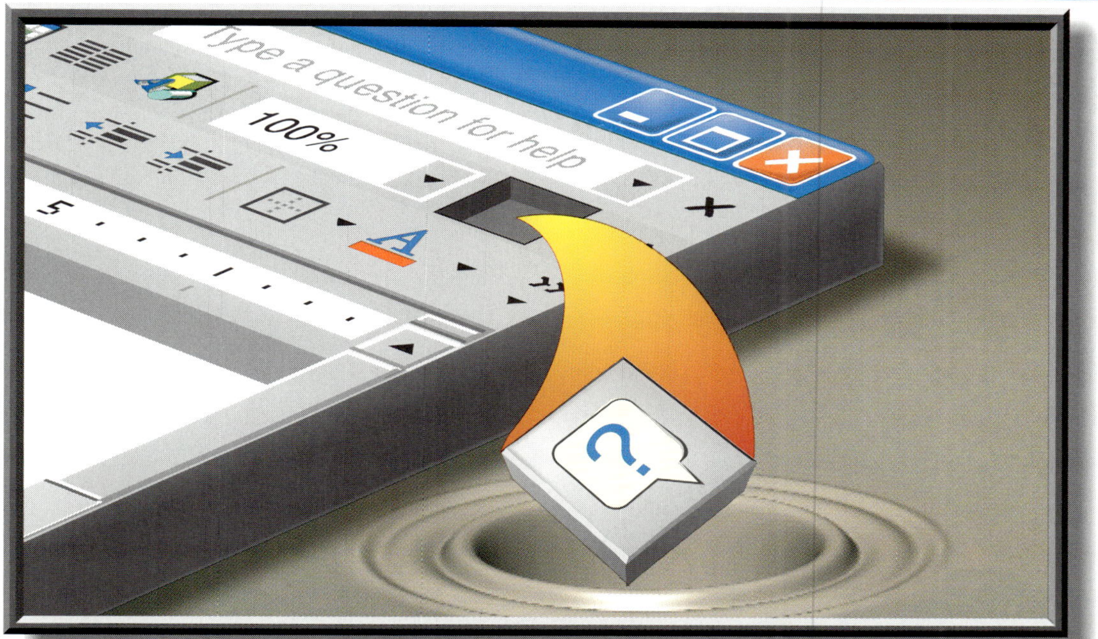

REMOVE A BUTTON

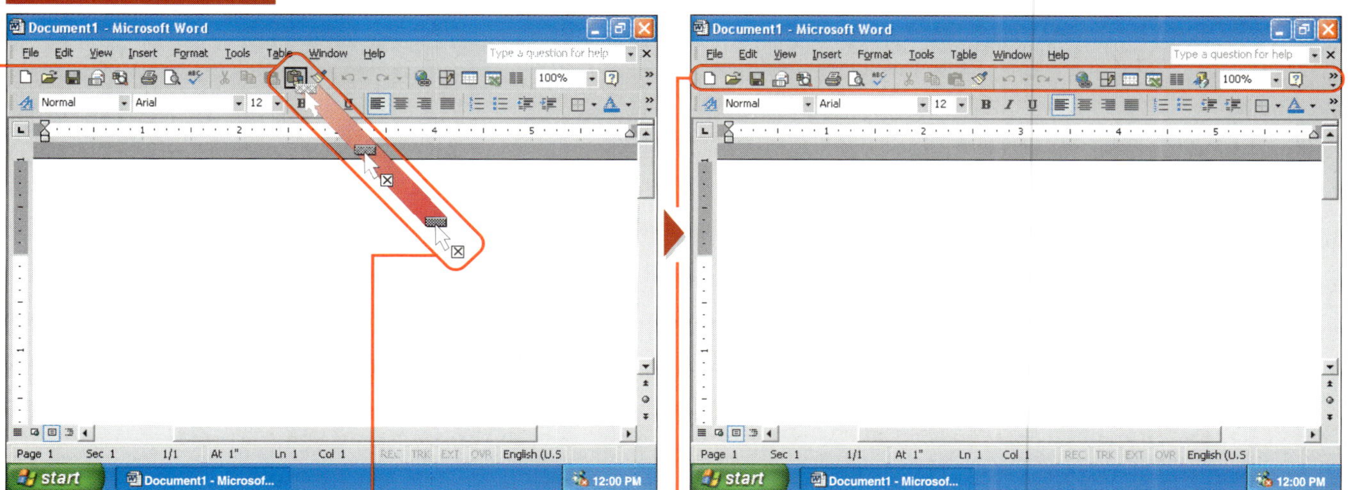

1 Display the toolbar you want to customize. To display a toolbar, see page 43.

2 Position the mouse over the button you want to remove from the toolbar.

3 Press and hold down the Alt key as you drag the button downward off the toolbar.

■ The button disappears from the toolbar.

CREATE A NEW TOOLBAR

You can create a new toolbar containing buttons you frequently use.

Creating a toolbar allows you to have a specific toolbar for a task you regularly perform, such as printing documents or adding AutoShapes.

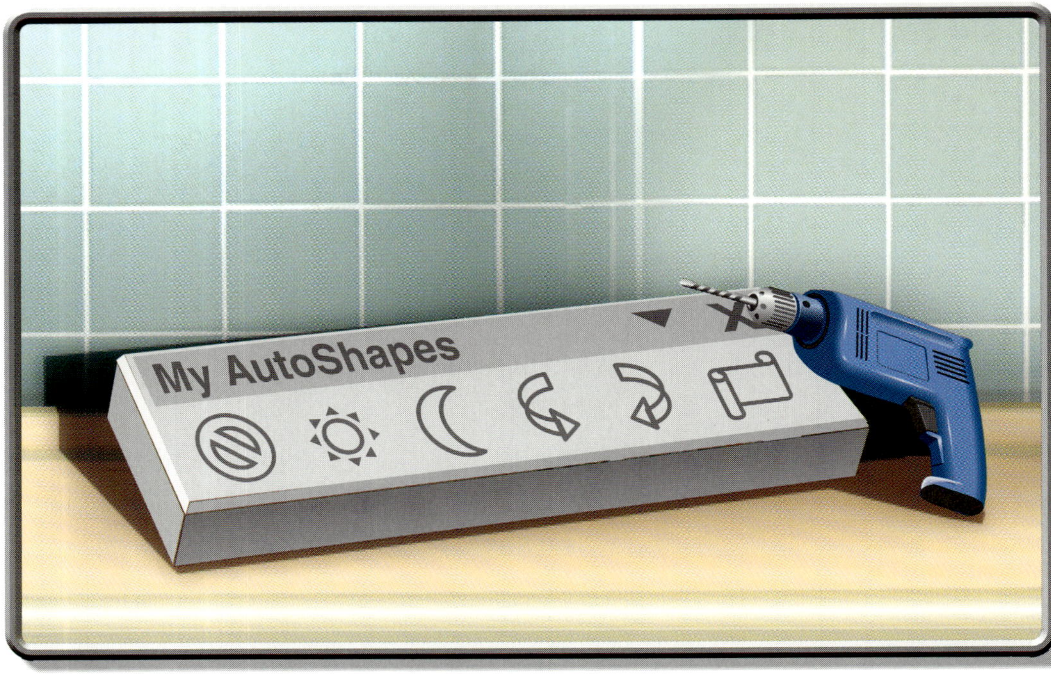

CREATE A NEW TOOLBAR

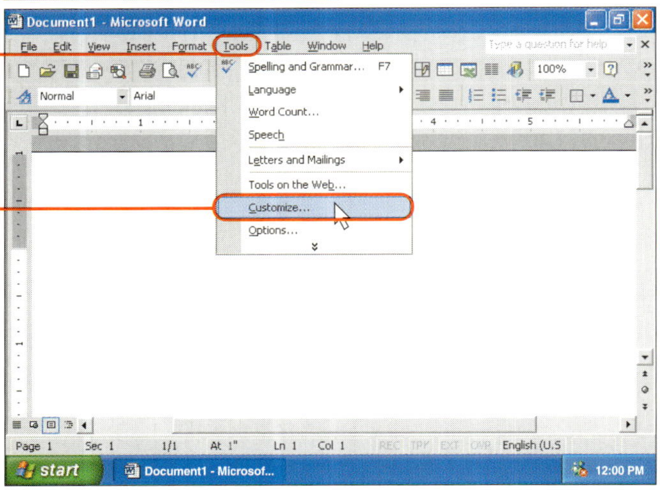

1 Click **Tools**.

2 Click **Customize**.

■ The Customize dialog box appears.

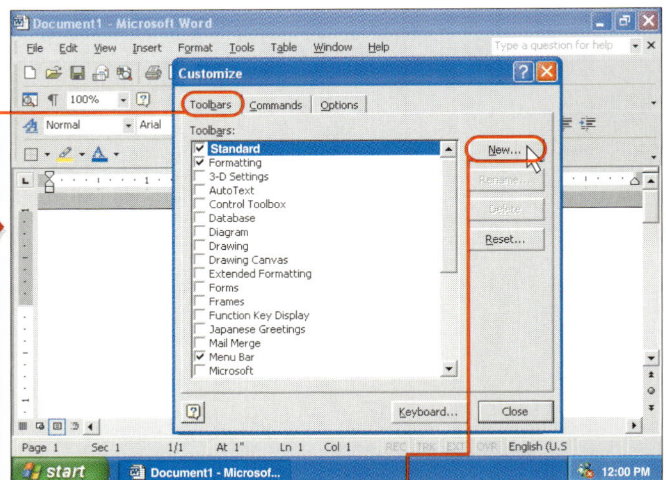

3 Click the **Toolbars** tab.

4 Click **New** to create a new toolbar.

■ The New Toolbar dialog box appears.

How can I move a toolbar I created?

After you create a new toolbar, you can move the toolbar to a new location on your screen. To move a toolbar, position the mouse over the title bar and then drag the toolbar to a new location.

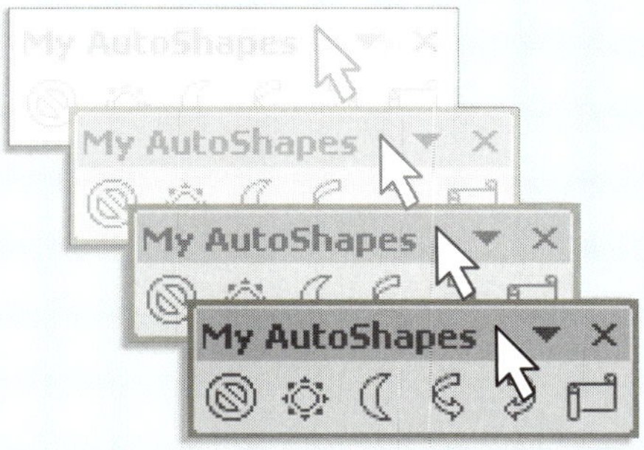

How can I hide a toolbar I created?

You can hide or display a toolbar you created as you would any toolbar. To hide or display a toolbar, see page 43.

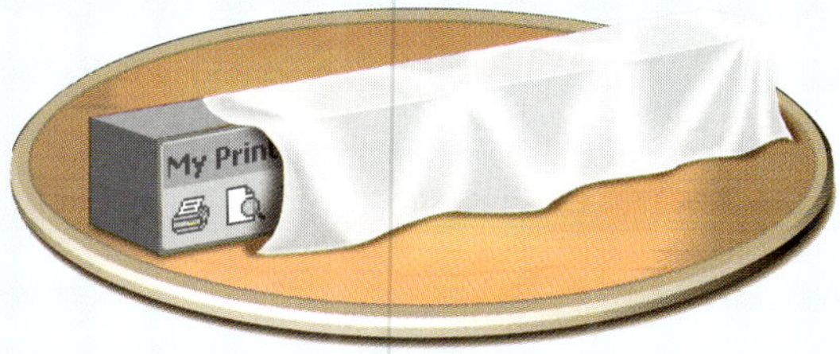

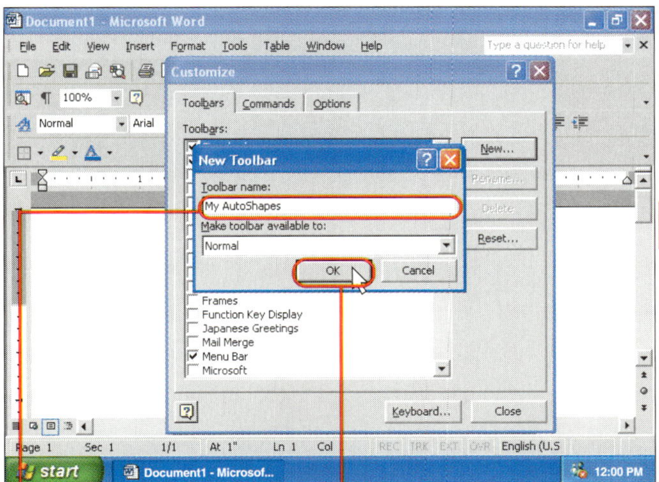

5 Type a name for the toolbar.

6 Click **OK** to create the toolbar.

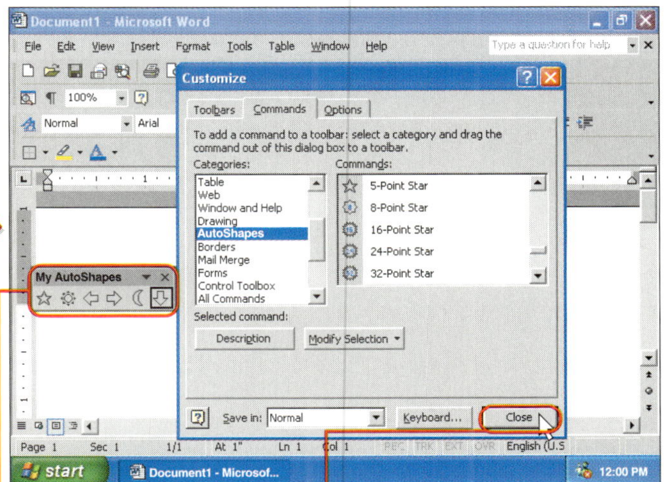

■ The new toolbar appears on your screen.

7 You can now add the buttons you want the toolbar to display. To add buttons to a toolbar, see page 246.

Note: You can move or remove buttons you add to the toolbar. To move or remove buttons on a toolbar, see page 248 or 249.

8 When you finish adding buttons to the toolbar, click **Close** to close the Customize dialog box.

RECORD A MACRO

A macro saves you time by combining a series of actions into a single command. Macros are ideal for tasks you frequently perform.

RECORD A MACRO

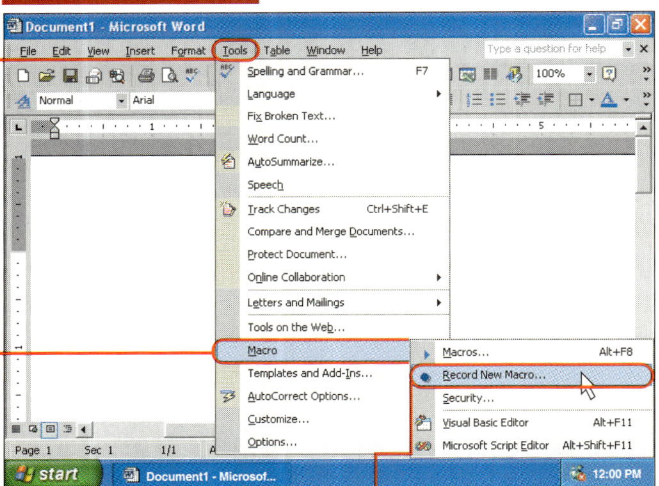

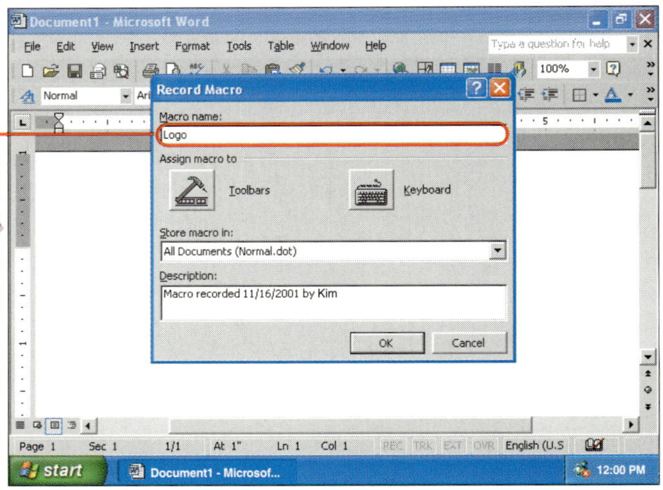

1 Click **Tools**.

2 Click **Macro**.

Note: If Macro does not appear on the menu, position the mouse over the bottom of the menu to display all the menu options.

3 Click **Record New Macro**.

■ The Record Macro dialog box appears.

4 Type a name for the macro.

Note: A macro name must begin with a letter and cannot contain spaces.

Why would I record a macro?

Macros can help speed up many repetitive formatting and editing tasks, such as removing extra spaces from text. Macros are also useful for inserting items, such as pictures or symbols, into your documents.

Should I practice before I record a macro?

Yes. Before recording a macro, you should plan and practice all the actions you want the macro to include. Word will record any mistakes and corrections you make while recording the macro.

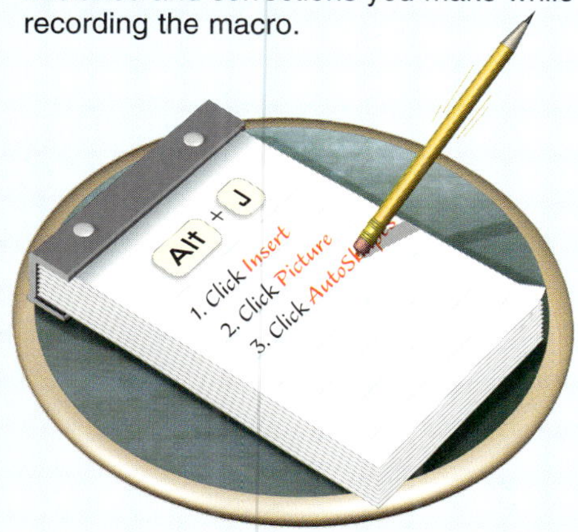

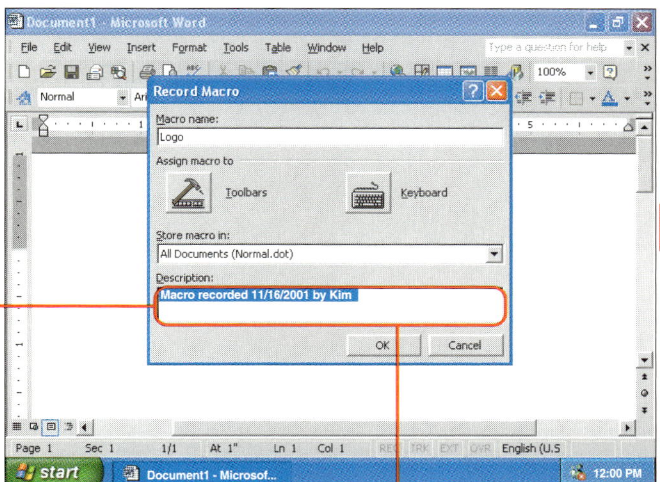

■ Word displays the date and your name as a description for the macro.

5 To enter a different description, drag the mouse I over the text in this area until you highlight the text. Then type a new description.

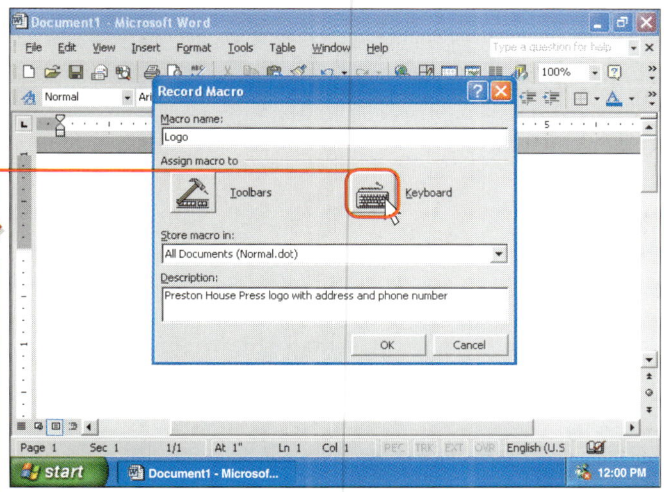

6 Click **Keyboard** to assign a keyboard shortcut to the macro.

■ The Customize Keyboard dialog box appears.

CONTINUED

RECORD A MACRO

You can assign a keyboard shortcut, such as Alt + J, to a macro you create. A keyboard shortcut allows you to quickly run the macro.

RECORD A MACRO (CONTINUED)

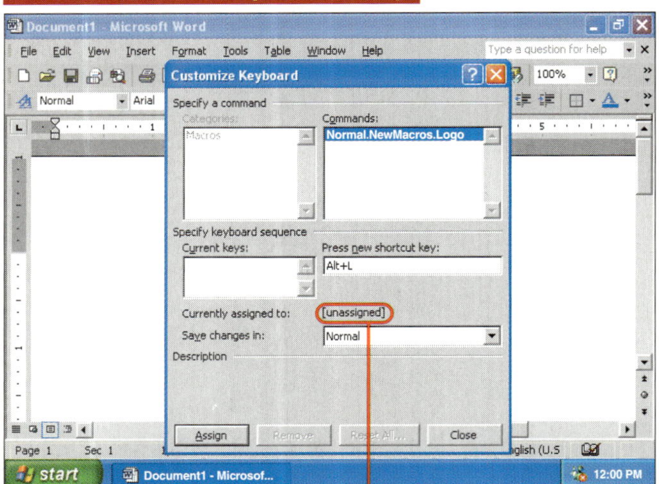

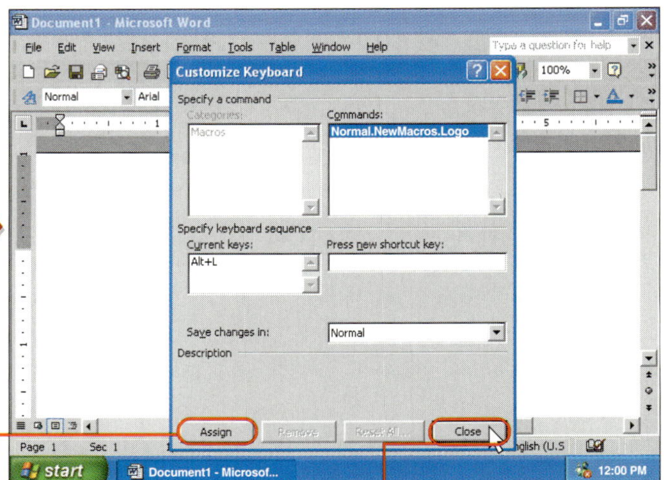

7 To specify a keyboard shortcut for the macro, press and hold down the Alt key as you press a letter or number key.

■ This area displays the word **[unassigned]**.

*Note: If the word **[unassigned]** is not displayed, the keyboard shortcut you specified is already assigned to another command. Press the* ←Backspace *key to delete the shortcut and then repeat step 7, using a different letter or number.*

8 Click **Assign** to assign the keyboard shortcut to your macro.

9 Click **Close** to continue.

Can I use the mouse while recording a macro?

While recording a macro, you can only use the mouse to select toolbar buttons or menu commands. You must use the keyboard to move the insertion point on your screen and to select text. To move the insertion point on your screen using the keyboard, press the ↑, ↓, ← or → key. To select text using the keyboard, position the insertion point at the beginning of the text you want to select. Then press and hold down the Shift key as you press the → key.

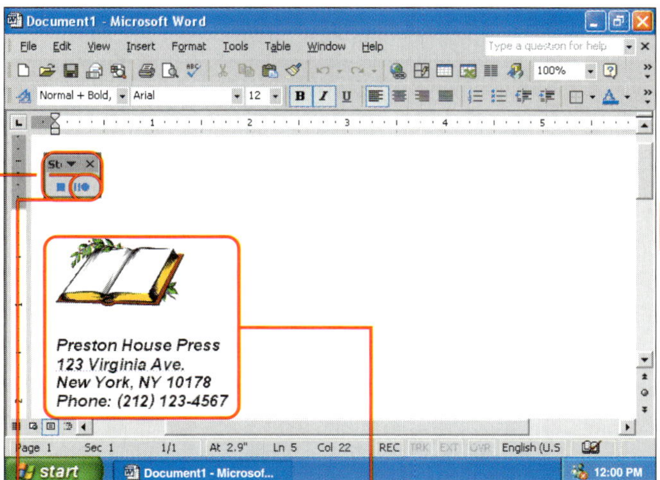

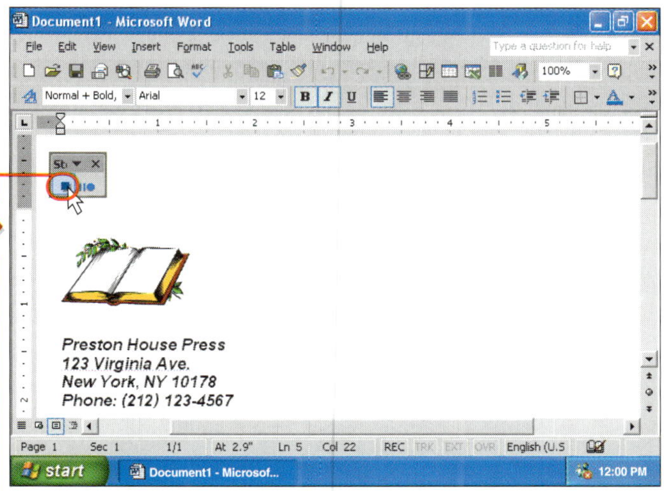

■ The Stop Recording toolbar appears.

10 Perform the actions you want the macro to include.

■ To pause the recording at any time, click [pause button].

Note: To once again resume recording, click [pause button].

■ In this example, a company logo is inserted into the document.

11 Click [stop button] when you have completed all the actions you want the macro to include.

■ You can now run the macro. To run a macro, see page 256.

RUN A MACRO

When you run a macro, Word automatically performs the actions you recorded.

RUN A MACRO

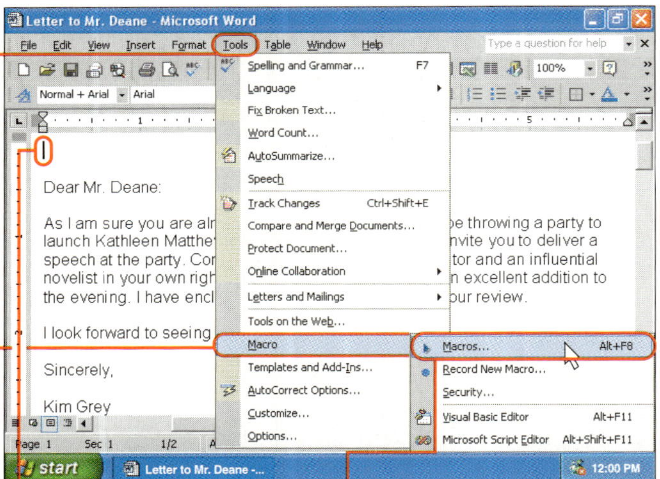

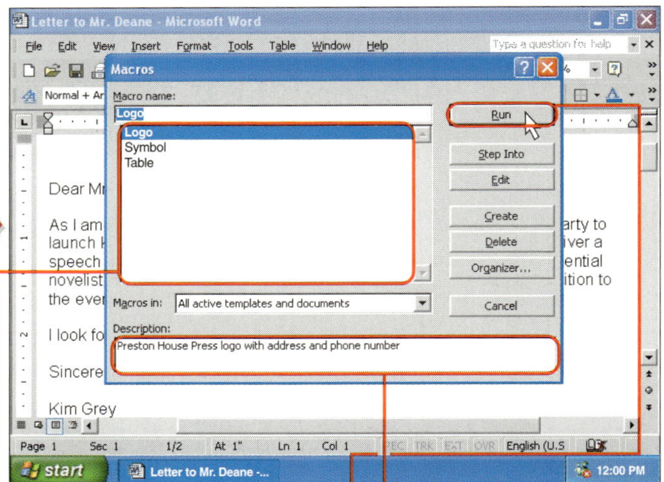

1 Position the insertion point where you want the results of the macro to appear.

2 Click **Tools**.

3 Click **Macro**.

Note: If Macro does not appear on the menu, position the mouse over the bottom of the menu to display all the menu options.

4 Click **Macros**.

■ The Macros dialog box appears.

■ This area displays the available macros.

5 Click the name of the macro you want to run.

■ This area displays a description of the macro you selected.

6 Click **Run** to run the macro.

Can I run the macro in all my documents?

After you have recorded a macro, you can run the macro in any Word document.

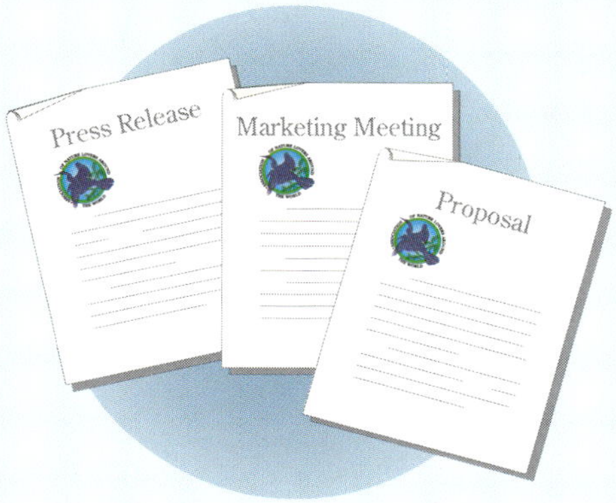

How do I delete a macro I no longer need?

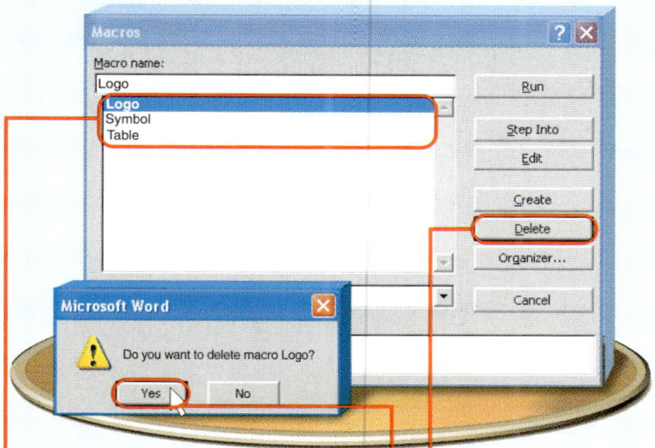

1 Perform steps **2** to **4** on page 256 to display the Macros dialog box.

2 Click the name of the macro you want to delete.

3 Click **Delete** to delete the macro.

4 Click **Yes** in the dialog box that appears to confirm the deletion.

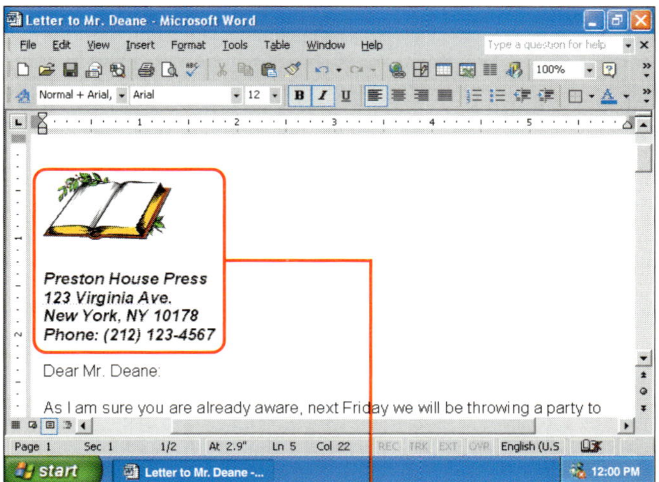

■ The macro performs the actions you recorded.

■ In this example, the macro inserted a company logo into the document.

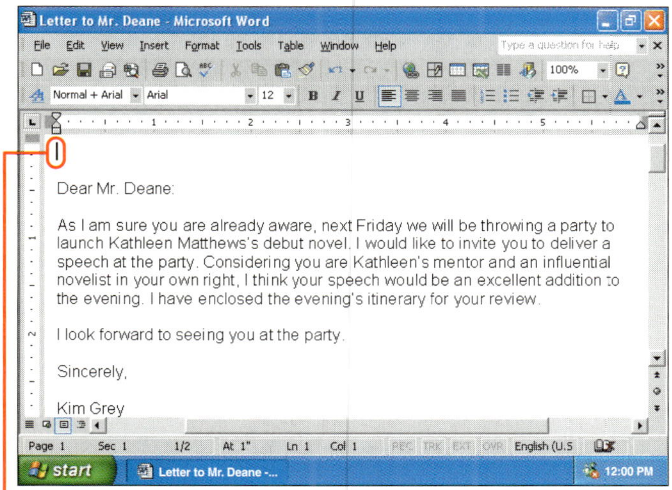

RUN A MACRO USING THE KEYBOARD SHORTCUT

1 Position the insertion point where you want the results of the macro to appear.

2 Press the keyboard shortcut you assigned to the macro.

■ The macro performs the actions you recorded.

MAIL
MAIL
MAIL
MAIL
MAIL
Mr. John Smith
11 South Street
Los Angeles, CA 90013
32
Mr. Jim Hunter
14 Willow Avenue
Los Angeles, CA 90028
32

CHAPTER 14

Using Mail Merge

Would you like to quickly produce a personalized letter for each person on a mailing list? This chapter teaches you how.

Create Letters Using Mail Merge 260

Create Labels Using Mail Merge 270

CREATE LETTERS USING MAIL MERGE

You can use the Mail Merge feature to produce a personalized letter for each person on your mailing list.

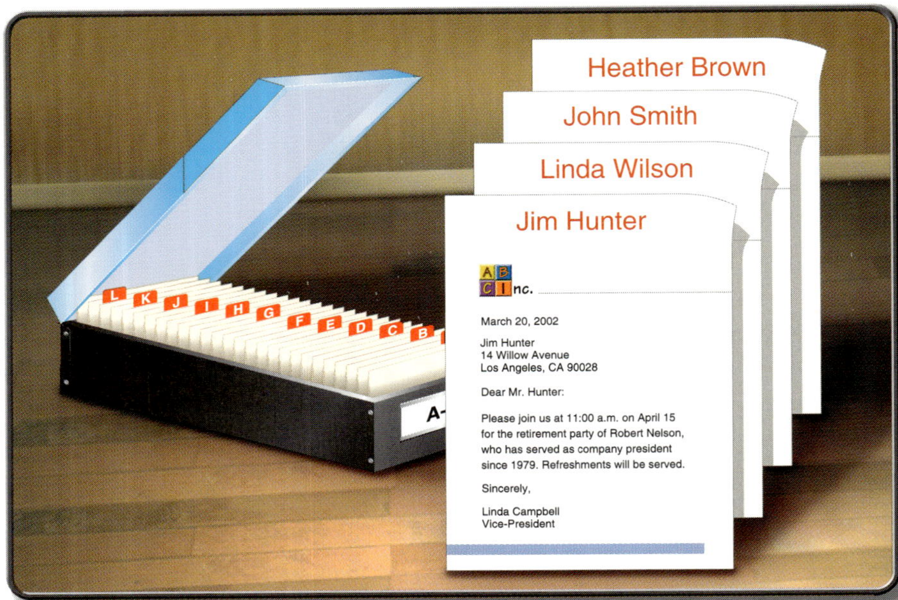

Performing a mail merge is useful if you want to send the same document, such as an announcement or advertisement, to many people.

The Mail Merge Wizard guides you step by step through the mail merge process.

CREATE LETTERS USING MAIL MERGE

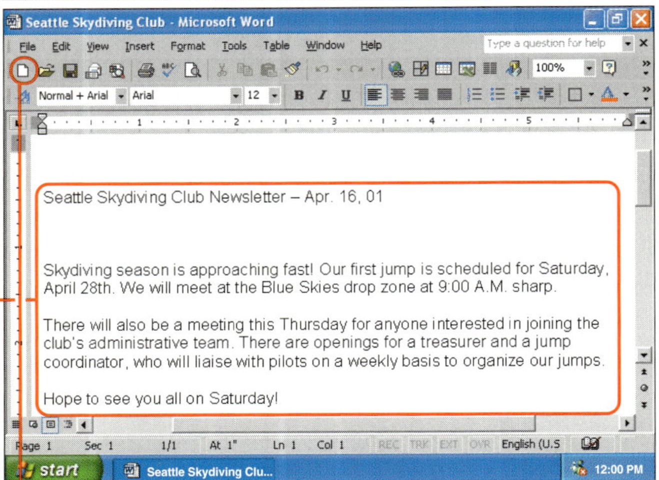

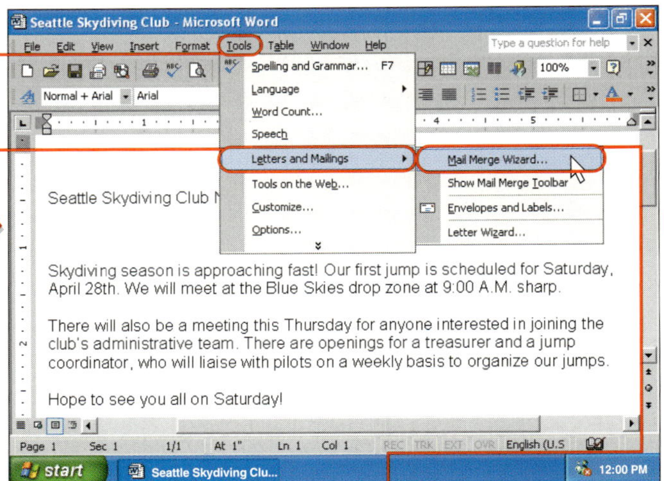

1 Click ☐ to create a new document.

2 Type the letter you want to send to each person on your mailing list. Do not include the information that will change in each letter, such as a person's name or address.

3 Save the letter. To save a document, see page 22.

Note: You can also use an existing document for the letter. *To open an existing document, see page 28.*

4 Click **Tools**.

5 Click **Letters and Mailings**.

6 Click **Mail Merge Wizard**.

What other types of documents can I create using the Mail Merge Wizard?

E-mail messages

Creates an e-mail message for each person on your mailing list.

Envelopes

Creates an envelope for each person on your mailing list.

Labels

Creates a label for each person on your mailing list. For information on creating labels using the Mail Merge Wizard, see page 270.

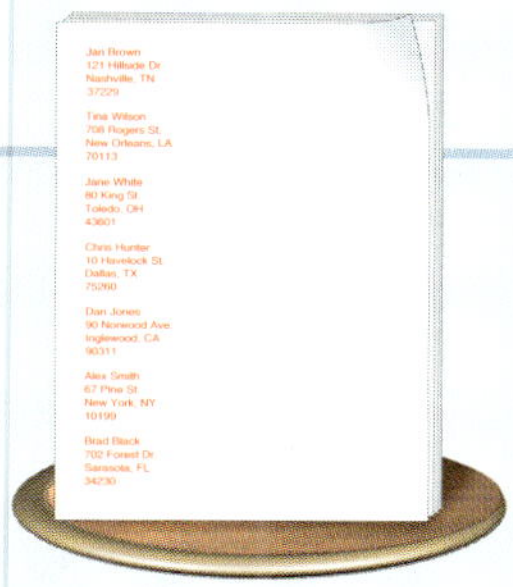

Directory

Creates a document that contains information about each person on your mailing list.

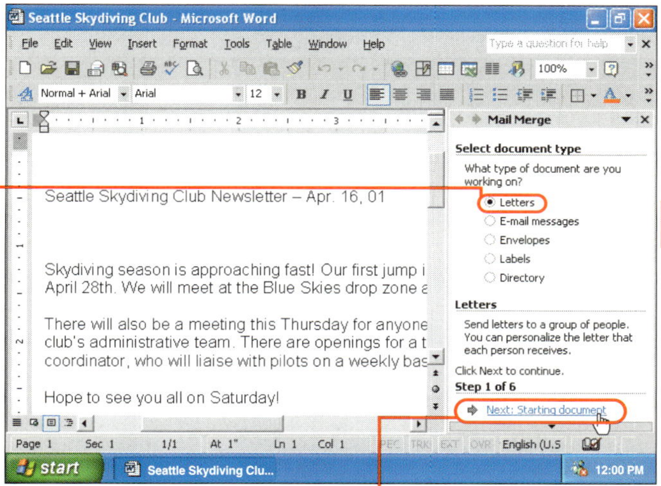

■ The Mail Merge task pane appears.

7 Click **Letters** to create a letter for each person on your mailing list (○ changes to ⦿).

8 Click **Next: Starting document** to continue.

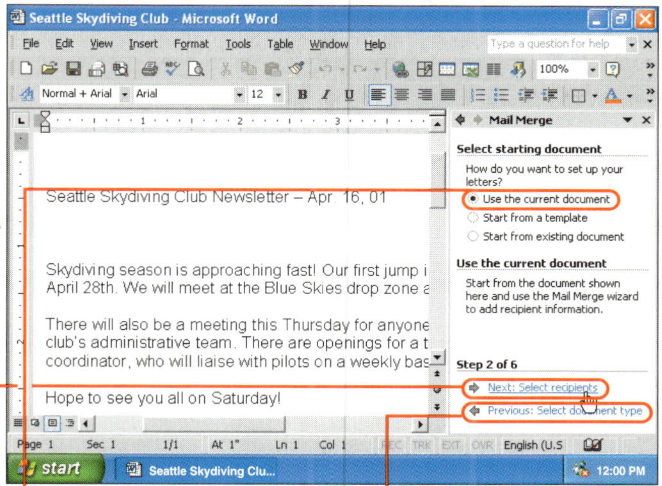

9 Click **Use the current document** to use the displayed document as the letter you will send to each person on your mailing list (○ changes to ⦿).

10 Click **Next: Select recipients** to continue.

■ You can click **Previous** at any time to return to a previous step and change your selections.

CONTINUED

CREATE LETTERS USING MAIL MERGE

You can specify the address information for each person on your mailing list.

CREATE LETTERS USING MAIL MERGE (CONTINUED)

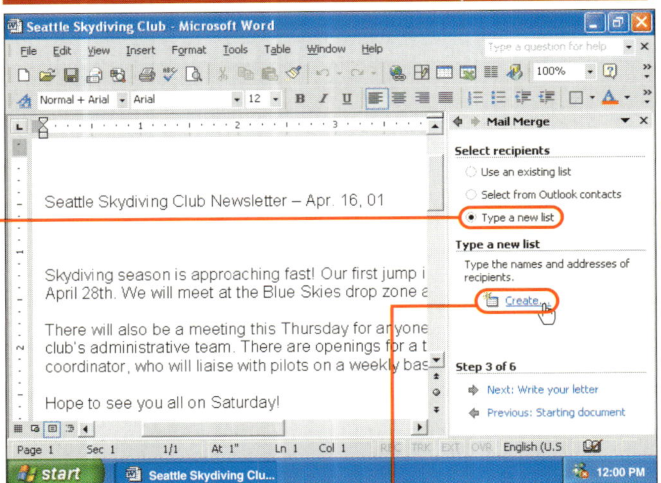

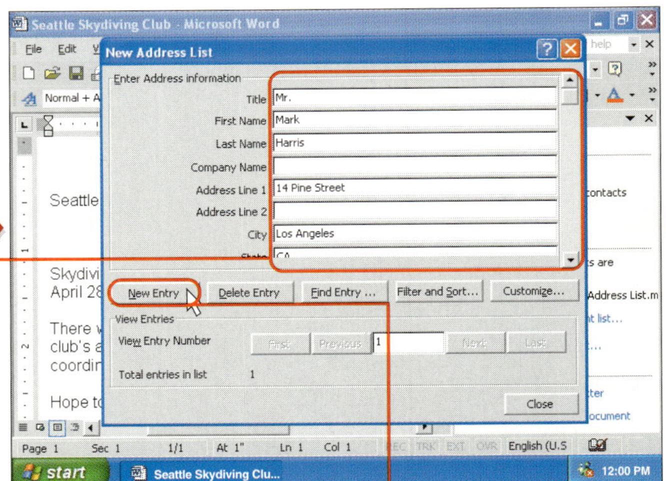

11 Click **Type a new list** to create your mailing list (○ changes to ⦿).

12 Click **Create** to enter the names and addresses of the people on your mailing list.

■ The New Address List dialog box appears, displaying areas where you can enter the information for each person on your mailing list.

13 Click each area and type the appropriate information for a person. You do not have to fill in every area.

14 To enter the information for another person, click **New Entry**.

How can I remove a person I accidentally added to my mailing list?

While creating your mailing list, you can display the information for the person you want to remove and then click the **Delete Entry** button. To confirm the deletion, click **Yes** in the dialog box that appears.

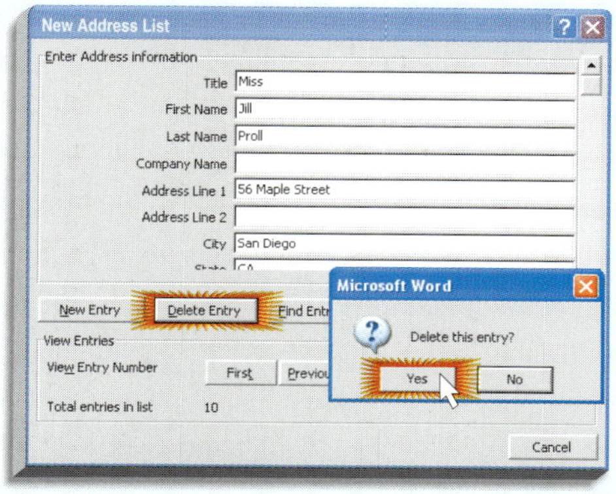

How do I use an existing mailing list to perform a mail merge?

Perform steps **1** to **10** starting on page 260 to begin the mail merge. To select the mailing list you want to use, perform steps **15** to **18** on page 272. Then skip to step **19** on page 264 to continue with the mail merge.

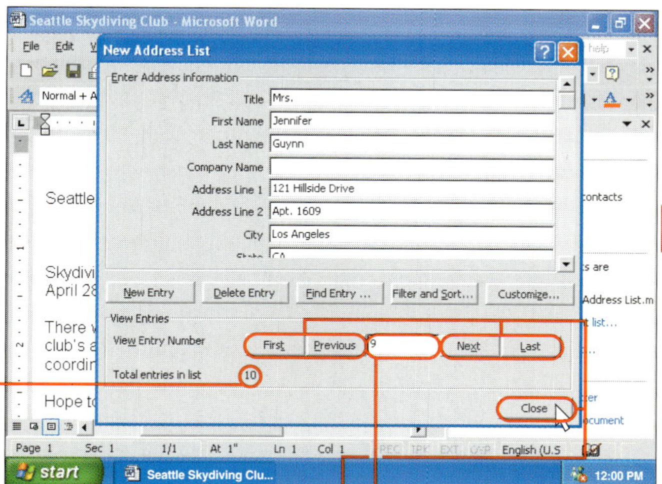

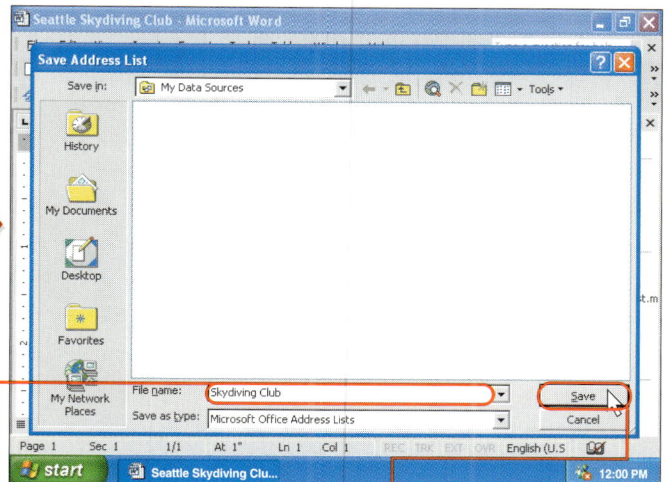

15 Repeat steps **13** and **14** for each person on your mailing list.

■ This area displays the number of people you have added.

■ This area displays the number of the entry that is currently displayed.

■ To browse through the entries, click a button to display the first, previous, next or last entry.

16 When you finish creating your mailing list, click **Close**.

■ The Save Address List dialog box appears.

17 Type a name for the file that will store your mailing list.

18 Click **Save** to save the file.

■ The Mail Merge Recipients dialog box appears.

CONTINUED

CREATE LETTERS USING MAIL MERGE

When you finish creating your mailing list, Word displays the information for each person on the list. You can select the people you want to receive a personalized letter.

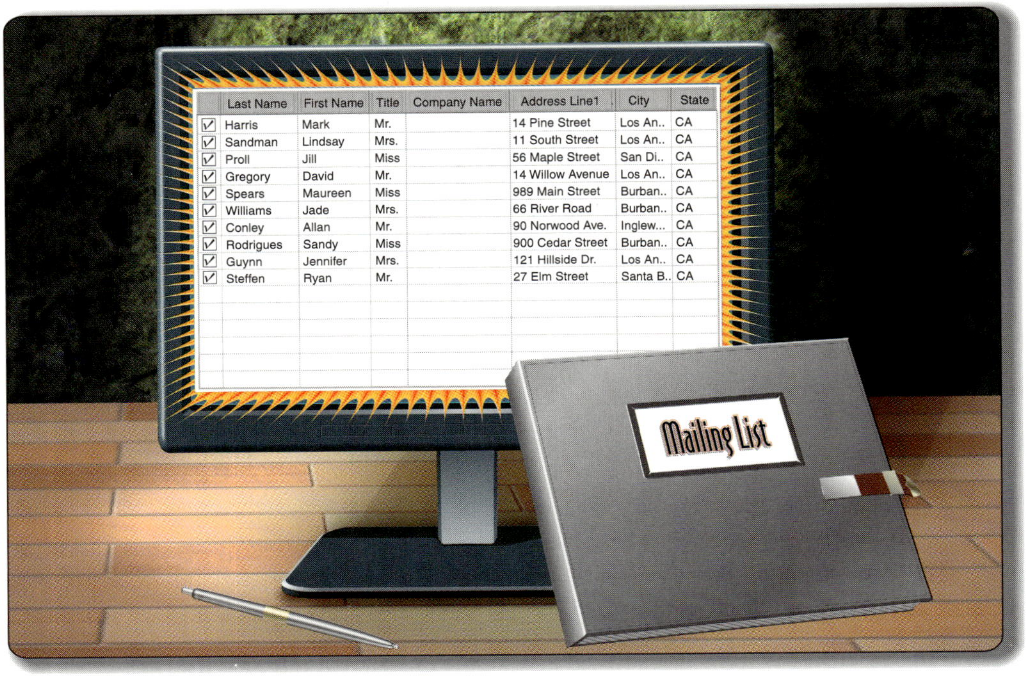

CREATE LETTERS USING MAIL MERGE (CONTINUED)

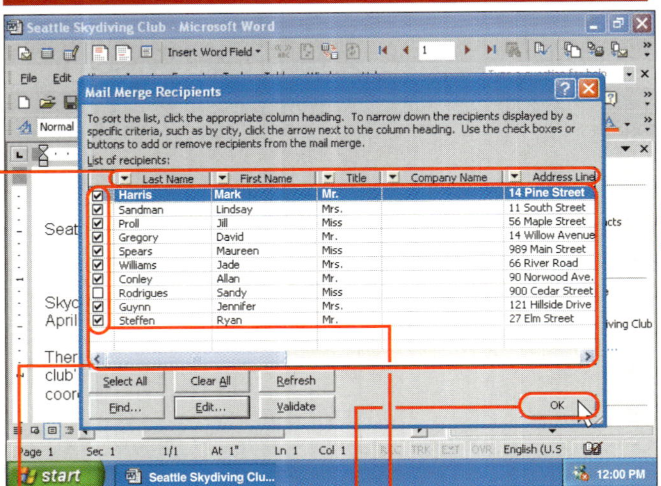

■ This area lists all the people on your mailing list.

■ To sort the list, click the heading of the column you want to use to sort the list.

19 A check mark (✔) beside a person's name indicates Word will create a personalized letter for the person. To add (☑) or remove (☐) a check mark, click the box beside a person's name.

20 Click **OK**.

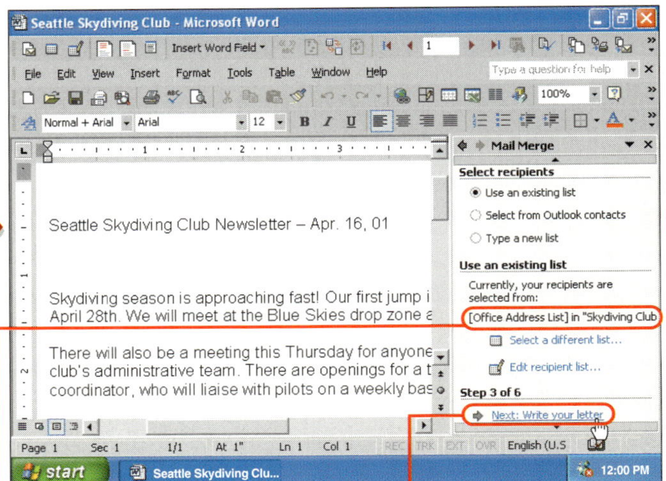

■ This area displays the name of the file that stores your mailing list.

21 Click **Next: Write your letter** to continue.

What type of information can I add to my letters?

Address block

Displays the address of a person on your mailing list.

Greeting line

Displays a greeting for a person on your mailing list.

More items

Displays a piece of information for a person on your mailing list, such as their home phone number or e-mail address.

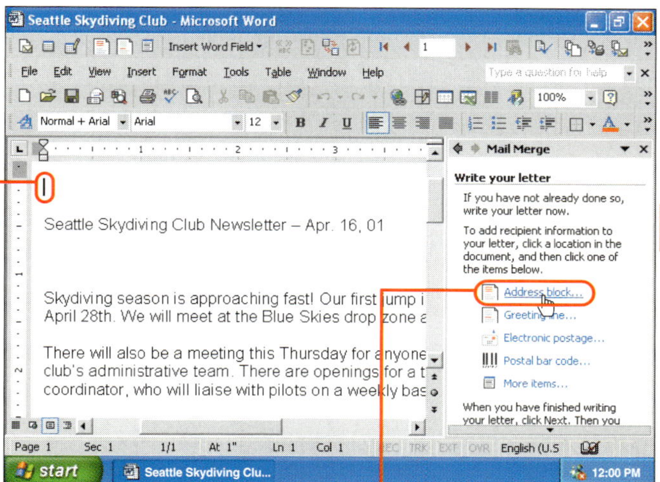

22 To display an address in the letter, click the location in the letter where you want to display the address.

23 Click **Address block**.

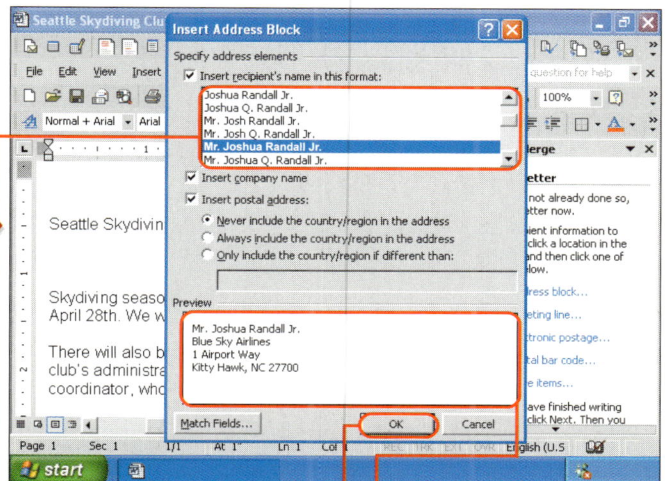

■ The Insert Address Block dialog box appears.

24 Click the way you want each person's name to appear in the letter.

■ This area displays a preview of how the address will appear in the letter.

25 Click **OK** to confirm your selection.

CONTINUED

CREATE LETTERS USING MAIL MERGE

Word helps you insert special instructions, called merge fields, into your letter. A merge field acts as a placeholder for information from your mailing list.

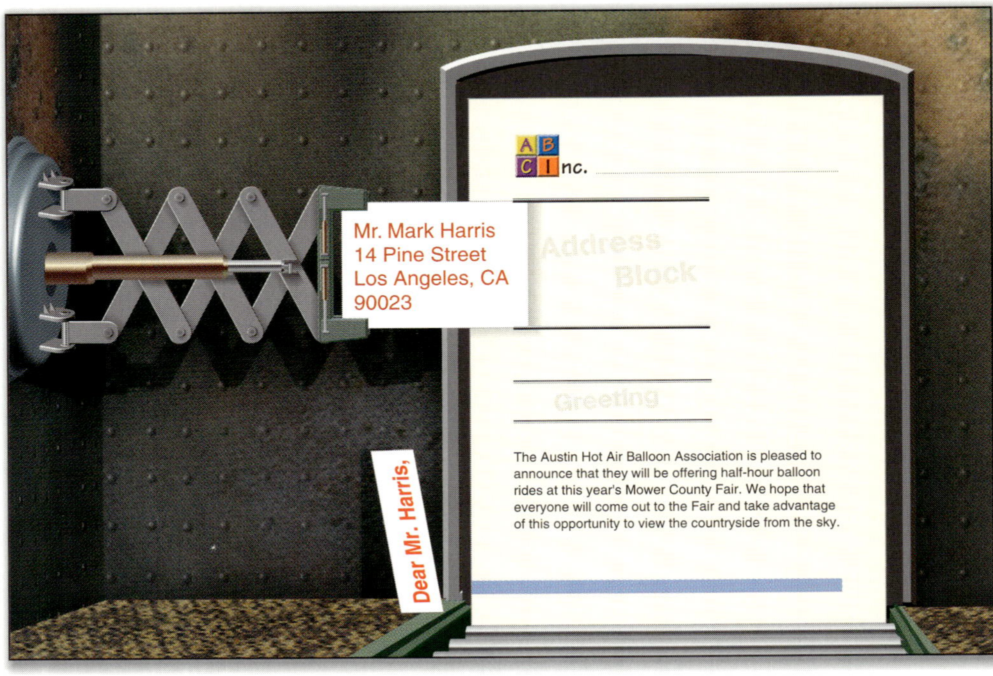

CREATE LETTERS USING MAIL MERGE (CONTINUED)

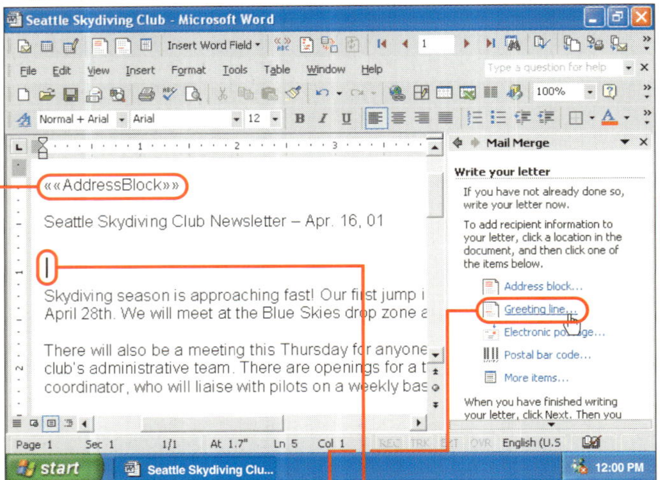

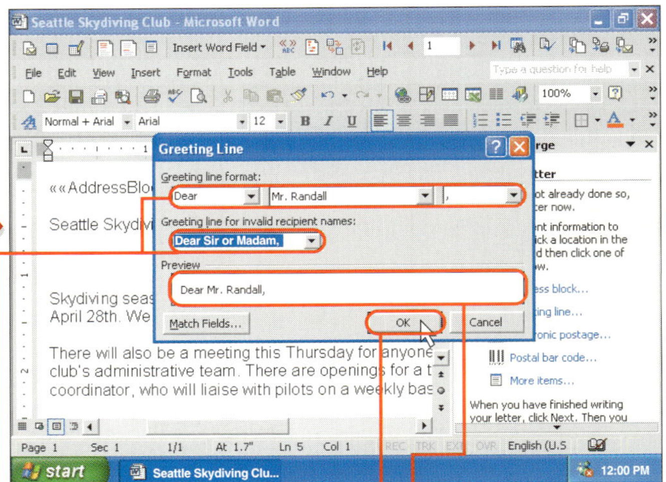

■ A merge field for the address appears in the letter. Word will replace the merge field with an address from your mailing list.

26 To add a greeting to the letter, click the location in the letter where you want to display the greeting.

Note: If you do not want to add a greeting to the letter, skip to step 29.

27 Click **Greeting line**.

■ The Greeting Line dialog box appears.

■ These areas display the available formats for the greeting. You can click ▼ in an area to select a different format.

■ This area displays a preview of how the greeting will appear in the letter.

28 Click **OK** to add the greeting to the letter.

TEACH YOURSELF

How do I delete a merge field I accidentally inserted?

To delete a merge field you accidentally inserted, drag the mouse I over the merge field until you highlight the field. Then press the Delete key.

TEACH YOURSELF

When previewing the letters, can I exclude a person from the mail merge?

Yes. When the letter you do not want to send is displayed on your screen, click the **Exclude this recipient** button on the Mail Merge task pane. Word will not create a letter for the person when you complete the mail merge.

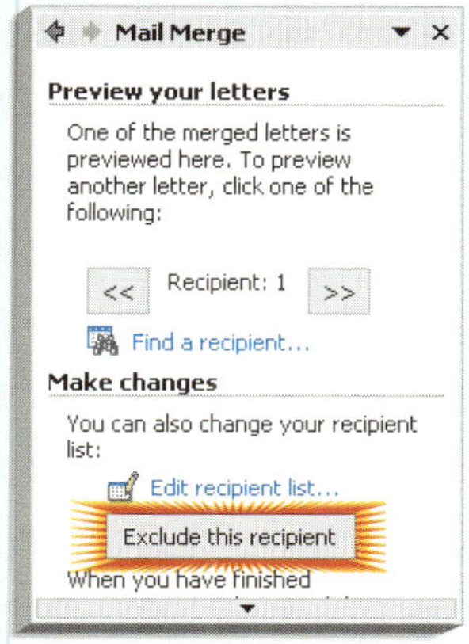

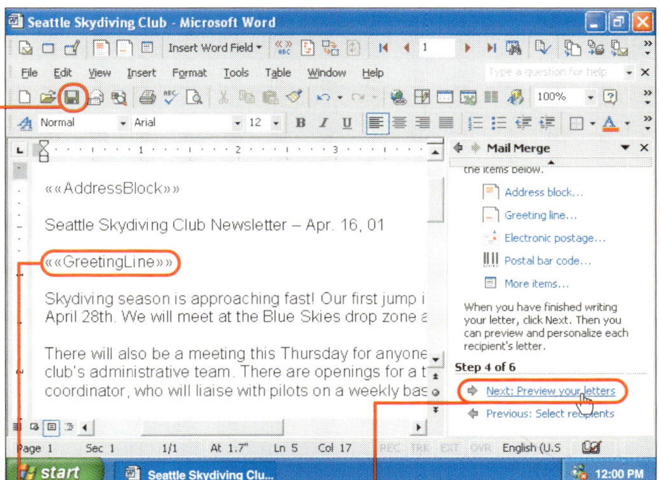

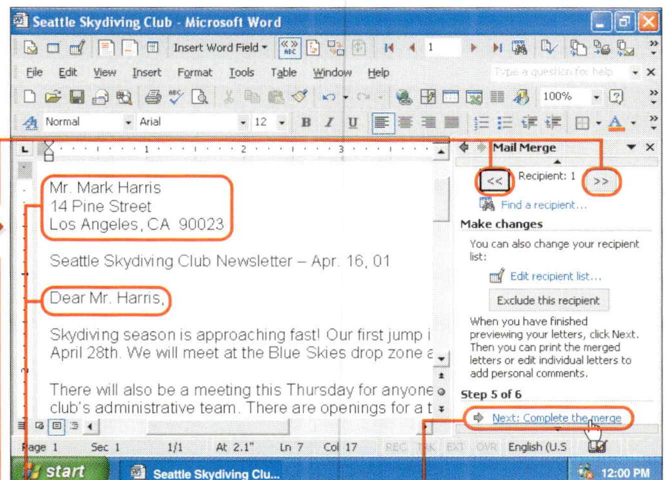

■ A merge field for the greeting appears in the letter. Word will replace the merge field with a greeting for each letter.

29 Click 💾 to save the changes you made to the letter.

30 Click **Next: Preview your letters** to continue.

*Note: If you cannot see the **Next** option, click ▼ to scroll down through the Mail Merge task pane.*

■ Word displays a preview of one of the merged letters. Word replaces the merge fields with the corresponding information for one person on your mailing list.

■ To preview another letter, click << or >> to display the previous or next letter.

31 When you finish previewing your letters, click **Next: Complete the merge** to continue.

CONTINUED

CREATE LETTERS USING MAIL MERGE

Once you complete your letter, Word can combine the letter with the information from your mailing list to create a personalized letter for each person.

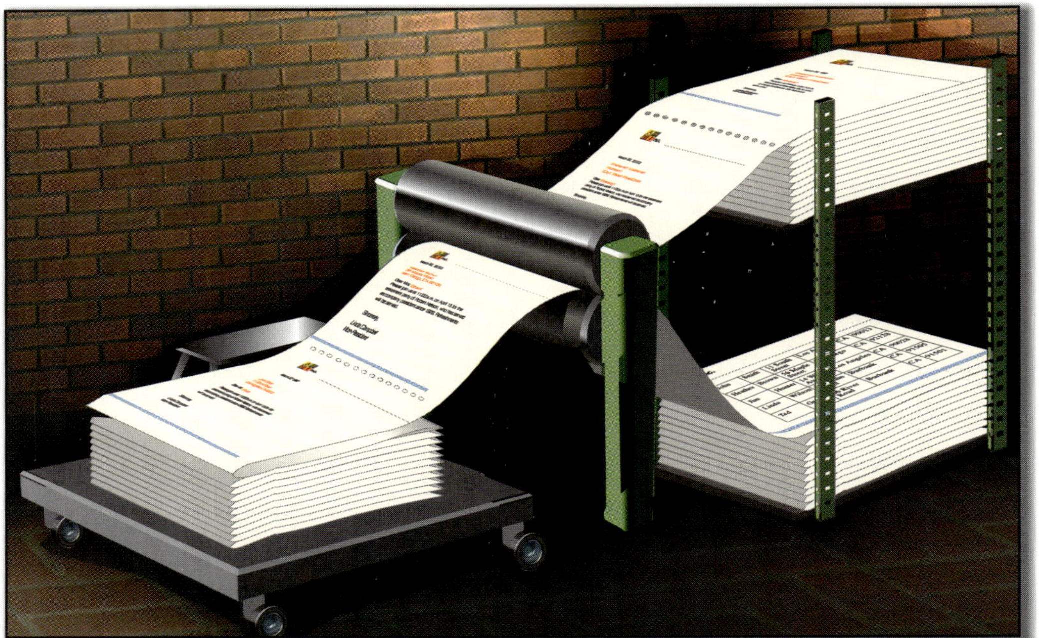

CREATE LETTERS USING MAIL MERGE (CONTINUED)

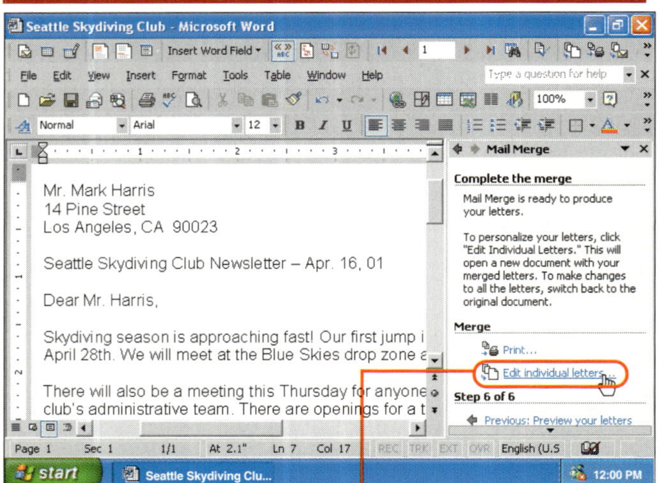

■ Word is ready to produce the letters.

32 Click **Edit individual letters** to combine the letter with the information from your mailing list.

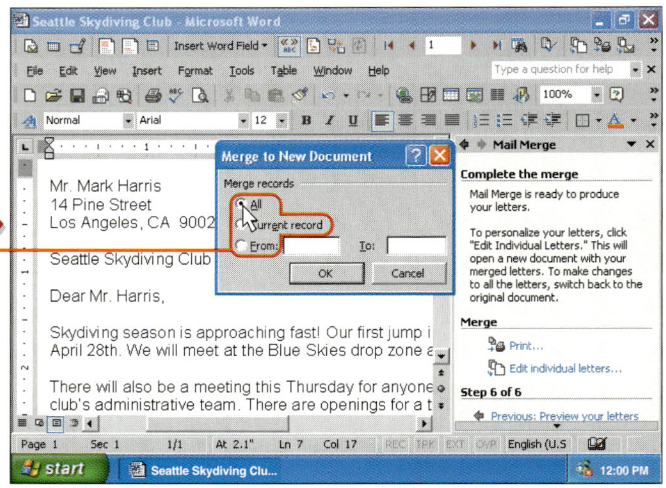

■ The Merge to New Document dialog box appears.

33 Click an option to specify which people from your mailing list you want to create letters for (○ changes to ⊙).

All
All people on your mailing list.

Current record
Only the displayed person.

From
People on your mailing list that you specify.

Can I print the letters from the Mail Merge Wizard?

Yes. Printing letters from the Mail Merge Wizard is useful when you know the letters are ready to print and do not require further editing. To print your letters from the Mail Merge Wizard, select the **Print** option in step **32** below.

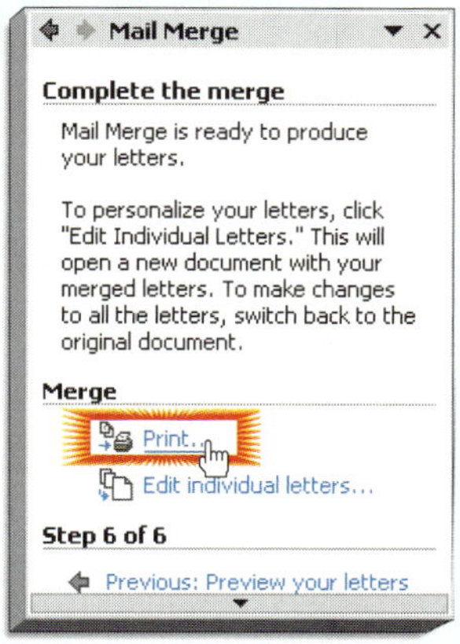

Should I save the document containing the personalized letters?

There is no need to save the document. You can easily perform another mail merge at any time to recreate the personalized letters.

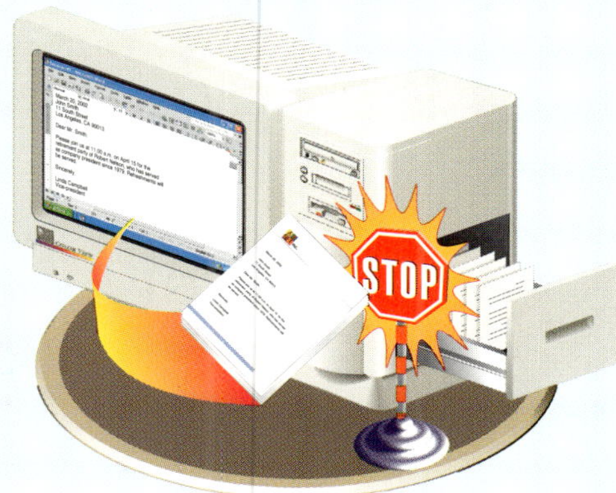

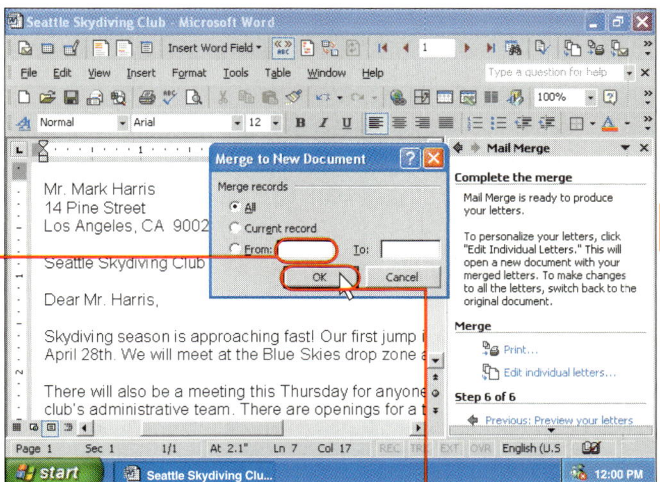

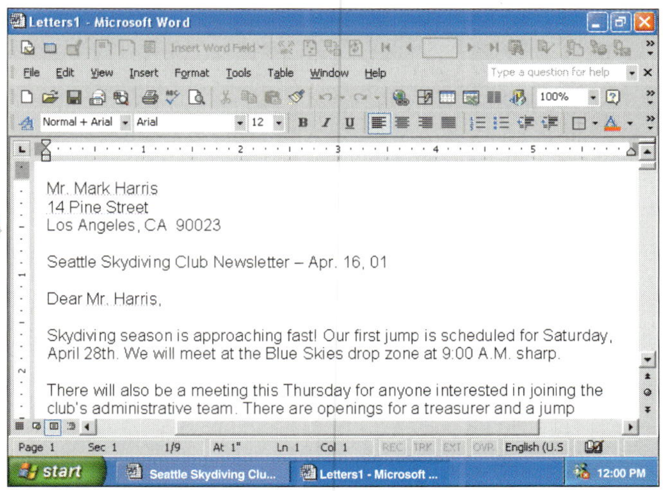

■ If you selected **From** in step **33**, click this area and type the number of the first person you want to create a letter for. Then press the Tab key and type the number of the last person you want to create a letter for.

34 Click **OK** to create the letters.

■ Word opens a new document and creates the personalized letters in the document.

■ You can edit and print the letters as you would edit and print any document. Editing a letter allows you to include additional information in the letter. To edit a document, see page 54. To print a document, see page 172.

CREATE LABELS USING MAIL MERGE

You can use the Mail Merge feature to print a personalized label for each person on your mailing list. This saves you from having to type each label individually.

You can use labels for addressing envelopes and packages.

The Mail Merge Wizard takes you step by step through the mail merge process.

CREATE LABELS USING MAIL MERGE

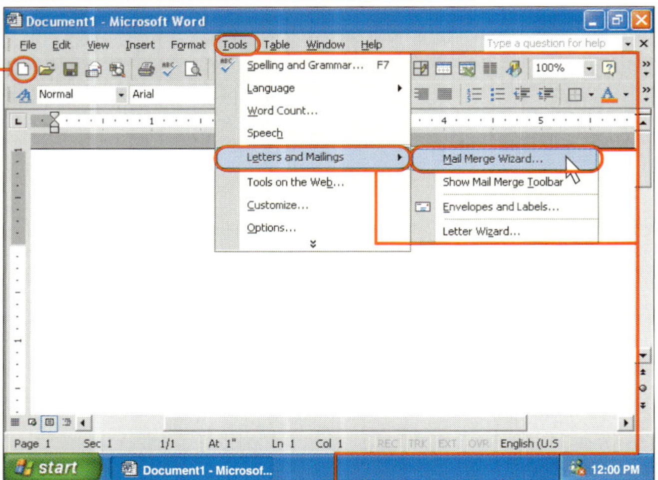

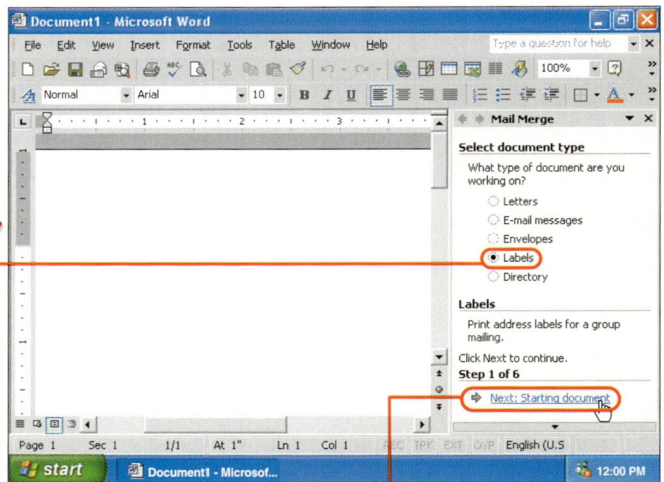

1 Click to create a new document.

Note: If is not displayed, click on the Standard toolbar to display the button.

2 Click **Tools**.

3 Click **Letters and Mailings**.

4 Click **Mail Merge Wizard**.

■ The Mail Merge task pane appears.

5 Click **Labels** to create a label for each person on your mailing list (○ changes to ⊙).

6 Click **Next: Starting document** to continue.

Can I use the Mail Merge Wizard to print envelopes?

Yes. You can use the Mail Merge Wizard to print a personalized envelope for each person on your mailing list. Perform steps **1** to **5** below, selecting **Envelopes** in step **5**. Then follow the instructions on your screen to set up the envelopes.

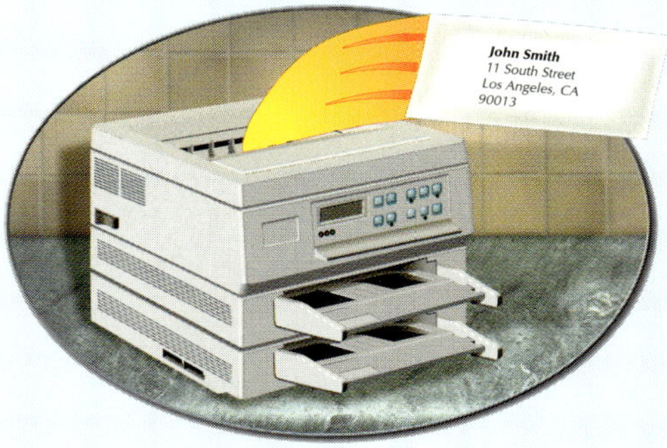

Can I create labels without using the Mail Merge Wizard?

Yes. If you want to create only a few labels, you can type the text you want to appear on each label yourself. For information on printing labels without using the Mail Merge Wizard, see page 176.

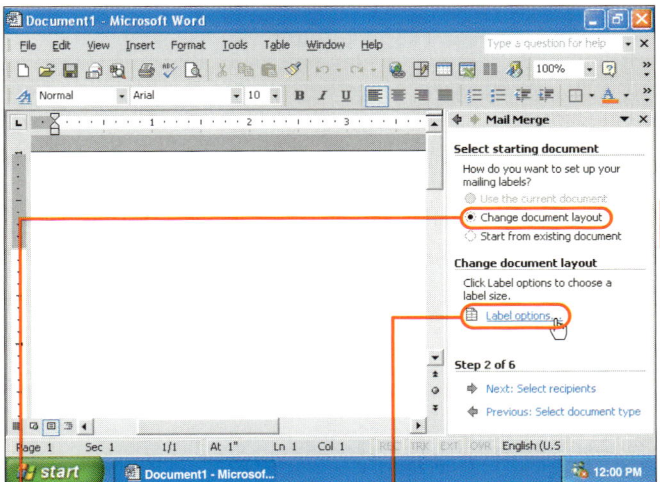

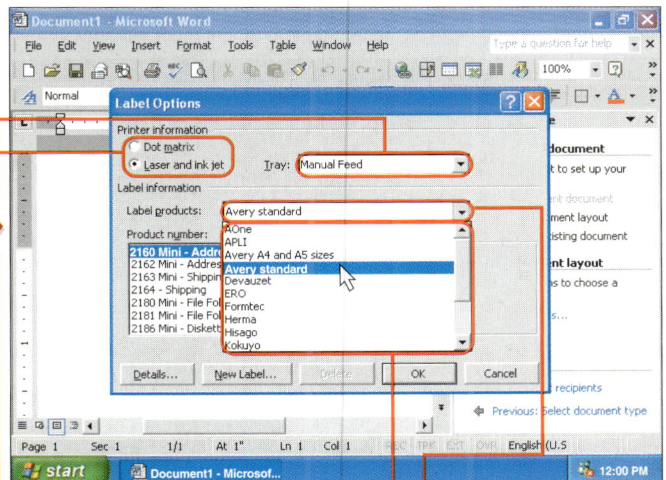

7 Click **Change document layout** to set up the current document for labels (○ changes to ⊙).

8 Click **Label options** to specify options for the labels.

■ The Label Options dialog box appears.

9 Click an option to specify the type of printer you will use to print the labels (○ changes to ⊙).

■ This area displays the printer tray that will contain the labels. You can click this area to specify a different tray.

10 Click this area to display a list of the available label products.

11 Click the label product you will use.

CONTINUED

CREATE LABELS USING MAIL MERGE

After Word sets up a document for the labels, you must specify which mailing list stores the address information you want to appear on the labels.

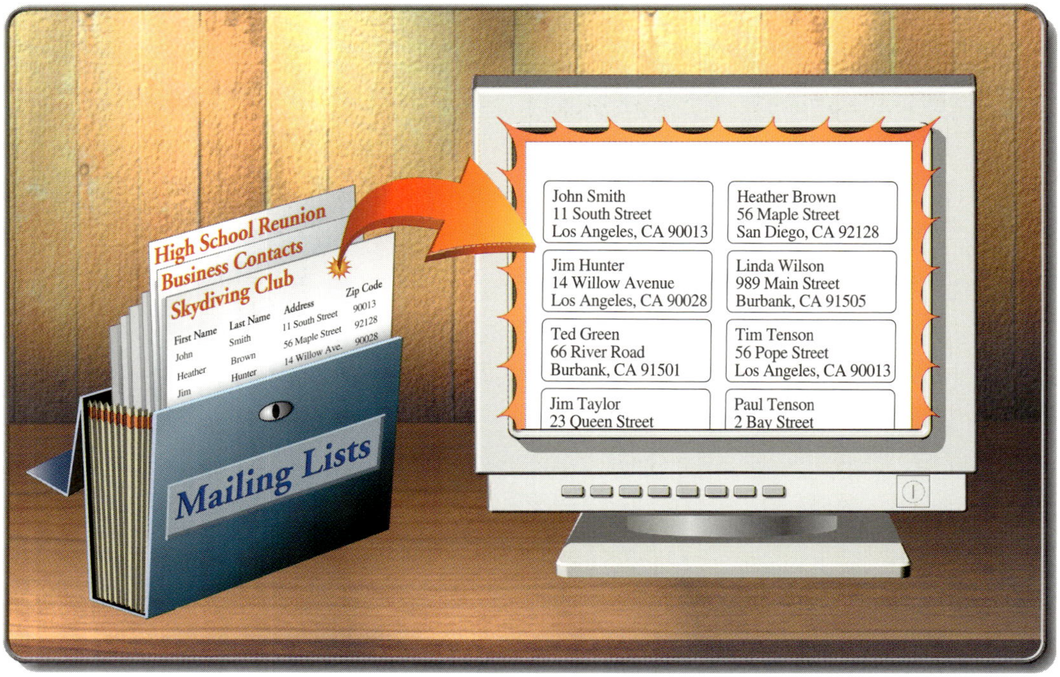

CREATE LABELS USING MAIL MERGE (CONTINUED)

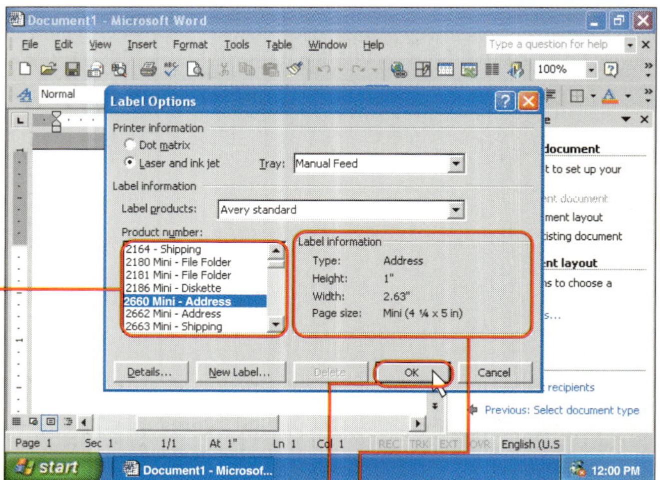

■ This area displays the types of labels available for the label product you selected.

12 Click the type of label you will use.

■ This area displays information about the type of label you selected.

13 Click **OK** to confirm your selections.

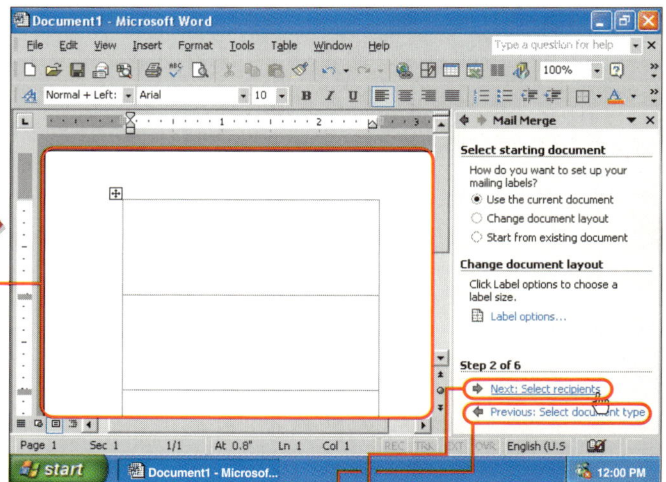

■ Word sets up the document for labels.

14 Click **Next: Select recipients** to continue.

■ You can click **Previous** at any time to return to a previous step and change your selections.

Which label product and type should I choose?

You can check your label packaging to determine which label product and type you should choose when printing labels.

Can I create a mailing list when I create labels?

If you have not created a mailing list that stores the address information you want to use, you can create a mailing list during the process of creating labels. After performing step **14** below, perform steps **11** to **18** starting on page 262 to create a mailing list for the labels. Then skip to step **19** on page 274 to continue with the mail merge.

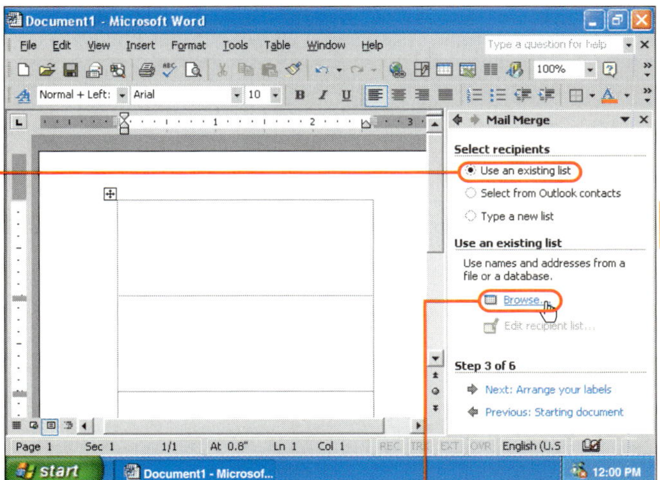

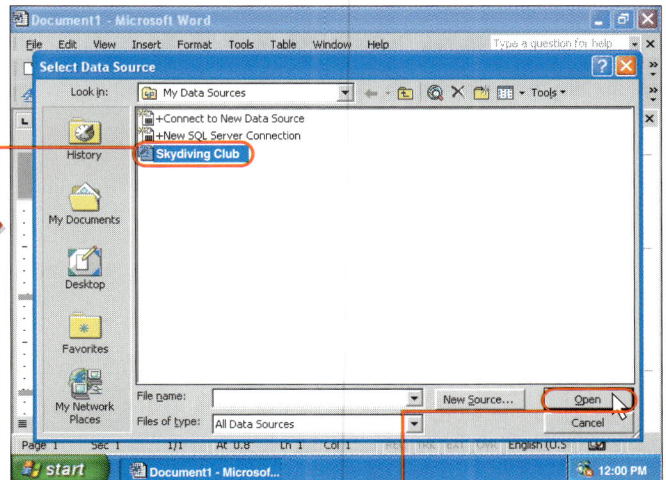

15 Click **Use an existing list** to use a mailing list you created in a previous mail merge (○ changes to ⊙).

Note: If you have not previously created a mailing list, see the top of this page.

16 Click **Browse** to select the mailing list you want to use.

■ The Select Data Source dialog box appears.

17 Click the file that stores the mailing list you want to use.

18 Click **Open** to open the file.

■ The Mail Merge Recipients dialog box appears.

CONTINUED

CREATE LABELS USING MAIL MERGE

Word displays the information for each person on your mailing list. You can select each person you want to create a label for.

CREATE LABELS USING MAIL MERGE (CONTINUED)

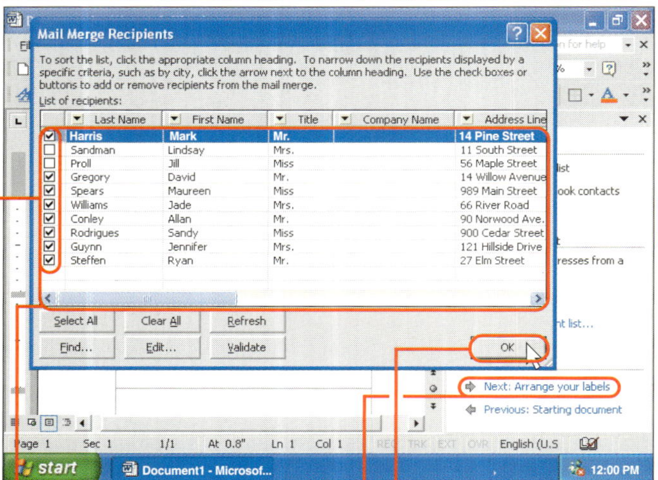

■ This area displays all the people on your mailing list.

19 A check mark (✔) beside a person's name indicates Word will create a label for the person. To add (☑) or remove (☐) a check mark, click the box beside a person's name.

20 Click **OK**.

21 Click **Next: Arrange your labels** to continue.

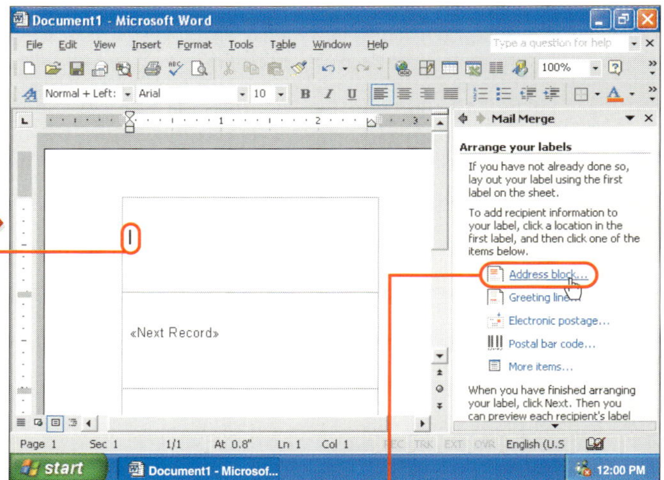

■ You use the first label to set up all of the labels.

22 To display an address on the first label, click the location on the label where you want to display the address.

23 Click **Address block**.

Can I sort my mailing list?

You can sort your mailing list when the Mail Merge Recipients dialog box is displayed. To sort your mailing list, click the heading of the column you want to use to sort the list. For example, if you want to sort the list alphabetically by last name, click the **Last Name** column heading.

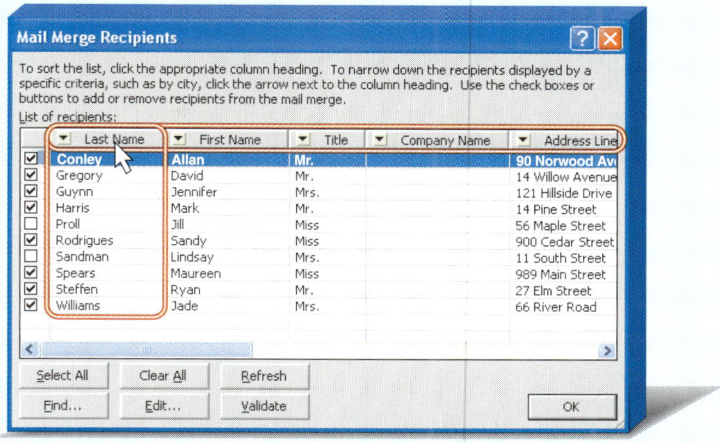

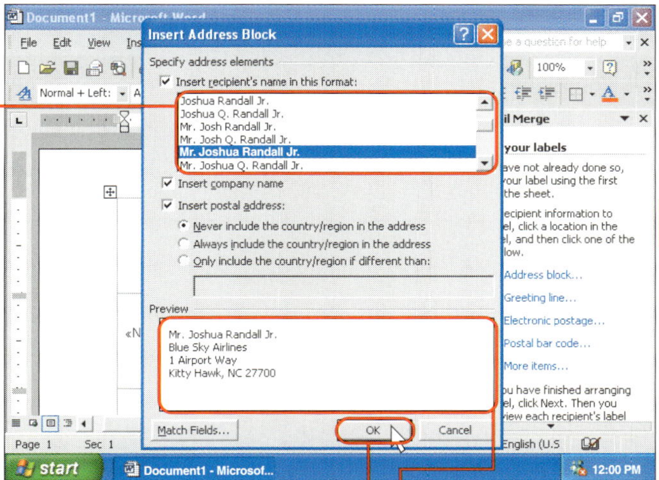

■ The Insert Address Block dialog box appears.

24 Click the way you want a person's name to appear on the label.

■ This area displays a preview of how the address will appear on the label.

25 Click **OK** to confirm your selection.

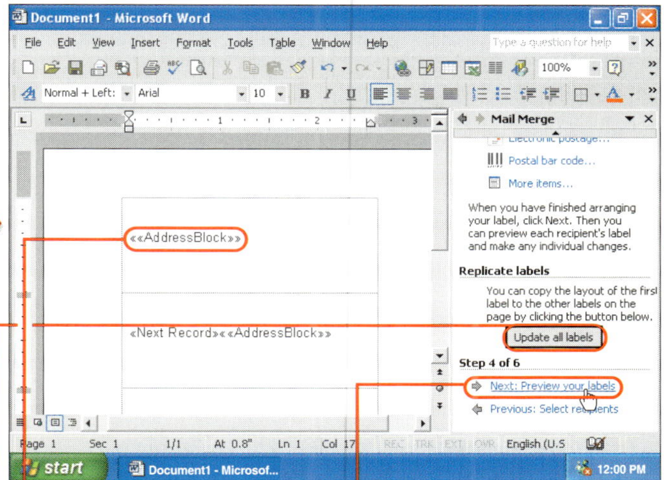

■ A merge field for the address appears on the first label. Word will replace the merge field with an address from your mailing list.

26 Click **Update all labels** to copy the layout of the first label to all the other labels.

*Note: If you cannot see the **Update all labels** option, click ▼ to scroll down through the Mail Merge task pane.*

27 Click **Next: Preview your labels** to continue.

CONTINUED

CREATE LABELS USING MAIL MERGE

After you finish setting up your labels, Word can combine the labels with the information from your mailing list to create a personalized label for each person.

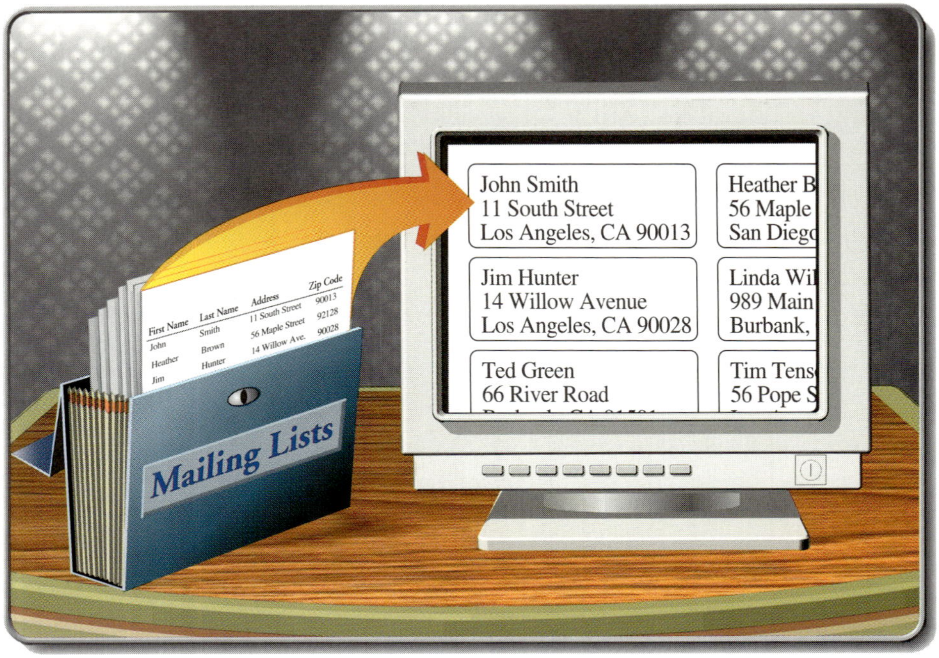

CREATE LABELS USING MAIL MERGE (CONTINUED)

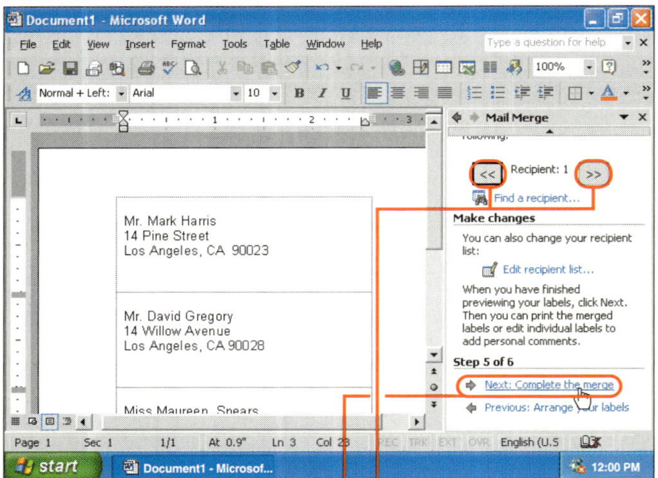

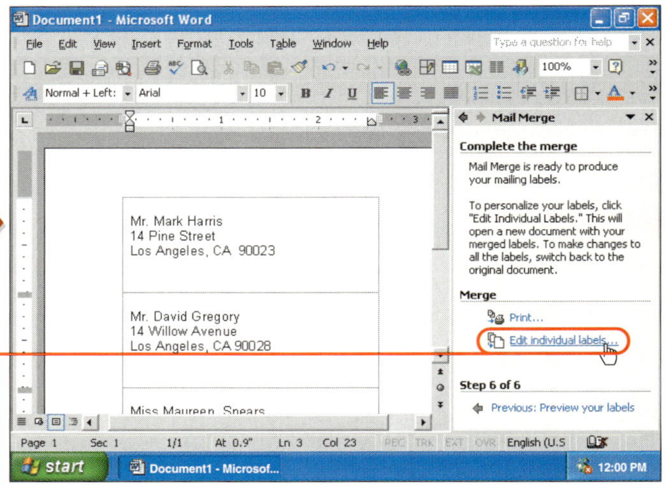

■ Word displays a preview of one page of the labels. Word replaces the merge fields with the corresponding information from your mailing list.

■ To preview other labels, click [<<] or [>>] to display the previous or next label at the top of the page.

28 When you finish previewing your labels, click **Next: Complete the merge** to continue.

■ Word is ready to produce the labels.

29 Click **Edit individual labels** to combine the labels with the information from your mailing list.

■ The Merge to New Document dialog box appears.

Which people on my mailing list can I create labels for?

All

Creates labels for all the people on your mailing list.

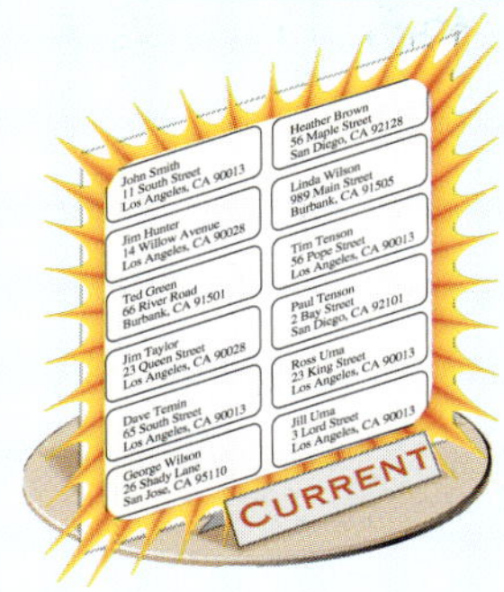

Current record

Creates labels for only the people shown on the current page.

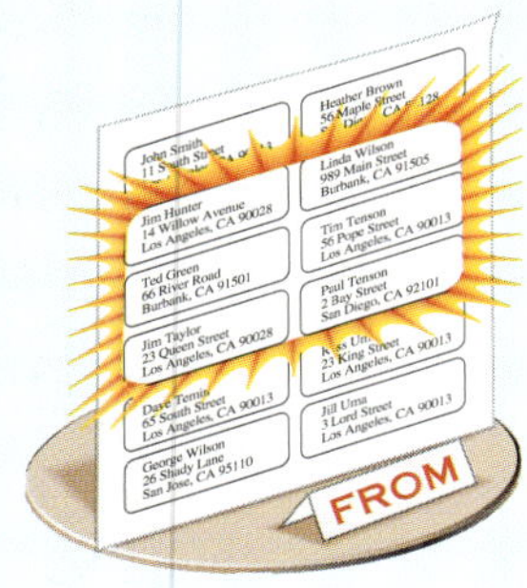

From

Creates labels for people on your mailing list that you specify.

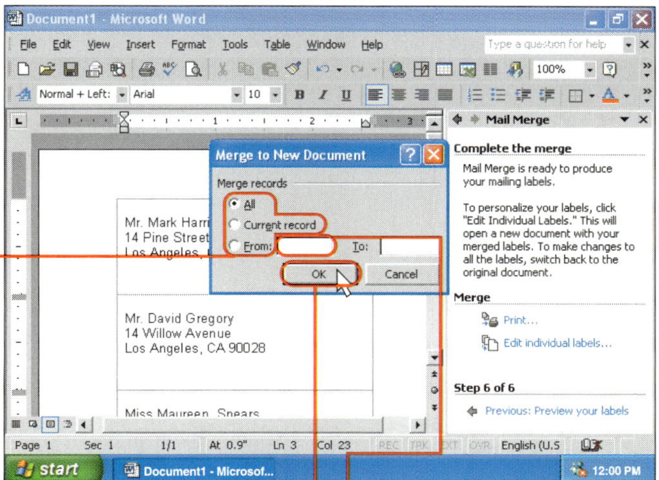

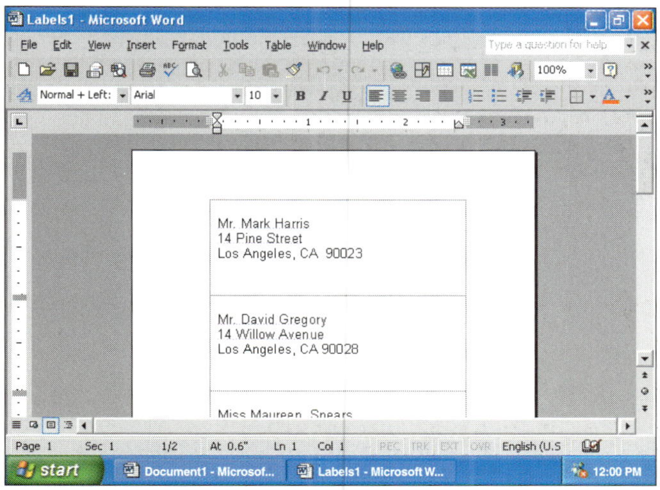

30 Click an option to specify which people on your mailing list you want to create labels for (○ changes to ⊙).

■ If you selected **From** in step **30**, click this area and type the number of the first person you want to create a label for. Then press the Tab key and type the number of the last person you want to create a label for.

31 Click **OK** to create the labels.

■ Word opens a new document and creates the personalized labels in the document.

■ You can edit and print the labels as you would edit and print any document. Editing a label allows you to include additional information on the label. To edit a document, see page 54. To print a document, see page 172.

Dictation Mode
Bass Treble On/Off
Bass Treble On/Off

ORDER FORM

TRADE & INDIVIDUAL ORDERS

Phone: **(800) 762-2974**
or **(317) 572-3993**
(8 a.m. – 6 p.m., CST, weekdays)
FAX : **(800) 550-2747**
or **(317) 572-4002**

EDUCATIONAL ORDERS & DISCOUNTS

Phone: **(800) 434-2086**
(8:30 a.m.–5:00 p.m., CST, weekdays)
FAX : **(317) 572-4005**

CORPORATE ORDERS FOR VISUAL™ SERIES

Phone: **(800) 469-6616**
(8:30 a.m.–5 p.m., EST, weekdays)
FAX : **(905) 890-9434**

Qty	ISBN	Title	Price	Total

Shipping & Handling Charges

	Description	First book	Each add'l. book	Total
Domestic	Normal	$4.50	$1.50	$
	Two Day Air	$8.50	$2.50	$
	Overnight	$18.00	$3.00	$
International	Surface	$8.00	$8.00	$
	Airmail	$16.00	$16.00	$
	DHL Air	$17.00	$17.00	$

Subtotal ____________

CA residents add applicable sales tax ____________

IN, MA and MD residents add 5% sales tax ____________

IL residents add 6.25% sales tax ____________

RI residents add 7% sales tax ____________

TX residents add 8.25% sales tax ____________

Shipping ____________

Total ____________

Ship to:

Name ____________

Address ____________

Company ____________

City/State/Zip ____________

Daytime Phone ____________

Payment: □ Check to Hungry Minds (US Funds Only)
□ Visa □ Mastercard □ American Express

Card # ____________ Exp. ____________ Signature ____________

Hungry Minds™

maranGraphics®

CHAPTER 15

Using Speech Recognition

Would you like to use your voice to enter text into a document? Read this chapter to learn how to enter text and select commands using your voice.

Set Up Speech Recognition 280

Using Dictation Mode 286

Using Voice Command Mode 288

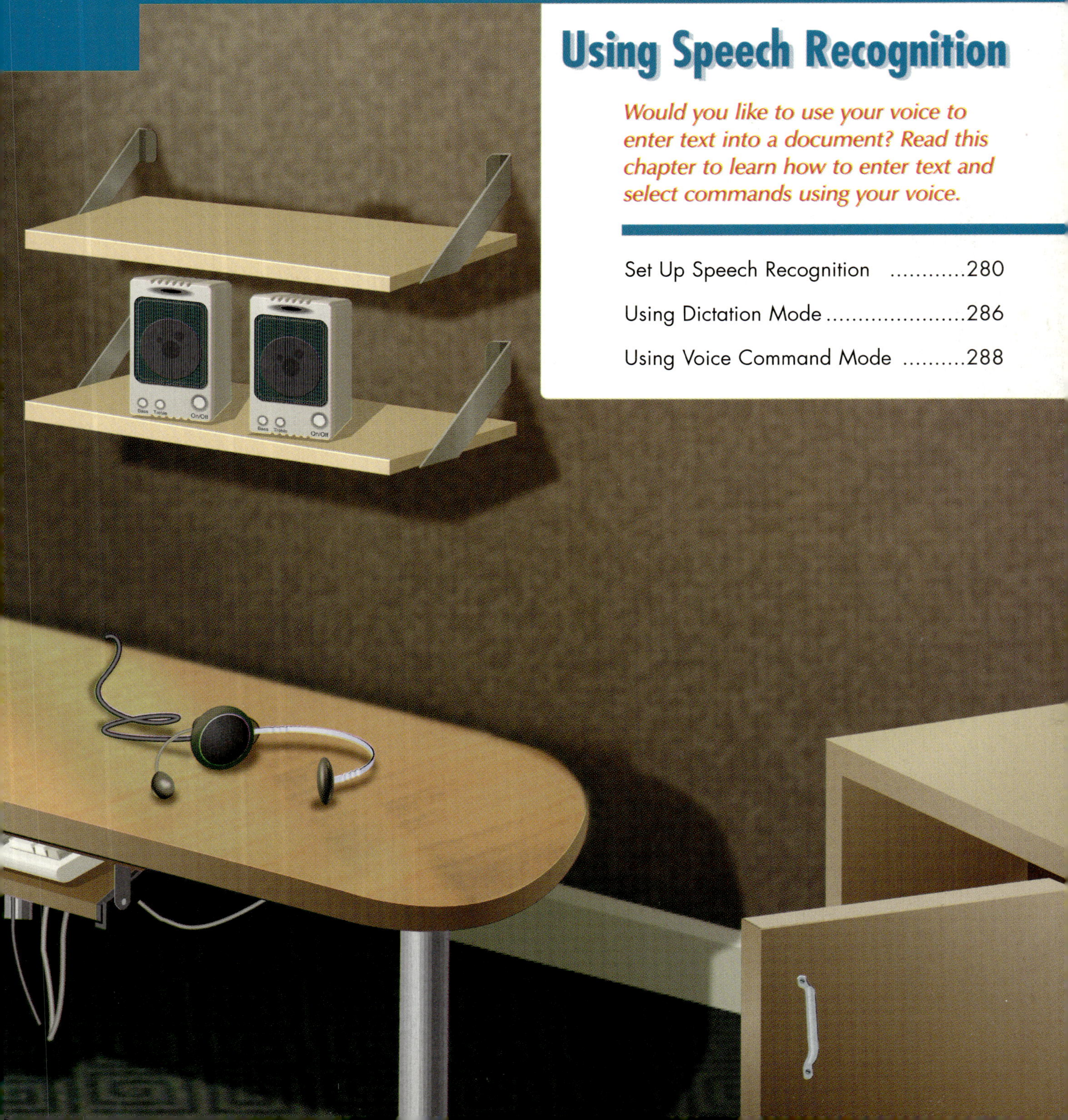

SET UP SPEECH RECOGNITION

Speech recognition allows you to use your voice to enter text into a document and select commands from menus and toolbars. Before you can use speech recognition, you must set up the feature on your computer.

Before setting up speech recognition, make sure your microphone is connected to your computer.

It will take you approximately 15 minutes to set up speech recognition on your computer.

SET UP SPEECH RECOGNITION

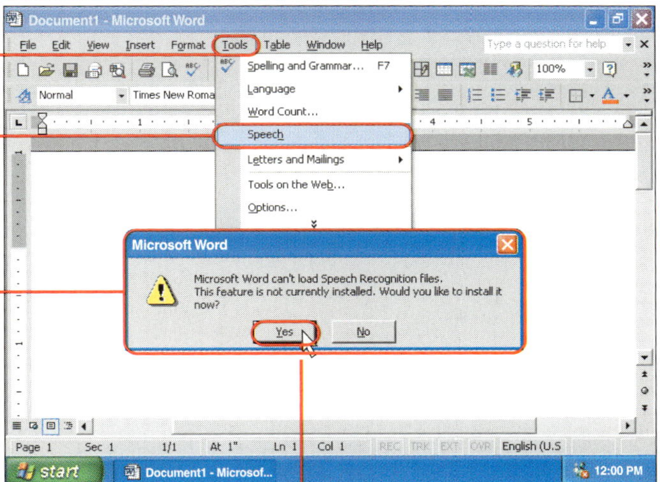

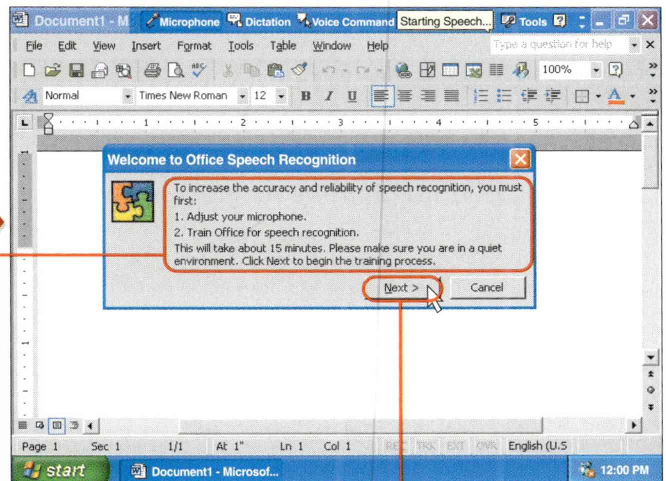

1 Click **Tools**.

2 Click **Speech**.

■ A message appears, stating that speech recognition is not currently installed.

3 Insert the CD-ROM disc you used to install Word into your computer's CD-ROM drive.

4 Click **Yes** to install speech recognition on your computer.

Note: A window may appear on your screen. Click ☒ in the top right corner of the window to close the window.

■ When the installation is complete, the Welcome to Office Speech Recognition dialog box appears.

■ This area describes the process of setting up speech recognition on your computer.

5 To begin setting up speech recognition, click **Next**.

Why does this dialog box appear when I try to set up speech recognition?

This dialog box appears if your computer does not meet the minimum hardware requirements needed to use speech recognition. You cannot set up speech recognition if your computer does not meet the minimum hardware requirements.

What type of microphone should I use with speech recognition?

You should use a headset microphone, since this type of microphone will remain in the correct position, even when you move your head. For best results, you should position the microphone approximately one inch from the side of your mouth so that you are not breathing directly into the microphone.

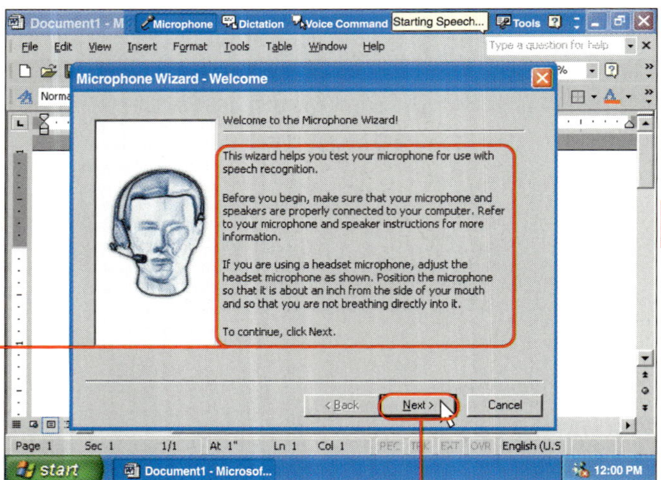

■ The Microphone Wizard appears. The wizard will help you adjust your microphone for use with speech recognition.

■ This area describes the wizard and provides instructions for positioning your microphone.

6 To begin adjusting your microphone, click **Next**.

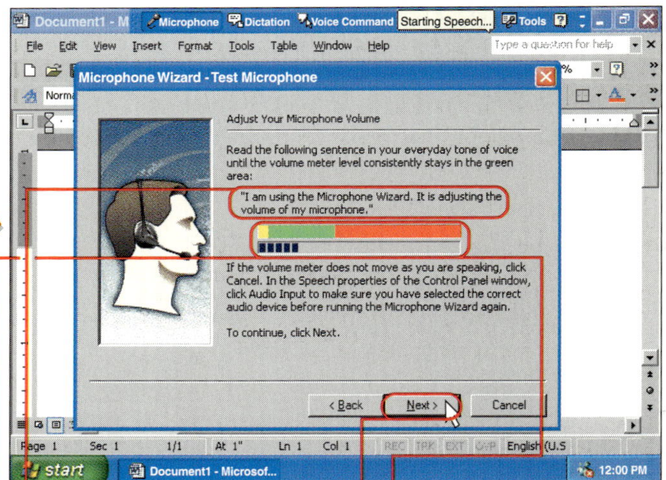

7 Read the text displayed in this area aloud to adjust the volume of your microphone.

■ As you read the text aloud, the volume meter in this area indicates the volume of your microphone.

8 Repeat step **7** until the volume level of your microphone consistently appears in the green area of the volume meter.

9 Click **Next** to continue.

CONTINUED

SET UP SPEECH RECOGNITION

You can train speech recognition to recognize how you speak. The Microsoft Speech Recognition Training Wizard takes you step by step through the process of training speech recognition.

You can listen to a sample sentence to hear how you should speak during the training.

SET UP SPEECH RECOGNITION (CONTINUED)

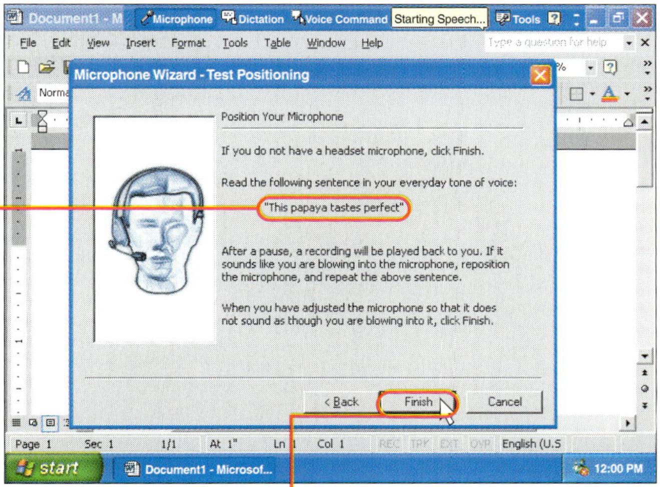

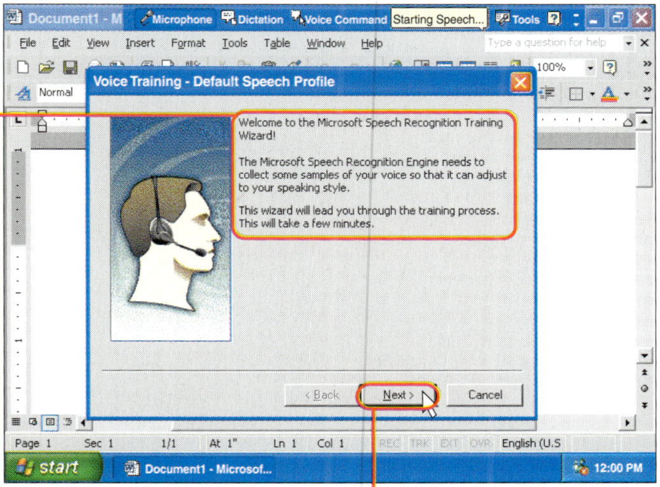

10 Read this text aloud to test the position of your microphone.

■ After a few moments, your voice will be played back to you. If it sounds like you are blowing into the microphone, adjust your microphone's position and then repeat step **10**.

11 When you finish positioning your microphone, click **Finish**.

■ The Microsoft Speech Recognition Training Wizard appears. This wizard will help you train speech recognition to recognize how you speak.

■ This area describes the wizard.

12 To begin training speech recognition to recognize how you speak, click **Next**.

Do I have to train speech recognition?

Yes. If you do not train speech recognition, the feature will not work properly. During the training, the Microsoft Speech Recognition Training Wizard gathers information about your voice. The speech recognition feature uses this information to recognize the words you say when entering text in a document or selecting commands.

How should I speak during the training process?

You should speak in your everyday tone of voice, pronouncing words clearly and not pausing between words. You should also speak at a consistent speed.

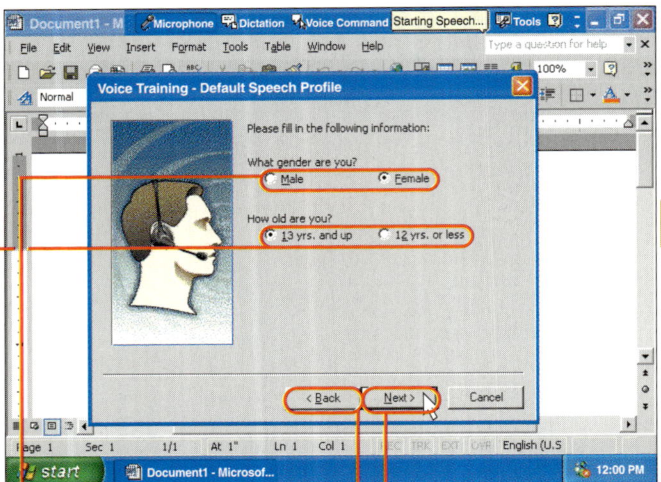

13 Click an option to specify whether you are male or female (○ changes to ⊙).

14 Click an option to indicate your age (○ changes to ⊙).

15 Click **Next** to continue.

■ You can click **Back** to return to a previous step.

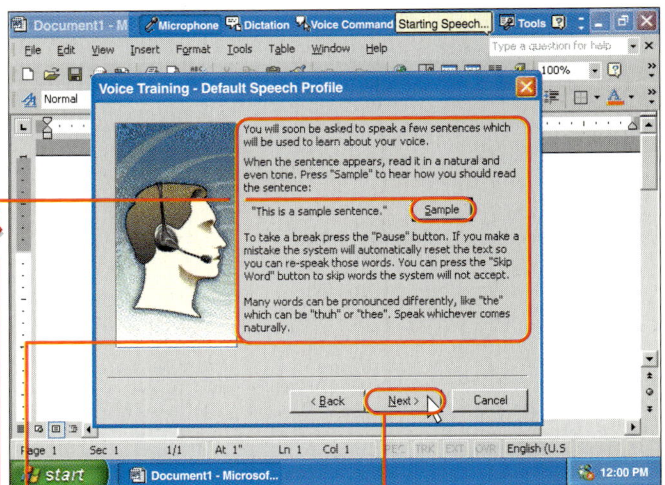

■ This area describes the training process.

16 To hear a sample of how you should speak during the training, click **Sample**.

17 Click **Next** to continue.

CONTINUED

SET UP SPEECH RECOGNITION

The Microsoft Speech Recognition Training Wizard provides text you can read aloud to train speech recognition.

You should train speech recognition in a quiet area so that background noise does not interfere with the sound of your voice.

SET UP SPEECH RECOGNITION (CONTINUED)

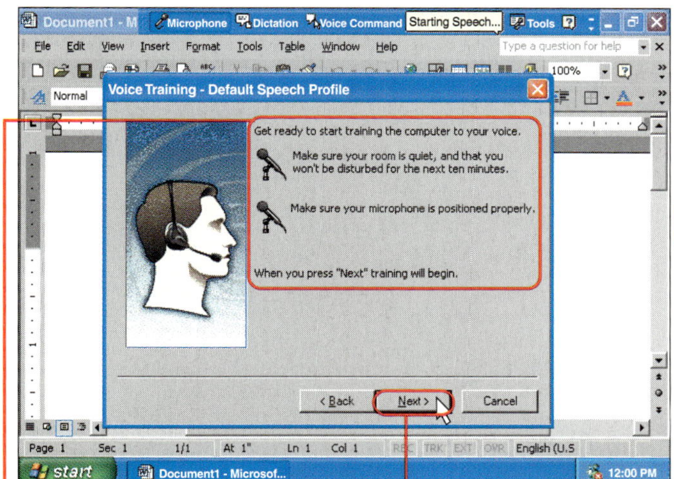

■ This area displays instructions about preparing for the training.

18 To begin the training, click **Next**.

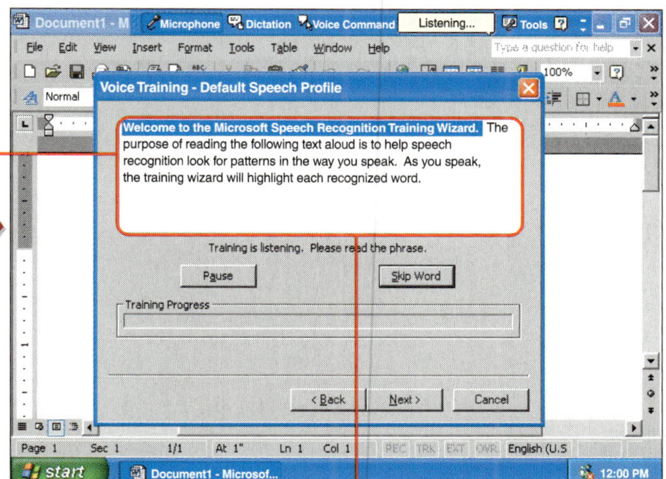

■ The wizard will display a series of screens containing text for you to read aloud.

19 Read the text displayed in this area.

■ As you read aloud, the wizard highlights the words it recognizes.

■ If the wizard does not recognize a word, it stops highlighting text. If this happens, begin reading again, starting with the first word that is not highlighted.

I have repeated a word several times, but the wizard still does not recognize the word. What should I do?

If the wizard cannot recognize a word you say, you can click the **Skip Word** button to move on to the next word.

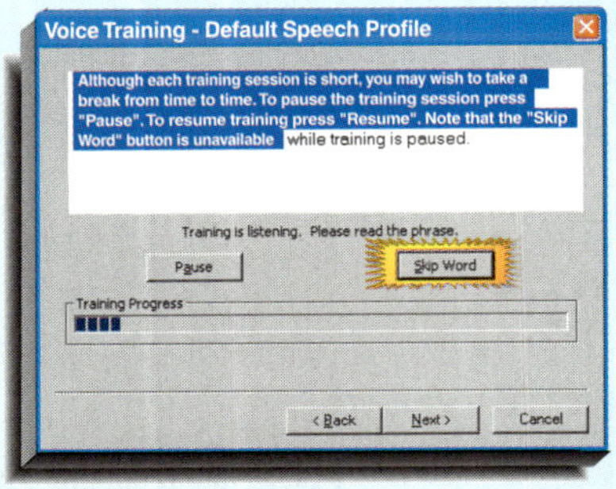

Can I perform more training?

The speech recognition feature provides additional training sessions you can perform to improve the accuracy of speech recognition.

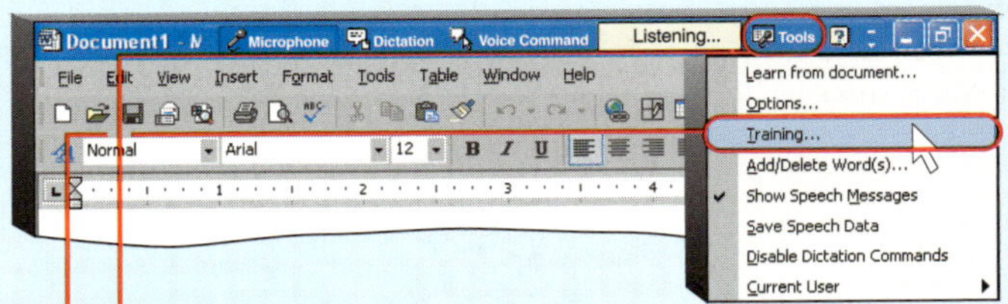

1 To perform additional training, click **Tools** on the Language bar.

2 Click **Training**.

■ The Voice Training dialog box will appear, displaying the available training sessions. Select a training session and then perform steps **17** to **21** starting on page 283.

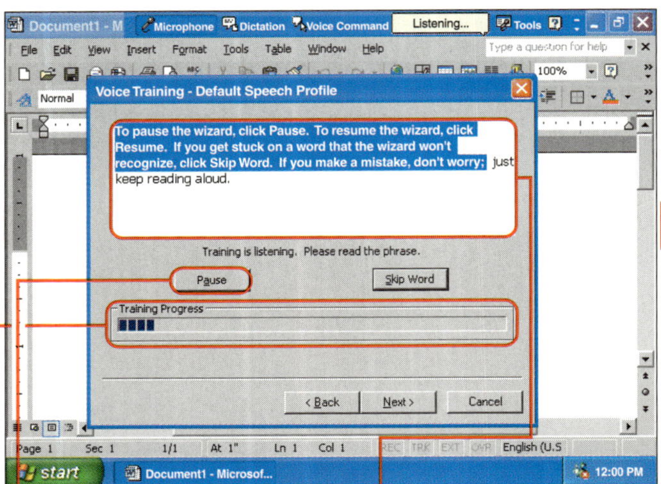

■ To take a break during the training, click **Pause**.

Note: To resume the training, click ***Resume****.*

■ This area displays the progress of the training.

■ When all the text in this area is highlighted, the wizard automatically displays the next screen of text.

20 Repeat step **19** until you have read all the training text.

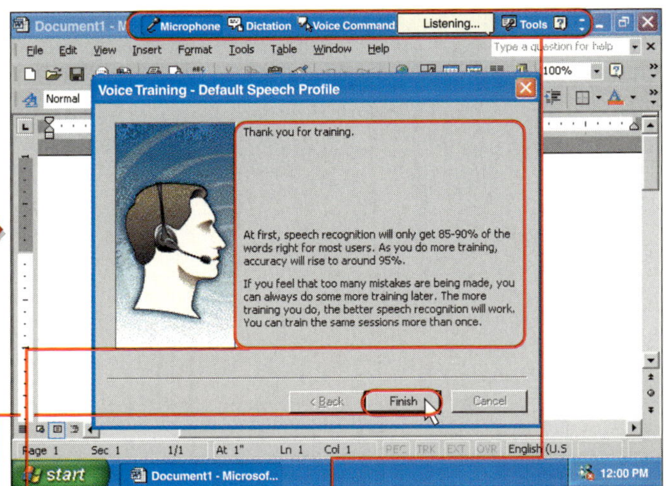

■ This message appears when the training is complete.

21 Click **Finish** to close the wizard.

■ This area displays the Language bar, which contains buttons you can use to perform tasks using speech recognition.

Note: A window will appear, displaying a video that introduces you to speech recognition. When the video is finished, click ✕ to close the window.

USING DICTATION MODE

Once you have set up speech recognition on your computer, you can use Dictation mode to enter text into a document using your voice.

Speech recognition is designed to be used along with your mouse and keyboard. You can use your voice to enter text into a document and then use your mouse and keyboard to edit the text you entered.

USING DICTATION MODE

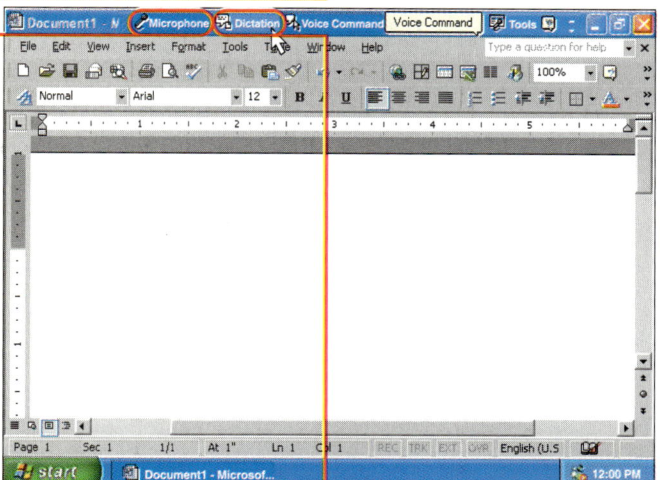

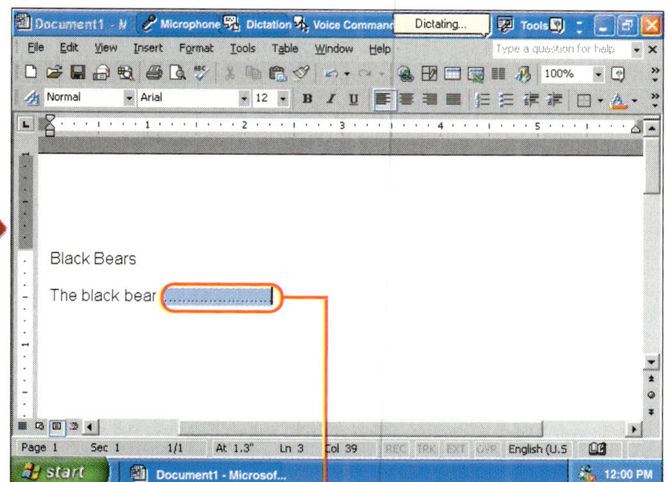

1 If your microphone is turned off, click **Microphone** on the Language bar to turn on the microphone.

Note: When your microphone is turned on, the Dictation and Voice Command buttons appear on the Language bar.

2 Click **Dictation** to turn on Dictation mode.

3 Speak into your microphone to enter text into the document.

Note: The text will appear where the insertion point flashes on your screen.

- As you speak, a blue bar appears on the screen to indicate that the computer is processing your voice. You can continue to speak while the blue bar is displayed on the screen.

- You should not use your mouse or keyboard while the blue bar is displayed on the screen.

What are some of the punctuation marks I can enter using my voice?

To enter:	Say:
.	"Period"
,	"Comma"
:	"Colon"
;	"Semicolon"
?	"Question mark"
!	"Exclamation point"
(	"Open parenthesis"
)	"Close parenthesis"
“	"Open quote"
”	"Close quote"
a new line	"New line"
a new paragraph	"New paragraph"

How should I speak when using speech recognition?

You should speak to your computer in your everyday tone of voice, pronouncing words clearly and not pausing between words. You should also speak at a consistent speed. If you speak too quickly or too slowly, the computer may not be able to recognize what you say.

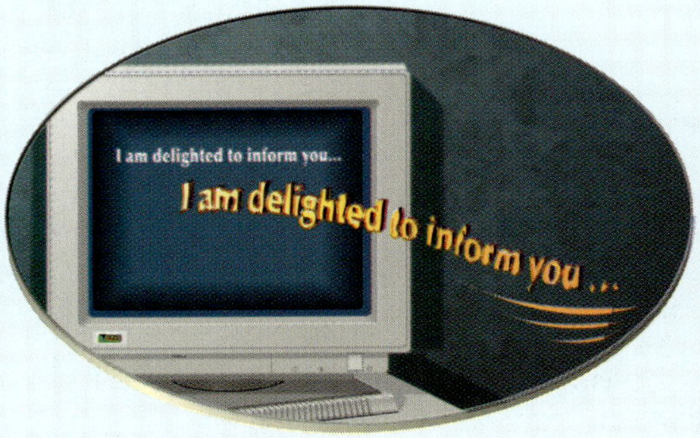

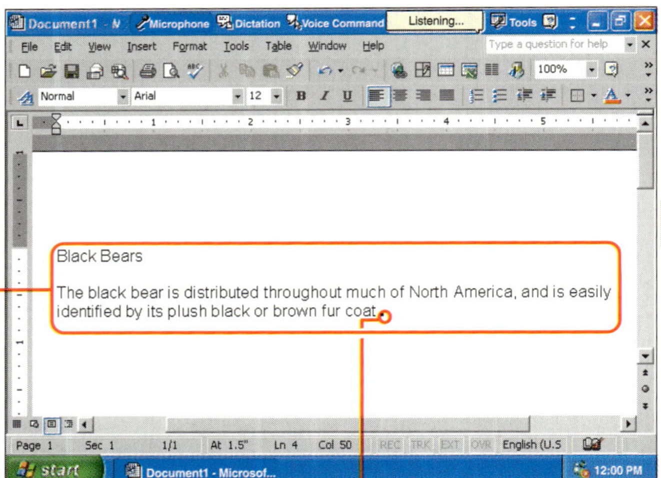

■ As the computer processes your voice, words appear on the screen.

4 To enter punctuation, say the name of the punctuation mark you want to enter.

Note: For a list of punctuation marks you can enter using your voice, see the top of this page.

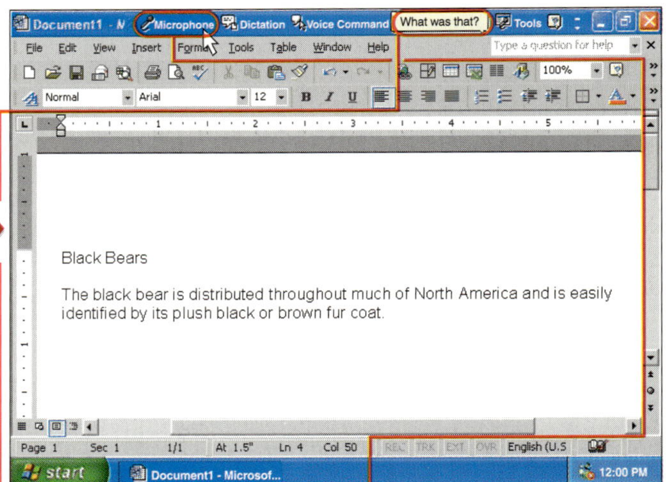

■ As you enter text using your voice, this area may display a message to help you use Dictation mode. For example, the message "What was that?" indicates you should repeat your last words.

5 When you finish entering text using your voice, click **Microphone** to turn off your microphone.

■ You can now edit the text you entered using your voice as you would edit any text. To edit text, see page 54.

USING VOICE COMMAND MODE

You can use Voice Command mode to select commands from menus and toolbars using your voice.

You can also use Voice Command mode to select options in dialog boxes.

USING VOICE COMMAND MODE

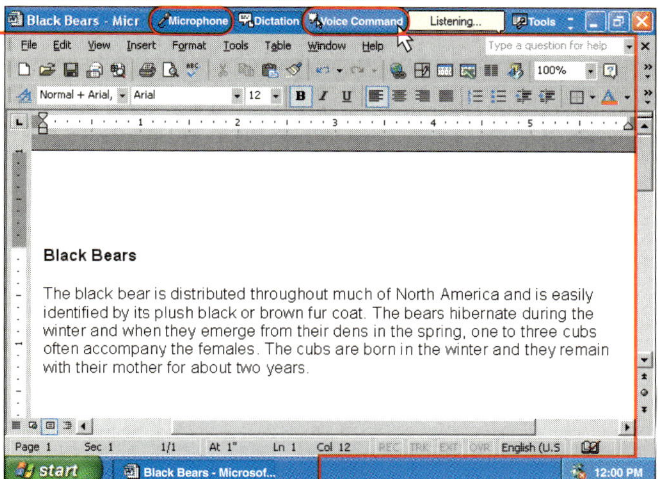

1 If your microphone is turned off, click **Microphone** on the Language bar to turn on the microphone.

Note: When your microphone is turned on, the Dictation and Voice Command buttons appear on the Language bar.

2 Click **Voice Command** to turn on Voice Command mode.

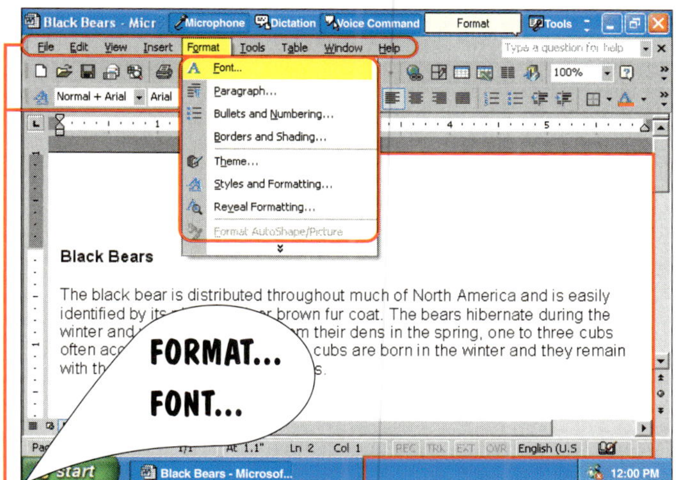

SELECT MENU COMMANDS

1 To select a command from a menu, say the name of the menu.

■ A short version of the menu appears, displaying the most commonly used commands.

Note: To expand the menu and display all the commands, say "expand."

2 To select a command from the menu, say the name of the command.

■ To close a menu without selecting a command, say "escape."

TEACH YOURSELF

Can I use Voice Command mode to select an option in the task pane?

The task pane displays options that allow you to perform common tasks. To select an option in the task pane using your voice, say the full name of the option. For more information on the task pane, see page 16.

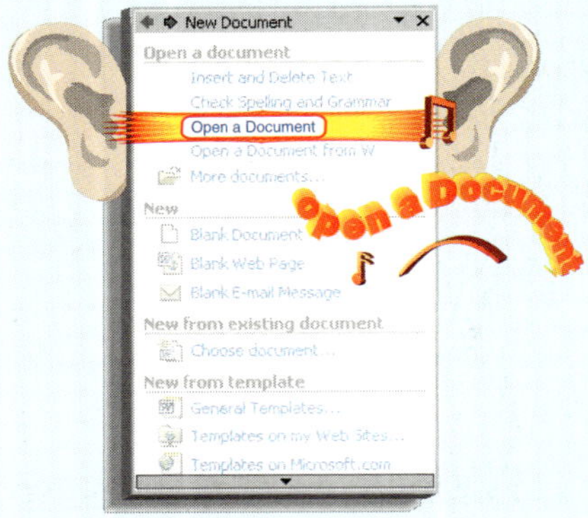

TEACH YOURSELF

Can I use Voice Command mode to perform other tasks?

Yes. In addition to selecting commands, you can use Voice Command mode to perform the following tasks.

To:	Say:
Move up one line	"Up"
Move down one line	"Down"
Move left one character	"Left"
Move right one character	"Right"
Enter a tab	"Tab"
Enter a blank space	"Space"
Delete a character	"Backspace"

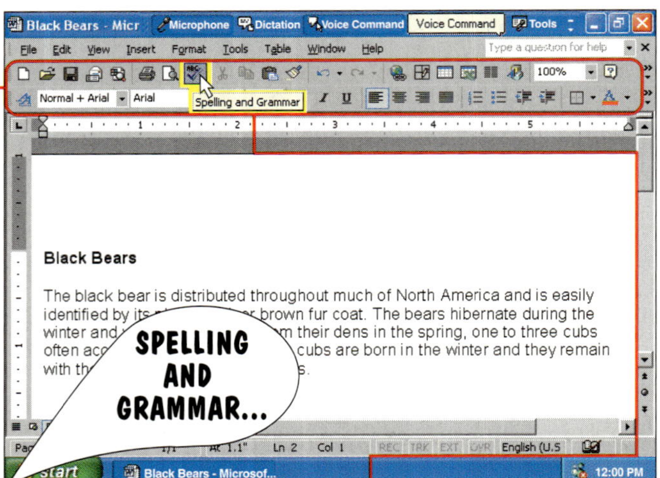

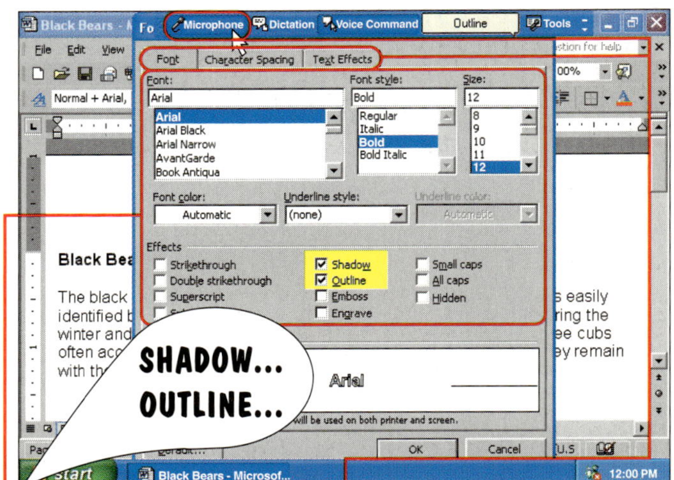

SELECT TOOLBAR COMMANDS

1 To select a command from a toolbar, say the name of the toolbar button.

■ To determine the name of a toolbar button, position the mouse over the button. After a few seconds, the name of the button appears in a yellow box.

SELECT DIALOG BOX OPTIONS

■ A dialog box may appear when you select a menu or toolbar command.

1 To select an option in a dialog box, say the name of the option.

■ If the dialog box contains tabs, you can say the name of a tab to display the tab.

2 When you finish selecting commands using your voice, click **Microphone** to turn off your microphone.

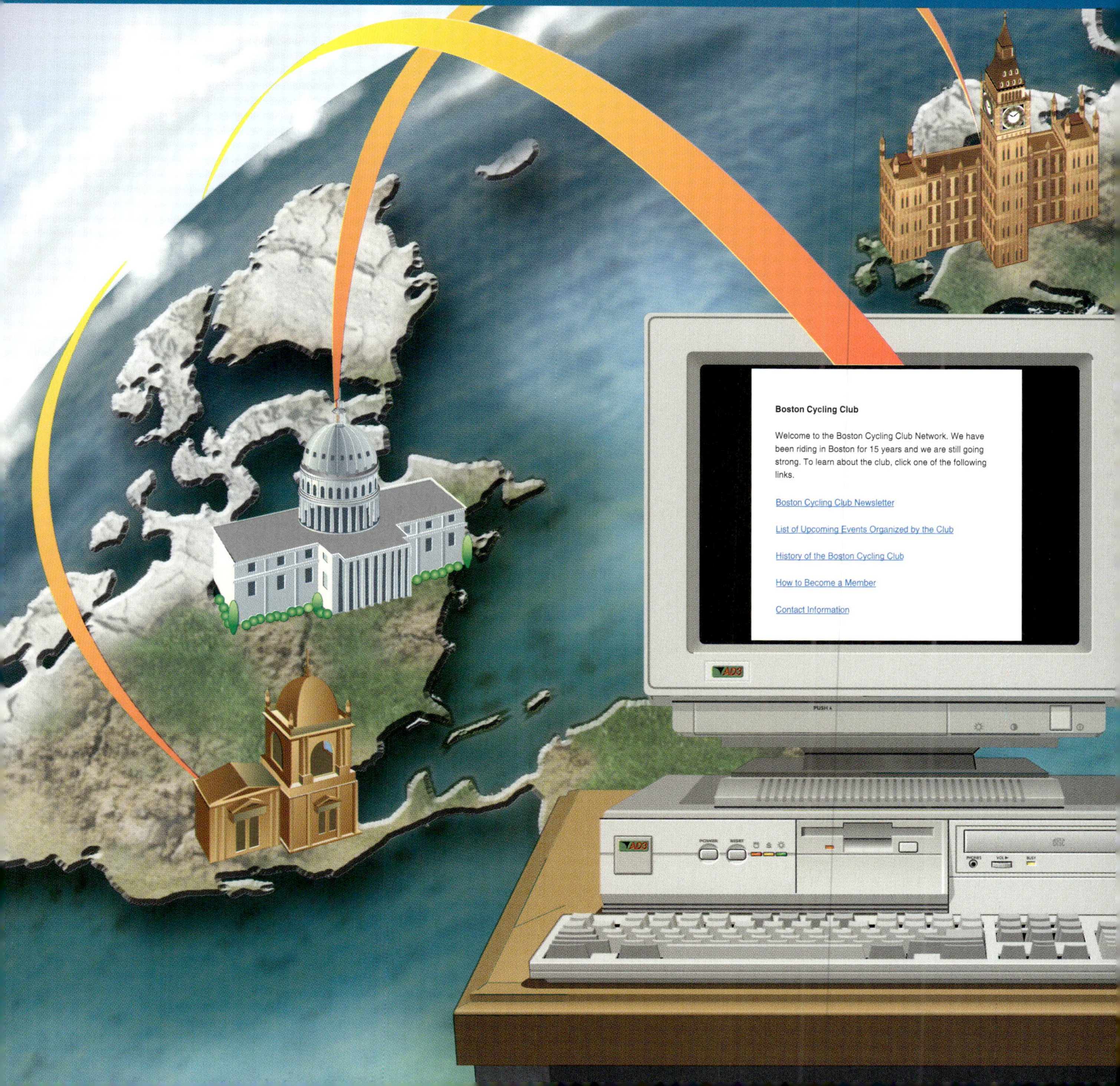
Boston Cycling Club
Welcome to the Boston Cycling Club Network. We have been riding in Boston for 15 years and we are still going strong. To learn about the club, click one of the following links.
Boston Cycling Club Newsletter
List of Upcoming Events Organized by the Club
History of the Boston Cycling Club
How to Become a Member
Contact Information

Word and the Internet

Are you wondering how you can use Word to share information with other people on the Internet? In this chapter, you will learn how to e-mail a document, save a document as a Web page and more.

E-mail a Document 292

Create a Hyperlink..........................294

Save a Document as a Web Page 296

E-MAIL A DOCUMENT

You can e-mail the document displayed on your screen to a friend, family member or colleague.

Before you can e-mail a document, an e-mail program, such as Microsoft Outlook, must be set up on your computer.

E-MAIL A DOCUMENT

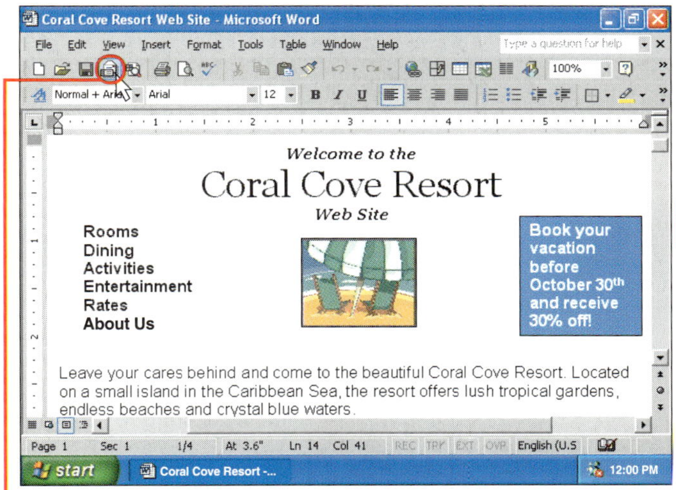

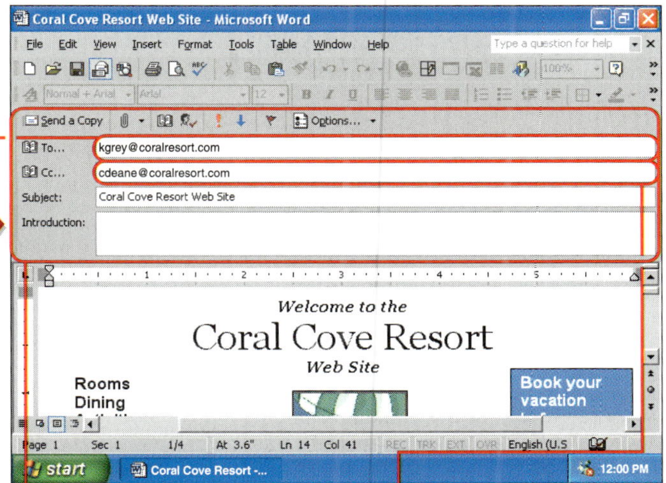

1 Click [icon] to e-mail the displayed document.

Note: If [icon] is not displayed, click [icon] on the Standard toolbar to display the button.

■ An area appears for you to address the message.

2 Click this area and type the e-mail address of the person you want to receive the message.

3 To send a copy of the message to another person, click this area and type their e-mail address.

*Note: To enter more than one e-mail address in step **2** or **3**, separate each e-mail address with a semicolon (;).*

How can I address an e-mail message?

To

Sends the message to the person you specify.

Carbon Copy (Cc)

Sends an exact copy of the message to a person who is not directly involved, but would be interested in the message.

Why would I include an introduction for the document I am e-mailing?

Including an introduction allows you to provide the recipient of the message with additional information about the document. For example, the recipient may require instructions or an explanation of the content of the document.

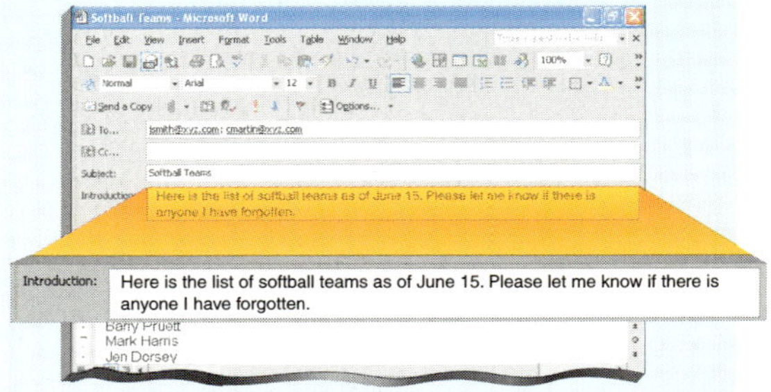

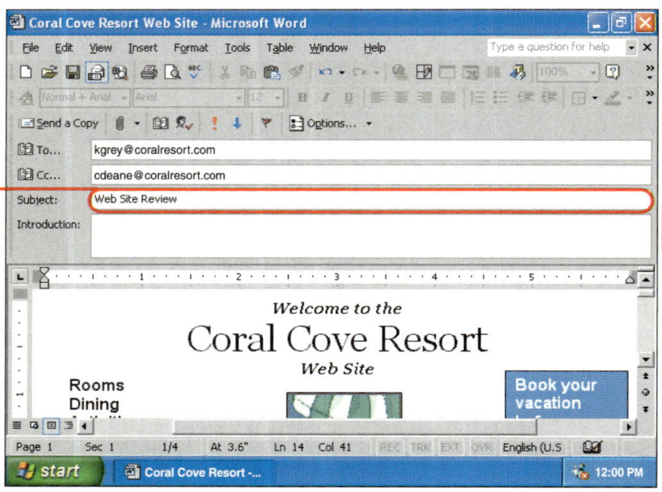

4 Click this area and type a subject for the message.

Note: If a subject already exists, you can drag the mouse I over the existing subject and then type a new subject.

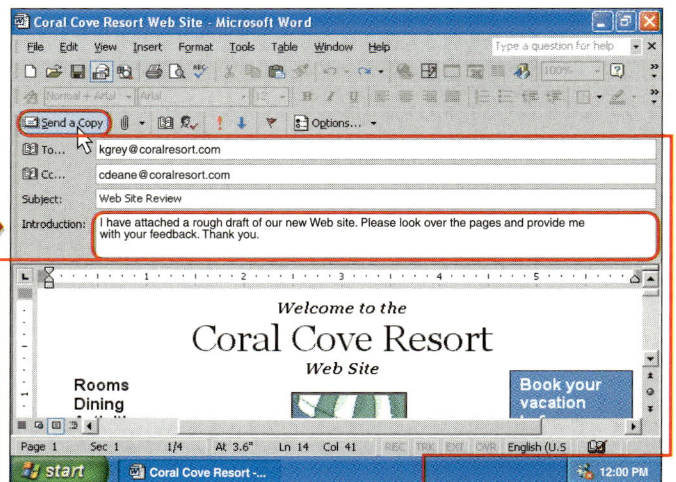

5 To include an introduction for the document you are e-mailing, click this area and type the introduction.

Note: You can include an introduction only if you are using the Microsoft Outlook e-mail program.

6 Click **Send a Copy** to send the message.

Note: If you are not currently connected to the Internet, a dialog box may appear, allowing you to connect.

CREATE A HYPERLINK

You can create a hyperlink to connect a word, phrase or graphic in your document to another document or Web page on your computer, network or the Internet.

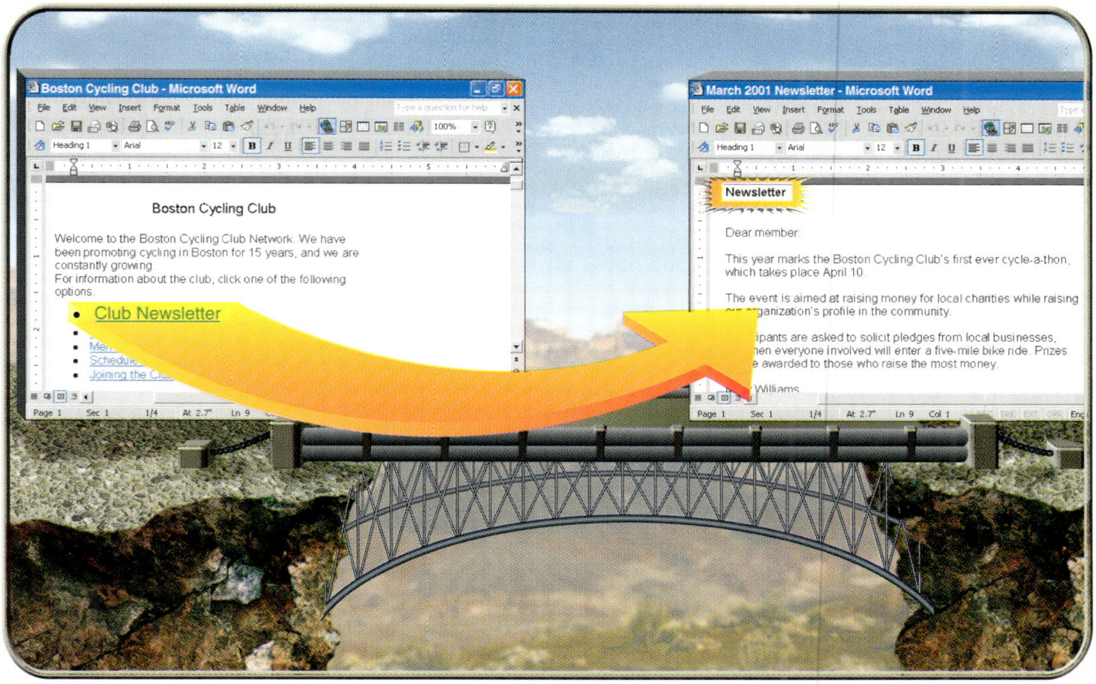

CREATE A HYPERLINK

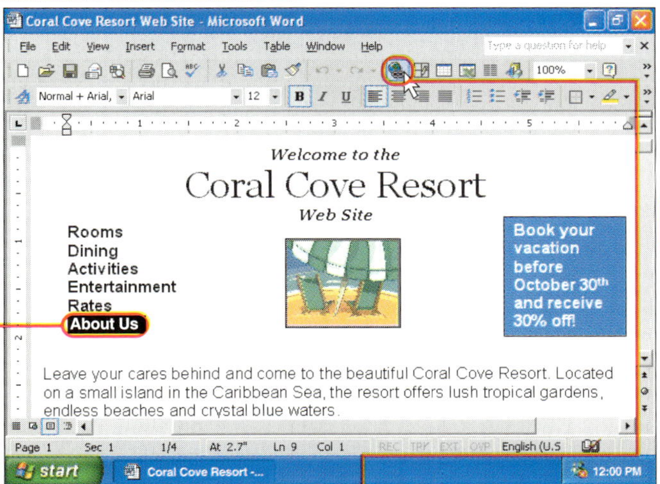

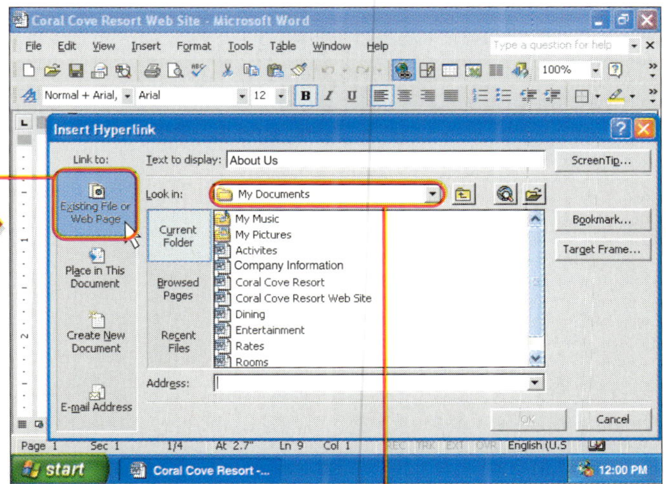

1 Select the text or click the graphic you want to link to another document or Web page. To select text, see page 10.

2 Click 🌐 to create a hyperlink.

Note: If 🌐 is not displayed, click » on the Standard toolbar to display the button.

■ The Insert Hyperlink dialog box appears.

3 Click **Existing File or Web Page**.

■ This area shows the location of the displayed documents. You can click this area to change the location.

TY TEACH YOURSELF

Can Word automatically create a hyperlink for me?

When you type the address of a Web page and then press the **Spacebar** or the Enter key, Word will automatically change the address to a hyperlink.

TY TEACH YOURSELF

How can I remove a hyperlink?

To remove a hyperlink completely, select the text or click the graphic and then press the Delete key. To select text, see page 10.

To remove a hyperlink but keep the text or graphic, right-click the hyperlink and then select **Remove Hyperlink** from the menu that appears.

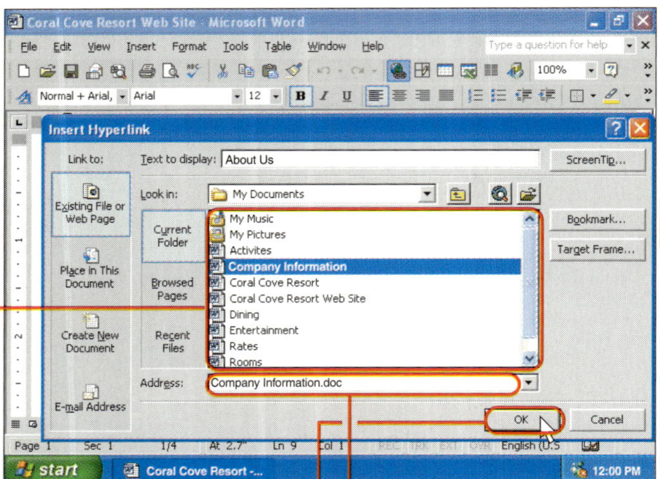

4 To link the text or graphic to a document on your computer or network, click the name of the document in this area.

■ To link the text or graphic to a page on the Web, click this area and then type the address of the Web page.

5 Click **OK** to create the hyperlink.

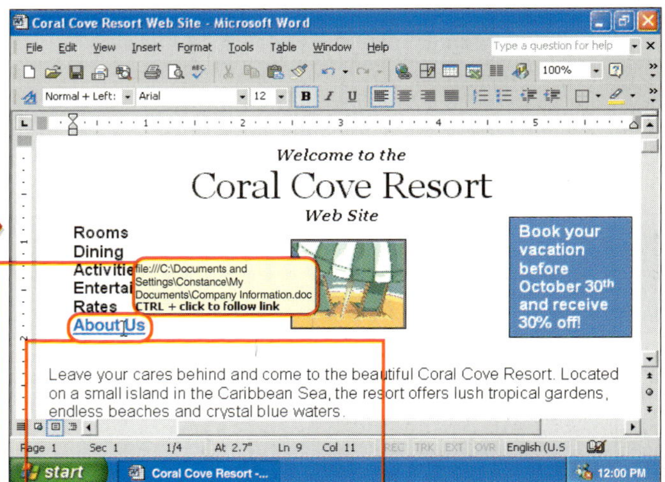

■ Word creates the hyperlink. Text hyperlinks appear underlined and in color.

■ When you position the mouse I over a hyperlink, a yellow box appears, indicating where the hyperlink will take you.

■ To display the document or Web page connected to the hyperlink, press and hold down the Ctrl key as you click the hyperlink.

SAVE A DOCUMENT AS A WEB PAGE

You can save a document as a Web page. This allows you to place the document on the Internet or your company's intranet.

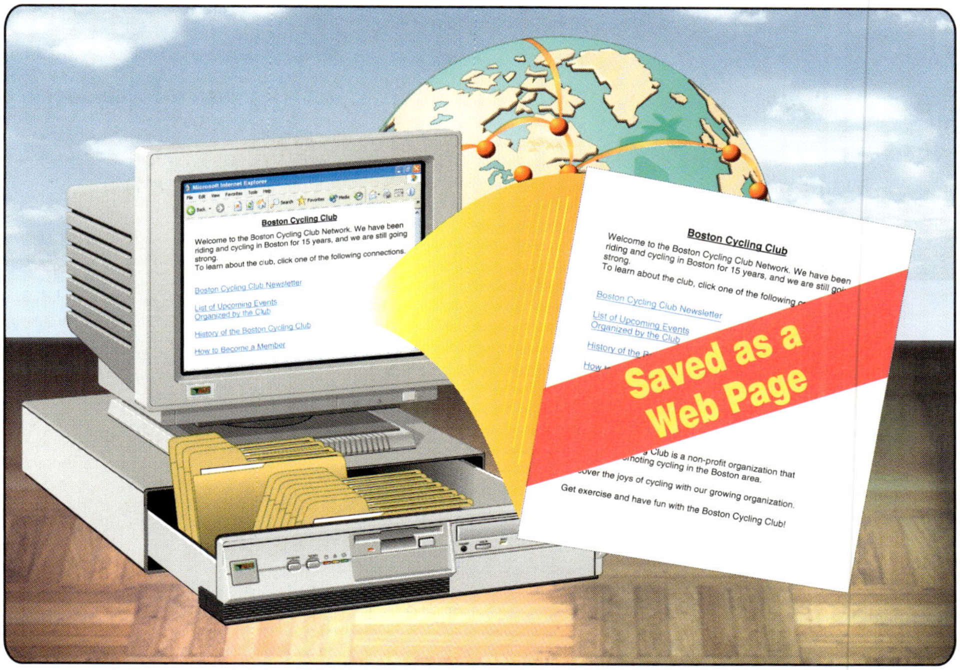

An intranet is a small version of the Internet within a company or organization.

SAVE A DOCUMENT AS A WEB PAGE

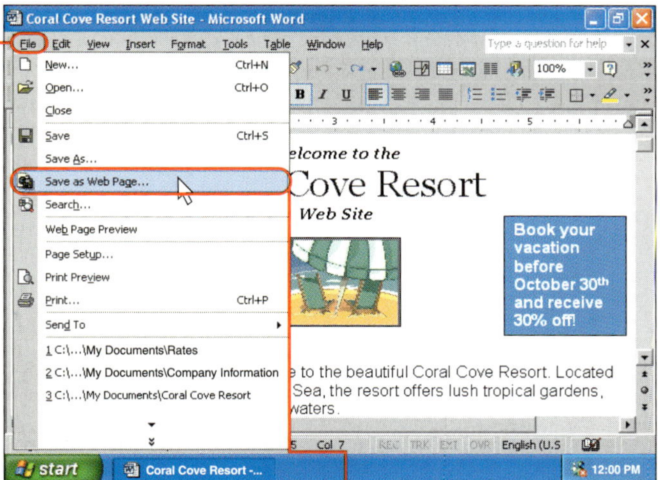

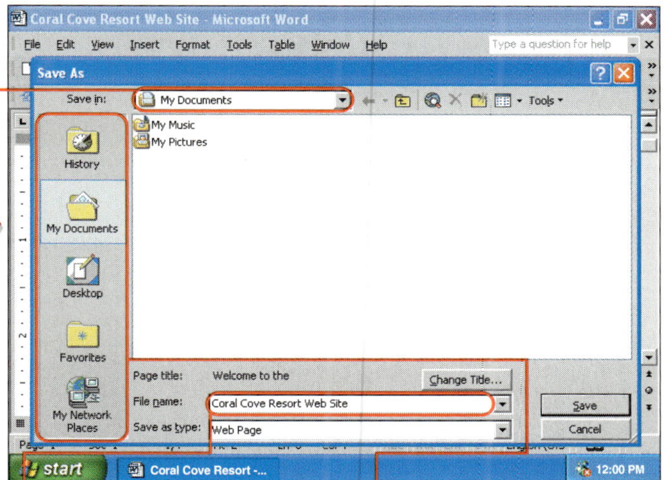

1 Open the document you want to save as a Web page. To open a document, see page 28.

2 Click **File**.

3 Click **Save as Web Page**.

■ The Save As dialog box appears.

4 Type a file name for the Web page.

■ This area shows the location where Word will store the Web page. You can click this area to change the location.

■ This area allows you to access commonly used locations. You can click a location to save the Web page in the location.

Note: For information on the commonly used locations, see the top of page 23.

What is the difference between the file name and the title of a Web page?

The file name is the name you use to store the Web page on your computer. The title is the text that will appear at the top of the Web browser window when a person views your Web page.

How do I make my Web page available for other people to view?

After you save a document as a Web page, you can transfer the page to a computer that stores Web pages, called a Web server. Once the Web page is stored on a Web server, the page will be available for other people to view. For information on transferring a Web page to a Web server, contact your network administrator or Internet service provider.

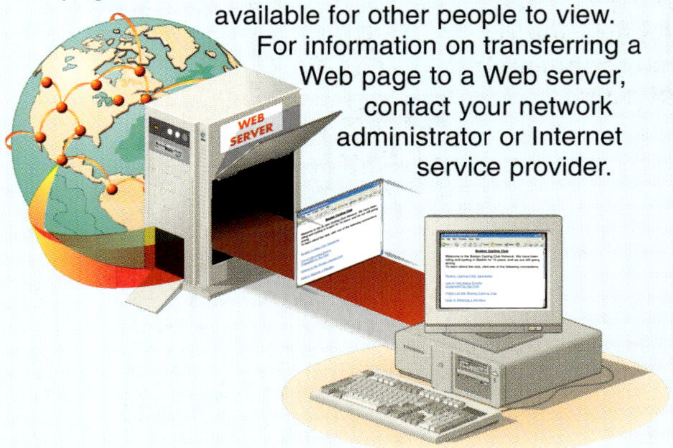

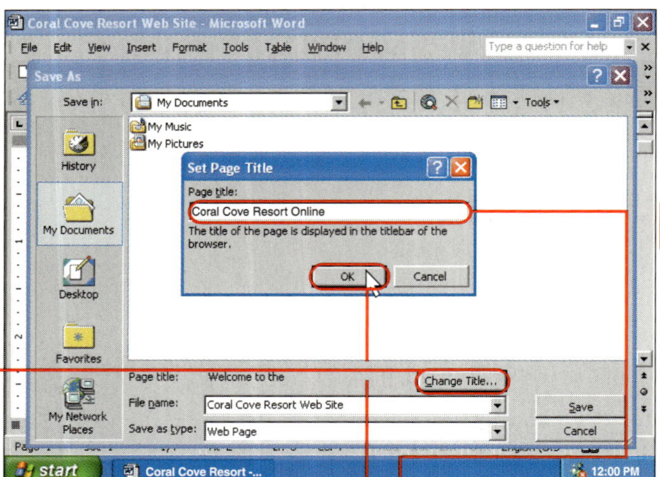

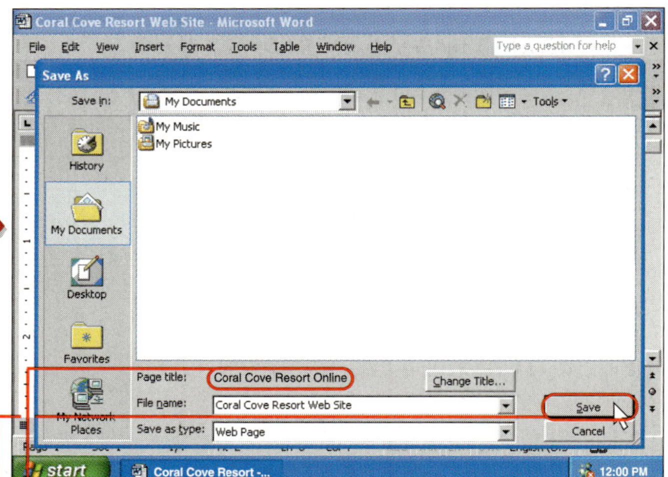

5 Click **Change Title** to specify a title for the Web page.

■ The Set Page Title dialog box appears.

Note: A default title may appear in the dialog box.

6 Type a title for the Web page.

7 Click **OK** to confirm the title.

■ This area displays the title you specified for the Web page.

8 Click **Save** to save the document as a Web page.

■ Word saves the document as a Web page and displays the document in the Web Layout view. This view displays the document as it will appear on the Web. For more information on the Web Layout view, see page 40.

INDEX

A

add
- animation to text, 100-101
- AutoCorrect entries to documents, 73
- AutoShapes, 212-213
- AutoText entries to documents, 75
- borders
  - to pages, 164-165
  - to tables, 206-207
  - to text, 136-137
- bullets, 124-125, 126-127
- buttons to toolbars, 246-247
- clip art, 220-223
- color
  - to graphics, 226
  - to text, 92, 96-97
- column breaks, 167
- columns to tables, 194-195
- comments, 78-79
- dates, 58
- diagrams, 232-233
- drawing canvases, 228-229
- drop caps, 134-135
- endnotes, 152-155
- envelopes to documents, 175
- footers, 148-151
- footnotes, 152-155
- formatting
  - to areas of text, 110-113
  - to tables, 208-209
- headers, 148-151
- highlight to text, 93
- hyperlinks, 294-295
- newspaper columns, 166-167
- numbers to lists, 124-125
- page
  - breaks, 142-143
  - numbers, 146-147
- pictures, 218-219
- rows to tables, 194-195
- section breaks, 144-145
- shading, 138-139
  - to cells in tables, 205
- shapes to diagrams, 235
- symbols, 76-77
- tabs, 130-131
  - with leader characters, 132-133
- text, 54-55
  - to AutoShapes, 213
  - to diagrams, 234
  - using Replace feature, 64-65
- text boxes, 216-217
- time, 58
- watermarks, 162-163
- WordArt, 214-215

address blocks, create using mail merge, 264-265
addresses, label with smart tags, 241
align. *See also* indent paragraphs; tabs
- graphics with text, 231
- page numbers, 147
- text, 94-95
  - in cells in tables, 204

animate text, 100-101
Answer Wizard, as a help feature, 19
appearance of text, change, 96-97
apply formatting, 110-113
- using styles, 115

arrange open documents, 186-187
art borders, add, 165
AutoCorrect, 67, 72-73
- Options button, 73

AutoShapes, 212-213. *See also* graphics
AutoText entries
- insert, 9
- use, 74-75

B

balloons
- for comments, 78-79
- for tracked changes, 80-81

blue
- rectangles, 73
- underlines, 108-109

bold text, 90, 96-97
borders
- page, add, 164-165
- tables, change, 206-207
- text, add, 136-137

breaks
- column, insert, 167
- page
  - control, 160-161
  - insert, 142-143
- section, insert, 144-145

bulleted lists, 124-125, 126-127
buttons
- AutoCorrect Options, 73
- Paste Options, 57, 189
- Smart Tag Actions, 240-241
- toolbar
  - add, 246-247
  - align text using, 94
  - move, 248
  - move or copy text using, 57
  - remove, 249

C

cancel changes, 59
carbon copies, for e-mail messages, 293
case of text, change, 91

cells in tables
  add shading to, 205
  align text in, 204
  borders, change, 207
  combine, 202
  overview, 193
  split, 203
  width, change, 199
center
  graphics, 231
  text, 94, 95
    vertically on pages, 158
changes
  review tracked, 82-83
  save, 23
  track, in documents, 80-81
  undo, 59
character styles, 115
characters. *See also* text; words
  count, in documents, 60-61
  delete, 55
    using Voice Command mode, 289
check
  formatting, 108-109
  spelling and grammar, 66-67
clear formatting, 105, 111
Click and Type feature, 9, 94-95
clip art, 220-223. *See also* graphics
Clip Organizer, 220-222
Clipboard task pane, 17, 57, 189
  move or copy text using, 57, 189
close
  documents, 26
  Print Preview, 171
  Word, 27
color
  of graphics, change, 226
  of shapes in diagrams, change, 237
  of text, change, 92, 96-97
  of text in diagrams, change, 237
column breaks
  add, 167
  remove, 167
columns
  newspaper, 166-167
  in tables
    add, 194-195
    delete, 196-197
      information in, 197
    overview, 193
    width, change, 198-199
commands
  select 14-15
    using Voice Command mode, 288-289
comments, add, 78-79
compare formatting, 120-121
Contents, as a help feature, 19
copies, print, 172-173
copy
  endnotes, 155
  footnotes, 155
  formatting, 102-103, 110-113
  text, 56-57
    between documents, 188-189
correct
  inconsistent formatting, 108-109, 120-121
  spelling and grammar errors, 66-67
count words, in documents, 60-61
create. *See also* insert; add
  address blocks, using mail merge, 264-265
  AutoCorrect entries, 72-73
  AutoText entries, 74
  borders, 136-137
  bulleted lists, 124-127
  documents, 184
    using templates or wizards, 242-243
  drawing canvases, 228-229
  drop caps, 134-135
  greeting lines, using mail merge, 264-265
  hyperlinks, 294-295
  labels, 176-179
    using mail merge, 270-277
  letters, using mail merge, 260-269
  macros, 252-255
  newspaper columns, 166-167
  numbered lists, 124-125
  styles, 114-115
  tables, 192-193
  templates, 244-245
  toolbars, 250-251
customize toolbars, 246-249
cycle diagrams, 233

D

dates
  insert, 58
    into headers or footers, 149
  label with smart tags, 241
default font, change, 98-99
delete. *See also* remove
  AutoShapes, 213
  borders
    from pages, 165
    from tables, 207
    from text, 137
  bullets, 125, 127
  buttons, from toolbars, 249
  characters, 55
    using Voice Command mode, 289
  clip art, 223
  columns in tables, 196-197
  comments, 79
  diagrams, 233
  drawing canvases, 229
  endnotes, 155
  footers, 149

footnotes, 155
headers, 149
leader characters from tabs, 133
macros, 257
merge fields, 267
numbers from lists, 125
page
breaks, 143
numbers, 147
pictures, 219
rows in tables, 196-197
section breaks, 145
shading, 139
shapes in diagrams, 235
tables, 193
tabs, 131
text 54-55
from tables, 197
text boxes, 217
watermarks, 163
WordArt, 215
Desktop folder, 23
diagrams, add, 232-233. *See also* graphics
Dictation mode, use, 286-287
directory, create using mail merge, 261
display
borders around text, 136-137
comments, 78-79
Document Map, 50-51
Drawing toolbar, 212
Find and Replace dialog box, 65
Footer area, 148-149
formatting marks, 49
Header area, 148-149
headings, for Document Map, 51
information for tracked changes, 82
previous or next
header or footer, 151
page, 12
ruler, 42
task panes, 16-17
toolbars, 43
Drawing Canvas, 228
Picture, 219
Tables and Borders, 204
Word Count, 61
WordArt, 215
white space, in Print Layout view, 48
Document Map, use, 50-51
documents. *See also* pages; text
arrange open, 186-187
check formatting for, 108-109
close, 26
compare formatting in, 120-121
connect using hyperlinks, 294-295
copy text between, 188-189
count words in, 60-61
create, 184
using templates and wizards, 242-243
display in Print Preview, 170-171
edit, 54-55
overview, 4
in Print Preview, 171
e-mail, 292-293
endnotes, add, 152-155
find, 32-33
fonts, change for all new, 98-99
footers, add, 148-151
footnotes, add, 152-155
format areas
many, 112-113, 103
one, 110-111
using styles, 114-115
grammar, check, 66-67
headers, add, 148-151
hide underlines under spelling and grammar errors in, 69
line spacing, change, 104
magnify, 46, 171
margins, change, 156-157
maximize, 187
minimize, 187
move
text between, 188-189
through, 12-13
using Document Map, 50-51
open, 28-29
in different formats, 30-31
protected, 37
page breaks
control, 160-161
insert, 142-143
pictures, add, 218-219
preview, 170-171
print, 172-173
overview, 4
protect, 34-37
review
formatting in, 118-119
tracked changes in, 82-83
samples used in book, 9
save, 22-23
in different formats, 24-25
as templates, 244-245
as Web pages, 296-297
search for, 32-33
section breaks, add, 144-145
select all text in, 11
spelling, check, 66-67
split, 47
styles, change, 116-117
switch between, 185
templates, create, 244-245
track changes in, 80-81
undo changes for, 59
unprotect, 37
views
change, 40
overview, 7, 41
zoom in or out, 46

drag and drop, move or copy text using, 56
Drawing Canvas toolbar, 228
drawing canvases, 228-229
    hide, 213
Drawing toolbar, 212
drop caps, create, 134-135

E

edit
    comments, 79
    documents
        overview, 4
        in Print Preview, 171
    text, 54-55
        in footnotes or endnotes, 154-155
        in headers or footers, 149
        in text boxes, 217
    WordArt, 215
effects
    animation, 100-101
    text, 96-97
e-mail
    addresses
        insert using mail merge, 264-265
        label with smart tags, 241
    documents, 292-293
    messages, create using mail merge, 261
endnotes, add, 152-155
enter
    punctuation, using Dictation mode, 287
    spaces, using Voice Command mode, 289
    symbols, by typing characters, 77
    tabs, using Voice Command mode, 289
    text, 8-9
        into tables, 193
        using Dictation mode, 286-287
        using Replace feature, 65
envelopes
    add to documents, 175
    create using mail merge, 261
    print, 174-175
Even Page Header/Footer, 151
exit Word, 27

F

Favorites folder, 23
File menu, use to open documents, 29
financial symbols, label with smart tags, 241
find. *See also* search
    documents, 32-33
    text, 62-63
First Page Header/Footer, 151
fonts
    change, 88, 96-97
        for all new documents, 98-99
    size, change, 89, 96-97
footers, add, 148-151
footnotes, add, 152-155
format
    documents, overview, 4
    footnotes and endnotes, 153
    open documents, in different, 30-31
    save documents, in different, 24-25
    tables, 208-209
    text
        in tables, 193
        in text boxes, 217
formatting
    apply, 110-113
        using styles, 115
    check, 108-109
    compare, 120-121
    copy, 102-103, 110-113
    marks, display or hide, 49
    remove from text, 105, 111
    review, 118-119, 120-121
Formatting toolbar
    display or hide, 43
    overview, 7

G

grammar, check, 66-67
    turn on or off, 68-69
graphics
    align with text, 231
    AutoShapes, 212-213
    clip art, 220-223
    color, change, 226
    diagrams, 232-237
    drawing canvases, 228-229
    move, 224
    overview, 5
    pictures, 218-219
    rotate, 227
    size, 225
    text boxes, 216-217
    use as hyperlinks, 294-295
    WordArt, 214-215
    wrap text around, 230-231
greeting lines, create using mail merge, 264-265

H

hanging indents, 129
Header and Footer toolbar, 148-151
headers, add, 148-151
height, of rows in tables, change, 198-199
help, 18-19
hide
    Document Map, 51
    drawing canvases, 213
    formatting marks, 49
    page numbers on first page, 147
    Reviewing toolbar, 83
    ruler, 42

task panes, 16
toolbars, 43
underlines under spelling and grammar errors, 69
white space, in Print Layout view, 48
highlight text, 93
History folder, 23
hyperlinks, 294-295

I

indent paragraphs, 128-129
Index, as a help feature, 19
insert
art borders, 165
AutoCorrect entries, 73, 77
AutoShapes, 212-213
AutoText entries, 75
borders
pages, 164-165
tables, 206-207
text, 136-137
bullets, 124-125, 126-127
buttons on toolbars, 246-247
clip art, 222-223
column breaks, 167
columns in tables, 194-195
comments, 78-79
dates, 58
diagrams, 232-233
drawing canvases, 228-229
drop caps, 134-135
e-mail addresses, using mail merge, 265
endnotes, 152-155
footers, 148-151
footnotes, 152-155
headers, 148-151
hyperlinks, 294-295
numbers in lists, 124-125
page breaks, 142-143
page numbers, 146-147
phone numbers, using mail merge, 265
pictures, 218-219
rows in tables, 194-195
section breaks, 144-145
shapes in diagrams, 235
symbols, 76-77
tabs, 130-131
with leader characters, 132-133
text, 54-55
text boxes, 216-217
time, 58
watermarks, 162-163
WordArt, 214-215
Insert Clip Art task pane, 220-223
insertion point
move, 12, 95
using keyboard, 54
using Voice Command mode, 289
when recording macros, 255
overview, 7
Internet
and Word, overview, 5
create hyperlinks, 294-295
e-mail documents, 292-293
save documents as Web pages, 296-297
intranet, 296
italicize text, 90, 96-97

J

justify text, 94

K

keyboard shortcut
assign to macro, 253-254
use to run macro, 257

L

label text with smart tags, 240-241
labels
create using mail merge, 270-277
print, 176-179
save, 179
landscape orientation, 159
Language bar, 285
languages, translate text into, 84-85
leader characters, add to tabs, 132-133
left align
graphics, 231
text, 94, 95
line borders, add, 164-165
lines
add across page, 137
count, in documents, 60-61
enter, new, using Dictation mode, 287
indent, 128-129
spacing, change, 104
links. *See* hyperlinks.
lists
add bullets, 124-125, 126-127
add numbers, 124-125
styles, 115
change, 116-117

M

macros
assign keyboard shortcut to, 253-254
delete, 257
name, 252
record, 252-255
run, 256-257
using keyboard shortcut, 257

magnify pages, 46, 171
mail merge
overview, 5
use to create
labels, 270-277
letters, 260-269
Mail Merge
task pane, 260-277
Wizard
use to create
labels, 270-277
letters, 260-269
mailing lists
create, using mail merge, 262-263
sort, 264, 275
margins, change, 156-157
maximize documents, 187
menu bar, overview, 7
menus
commands
add to short version, 15
select, 14-15
using Voice Command mode, 288
shortcut, use, 15
merge
cells in tables, 202
fields, 266-267
microphone, turn on or off, 288-289
Microphone Wizard, 281-282
Microsoft
Outlook, 292
Speech Recognition Training Wizard, 282-285
minimize documents, 187
mouse
use when recording macros, 255
wheeled, 13
move
between
documents, 185
footers and headers, 151
buttons on toolbars, 248
drawing canvases, 229
graphics, 224
insertion point, 12, 95
using keyboard, 54
using Voice Command mode, 289
when recording macros, 255
tables, 200
tabs, 131
text, 56-57
between documents, 188-189
through
documents, 12-13
using Document Map, 50-51
using keyboard, 13
headers and footers, 151
toolbars, 44, 251
buttons on, 248
My Collections folder, 221
My Documents folder, 23
My Network Places folder, 23

N

name
documents, 22
macros, 252
templates, 244-245
Web pages, 297
names, label with smart tags, 241
New Document task pane, 17, 243
newspaper columns, add, 166-167
Normal view, 40-41
number pages, 146-147
numbered lists, 124-125

O

Odd Page Header/Footer, 151
Office Collections folder, 221
open
documents, 28-29
arrange, 186-187
in different formats, 30-31
protected, 37
organization chart, 233
add shapes to, 235
orientation of pages, change, 159
orphans, control, 161
Outline view, 40-41
Overtype feature, 55

P

pages. *See also* documents; text
borders, add, 164-165
breaks
control, 160-161
insert, 142-143
center text vertically on, 158
count, in documents, 60-61
display previous or next, 12
footnotes or endnotes, add, 152-155
headers or footers, add, 148-151
magnify, 46, 171
margins, change, 156-157
numbers, insert, 146-147
into headers or footers, 149
orientation, change, 159
print, 172-173
section breaks, insert, 144-145
shrink text to fit, 171
watermarks, add, 162-163
Web, save documents as, 296-297
paper
size, change, 180-181
source, change, 180-181

INDEX

paragraphs
  add drop caps to, 134-135
  count, in documents, 60-61
  indent, 128-129
  select, 11
  styles, 115
passwords, protect documents using, 34-37
Paste Options button, 57, 189
phone numbers, insert, using mail merge, 265
picture
  bullets, add to lists, 126-127
  watermarks, add, 162-163
Picture toolbar, 219
pictures, add, 218-219. *See also* graphics
places, label with smart tags, 241
point sizes, 89. *See also* fonts
portrait orientation, 159
preview documents, 170-171
print
  documents, 172-173
    overview, 4
  endnotes on separate page, 155
  envelopes, 174-175
    using Mail Merge Wizard, 271
  labels, 176-179
  pages, 172-173
  selection, 172-173
  text, 172-173
  tracked changes, 81
Print Layout view, 40-41
  display or hide white space in, 48
  use to change margins, 157
Print Preview feature, use, 170-171
protect documents, 34-37
punctuation, enter using Dictation mode, 287
pyramid diagrams, 233

R

radial diagrams, 233
record macros, 252-255
remove. *See also* delete
  animation effects, 101
  AutoShapes, 213
  bold, 90
  borders
    from pages, 165
    from tables, 207
    from text, 137
  bullets, 125, 127
  clip art, 223
  color from text, 92
  column breaks, 167
  comments, 79
  designs from tables, 209
  drop caps, 135
  endnotes, 155
  footers, 149
  footnotes, 155
  formatting from text, 105, 111
  headers, 149
  highlight from text, 93
  hyperlinks, 295
  italics, 90
  leader characters from tabs, 133
  merge fields, 267
  newspaper columns, 166
  numbers from lists, 125
  page
    breaks, 143
    numbers, 147
  pictures, 219
  section breaks, 145
  shading
    from cells in tables, 205
    from text, 139
  smart tags, 241
  splits from documents, 47
  symbols, 77
  tabs, 131
  text
    boxes, 217
    from tables, 197
  underlines
    from spelling and grammar errors, 69
    from text, 90
  vertical centering, 158
  watermarks, 163
  WordArt, 215
replace text, 64-65
  using Overtype feature, 55
  using thesaurus, 70-71
  with translated words, 84-85
resize. *See* size
Reveal Formatting task pane, 118-119, 120-121
review
  formatting, 118-119, 120-121
  tracked changes, 82-83
Reviewing toolbar, 78-79, 80
  hide, 83
right align
  graphics, 231
  text, 94, 95
rotate graphics, 227
rows in tables
  add, 194-195
  delete, 196-197
    information in, 197
  height, change, 198-199
  overview, 193
ruler
  display, 42
  hide, 42
  overview, 7
run macros, 256-257

S

sample documents used in book, 9
save
  documents, 22-23
    in different formats, 24-25
    as templates, 244-245
    as Web pages, 296-297
  labels, 179
scale drawing canvases, 229
scroll
  through documents, 13
    in Print Preview, 170
scroll bars, overview, 7
search
  for clip art images, 223
  for documents, 32-33
  for text, 62-63
  for words, 62-63
Search task pane, 17, 32-33
section, breaks, insert, 144-145
select
  commands, 14-15
    using Voice Command mode, 289
  dialog box options, using Voice Command mode, 288
  entire documents, 11
  text, 10-11
    when recording macros, 255
  toolbar commands, using Voice Command mode, 289
selection, print, 172-173
sentences, select, 10
set up speech recognition, 280-283
shading, add, 138-139
  to cells in tables, 205
shapes
  add to diagrams, 235
  color, change for diagrams, 237
  delete from diagrams, 235
shortcut menus, use, 15
  to correct spelling and grammar errors, 67
shrink, text, 171
size
  drawing canvases, 229
  graphics, 225
  of paper, change, 180-181
  tables, 201
  text, 89, 96-97
  toolbars, 45
Smart Tag Actions button, 240-241
smart tags
  options, change, 241
  use, 240-241
sort mailing lists, 264, 275
source, of paper, change, 180-181
spaces, enter, using Voice Command mode, 289
spacing, between lines, change, 104
speech recognition
  Dictation mode, use, 286-287
  overview, 5
  set up, 280-283
  Voice Command mode, use, 288-289
spelling, check, 66-67
  turn on or off, 68-69
split
  cells in tables, 203
  documents, 47
Standard toolbar
  display or hide, 43
  overview, 7
start. *See also* open
  Word, 6
status bar, overview, 7
stop, tracking changes in document, 81
styles
  add to diagrams, 236-237
  apply, 115
  change, 116-117
  create, 114-115
Styles and Formatting task pane, 103, 110-113, 114-115, 116-117
switch between
  documents, 185
  headers and footers, 151
symbols, insert, 76-77

T

table styles, 115
tables
  borders, change, 206-207
  cells
    add shading, 205
    borders, change, 207
    combine, 202
    overview, 193
    split, 203
    width, change, 199
  columns
    add, 194-195
    delete, 196-197
      information in, 197
    overview, 193
    width, change, 198-199
  create, 192-193
  delete, 193
  format, 208-209
    text in, 193
  move, 200
  overview, 5
  rows
    add, 194-195
    delete, 196-197
      information in, 197
    height, change, 198-199
    overview, 193

size, change, 201
styles, change, 116-117
text
align in cells, 204
enter into cells, 193
Tables and Borders toolbar, 204
tabs
add, 130-131
with leader characters, 132-133
enter, using Voice Command mode, 289
move, 131
remove, 131
use, 131
target diagrams, 233
task pane
Clipboard, 17
use to move or copy text, 57, 189
Insert Clip Art, 220-223
Mail Merge, 260-277
New Document, 17, 242-243
overview, 7
Reveal Formatting, 118-119, 120-121
Search, 17, 32-33
Styles and Formatting, 103, 110-113, 114-115, 116-117
Translate, 84-85
use, 16-17
to open documents, 29
telephone numbers, label with smart tags, 241
templates
create, 244-245
defined, 242, 244
use, 242-243
text
add
to AutoShapes, 213
to diagrams, 234
align, 94-95
in cells in tables, 204
graphics with, 231
animate, 100-101
appearance, change, 96-97
apply formatting to, 110-113
bold, 90, 96-97
borders, add, 136-137
case of, change, 91
center, 94, 95
vertically on pages, 158
change style of, 116-117
check for formatting inconsistencies, 108-109
color
change, 92, 96-97
in diagrams, 237
compare formatting, 120-121
copy, 56-57
between documents, 188-189
delete, 54-55
from tables, 197
edit, 54-55
in footnotes and endnotes, 154-155
in headers or footers, 149
in Print Preview, 171
in text boxes, 217
for WordArt, 215
effects, add, 96-97
enter, 8-9
into tables, 193
using Dictation mode, 286-287
using Replace feature, 65
find, 62-63
fonts, change, 88, 96-97
format, in text boxes, 217
formatting, remove from documents, 105, 111
grammar, check, 66-67
highlight, 93
hyperlinks, create, 294-295
indent, 128-129
insert, 54-55
italicize, 90, 96-97
justify, 94
label with smart tags, 240-241
left align, 94, 95
move, 56-57
between documents, 188-189
orphans, control, 161
print, 172-173
replace, 64-65
using Overtype feature, 55
using thesaurus, 70-71
with translated words, 84-85
review formatting of, 118-121
right align, 94, 95
search for, 62-63
select, 10-11
when recording macros, 255
shading, add, 138-139
shrink to fit on pages, 171
size, change, 89, 96-97
spelling, check, 66-67
track changes to, 80-81
translate, 84-85
underline, 90
watermarks, add, 162-163
wrap around
drawing canvases, 230-231
graphics, 230-231
text boxes, 216-217
thesaurus, use, 70-71

time
    insert, 58
        into headers or footers, 149
    label with smart tags, 241
title bar, overview, 7
titles, of Web pages, 297
toolbars
    buttons
        add, 246-247
        align text using, 94
        move, 248
        move or copy text using, 57
        remove, 249
    commands, select, 14-15
        using Voice Command mode, 288
    create, 250-251
    customize, 246-249
    display, 43
        Picture, 219
        Word Count, 61
        WordArt, 215
    Drawing Canvas, 228
    Formatting, overview, 7
    Header and Footer, 148-151
    hide, 43
    move, 44, 251
    Reviewing, 78-79, 80
        hide, 83
    size, 45
    Standard, overview, 7
    Word Count, use, 61
track changes
    in documents, 80-81
    review, 82-83
train speech recognition, 282-285
Translate task pane, 84-85
translate text, 84-85
turn off spelling and grammar check, 68-69

U

underline text, 90
underlines
    purple dotted, 240-241
    under
        formatting inconsistencies, 108-109
        hyperlinks, 295
        spelling and grammar errors, 8, 55, 66
            hide, 69
undo changes, 59
unprotect documents, 37

V

venn diagrams, 233
vertically center text on pages, 158
view. *See also* display
    comments, 78-79
    of documents, change, 40-41
    headers or footers, 148-149
    menus, 14-15
    ruler, 42
    text for footnotes or endnotes, 154
    toolbars, 43
Voice Command mode, use, 288-289

W

watermarks, add, 162-163
Web. *See also* Internet
    pages
        connect to documents, 294-295
        save documents as, 296-297
    server, 297
Web Collections folder, 221
Web Layout view, 40-41, 297
wheeled mouse, 13
white space, display or hide in Print Layout view, 48
widows, control, 161
width, of columns in tables, change, 198-199
wizards, use, 242-243
Word
    and Internet, overview, 5
    exit, 27
    overview, 4-5
    start, 6
    window, parts of, 7
Word Count toolbar, 61
WordArt, 214-215. *See also* graphics
    toolbar, 215
words. *See also* text
    count, in documents, 60-61
    replace, 64-65
    search for, 62-63
    select, 10
    translate, 84-85
    use as drop cap, 135
wrap text around
    drawing canvases, 231
    graphics, 230-231

Z

zoom in or out, 46